LETTERS
from the
GOOD WAR

Also by Hugh Aaron

Essays
Business Not as Usual

A novel
When Wars Were Won

A short story collection
It's All Chaos

LETTERS
from the
GOOD WAR

A Young Man's Discovery
of the World

by
Hugh Aaron

Stones Point Press
P.O. Box 384
Belfast, ME 04915

COVER by Tim Seymour Designs
EDITED by Ramon de Rosas

FIRST EDITION

Aaron, Hugh
Letters from the Good War: A Young Man's Discovery of the World
Library of Congress Catalog Card Number: 96-68798
ISBN 1-882521-04-8

$20.00 Softcover
Printed in the United States of America

This book is dedicated
to the memory of
my mother and my father,
who saved these letters
out of love for a son
who may never have returned.

The Song of the Seabees

Introduction
The Navy wanted men
That's where we came in
Mr. Jones, and Mr. Smith
The Owens and Cohens and Flynn.

The Navy wanted more
Of Uncle Sammy's kin
So we all joined up
And brother we're in to win.

Chorus
We're the Seabees of the Navy
We can build and we can fight
We'll pave the way to victory
And guard it day and night
And we promise that we'll remember
The Seventh of December
We're the Seabees of the Navy
Bees of the seven seas.

Contents

FOREWORD

Writing a foreword to Hugh Aaron's letters is like saying a few words after Lincoln's Gettysburg Address: It's a tough act to follow—but a privilege, too.

One of life's deepest regrets is that of neglected opportunity, especially in expressing love for parents, to whom—once they are gone—words of praise prove futile, gestures of affection mute. In these letters, however, Hugh, as a World War II Seabee, tells his mother, his father, and his brother, too, how much he loves them, admires them, misses them. There are conflicts, also: old grievances aired and new ones erupting, though nothing this family couldn't handle. And this is a family of immigrant stock, molded by the Great Depression, tested in a frightful world war. To Hugh's traditional Jewish parents his letters must have reflected the biblical observation that a loving son gives his mother joy; a devoted son gladdens his father's heart.

These splendid letters also represent a journey both literal and cerebral, revealing the growth of a young mind—calm and turbulent, rational and imaginative—searching for truth as it thirsts for knowledge, groping for answers to life's problems as it grapples with life's perplexities. It is a mind in transition, an uncommon mind responding to upheaval and uncertainty, to kindness and insult, to literature and music, to God and man.

Socrates says that the unexamined life is not worth living. Hugh's letters, then, can surely be classified as Socratic. Had Hugh placed himself under a microscope, he could not have examined himself—nor others, nor events—more closely. Though, on occasion, he can be hard on others, he is harder on himself. His self-honesty is as painful at times as it is refreshing. He never forgets a kindness, always grateful to good people good to him—and good for him.

These articulate reminiscences resurrect the times when names like Anzio, Casablanca, the Coral Sea, and Normandy dominated the news; men like Roosevelt, MacArthur, and Churchill dictated—if not controlled—events; entertainers like Bing Crosby, Bob Hope, Jack Benny reigned supreme in films, in the theater, on the radio in what was then called the Home Front, for which Hugh, the young Seabee, yearns and to which he addresses his soul-searching correspondence.

ix

These are letters of reflection, a progress of the soul, in a world in turmoil, changing dramatically, rapidly, and irrevocably.

Hugh writes that he wants to be a writer; he *is* a writer, but he doesn't know it (his father does, however). His eye for detail is well nigh photographic, his expression both powerful and lyrical, whether discussing abstract ideas or describing a city or a sunset. In his developing and fertile mind he maintains a balance between thought and mundane living. Hugh impresses people as much as they impress him. His letters reveal a discriminating, headstrong young man without affectation, friendly without condescension. Sense of humor? Check his epistolary sign-offs. His work record as a Seabee matches his work ethic—extraordinary. The reader likes him, for he has a good heart. He has character.

Yes, his mother saved every letter he ever wrote home. Well, Jewish mothers did not get their reputations lightly; but isn't that what women do when receiving love letters?

Ramon de Rosas
Arlington, Massachusetts

A DAUGHTER'S THOUGHTS

These letters are unique! With each passing page, and therefore, with each passing day, I learned more about my father...as he learned about himself. I found it fascinating to witness an adolescent consciously, yet innocently engaged in the process of assessing and documenting his own development into manhood. His introspection was obviously subjective in its execution, but he understood himself and his world with staggering clarity. Through words written for those dear to him, my father boldly revealed his character: articulate, intensely driven towards success and growth, inquisitive, and charmed by all that is new. Such depth of character, such an exquisite eye for detail! All this makes *The Letters* an enlightening read.

A generation ago, my father's letters helped maintain an intricate bond with his family by allowing them into his everyday experience of the war. Readers today will be transported to that time and will participate in a world of patriotism, anti-semitism, and close familial kinship, an account much more personal and revealing than any historical reference. To meet young Hugh is to glimpse, and ultimately respect, the tremendous chasm that exists between the experiences of his and subsequent generations in the U.S.

For me, reading the letters was a personal, emotional journey; there were moments of sharp identification and moments of disbelief. Reading was frightening because of the purity with which I met and beheld the man who would become my father. Reading was joyous because of what I discovered about his love for and devotion to his family, and for his passionate character. I feel as though the letters are a gift to me from my grandmother who so meticulously saved and cared for every one. I am changed; my vision of my father is forever altered.

Reading this book is a commitment. It is an honest glimpse into the past, and in that way it is a gift to all of us in the present.

Suzanne A. Holmes
Boulder, Colorado

PREFACE

Thanks to my mother (who was in her mid-forties when I was in the service), who saved every letter I had written to her and my father (about 50) and my brother (about 15) during the war, I'm able, in my seventh decade, to recapture what it was like to be an adolescent crossing into manhood in those dark days. Perhaps "recapture" is the wrong word, because the letters really fail to bring back the feelings I had then, or remind me of the incidents I describe. I remember virtually nothing. Indeed, that wide-eyed 19-year-old is such a total stranger to me, that I'm more comfortable referring to him in the third person. But from these letters I can see, with some objectivity, what I was like during those formative years, and how I became the adult who both failed and succeeded in various aspects of my later living. I'm most fortunate. Few are given the opportunity to have a clear picture of what they once were and whence they came.

At times, as I transcribed the letters into the computer, I felt like shaking this Hughie and telling him to loosen up, get with it. He was compulsive about many things, grossly immature about many others, and he lacked the wisdom of patience. He allowed many opportunities to pass him by. I was shocked to see how blatantly Freudian his ties to his mother were. And I confess being surprised at the relentlessness of his drive for recognition and advancement, derived in large part, it seems, from his need to please his parents. But I also found myself admiring his willingness to admit error and look at himself with some objectivity. And I saw in him qualities, such as love for family and respect for others, a resilience, and a strong moral sense, that a mother and father could treasure in a son. Actually, as the transcribing progressed I found myself feeling like a father to that lad who was, incredibly, myself.

As you move into the letters, I believe you will get to know the personality of the writer as he can rarely be known in a novel or poem. You will be observing the writer develop into early manhood, and, perhaps, note a certain maturing of his writing style during the two years and nine months that the letters cover. But more fascinating, I think, you'll gain from these letters a feel for the times that were so different from the way things are today, through the eyes of an adolescent who misses no detail, no nuance, in his observation of the world around him.

By the time the transcribing was completed, I was overwhelmed with feelings of loss and regret, loss of the youthful spirit that has gradually ebbed during the years of my life's tribulations, and regret that after the war I didn't maintain contact with the many kind, dear friends (described in detail in the letters) that I had acquired during my wartime travels in the U.S. and overseas.

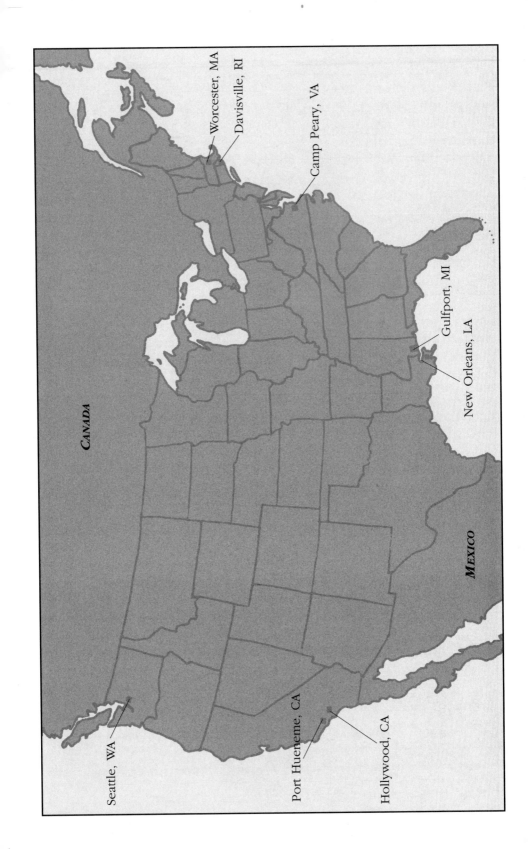

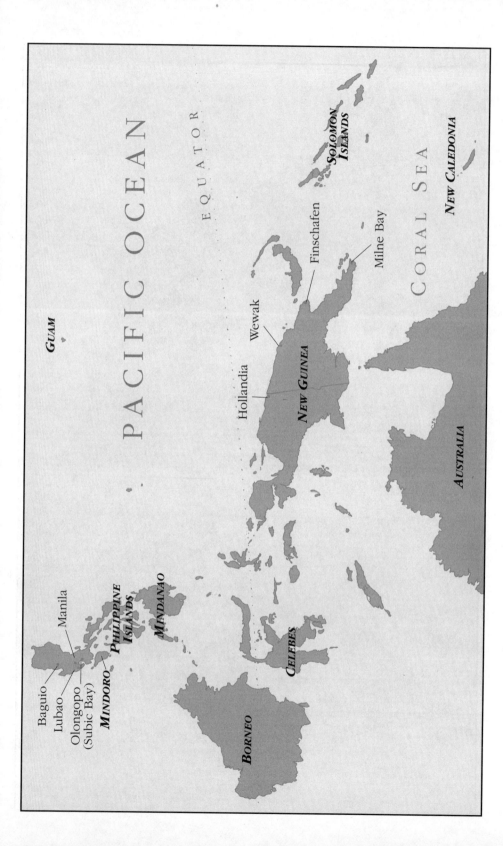

SOME STATISTICS

Born November 30, 1924 in Worcester, Massachusetts.

Inducted directly from high school into the U.S. Armed Forces at Camp Devens, Massachusetts July 5, 1943. Service number 802-14-676.

Assigned to the 113th Naval Construction Battalion at Camp Peary, Virginia August 1943. Issued Springfield rifle 02 number 3929572

Trained at Camp Peary, Virginia; Davisville, Rhode Island; Camp Holliday, Mississippi; Camp Rousseau, Port Hueneme, California.

Shipped across the Pacific aboard the USS *West Point*, formerly the *America*, February 1944

Performed duty overseas at Finschaven, New Guinea; Hollandia, New Guinea, Mindoro and Subic Bay, Philippines, Guam.

Shipped home aboard the aircraft carrier *Hornet*. Debarked at Seattle, Washington November 1945.

Honorably discharged from service at Boston, February 1946.

Graduated University of Chicago 1951.

Married June 1955.

Daughter born February 1958, son born December 1960, daughter born July 1965.

Entered business 1966.

Sold business 1985.

Divorced 1987.

Remarried April 1989.

STATESIDE

Williamsburg, Virginia

Inducted into the U.S. Armed Forces July 5, 1943.
Service number 802-14-676.
Issued Springfield rifle 02¹ number 3929572.

7/6/43
Camp Peary, Williamsburg

Dear Mom,

Well, here I am at Camp Peary after traveling over twelve hours. Boy, what a trip!

We started from Boston, as you know, at 6:00 PM and passed through Providence, Cranston, and Westerly, Rhode Island, then across the length of Connecticut via New London and New Haven to New York City. We had our own private car which was only fairly comfortable. When we reached Penn Station at midnight, I was pretty tired, but, with everything so rushing and enormous, I became wide awake.

We changed trains for Washington, our next stop. This time we had a better coach, but much to my disgust, it wasn't a Pullman. I slept sitting up most of the way to Philadelphia which was more than most could do. To top it off, the guy sleeping next to me was using my shoulder as a pillow, and, when I awoke, I was stiff all over, not to mention sticky and sweaty. I dozed intermittently from Philadelphia to Washington.

After reaching Washington at dawn, about 5:00 AM, we had about fifteen minutes while waiting for a connection. Two others from Worcester and I roamed around. Washington's depot is certainly beautiful, a little smaller than (Boston's) South Station. But Penn Station, by the way, dwarfs even South Station. The trolleys in Washington are elegant with venetian blinds. They run on diesel as well as electricity.

The train left Washington slowly so that I had a beautiful view of the Capitol, the Washington Monument, Lincoln Memorial, the Pentagon Building, the War Department, and the new Jefferson Memorial. Boy, what buildings—enormous and beautiful.

All the way from Boston to Washington we had only clean streamlined diesels. But we had a coal-fired steam engine from

Washington to Richmond. Because it was hot, we opened the windows and were covered with soot. Listen [brother] Ronnie, I tried to keep my trousers as clean as I could, but it was impossible. All my clothes were filthy by the time we arrived at camp.

We passed through small towns in Virginia, including Quantico,[2] where we saw a part of the naval base. Richmond seems to be a fine city. Though it appears to be about the same size as Worcester,[3] I think it beats it by a mile. We took a trolley down Richmond's main thoroughfare. Then we switched trains for a third time and boarded a fine coach to Williamsburg, which I haven't explored yet. Camp Peary is a good five to eight miles from that town. I got about three hours sleep all night and that was doing well. I forgot to mention that we picked up other Seabee recruits along the line.

By the way, don't write until I tell you where my training area is. I'll know in a day or so.

I must tell you about the food. Soon after we departed Boston, we had hamburg as usual, but a full meal. Next morning at 7:00 we had a wonderful dollar breakfast, including oatmeal and cream, thick slices of bacon and plenty of scrambled eggs, grape juice, coffee or milk and ice water, all at government expense, mind you. Oh, yes, a colored waiter kept passing an empty silver plate under our noses saying, "Don't forget this, fellows." Every time he came by, he brought the plate to our attention, so each of us tossed twenty cents on his plate.

I'm writing to all three of you at once. I hope you will overlook the deplorable condition of my clothes when they arrive, but under the same conditions, I'm sure you could do no better. I'll want a few things, but I'll mention them in another letter.

Love to you all, Mom, Dad and Ronnie.

Hughie

Camp Peary 7/8/43

Dear Folks,

Well, I'm settled now. I'm an apprentice seaman, which means I drill and drill. Yesterday was a tough day. We had a thorough physical. Many were turned down and returned home. Then we were outfitted with clothes, all 115 pounds of them. See the list enclosed. Add to it another dress suit, bedding, shoe shine kit, toothbrush and case, buttons, a soap case, two duffel bags, knife, comb, puttees[1] and some items I haven't examined yet. After boot training, we'll be given a rifle. All belongings were stencilled with our names.

Our pictures were taken, and what pictures they are. Really, we are the cutest boys with that G.I. clip that takes about thirty seconds.

We laughed at each other at first, but now we're used to our appearance. Our heat is like the heat you had some weeks ago, only worse and more humid. We swelter all day. Lately we've been lucky with the skies overcast. When the sun comes out, it's twice as hot as in Worcester.

The food here is good and more than enough. I have milk only once — in the morning with cold cereal, which isn't quite a glass. I miss it. Coffee is served, but I drink water. You ought to appreciate your water up there. Here it's lousy — clear but chlorinated with a peculiar taste. I hold my nose when I drink it. Unfortunately, I must drink a lot because I sweat so much.

I'll be here for four weeks of drilling and primary training, then a short leave, and back again for four weeks of advanced training. We've started basic which consists of drill, drill and more drill, practicing all sorts of formations, positions and turns. We do this with rifles.

We have four pairs of shoes: low dress, two heavy G.I. for work and drill, and high black dress.

The camp is enormous, more than I could ever see. It covers miles and holds many thousands of men. We sleep in wooden barracks, sixty to a barracks. Each side is divided into platoons of thirty men. We have double berths; mine is a lower bunk.

We ourselves packed the clothes we sent home. Packed is the wrong word. They rushed us so that we only had time to throw them into a container. We couldn't keep any civilian material, including extra handkerchiefs or stockings, because they issue us plenty of everything.

I hope you like the writing paper I bought. I thought it looked rather official. I get fifty dollars a month. About seven dollars is taken out for my $10,000 life insurance policy. You, Mom, are the beneficiary. One year and not later than five years after discharge, I may convert it into a civilian policy. Do you want me to send all but ten dollars a month home or buy war bonds? Either way, they'll do it automatically at my request. I kept only this month's pay for myself.

I want all three of you to write often. Send me my watch and some shower klacks[2] when you have time.

> Love to you all,
> Hughie A.S.
> Area B9 Platoon 4734, Barracks 123
> N.C.T.C., Camp Peary
> Williamsburg, VA

P.S. I hear all kinds of accents in my barracks. The men come from every state in the union. Don't be surprised if I acquire a Southern accent.

Camp Peary 7/9/43

Dear Folks,

I haven't written anyone else but you because I'm so busy. I have all I can do to find time to write this.

We get up about 5:00 AM and do setting up exercises. Then we have breakfast, what we call "chow" or "eats." After chow we raise the flag, a ritual called "colors."[1] Then drill starts and continues for hours. After drill we have lectures on combat and warfare. Then chow and more drill and lectures though the afternoon. Finally we have supper, after which we have the remaining three hours of the evening before taps to ourselves.

I must cut this short. I'm busy rolling up my clothes. This automatically presses them and has to be done just so. I should mention that this is boot training which ordinarily lasts six weeks but is being accelerated to four. After the course is done, we have a 62 hour or three day furlough. Do you think I should come home? It takes about seventeen hours each way by train. I would like to. However, I don't want to return a minute late. The penalty for AWOL[2] is a thirty-six dollar fine. That's no lie. The discipline is very strict.

Camp Peary 7/10/43

Dear Folks,

Today we had our first combat training. I'm dead tired and still have half a day to drill. We are learning various combat formations and how to crawl in the dust. Luckily we have forest green coveralls, a Marine uniform,[1] but are they hot! We drill in the broiling sun; still our uniforms, which are either coveralls or dungarees, have to be just so. The heat is terrific. Many are complaining of sore feet, but luckily mine are fine, although my legs are a little sore. After a shower I feel fine. I usually take one before going to bed at 8:30 — 21:30 navy time. It's no cinch, the Seabees. You certainly keep hopping. Some don't have enough time to eat, but I am able to get in every meal.

By the way, I can buy a waterproof, shockproof watch at the ship's store here for about thirty dollars. Ordinarily it sells for much more outside. Can you get me a pair of sunglasses that would clip over mine? Do you think I should buy the watch?

When I arrived Tuesday morning, I had had only three hours' sleep. That night I got only five hours and have been exhausted. But now I've caught up on my sleep and feel much better.

Boy, are they fussy about bedding and clothing. If our shoes are placed a little out of line, we don't pass inspection; if our blanket is facing the wrong way, if even a speck of paper is on the floor, or our duffel bag is tied with the wrong knot, we flunk inspection. We must wear our white sailor hats at all times, and if anyone has a speck of dirt on his, he is told so. Everything must be just so, and I mean just so.

Just got back from drill, drenched. The same yesterday —drenched. I'm learning to take it. When we step in the mud we must keep our heads up. This is certainly an all work and no play outfit, but I don't mind. I think I'll like it—for a while anyway. Buy *Pic* magazine. I'm told it has quite an article about the Seabees. (I'm using both sides of paper to conserve.)

The base offers such recreation as movies, USO shows,[2] swimming in a pool, and radio shows but I never have time to take advantage of any of it. I hear Bob Hope[3] and Fred Astaire[4] were here. The camp is about a year old. The Seabees are eighteen months old. As far as ratings go, I fear it will be a long time before I advance.

Just learned that Sicily is being invaded.[5] We get newspapers here, but the chaplain told us at a recent assembly what to write while we're in camp. We must watch our step and not give out any crucial information.[6]

Everybody addresses everybody else here not as "friend" or "Hey, you," but as "mate." This and our uniform are the only similarities to the regular navy. Oh yes, the floor or the ground is referred to as the "deck." And the swearing is terrific.

Camp Peary 7/12/43

Dear Mom,

I insisted that you leave last Monday (in Boston), because I really was embarrassed in front of the other fellows. I wanted you both there with all my heart, but it didn't seem proper that you remain. After I returned from the mess hall, I looked for you, feeling sorry that I couldn't give you a more fitting goodbye. I had a lump in my throat.

The course I'm taking will be over the first of August, and we move the next day. I'm not sure that I'll be given that sixty-two hour leave now. But I'm glad in a way, because it will be added to my ten day furlough after the four weeks of advanced training. I hope I'm shipped to Davisville, R.I. for that training.

I think they'll send me across after advanced, but I'll never see combat. I'm "special assignment" because of my bad eyes.

I've made a few acquaintances in the barracks: a boy named Gagnon from Springfield, another boy named Goldstein (not Irish) from New York. Both are nice. I also have a clean[1] friend from Los Angeles. There's a man named Anderson from Worcester. He was on the train from Boston. Just today his wife sent him a clipping from the *Telegram*[2] in which both his name and mine appeared on the induction list. That very dark boy you saw in Boston is in the next barracks. He is very homesick. If we go home, we shall go together. I get along very well with all the fellows. They admire my physique.

We had vaccinations, typhoid and yellow fever jabs today. Four more shots yet to come. At the hospital they all ask if I'm a weight lifter.

We're learning combat tactics with unloaded rifles. We also learned a little about hand grenades and Springfields (rifles). We do all sorts of close formation marching from dawn to dusk. No rest for the weary, but I like it just the same. We crawl in dirt and walk through mud; what a wash I have. We must do all our own dungarees and coveralls. Only our dress uniforms and whites are sent to the cleaners. But we won't wear these until after boot training.

Our barracks had KP[3] yesterday. Every four days each barracks has either KP, guard duty, or clean up duty. As luck would have it, I landed the worst job in KP—washing and greasing big pots and pans. We worked in the kitchen from 4:40 in the morning until 7:00 that night with only time off to eat, while others, who had easier jobs, went swimming. Then after 7:00 we had to do the pans all over again, because the previous KP detail had put dirty pans in the rack. We got blamed for it and had to work until 10:30, in all about eighteen hours straight. We went to bed without a shower, only to awake at 5:00 AM for more drill. What a day; I'll never forget it. Thank God, I'll never land KP again.

I hear that while I was at KP, the ambulance kept going back and forth to the drill grounds to retrieve some of our boys who had fainted from the heat. They're really working us to toughen us up. When we fall to the ground to fire our rifles, they order us to "bust the deck" or "break the ground wide open." Some of our instructors are Marines. There's a detachment of them on the base. It's truly Marine training.[4]

I hope Dad doesn't have any high hopes for me because there are hundreds of thousands of men here. The navy or the army doesn't give a damn about the individual.[5] My chance of getting anyplace at my age is pretty slim.

I'm feeling fine and am as healthy as could be. The hard work has done me good. As I said, I like it so long as I know it's going to end in a few weeks. If it were to last forever, I'd go nuts.

Camp Peary 7/13/43

Dear Dad,

I'm very busy. We're still drilling and attending lectures about rifles and hand grenades, navy laws, and Japanese and German fighting methods. You'd think I'm in the army. I often wonder myself. We are given this training so that we can defend ourselves, if we have to, against the enemy while on a construction project. It's really good. The Marines that generally accompany Seabee outfits do the fighting. I doubt whether I'll ever see combat, but the training is worthwhile just the same.

Remember how strict the Army Air Corps was in the Clark Gable[1] movie?[2] Well, they're just as strict here. Shoes cannot extend beyond the side of the bed; blankets must be folded in just the right way and our duffel bags must hang only so far from the floor. And it's a MUST that our barracks pass inspection.

After receiving three shots in the arm yesterday, I felt sick all day—a headache and a swollen arm. Since none of us were fit to shoulder a rifle, we drilled without one. Today I learned about the latest U.S. carbine.[3] Quite a piece. The enemy has nothing like it.

The weather has been lousy—rained three times today. In fact it has rained every day since I've been here. You can give Virginia back to the Indians.

Just got back from a USO show. Boy, was it swell! It consisted of dancing, singing, comedy, and music, all directly from Broadway and Hollywood. Some of the performers were stars from Deanna Durbin's[4] latest picture.[5] I'd like to see more of this.

I'm so busy that I haven't had a chance to get homesick. Still, I'll be glad to get home. Please write. I'd appreciate getting a letter every day. I feel dejected when no letter arrives. We all feel the same way.

Camp Peary 7/14/43

Dear Folks,

Norman[1] is to be pitied, poor boy. But he has it easy compared to this boy. I'm doing a three month course in military training in four weeks. Take today. I shouldered a gun in the hot sun while wearing heavy coveralls that, drenched with sweat, stuck to my back. I stood at attention, looking straight ahead without moving an eyelid while streams of sweat, dripping off my face, burned my eyes.

Down here when it's hot, it's really hot. And it usually pours every day. No matter, we drill in the rain just the same. By the time we march back to the barracks, a good distance from the drill field, we are soaked to the skin. Fortunately, I don't have a cold. I seem to stand the strain as well or better than most.

So you think you know all about the Seabees, eh Dad? That's what you think. Even our officers don't know everything there is to know. The Seabees are the toughest, fightingest men in the service. We fight for what we build. Our motto is "Can Do." A comedian at the USO show last night told of a Seabee who, meeting a Marine, said, "Where have *you* been?" Oops, some sweat just dropped off my forehead onto the paper.

After questioning a CPO (Chief Petty Officer), I learned I will not be given an IQ or aptitude test. I feel downhearted. How can I show my ability? I doubt whether I'll be sent to a school; they don't have enough time to train men. I'm disappointed. I'm on the lookout for the first opportunity. Right now I'll look into doing swimming instruction. They do that here. I'm making the best of it, and I'm determined to become something, in spite of it all.

There are some fine clean boys in my barracks. In fact most of my bunkmates are pretty nice fellows and I get along with all of them. We'll probably be separated in advanced training, but I hope not. There are also a couple of wise guys here, but they don't bother me.

On Sunday after church services we drill. My feet are holding up well, but the others are complaining. I've used the safety razor three times for practice, but I prefer the electric razor. The wash room has electrical outlets, five showers and flush toilets which are kept spotless.

My eyeglasses don't interfere with my drilling. When they become covered with sweat, I merely take them off and wipe them clean with a handkerchief. I really would like sun glasses. The sun bothers my eyes a lot.

There are five boys my age in the barracks. Most of the men are in their middle twenties or early thirties and married. When someone meets a boy from his own state, is he happy! When we see a group marching, we yell out the name of our state to see if there's anyone from home among the marchers. All the men are as green as I am. The older men can't keep up with the younger fellows.

Ronnie can have my bathing suit. The navy gave us a black one. I also have five pair of dress pants.

You can't know what it feels like when a letter arrives. You feel warm inside. I find little time to write you, but I make time unless due to orders it's impossible. I write before I do my duties.

It's been a while since I've heard Dad's sort of humor. His three P.S.'s put me in stitches. Send me more, Dad. And Ronnie had better write, or, when I'm home on leave, I'll practice a few combat tricks I learned on him. Incidentally, Dad, there are many here who don't drink coffee or smoke, so there.

Since I have more time than usual to write tonight, my letter will be long. I like to write now. It feels good to write to someone, especially your folks.

I'm attending lectures, but I can't tell you what they're about. We can't tell our friends what we're doing, even on the drill field.

Our barracks is located near some woods. About ten feet from my window are five trees, and a couple of hundred yards beyond is a beautiful river, the York.[2] It's the largest river I've ever seen—about a mile across. It's a beautiful sight to catch the sun rising out of the river in the morning. Because steamers don't use the river, it's unspoiled. We are about sixty miles from the sea.

We have two fine woolly white blankets to keep us warm during the cool nights. When I awake at five in the morning for exercises, I hear all sorts of birds singing in the woods. I hear the whistle of bob-whites.[3]

With washing yet to do for inspection Friday, I must quit.

P.S. I've learned to appreciate home after being here. Worcester is a fine town, and you are certainly fine parents after hearing what others have to say about their parents. By the way, in case you're wondering, the letters N.C.T.C. on my letter don't stand for "No Cards Till Christmas," but rather "Naval Construction Training Center."

Camp Peary 7/15/43

Dear Ronnie,

I haven't received any letter from you yet. What's wrong? Let me know what you're doing. Have you done much swimming? Even though we have an outdoor pool, I never get a chance here. Our barracks had KP today, but this time my job was easier than last Sunday.

The weather has cleared—not a cloud in the sky. But it's still hot.

I don't think you'd like the Navy. If you so much as make a squawk to an officer, well, it's just too bad. Navy punishments are severe. The primary purpose of boot training is to learn discipline.

One fellow already broke his ribs following orders. Even though he knew what he had to do was dangerous, he did it nevertheless.

This camp, about twenty-six miles square, has seventy to eighty thousand men. It's so large that it's almost impossible to locate anyone here. I'll be glad when I'm through boot training. Although it doesn't bother me, it's a physical grind. Now I know why sailors go wild during liberty. Although we are plenty busy, being cooped up is monotonous.

Camp Peary 7/16/43

Dear Dad, the best one I ever had (it rhymes),

The weather is beautiful now, but it's terribly hot and humid. I understand that the land here isn't typical of the Virginia landscape. The Navy bought it for very little.

My glass frames broke, due to the terrific heat and sweat and banging around. But the lenses are intact. The GI glasses are made of steel and uncomfortable. Moreover, I couldn't have them sooner than two weeks. I'm sending the lenses home for new frames. I guess I can get along without a shock proof watch. By the way, no cameras are allowed on the base, so I can't send you pictures.

I've stopped shaving with the safety razor and use my electric. You mention that Seabees can take the V-12 test.[1] I'll be on the lookout for any tests offered. However, even if I passed, my eyes would hold me back.

I'm glad that you look forward to my letters. It makes me feel good. You can't realize how I look forward to your letters. I feel wonderful all day after receiving one.

I doubt whether this life will build me up more. I took better care of myself at home where I got more milk. Boy, do I miss milk. It sells like beer down here. By the time I get to buy some, it's all gone. I buy it at every opportunity. I think I got better food at home.

I forgot to mention they took my picture right after I had my butch haircut. It will be on my identification card, which I haven't received yet. They say the picture never resembles you, but rather some missing link. Anyone seeing the picture would think you had just escaped from Alcatraz.[2]

Ronnie's letter just arrived. Yes, A.S. stands for Apprentice Seaman. Yes, it's so hot down here that when you spit, it immediately starts boiling.

I wouldn't advise you to buy a '38 Chrysler, Dad. They're gas burners. Anyway, a '38 is too old. Yes, I do get up early in the morning and if I don't, it'll be just too bad. They serve butter, but not enough for me. I often go back for seconds, and, when they can't spare any, I go to the store and buy something. I was tempted to buy a whole pie today, but, not having had enough time to eat it, I didn't.

Camp Peary 7/17/43

Dear Mom,

I just received Dad's letter, with his salutation, "Hi Mate." I got a great kick out of it. When the fellows saw it, they laughed too. Ronnie's joke about sailors made a hit here.

They are letting up on us a little. We had another inoculation today which knocked most of us for a loop. Some got dizzy and fainted; others came down with a fever and went to the hospital. I have only a sore arm. I guess now I'm too tough for the stuff. This training is doing me good and teaches me a lot.

Oddly enough, I'm not as homesick as most of the fellows, but I'd still crawl back home on my hands and knees. I haven't the faintest idea what's going to happen to me and neither do the officers.

Our officer is a Mr. Ruppert, a Warrant Officer, and by coincidence a neighbor; he comes from Holyoke. He's a swell fellow. Since I'm not allowed to talk to him directly, I'll ask the two CPOs in charge of our platoon for permission to do so. Chances to get college training are slim, because, as I've said, we're a construction outfit. But don't worry, I'll speak up.

I train with my glasses on except when it's very hot. We don't have to watch our drill master anymore. We only have to hear his commands.

Although my instructor told me that S.A. means I won't be sent across but will remain here on special duty, I'm not so sure. It seems that the officers themselves don't know what S.A. (Special Assignment) means. I'm still trying to find out many things.

The population of this camp is 65,000. Today's temperature was 111. It was 110 two days ago. What a climate!

I hear I will get weekend leave and every fourth night off in advanced training, so pray for Rhode Island. You see, in boot we are in quarantine.

This morning was tough. We had sham battles in the woods with real but empty Springfield rifles. The woods are dense; you can't walk any distance without having to clear a path. It's real jungle and we sink up to our knees in the mud. We also crawl in it. It's like quicksand, worse than Guadalcanal.[1] One fellow had to be pulled out. My squad won a battle and lost one. I was taken prisoner twice. You'd like it Ronnie: it's like playing cowboys and Indians. We say "Bang, I got you, you're dead," and the "enemy" comes out with his hands up. It's a scream but it teaches us a lot. I was hiding in dense undergrowth when I heard a twig snap. I took a leap, sinking above my ankles in oozy mud, and screamed "Hands up." Just as I suspected, they were from a gang we weren't even fighting. I "killed" one fellow three times.

I received some letters from Aunt Henrietta[2] in which she graciously offered me anything I wanted and asked me not to be bashful. She suggested cookies. Also Sadie[3] sent me an informative letter. She said that were I to write to Bill[4] or Grandma,[5] she too would read the letter. That way I could cover the three of them.

I love you for writing so faithfully. I look forward to mail time.

Just remembered: Southerners treat us Yankees pretty well but hate Negroes.[6] Negroes are kept separate in another part of the camp.[7]

Don't worry about my getting enlarged muscles. This training will break me before it will build me, so don't get funny, seeeee.

It's about time Dad did some typing. It's good exercise.

So long, *hasta la vista, au revoir, gesundheit* and good luck,

Camp Peary 7/18/43

Dear Dad,

Is Mother in the hospital yet? If not when does she go? When she's there, let me know how things are going.

I had an interesting morning. I slept until seven. Boy, it was heaven. We were allowed to sleep late because of church and our inoculations; doggone it, if I didn't wake up at five as usual, but I was able to fall back to sleep. Well, after a good breakfast of Wheaties, milk, bacon and eggs, two plums, apples and coffee (I had water), we loafed around until nine-thirty when a four wheel drive truck picked up the Jewish boys and drove us to a synagogue eight miles away. I saw more of the camp on the ride; the landscape was beautiful. We traveled along the York River; on the opposite shore was historic Yorktown.[1]

We finally arrived at a cute little synagogue surrounded by green lawns and maple trees. It was simple, clean and new inside. Services lasted about an hour and a half; they were quite good. A few distinguished speakers conducted dedication exercises. The program is enclosed. The camp's captain and the senior Jewish chaplain of the navy spoke. Fine speeches.

From my barracks, Goldstein, a native of Manhattan with a "toidy toid" street accent came with me. I was amazed to see that there were sixteen Jewish fellows in my area. There were hundreds of Jewish Seabees attending so that many had to stand. The Newport News B'nai Brith[2] donated a Torah.[3] Only three women were present, two from New York. Boy, were they popular. It has been so long since anyone has seen a woman, everyone wanted to shake their hands. It was pretty funny. We were given USO post cards afterwards and a Mazuzah by the Jewish Welfare Board. It's a small locket containing a part of the Torah to be hung around the neck.

I went swimming in the pool and enjoyed it. They wanted me to do handstands. Got it down to a T now.

Camp Peary 7/19/43

Dear Mom,

I must tell you about a few things I learned from a CPO. It seems that in boot training I can't do much to improve my rating, but I must keep my record clean which is fairly easy. In advanced training I can apply for an officer's commission. Of course, my eyes aren't good enough and I'm too young to qualify for a commission. However, I could be a CPO. For this I'll have to work hard and speak up. I'm going to investigate various opportunities while I'm still in boot training. Things seem brighter after learning about this.

I'm getting to like this life more every day. I don't mind taking orders, but someday I'm determined to give them.

I saw a really wonderful USO show. Although I was sick in the head and stomach and had a sore arm from the jabs, I wasn't as sick as the others, and I was able to stick it through. Three more jabs to come, darn it. I'm sure to remember about my clothes because every night I dream of putting them away according to regulations. Please, when I get home don't let me ever see a pot or pan. I count them at night instead of sheep. And when I get home, I want to sleep until two in the afternoon. I want to eat without waiting in line. I want to rest and do just what I want. That would be Utopia.

In inspection our barracks ranks among the highest. I personally have a clean inspection sheet. I'm beginning to like Virginia more. The weather has been beautiful for several days.

When you are in the navy, promises mean nothing. The navy does what it wants with you no matter what any pamphlet says to the contrary.

Today was supposed to be a duty day for our barracks. I got up at the usual five o'clock hour ready for exercises. But since the officer who conducts them didn't show, the fellows asked me to put them through a workout. They know my athletic background from my physique, visible when we take showers. With the CPO's approval I put them through a few simple exercises. Afterward, my detail was assigned to cleaning the officers' quarters, which included an hour spent cleaning the floor (or swabbing the deck in navy language). Hitting the deck means falling to the ground; cracking the deck wide open means falling to the ground so hard that you break a rib or two. Then with another detachment we were ordered to load bags on a truck which never showed up. We loafed for an hour, until I was ordered to relieve a guard on guard duty. After putting leggings on, I stood guard from 10:30 to noon, when the corporal of the guard ordered me to eat and dress into my whites by 12:20. I suspected a catch, but one thing you must remember in the navy above all: keep your mouth shut and don't volunteer. Even the officers tell us that.

At the appointed hour I was on a bus with most of my shipmates on the way to Williamsburg. I learned later that the commander received instructions to find forty men immediately for a tour of that town. Since our barracks was nearest to the commander's office, we were the handiest and therefore chosen.

We arrived in Williamsburg with six buses from other sections of the camp. The weather was beautiful, not too hot, not a cloud in the sky. We were immediately ushered into a small, attractive, air-cooled theater. There we were informed that we were guests of Mr. & Mrs. J.D. Rockefeller, Jr.[1] and that we would be divided into groups of thirty with a hostess assigned to each to show us the town. We were shown a short film on the town's restoration to its original state in 1705. The tour, which was to last four hours, was only an introduction.

The tour began with the Governor's Palace, absolutely the most beautiful home I have ever laid my eyes on. It had the original chandeliers of sterling silver and English cut glass and the most beautiful antiques you ever saw. We went through every room. It would take pages to describe it all.

The garden, the terrace and the private canal were also beautiful. All the governors from the late 1600s through the early 1700s lived here. Then we visited the museum which was the original courthouse. Next we saw the old powder magazine where we saw the real guns that were used in the early days. We toured the George Wythe house in which Washington and Jefferson had lived. It was truly beautiful. It would take a week to go through the entire town.

We didn't get to see William and Mary College[2] or the Old Capital, but we saw the old church with its old graveyard. The interior of the church was beautiful. Everything was restored to what it had been in

1700. Even the women guides were dressed in costumes from the early times. When the tour was over, we had seen only a fraction of what we wanted to see.

After the tour, we visited a beautiful drugstore where I had my first chocolate malted in a long, long time. Boy, it tasted like ambrosia. The other fellows were too excited over seeing girls to join me. It has been so long since they've seen them that they went nuts. Boy, it was funny. Although I've only been away two weeks, it felt strange to see men and women in civilian clothes and cars, and to sit in a drugstore drinking a milk shake. What a wonderful experience. Someday I'd like to return and see more of the town. The hostess said that the USO could make the arrangements if ever I decided to visit. Before the war the town had a population of only two thousand, but due to the existence of Camp Peary it has grown three fold. When I asked the hostess what she thought of northerners like me, she said she sees so many that they don't bother her.

I'd like you and Dad and Ronnie to visit Williamsburg when you can afford it. You'd love the beautiful furniture and the old styles. Ronnie would like it because of the historical interest. The English lords lived here after Jamestown[3] as did the American troops during the battle of Yorktown across the river. Let's hope you'll visit someday.

Camp Peary 7/20/43

Dear Dad,

I have some good news. Today I was promoted to Seaman 2/c. My pay will only be increased $4.00 a month to $54.00, but this should pay for most of my insurance. I wasn't promoted on merit because I didn't do anything to deserve it. Every apprentice seaman in my area received the same promotion. Personally, I suspect something is up. I smell a rat. Under the new rate I wear two stripes on my sleeve.

Do you remember how I used to dread writing letters? Well, now I really love to write and tell you about my experiences.

Camp Peary really can be beautiful. My spot is beautiful as I look over the river—which is wider than any lake I've ever seen, including Webster Lake[1]—and see the reflected rays of the sunrise coming out of the shimmering water. It's so gorgeous I'm held spellbound every morning. The fellows think I'm nuts. Now it's about sunset, and I'm sitting in the woods against a big black walnut tree that overhangs the river's edge. I'm completely relaxed. I often write here.

I can't figure out how I'm able to get up in the morning. At the beginning they had a hard time waking me, but now I get up promptly myself.

We are allowed no excessive baggage, not even a hanky. They give us everything we need. I love the toilet kit you bought for me. They give us sewing equipment.

I don't have much time to spend money. Today I bought a pint of vanilla ice cream—good stuff, only 15 cents. I keep my money in a money belt which I wear at all times, even at night. The zipper on the money belt is rusting due to my perspiration, but it still works. There are many boys here my age so I don't lack for friends. I made friends with one fellow in his late twenties from LA. He had studied engineering at the University of California for five years, the last two on scholarship, and he was only an apprentice seaman until today when he was promoted to Seaman 2/c. He couldn't get a commission because of his bad eyes. What a shame, a man of his knowledge and ability. But he's taking it well. He speaks intelligently, has traveled a lot, and he's clean.

There's another fellow here who was in the plumbing business in Detroit and invested $8,000 to fulfill a plumbing contract. He was only able to take on the contract after he was reclassified from 1A to 3A, but then he was reclassified again to 1A and inducted into the Seabees. He lost his entire investment. I've seen pictures of his home and car. To top off his bad luck, he had a fall resulting in internal injuries and was laid up in the hospital here for a couple of weeks. Compared to him, I feel fortunate.

The mosquitoes aren't so bad here because of insect control. I'm sorry to hear about the Hotel Bancroft.[2] My suntan is fading. Boy, do I wish I could strip to the waist when drilling but no can do.

We had drill competition today. Our outfit came in second, losing by only one point because one fellow fumbled. We'll have another opportunity next week, and we'll do our best to win.

Well, Dad, I've run out of writing material tonight. (Aunt) Pearl[3] just sent me another letter. Damn swell of her.

Camp Peary 7/21/43

Dear Ronnie,

I received four letters today, a new high: a card from Dad, a letter from you, one from Aunt Ida[1] and a letter from the Gallants.[2] I really deserved them because I was worn out. I had the worst day yet. We began the morning as usual, rising at five, then chow, then raising the colors. We got our rifles and marched to the drill field. The sky was cloudless. We drilled under the broiling sun for two hours without a break for water or relief. Boy, were our mouths dry. Three fellows passed out, one while marching, and two while drinking water during a rest. Actually we all felt like passing out. Our heads ached, our bodies were drenched with sweat, and our clothes were soaked.

We were then given extended order drill—combat practice. We had to run, throw ourselves on the ground and crawl on our bellies. That's all we needed to be finished off. When we fell in the dirt, it became mud from our wet clothes. Our heads were swimming. One big bruiser fell into a bawling fit and passed out. After an hour and a half of this, we were too tired to march home; nevertheless, we were ordered to do so on the double. I was the only one who had enough pep to run. I tried coaxing the others, but they could only walk. If they had run, I'm sure they would have dropped.

This afternoon we attended a few lectures which enabled us to rest up a bit. As I'm writing this, I feel fine. It's about 5:30 PM. I have the rest of the evening to myself—yeah, to wash the soiled clothes I wore today. It's just like cowboys and Indians, Ronnie, except you can't stop when you want to.

I hear Uncle Louie[3] is moving near (Aunt) Ida. Ida is ambitious for (Cousin) Bob[4] and me. I wish she weren't, because I think she's due for a disappointment. By the way, I learned semaphore signaling[5] today.

Say Dad, it's sure swell of you to send me a card, even though Mother and Ronnie wrote. I got a great kick out of it. It's your grand sense of humor that keeps my chin up.

P.S. #1: I don't swear yet.
P.S. #2: I don't smoke yet.
P.S. #3: I don't drink coffee yet.
P.S. #4: I still like your food better, Mom.

Camp Peary 7/22/43

Dear Dad and Ronnie,

Received your letter and I love you both for it. Swell letters, all of them. I cried with joy when I heard the operation[1] was all over and Mother was doing well. I have KP tomorrow so I don't have time to write much. I'm feeling wonderful and carrying on in good spirits. Received five letters today, including yours, one from Aunt Pearl, and one from Johnson Fulgoni,[2] an acquaintance from the Y.

Camp Peary 7/23/43

Dear Folks,

Women are supposed to have intuition, a way of knowing things that are happening without being told. Well, some men do too. While I was in the synagogue Sunday morning, the idea that Mother was in the hospital came into my mind like a flash. I was stunned at the coincidence last night when I learned from your letter that she was in the hospital, and I was overjoyed to hear that she was doing well, well enough, I hope, to read and answer this letter.

The mails are treating me gloriously. Five more letters last night: from Ronnie, Aunt Sadie, my friend Lionel,[1] from another school chum, and a lovely letter from Aunt Anna.[2] But your letters are the first opened. The day isn't complete without hearing from you.

Yesterday we drilled, attended a few lectures, and participated in a sham battle. It was a tough day and terrifically hot. Today I have KP, serving food and swabbing decks. I must return to work in an hour.

I had two more jabs today, the last of them. They affected me less than the earlier three. My arm is only slightly sore. I'll have one more at the advanced base. I was lucky to visit Williamsburg because technically, as I've said, I'm in quarantine and am not allowed to leave the area.

All of us talk about leave.I'm really not anticipating leave with as much anxiety as others. Being cooped up is hard, I admit, but it doesn't bother me much. I don't want to give you the impression that I think only of leave. No siree. I've had enough disappointments now to expect anything without feeling sorry. In the Navy I've learned that it's best to expect nothing and await everything. I'm taking things just as I promised I would: accept them as they come. I can take it and I'm taking it. There are many others in far worse straits. Truly I'm fairly happy and in good spirits.

I'm glad that you met and talked with a Seabee. I don't know why he should be surprised that I was inducted. Many here have told me they were inducted into the Seabees against their will, and some never got ratings they were promised.

You've written me some marvelous letters, Dad. I hadn't realized how well you write. I'd as soon wait around for the mail to read one of your letters than to go to one of the shows. No kidding. I see that your English is improving when you use words such as "respite." Quite the guy, I must say.

Every time I read your letter about Mother doing well, I could cry with joy. I hope she can write soon. How is your leg holding up? From one of your letters I see you are still working late. After Mother's released from the hospital and fully recovered, why don't you get away, Dad? I was invited to visit a friend of mine from New York City while he's home on leave. Of course, I'd rather go home, but wouldn't it be swell if we could meet in New York while I'm on a long leave this summer—if I have one?

Well, Ronnie, in answer to your letter, no, we don't feel silly doing those sham battles. We see them as serious business. It's the strategy that counts and not the capturing or killing of men in themselves. In reply to your question, there are thirty men to a platoon.

I never realized I could put down such a big breakfast myself. It's the size of a dinner. You see, people from the west like big breakfasts, so it's served to us all.

Perhaps, Dad and Mom, you think I'm getting religious. Not at all. I have nothing to do on Sundays except to attend the synagogue. I find I also enjoy it. The service is liberal, more or less reform.[3]

My good night parting: a kiss for Mom, a handshake for Ronnie, and a bit of skin[4] for Dad. Blow it off and into my pocket.

Camp Peary 7/24/43

Dear Mom,

I'm really thrilled about your quick recovery. I can't wait to see you. If I could, I'd crawl back home on my hands and knees to visit you.

Dad and Ronnie have been prompt and dependable in writing letters. I guess we have a few authors in the family. Dad has also been sending cartoon postcards. Both I and the fellows in the barracks get a great kick out them. Dad and Ronnie's sense of humor is unsurpassable.

Today was the easiest I've had so far. We loafed all morning, received our dog tags and dress blue jumpers (the blue uniform top). Next week we break camp. I talked to an officer about my predicament. He told me to make my aims and background known to my platoon officer in advanced training. He also said that boys without trades were drafted into the Seabees for pick-and-shovel work, but I'll try to avoid it. As for recognition, I'm only a second class seaman and observed no more closely than anyone else. By the way, you're still using A.S. after my name. Please use S 2/c.

Dad suggested I bring his business cards[1] to Williamsburg. Well, Dad all the antiques were in good condition. The upholstery looked perfect, so no soap.

I want to send you a letter that I received from the artist friend whom I know from the Y and the Art Museum. He is a learned man, a cripple, and a graduate from the Massachusetts College of Art.[2] Please return the letter because I keep them all and read them over.

Camp Peary, Sunday AM 7/25/43

Dear Ronnie,

Today should be a fairly easy day. We'll drill a little this afternoon. The weather is beautiful, with a wonderful breeze.

I went to bed at 10:30 last night and was allowed to sleep until 8:00 this morning. But for the life of me I couldn't sleep beyond 6:30 which is still an hour and a half later than usual.

I'm feeling wonderful and am beginning to enjoy things now that it's getting easier and the hubbub and confusion of the early days are over.

Another unit is leaving for California this week so chances are we won't go there. I should know where sometime next week.

It seems that the Seabees are becoming better known. I heard that one of our officers, while walking the streets of Washington, was stopped by a distinguished civilian who asked what part of the navy he was in since he wore unfamiliar tans. Well, when the officer replied that he was a Seabee, the civilian was impressed. Seabees are all set; they're welcome in all circles.

There's the story about the Seabee who, while walking along a street in New York, was stopped by three Marines. Expecting a fight, he was surprised when the Marines asked to shake his hand. They noticed the Seabee emblem on his arm. The Marines had seen the splendid work and fighting by the Seabees at Henderson Field on Guadalcanal. As the field was being bombed the Seabees filled the bomb craters with their bulldozers as fast as the bombs fell. This is a true story and official.

There's also the story about a scheduled attack on one of the Solomon Islands that was supposed to pave the way for the Seabees' arrival. Well, the schedule got mixed up and the Seabees arrived first. By the time the Marines arrived, the Seabees had already cleared out the Japs. The Marines confess that the Seabees are the toughest fighters they've ever seen. When the Marines finish a battle, they rest; but when the Seabees are done fighting, they return to work repairing the damage and working at construction.

Well, it's just as the Commander told us: "If you keep your mouth shut and your bowels open, you'll do all right in the Seabees."

Camp Peary 7/26/43

Dear Folks,

It poured last night and washed the air clear. Today was beautiful, ideal for a hike. We walked all morning at any easy gait. First we went along the river, which I learned is three miles wide at this point, not the two miles I had thought. What a beautiful view. Then we went through a wonderful, cool forest and later passed the rifle range where I heard all kinds of firing from rifles, machine guns, and so on. It sounded like a battle was going on. I saw a young doe trotting through the woods. I hear the game was abundant here before this place was built only last October. We had a pleasant seven mile jaunt with rifle and pack, a mere introduction to longer hikes in the future.

We returned home in time for chow when I found Mom's letter waiting. It was packed full of news that made me feel fine and dandy for the rest of the evening. I also got two swell post cards from Ronnie. Mom, I'm so glad you went through the operation well; most of the fellows here know about it. I just couldn't keep it to myself. Oh, I'm so happy to know that my letters help you. You've all been wonderful writing. Dad and Ronnie were swell during your crisis. If it's inconvenient for you to write, Mom, I'm sure Dad and Ronnie will do their best to compensate. But I suppose by the time you receive this letter, you'll be fine and strong.

I also received a letter from (Cousin) Lil[1] at Pocasset (Massachusetts) and one from Aunt Pearl who has certainly been swell. I also got a very nice letter from Mr. Riccius,[2] the old man whom I met at the Y. He offered to help me at any time. I received a card from Barnett L., another friend who is going into the army. The eyeglasses you sent me are fine and so is everything else, except for the food which could be better, but I'm not complaining because we leave Sunday.

Enclosed is a money order. Please use it for yourselves, just this once. Dad should take at least five dollars as his birthday present for last July 10th. Use the rest for hospital expenses or clothes.

Camp Peary 7/27/43

Dear Dad,

Sorry, but the chrome bolt that held the head of my electric razor fell down the drain. I really treated it carefully, but it was an accident. Please send to Boston for the Schick Colonel part. Let me know when you receive it, and I'll tell you where to send it.

Camp Peary 7/27/43

Dear Mom, Dad and Ronnie,

Things are routine around here, so I don't have much to write about today, but I'd like to mention the food we had today.

For breakfast I ate the following: one bowl of Rice Crispies and milk, an apple, two pieces of some kind of meat (They tasted like lamb chops) and potatoes, bread and butter, and water. But since I was still hungry I returned to the cafeteria line and had a bowl of Quaker Puffed Sparkies with milk, a ladle full of Farina[1], and another apple. After breakfast I bought and drank a pint of milk. And when one of my buddies also bought me a pint, I drank that also—which makes about 1 1/2 quarts for breakfast.

For dinner I had lettuce, tomatoes, roast beef and gravy, some sort of beans, bread and butter, water, and cake and ice cream. The others had coffee or tea but, of course, I won't touch it. Before dinner I bought a pint of milk and a full sized apple pie to add to my meal. So I drank the milk, ate three quarters of the pie and sold the other quarter.

I haven't had supper yet. Who knows what we'll have? I'm not getting any heavier due to the hard work and heat. I do feel fine. However, most of the others say they feel lousy. They complain they don't get enough sleep. To be sure, 9:30 to 5:30 isn't much sleep after such hard work. It's not easy for most to fall asleep as soon as lights go out, but I'm under as soon as I hit the pillow. I guess I'm taking the activity pretty well, because I feel none the worse for it. When I awake in the morning I'm alert, but the others are half dead.

Our dog tags are metal strips attached to a neck chain. They are marked with name, ID number, blood type and the letters USN. I also have an ID card with my picture on it, if you want to call it my picture. If I really look like the picture, I pity the poor photographer.

I'm sad today because I received no letters. I hope you had good reason for not writing. It's an awful let-down when you're used to getting a constant stream of letters from home. I'm sure that you were all so busy that you couldn't write, and certainly I'll excuse Mother. I realize it must be hard sometimes. I find it so, too. Usually I write two or three letters a day, and always the letter home is the first one.

Say, most of the fellows are receiving candy or cookies. How about sending a little chocolate or something? It's hard to get such stuff here in boot camp. I guess you think it's nervy of me to come outright and ask you. But I'm sure you understand that if it's inconvenient, you don't have to. It doesn't have to be much. Only a little would satisfy my craving.

Let me tell you a little about the fellows I live with. Most keep themselves personally clean. However, one fellow from Tennessee in the next barracks was dirty and was warned by his officers to clean himself and his clothes. When he didn't, before the officers got the chance to punish him, his shipmates jumped him, took him to the showers, poured Rinso[2] over him and scrubbed him, clothes, shoes and all, with a stiff brush.[3] Boy, has he been clean ever since!

We have three or four college graduates here. They were tricked just like me and drafted. Even our officers admit that the recruiting stations are misleading and unfair. There are a few boys my age; we get along well. We have many discussions. I avoid arguments, haven't had any yet and don't intend to argue with anyone.

The worst punished offenses in the navy are fighting and gambling: solitary confinement, bread and water for thirty days at the Commander's option. Since we don't have liquor there's no drunkenness. Swearing is prevalent, but it's not as bad as it was at first. In fact, there are several men in my barracks who don't swear, and they openly admit that they hate it when others do. Of course, there are always a few rotten eggs. The only one we had in our barracks was discharged weeks ago so now everything is fine.

Love, love, love, to the three of you.

Camp Peary 7/28/43

Dear Folks,

In tonight's mail I received one letter from each of you, so I'll start with Ronnie's.

You certainly have a swell sense of humor, Ronnie. I enjoy your letters very much. I can always count on a good laugh when your letters arrive. I'm glad you had a chance to see a stage play. I've never seen one, even a lousy one. So Dad thinks the ones in Boston are better. You just stick to your opinion about our modern plays even though Dad says the ones in his day were better. All Dads are alike. They all say the same thing.

You ask what I do in my spare time. All I seem to do is wash clothes, write letters and clean up. I'm so tired that I don't want to go anyplace, even to a show, during my free time from five to nine-thirty PM. I have no chance to get a tan because I can swim only after sundown. Anyway, I'm not crazy about the pool. It's small and overcrowded. So my tan is fading rapidly even though we have glorious sunny days. That one time I saw a USO show was an exception. I expect to see no more for a long time.

And now for you, Dad. On the drill field we are allowed to drink water only once in the morning and once in the afternoon. Too much water makes you sick. Don't worry, they don't give us ice water. It's that lousy chlorinated water, nearly warm. I don't mind it now. On the seven mile hike we were allowed no water. We're told to drink as much water as possible at night and in the early morning.

I'm glad that you're not concerned about how I'm taking the physical strain. I really don't mind it at all. I don't know whether I'm losing weight or not. We have no scales here. I doubt that I am.

Semaphore is not code, Dad. Different positions of the flags stand for letters.

So Garbo[1] told you a few things about volunteering, eh. Well, I knew that already. The officers themselves tell us we'll be safer if we never volunteer for anything.

They have incompetent medical help here who do things in a slack manner. I learned this from my bunkmates who have undergone treatment. It's because the camp is new.

A little sad news. A CPO told me today that after boot is over on Sunday, I face two possibilities. Either I'll remain here for advanced training or be assigned to Ship's company which is simply maintenance work at this camp. I felt pretty down about it, but now I'm over it. I guess I'm having some bad breaks—for a while anyway.

Now for you, Mom. I'm still thrilled over your quick recovery. I'll write twice a day if it would make your days shorter. To answer your questions, no, I don't think I'm thinner, but my hair is coming back. There'll be no waves for a long time though.

Mom, your letters are wonderful, so don't feel that because you don't have Dad's brand of humor something is missing. When I finish reading either of your letters, I'm deeply affected. I feel wonderful all day. I had never realized that the three of you could write such fine and loving letters. It truly touches me. When I read each letter, though I sense the different styles, I can tell that each one has the same sincerity and love behind the words. It's swell of you to write that you wish me the tops and offer your love. Tears came to my eyes when I read that you wished Ronnie and me to be the tops. I have plenty of time to think, and I'm not the type of boy to cry over being homesick. I'm proud to say, without bragging, that I've taken on responsibility for myself like a man.

But often I lapse into memories of home, of how I showed disrespect for you both, even for Ronnie.[2] Being away, I can look back and see myself as you and Dad saw me. I never realized how blind I was. It takes being away from home to learn how wonderful you were to me, how much you both worked for me. I have the swellest folks in the world, and nobody knows it better than I do. I can never repay you, I know, but I also know that you wouldn't expect any material repayment. My love and devotion will, I am sure, return to you what you gave me.

These are big words in meaning, but to me, as I sit here, they seem simple and easy to fulfill because I know I have what I must give. Please understand that I have not wasted time thinking up beautiful ways to write my thoughts. This is written in the heat of my deepest emotions. Let's live again amid the happiness of the past that I hadn't realized existed until I left.

My sincerest love to you all,

Camp Peary 7/29/43

Dear Dad,

Since we weren't cautioned [not to tell], I guess I can tell you what we did today. We had hand grenade practice; that is, we were taught the current way to throw one. We also learned how its mechanism worked. There's much more to it than I imagined. We were told about the various types of gases and their effects. After being given gas masks, and shown how to put them on, we were led into a chamber filled with tear gas and asked to remove our masks. The gas burns your eyes and makes them tear and your nose run, but it's harmless otherwise. It was awful and I hope I never have to go through such an experience again.

Don't be alarmed about what I'm going to say. I want you to know so that you won't be surprised when it happens. My chances of going overseas after advanced training seem assured. That's what they're telling us. We've been issued Marine helmets, but this doesn't necessarily mean that we'll be assigned to a combat area. The helmets are merely precautionary. You should know that I'll be sent across despite my nearsighted eyes. It's silly, of course, to be concerned, because I couldn't fight with my condition. I doubt if I'll have to. Furthermore, I made it clear to my superiors that I'm helpless without my glasses. When I didn't have them for a few days, I refused to participate in one of the sham battles. The officer understood so he made me a messenger. You see, Dad, I've done just what you suggested about my eyes.

I'm glad to know that Ronnie helps you so much. I guess he's becoming strong lifting all that furniture. He's a swell kid all right. I hadn't realized I'd miss him so. It's too bad we squabbled so much before I left, but that's forgotten. Our arguments were silly and meaningless. I love him plenty. When I am home on leave, we'll try to have swell times together. And when I'm home I'd be glad to help you at the shop.

No, I haven't done any handstands around here. The guys would think I'm nuts. I can imagine you doing a handstand. Boy oh boy!

After finishing yesterday's letter, I saw a muskrat sitting a few yards away and eating weeds. It even looked up at me. I usually write my letters while sitting on a carpet of pine needles, my back against a tree, in the woods behind the barracks. Here, where it's cool and beautiful, I'm alone and at peace. My awkward position and the fact that I'm writing on the small cardboard box in which I keep my paper, will explain my poor handwriting. I look forward to this time after eating when I'm relaxed and free to think of all of you, with no one to bother me. I hear only the birds singing. It's truly a delightful spot with the river in full view across the field to my left. Well, I must stop waxing poetic, and come back to reality. We're going on a long hike tomorrow.

Camp Peary 7/30/43

Dear Mom,

My dress uniform has been altered, with my rating sewn on the shoulder and sleeve: two stripes at the wrist, and one stripe around the right shoulder.

Went on a nine mile hike today carrying a rifle. I'm pleased to say that my feet fared well, feel as fine as they did when I awoke this morning.

Today I heard so many wild rumors from supposedly authoritative reports about whether we'll go across or not, that I'll just wait and see what happens. Nobody really knows anything. Today is our last day of rigorous training. Tomorrow we get KP again—my fourth time. Sunday we'll be in our dress uniforms for a thorough inspection. Monday we break camp. We know that some of us will go to Rhode Island, some will be assigned to battalions elsewhere and some kept here for camp maintenance.

Camp Peary 7/31/43

Dear Mom,

First they tell us one thing, then another. The C in CB stands for "confused." We're just flooded with rumors—scuttlebutt we call it—about where we're going. God only knows whether I'll be here for only a few more days or a few more months.

I was on KP today and, in addition to my regular meal, ate five pieces of apple pie with five squares of ice cream. Although I eat a lot, I don't look it. When I'm on KP I'm sure to get plenty of good food.

Had a haircut today—sides trimmed only. Now my hair is as long as if I had a close haircut. In a couple of weeks it will be back to normal length. The barber did a good job for fifteen cents.[1]

I'm dead tired. We're allowed to sleep until 6:30 tomorrow. Oh, boy.

Camp Peary, Sunday 8/1/43

Dear Folks,

Good news folks. I think I'll be having advanced training in Rhode Island and will be there in a few days. Tomorrow I'll move to another area where they're making up a battalion. Of course, my orders could be changed, but chances are I'll be assigned to the 113th battalion, headquarters company. A battalion consists of 1080 men. I don't know what "headquarters" means yet.

Since very few are assigned to this battalion, I consider myself fortunate. Some of my friends are coming too. But the Worcester man, Ted B., the dark haired lad who came here with me, has been assigned to Ship's Company which involves clerking, KP or mosquito control. Too bad. He won't be allowed home on leave. He feels pretty bad and has asked me to get in touch with his folks when I get to Worcester. Some were sent to a replacement center where they may have to wait months before being assigned to a unit. Others were assigned to a Super 7 battalion which means they go across immediately.

No doubt, I've got the best deal. Now I'll get good training and have a chance to show what I can do. From men who have been there, I've heard only good things about Camp Endicott in Davisville, R.I. They say it has modern conveniences, plenty of entertainment, and that I'll enjoy the place—although it hasn't been so bad here, after all. By the way, I've already worn out the soles of my GI shoes.

Camp Peary 8/1/43

Dear Cousin Lil and Sol,[1]

It was certainly swell to hear from you. Life would be very monotonous if I didn't have letters like yours to break it up.

I was glad to hear that you were able to get a little vacation. I know that Sol could use the rest. It's too bad that the weather wasn't a little better. You ought to have our weather down here. It's beautiful, but hot.

I guess Harold[2] has been able to see quite a bit of the country by now. I have seen only a few cities in the east, such as New York, Philadelphia, Washington and Richmond, but probably will see more before the war is over. I have already toured Williamsburg, that old, historic town. It is, without a doubt, the most beautiful town I have ever seen.

So you saw one of those camp shows, eh. I, myself, haven't had time to see a movie, but I did get away to see one swell USO show. I don't remember if I told you in my last letter.

Where you were is all army, and where I am is all navy, and boy, am I sick of seeing navy uniforms. Civilian clothes would be heaven right now.

Today we are breaking our boot training, and then I go into advanced. When I look back at this past month of July, I am glad that it is over. Between military drill, combat tactics, inoculations (7 of them), lectures, and last, but not least, KP, I was going just about nuts. However, I came through it beautifully and am just waiting for more to come.

I have been kept well informed through daily letters from Dad and Ronnie as to my mother's condition. You can well imagine how thrilled I have been to hear how well she is doing. I guess before long she will be home if she isn't already.

There isn't much more to say right now, so give my best regards to Aunt Eva[3] and the kids. Remember me to Shirley,[4] Eddie[5] and Joe Ducharme.[6]

Your loving cousin, Hughie

Camp Peary 8/3/43

Dear Mom,

I'm now in the biggest bedroom in the world, temporarily stationed in a gigantic drill hall 600 feet wide and 150 feet long with bunks enough to hold a complete battalion of 1100 men. The hall is so large that it has a speaker system. It contains clothes washing facilities, a vast area of clothes lines, and hundreds of spotless toilets and wash basins, even nicer than the ones we have at home.

Tomorrow we prepare for leaving on the troop train the following day. My company is the first to board the train. By the way, the food here is better than at the boot area. This morning we had close order drill, but mostly we're getting ready for the trip.

Last night while I was washing clothes—what else? it never ends—I looked up and across the table saw an old friend[1] from

Worcester. I knew him from the Y; he's quite an athlete. Occasionally he used to drive me home. He's assigned to another company, but I plan to keep in touch with him. He plans to bring his new Ford to Camp Endicott—sailors are allowed cars in advanced training—and since he expects to visit Worcester often, he's offered to let me join him if we have liberty at the same time.

I learned that Headquarters Company to which I'm assigned isn't considered a fighting unit. Our men are the cooks, musicians, draftsmen, signalmen, athletic and swimming instructors etc., men who provide services to the battalion. So far everything seems rosy.

We leave at 10:45 AM. If we stop in New York, I'll call either home or the store.

Camp Peary 8/4/43

Dear Dad,

I know you won't get this in time, but the call you expected tomorrow, Thursday didn't happen because I've since learned that troop trains never stop. Luckily, being in Headquarters Company, I'll be on the best car in the train. We'll be using the dining car while the men in the other cars get box lunches. Headquarters always gets the cream.

More good news: when we arrive in Davisville I'll get liberty. If its for more than 12 hours I'll go home. Perhaps, I'll be home by the time you get this letter.

I'm expecting a swell camp in R.I. compared to this one. It's on the ocean, only 18 miles from Providence.

I received a wonderful letter from Aunt Pearl. Besides you folks, she's, without a doubt, my most loyal correspondent.

Latest word is that I'll get a 12 hour liberty every fourth night, train at Camp Endicott for three weeks after which I get a ten day leave, then go overseas.

I'll be seeing you soon.

Camp Peary, 9:00 AM Thursday, 8/5/43

Dear Ronnie,

Today we leave. Boy! Got up at 4:00 AM, packed, and put on my dress whites. My company is the first to depart. We'll be on our way at 1:00 PM. Two troop trains will take us to R.I. I hope it's cooler up there. Here the heat is terrible.

As I write I'm watching some entertainment on the drill hall stage—a banjo and a chorus, and a short fellow with a fine voice. Song sheets have been passed out for some community singing.

Davisville, Rhode Island

113th Batt Co Hdqrs Plat A-B
NCTC Davisville, R.I.
Camp Endicott   8/7/43

Dear Folks,

Well, here I am in Rhode Island. There's no sense in writing a long letter because I expect to be home before the week is over. The camp here is beautiful—like paradise compared to Camp Peary. I'm fifteen minutes from the ocean where I can swim. There are plenty of places for good times and the food is plentiful. It's like living on a college campus. We have Marine instructors here. There are also WAVES.[1] The barracks are beautiful two story structures with loud speaker systems. And, boy, is the weather and air swell compared to Virginia's. Give me New England any day. Be seeing you.

Camp Endicott 8/7/43

Dear Mom,

Your letters of Tuesday and Thursday were waiting when we arrived Friday night. I never enjoyed letters more. For a woman just recovering from an operation I'd say you're all right.

The weather and climate here in New England is so much better than the blasted climate of Virginia. It was enough to drive a man nuts. You can't walk without your clothes becoming soaked with sweat. And when you were thirsty, you had only that lousy lukewarm, chlorinated water to drink. We're on the ocean here—I saw the beach last night—and the nights and mornings are cool. You keep your hands in your pockets to keep them from freezing. The afternoons are warm, and sometimes hot, but not the way it is down south. You don't perspire nearly as much. I like this climate much better.

I'm happy to know that my mail entertains you. If you can't figure out where I put all that food, you'd know if you were out here drilling with me. By the way, the day I bought five pieces of pie and ice cream, I also bought a pint of ice cream that night. The food here is wonderful, one hundred percent better than at Camp Peary. And milk is readily available.

By the way, Ronnie ought to see the beautiful gym we have here. I must cut this letter short—muster call in a few minutes. I have $4.00

which I think is enough to get me home. I had expected to get paid Thursday but didn't. I sent you a telegram because I couldn't phone.

Camp Endicott 8/8/43

Dear Folks,
Now I'm sure to be home Thursday. They're all mixed up here. Won't eat here so expect me home for chow. Have watch strap ready.

Camp Endicott 8/9/43

Dear Mom,
Never in all my life did I enjoy myself more than when I was with Dad and Ronnie yesterday. It's too bad you couldn't come, but I realize the trip would have been too strenuous.

Camp Endicott 8/10/43

Dear Mom and Dad,
Tough breaks are hitting me smack in the face again. True, I'm near home and in a fine camp, but I'd rather be back in humid Camp Peary than endure what's ahead of me. I've been assigned to twenty-one days of KP, twenty-one of what will be the most miserable days of my life. It's the dirtiest, rottenest deal in this navy. I'll never be recognized or become anything. Even after putting in the twenty-one days, I'll not be trained for anything except KP. You might wonder why I'm being so blunt. Well, I want you to understand my predicament, and abandon those sweet dreams that both of you have for me. I've already given up any thought of being given an opportunity to advance. All I can do is wait for this damn war to end, then further my education. So long as I'm in the navy, I have nothing promising in store for me.
When I learned about my going on KP prematurely, I couldn't help letting a few tears drop. But I kept all my feelings to myself and kept quiet. After I contained myself, I thought more clearly and went to see my company chief, CPO Tretter, a man about Dad's age.
When I entered his office he could easily see that I was blue. After he kindly asked me to sit down, I talked plenty. He told me that twelve boys were chosen to be swimming instructors, boys, I saw, who didn't have nearly the experience I had. I explained that I had more training than most of them, and that I could secure a recommendation from one of the foremost physical directors in the country. I told him I had been enrolled in college before I was drafted, and that my high school record was all A's. As he listened to me attentively, I suppose my voice

broke somewhat, but I kept calm and cool. I ended by asking, "What can I do?"

He answered thoughtfully, weighing his words. He said that he was an insurance man back in Oregon, and that he could be cleaning up thousands if he had stayed there. He said that this war is to be won by all of us, and that whatever each of us does will help. Although he realized my term on KP seemed like an eternity, it's my job, and I should reconcile myself to it. Then he said, in all sincerity, from the bottom of his heart, he feels I have been one of the foremost boys in the battalion. Right from the beginning he saw I had initiative. He said he admired me for coming to him, of facing him; there aren't many boys who would have had the nerve.

He gave me some final words of advice: don't make a scene, don't go to my commanding officer, let him, the CPO, take care of my complaints. After we're at the base for a while, and the commanding officer isn't so busy, he'll obtain an interview for me because he felt I have something. I agreed to cooperate because I really have confidence in him. I like him very much and I think he feels the same way about me. However, I think he said what he did only to console me. He can't really do anything for me because he has no authority. Believe it or not, there's a man with a college degree in my KP detail. So what chance do I have? I'll have to be satisfied—but I'll be damned if I will. I'm determined more than ever to become something—even if I have to make the opportunity myself. I'm not afraid to go the limit. I'll wait a few weeks to see what happens and if nothing happens, I'll make it happen.

Without going into the details of KP duty, which in itself is easy, it's the lack of sleep that gets me. Although I wasn't getting enough sleep before, with KP I have to awaken an hour earlier than usual. I guess I'll just have to get used to it.

I know I don't have to tell you these things, and instead I could glorify what I'm doing in the navy, and you wouldn't know the difference. But I realize you are broad minded enough to understand. Although you will probably feel bad, you'll get over it. I feel better for not hiding anything from you.

There's one good thing about my detail: I'm safe and subject to no danger. After all, that's the main thing. This war is merely transitional, and every transition is really unimportant. It's the outcome that counts; it's the outcome I'm interested in. I expect to come out of this a better man than when I went in. That is my ultimate aim whether it's KP or college. My ideals have been raised all the more as a result of the breaks, whether good or bad, and from my association with all sorts of men here.

Your faith in me has really encouraged me in whatever I do. When I met Dad and Ronnie at the guest house, I could feel their understanding and love.

I feel relieved after writing this letter. I'm keeping my chin up.

Camp Endicott 8/11/43

Dear Mom,

Received your letter and Dad's last night. I'm sorry that Dad and Ronnie found it so inconvenient to get home,[1] but neither of you need visit me any more because I can get home every four days.

When your letter arrived I was on my way to a swell show. Coincidentally you asked me to have a good time so I had one last night. The show consisted of a battle between the Seabee orchestra and the one from the Newport naval base. They played hit tunes, semi-classical and jazz. There were some fine singers, among them a man with a marvelous voice. There was also a remarkable violinist. Boy, could he make the fiddle talk. Some Waves also sang. One of them, without a doubt the most beautiful girl I ever saw—a dead ringer for Hedy Lamarr—was in an evening gown. A magician cracked a few jokes. Here's one: A second class seaman, saying that he wanted to go home because his wife was going to have a baby, asked his commander for liberty. Of course the commander graciously consented. After liberty the seaman came marching in to thank the commander. The commander asked, "Well, was it a boy or girl?" The sailor replied, "Now Commander, you know those things take time."

As the chaplain said, you need liberty to lay the keel but not to launch the ship.

I realize you're a little shaky yet, so I don't think I'll bring anyone home with me.

I'm raring to eat corned beef and potato salad. Lead me to it. Boy oh boy.

My chief, Mr. Tretter, has already spoken to the company commander about me. I'll have an interview in two or three weeks. He told me to stay on the ball at KP because I'm being watched. If I do well, I'll be all set. I've really found a friend and booster in Mr. Tretter.

Home, here I come.

Camp Endicott 8/13/43

Dear Folks,

I was really worried last night when the guys were late to show up. They said they were delayed because they had long goodbyes.

We left Worcester about 1:30 AM after stopping for a bite in a lunch cart. I slept all the way into Providence. Boy was it pouring. When I awoke it was still coming down in torrents. Strangely, we didn't know the way to Camp Endicott from Providence. We asked one man for directions, but he spoke so fast and left so quickly that we didn't know what in the world he was saying. By luck, we ended up at the bus terminal where we met a sailor — coincidentally a Worcester boy — who was going to Endicott and who knew the way. We arrived in camp at 3:30. I slept for only three hours, but I don't feel in the least tired. Tonight I'll probably go to bed at eight so I'll be rested for Saturday night.

I'm going with the sailor to Worcester Saturday night, but will probably return by bus because I have tickets and can get back early. After being home, I feel wonderful today, and now I have the weekend to look forward to.

Camp Endicott 8/16/43

Hi Ya Folks,

Made the last bus on time last night. It was fortunate that I got a seat so that I slept mostly all the way. A pharmacy school grad, stationed at Newport, sat next to me. He gave me a few tips about the navy; I really enjoyed hearing what he had to say. He thought that for Dad to go to the Red Cross was a swell idea. He said he had passed the physical for the V-12 program, and despite being a college boy, still couldn't get in.

When I arrived in Providence, there was another bag on the bus in place of my blue bag. Since there was a name on the other bag, I dashed into the terminal and located mine. My paper bag was also gone and another in its place, but I hadn't realized it wasn't mine until I heard a fellow exclaim that the bag he had contained whites that weren't his. I then discovered that he had my bag and I his. Boy, what luck. I learned a real lesson. Evidently while I slept, the other fellows took the wrong bags. From now on, I'm going to keep my bag under the seat instead of on the rack.

At 1:00 AM the line waiting for the bus to Endicott was blocks long, and I got at the end and settled down for a long wait. Fortunately, when I reached the half way mark in the line, a second bus came and took us. However, I had to stand all the way from Providence to Davisville. But I didn't mind and arrived at camp at 2:00 AM. Although it was short, I had a good sleep last night and I feel rested. Tonight I'm going to bed early, though.

It's official: My ten day leave begins September 2.

Camp Endicott 8/18/43

Dear Folks,

Got in last night about 4:00. We were late because we lost our way in Providence and landed somewhere in the sticks. We came down in a different car than usual, this time with the two fellows' wives so they could drive the car back to Worcester. I slept most of the way.

Bud[1] was impressed with Worcester, and he really enjoyed himself. It turned out the supper you served was his favorite. He said, it couldn't have been better, and he can't get over how you knew that he loved french fries.

Camp Endicott 8/20/43

Dear Folks,

It's still the same old routine around here—very monotonous. I just tolerate it. We're leaving for a week of rifle practice at Sun Valley. We'll live in Quonset huts, ten or twelve to a hut. That will be a welcome change.

Posted on the bulletin board was a notice asking for V-12 applicants. I had all but one of the qualifications listed—my eyes, 18/20. Though I knew that, I hadn't given up hope. Now, however, V-12 is out of the question. When I went to the Red Cross yesterday to pick up my papers, I was told that they weren't able to contact my commanding officer. Don't be too hopeful; I'm not.

The fellow in the bunk next to me sleeps with his glasses on. One day I asked him why, and he answered that he can see his dreams better when he wears them. He also wears his watch so that he'll know when to awake. I'm not kidding.

Sun Valley 8/22/43

Dear Folks,

From here my letters will be slow in getting to you, so have patience. It's much more primitive here than down in Virginia. The toilets are chemical and everything is done in rough fashion. I believe we're living under conditions similar to an overseas base. We're about six miles from Camp Endicott. When we return to Endicott, we'll be in a different location from before.

As usual, I'm on KP here at Sun Valley, and I doubt if I'm going to get in any firing.

I received the pictures and am returning them with this letter, much as I hate to. The picture of me alone is lousy. Tear it up. But I rather like the one of us all together.

Nice of Lil and Sol to take you to Boston. What sort of operation did Yetta [Henrietta] have, or shouldn't I know?

Bud, the boy who came to Worcester with me, sleeps in the next bunk (We have cots).

Ray[1] is lucky getting a six day leave. The regular navy gets everything anyway.

Sun Valley 8/23/43

Dear Mom,

I have more time to write here at Sun Valley because we finish KP sooner than at Endicott. The sad part is that we have to awaken at 3:30 AM Of course, I have to go to bed at 8:00 or 8:30, but the others stay up until 9:30. I don't know how they do it.

I've been officially appointed M.A. (Master at Arms) of the galley. With fifteen men under me, I'm in charge of serving the food, and cleaning the galley and two mess halls. The responsibility is fairly heavy, and it really keeps me going. The part I don't like is having to drive the fellows to keep working. But we're getting better organized now, and by this afternoon I expect to have a cooperative unit. I try to be diplomatic with the fellows, and I pitch in and work along with them so all do as I say. I'll have this job for only the week, then back to the serving line again. I've had no interview yet with the commanding officer and the Red Cross still has my papers. I think the deal fell through and that I'll be on permanent KP.

I've heard some confidential information from an officer (which means it's official) who says that after our ten day leave, we go to Gulfport, Mississippi, for four days then on to California, arriving there by the 28th of September. I won't believe it until we're there, although the information did come from an authentic source. Whether it's true or not, don't tell anyone about this until I'm home. I don't know whether I'm even supposed to tell you, but since I wasn't cautioned, I guess it's okay.

I just learned that a dozen boys are going to swimming school. They're learning everything about swimming, including theory. I certainly envy them.

Send more letters if you can, even though I'm near. The day seems much longer when I don't get any. I hope you're restraining yourself. I bet Dad is working day and night. I can help him inside the shop and on the truck when I'm on leave. I can wear my dungarees.[1] I'm quite sure it's allowed. It's still a navy uniform.

Sun Valley 8/24/43

Dear Dad,

My new KP assignment really keeps me running around like a chicken with its head cut off. I must see that all my men are well supplied and kept busy. I rather like the job, though. Of course it's only temporary. The position might help me in future ratings—who knows?

I basked in the sun for 2 1/2 hours yesterday afternoon and have a pretty good tan. I have plenty of time off. I was just playing horseshoes, and I'm so rusty that I lost three out of four games.

I'm still rising at 3:30, but I don't feel the least tired because I rest during the day. Although I don't get as much milk here as I did at Endicott, I have a half pint of ice cream every day. Had six pieces of wonderful, delicious apple pie last night and I still didn't get full. I'm in a position to get plenty to eat, and boy, do I.

How is business? Has the fall trade pickup begun? I hope the weather is warm when I get home so I can get some swimming in. When does school start?

Sun Valley 8/25/43

Dear Folks,

Had a pretty good day yesterday—two more hours of basking in the sun and wrote a few letters. I received a long letter from Lionel Gallant. He's going to send me a picture next letter. He expects to have a seven day leave while I'm having mine.

I also received a letter from Mr. Aldrin (Assistant High School Principal) giving me the same advice as Mr. Beeber (the Principal). He can't do anything for me, but his letter was much finer than Mr. Beeber's.[1] I really enjoyed it. You should read it so I'm sending it along.

As far as I know, today is my last day on KP. Oddly enough, I was beginning to like the KP job, because each day I gained more prestige and authority. I had built a real working organization, and ran it more efficiently than the other M.A.'s. In fact, I was beginning to get some recognition. The head cook asked my name, and remarked to one of his men that I was the best man they've ever had on KP. I kept things moving, and ran an efficient organization.

I'm sure that if I stuck to KP, I'd be assigned a higher position possibly head M.A., especially since the present head M.A. is becoming a chief petty officer. Still, I refuse to take credit for the efficiency of my men, for they are really a fine set of boys. They seemed to take to me; I'm one of the few M.A.'s that is addressed by the first name.[2] They willingly do everything I tell them to do, while other M.A.'s have trouble with their men. Truly, I was beginning to make a success of KP.

I've now been assigned to signaling school, where I'll be taught semaphore and other works in signaling. I'll also be a messenger, whatever that entails. I don't know whether the signaling schooling will lead to a temporary or permanent position. At any rate, Chief Tretter is responsible for this assignment which should give me an opportunity to secure a rating. If I do well at this, I'll be more enthusiastic. At least I'm getting a better deal than some other fellows still on KP. So you see, my speaking up did at least retrieve me from KP. I've not had the interview yet.

I'm catching up on my sleep: slept two hours in the sun yesterday afternoon. I wasn't tired enough last night to fall asleep right away so I sat up and talked. I get paid Friday and have made out an allotment for $30.00 which you will get for September. Mother is the beneficiary. If you need the money, take it. It's yours.

I hear a new law has been passed that grants members of the armed forces who wish to enter college, tuition and living costs at government expense. See what you can learn about it. Maybe it's only a rumor.

As Lowell Thomas[3] says, "So long until tomorrow. Take it Hugh."[4]

Sun Valley 8/26/43

Dear Mom,

Even though I'm near home, I look forward to letters, anyone's. We have a man here whose home is only twenty miles away. You can't imagine how low he feels when he doesn't receive letters. I can't explain it, but somehow letters alleviate the desire to be home, at least to a degree.

Henry Wolf, a Jewish boy from Philadelphia, is planning to go to Providence with me on a twelve hour liberty Saturday night. Because he doesn't drink, we expect to have a swell time together. You see, one should only go with a mate having the same habits as yourself. If you don't, you'll have a miserable time.

I'm still on KP despite learning signaling. Signaling school is taught at night after KP. We're learning only semaphore, and if we succeed at it, we'll be given a signal man's rating and taught blinker dot-dash (Morse and International codes). A signalman is always visible to the officers, therefore he has a better chance to get a higher rating.

Now I must tell you about the compliment I received. The commissary Chief Petty Officer and head cook offered me a cook's rating. They'd send me to cooking school or teach me themselves. I'd start at $78.00 a month, in a few months be raised to $96.00, then to $126.00. Of course, I refused because cooking doesn't appeal to me, nor does the money interest me very much, and I don't care for a cook's rating. They approached me twice. The CPO said that I was a wonderful little worker and that nobody has come up to me yet. It made me feel really good. Instead of a detriment, now I've made my KP duty an asset. You can't imagine how many boys would like to become cooks. Many have applied, yet I was asked. When the Lieutenant interviews me, this will give me a boost.

Sun Valley 8/27/43

Dear Dad,

Mom wrote on the 25th that my letters didn't sound very cheerful. Well, that may be, but I really was; I'm in good spirits and not moping around. Really, I'm too busy to think of myself. It's only when I write home that I begin to think of myself. If I were brooding, would I be praised for my work? Not only do I take everything with a smile, I also do plenty of singing.

Confidentially, I'm not concerned about the Red Cross or a future interview with the commander. From a most reliable source, I learned how I stand in the eyes of the officers. As a matter of fact, I was told by two people that Mr. Tretter has been praising me highly, saying that I'm number one man in the physical education field. Unknown to myself, I was watched on KP and favorable reports were made. The officers are considering making me an instructor in physical education. I'd like that. So long as I keep "on the ball" (navy language) my chances will improve. I'm keeping my fingers crossed. After the war, I could go to college and secure a more thorough training in physical education. In physical education I'd have a chance to get a good rating. It's odd how things look black one minute and bright the next. I guess I don't have enough patience. In a recent book I read, there was a character who believed that things would come his way if he waited — and they did.

If I get to Mississippi I'll not be there long before I go to California. It's not hot there now. My ambition is to stand on the corner of Hollywood and Vine — if I get there.

You needn't explain that somebody else's grass looks greener etc. I realize what I have to go through and the disappointments I'll have to endure, so don't worry about my morale, Mom.

Since school starts the week I'm home, I'd like to visit a few of the teachers. I want Dad to take it easy when I'm on leave. I can help a lot in those ten days. Don't think that I'll be deprived of any pleasures. I'd rather work at the store. I know there's no sense in saying this to you, Dad, so I'm writing to Mother.

I haven't fired a gun yet and don't expect to for some time. Since I began this letter, I've seen Chief Tretter, who told me to be patient and that something will break soon. This corroborates what I heard yesterday. He said he's boosting me one hundred percent and that he's heard some fine reports about me. Now I'm sure things will improve.

I didn't complete this letter this morning because I had to fry some fish, halibut, the rest of the morning in the kitchen. Now I'm quite expert at it, even to regulating the temperature. Let me know whenever you'd like me to fry some, or just send ten cents in stamps, and I'll send directions free.

Sun Valley is a flat area about a quarter mile square. It's situated near the main highway at the bottom of a small incline surrounded by thick woods. No fence separates the place from the road. All structures are Quonset Huts, even the kitchens and mess halls. The entire battalion is housed here. The Marines, who train the men in gunnery, live on the outskirts. The ground is sandy, and dry under the sun which has shone every day until today. Now it's cloudy, and fairly cool. At night it's freezing. After taking 2 1/2 hour sunbaths daily, I'm as dark as the day I left Virginia. The latrines are so clean they have no odor. The hot and cold water showers are fine. While everything is crude, it's serviceable. I like roughing it. Even though it's rougher than Peary, I'd rather be here.

Camp Endicott 8/29/43

Dear Ronnie,

I'm now back in Camp Endicott and doing the same routine as before. My change of status was only for the duration of our stay in Sun Valley. Anyway, I have only three more days of mess detail.

Henry (Wolf) and I had a fairly good meal in the Waldorf[1] in Providence last night. Then we roamed the downtown until dark. Say, is that a busy place. Worcester is quiet compared to it. There are many tall buildings there, much taller than any in Worcester. We went to see "Hi Diddle Diddle"[2] with Adolph Menjou[3] and Martha Scott.[4] It was a beautiful theater, and enormous.[5] Even though the picture was fair, I enjoyed it and had a few good laughs. I preferred to see "Hers To Hold"[6] with Deanna Durbin, but Henry said he wanted a laugh.

At eleven after the show, we walked around the downtown again and saw people in every kind of uniform and girls wolfing.[7] Boy, are the girls hard up, despite the fact that the city is jammed with servicemen. I called up one of my mates who lived in Providence. He picked us up in front of the Biltmore Hotel, the swankiest hotel in town. Boy, is it beautiful inside and out. My friend showed us some sights, including the state capitol. This same fellow is driving me Thursday into Providence, where I'll meet another fellow who will travel with me to Worcester.

Camp Endicott 8/30/43

Dear Folks,

Yesterday was like a real Sunday even though I had KP. I read the *Globe*[1] and listened to the Sunday programs on the radio. Last night. I saw a USO show in which three performing artists sang and played. One singer who was famous (I don't remember his name) sang some operatic and classical pieces. He truly had the most beautiful tenor voice I've ever heard. Then a lady played a Stradivarius violin[2] Never before have I heard such a sweet tone from a violin. Then a beautiful girl from Australia sang some more opera and classical pieces. The three of them entertained us all evening. I certainly enjoyed all the beautiful music. I'll never forget "Ave Maria"[3] on the Strad, or the songs from *Carmen*.[4] I wish I could remember the performers' names. All are radio and screen stars. One of the singers played opposite Grace Moore[5] in a recent picture.

I'd like to see Fred Waring's[6] group which is due here on the 14th.

I stopped by the Red Cross today to pick up my papers. They told me they had written you and also got in touch with Lt. Henry. He told them that he was still busy organizing the battalion, but that he would watch me. At least I'm getting some attention but who knows what will come of it.

I'm bringing a few whites and blankets home to wash and have dry cleaned. They need it badly. Now that I'm experienced, I can do the wash myself. I'm also bringing work clothes so I can help in the store. They also need washing. I'm bringing only one pair of dress shoes, and I hope my old shoes will still fit. This is my last letter until I get home. So long until Thursday.

Camp Endicott 8/31/43

Dear Mom,

I didn't expect to write, but after receiving your letter I decided to anyway.

Our company commander bid goodbye to the company. It's a tough break for me, but still I have Chief Tretter behind me. There's still plenty of hope left even though I return to KP after my leave. I hope I'll be relieved of it. Since Mr. Tretter keeps my hopes up, I feel I'll be taken off KP sooner than the others. Why, I even have KP the morning of my departure, while everyone else in the battalion gets the time off to pack.

My mail isn't censored,[1] and I'm sure, neither is yours. You may rest assured that I refused the cook's position with tact. I'm sorry that you have the impression I have a chip on my shoulder. I don't. I'm taking things good naturedly. I'll get target practice at my A.B.D. (Advanced Base Depot).

I don't know when the Red Cross contacted the commanding officer who was at Sun Valley. What Dad said or did at the Red Cross, or what impression he made on the listener, doesn't bother me in the least. No harm has been done, only good.

I'm so glad you're getting your teeth fixed. I was about to insist on it when I got home. Speaking of teeth, I'd like to have an examination when I'm home. The dentists here are inefficient, and would as soon pull a tooth as fill it. I've also found that glasses here are no cheaper than at home. They sent us to a doctor in Providence and we paid full price. I think it would be good to have an extra pair of glasses on hand, especially in this outfit. They even recommend it. I learned that waterproof watches that regularly sell for forty or fifty dollars can be bought at ship's store for eighteen to twenty dollars. At those prices I'll buy one because it will last forever. A foursome Remington electric razor selling for $19.50 retail is $12.75 here. They're better than the Schick. I can't bring blankets home to be washed: not allowed.

So long. Be seeing you.

Camp Endicott 9/11/43

Dear Folks,

Arrived at camp about 3:00 AM and found my new quarters easily. To my utter surprise, I discovered my blankets, mattress and duffel bags on my bunk. Fortunately I was able to sleep immediately, sleeping until 7:00 and a hearty breakfast.

My mates were waiting for me at the corner. The driver was familiar with the route, and I thoroughly enjoyed the trip. We took our time driving down at about thirty miles an hour.

I think we leave Tuesday for Gulfport. As I've said, we'll stay there a while then go to California. Remember though, that none of this is official yet and may not be valid.

I bought the electric shaver today for $12.85 (with a year's guarantee) and have sent it to you today. I have doubts about buying the watch. The battalion allotment is limited. Watches are only granted to the most important men in the outfit. I'm back on good old KP, but for only two more days — I hope.

9/12/43

Everything fine. Expect to leave for Gulfport tomorrow afternoon. Will try to write en route.

9/13/43

Leaving at 5:00 PM for unofficial destination. We'll ride for more than two days. I think it's Mississippi. Bought Bulova waterproof watch for $18.65. Very lucky. Will write on train.

En Route to Parts Unknown

7:50 AM 9/15/43

Dear Folks,

I'm on my way and still not sure where I'm going. Went through a treacherous night sleeping in the day coach. Unfortunately Pullmans weren't supplied. As soon as we left Endicott I knew, after passing through New London and New Haven, we were heading for New York City. Then we followed the Hudson River to Albany. About 3:00 this morning we were in Syracuse. We just passed a small town called Jordan, and we're headed for Buffalo as we follow the Erie Canal across western New York state. After Buffalo we expect to hit Cleveland. It's fun trying to figure out whether we're going to California or Mississippi. If we go to Mississippi, we'll probably follow the Mississippi River down. For now, we're buffaloed in Buffalo. (Some quip, eh.)

This morning had a fine breakfast consisting of oat meal, scrambled eggs with ham and potatoes, rolls, milk and a plate for the tips.

Boy, do these trains move. However, their wheels are always being checked for hot boxes. One hot box was discovered, and the car was left behind. The country here in western New York is pretty, fairly flat with gently rolling fields and woods. Although I didn't get much sleep, I feel wide awake, and I'm enjoying the scenery. We had on our dress blues when we boarded the train, but we immediately changed into coveralls which are much cooler and more comfortable.

My new watch is a peach. Boy, was I lucky to get it. I was smart and secured it through a CPO, a man from Rochester. We get along well, so he purchased the watch under his name, letting me choose the one I wanted, and even paying for it until we left camp when I reimbursed him. I'll continue later. Can't help noticing how perfectly flat it is around here.

1:50 PM

I sort of rushed through the last letter so please excuse the penmanship. I'm enjoying the trip immensely, much more so than the two previous train rides. Let me review my route so you can follow me this far.

Crossed Rhode Island, hit New London, New Haven, then New York City. Traveled north along the Hudson to Albany, sleeping most of the way, then traveled due west to Utica, Schenectady, Palmyra, Rochester and Buffalo. The countryside is beautiful, amazingly flat and very fertile, consisting of enormous fields with wooded areas scattered here and there. When we passed through Rochester I was amazed at its size and beauty.

At Buffalo we had a wonderful fresh water fish dinner in the diner. Our route is called the Nickel Plate Road. It follows the shore of Lake Erie; I've now seen the lake several times. It resembles an ocean, having white caps and breakers, extending as far as the eye can see, fading off into the horizon. You can see the countryside for miles around because it's so flat and rolling. It's more beautiful than Massachusetts. This is big farming country, you know, with enormous apple orchards, pastures where cows and horses graze, and vast acres of all kinds of vegetables. I'll continue this as we travel. I believe my previous letter was mailed in Buffalo.

4:20 PM Bulova watch time

Well, we're passing through northern Ohio, having stopped in Erie, Pennsylvania, a pretty good size city. It's a large manufacturing center and full of smoke. After sleeping for an hour, I awoke in Conneaut, Ohio. Dad, didn't you buy some leather from the Conneaut Leather Company? We still don't know where we're going.

The land in Ohio continues flat, not as pretty as New York state. All about are extensive farms; most of the crops appeared burned from the sun. It's very hot in the car and the ride is becoming tiresome. Just learned that we'll have a shower when we arrive in Cleveland an hour from now. Just pulled into the small town of Perry. A train load of tanks and tank destroyers passed on the other track. We've several days of travel still ahead of us. I'm really seeing the country now.

6:40 PM

Leaving Cleveland where I saw enormous, indescribable steel mills. Boy, what a city! We debarked here for fifteen minutes to stretch. Had fried chicken, vegetables, ice cream and milk for supper. The meals are wonderful. We couldn't take a shower in Cleveland after all, but I washed on the train and feel fine. My penmanship is uneven because the car rocks; we're doing at least sixty-five or seventy. Boy, are we moving! Still don't know our destination, but think Cincinnati is the next stop. The farther west we go, the nicer the land becomes, the more fertile it is. The steel and industrial plants are enormous, extending as far as you can see, their parking lots covering hundred of acres. I saw a lot of Lake Erie[1]. This very minute I'm watching a large ore carrier not more than one hundred yards away. I'll try to get some sleep now and will continue later. We've been riding for twenty-five hours.

9/15/43

Dear Folks,

Just entered Bellevue, Ohio, in the north central part of the state. The country is amazingly beautiful and fertile. All you see is flat plain and more flat plain. Farms, hundred of acres in size, grow corn, vegetables and soy beans. The plains are dotted with beautiful trees everywhere. We're following the curve of the Great Lakes, sometimes only a few feet from the shore. Now that it's getting dark I won't see much until morning.

Just turned my watch back to 7:10 and it's pitch dark. Your time, Eastern War time, is 8:00 time.

En Route, Thursday, 5:30 AM Central Time 9/16/43

Dear Folks,

I just awoke from the craziest sleep ever. We removed the seat backs and laid them over the seat platforms to form a level place, making our beds for the night. There was a body curled up in every available space. We resembled piled dead with heads and feet in every direction. I must say I slept much better than the previous night.

On awakening briefly at 3:00, I noticed we were in Frankfort, Indiana, right plumb in the middle of the state, the corn belt, and heading southwest. The moon was so bright I could see the land as clearly as if it were day. Corn fields extend in all directions for miles, with an occasional stand of trees here and there. This is real country. Since we're covering so much ground, the train must be doing sixty-five or seventy.

After passing Fort Wayne, Indiana, we're now in southern Illinois. I suppose we're going to St. Louis, but who knows. Personally, I think we're headed for Mississippi, but the anxiety of not knowing for sure is fun. Many fellows are getting restless and feeling nervous. As for me, I'm enjoying it. It's an entirely new experience. I'm really seeing the country. Just stopped at Hilge, outside Charleston. I'm certain now we're headed for St. Louis.

9:30 AM Central Time

Got off the train at Centralia, Illinois for a stretch. We're now heading due south. Having changed tracks, I know now we're not going to St. Louis. We're on the Illinois Central railroad. This land of corn fields and apple orchards, with a scattering of colorful woods spreading to the horizon, is beautiful. This is not the Great Plains, nevertheless it's rich table land. The sky is as blue as any sky I've ever seen. We had a storm each of the past two nights, but each time we rode out of them. So far, I've passed through seven states.

12:00 M Central Time

Just entered North Cairo on the border between Kentucky, Missouri, and Illinois. The terrain is similar to New England's, perhaps a little less hilly. This is really big country, let me tell you. The farthest west I've been so far is Carbonsville, Illinois. In case you're interested in following my route, we passed Defiance, Ohio; Logansville, Indiana; and Desota, Illinois. This minute, we're on a bridge crossing the Ohio River, about a half mile wide here. I saw a river boat with a rear ferris wheel going up the river. The river is bordered on both banks by a thick forest. What a sight!

I think this letter will be mailed in Cairo. I've seen some cotton fields already and cypress trees growing in a swamp.

2:10 PM Central Time

We're in western Kentucky now, passing through Bardville and Fulton (506 miles from New Orleans, 406 miles from Chicago). Fulton is filthy, looks like an outpost. My previous letter was mailed in Fulton because we didn't stop in Cairo as expected. This country, rolling fields and wooded, isn't as pretty as the blue grass section. There are corn fields everywhere and some cotton fields. It's warm outside. You must realize that this is a very poor section.

Ten minutes ago I had a dinner of creamed chicken, fruit, rice pudding and milk. The meals are still excellent.

5:10 PM Central Time 9/16/43

I'm writing this behind the rail station in Memphis. We've just left Dyersburg and Henning, Tennessee behind. This is cotton country. I saw pickaninnies[1] in the fields picking cotton — low plants that grow to knee height. The landscape, covered with white dots, is pretty. I viewed the junction of the Mississippi and Wolf rivers. We were near enough to see the current. At Memphis the Mississippi is about a mile wide. River boats and barges can be seen plying the river.

Memphis is large and surprisingly clean and new. Its downtown has many tall, modern buildings and its streets are well paved. This is the largest city we've been in since Cleveland.

We've been traveling 48 hours now and expect to spend another night and morning aboard. By the way, we have two mascots aboard: two kittens named "Scuttle" and "Butt." Together they spell scuttlebutt, the navy word meaning rumor. They deposit their waste, ahem, in a candy box filled with dirt and do pretty well.

The train just started up as we continue through Memphis. Here's what I see as we ride: Lots of Negroes. Street cars more modern than Worcester's. A big iron works.

We're still on the Illinois Central. You should see the awful places the pickaninnies live in — worse than shacks.

The battalion is travelling on three trains by different routes. Our train, section one, is, I think, traveling the longest route.

I see cypress trees on both sides of the tracks, craziest trees you ever saw growing in swamps. I'm filthy and black with grime but feel swell. Because the car gets stuffy, we keep the windows open but the smoke and soot seem not to blow in. Still, though I wash before every meal, I'm dirty again in ten minutes. There's a levee and a Negro shack with a rag for a door.

Now we're in Mississippi. Coldwater is our first town on our way to Jackson. We expect to reach Gulfport, our new base, by morning. It's located right on the Gulf of Mexico. There are cotton fields everywhere. It's getting dark so I'll try to get some shut-eye.

Friday, 2:00 PM 9/17/43

Dear Folks,

At eight this morning we arrived in camp (Don't know its name yet) which is just outside Gulfport, a small city with many tall hotels for vacationers. I've only seen the city from a distance. The camp is only about a fifteen minute walk to the Gulf. We have beautiful, brand new two story barracks with toilets and showers. The barracks are finer than those at Endicott, which were pretty good. At the first opportunity, I'll describe the camp more.

I slept most of the way though Mississippi, but awoke when we went through Jackson, a good sized city. Some areas of the country here are flat, others hilly like home, but the trees are different. I noticed that the tall pines, which are common here, are being tapped for their resin to make turpentine. The soil is red in spots, light brown in others, and very clayish.

2:30 PM

I have some time so will continue. At 6:00 this morning we were three hours below Jackson. The countryside is far from beautiful: red clayish soil, woods of tall pines and occasional fields. The shacks in which the Negroes live appear ready to fall apart. And talk about the filth; it's disgusting. This is big turpentine country, you know. I saw forests tapped for the resin.

On the way down we passed two big army bases, an air base in Kentucky and another in Tennessee. Hundreds of planes filled the fields.

The weather is awful. It's pouring now and I hear it has been doing it for the past three days. While our train was entering camp, we were ordered to take off our coveralls and put on dress blues over our filthy underwear. You see, the train comes right into the camp. They kept us standing in the rain for a good long time. I think I'm dirtier now than I have ever been in my life. And I can't take a shower until I have a bunk assignment which will be God knows when.

As I wrote earlier, the barracks are fine, and so are all the other structures, including the chow hall. The camp is set on a flat field that extends as far as the eye can see. It's far superior to Camp Peary, although not quite as elegant as Camp Endicott. I don't believe this camp is as large in area or population as either Peary of Endicott, but it's still plenty big. It seems they have lots of entertainment here. I noticed from last week's posted bulletin that the Camel Caravan[1] and the Spotlight Band[2] had performed. You probably know them. Both are on the radio.

There are few places to visit on liberty and not much doing in Gulfport. Most of the boys go to New Orleans, about seventy-five miles from here. I'll try to get there on a long liberty. I'd also like to do some swimming in the Gulf. I hear there's a city frequented by tourists about ten miles away. This section of the Gulf is a resort area. Gulfport is also a port where many ships unload and it's an embarkation point for the Seabees (so was Endicott). As I understand it, we'll stay here a couple of weeks then move on to California. I'm just waiting to see what my duties will be.

Here at camp I've already had two meals — not half bad. The water is better than at Camp Peary, although it's slightly chlorinated. But it's cooled by water coolers. (By the way, Endicott's water couldn't be beat). I think I'll like it here better than Camp Peary.

I've been traveling continuously for three nights, two days and a morning, in all over two thousand miles. And I certainly enjoyed every minute of it, even though I was dirty and had to sleep like a kitten curled up on the hard seats. Since I could sleep on a picket fence, it didn't bother me. And the food was good.

We passed through the following states: Rhode Island, Connecticut, New York, Pennsylvania, Ohio, Indiana, Illinois, Kentucky, Tennessee and Mississippi, ten in all. Before long, I'll have been in every state east of the Mississippi. I have only North Carolina, Florida, Georgia and Alabama to see yet. Oh yes, I saw the Canadian border just outside Buffalo.

Of the three trains that brought the battalion here, my train took the longest route so I saw even more than those on the other trains. Right now, I'm so sick of traveling and trains that even the sound of a train whistle drives me nuts.

I'll certainly need a couple of weeks to rest up a bit. Then off we go again. In spite of everything, I'm enjoying the experience and expect to keep on, and continue seeing whatever I can.

Now let the letters flow. Boy, can I use some!

7:40 9/17/43

Hiya Folks,
I chose this postcard to give you an idea of what Gulfport looks like. I expect to be stationed at Camp Holliday (found out the name) for a month. I think I'll like it here very much. The camp is very nice, very modern. Some regular navy and Marines are stationed here too.

Gulfport, Mississippi

Dear Mom,

I just returned from breakfast. The chow's pretty good. In spite of an acute milk shortage here, we get plenty of it.

We've had morning exercises, the first since Peary. I don't know what my duties are yet. As usual, everything is in a confused state, but that's to be expected right after a move. I hear we're a half mile from the ocean. If I get a 36 hour leave, which I expect to get soon — maybe tonight — Henry Wolf (the boy from Philadelphia) and I will go to New Orleans.

After securing a New Orleans newspaper, I discovered why the weather has been so poor. We're at the tail end of a severe hurricane that hit Galveston.[1] Hurricanes occur frequently here. I forgot to mention that I saw sugar cane growing on the way down.

You may have wondered why we took such a roundabout way to get here. Well, there are several possible reasons: to prevent sabotage,[2] maybe this was the only available route open or they had to stall for time. You can never tell.

Anyway, I never thought I'd see the Mississippi River or the Ohio for years to come. I'm certainly a long way from home, and by next month I'll be even farther.

I'm struck by how well this camp is laid out. The buildings are remarkably well constructed. They're heated by gas blowers. Our chow hall exterior resembles a Howard Johnson's road house. No kidding.

I'm crazy about my watch. It has a round case with a chrome finish and a black face with white hands and numbers. It also has a sweep second hand that points to designated second marks around the edge of the face. The strap is gray and the most comfortable one I've ever worn. The watch winds easily. It's also a stop watch; pull out the winder and it stops automatically. So far it has kept perfect time. Although it has a glass crystal it's supposed to be unbreakable. The retail price was $47.00; that's the truth. But the Ship's Store is only allowed to make a ten percent profit on such articles. So, you see, it was a swell buy. Why, I noticed that even the commander wears one.

I'll continue to write regularly. I know you'll do the same.

Sunday 9/19/43

Dear Mom,

Of course what I'm about to say is more applicable to a girlfriend, but I want you to know that you're the only one. No doubt, you're mopping the hall or the kitchen today. I hope you enjoy it, ha, ha.

Dear Ronnie,

I'm seeing the world alright, or at least the country. I'm getting a great kick out of this life alright. Wish me lots of luck.

Dear Dad,

I'm dressed now for a visit to Gulfport and Biloxi. Memories of KP; I've been assigned a day of KP for next week. What's that radio program mean, "Life Can Be Beautiful"?[1] Like a true Seabee, I'm still in a confused whirlwind. As far as I know, I'll receive all my military training at this base.

A.M. Monday 9/20/43

I went to Gulfport at 9:30 in the morning and didn't have a chance to complete my letter. This continues it.

Here is where we get our real Marine military training, even more strenuous than the training in Virginia. They say we're due for a fifteen mile hike tomorrow to warm us up for the coming two day hike of thirty-two miles. I'll be getting firing practice. The firing range camp here is more primitive than the one at Sun Valley, R.I. There are no lights, no chemical toilets, no showers or places to shave. They say it'll be hell.

Toward the end of training we'll launch an attack on Easter Island off the Gulf coast and land in barges in waist deep water while under actual (blanks) fire. There hasn't been a casualty yet so you needn't worry. We'll have to crawl on our stomachs while actual machine guns are firing (real bullets) over our heads. Some fun, eh? But it's done in such a way that casualties are impossible. They've worked it out with perfect precision. You needn't be concerned because this is a part of everybody's routine training. Actually I'm looking forward to it. You might think we were a combat unit. But, more than ever, they're stressing that we're not. They tell us we're learning how to defend ourselves and how to keep cool under fire.

All the CPOs in my company are aware that Phys Ed is my line and they're pulling for me one hundred percent. Although it's now definite that we'll go to California, we will be staying here longer than planned. The original schedule called for us to spend two weeks here, but it has been extended to five or six weeks because ten more battalions are ahead of us waiting to go to California. I hear we'll go to Camp Parks, south of San Francisco.

Yesterday I had a wonderful day. As you know, I visited Gulfport and Biloxi. I went with a friend, twenty-six years old, from Cleveland. This fellow neither drinks nor chases women and he's an ardent bowler so we get along swell. Wolf, the Jewish boy from Philadelphia, couldn't join me because my liberty night was changed from his. It's too bad because we get along so well. He's in a different company, but we see and talk to each other often.

The streets in Gulfport are jammed with sailors, so in the afternoon we went to Biloxi, fifteen miles up the beach. We went in a trailer bus which resembles a trailer truck except that the trailer portion has windows and seats just like a regular bus. Though the trailer was made of wood, it was modern and comfortable. Following the shore road to Biloxi, we saw beautiful homes one after the other set among tropical trees and plantings. I'm sending you a picture postcard of one of the hotels on the beach to give you an idea of how beautiful the buildings and grounds are.

In peacetime, Biloxi has about fifteen thousand people, but now it must be nearer twenty thousand. Being strictly a resort city, the stores get resort prices. There are several yacht clubs here. The place is always jammed with soldiers from the surrounding camps and Keesler Airfield. Rarely is a sailor seen, so my friend and I were novelties. The streets were crowded with both soldiers and civilians since a bond parade[1] in progress was coming down the street. Boy, what excitement. Luckily, we were able to buy a couple of milk shakes. We also found a beautiful bowling alley with automatic pin setters. After an hour at the alley, we went to see a movie, "Watch on the Rhine"[2] which I enjoyed very much. After returning to Gulfport we ate supper in a restaurant then took a taxi back to camp. Since three other fellows joined us, the cab fare cost each of us very little. So you see, after spending only $2.50 for eats, amusement and transportation, I had a swell day.

I plan to do it again on another liberty. Have received no letters yet.

Tuesday 9/21/43

Dear Folks,

Now the real training starts. Yesterday afternoon we learned how to take apart and reassemble a Remington 03 rifle. What a gun! Our intelligence department claims it's the best rifle in the world. Last night I saw "Pride of the Yankees"[1] with Gary Cooper[2] and Walter Brennan,[3] a swell picture. If it comes to Worcester, you ought to see it, Dad.

I'm getting plenty of sleep now, turning in around 9:30 and awakening at 6:00. Often I even go to bed before 9:00.

This morning I awoke at 6:10 and on my way to the washroom a CPO, having heard that I had experience, approached me to ask that I give his platoon a morning workout at 6:15. That gave me only five minutes to review the exercises I had learned at the Y, at school and at boot camp. Well, I agreed to his request, thinking that this was a good opportunity to show what I can do. I put the men through only a fair workout because I had to recall the exercises as we went along. At least, I got a few groans from the fellows and some felt sore afterwards. I think I was successful at doing it.

While in chow hall this morning, Chief Tretter sat down with me and talked about my situation. He explained that since I had been observed showing satisfactory conduct and performance, he had recommended me to several officers. However, it has been very hard to find a place for me. He said that I must keep waiting. I've done plenty already, but I suppose I'll have to do more. I hesitate to act on my own initiative for fear that I'll interfere with Mr. Tretter's efforts. He would like to see me in charge of Welfare and Recreation for the battalion, or possibly have me leave the battalion in California for a similar job at the base there. The CPO presently holding the Welfare and Recreation position is bound to leave that job at any time. They say he's a pretty nice fellow, quite wealthy and a tennis player. He used to live in swanky hotels where the movie stars stay and made hundreds, possibly thousands each week. Although he was eventually due for an officer's commission after he got his CPO rating, he was caught performing an illegal transaction with a first class boatswain's mate and demoted. So, you see, I must wait.

This afternoon, after hours of marching and running through the obstacle course, (Boy, what a workout!) our platoon went swimming in the Gulf. The water was calm as a lake and warm as toast, far warmer than our northern waters, even warmer than our lake water. I stayed in the whole time without getting cold. The ensign appointed me life saver while we were in the water. I very much enjoyed the afternoon.

Though I'm not sure, I believe I'll have a swimming instructor's position soon. They've arranged for a pool in Gulfport in which 245 non-swimmers in the battalion will be taught how to swim. I heard from a reliable source that the ensign who went swimming this afternoon submitted my name for the job of swimming instructor.

Our new company commander hails from Brockton, Massachusetts. He's a tall, swell looking fellow, named Liberty. I hear he's a pretty nice guy. He and the ensign, who's in charge of military training and physical education, talked with me this afternoon. They asked if I had attended Springfield College. I explained that I was a swimming instructor back home and that I was admitted into Worcester Tech.[4] They seemed impressed. You see, the lieutenant (our new company commander) had overheard me remark about the cold ocean up north, and he asked whether I was from Massachusetts.

Tomorrow night I'll attend a USO show. I'll welcome the coolness of the theater. The heat here is worse than that of last summer at Camp Peary, but I got used to it in a couple of days.

To date, no letters have arrived from home. One came from Ted Bagdikian[5] who's still at Peary and has been home only one day during a three day leave. He's now more or less reconciled to his lot and expects to be transferred to another base soon.

I've rambled on long enough.

Lotions, and a Gulf of Mexico, (Don't think I didn't swallow plenty) of love to all of you,

9/22/43

Dear Ronnie,

I'm really learning something here. I spent the morning listening to lectures and seeing demonstrations on camouflage and field fortifications. A speaker that just came over from Africa gave a very informative and interesting talk. Have you wondered why submarine warfare has been reduced to a minimum? Well, according to this speaker, radar[1] is why. Our country has developed radar which works even through water.

Today they made up the list of non-swimmers, so I expect that instruction will start soon. I don't know yet how I fit in.

After chow they took us swimming at the beach. It seemed too good to be true that we'd get swimming two days in a row. After our swim, they marched us a few miles then made us do the obstacle course. Boy, what a day! My clothes were drenched in sweat and my body was red from the sun and heat. Many fellows had to visit sick bay to receive treatment for their feet and aching bodies. But I took a good shower, packed down a swell supper, and bought a milkshake at the store. Now I feel tops.

I can feel myself getting hard. The training is so strenuous that men over thirty-five are not permitted to go through the whole program. Believe it or not, we're asked not to go through it if we feel we're not capable. Usually, only a few weak ones step out, but there are plenty of huskies left to make up for them. Truly, I'm enjoying the training. It doesn't bother me in the least, and what an appetite it gives me.

I imagine you folks have been wondering what I use for money after spending $30.00 for a watch and razor. Well I got $13.00 pay before I left Endicott giving me a total of $21.00. Now I have $17.00 left which is more than enough spending money. By the way, there'll be no more KP for me. My KP duty days are over. Headquarters company has been excused from any more KP or cleanup. You can imagine how happy this makes me.

The truth is, with swimming in the ocean and learning interesting things, I'm enjoying life here. Before long I expect to be an instructor which will assure me an advanced rating. I'm keeping my fingers crossed and my eyes open.

As yet, I've received no mail. I guess it takes quite a while for mail to reach here. I know that you're writing, so I'm not worried. It's too bad you can't join me. It's like summer all over again. How's school coming? I bet South High has the best football team this year.

To be continued in serial form tomorrow.

9/23/43

Dear Mom,

We're still doing the usual rigorous routine. We had a morning of extended order drill[1] and mock warfare. Our guns had blanks, but, unfortunately, I didn't get a gun.

It's mid-afternoon now so I'll delay this letter to see whether I receive any from you. Mail just came: none for me. I'll wait in case some arrives tonight.

Now it's evening and I'm sitting in the theater waiting for the USO show to begin. I received no night mail either. It has been two weeks without mail; yet, I know you've been writing.

This afternoon we did dry firing, that is we were taught how to hold a rifle, how to pull the trigger[2] (There's a trick to it), and the various firing positions. I was surprised to see how much there is to firing a rifle.

Well, tonight I've been officially informed that I'm a swimming instructor. Mr. Tretter told me that I was definitely appointed by Mr. Liberty, our company commander. If I do well, and I think I can, I can, and will, go places. Tomorrow I'll tell you how the show was. The way it's going so far, it should be swell. Good night and love to you Dad and Ronnie.

12:30 PM Friday 9/24/43

Dear Mom,

Just this minute your marvelously long letters of Tuesday, Wednesday, Thursday, Friday and Saturday arrived. It's wonderful of you to write every day even though you couldn't mail the letters. I also appreciate you're sending them by air mail. At Endicott the southern boys found that air mail was no faster on the north-south route. From the postmark I gather that your letters take three days to reach me.

I'm anxiously awaiting the arrival of pictures in the next mail. Maybe Dad isn't a photographer; so what. Listen, any picture of you folks is beautiful to me. The clipping you sent had both me and the fellows roaring.

6:00 PM

I'm glad to see that Ronnie is buying bonds. I believe I'll have a few myself when I get back. Has Mr. Cleavitt [a gym instructor at the Y] sent in that letter of recommendation? I can use it. I'm sure Ronnie's toe will heal well. Here such an injury would seem trivial compared with the injuries the fellows have while drunk or fooling around.

The fellow who secured the watch for me, interviewed me just a few minutes ago. He's going to recommend me for a cockswain third class rating which would make me a third class petty officer, quite a jump from Seaman Second Class. I'd be in line for physical instructor with that rating.

Thanks for complimenting me for being a son who writes often. I don't understand why I like to write so much. I guess it's due to a longing to stay in touch with those closest to me.

If "Yanks Ahoy" comes here, I'll be sure not to miss it. Boy, Ronnie rates high if he can go out at night to see a movie. I'll bet he'll be a man about town before long. When will he start going out with girls? I suppose pretty soon. I hope he isn't like me. I know you'd like him to date. I'm sorry I couldn't have met your wishes on that score.

We had more mock warfare this morning. The guns had blanks. It's a scream to see me firing. Whenever I do, I can't help flinching and closing my eyes. We were fighting in a heavily wooded, swampy area where we sank to our ankles in muck. There are alligators, but I didn't see any. I encountered some water moccasins, slimiest looking snakes I ever saw. Our legs were well covered to protect us against them. One fellow ahead of me, trying to jump a ditch, missed and fell into the slimy mud up to his waist. I just stood there laughing. You should see the dirty look he gave me. I got out of there fast.

After cleaning up we went to the firing range this afternoon. There we got the feel of the rifle shooting at temporary targets. From yesterday's training we were supposed to be familiar with a rifle and know how to handle it. We were given Enfields this time, a powerful rifle with a kick when fired. When my turn came, I was instructed to go to the firing line and load the piece with five cartridges. I was nervous as the devil. After some fumbling I managed to put on my sling, then loaded the chamber, pushed in the cock, and removed it from safety. Our targets were one hundred feet away. As I lay in a prone position, my heart was beating like a trip hammer. When the signal to commence firing came, like a rookie I closed my eyes and pulled the trigger. But nothing happened. Then I became more nervous. I called the instructor over to see what the problem was. Apparently, I was so tense that I wasn't pulling the trigger correctly. I then pulled it once more and the rifle fired. I have no idea where the bullet went, but I thought my shoulder would fall off.

Now, more at ease and determined, I reset the elevation on my sight, tightened the sling, opened the cock and closed it, and fired again. The bullet hit the target a bit too low. I had three more shots left. After raising the elevation a bit, I fired again. This time the kick didn't bother me because the gun was tight against my shoulder, offering it no give. You see, I had learned the secret of avoiding the brunt of the kick. Although nearer the bullseye, the shot was still too low. Since the rifles are high powered, the noise is deafening, but if you keep your mouth open it won't trouble you. By the fourth shot, which was nearer the bullseye, my nervousness had disappeared. I was determined to make a bullseye on the last shot. After checking everything, I fired and darned if I didn't hit the bullseye. Boy, was I elated. I wanted to keep shooting, it was so much fun, but my time was up, and we had to leave.

From now on just call me William Tell the Second, ahem. Enclosed is the target with the actual bullet holes I made. The target looks pretty small from one hundred feet away. For having fired a gun the first time, I did excellent, even better than some veterans. I can't wait to visit the range again and get all bullseyes.

When we go to the big range, we'll have automatic targets like those you see in the movies. They're close range targets.

I suppose this is the grandfather of all letters. It's about time to close.

2:30 PM Saturday 9/25/43

Dear Folks,

I received your letters of the twenty-second and twenty-third. Both went airmail which I appreciate. But you needn't spend six cents a day when regular mail at half that gets here in three days anyway. If you continue using airmail it would cost about $23.00 in a year.

I'm glad to hear that you don't become tired, Mom. I always knew you were a super-woman. It would do you good to baby yourself once in a while.

I don't see why you must apologize for a few mistakes in grammar. I beat you by a mile. I write as thoughts pop into my mind which doesn't lend itself to good writing. I believe I understand everything in your letter. The question is do you understand everything in mine.

Today we went on a twelve mile hike. After six miles we reached the Wolf River, our destination. Since we had brought our bathing trunks, we all went swimming, even the officers including the skipper (the Commander) himself. The river, about sixty feet wide and wooded on both sides, was deep, well over our heads, with a sandy bottom. The water was wonderful. The trees, weighted down by Spanish moss, bend over the river. What a beautiful spot. As you can imagine, I enjoyed myself. We did quick time on the way back and occasionally ran. Try that for six miles without a rest sometime. So many fellows were knocked out, the battalion was given the afternoon off.

Sunday AM 9/26/43

Dear Dad,

Today is a day of rest and leisure. Later I plan to go swimming in that water of waters, the Gulf. Last night I saw the movie "Stormy Weather"[1] with Lena Horne.[2] It was a swell musical and plenty entertaining. I expect to see another movie tonight as well.

I'm receiving letters from home faithfully now. It's a supreme pleasure to know that there's always a letter waiting when we have mail call. I'm farther away from home than I've ever been. Somehow Virginia felt so much nearer. Of course, the ride was much shorter. However, I'm far from homesick. As a matter of fact, I think were I home for a couple of days, I'd want to be back here again.

Camp Holliday Monday 9/27/43

Dear Dad,

Quite a day today; yes, very interesting, too. The skies were overcast and rain threatened. After being given weapons, off we marched about a mile outside the camp grounds to a field surrounded by woods. We assumed battle formation and prepared to attack an enemy hiding in the woods. I was appointed the leader of my squad and given the responsibility for its advance. After an hour of advancing, we couldn't locate the enemy. Then the officers called a meeting of both sides, but only our side appeared and congregated.

There was still no sign of the enemy even after another signal was given to cease maneuvers, summoning the other side to meet at an appointed spot. After much calling and signalling, the enemy still failed to reply. Meanwhile it began pouring. So there we were, dressed in our green coverall fighting attire, wearing helmets, rifles slung over our shoulders, gathered in the middle of a field in the pouring rain waiting for the enemy to appear so we could all return to camp. One fellow remarked that we looked more like Marines than they themselves. Eventually, we decided to send a scout to find the enemy and instruct them to return to camp. Wouldn't you expect it? When I saw our officer eyeing me, I knew I was the one chosen to be scout.

There I was in fighting uniform, rifle slung over my shoulder, soaked to the skin, trudging over field and woods, hollering wherever I went, to attract attention. After about a half mile I saw ten men approaching, their guns raised ready to attack. It took a while to convince them that my mission was no trick and that they should report back to camp. Hearing of yet another lost platoon, I searched for and soon found them. Their CPO in charge began cursing like the devil. "Where in hell is the enemy?" When I explained that the enemy couldn't be located by our side either, and that he should return to camp, he exploded, "Do we even have to chase the enemy to make them pursue us? For crying out loud, we're supposed to be the defense. Why in hell is the other side running away?" As he griped, I merely trudged alongside him not saying a word. Then he mentioned that one of his platoon squads was still missing. Oh, Oh. That's all I had to hear, and I'd have to keep searching. But fortunately they met up with us on the main road.

I was so filthy and wet you'd think I was on Guadalcanal. The rain continued coming down in torrents and splashing off our Marine helmets. After we walked some distance, we met an officer who informed us that we'd have to go through a swamp before returning to camp. You see, he said that we had had it too soft, that it was time we roughed it. We bound up our legs and arms to protect us against the very poisonous cottonmouth snakes that inhabit the swamp. By then we were so wet and tired, we didn't care where we went so no one protested against going through the swamp.

At first there was only mud, ankle deep, but as we moved further into the swamp, water was everywhere underfoot. The boughs of gigantic trees hanging with Spanish moss arched over us. Rain beating on our faces, we waded through the water as our shoes oozed with cool slimy mud at every step. Oh, it was just ducky. Occasionally we'd sink up to our waists in the muddy water.

Toward the end of our trek we had to cross over a log. A man stood at each end of the log encouraging us to cross one at a time. When I reached the middle of the log, I noticed that the fellows at each end were shaking it, causing me to topple into a ditch up to my armpits in mud and water. Holding my rifle over my head to keep it dry, I succeeded in wading to the road. The same thing happened to every man who crossed on the log. But you had no choice: it was the only way to reach the road. It seems, you see, that tipping us from the log was done intentionally to make things tough. Finally the entire platoon assembled, bedraggled and covered with mud, and marched a couple of miles back to camp. What a morning! And what a washing I've got, oh boy! Oh, well. It's only one day in the life of a Seabee.

It's still pouring. We had instruction on booby traps this afternoon—very interesting. Also an unusual thing happened. While I was standing in the ranks, an officer approached and drew me aside and asked my name and grade. After I answered him politely, he asked if I had been a swimming instructor and for what organization. After I gave him the information he said, "I've been watching you for some time, and I've noticed that you've done everything very well. I'm going to recommend you for Seaman First Class." But he cautioned me not to repeat what he had said. After thanking him, and keeping a blank face, I stepped back into the ranks.

Well, this is a paradox. A CPO has already said that he had recommended me for a cockswain rating, one step higher than S 1/c. Since I'm friendly with the CPO, I informed him of what the officer had said. After pondering a moment, he said that the officer's action was wonderful, and he would see to my being advanced one rate higher. Apparently the officer knew nothing of the CPO's recommendation and felt that a jump to S 1/c would be sufficient. But knowing me better, the CPO felt I deserved a higher rank. So, you see, I'm really being observed and recognized, even by officers with whom I have no direct contact. From all this, I ought to go places. Things certainly look rosy.

Even the fellows are showing me more respect than ever. They think I'm quite clever and always request me as their leader. Many of them come to me with their personal troubles, and show me pictures from home. A few have asked that I read letters from their girlfriends and seek my opinion. It's a scream. They're really swell guys. In the morning, I'm greeted with "Good morning, Aaron," by whomever I meet. This has been quite recent, and I'm not sure why it's happening. I know my good physique has something to do with it. When swimming is discussed, and it's discussed often, I'm the ultimate authority.

Boy, I've written more than I intended. Although it might appear that some of the things I've written are exaggerations, I assure you they're not. I don't mean to brag, either.

1:00 PM Tuesday 9/28/43

Dear Folks,

We had firing practice all morning. I made a fair score. Of course, all this is preliminary to much more firing in the future. This afternoon we'll have gas mask drill.

I browsed through the library the other night and was amazed to find such a collection of fine books. I checked out Taylor Caldwell's[1] *Dynasty of Death*[2] which I've already begun and think I'll enjoy.

How's school coming Ronnie? I hope you're taking it easier, Dad. After all, you now have one less person to support.

My pay would be $66.00/month if I get a S 1/c rating, increasing my allotment home. A cockswain gets $78.00, but I feel the S 1/c is more probable.

7:15 PM Tuesday 9/28/43

Dear Mom,

This is my second letter today because I received three of your letters and just had to reply. I've decided not to go on liberty because the weather has turned bad. So I'm writing you instead and enjoy it as much as if I had gone out.

I received a card from Aunt Sadie and she wrote all about Uncle Bill. I wrote Aunt Anna a week ago.

Special arrangements have been made for the Jewish boys to attend Rosh Hashanah[1] and Yom Kippur[2] services in Gulfport tomorrow night. I think I'll attend.

Say, that picture of you is wonderful, Mom. Boy oh boy, am I proud of you. The two pictures of Dad and Ronnie are also swell even though they aren't too well centered. I showed them to the fellow who's sitting writing beside me. He said, "Boy, your father looks awfully young. What's he, about forty?" When I told him how old Dad really is he almost fell through the floor. I must confess though, that I feel none of these pictures do you justice. Ronnie's handsomeness doesn't show up well. Dad is younger looking yet than the picture shows and more jovial, and you are much sweeter.

I'm happy to see that you are at last buying things for yourself. It's about time that you started enjoying life. I only wish Dad wouldn't work so hard. My main incentive to get a better rating is to make more money so that I can contribute to the family. I'll not be happy until you accept my contribution. Bear that in mind. I figure the more money I make, the less you'll feel that by taking some you'd be depriving me of savings.

Being in Platoon 4 is a lucky break. Mr. Tretter, being the company chief, is head of all the platoons, as well as my platoon. It is as my platoon chief that he's recommending me for a rating.

Have no fear of my raising my head while under fire. The Seabees haven't had a casualty yet. The army is far more dangerous. The Seabees have only excellent marksmen. I enjoy roughing it; I think it's fun. I'm lucky being young because the older fellows really suffer.

I'm spending my money wisely. I realize you know I wouldn't splurge. It's wonderful of you to tell me to spend as I like, and you can be sure I won't spend like a trooper when on liberty.

I'm finding it hard to secure a Camp Holliday banner. How would you like a soft pillow cover with the Seabee emblem on it?

Our Mr. Liberty isn't related to the leader of the Boy's Club in Worcester. He's light complexioned and tall. The one in Worcester is Italian. Our Mr. Liberty is either Irish or Scotch.

2:30 PM Wednesday 9/29/43

Dear Dad,

This morning we had hand grenade drill and two runs through the obstacle course. Since five men are already giving swimming instruction, I won't be. It seems that no swimming instruction will be given to our company. What a system! It's a scream. I don't think of such things any more. In fact I'm just as happy receiving training as giving instruction.

This afternoon I received a letter from Aunt Pearl and one from John Fulgoni — six interesting pages packed full of laughs. Mom's humor gives me fits too. I get a great kick out of her quips and sarcasm,

Tonight, under special liberty, I'm going to services with Wolf.

Friday 9/31/43

Dear Folks,

I have a few hours of spare time before leaving on a thirty-two mile hike to the rifle range. The trip will take two days and will require that we bivouac at the half way mark. We'll be doing it by night which classifies the hike as a maneuver.

Although not official yet, I heard this morning from a reliable source that only eleven members of the battalion will be granted rerates. Just think, only eleven promotions in the entire battalion and fortunately I'm one of the chosen. I'll be promoted to Seaman First Class, which I consider an honor in view of how few promotions are being given. Although I was aiming for cockswain, it would be quite a jump from my present rank. In a month or two I can put in for the higher rating, and with my new rating I'll have a better chance. I'll get a $12.00/month increase in pay which I'll allot home.

Night before last I learned that there are twenty Jewish boys in the battalion, among them a Jewish lieutenant and a dentist. Gulfport Field is a large army air base about fifteen miles from camp. We visited the base to attend Jewish services at a large theater there. I was surprised to see so many WACs attending the services. I enjoyed it; the services were nice.

The camp is not nearly as nice as our Seabee camps. They tell us the food isn't so hot and the water is lousy, like Camp Peary's. And worse than us, they're so confused nobody knows what's happening. Every air corps man I talked to was disgusted. I guess everybody else's grass always grows greener. One fellow told me that KP is a wonderful job, just imagine. And that several men after being sent to radar school are on KP detail. Boy, I don't regret being in the Seabees after listening to them and seeing their base. I'll take the Seabees any time. Enclosed is the program for the services. I would have liked to attend tonight's services but it's impossible.

I would like you to meet John Fulgoni. Besides you folks, he's the most loyal letter writer I have and his letters are wonderful. It's rotten of Mr. Cleavitt[1] not to send a recommendation. Certainly I can do without it. But he burns me up. When I get back I'm going to advertise his rottenness.

The navy doesn't allow cameras so I can't take pictures. Some day, I'll have a portrait photo made. During our first few weeks we were allowed a radio, but now they're banned. I don't know why.

It's a shame Ronnie has to work so much. If he doesn't watch out he'll become like me. He should have more time to mingle with school friends. I didn't and now regret it. Still, he shouldn't neglect his studies, either.

Well, Ronnie your sense of humor certainly hasn't deserted you. Boy, were the fellows staring at me while I was laughing reading your letter. They thought sure I was nuts. I knew South High would trim Classical. South is the best all around school, ahem. Of course, the reason is I went there. When are you going to learn how to spell? I had to send your letter to Washington to have it decoded. Better keep on the good side of Miss Phillips.[2] If she remembers me, I pity what she'll do to you. How did the game go between Holy Cross[3] and Dartmouth?[4] You ought to come down and see me some time. We have good seafood, shrimp. Get it?

7:00 PM Saturday 10/2/43

Dear Folks,

So much has happened in the past twenty-four hours, that I don't know where to begin. I'll start at the beginning: 8:00 last night. After assembling, the 113th battalion marched a distance of thirty-two miles during twenty-one hours. It was so dark no one could discern the man ahead of him. The fellows began singing rollicking songs such as "Inky Dinky Parlez Vous," "My Darling Clementine," some Seabee songs, and other popular pieces, which put us all in a marching mood. After two miles we had our first five minute rest. This allowed us to tighten our shoe laces, put on two pairs of stockings and relax a bit. Five miles later, when we stopped to rest, the marching began to take its toll. Several fellows complained that their bodies were in pain. Unable to lie on the grass beside the road due to the night dew that had saturated the ground, we instead lay prone on the cool road for relief.

It's getting dark now. We have no electric lights so I'll have to finish this tomorrow. All's well; I arrived here in remarkably good condition.

11:30 PM 10/3/43

I apologize for dating last Friday's letter the 31st. I had forgotten that September has only 30 days. The joke is on me.

To continue my account of the hike, we had our third rest at 1:00 AM, lasting about fifteen minutes during which we were served K rations and water. These were supplied by trucks that had been following us. You've probably heard of the new K rations. We had the supper unit packed in a four-by-six-inch box in which the food is wrapped in cellophane. In order to see, we made a fire of the boxes. The food consisted of a beef mixture to which was added pork and various nutritional ingredients. It was packed in a sardine like can. Though it resembled cat food it tasted pretty good. There were a couple of packages of what looked and tasted like cookies called K1 and K2, but were really various grains rich in certain vitamins. Included was a thick stick of chocolate that looked rather like shellac but it didn't taste at all bad. Some dry powdered bouillon to which we added water came in a cellophane packet. It also tasted good. There were also three Fleetwood cigarettes, a stick of gum, and three lumps of sugar.

After hiking six more miles we reached the bivouac area at 4:00 AM. Everybody was dead tired, with blistered feet, aching legs and drooping heads. I felt fine except for a little weariness from lack of sleep. My legs were in good condition and I can't get over how well my feet held up. I had none of the problems with my arches that I used to have. In all, we had hiked eight hours. During the hike we were warm, often even sweating. We didn't carry a pack or a gun, and wore only helmets and fighting coveralls. Much of the trip was on dirt roads, but eight miles were paved. They were a tough eight miles, because each step on the pavement was a shock to our feet. Well, in the morning we still had fourteen miles to go.

Fortunately, with our bedding and tents shipped ahead, all was set up and ready when we arrived at bivouac. We simply plopped on our cots, seven men to a tent, and slept through until 9:30 in the morning. After about five hours sleep we had more K rations for breakfast, the dinner unit, consisting of American cheese, more cookies that were marked with different symbols than the K1 and K2, sugar, gum, cigarettes, a box of malted milk, dextrose tablets, and a package of imitation lemon powder which was supposed to be rich in vitamins when dissolved in water. These K rations were surprisingly filling. In fact, after a meal you want no more. Anyway, knowing they contained energy, I ate plenty of Hershey chocolate bars before we left.

When I awoke that morning, since I had a towel and soap packed in my bedding bag, I washed in a cool, clear stream nearby. Boy, did it feel wonderful. There was a spring but it contained sulphur. Being very thirsty, we drank it even though it tasted terrible. Anyway, they say sulphur water is good for you.

After we got going at 11:00 AM, the sun was really beating down on us. The weather was remarkably beautiful; the sky was cloudless blue. Although it was terribly hot in the sun, there was always a pleasant breeze, and it was comfortable in the shade. Everyone stripped to the waist and several got sunburned. My own back is brown now and my face is a healthy red.

After resting two or three times on the way, we pulled into the range at 5:00 PM. The last five miles were really tough. We arrived dead tired, hot and filthy with sweat and dust. Many sang trying to keep up their spirits, but several fell out along the way and had to be picked up by trucks. The one thing that kept most of us going was that our mates were making it. The thinking was, "If the other guy can do it, so can I."

You should have seen how some of us limped along with hot, blistered feet, tired legs and exhausted bodies. We kept a fast walk pace for several miles, the last fourteen to be exact, and I mean fast. Sometimes you had to run to keep up. Occasionally the pace would slow down to an easy walk for four or five miles then speed up again. But surprisingly, once we were in a fast pace we didn't want to slow up. You see, eventually our walking rhythm became mechanical and any change made us conscious of our pace. In fact, fast walking somehow offered some relief to our feet and our minds as well. Most of us walked like automatons; one foot followed the other of its own accord.

I must say the country here is beautiful. Mississippi may be noted for its swampy terrain, but not here as we hiked through a rolling countryside of occasional fields and tall pine forests on both sides of the road. I couldn't get over how starry the night was; I never saw so many stars in my life. Boy, is the night cold! We were always comfortable while walking, but after we stopped for a five minute rest, we'd be freezing.

We were really in tough shape when we pulled into the range. The range camp is small, consisting of a street of barracks similar to Camp Peary's, sufficient only to house one battalion. The battalion that occupied the place before us left it filthy, and did we have some cleaning to do. The water here also contains sulphur, but it didn't taste too bad, not as bad as the spring at bivouac.

Not until I sat down did I realize how tight my legs had become, and how sore my feet were. Still my arches felt wonderful. I took a cold water shower, which is all that was available, and it did wonders for me. After being cooled my feet felt better and my body aches disappeared. Our clothing and bedding had already arrived before us by truck.

I guess if I can walk thirty-two miles with my feet holding up as they did, I don't have a foot problem. No doubt, wearing two pairs of socks had something to do with it. But everyone else also wore two pairs. Why, I didn't even have one blister while everyone else had one or more. The sick bay was jammed last night by men having their feet attended to.

I went to bed about 8:30 and slept through to 8:00 this morning. We were allowed to sleep as late as we wished. I awoke without an ache or pain in my body and my feet felt as if I had never been on a hike. Last night we had swell chow, and this morning's breakfast was wonderful: hot cakes being one of the main dishes. Everyone went through the serving line two or three times.

This afternoon we can go swimming in the stream (There's diving there too) but I prefer to lay around and get a sun bath. The sky is cloudless, as it has been for several days, and it's like a typical June day. I learned that our company commander is from New Bedford and at one time, lived in Worcester. At least Dad's age, he walked every mile with us. He's the sort of man who would never send his men through something that he wouldn't go through himself. The fellows are crazy about him. Oh, yes, I'm sending you some of the packaging and literature from the K rations that may be of interest to you.

Mom, your letter of the 28th was waiting for me when I arrived here. And another letter from Aunt Ida. Thursday we expect to march back to the base the same way we came. It appears we'll have very few days of rifle practice. Now that we're hardened to it, I don't expect we'll mind the hike back as much as we did coming here. After twice making use of the toilets, I find them terrible.

It looks like I'll be getting a thirty-six hour liberty to attend Yom Kippur services Friday and Saturday. All the Jewish boys are planning to attend Saturday's. I've been asked to go with them, and I said yes, by all means. So you see, it's quite a break, and I know I'll enjoy myself as well.

This is really a long letter, boy oh boy.

I'm afraid you misunderstood what I wrote concerning my rerate. According to Ida's letter, she thinks I'm a third class petty officer—which I'm not. As I explained, I've been promoted to first class seaman and I'm only in line for third class petty officer in a month or two. As I indicated, I consider it an honor to have received a rerate in view of the fact that only eleven rerates were granted in the whole battalion of over one thousand men. I realize you feel proud because I received a rerate, but please don't advertise it until it's officially announced. I'm sorry that I led you to believe I'm getting a cockswain rating. Remember a recommendation for rerate doesn't mean I have one.

Now, I'll have to make sure I get a third class petty officer's rating in order to justify myself in the eyes of those who think I have one. Give me a month or two and I'll be a cockswain. Bear in mind, since I've been advanced to S 1/c, I've been recognized. Many college men are still only second class seamen and I'll be a rank above them.

If I had more time, I'd discuss Ronnie's relationship with girls. All he needs is a start. Thanks for Uncle Bill's address. I wish I could get over to his camp to see him.

P.S. My new rating is equivalent to an army corporal. Pardon my penmanship. I'm sitting in a awkward but comfortable position.

12:30 PM Monday 10/4/43

Dear Mom,

We're still at the range camp. This morning we had cut a field of grass with a scythe. I looked like Father Time and learned how to wield the scythe pretty well. Since it's so hot, we worked stripped to the waist. I'm getting a swell tan. Don't know when we'll start rifle practice.

I had a glorious afternoon Sunday, having gone swimming in a cool stream in the woods about a half mile from here. The bank and river bottom were sandy just like our ocean beaches. Most of us swam in the nude, including me. I basked in the sun and felt like a million.

6:30 PM

It's a bit late but I wish you all a happy new year. It's 5704.

I sometimes write as many as five letters a day. You do pretty well yourself.

There are twenty-three Jewish boys in the battalion. I'm in close contact with two, both decent fellows. We talk and go to shows together often. I'm the only Jewish boy in my company, but it's not a problem because the battalion sticks together. The battalion has approximately 1200 men, 200 to a company, 30 to a platoon and 10 to a squad.

All petty officers wear regular sailor uniforms. A third class PO has one chevron on his arm, second class PO two chevrons, and a first class PO three chevrons. Above the chevrons there's an eagle. A cockswain (The rating I didn't get) has his chevrons on the right arm, indicating more authority than chevrons on the left arm. I'll have to be a Chief Petty Officer to satisfy your desire that I wear a uniform like an officer's. A CPO must be at least twenty-eight years old. However, in phys ed, age is not a factor. It would take at least eighteen months to become a CPO, a difficult thing to do.

10/5/43

Dear Dad,

This morning, stripped to the waist under the hot Mississippi sun, I dug ditches with pick and shovel. But, oddly enough, I enjoyed it. While sweating, you feel pretty good. Truly, digging the ditch has been my only real accomplishment since I've been in the service. Here at the range, I haven't fired a gun yet.

This morning I read in the *Reader's Digest* an article by Eric Johnston of the U.S. Chamber of Commerce concerning our postwar relationship with Great Britain. I marveled at how well he presented the American point of view. By all means, read the article; it's excellent.

I'll hold up on mailing this until mail call at 7:00 PM, the only one here at the range.

I received three letters, one from Aunt Pearl, one from Mrs. Gallant, my friend Lionel's mother, and, best of all, one from you — a fine letter too. I marvel at your ability to write such letters.

I realize that Mom's letters express the thoughts of the whole family. After all, she's the natural spokesman since she has more time than you or Ronnie. However, I certainly appreciate receiving yours and Ronnie's letters too.

Yes, I'm sure I've gained self-confidence and acquired independence since I've been in the service. I've learned the ropes pretty well and have met a cross section of people from all over our nation. My ideals are as pure as ever despite the effort of many here to corrupt any young man's ideals. I've been taught to be level-headed, and to keep learning, and I haven't grown the least bit cocky over what I have learned. I've already witnessed a change in attitude in some who submitted to contaminating influences. I'd never yield to the small but unavoidable rotten atmosphere that's bound to exist in any organization of this kind. I'm proud of the fact that you have more confidence in me than ever. I really had to smile when I read that you've redoubled your faith in my ability to handle myself. And such confidence in me has only caused me to redouble my faith in myself.

I understand that it's much more difficult for you to find things to write about than I. So long as I hear from you, I don't care what you write. Your letters need not be lengthy; merely a word would suffice.

I fired a carbine this afternoon and got a pretty good score. It's the first time I've handled this rifle. Boy what a gun!

Well, I'd better knock off now, as they say in the navy.

12:30 PM Wednesday 10/6/43

Dear Ronnie,

Well, I was firing all morning, thirty rounds to be exact, and got a fairly good score. This afternoon I'll be taking the final test. If I pass, I won't need any more practice until I'm issued my own rifle. At present we're firing carbines, automatic rifles whose trigger you only need to pull once to fire more than one bullet.

6:15 PM

After being on the range all afternoon, I didn't pass, as expected. I guess I wasn't born to be a marksman. However I'll have another chance. I'm sure I'll make good. I had a little trouble sighting at the beginning. After a while I caught on but too late to rescue my score. You see, no two guns fire alike, and I used two different rifles.

7:30 PM

Along with your letter, Mom, I received one from John Fulgoni just packed full with his wonderful humor. He sent a picture which I'm forwarding to you so that you can see what he looks like. Please return it. I wish you folks could meet him. He's Uncle Bill's type.

Last night Chief Tretter informed me that I'm officially a S 1/c and that he was indirectly responsible for it. But I can't announce that I'm S 1/c until I get it in writing. Now they're seeking applicants for officers' candidates school. But I'm out of luck because I can't satisfy the age and education requirements. Mr. Tretter said that he feels I'm officer material, quite a compliment. It's rare that they give a rerate to boys my age when men who are much older remain in their old categories. Frankly, I'm just another man here too, but I spoke up and attracted attention. Otherwise I'd have never been noticed.

So far, I've been receiving all your letters daily with amazing punctuality. Say, if you think you're anxious to receive my letters, you can imagine how I feel about yours. I almost kill the mailman before my name is called. I sit outside on the steps from 5:30 to 7:00 reading or writing letters so that I'll know firsthand when the mail arrives.

From the time the first name is called until mine is, I go nuts, ringing my hands and jumping around. And, boy, I pity the poor fellow in my way when my name is called as I dash for that remarkable morale lifting epistle.

I use this stationery instead of the Seabee paper because this comes in a convenient folder. All kinds of stationery are available here, and quite reasonable too. Facilities for buying are fine so there's no need to send me bonbons. Get that word? Boy, am I sharp!

So you laughed at my experiences on maneuvers, eh. Well, frankly we laugh ourselves. As we discuss them afterwards we laugh so hard our stomachs ache. I'll never forget pulling my saturated wallet from my pocket after wallowing in water up to my waist. The money in my money belt got pretty wet too. But after drying out, everything remains in good condition.

By the way, we lost Scuttle, the cat, but I often see Butt climbing a tree or chasing insects.

Thursday 10/7/43

Dear Mom,

So at last you received my first allotment. Before long it will be increased $12.00. By all means use it for whatever you need. It's yours so far as I'm concerned. It makes me happy when you write that you look forward to the day when I'll have a good position to enable me to bring money into the house. If only you could know how much I want to contribute to the family welfare.

I was unable to finish reading *Dynasty of Death* before leaving for the rifle range, and I couldn't take it with me. I'll try to take it out of the library again.

Today was a thrilling day. We awoke especially early at 5:15 AM to dynamite blasts, whistles blowing, and shrill shouting. I was startled. The barracks erupted into an uproar. Immediately I put on my coveralls (We sleep in our underwear) and after slipping into my shoes, dashed for the woods to hide. It was a surprise raid. Talk about realism. Why, you could feel the concussion of the almost deafening explosions. I'd swear they were real bombs. In half an hour it was over, our normal awakening time. Some fellows even went back to bed for ten minutes. What fellows!

After breakfast we hiked through the woods until 10:00 AM. After that we went through the "combat course," a half mile of territory consisting of woods, fields and hills. Each man in our company was given a carbine with twenty rounds of live ammunition. I'm not kidding. We were wearing our fighting green gear including steel helmets. After our squads formed a battle formation, we advanced toward the enemy somewhere in the woods. Everyone must run, and boy, you don't stop. After entering the woods, as we were advancing in a line, dynamite charges went off about 100 yards from the line of fire. Everyone dropped to the ground, rifles cocked and in a firing position. Suddenly a number of dummies popped up from the ground about 100 yards ahead of us. Simultaneously we fired ten rounds of ammunition. Boy, what a racket. We got up and advanced again, then dropped to the ground and infiltrated the area by crawling one man at a time until a firing line was formed. Again more dummies appeared in all directions and we unloaded our remaining ten rounds.

This afternoon we returned to the combat course again with carbines and twenty more rounds of ammunition. After again advancing at a good clip in battle formation, dynamite charges went off all around us. Boy, did we hit the deck. I was almost scared out of my pants. My heart was pumping like a trip hammer and my face from head to chin was covered with beads of sweat. As more dummies appeared, all of us fired. But this time machine gun bullets were whizzing through the air, mortar shells were exploding and B.A.R. automatic rifle fire was coming from all directions. Dynamite was exploding everywhere, bursts of fire erupted and dirt flew. And we hugged the ground for dear life, let me tell you. As I peeked beneath my helmet to fire from a prone position, I saw a bullet hit a tree about seven inches in diameter and come out the opposite side, pulling a chunk of the trunk along with it.

You've probably seen moving pictures of battles. Well, they don't simulate the real thing. It's really much louder and the concussion from explosions shakes every inch of you and knocks the wind out of you. I even saw some men knocked down by concussions. After things quieted we got up and advanced. No longer afraid, and no longer giving a damn, I was only determined. After advancing a couple of hundred yards on our bellies, the excitement began again. One charge went off not more than fifteen yards ahead of me. Now I was really mad and I just kept pulling the trigger at the dummies. Ahead of us bullets were flying everywhere. Then just as suddenly as it began, it stopped.

So this was the real stuff. Of course, you're safe if you do what you're told and keep within limits. But while you're being watched, the people operating the course try to scare you as much as possible by exploding a charge when you're near it, not so near as to hurt you but near enough to give you an idea of what the real thing is like.

Well, it's over now. Afterward I was surprised to find myself drenched with perspiration, but until then I was unaware of it I was so involved in the shooting. What an experience.

This was the nearest thing to actual battle that I'll ever experience. Bullets were fired in such a manner so as not to hurt us, but, of course, it won't be that way on a real battlefield. Yes, it's dangerous with live ammunition flying everywhere, but if you hug the ground, mind your squad leader and tend to your task, you'll be safe. They really scare the pants off you, no kidding. At first, my mouth was so dry I couldn't swallow. By the time you're in the midst of battle, you get over being nervous. This is real training, boy oh boy.

All this sounds dangerous, I know, and can be dangerous, I admit. That is, if you make a false move, you'll know it. Even the trees were planted with booby traps. However, keep one thing in mind: the navy can't afford to lose men. If you keep your head and follow directions, you're as safe as a babe in the woods. It's just that the training has to be made as realistic as possible. Well, anyway, it's over and no harm has been done. The only guys who were hurt were wise guys who thought they knew it all and ignored directions.

Telegram 10/8/43

In New Orleans for holidays. Will stay here Saturday. What a town! Really having fun. Write. Hughie

USO
Camp Street
New Orleans
11:00 PM Friday 10/8/43

Dear Folks,

Who would have believed that when I heard Mrs. Mann [a neighbor] talk of her brother once being in New Orleans, that in the near future I'd be there myself? It's certainly a funny world and for me, luckily, life is fascinating.

A truck brought us Jewish boys from the rifle range this afternoon so we could go on liberty at 5:00 PM. The battalion is still on the hike back and won't arrive at Camp Holliday until tomorrow afternoon. I don't have to return to camp until Sunday morning.

I'm with Henry Wolf, the boy from Philly who went with me to Providence. I like him more and more. Another fellow, George Chast, is also with us. He's in his late twenties, formerly a high school and college teacher of languages in New York City. He's a clean fellow, married and doesn't drink. We three traveled to New Orleans together, and, once here, found a USO in which to sleep for only thirty cents a night. The people treat us wonderfully. Food such as snacks, pie, coffee, milk and doughnuts cost practically nothing.

We've already visited two other USOs to see what's going on. We learned where the Yom Kippur services will be held and will attend them tomorrow morning at 9:30. We arrived too late this evening to attend Kol Nidre[1] services.

We had departed Gulfport at 6:00 PM and arrived in New Orleans at 8:00. On the way we crossed a bridge that was built right over the Gulf. What a sight! It was dark when we reached New Orleans, but there was no dim-out. It seems strange to see store windows, lit up, bright street lights and autos rushing in all directions. This is one big city, let me tell you.

Canal Street, wide and long, is the main street. On each side extending for a good distance are beautiful stores. Their classy facades and bright windows amazed me. The buildings are elaborately designed, most of moderate height with a fifteen or twenty story hotel here and there.

I've been walking up and down the main street listening and observing. There's a constant hubbub. I saw men in uniforms of every description: English, French, Dutch, from every United Nation. Some were officers in full regalia. I heard Spanish and French Creole spoken, and English with that slow southern drawl that I found oddly fascinating. I've just been enchanted by the whole thing. This is a new experience for me. Providence and Williamsburg were never like this.

I wore whites because it's quite warm, but the weather is beautiful. Tomorrow we plan to visit the French Quarter and take a boat ride on the Mississippi. Having been here before, Henry is showing us the town. I just had a few pecans New Orleans style and a swell milkshake. Now I'm going to bed. I'll write tomorrow, as always.

6:00 PM Saturday 10/9/43

Dear Mom,

Today has been wonderful. I'm overwhelmed with seeing things, eating ravenously and just enjoying myself. This experience has given me many things to remember.

We slept well, awakening at 7:30. After breakfast we strolled along Canal Street until about 9:30 then we went to Yom Kippur services conducted by an Army Chaplain at the YMHA.[1] The service, which was interesting and pleasant, lasted about two hours. There were men dressed in all kinds of uniforms in the audience. I was surprised to find that the YMHA was such a beautiful, modern building.

After the service we visited the French Quarter which consisted of structures, some over 200 years old, with elaborate porches and facades. The ornate ironwork was exceptionally pretty. There were antique shops everywhere, and some of the furniture they showed was beautiful. I saw a few sofas that almost knocked my eyes out. We also visited a few museums and cathedrals, some parks and a few old buildings. As you can imagine, it was most interesting.

A big bond parade was in progress on Canal Street. The streets were jammed. People everywhere were wearing costumes. Many were buying trinkets and gifts. It was all so exciting.

The people here are very nice, very cordial, especially the girls. Believe it or not, one waitress tried to date me. We had a full course meal of lamb with macaroni, soup, spinach, potatoes, lettuce, milk and apple pie, in a beautiful, modernistic grille. The food was exceptionally tasty and plenty of everything. In the background we could hear popular songs playing, making it all very enjoyable. Including booth service and cloth napkins, it cost us only seventy cents.[2]

In the afternoon we went on a river steamer excursion. It was most enjoyable. Over a loud speaker system a man explained the sights that we were passing, among them the four and one half mile long Huey Long bridge. The trip lasted two and one half hours.

We'll have supper now and at 8:00 take the train back to camp.

4:00 PM Sunday 10/10/43

Dear Mom,

We took the 7:55 PM train back to Gulfport arriving here at 10:00. Our car was air-conditioned too. I'm really an old hand at travel now. No longer do I feel nervous as I used to before I went into the service. In fact, I feel more confident in everything I do. I don't feel awkward when going into a restaurant the way I used to. As a matter of fact, I hold a pretty good conversation with the waitresses. Of course they always start the conversation.

Before catching the train I had a wonderful supper: veal chops and French fried potatoes. It cost me only $1.10. I confess the trip cost $6.00 and some change, including eats and all. But it was worth every cent. Liking food, I couldn't help buying something good. You know, New Orleans is noted for its good cooking. Oh, how I wish you folks could have been with me to see the sights. They were marvelous. I'll never forget it.

You know, it's funny: during supper one of the waitresses remarked about our northern accents. She was from Ohio and came here to be with her army boy friend who was on maneuvers. So she took the waitressing job. I remarked, "Too bad he didn't join a good outfit." "Yes," she said, "I wanted him to join the Marines." Boy, did I shut up like a clam. The Marines are the Seabee's bitter rivals. Well, it was all in fun anyway.

On the train I met a sailor from Worcester. The soldier who sat with us had a portable radio. He let me fool around with it a bit and I got WBZ from Boston. Excited, I exclaimed aloud about getting the station from back home. Overhearing me, a sailor nearby asked if I ever listened to WTAG, WORC or WAAB. I knew then he was from Worcester. We were both so thrilled that we talked about the city practically all the way to Gulfport. He lived on Lincoln Street near Perkins. He was also a great friend of Ralph Mayo's, a teacher at South High, and also a friend of Mrs. Joyce.[1]

Another coincidence: when I was on the river steamer, I heard a radio broadcasting news over the loud speaker, including Holy Cross football scores. Worcester Tech was also mentioned. Boy, was I surprised.

Do you remember "Stage Door Canteen,"[2] the movie we saw together in Boston before I took the train to Virginia? Well, I heard the theme[3] song playing as I entered the USO the other night.

I'll be sending along a few circulars and a picture taken of the three of us by a street photographer while we were walking through a park in the French Quarter. The picture's not so hot, but it's a good souvenir of my trip to New Orleans.

Thanks for your letter, Ronnie. So you wouldn't want to be in my place, eh. Boy, you would if you visited New Orleans. I noticed that you added "yet" when you wrote that you're not going out with girls. You should be here to let some of our Seabee wolves teach you.

By the way, I didn't fast Saturday because I couldn't pass up the good food in New Orleans. I had butter, plenty of milk and ice cream too.

P.S. Quote from Kate Smith:[4] "If you don't write, you're wrong."
P.P.S. We're living in Quonset huts now instead of barracks.

10:00 PM Tuesday 10/12/43

Dear Mom and Dad,

I don't mean to omit Ronnie in this letter, but I'm sure what I have to say wouldn't interest him. I received three letters today: from Cousin Lil, from Mr. Ringer, and of course, yours. I'll answer only your letter tonight because I have something important to say. No nothing bad has happened. I'll begin at the beginning.

I saw "Hers to Hold" with Deanna Durbin tonight. By chance, I found myself seated beside a member of my battalion, a fellow about twenty-three years old who had two years of college. After the show we got to talking about the finer things in life: about parents back home, families and even girlfriends. As you may guess, very few men in an organization such as ours discuss or even think of the pure and wholesome things in life.

We then discussed the relationship between men in general. Here I am, a S 1/c, a mere high school graduate while many men much older than I with abilities superior to mine hold lesser ratings. Here I am, a mere boy with a rating that many men who believe they are superior to me and probably are, long for. No doubt these men resent me. It's human nature. Some men dislike the success of others. Some men mutter and gripe, and despise those who have earned their place as a result of their accomplishments.

Here, men use profanity to express themselves and their diction is limited. They envy those who can speak clearly, distinctly and with decent diction. This makes them feel inferior so they curse more. You may well wonder why I received a higher rating when so few were granted, when men more deserving than myself failed to get one. You may wonder, but I don't. Frankly, I talked my way into getting that rating. I saw the proper people and talked loud and big, and, I suppose, brazenly. But what choice did I have? I hold no qualifications for a high position compared with the other men who have trades. Big talk is my only tool while their tool is their skill. I now realize that many that failed to get a rerate resent me for getting one.

Then there's something else. Not until the holidays did the boys realize I was Jewish. Since entering the service I've encountered no anti-semitism. Since boot camp I've felt secure against this evil. But today, for the first time I felt it. While we were in the ranks, a fellow, whom I bunked with and laughed with and liked somewhat, told me in plain words that he and others resented the fact that I got liberty to go to "church." Why should I be allowed to go to New Orleans when he and his like weren't. I was dumbfounded and at first didn't know what to say. I suspected my rerate provoked him and was partly responsible for his anti-semitic attitude. My face reddened with anger. I called him an "ignorant damn fool" and I told him if he bothered me anymore I'd lay him flat. He shut up like a clam. Afterwards, he became more friendly, and I went along to some extent, but a feeling of distrust was still there. I'll never forget this incident. So you see, being Jewish brings on resentment.

I discussed this with the boy that I mentioned earlier, the one I met in the movies. He's broad-minded, so he offered some advice because he thinks I'm decent and have ideals similar to his. (By the way, he's applied for OCS — Officers' Candidate School). He said, "You have the hardest job in the battalion. I don't envy you a bit." He explained that the curse of anti-semitism is a result of resentment by gentiles of the success of the Jews. (He's gentile himself.) He went on, and I quote, "Being Jewish is the greatest curse in the world." He cautioned me about the way I talk. "Don't swear," he said, "but don't speak over their heads as you're apt to do. They resent your decency." He warned me not to try to rise in rank too quickly because the fellows won't like it. It's better to have a title with the word "assistant" before it. It's better to be popular rather than have a "head" title and be envied and disliked. He said he realized that to tone down my enthusiasm, my desire to achieve and my ambition to advance, is a most difficult thing to do, but it has to be done if I wish to remain popular and have friends. Oh, our talk went on for hours, and what I've written here is only a small portion of the advice he gave me. Don't get me wrong. I get along swell with the fellows, and they like me. However, this fellow observed a tiny spark of feeling against me, and he's been wanting to speak to me about it. He chose his words carefully not to offend me, but he was candid.

So, you see, I must restrain my ambition and not make myself too conspicuous. I'll just have to watch myself. So far, I think I've done fairly well in this respect, but I fear I've kindled a tiny spark of resentment since my rerate. I must smother it before it spreads.

I do hope that this letter will be taken in the right way, and not give the impression that I'm unpopular with my mates. I'm not surprised at what happened because I expected it would sooner or later. It seems that resentment is the burden every industrious Jew must endure. Since, in the service, I'm in closer contact with people than in civilian life, I must be especially careful. Let's hope for the best. Please realize that if I'm slow in gaining the limelight, it's not because I can't. It's because for the sake of my security and happiness, I must remain obscure lest my achievement bring on dislike and resentment. So it's a curse on youth as well as the Jews.

No doubt, you're wondering why I wrote this at such a late hour. Well, I had to get these thoughts off my chest. I've had — oh, what would I call it—an intuition that something unpleasant was up. Not until I talked with this fellow did I fully realize the situation facing me.

As always, Hughie

Wednesday 10/13/43

Dear Mom,

I've just increased my allotment home by $10.00, effective December 1st. On getting a $12.00 a month raise, I've increased my personal allowance by $2.00. I don't really need the $2.00, but since you insist that I have more spending money, I'm submitting to your wishes. Ten Dollars is ample for my needs and now, with an extra two, I'm extravagant.

Cousin Lil informed me of Joe's[1] illness. It's too bad; he's such a lovely man. Remember Mr. Lazott[2], my physics teacher at South High, who died from a brain tumor? Let's hope Joe's fate will be different.

The natives here are fairly friendly and hospitable. But because the service men easily outnumber the civilians, the poor civilians can't get on buses, eat in restaurants or walk the streets without feeling out of place. If they should treat service men badly, I don't blame them. In spite of the situation the locals are still nice to us.

The winters here are like your autumns. Today was as warm as any summer day at home. Why, I even went swimming yesterday and today. It seems strange that you're worrying about having enough coal while I'm swimming in the surf of the Gulf. They use coal down here only for heating water, and they heat their homes by natural gas.

I feel wonderful, in the top of condition. I'm thankful that I'm getting enough sleep. My body is tanned, my face a reddish brown from the sun and the ocean.

Mr. Ringer[3] sent a check for $31.50, after I had written him that I could purchase an electric razor for him now, but not a watch. The stores are out of them. Tell him that once a new supply of watches arrives I'll buy one. I'll send the razor in a day or two. By the way, a special office on the base cashes checks.

It's good when you write about trivial happenings at home. To me, they're important.

I should tell you what's happened to me these past three days. We were taught Judo, a modified jiujitsu, Monday afternoon. We learned how to break necks, backs, arms, and legs and how to paralyze a guy. It was very interesting. Say, Ronnie, how about a fight sometime?

I had liberty Monday evening with a very fine fellow from Natchez, Mississippi. We visited the GCM, the Gulf Coast Military

Academy, one of the finest of its kind in the country. Every year it sends two boys to West Point. We brought our bathing suits hoping to swim in the swell pool there, but the trip from Gulfport took so long that darkness had fallen by the time we arrived and couldn't swim. We called on this fellow's grand aunt who had been a teacher at the Academy. Although she's in her seventies, she's quite sharp and modern-minded and even likes boogie woogie.[4]

She showed us the children's dormitory where the kids are six to twelve years old, and remarkably well mannered, always addressing us with sir or m'am. On being introduced, they even saluted. Sons of naval officers, diplomats and wealthy folks, they're from all over the nation. The kids were so thrilled to see us that they offered us candy and gum and talked to us about their folks, showed us pictures of them, and showered us with questions. They asked us to help them with their homework. especially math. I helped a few boys. One boy, after seeing my left arm suddenly cried out, "Look a cry baby," and they all yelled, "Yeah, a cry baby." "What's a cry baby?" I asked. One of the youngsters replied, "That's what the CB on your arm stands for." Well, I just died from laughing. We sure had one swell time with those kids. They were so lively and healthy looking that you couldn't help liking them.

Later we sat in the grand aunt's apartment talking about everything from politics to snow. She admires Roosevelt.[5] From our conversation I discovered the southern point of view on many subjects. I also learned about the local area and its people. She was nice as pie to me and offered us refreshments. Before we realized it, several hours had passed, and it was time to return to camp. So I had spent a very enjoyable evening with a seventy year old woman. As we walked back along the beach under a full moon and beside a glistening sea, I felt swell.

Yesterday, after a morning of drilling, I went swimming in the Gulf again. The sea was especially rough, and I never enjoyed myself in the ocean more. Riding the high waves and the warm surf was just extasy (even though I just misspelled the word).

I've now been appointed head of my company's recreation department and have charge of swimming instruction, physical education, sports and leisure. At the moment, I'm forming a softball team.

This morning, for the first time, I performed the job for which I'm trained. With an aid, I instructed swimming at a marvelous outdoor pool that belonged to a swanky hotel in Gulfport. And I made some real headway with the fellows. They cooperated miraculously, becoming so enthused over what they had learned in so short a time, that they wanted to return in the afternoon. They are even asking the officers for lessons in addition to those regularly scheduled. Normally, I'll be giving lessons once or twice a week. It was a great success, and, it seems, the fellows were greatly impressed. Now they have a world of faith in me as their instructor. Many have personally thanked me for teaching them so earnestly.

This afternoon we marched in a pouring shower and got drenched to the skin, but it was fun.

Last night I saw "Hers to Hold". It was swell, both musical and dramatic. This evening I saw "Two Tickets to London"[6] with Michele Morgan.[7] Not bad either. Boy, I'm really enjoying myself. I guess it isn't hard to see it in my letters. This isn't so bad, after all, eh?

Thursday 1:00 PM 10/14/43

Dear Dad,

I just received your lovely letter of the ninth. Your letterhead is ideal. You may also add before my title, "A son proud of his parents."

How's Ronnie now? All better? To tell the truth, I believe he came down with the grippe, because last summer he didn't get enough sunshine. A sudden change in weather is apt to weaken one's resistance not already strengthened by the summer sun. How I wish he was down here swimming in the surf in the sun.

After the war, you'll probably travel more. I find many of the places I've seen so attractive, that someday I'd like to see them again. Maybe during vacations after the war we can travel together. I'll have some money by then, and you'll no doubt be able to afford it. Oh, I know, right now it sounds like a pipe dream. But who knows? I haven't come in contact with any Jewish families here. Oh, there are plenty of them in Gulfport and New Orleans, but I never bother to contact them. However, I have met several Jewish boys who come from the South. It's odd hearing them speaking Yiddish with a southern accent.

Say, would you send me a *Worcester Gazette* occasionally? I don't mean daily or weekly, just once in a while. A newspaper from home would feel good.

I know you civilians are also having it tough. If only you could get more help for the business. "C'est le guerre." (Meaning "It's the war," in French.)

6:30 PM

I'll be on liberty in Gulfport tonight and plan to attend a dance.

P.S. My swimming instruction was such a success that it was reported to the commander. It could lead to something. Who knows?

Friday 4:30 PM 10/15/43

Dear Folks,

You know, those damn helmets are really annoying in the rain: the water drips off them onto your clothes. Private Berger has a bright idea.

The clipping you sent me of the football game is swell. I know each one of those players from last year.

Mom, in answer to your question why other boys my age are given the opportunity to go to college, I can only urge you to give up any hope of my going to college under any program while I'm in the service.

10/16/43

Dear Folks,

This continues yesterday's letter. As I was saying, you must give up the idea of my ever going to school while I'm in the service. Frankly, I'm getting whatever I can out of this outfit, and it isn't so bad. As you know, I've made much progress in gaining recognition.

I've been in Mississippi a month today. Boy, does time fly. It seems as if we arrived here only yesterday. We've gone through plenty here and I've enjoyed it immensely. To tell the truth, I actually like it here. The weather has been beautiful.

Night before last, I went on special liberty to Gulfport. I say special, because my CPO secured it for me at my request. I was the only one in my company having liberty. I went with a friend from Denver who had often tried to go on liberty with me without success. Since he had liberty, I took the opportunity to request it. Not many fellows are allowed this. He wanted to go to a dance, so I tagged along. I don't know why, but the dance was a failure, a very unusual outcome at a USO dance. Anyway, I enjoyed the sights, but it wasn't the best time I've ever had.

But last night, my regular liberty night, I went out again. I had planned to remain in camp, but since our company was going to have a sham battle late in the night, I figured that I'd better leave camp while I could, or I'd be pulled into the battle. It wasn't that I wished to get out of anything, but I'm so sick of these unimportant sham battles. Whenever anything important comes up, all liberties are canceled. Since liberties weren't canceled last night, it proved that the maneuvers were unimportant. This morning I learned that the battle was a farce; I didn't miss anything.

Well, I was joined by the fellow from Natchez. Only twenty-nine, and the father of three children, he's one of the nicest, cleanest fellows you could ever meet. He won't touch a drop, a rare thing among Seabees. After roaming around Gulfport trying to find a decent show and finding only lousy ones, he decided to look up a distant cousin that he hadn't seen in fifteen years. While we were in a drugstore looking up his cousin's address in the telephone directory, his grand aunt appeared by sheer coincidence and drove us to our destination.

We stopped before a beautiful colonial style cottage set off the boulevard that bordered the beach. It almost knocked my eyes out. Inside was as cozy and quaint as could be. Mrs. Linfield, a handsome woman about your age with a magnetic personality, greeted us. Of course, she was college educated. Immediately, I knew I would enjoy myself. I couldn't get over her attractiveness.

Well, we settled down in the living room which was furnished with some practical furniture and a few antiques. The wallpaper on three walls was beautiful, and the fireplace wall was all white. Was I surprised when two girls, one eighteen and the other seventeen, walked into the room? They greeted me as if they had known me all my life. Actually, I was taken aback by their friendliness and charming personalities. Of course, these were the daughters, possessing the same beauty and personality as their mother. I couldn't help but like everything about them. We talked for several hours, discussing everything from why we Yankees say "you all" instead of "y'all," to Eleanor,[1] as they referred to Mrs. Roosevelt.

The older daughter graduated high school the same day I did. She's now attending college, majoring in art, commercial art, that is, similar to what John Fulgoni does professionally. She was surprised when I told her that I used to model in an art school for the students. We had plenty to talk about concerning art and high school.

The younger daughter is a senior in high school and full of the devil. She's interested in chemistry, and would like to be a laboratory technician. When I told her that I too was interested in chemistry, she was impressed and we had a long discussion.

Both girls are football fiends. By coincidence I had your letter with me and the clipping reporting South High's undefeated football team. When I showed it to them they went almost nuts.

After an hour, the younger girl's beau came to take her out. He was a high school senior. After we began talking about football, it turned out that he was a Holy Cross addict (Holy Cross is popular down here), and he didn't want to leave. Finally, his date got him out of the house. It was really funny. The mother remarked that she is reliving her high school days, for now her house has become more or less a club house for all the boys and girls.

I had to laugh when I revealed my age. They thought I was about twenty-three because my chum, their cousin, is twenty-nine. Furthermore, in their opinion I didn't talk like a recent high school graduate.

I should mention that the family has no father. He was a well known doctor, and, while stationed in a hospital in the hills of New Mexico, was killed in an auto accident.

In all, I had one of the most enjoyable evenings I've had since I've been in the service, and as a matter of fact, in my life. When we left, they extended an earnest invitation for us to come back. Maybe, someday we will. With chocolate so scarce for civilians, and so plentiful for soldiers, we promised to send them some.

Today I received a letter from you, John Fulgoni, Ted Bagdikian at Camp Peary, and Lorraine Gallant, Lenny's sister. What a friend I have in John. They don't come any better.

Today is the first cold day we've had: below fifty. Being used to warm weather, we're freezing. But this is only a temporary cold snap.

Yes, George Chast, the fellow who went to New Orleans and attended services with me, is Jewish. He holds a lower rating than mine. You see, even though he's brilliant, his knowledge is worth nothing in the Seabees. Therefore he has a low rating. It's a shame.

Saturday 8:30 PM 10/16/43

Dear Mom,

This is my second letter home today. Since I have the rest of the evening with nothing to do, I feel like chatting with you.

At 9:00 tomorrow we're supposed to invade a sandy island about twelve miles out in the Gulf. I've just finished packing, according to the way we were taught, the regulation seventy-five pound pack we'll be wearing on our backs. Also, as we were taught, each man will set up a pup tent to live in all next week. It's wonderful training and I'm looking forward to the experience.

The day after I gave swimming instruction, everyone congratulated me. I was baffled as to why until one fellow mentioned that word of my ability as a swimming instructor had become widespread. Many had admired the beautiful job I had done. The men told the CPO and the CPO told the officers. Soon the head of Welfare and Recreation got wind of it. Even the skipper himself, Commander Nowell, received a report, saying that I gave the most successful swimming instruction in the entire battalion. You see, there are other instructors. Mine weren't the only swimming instructions given. My instruction aid, who is twice my age, is a prince of a chap, and an excellent swimmer. But he knows nothing about instruction. After observing my teaching technique, he was able to help me a lot. I used Jack Manning's method. Manning is a New England aquatic director. I learned his method when I helped him teach at the "Y" last June. He has a good system, and it worked perfectly.

Mr. Tretter informed me of all this and said that there was talk of making me the physical education and swimming instructor for the entire battalion. As you know, I'm now head of my company's recreation department and I've organized a crack softball team.

Enclosed is the second edition of the battalion newspaper. Note the publicity I received at the bottom of page five. I have no idea who submitted the news about my swimming party. Ours is the only one mentioned among all the swimming parties given by instructors in the other companies.

Yes, I may have been given all the credit, but it wasn't wholly deserved. I really wasn't responsible for the success of the session. The fellows I taught were. Every one of them put their heart and soul in learning how to swim. Their cooperation and total response was marvelous. That's why they caught on so well. I'm not being modest when I say that they truly deserve the credit. They were so happy at doing well that they attributed it to me. This swimming incident has certainly won over several of the fellows who didn't approve of my rerate.

So you see that things are working out well. The trouble is that unlike the regular navy, the Seabees consider their swimming program as secondary. If I gain a responsible position, I'll try to change their attitude.

There's no doubt in my mind that I'm content being where I am. I'm sufficiently reconciled to say that I'm happy.

By the way my friend from Natchez phoned the family we visited last night and they said they'd like me to join them for dinner from time to time. I'd really like to but I fear that I'd be imposing.

A week from this weekend, I get another thirty-six hour liberty. I don't know what I'll do or where I'll go as yet.

Cat Island, Gulf of Mexico

Dear Folks,

Would you think, say five months ago, that I would be writing a letter while basking on the sands of a semi-tropical isle in the Gulf of Mexico?

I can veritably say that this is the most beautiful morning I have ever seen in my life. The sky is as cloudless and blue as one can possibly imagine. The sea is a calm silvery aqua as the light morning breeze carries the sound of small rollers breaking on the beach to my ears. There I go, getting poetic but the serenity is indescribable. The nearest people are about a mile down the beach.

No doubt you'd like to hear about everything that's happened, so here goes. About 6:30 yesterday morning, (That's Sunday) each man made up his regulation pack consisting of clothes, personal gear and pup tent, the sum total weighing about seventy-five pounds. We marched about three miles along the boulevard to a navy reservation where barges awaited us. Since this was the first time we had to wear packs as well as carry rifles, many men dropped out due to weariness.

We boarded the barge about 10:00. To give you an idea of its size, here's what one accommodated: two companies of about 150 men each, a crane the size of a steam shovel, a jeep, a large army truck, a bulldozer, and food and construction supplies. The trip to the island took four hours in a moderately calm sea. At two o'clock when we arrived at the island, the plank was lowered, and by squads, waves of men leaped into knee deep water and rushed to meet the opposition planted ashore. (The island, six miles long and four miles wide, is shaped like a T; we landed at the T end.) The enemy was so well concealed that I couldn't see anyone, yet shots were coming from all directions.

When the sham battle was over we settled down to setting up our pup tents in the sand some 200 yards in from the beach. (The sand extends about 400 feet in from the shore.) We slept two to a tent. My bunk mate was a very fine fellow from Chester, Pennsylvania. Luckily I was assigned guard duty, four hours on and eight hours off. My watch began at midnight and ended at 4:00, and I had time off until noon next when I was on watch again until four. During time off I was on my own, so I had plenty of time to swim and sleep and just plain bask in the sun.

I had several funny experiences during my watch last night. After being awakened at midnight to go on duty, I had the usual sandwiches and coffee—water or milk for me. I was transported by jeep to my post about a mile into the woods. That was my first jeep ride. The driver sped like the devil over the soft, bumpy, primitive roads. Boy, talk about bronco busting. This was twice as bad.

10/19/43

This continues yesterday's letter. While on duty we guards challenged five cows, two pigs and some horses. Weren't we surprised to find animals instead of people rustling the bushes? But it certainly kept us on our toes.

The island, called Cat Island, is privately owned and lies about twelve miles out. Because it's beyond the five mile limit, we're technically overseas. Fringed with sandy beaches, as I've said, it's semi-tropical interior is heavily wooded with pines and low branched trees that are draped with Spanish moss, giving a nice effect. A part of the island is devoted to an army dog training camp, having about 200 personnel. I've already met a few trainers and their dogs which I've enjoyed patting. Most of the dogs were German Shepherds and Collies with a small variety of other breeds. They were the most beautiful dogs I've ever seen.

I've become black as a Negro. Folks, I can't describe the serenity and mood of these surroundings. This is the most beautiful beach you would ever lay your eyes on. Pure white sand and white foam breaking on the shore extend as far as the eye can see. You need only walk out twenty feet along a gradual slope for deep water even at low tide. The water is the clearest I've ever seen and there's not a rock to hurt your feet. The temperature of the water is soothingly cool, neither warm nor icy cold like the water up north. Again today the sky is absolutely cloudless. This is truly like a South Sea isle. I could spend the rest of my life here. Although the sun is strong, the days are comfortably warm and with little humidity, but the nights are freezing. Even wool isn't enough to keep you warm. If only Ronnie could join me, he'd go nuts with pleasure.

So I work nights and play during the day. This paradise will come to an end on Friday when we return to Camp Holliday. I just learned this letter can be mailed from here. Forgive the delay. I've put a bit of sand in the envelope.

Wednesday 10:00 AM 10/20/43

Dear Mom,

Here, as usual, I'm on the beach just absorbing the sunshine and salt air. As you know, this is the farthest out in the ocean I've been, and it's the first time I've been on an island. All I can say is I'm having one darn swell vacation.

I've been receiving letters regularly, among them yours and a card from Dad. Yesterday I received a letter from Jack Brierly, the former president of our high school class. He enrolled at Worcester Tech, you know. He wrote that I'm lucky I'm not there, because he and all the boys our age who are attending the college are being drafted. He wrote that he never had a chance to learn anything in the short time he's been there, and that he'd be ahead if he had gone into the service sooner.

I also received a letter from my good friend, Lenny, who is now a third class petty officer in the navy and getting $78.00 a month. He's now going to advanced school for training in radio, electricity, and sound. Lucky, eh? There's nothing better than the regular navy. He sent the enclosed picture to me. Would you please send the slides to his home?

Why are you copying my letters on a typewriter? Why don't you just keep the letters themselves? Copying them is a big job. Well, I'm going to try and get some shut eye. So long.

Thursday 10:30 AM 10/21/43

Dear Folks,

Everything has been so grand out here on the island that I can't stop talking about it. Again today is cloudless and a swell surf is rolling in despite the calmness of the sea. I don't see how any other beach can beat this one, neither Miami nor Waikiki I'm sure.

At night, when not on duty, I sleep on the hard ground in the pup tent, with one blanket under me and another over me. The first night was tough, but I'm used to it now and sleep as if I were on a feather bed. Let me tell you, this is really roughing it. I remember that when I was a Boy Scout you didn't allow me to go on an overnight hike. I guess I've fooled you, after all. So far I'm about the only guy around here that hasn't got a cold or a sore foot or something. I'm keeping my fingers crossed. I'm quite surprised at how much I can take. Everything is so soaked from dampness in the morning that you'd think it had rained during the night. When I'm on duty from 4:00 AM to 8:00 AM I have to wear foul weather gear to keep dry. At sunrise a two foot thick layer of mist covers the ground. The effect is quite odd. Guard duty is really boring, but I don't mind since I have the daytime hours off.

You know, while we're on the beach swimming and running around we're completely naked. I'm naked most all day.

Well, we break camp tomorrow. I certainly hate to leave this place. It's only bad feature is the toilets. Before I forget, would you send me my Boy Scout flashlight? I sure can use it.

Rumors are flying thick and heavy around here that we'll leave for California before the first of the month. And I have a very faint ray of hope in the statement that we might return to Endicott after California.

The picture of me in New Orleans wasn't so hot, because the guy who took it was only a street photographer. But he was handy, so I thought I'd have the picture taken for the fun of it. I wouldn't be surprised that I put on weight. I'm more active and in better condition than ever. I should be in top condition with all this swimming, fresh air and daily sunshine.

Say, did I tell you that the ocean is just full of fish? And what fish! The fellows catch crabs, oysters and shrimp and all kinds of sea fish. I ate my first oyster yesterday—raw, right from the shell. I also ate a crab. Boy, are they good.

You probably know about porpoises. They are black fish, about five feet long and exceptionally friendly. You can see them jumping into the air every so often. While you're swimming they come right up to you and actually play with you.

The other day I went swimming with a CPO who had waded out to his hips to wash. Suddenly, he saw a fin sticking out of the water coming lickety split towards him. He yelled, scared stiff, thinking it was a shark, and fell over backwards. It was only a porpoise, which missed him only by inches. They can maneuver themselves in shallow water, big as they are, often coming within a few feet from shore. The water is abundant with flounder, too.

By the way, the island is of some historical interest. It was a pirate hideout. Well, now I must return to the lazy life of reclining and end this hard labor of pen pushing, ho hum.

Gulfport, Mississippi

Dear Folks,

My vacation at the seashore is now over. We returned to camp from the island yesterday. Tonight I have a thirty-six hour liberty.

I've been falling behind on letter writing due to my many duties. Ten letters arrived between yesterday and today. That's quite a record. Four are from home, two from the Gallants, one each from Mr. Riccius, Cousin Lil, Aunt Sadie and Grandma. It's funny, just when I'm writing the least, I receive the most letters.

Your letters mostly concern my letter of a week ago Tuesday. I never realized that my letter would bring on such a clamor of advice. You people took my letter much too seriously. I wish to discuss the problem so we can get things straight.

As long as I've been in the service, until the incident I wrote you about, no one has remarked about my being a Jew. As far as I can see, there is little or no anti-semitism in the battalion. The fellow that taunted me didn't even mention the word "Jew." It was only inferred. I fear my letter was a bit too strong. I was anticipating trouble. I'm treated no differently than any of the other fellows. I didn't swear at the fellow but merely told him to shut up. If I had ignored him, he'd have only kept on. Coincidentally, he was in my non-swimmers' class, and he saw that I gave him as much attention as the others. Today he is nicer to me than many of the other fellows. Of course, I can never trust him. As far as my looking for fights is concerned, have no fear. When I get mad at someone, I try to avoid him, and I watch who I get mad at. We didn't resort to fisticuffs. There were only words between us. Fights are rare here. I'm sure you can have confidence in how I conduct myself. There's no need to remind me. You needn't worry: my record is foremost in mind whenever I'm in a predicament with another fellow.

I appreciate your wisdom and words of advice. But you haven't told me anything that I don't already know. Rarely, if ever, do I express what I really think. I gripe very little, and I try not to antagonize anybody. I never discuss religion. So you see I know what's right and what's wrong. I've seen and heard much these last few months, in particular the last month. I feel—and I'm sure you will agree—that I have enough common sense to act correctly. I have kept my head in every instance. If I hadn't, I'd have let you know. From your letters I know how sincere and heartfelt your wishes for my welfare are. I read each one carefully, absorbing every word. Your words are true, and they're also a part of my personal doctrine. I'm willing to admit that I have a quick temper, but to a large extent I've overcome it. I think more before I speak than I used to.

Regarding my statement about my future advancement, I agree with you completely. I didn't mean to say that I plan to remain where I am now. What I meant was that I don't want to be a loud mouth as so many are when seeking a rerate. However, it's slower if you only wait for the officers to consider you for a rerate. You've got to make a noise and build yourself up. Oh, don't worry, I'm aiming higher but I'm doing it without antagonizing and bringing on resentment.

As I feared it would, my letter gave you an impression of things that I hadn't intended. Nothing bad has happened. My status is unaffected. I merely told you what the possibilities were and not what actually happened. I admit that the advice that fellow gave me wasn't necessarily correct, but he said the things he did for my own good. I wish we could have talked, then I could have made things clearer. As a matter of fact, after I had written the letter, I forgot it. I don't harbor such thoughts. I'm sorry I caused you worry and to have doubts about me. So be at ease; I am. I'm surprised at my self-confidence. As long as I'm confident, there's no need to worry. So far I've handled everything that's come up quite well without help. Give up? Why, I would never give up trying, no matter how much I'm insulted. But nobody has hurt me either mentally or physically. I'm not moping. I'm enjoying life and don't have a worry in the world.

I wish you hadn't told others about my letter. I prefer my letters to remain between us only. I write you about things that happen that I would never tell anybody else. And there are many things that I can't write about for obvious reasons. As a parent, you no doubt know that. You may broadcast the facts I write about, but not my problems. Lil has already written me on the subject. I don't like receiving such letters from relatives. People have been given a false impression over a letter that I've forgotten. I know Lil meant well, and so do you as a parent, but you should know that by now I can solve my own problems. I'm not a child. I can think straight and act wisely. Not that I don't welcome your help. Civilians can't possibly understand the situation facing every intelligent serviceman. I don't mean to suggest that our way of life is so vastly different from yours or that we are better than civilians. But I have heard stories of men in the service who have endured the most disappointing experiences you can imagine. I wish I could say what I mean better than I have. It's so difficult. It's my fault that in the letter I didn't make myself clearer. Unfortunately, I'm not a writer. And I hope I didn't say anything in this letter that would hurt you. I don't mean to. I love every one of you for taking such an interest in my thinking and my problems. I'm sorry now I ever wrote that damn letter. Even now, I feel I haven't communicated well. Boy, I wish I could talk to you.

Gulfport, 10:00 PM

Dear Folks,

Here I am again in Gulfport on a thirty-six hour liberty. I'm in a USO where plenty is going on. It's quite a dance, they're having. I feel sorry for the poor girls. Boy, do they get tossed around.

I had a swell T-bone steak for supper in Angello's, a classy restaurant. Best I ever tasted. Guess I'll sign off now. Will write tomorrow.

Sunday 2:00 PM 10/24/43

Dear Mom,

Since the usual way to open a conversation is to talk about the weather, let's talk about it. Were I to close my eyes, I'd swear we're having a beautiful June day back home.

In a way. I'll be sorry to leave this place. I've really enjoyed myself here more than Virginia or Rhode Island. The people are cordial in spite of the difficulties the servicemen bring on. Although I was planning to visit Mobile, Alabama this weekend, I'm rather weary after the ordeal on the island and the trip back so I don't feel much like traveling.

Just think, November is almost here. This month has gone by like a whirlwind. We expect to remain in Mississippi at least until November second, possibly longer. Orders for our destination or our time of departure have been changed. It seems I have roving fever: after a month I want to move on.

The USO dances are really funny. No sooner does a sailor or soldier and his girl get out on the floor, when someone cuts in. I timed one girl. Without exaggeration she was out six times in thirty seconds. The servicemen practically kill the girls during a jitterbug[1] number. I can't figure out how the girls, all townspeople, stand it. Their faces are expressionless when they dance. They slip back and forth from one fellow's arms to another fellow's automatically without bothering to look at their partner and see what he looks like. I can't figure out how the men enjoy it. They never dance with one person more than a few minutes. Oh well, that's the service for you. It's the soldiers that jam these places. If there were only the Seabees and sailors it wouldn't be so bad since there aren't as many of us.

Enough said. Knocking off now.

Monday 4:15 PM 10/25/43

Dear Mom,

I plan to see "Five Graves to Cairo"[1] tonight.

I'm way behind on letter writing. I don't know why, but I've lost all ambition to write anyone but you folks. I guess I'm too used to having fun and enjoying myself. Instead of writing I go to shows.

So you thought I'd learn how to dance. Frankly, I'm not looking for any opportunity to learn. If one comes up, I'll take it, but I'm not going to go out of my way.

I'm so happy that you are having your hair done and that you're buying clothes. According to Yetta, you were simply stunning when you visited her in Boston. That's what I like to hear.

Rumors are flying thick and fast about the battalion's next move. I suspect that we'll be here another two weeks. Don't be surprised if I land back in Rhode Island again. To tell the truth, I'd rather go to the west coast. Oh, by all means I'd like to see you folks, but if I saw the west coast first then went home my wishes would be complete. You see, if we go to Rhode Island for our advanced base depot, we'll be assigned to the European theater. I prefer that. As you may have noticed, the heading on my stationery refers to Camp Holliday as A.B.D., Advanced Base Depot. Battalions only ship out of Advanced Base Depots but it doesn't apply to our battalion. We are receiving only modified training here. I doubt whether we'll ship out before next year.

Boy, would I like to get into Gene Tunney's[2] program! But now that I'm assigned to the battalion, it's hard to transfer, especially with all the training I've had. Furthermore, each battalion has its own particular kind of training. You see, they couldn't find anyone with my training to replace me. If we end up in Endicott, I'll see what I can do, but down here I can do nothing. If we go across, I'll undoubtedly be in the recreation department. Fortunately several chiefs and officers are boosting me.

Say, do you ever get sick of my egotistical letters? Doggone it, I use the word "I" more than any other word. Actually, I'm getting sick of talking about myself. Enough said. I'll be hearing from you. If you don't write you're wrong, or something like that.

5:30 PM

I just received two more of your letters. They contain things that I deem it imperative to answer. Here goes. Often I'm unable to complete a letter, because I must leave camp to catch a bus or I'm called to muster or some other reason prevents me. I usually write after dinner, but time flies so, that I usually have to dash out to roll call. Please don't think I cut things short on purpose, and I'm sure you don't. I've never ended a letter because I attended to my own pleasures. Not on your life. Often, I have an uneventful day and as a result, have little to say. This past week I didn't write for two or three days because it was impossible to mail letters while traveling to the island. I probably don't always explain things as well as you'd like, but that's because I don't place as much importance on an event as you would. Folks, I live by and for your letters and my replies are the most important thing I do throughout the day. Please remember that.

It's too bad Uncle Bill has it so tough. I don't see the sense in such strenuous training. It's not a training course; it's a break down course. A man must have his sleep. It's too bad he found the five mile march so hard. It would be merely a jaunt for us.

Yeah, if you want to send me some figs and raisins, please do. We get plenty of candy here but not the above. However, if you can't spare the points,[3] forget it. I'm looking forward to getting the newspapers.

I received a lovely letter from Mrs. Mann.[4] I hope you didn't get the idea that I govern my behavior by that man's[5] advice. I listened, but I came to my own conclusions. Don't worry, I'm man enough to think for myself. By the way, I've applied for another rerate. They probably think I have plenty of nerve, but who the hell cares.

Tuesday 10/26/43

Dear Dad,

Our training schedule in Gulfport is now completed. We're only stalling for time, waiting to be assigned to another base for more training. Our departure date may be in a week, a month or six months. Who knows? They're actually looking for a way to keep us busy. I'm not doing a darn thing except a few petty tasks.

Today, the battalion received no mail. We don't know why, and speculate it's due to a train wreck or maybe we're moving. The uncertainty is fun. I'm fascinated waiting to see what will happen.

It's chilly enough today that most of us are wearing sweaters and pea jackets. We're all so sensitive to sudden changes in temperature. Our blood must be plenty thin. Anyway, this life agrees with me. I feel better and look better than ever in my life. It's due to getting plenty of sleep, eating good food, having good times and being in the fresh air. I don't have that lazy, sluggish feeling anymore. (I take Carter's Little Liver pills,[1] that's why.) I'll bet you're freezing up there now. Brrr, talking about it makes me shiver. I just heard that the government debt is $104,204,022,068.70, and two army privates sent thirty cents to the treasury department to round off the figure. That's being on the ball, eh.

Here's a joke that you may or may not have heard. A Seabee went looking in the Solomons jungle for Japs, yelling "Down with Hirohito." Finally, a Jap yelled back, "Down with Roosevelt." "Did you kill the Jap?" someone inquired. "Of course not," replied the Seabee. "How could I kill a fellow Republican?" Not bad, eh. Okay, okay so it was lousy.

I must tell you about the embarrassing experience I had while on guard duty on Cat Island. I was one of three guards, with loaded rifles and cartridge belts, patrolling a 300 yard line in the woods. We were on the midnight to 4:00 watch. Each guard had orders to allow no one, but no one, to pass through his 100 yard sector.

At about 2:00, we heard a rustling in the bushes some distance away. However, we weren't allowed to leave our posts to investigate. As we waited, we brought our guns to port arms, the challenging position. I being the center guard, I crept slowly to consult each guard on what we should do. We decided to lay low and wait some more. We waited about forty-five minutes in stygian darkness while the rustling grew louder. Soon we heard the sound of footsteps in water coming from all sides. Becoming worried, I crept over to the guard on my left and suggested that we release our safety and be prepared to shoot. (You see, our orders were to be ready to shoot, and to do so if need be.) As we talked, we heard a cough which confirmed our suspicion that men were approaching. Suddenly, we heard something break through the undergrowth nearby, and the rustling continued around us. Boy, were our hearts in our mouths! The other guard whispered "ambush," but I told him he was crazy. An ambush couldn't happen in this place.

Then suddenly we saw creatures coming from under the trees into a moonlit opening. We could make out a half dozen cows, some pigs, and a couple of horses. We could hardly stop laughing. Later we learned that all the guards on watch that night had a similar experience, but they wouldn't pass it on to their reliefs just to have fun.

I'm ending this letter in the theater where I'll be watching "Holy Matrimony"[2] with Monty Wooley[3] and Gracie Fields.[4] I saw "Five Graves to Cairo" with Franchot Tone[5] last night. Excellent. It's a pleasure to see a movie and not have to pay a cent. And we are shown the latest pictures.

I just returned from the movies. "Holy Matrimony" was a fine picture, packed full of wholesome humor. It was swell.

Wednesday 4:30 PM 10/27/43

Dear Ronnie,

We're still stalling for time, doing nothing important. No mail again today. Maybe our mail is being sent elsewhere by mistake.

They tell me you folks at home are dying from starvation, that you're having a terrible time with eggs. You mean, you can't even get powdered eggs? Well, I guess you have to resort to the old fashioned kind, the kind you break open, after all. I understand that during blackouts, a Worcester Scotch man runs around developing his film. Is the butter situation any better?

With nothing else to do, I expect to see a USO show tonight. I can't think of a thing to write about. Oh, well, maybe somebody will commit suicide. Enclosed, is the third edition of the battalion newspaper that tells all about what we did on the island last week.

Your favorite "pin-up" Seabee,

Wednesday 8:15 PM 10/27/43

Dear Mom,

There's no need to send me anything for my birthday. I have everything I want and need. I won't feel hurt in the least if you don't send anything. Your faithful and swell letters are my birthday present. They mean more to me than any tangible object.

You ask if I know E.C, Poske, the Master at Arms of Company A. Before the war we used to work out together at the "Y." We met again at Camp Peary when the battalion was being formed. He's the fellow who used to drive me home from Endicott. We see each other often and talk about the good old days back home. He's a swell fellow and has quite a bit of influence in his company. Yes, I know him: we're the best of friends.

We servicemen can get all the candy, stationery and jewelry that we wish. In fact, we can buy the finest Bunte's chocolates and other famous brands to send back home. Seems funny, doesn't it.

Just returned from the USO show. It wasn't bad, but too short.

10/28/43

Dear Folks,

We arrived in Gulfport six weeks ago today. Four months ago today I was inducted into the Seabees at Fort Devens.[1] It seems like yesterday.

Yesterday was a gala day. We had all kinds of parades to celebrate Navy Day.[2] Perhaps the V-12 students held a parade in Worcester.

It's now a month since my embarkation leave, and I'm still in the country. It seems odd that I'm here. I'm sure our schedule has been changed. A battalion ordinarily leaves the country within a month of embarkation leave.

I'll write again after the noon mail arrives so hold the phone for a while.

Friday 7:30 PM 10/29/43

Dear Mom,

We're having a big dance at the base tonight to celebrate Halloween. I had liberty last night and since I had a standing invitation to visit the Linfields, my friend and I went there, a box of candy under our arms, and partook of their Southern hospitality. And, indeed, what hospitality it was. We were greeted with the same friendliness as was bestowed on us during our last visit. Only it was yet more casual. "Hello Huey," Mrs. Linfield said when she opened the door. My name is associated with "the honorable Huey Long."[1]

As expected, I enjoyed every minute. We talked and talked all evening about just everything. They played some Gershwin[2] records, particularly "Rhapsody in Blue."[3] The subject of fruit came up, and they asked if I knew what a pomegranate was. Not aware that what we call Indian Apples were actually pomegranates, I said that I hadn't the faintest idea what they were. They led me into the darkness of their back yard where we picked a pomegranate of a tree. We stood there having a swell time eating the darn things. You know how messy eating pomegranates is. Before long we were ready for a bath, well, at least a face wash.

I saw a fig tree there for the first time in my life and several other Southern trees and shrubs that were unfamiliar. To make up for the difficult job we had eating the delicious but seedy and juicy pomegranates, Mrs. Linfield served us cake which we devoured in true Seabee manner. Luckily, Mrs. Linfield doesn't subscribe to Emily Post's[4] dictums. Even Ann, the older daughter, enjoyed the crumbs. I suppose everybody likes the bottom of the pan. Of course, in order not to offend Mrs. Linfield, we did this on the sly.

Later in the evening it was the younger daughter that added a kick to the conversation. Although she's frivolous and full of the devil, she's also a brilliant student, especially in chemistry. Soon the girls showed us their Gulfport High yearbook. What a beautiful school they attend. I was surprised to learn that Ann was the belle of the senior class last June. Her picture was on practically every page for every social event and major office. Why, I was visiting the most popular girl in Gulfport. The idea actually frightened me. It seems that Ann walked away with every honor that could possibly be given to a student graduating her high school (the only one in Gulfport). Soon I also learned that the younger daughter was similarly involved and honored in her class.

I sure had a fine time last night. It brought back memories of long ago when I was in high school.

When I read your Monday's letter about having company on Sunday, a smile crossed my face. I remember well those family gatherings, although they seemed so insignificant at the time. I pictured you rushing about, doing your best to please everyone and making sure that each morsel of food was "la pièce de resistance" (French for "a perfect thing"). Which reminds me where are those raisins I asked for?

You know, by writing regularly, I fear that you'll expect that I'll continue indefinitely. But, the time will come when I won't be able to write letters home every day. Emergencies are liable to arise so please don't be disappointed when you receive no letters for a time. By the way, I just learned that I can call home for $3.00.

I heard some good news this morning. I never told you that our training in Mississippi was to prepare us for becoming a combat battalion, that is we were slated for combat duty. But since we've performed so marvelously in construction, we'll be assigned to strictly construction work. Of course, there's always a chance we'll see some combat. We expect to remain stateside for some time, yet.

Many men have requested and been given ten day leaves. I've not asked for one, because if we go to Rhode Island before leaving the country, I'll take it from there. I heard that since we've remained in the country for thirty days after our embarkation leave, it's no longer valid. So legally we're due another leave, but, if necessary, the order can be retracted and leave refused. However, the president just signed a law requiring that all men be granted a twenty-one day leave before embarkation. I hope it applies to us.

Saturday 10/30/43

Dear Dad,

Leaves are being handed out left and right. A bus load of fellows from the 113th is going to Baton Rouge, 165 miles away, to see LSU, the home team, play Texas Christian. It's going to be quite a game. I suppose Holy Cross is playing this afternoon. Gee, do I wish I could see a good football game. I bought the *New Orleans Item*, the leading New Orleans newspaper, and was surprised to see the sports page plastered with stories about Holy Cross. I see they're undefeated, eh. Holy Cross is very popular down here.

These days the inactivity is boring. I'm anxious to get moving. We've been down South long enough. Tomorrow is bag inspection; all our clothes are inspected in order to see what we lack and to make sure we have only our own.

I'm sorry that this letter is so uninteresting. If only we'd have a murder that I could write about. Oh, well, that's navy life for you. Excitement has its ups and downs.

With lotions of love to all of you, and, in closing, remind you that "we Seabees are very congenial people. We greet the Marines at every invasion."

Sunday 10/31/43

Dear Mom,

Since Sunday is a day of leisure for all those not on duty, I did nothing today. I passed inspection with flying colors.

Yesterday I had a haircut. (The battalion has three barbers.) The barber that cut my hair, had attended a barber's college and does things scientifically. Because he was one of my swimming students, he gave me special treatment. You should see how he groomed my hair. Believe it or not, he even matched my waves. He was so thrilled with the swimming lessons I gave him that he offered to give me an egg facial massage to improve my skin. So this afternoon he spent hours doing it. He used the whites of raw eggs, cold cream and a facial shampoo. Now my face feels like a million dollars. Although it's been quite clear compared with the way it was when I was home, now it's as smooth as a girl's. He certainly knows his stuff.

I received your letter of the twenty-seventh this morning. It's too bad you're having such lousy weather while we're having weather that's like the best days of June. Gee, I wish I could see you in your new coat. Ninety-six bucks doesn't seem very much for a coat. Couldn't you have bought something better?

No goodies from anyone yet. I'm sorry to hear how miserable Uncle Bill's camp is. Even Camp Peary sounds better. The navy is strict on cleanliness, anyway. I can't get over our wonderful food. For three consecutive Sundays we each get one half a chicken, prepared differently each time. Last Friday we had shrimp. And we can have all the butter we want.

For dinner we had half a creamed chicken, creamed carrots and peas, mashed potatoes, chicken soup that was excellent, stuffing, apple pie, cocoa, all the fresh bread and butter we'd like and an optional second piece of pie. Tonight we had swell cold cuts with potato salad. The bakery products are the best I've eaten. And even though the milk comes from Wisconsin, it tastes fresh. So you see the food is as good as at home. Every afternoon I have a chocolate malted or a sundae at the fountain. My stomach is sure getting swell treatment.

I guess I forgot to explain why I returned Mr. Ringer's check. It seems only navy personnel checks can be cashed, which I didn't know. The store still hasn't received any watches, but they do get them from time to time. I hope the Ringers will have patience. They got a wonderful bargain on the razor I sent them. I bought it through the same guy that gave me the massage.

So you think my steak dinner was expensive. Well, it was but please notice, I'm never broke, and I'm even planning to send ten dollars home. Better still, I'd better keep it, because we've been officially told that we'll be moving within the next two weeks. Although the meal cost $1.50, it was well worth it. I know it may sound like I'm splurging and going high class, but I like food and have no regrets over buying a good meal once in a while. I don't do this every week, mind you. Most of the fellows blow $15.00 away in one evening. That's more than I spend in a month. Because I budget myself, I always have money, more than most fellows, and they know it. But I never lend money, and I'll never have to borrow it. If I run low, it'll be my own fault, and I'll just have to suffer. Last weekend I spent only the day in Gulfport, returning to camp to sleep. It cost me only five cents, the fare from camp to Gulfport and return.

I plan to see "Wintertime"[1] with Sonja Henie[2] tonight. So long until tomorrow.

Monday 7:17 PM 11/1/43

Dear Dad,

Here it is, the first of November, and it's unusually hot, just like a humid August day. With training over, we've been assigned to work details. I've been tearing labels off tin cans and crushing them, an especially boring job. It appears that the swimming program has fallen through. Instruction hasn't been given for weeks.

Thanks for the newspapers of the 18th and 19th. Everybody from central Massachusetts wants to read them. Quite a few articles in those issues were about people I know. I read the news, even though it's old. Only occasionally do I buy a New Orleans paper. I'm not informed on the war news. You know more about what's happening in the war than I do.

Our mail has gone haywire again. Few of us received letters today; none for me.

I enjoyed the sets and the music in "Wintertime." I notice in the paper that the picture showed in Worcester a week ago. Of course, here we see it free. Boy, I see some swell stage shows have come to Worcester. Do you take advantage of them? Have you gone to the opera, Mom? Have you seen "For Whom the Bell Tolls?"[1]

Are you working hard as ever? Why don't you let up some. After all, you haven't as many to support.

How did Holy Cross make out? LSU beat Texas Christian, but Navy lost to Notre Dame, darn it.

All of us are beginning to feel restless. This waiting and killing time are nerve racking. I'm not too bothered by it, but some of the fellows are griping something awful.

12:30 PM 11/2/43

Dear Folks,
I'm still on the same rotten detail as yesterday.

You're wrong in thinking that I'm tired of writing. Truly, I enjoy it, especially to home. Once in a while I don't feel like it, so then I write to no one but you. Liberties take more time away from my letters than anything else.

Tonight I plan to see "Sweet Rosie O'Grady"[1] with Robert Young.[2]

9:00 PM

I received your letter of the 29th tonight, but I'm tired so will postpone answering until tomorrow.

Wednesday 10:00 PM 11/3/43

Dear Mom,
Tonight I'm on liberty in a USO in Biloxi and took in a show, "The Sky's the Limit"[1] with Fred Astaire and Joan Leslie. It was pretty good. I also took in more sights, in all an enjoyable evening. The show I saw last night, "Sweet Rosie O'Grady" was a swell musical.

I think the mails are so freakish these days because of the Christmas rush. By—this blankety blank ink. As I was about to write: By the way, the weather is still fine and dandy. We're almost sure now that we're headed for California near Los Angeles.

I think my next rerate will come slowly. They're reluctant to hand out petty officer ratings. Furthermore, I haven't been given the chance to prove myself. I doubt if I ever will. The Seabees aren't interested in swimming instructors, at least not this battalion. Find out what you can about the Gene Tunney program. If I pursue it, I can make it hard for myself. I realize this is a big order, and I won't be disappointed if you have no luck. After we're at our new base, I'll investigate.

I bet you look like a million dollars all dolled up in a new hat, dress and coat. I'd give a million to see all of you.

I can't figure out how a penny and a slug got into the envelope I sent. I don't have any slugs. Doggone it, maybe my letters are being censored. I put in an order for battalion pictures weeks ago. When I get them I'll send them home.

It's too bad Dad finds it tough to get fabrics and upholstering supplies. I wish something could be done. You've been fortunate so far.

I may go to Mobile over the weekend. I think it's time I headed back to Gulfport so I'll close.

11/4/43

Dear Dad,

Due to the confused mails, I received no letter from home today but a swell letter arrived from Aunt Anna. She rather liked the last letter I sent her.

I lost a little sleep due to liberty last night so I plan to retire early tonight. Although liberty is up at 7:00 AM, I usually start back to camp at 11:00 PM and I'm in bed by midnight.

I went out with Al Martin who hails from near Pittsburgh. He's a swell fellow and has good habits. His only trouble is that he's madly in love with a girl named Lorraine back home. He's twenty-three and was a movie projectionist like Uncle Max. I enjoy his company, especially when we go to a show and he points out the flaws in the projection. I've already learned quite a bit about theaters from him. It's very interesting.

Still assigned to the tin can detail, I'm pretty disgusted, but what can you do? No doubt, you've noticed that the mood of my letters varies. Right now, I'm feeling pretty low because of the way I'm assigned menial tasks and dirty jobs. No one is to blame. It's the way of the Seabees. I'm tempted to complain to the commander. I haven't yet been given a fair chance to show what I can do. The only thing I have to look forward to is to get this damn war over with, return home, and go to school.

As you saw from my letters, a month ago I was ambitious and optimistic. No longer. Now, all ambition has faded. It isn't that I've given up, not that. It's that I feel so constricted in this outfit that I can't turn. I feel they have me under their thumb. As I said, a petty officer rating which would release me from their hold, is rarely given. No doubt something will come up and I'll feel better again. I usually get over my frustration sooner or later. If it weren't for liberty and the shows, I'd go crazy.

You see, I'm doing the same job that the Negro prisoners are doing. Can you blame me for kicking?

Don't let this letter of dejection bother you. I've got to blow my top to someone. If I were to do it here, I'd get into trouble. You folks provide a safe place. You know me well enough to be familiar with how I react to disappointment. I await your longed for letter tomorrow. Boy, I sure can use one.

With all my love to the three of you,

                                                    7:00 PM 11/5/43

Dear Folks,

The mail was kind to me this morning: a letter from you, Dad and you, Mom and the flashlight. They are all a sailor boy could ask for from the mail. Today I'm in much better humor. In fact I feel pretty good, the reason for which I'll explain later.

Say, Dad when do you plan to write a book? No kidding, I never knew you could write so well. If I were to overlook a few misspellings, I'd swear that you were Shakespeare the Second. I glowed with appreciation when you wrote "a letter that you receive from home is as important to you as a day's work is to me."

It looks like we'll be here longer than two weeks, after all. Orders can change overnight, of course. I wouldn't be surprised if we stayed here another month. We aren't moving because we have to wait for an opening while the California camps are filled to the brim with battalions waiting to ship out.

The only hint that it was Halloween here is an occasional party and a dance. None of the windows in Gulfport or Biloxi were marked. I think up north celebrating Halloween is a bigger thing. I like your "barer and barer like Sally Rand." Why, Dad you surprise me. I'm reminded of Bob Hope's definition of a Seabee: "An old salt looking for a piece of sugar." Yeah man.

Although I've been low the past few days, brought on by my work, I got over it today, and I've been able to keep my head high. I've been doing some thinking and have come to a few conclusions.

I spoke to a CPO and he's trying to get me off that work detail. After telling him that I had a couple of years of mechanical drawing in school and that I majored in mathematics, he was surprised, saying, "I never knew that. Why didn't you tell me. I thought you were interested only in phys ed." I explained that since they don't need me for phys ed, I'd welcome doing drafting or surveying instead of the dirty, rotten detail I'm on. So he's doing what he can for me; meanwhile, if they still need a swimming instructor I'm available.

I suspect I'll have difficulty getting into Tunney's naval program. A recent announcement cautioned the men not to correspond with the navy to seek a transfer from the battalion. You see, several men have tried. It's apparent that I still don't know what my status is in this outfit. When they need men to do drafting and surveying I'm available, and, when they need swimming instructors, I'm also available. I expect they'll soon think I can do anything. If they ever need steeple jacks, I'll inform them that I used to climb trees as a kid.

I haven't noticed any changes in myself other than my darker skin color. It difficult to see such changes. I haven't grown any taller and I have no idea of my weight. All I know is I feel swell and I'm in good condition. I received the usual comments on my physique. I'm bound to with all the 4-Fs around here. They ask the usual questions concerning developing their own bodies. The older men tell about how good they looked when they were young.

When I'm in California I'll have some pictures taken. I don't care for the photographers here. Los Angeles should have some good studios.

It was fine of you to send Aunt Anna some money.[1] Now I understand why she wrote me that "Your mother and father were very wonderful to me while I was sick and some day I hope to repay them both for their kindness."

No doubt, Dad with his poetry and I with my experiences, could well combine and become a second Longfellow.[2]

Doggone, Mom, do I wish I could see you all dolled up. Do you wear your teeth all the time? How are your eyes?

Ronnie, give Miss Phillips my worst regards.

Mom squealed on you, Dad, and told me that you spent two hours writing your letter. I'm not surprised. A letter as fine as yours couldn't be composed in less time. Remember how I used to spend hours writing a letter with the aid of a dictionary? Now letters come off my pen as if prefabricated. In fact, my writing doesn't keep up with my thoughts. Now it seems I can write without even thinking.

Love to each and every one of you, Hughie (Expert tinsmith. Specialty: tin cans.)

Saturday 8:00 PM 11/6/43

Dear Mom,

I got three letters in tonight's mail: yours, one from Aunt Sadie and one from a school chum who is an air cadet in Alliance, Ohio.

You seem pretty happy about my experience with the Southern family, only you'd like me to meet Jewish girls. To be honest, Mom, Jewish girls are rare down here. And for that matter, I don't bother much with any of them, Jewish or Gentile. I simply met these people and we talked, that's all. I'll probably never in my life see them again. To tell the truth, I don't care whether I ever see or talk to the opposite sex. I don't know why, but I'm still the way I used to be, but I know it isn't exactly right for a fellow my age. My education is foremost in my mind so I'd never allow myself to get friendly with a girl, Jewish or otherwise. So many fellows become attached to some girl they meet somewhere and forget about the girl back home. You'd be surprised at how many love affairs develop. In my opinion, it's sort of silly.

Yes, I know I had given you the impression that the Seabees are a non-combatant outfit. However, about a month ago I learned that some of our battalions are used strictly for combat. The 113th was chosen to be a combat unit, but, as I wrote you, that's been changed. Now we're strictly a construction outfit.

You are mistaken believing that I'm anxious to go across to fight. You can't mention an instance when I even hinted at such a thing. Please believe me; I don't want to fight unless I have to, and above all, I don't want to go across. I'm sorry you got the impression I do. Had I implied such a thing, I'd only be trying to act big and brave and cocky. Don't worry, I've seen enough of what warfare is like to know it's not fun. The real stuff is one hundred times worse, and don't think I don't know it. I admit I'd like to see California, but I dread the day when I have to leave these shores. Please understand that these are my sincerest sentiments.

Many of the fellows are receiving some packages a month after being sent and others a week after. You see, the Fleet Post Office balls everything up. I'll wait a while longer for the package Aunt Ida sent before I say anything.

I hear the dim-outs have been lifted. I'd like to see Worcester again the way it used to be.

I'm no longer on the can detail, but I'm on something almost as bad. I'm making bricks from tar and dirt. What a dirty rotten deal this is. Chief Tretter can't help me at all. I don't blame anybody but the Seabees. I like the training, but now that the training is over, I'm strictly a common, ordinary laborer that isn't expected to think for himself. I have to take it, though. I go out as much as possible to enjoy myself; it's something to get my mind off what I'm doing. I'd do anything to get back to thinking tasks and studying again. It isn't that I mind doing hand labor, but Chinese coolies[1] would do the sort of work I'm doing. I want to feel that I'm accomplishing something. This is definitely the wrong outfit for me, but there's nothing I can do about it.

Anyway, I'm not brooding and I feel well and, in a way, happy, since I'm seeing things. I weighed myself this evening; in uniform I weigh 173 pounds. Was I surprised? My uniform doesn't weigh more than five pounds. I guess I'm putting on weight, alright, but I'm not fat. My waist is still the same because my underwear still fits just right. I don't do my own washing anymore. Now I send my clothes to the laundry every week, and they do a fine job.

Sunday 5:00 PM 11/7/43

Dear Folks,

It's raining, ruining what could have been a swell day.

Liberty began at 5:00 yesterday evening, so I went to Gulfport and later returned to camp to catch some sleep and breakfast. My friend and I planned to leave camp by catching the 7:30 AM bus to Gulfport, and taking the 7:55 Greyhound to Mobile. But everything seemed to go against us. Although the sky was overcast, we figured it would clear up. Why not take advantage of a whole weekend of liberty? We then discovered that 9:00 o'clock was the earliest a bus would leave camp which meant that we'd have to wait in Gulfport for the next bus at 10:00 which wouldn't give us much time to spend in Mobile. So we hiked about a mile to the gate hoping that someone would pick us up. It started to pour and there wasn't a car in sight. But we were so determined to have this weekend that this didn't discourage us. Suddenly out of nowhere a car appeared driven by a middle-aged Mississippi woman native. She picked us up and was willing to take us out of her way to the bus terminal. That was at 7:50, giving us only five minutes to buy tickets and board the bus. Soon we encountered a troop train that had stopped, blocking our way. The woman turned the car around, and raced through several blocks to avoid the train and brought us to the bus terminal just in time to make the bus as it was readying to pull out. Fortunately, we had wonderful seats during the three hour ride.

I ate dinner in the most beautiful restaurant I ever saw. It was like a movie set. On entering, I gasped in amazement. It was so beautiful, that it's beyond description. By comparison, the Waldorfs back home look cheesy. The entrance is all chromium and marble and the doors open in such a different way that I can't rightly explain it. As you push, the door seems to go with you. The ceiling is very high, supported by square columns the entire length of the spacious room. The atmosphere was subdued, and the light dimmed, but not so much that you couldn't see well. The restaurant was decorated light purple or violet, similar to the color of the antique velvet you use. Both the walls and columns glistened as if wrapped in cellophane or some smooth, transparent plastic material. Hidden purple lights played on the ceiling. The floor was thickly carpeted and the chairs comfortably upholstered. The tables were like colored marble; the plates and utensils were marked consistent with the rest of the decoration.

You first enter a reception area separated from the main room by a modernistic chromium rail. From there you step to a beautiful case full of food that runs the length of the room. You take a tray, place it on a shelf that runs in front of the case and push it along, stopping to select whatever you wish. Girls dressed in white across the counter politely ask what they can serve you. The beginning of the line has desserts and continues right down to the main courses. Each item has the price marked and is served on a separate plate. There's milk galore and all the butter you want. At the end of the line two girls check what you have at a glance and place a check on your tray. A colored waiter then takes your tray, finds a place for you to sit, and hands you the eating utensils wrapped in a cloth napkin. You don't have to do a thing.

The ladies' powder room and men's restaurant is upstairs in the mezzanine that runs along one side of the room. The men's room is also beautiful, with walls of colored tile, and immaculate. I never saw such fancy toilets in my life. When the seat is vertical it's in a casing of sorts. To bring it down, you pull a lever attached to it; the seat goes back into the casing automatically. Perhaps you wonder why the seat is encased. Well, there's ultra violet light inside the casing that immediately kills any bacteria on the toilet seat. Ingenious, eh.

We spent the afternoon in a theater watching "Thank Your Lucky Stars"[1] with Eddie Cantor[2] and several other big stars. It was pretty good. Despite the rain, I've enjoyed the day, but I'd like to visit this place again in good weather.

Believe it or not I ate too much, and the whole meal cost only sixty-six cents. I'm not kidding. Was I surprised, especially since the food was so wonderful. Reasonable isn't the word. I don't know how they do it.

Monday 11/8/43

Dear Mom,

As of now, I've accumulated sixty-three letters cards, more than forty of which were from home. Pretty good, I think. I tied them up neatly and put them away.

I'm now off the brick making detail. At 3:00 this afternoon I'm supposed to help build a new chow hall. The hours are lousy: 3:00 PM to 11:00 PM. Soon I'll probably be digging ditches.

We returned early from Mobile, taking another beautiful bus, the same one that follows the Gulf coast from the southern tip of Florida to New Orleans. The day was inexpensive, and I have more money than I need.

The lousy weather disappeared this morning. Now the sky is cloudless and deep blue. Just think, we've had only one day of rain during a whole month. Since today is quite cool, I'm wearing the wool sweater issued by the navy.

So I have another city and another state to add to my list. It's interesting to visit various cities. But the people are alike wherever you go. People never change from one place to another. Some are friendly and talkative, some are cold and silent. On the whole, the people here are friendly and helpful. Compared to New Orleans and Gulfport, Mobile has few servicemen on its streets. Seabees are rare, and the sailors that are here mostly come from Pensacola, Florida. However, there's quite a lot of gold braid.

Next to Biloxi, Mobile is the oldest city on the Gulf coast. The streets are narrow, mostly lined with old buildings and here and there a new one. Liggetts has quite a store downtown, and there are several fine hotels and restaurants. There's also another chain of drugstores — offhand, I can't remember the name — that's more elaborate than Liggetts.[1] The chain also has a large store in New Orleans. They say their store in Miami is a wonder. The stores are modernistic and carry everything under the sun. The store in Mobile has a cocktail lounge, and a restaurant upstairs. What a place. I just remembered the name of the chain; it's Walgreen's. It seems the North doesn't have as many fancy places as they do down here. I suppose, I think so because when I was back home, I never went out enough to see what there was.

I'm more anxious than ever to see what California is like. I hope we'll go to Endicott after California. We still don't know when we'll leave the South.

Love to you all, Hughie, the liberty hound

Tuesday 1:00 PM 11/9/43

Dear Mom,

Well, I'm on what is called the swing shift. So now I have to write letters in early afternoon before the evening mail arrives but after the noon mail.

We're building a chow hall from Quonset huts. They have us doing everything and anything, from installing window frames to lining walls with Masonite, to pushing a wheelbarrow. I actually enjoy the work. At last I'm accomplishing something. I get a kick out of reading the blueprints, which, oddly, I find easy enough to understand. I suppose my training in mechanical drawing has helped. I feel much better now that I'm doing something worthwhile. I'd like to do drafting, though, where I can use my head a little.

Last night, one of those swell letters from John Fulgoni arrived. No kidding, each of his succeeding letters gets better. I so look forward to them. Funny, isn't the right word to describe how comical he writes. He answers mine very promptly and asks me to keep writing since he can't be in the service. I'm doing it for him. He asks how you feel. About the same time as you, his mother went through the same operation.

You still ask what I've been doing. Well, you know. You know what I did last week, and what I'm doing now. No longer do I give instruction, and I do the same thing as the other fellows. I'm merely a cog in the gear and am unable to use my initiative. In the service you do everything under orders. I would only cause confusion in the officers' plans were I to try anything on my own. As for my being restless, I'm not as restless as I may sound. Anxious to move on, the other fellows are always griping. It doesn't matter where we go so long as we move. For sure, the navy has taught me how to wait.

You write, "My only caution is for you to keep mind and body clean." Let me tell you what I do. I shower every evening before retiring, although now since I'm working nights, I do it in the morning. We have plenty of running hot water. As for having a clean mind, that I'm Hughie should be guarantee enough. After all, I have to live up to the Aaron family's reputation.

Although the food here isn't bad, I'd just as soon eat the food you serve. We don't get the foods that we have at home. Furthermore you cook 1,000 times better. We don't have black bread, sweet butter, cottage cheese, sour cream, bagels, french fries, tasty beef stew, and eggs the way I like them. The little things make the difference. And never can anything replace the home atmosphere.

So long as I'm on this job, I won't have any liberty or see shows. However, we're told we'll be compensated for the loss of leisure. Frankly I don't care so long as I'm working.

I plan to phone you when we leave. Should I call collect? I can afford to pay for the call, but I know you didn't like that I paid for the telegram. I suppose this is asking a silly question. You'd say yes, anyway. I hear that collect calls go through faster.

11/10/43

Dear Mom,

I hear that our company will be given a special sixty-two hour liberty some weekend — that's three days. I'll probably spend the time in New Orleans.

The weather is still gorgeous although rather cold or perhaps it only seems that way because we're so used to warm temperatures. Even though I run around in a woolen sweater and pea coat, I still don't feel warm. Even my feet feel cold despite woolen socks and heavy GI shoes. I can imagine how cold I'd feel if I were home now.

For a time, I was busy forming softball and football teams, but I didn't succeed because my regular duties interfered. I'm letting things take their course. By the end of December, if I don't receive a rerate I'll act.

I just returned from afternoon muster where it was officially announced that we'll be getting a sixty-two hour liberty as a result of our company's showing in its contribution toward the National War Fund drive. The date isn't set for my liberty section: the company is divided into four liberty sections, and only one section is allowed out at a time. We were told that some will have to take liberty in California, so from that I gather we'll be leaving soon, contrary to appearances.

Thursday, Armistice Day, 11/11/43

Dear Mom,

Last night I did some carpenter work making frames for screens. What beautiful equipment we have: band saws, circular saws, planers, all new. Say Dad, after the war you should be able to pick up some of this stuff pretty cheap.

Now that I'm working nights, I haven't seen a show in some time. I've got to write Uncle Bill soon. I've always felt that Cousin Bob was egotistical, so to the devil with him. Mrs. Mann has raved so much about her brother that you'd think he was something marvelous. People are never what others rave about. No doubt, some would be disappointed in me.

The main subject around here is when do we move. It's fun listening to the various opinions. Yesterday I sent the battalion pictures with brief comments. The lot cost only fifty cents. They'll be sweet memories of when grandpa was a Seabee for some child.

I laughed over your episode with, Mr. Marston. He took Mr. Lazotte's place, you know. The students also find him quite boring, but he does know his stuff. Although I never had him, I personally don't think he teaches a heck of a lot. He means well, and he isn't a bad sort of chap at heart. He has always been swell to me. If he writes to me the way he talks, I'll need some new specs. Since there's nothing else to do, I think I'll write to a few teachers.

By the way, do you recall the fellow that stopped in the store and asked for me while I was at Peary? He had asked me to write him but I forgot his address. His name is Chester Allison, a friend from the Y. He lives in the Burncoat section. Would you send me his address?

Next week, I'll be having so many liberties that I won't know where to go. I've seen everything I want to see. And liberties cost money. You know I don't enjoy spending it.

Friday 11/12/43

Dear Ronnie,

Your letters are good for exercising the stomach with belly laughs. Have you heard these? "I sent you a coat, but it was overweight and was returned, so I cut off the buttons and sent it again. You'll find the buttons in the left hand pocket." Or, "My brother died last night but he's doing well. I hope you're doing the same."

I got over the blues long ago. Frankly, I don't care what happens to me now. I'll take advantage of anything that comes my way, but I'm not worried about it. The chaplain can't help me. He's been unable to help many others, including men more qualified than myself, who have gone to him for similar reasons.

Now that watches are in stock, getting them involves the same rigamarole as at Endicott. Since they know that I already have a watch, I can't get papers without getting the CPO who bought me my watch, in trouble.

The latest scuttlebutt is that the battalion will be split up, but that's improbable. We usually make fun of rumors. "What's the latest scuttlebutt," someone asks. A guy answers, "We're going home on leave tomorrow, then returning to base to ship out to build summer huts at the South Pole." Or we say something else just as ridiculous. We say, believe half what you read, and none of what you hear, and you'll know the truth.

Saturday 11/13/43

Dear Folks,

Look at this date. We just missed Friday the thirteenth. I have Lenny Gallant's letter of the eighth. Lenny seems to be doing pretty well. Do you remember a Greek boy named Nick that used to shovel snow with me? He lived on Woodland Street. Well, he's at the same place as Lenny and going to school, too. How I envy those boys. I guess you can't expect all the breaks.

So you'd rather have me stay where I am if it keeps me in the country. To tell the truth, I wouldn't be surprised if we never left the country. Many battalions with numbers lower than ours are still here and have to leave before us.

I'm still with the construction project. It's costing the navy $50,000 to build. We should be finished Monday.

I've been buying the New Orleans newspaper lately. It favors Holy Cross over Vilanova today.

Remember what I was doing last year at this time? After quitting work in the drugstore near Holy Cross College, I went to work in the chemistry lab. I never dreamed then what the future would hold in store for me.

Next installment tomorrow.

Love to you all, Hughie, the construction worker.

Sunday 11/14/43

Dear Mom,

Before I get into the letter proper, I must ask how do you like this stationery. I use it only when I wish to make an impression, ahem.

At long last I've received the bonbons, the figs and the nuts. Thanks a lot. I'm really enjoying it all. Eating nuts is rare for me and I can't remember when I last had figs, boy oh boy.

The building project is now finished. Remember what I told you it cost? Well add $20,000 for kitchen equipment to give you the total cost. The equipment, which includes ice making machines and refrigerators, is beautiful.

The project was more or less experimental to see what the men could do. As a result, many of us are up for rerates, I being one. Even though I don't know a heck of a lot about construction the CPO recommended me because I'm a willing, ambitious, and good worker, so he said. Last night an officer approached me and asked what my present rate was, and how long ago did I get it. He mentioned that he was glad that I'm S 1/c because I deserved it. Maybe his noticing me will mean something. Keep you fingers crossed for me.

I've decided to take a correspondence course in advanced mathematics, probably analytical geometry. It's designed especially for servicemen and costs only a few dollars, according to our personnel department. I may as well spend my spare time learning something useful and that will prepare me for college. I understand the course gives college credits, but I don't care about that. I'll be sending my application to Washington tomorrow.

Tonight I plan to see "Above Suspicion"[1] with Fred MacMurray[2] and Joan Crawford.[3] This will be my first night off in a week. If only I were in Rhode Island. I'd be home often. I have much more time to myself here than when I was in Rhode Island.

I had my blues pressed and the stripe on the shoulder changed to the other arm. Remember, it was on the right shoulder, but Washington ordered that all Seabees have the stripe on the left shoulder. Do you have an extra picture of me in uniform? John Fulgoni would like one. If you have one, send it to me, and I'll forward it to him.

There's a chance I'll have two sixty-two hour liberties consecutively. If that happens, I'd have six days. Since it takes forty-three hours to travel from Gulfport to Worcester and costs only $35.00 round trip, I'd have a couple of days at home. Don't you think it would be worth it? Of course, if we get ten days off for Christmas, I'll certainly go home.

Many fellows go to Keesler Field, the army air base in Biloxi, and hop on any bomber going near where they live. To make it legal there's a charge of one dollar. Many bombers leave here for New York. I think I'll investigate. Of course, if I do get two consecutive sixty-two hour liberties, it'll be by sheer luck.

Love to every one of you, Hughie, the bonbon king

Monday 9:00 PM 11/15/43

Dear Folks,

I have good news for you today, first I'll answer your letter and card. I also received a letter from Lionel's sister. I wish she wouldn't write so often. Not that I don't like her. She's a swell kid, but I feel obligated to answer her every time.

The day Uncle Bill wrote you, I was in Alabama. Since I have a couple of lengthy liberties coming up, I considered visiting him at his camp, but after finding that Galveston is in the northern part of the state, I saw that it would be too lengthy a trip. However, I could change my mind. I do plan to visit Baton Rouge, the capital of Louisiana, some weekend. They say it's a beautiful city and practically void of sailors. I'd also like to take in a football game there.

My friend, the cousin of the Linfields, called them and they invited us to visit Wednesday night when we get liberty. I rather enjoy visiting them because it reminds me of home and puts me in touch with home life.

Isn't Al Barios[1] a lucky fellow, becoming a pilot? If it weren't for my blasted eyes, I'd have had a similar opportunity.

Confidentially, I was assigned the dirty work I mentioned a week ago, because there was nothing else for us to do. Everybody shared in it. Don't worry, I didn't put my foot in it. Kicking does no harm so long as it's done at the right time.

If we move while we have a wash in the laundry, it would be sent to wherever we are. Have no fear.

I took your remark about Jewish girls lightly, but I suppose I reacted a bit too strongly. I thought you were also referring to having an innocent contact with a gentile girl. I'll forget the subject if you will.

I think Dad's advice concerning what course I should follow during the duration is fine. As a matter of fact, I have always had his idea of making the best of it, then college after the war. As happened last week, occasionally I become disgusted, and I try to formulate ideas for getting out of this outfit. But no more of that stuff, for things seem to straighten themselves out soon enough. I'm sorry I bothered you with such foolishness. It won't happen again. I've had an informal talk with the chaplain, but he offered no advice because his hands are tied.

I now have literature on the correspondence course and will send away tonight for an application. I also have *Dynasty of Death* again.

Today I was assigned to the recreation department as an aid in devising a physical fitness program. If it's successful, I'll have a steady position. This could well be my chance. Who knows? The program consists of calisthenics, relay races, sports, boxing instruction, and so on.

Now that our training is over, we do little or no drilling. My work in recreation is similar to my work at the Y and extremely pleasant.

This is the sort of thing that Mr. Cleavett does at the Y. Although officers are usually in charge of such a program, enlisted men were chosen to do the job due to unusual circumstances.

Last night for the second time I saw "Stand by for Action" with Robert Taylor[2]. You may remember I saw it with you folks last spring when I was a civilian. It's the picture in which a boat load of babies was found. I enjoyed it even more this time. Tonight I saw "Above Suspicion" and found it thrilling and good entertainment but both Crawford and MacMurray have had better roles.

The lights are about to go out, and I have yet to take a shower.

Love to the three of you, Hughie, holder of a new job every week.

Tuesday 9:00 PM 11/16/43

Dear Mom,

I just returned from seeing "Paris after Dark"[1] with George Sanders,[2] Philip Dorn[3] and Brenda Marshall.[4] The movie is about the underground in Germany. It was boring, just lousy. It should be called "Blackout after Dark." Don't see it.

The correspondence course will cost $2.00 a month for nine months. It's sponsored by the Army Institute, a government agency in Washington. My money order was made out to the Treasurer of the United states. It's designed for ambitious servicemen and is supposed to be an excellent course. Now the rest is up to me.

So Bill Hannon[5] did alright for himself in the army. He had a wonderful rating, and it's too bad he couldn't stay in. Won't he be conspicuous at home?

I doubt if I'll start swearing because the passwords require it. Well, if I have to, I guess I'll just have to. Can you picture me swearing? Oh,yeah.

So you discovered my misspelling of "facilities" after all. When I write hurriedly, I spell without thinking. Did you notice that I spelled the word correctly in subsequent letters?

When I'm in New Orleans I'll try to take in an opera or stage show, as you suggest. I had often considered it, but didn't have enough time when I was in Mobile. There isn't a decent movie theater in either Gulfport or Biloxi, let alone a stage for live performances. However, the theaters at the base are very nice and I enjoy watching pictures in them. The sound and projection are excellent.

I read that Robert Taylor is stationed in New Orleans and that Wendell Willkie[6] is also there.

I'll be doggoned if Uncle Bill isn't hooked. Already, he can't seem to get along without a girl. I'm glad I never had any girlfriends. I have enough people to write to as it is. And I don't have to worry that some 4-F[7] will take her from me as so many fellows here do.

The clothing situation in the navy is much different from the army. In the navy we can keep as our own all the clothes issued us except for the GI shoes (training shoes) and fighting coveralls. That includes our dress uniforms and dress shoes, blankets, and even our helmets. We can bring them home after discharge. Of course, in the army the government owns everything and keeps them after discharge. Also soldiers have to buy their own dress shoes.

The navy allows each man $125 for clothes. When our GI shoes and coveralls wear out, they are replaced free of charge. However, we must pay for the cost of replacing our dress blues and white after they wear out. We can buy beautiful raincoats, the same ones that officers wear, for only ten dollars. They're worth at least three times that much. I don't think I have room for one. Should I buy one? What do you think? I've considered it, but my sea bag is already quite full. By the way, rubbers are the only thing that's issued a sailor to protect him from the rain. At least, the navy cares about your feet getting wet.

Those who built the new chow hall will be the first to eat in it. They say we'll have porter house steak just to start off the meal. I'm now not the least bit sorry I took that job, yum, yum, even though we had to forgo our liberties.

Forget sending me anything for my birthday. It would probably get lost in the mail, anyway. Thanks. I know the sentiment is there. After all, a present doesn't matter so much as the thought behind it.

Love, Hugh, can't spell physillyties

Wednesday 11/17/43

Dear Mom,

Tonight I'm in Gulfport on liberty again. As a matter of fact, having brought my writing tablet with me, I'm writing this letter in the Linfield's home. I'm rather enjoying the discussions we've been having about almost everything imaginable.

Today, the physical fitness program went over with a bang. I like the work a great deal and I hope I'll be able to keep at it. I'm working from 8:00 to 4:00 with time off for chow.

While working we were undress dungarees, and during leisure, on liberty that is, dress blues. I'm getting used to the cold; my blood must be getting thicker.

Don't worry about my getting short of money. I always have plenty on hand. I don't play craps either. Of course, I haven't forgotten our phone number. Madame, your suggestion that I have is an insult—or maybe you know me too well. I'm sorry to hear about Mr. Kanef's suicide. Would you send me his wife's address so I can send her a card?

I could go on, but I must cut this short out of politeness to my hostess.

Love to every one of you, Hughie—stepping out a bit, now.

11/18/43

Dear Folks,

The mails graced me with your very funny card, Dad, and a letter from Fulgoni, also full of the devil. Where did you find those Private Breger cards.[1] They're sure swell. I hear that Holy Cross has three All American players.

With two other fellows I'm planning to see LSU play Tulane this weekend on a forty-five hour liberty then, that evening or the next morning, go on to Baton Rouge after the game.

I'm amazed that I wish to see so much. Not long ago I'd be afraid to go to Boston alone. Now I visit Mobile and New Orleans, twice the distance from Worcester to Boston, without a second thought. And I do most of the inquiring and locating of places rather than my companions.

I just returned from having one of the best suppers I've ever had in my life. You see, the new chow hall was christened this evening. Each man that built the chow hall received an exclusive written invitation to attend a gala dinner. Well, it was gala alright. To attend we had to dress up, but it was worth it. The men was as follows: a big, juicy, mouth- watering porterhouse steak, crispy french fried potatoes, one bottle of beer (Schlitz) to each man, or coffee, (As you'd expect I had neither to drink.) the best lemon meringue pie I ever ate, raw carrots, celery, peas, two thick slabs of butter, hot buns, fresh bread, pickles and soup that was very good.

For a job well done, we received a thank you from the commander himself. And on top of all that, we were granted a special liberty weekend. So our work was well rewarded after all. It was really something.

We did nothing today. The company we were supposed to give instruction to was detained in barracks all day because they had kept an unclean barracks. As you can see, our battalion is strict. The wayward company now had to do a general house cleaning. Our own barracks is spotless. A cleaning detail scrubs down the decks every morning, keeps the windows shining bright, and the sills white without a speck of dust. Although I loafed, I was not allowed to write. Regulations prohibit it, but I won't explain why in this letter. It would take too long. That's the navy for you.

We had another interesting happening today in the battalion. While the men were sleeping in Company B barracks, six wallets and several watches were stolen. As a consequence, there was a big row this morning, and I mean big. All the officers and SPs got on the job of finding the culprit right away. Several wallets, all empty, were found in various men's bunks. Of course, they were planted. Every man in Company B was confined to barracks; they weren't even allowed to leave to eat. A special investigating party required that all clothes be unfolded, and all personal property be laid out, including each man's wallet. The men were made to strip to the skin and have the clothes they were wearing examined.

After this was done, nothing revealing turned up. As a consequence the entire battalion was confined to barracks and all our clothing and personal gear, including bed covers and pillows, were unrolled and inspected. I was lucky enough not to have to strip although I was frisked. My bag contained two empty wallets, but I had some identification in each. Eventually, they discovered that one fellow in another barracks had exactly the same amount of money that was stolen on his person. They also learned that he had replaced the Company B guard that was on duty last night. They concluded that it was him based on the circumstantial evidence and recovered everything that was stolen. He's sure to receive a court martial.

So you can see to what lengths the Seabees will go to prevent stealing and to recover what would be stolen. Most of the men are pretty honest, I think, and after what has happened, even the dishonest among us would try nothing. You can imagine how boiling mad most of us were. If we would ever confront the culprit, I'd pity him. Thank God, I always wear my watch and my money belt when I'm sleeping. After the dull time we've been having, we made up for it with today's excitement.

On my new job I conduct calisthenics and supervise relays and various games. I also serve on the so-called Committee for Physical Fitness Program.

Yesterday evening I had the most enjoyable twelve hour liberty since being down South. When I visited the Linfields, I had my writing folder with me. In it were several items from home, including the school paper which I knew would be of interest to the girls. I had also brought along some of John Fulgoni's letters in which he discusses art and the museum in Boston. Of course, this interested Ann, the art student. Everyone got a great kick out of the school paper, especially the girls' section. You had cut out a few sections in this issue where my name appeared as a Horace Mann honor student. I had a devil of a time explaining what had been cut. They thought I was keeping secrets from them.

After I had read a portion of John Fulgoni's especially humorous letter to them, they asked me to read the whole thing. In fact, they were laughing so much that the younger daughter and Mrs. Linfield came close to rolling on the floor. What amused them so was John's description of an opera that he went to. They asked for John's address in order to correspond with him and receive similarly humorous letters.

Spying the pictures of you folks, they insisted on seeing them. So I had to and was darn proud to do it. They were just crazy about you, Mom, and said that you had the nicest, the most pleasant face they ever saw. I assure you they weren't throwing it. Mrs. Linfield gazed at your picture a good three minutes. And you, Dad, came as a big surprise to them. They figured you were in your early forties, and, when I told them how old you really were, they refused to believe it.

When they saw your picture, Ronnie, boy, did I have my hands full then. The younger daughter, just eighteen, couldn't get over how good looking you were. When I told her that you were tall, I thought she was about to fall in love with you. She kept questioning me about you and looking at your picture. When she asked how old you were, I sort of exaggerated your age, just as Dad always does about you and me, to make you even more impressive. I said, "Well, he'll be sixteen soon." I wish you could be here. You're becoming competition, kid. I had better watch out. She's really a humdinger.

I was alone in the den while writing you from the Linfield's last night when Mrs. Linfield called out, "Be sure to include in your letter that we are crazy about your folks. They look like lovely people." That was awfully nice of her, I thought. Not everybody would say that.

When we said goodbye, she said, "I don't wish you boys any bad luck because I know you want to move on to California, but I wish you could stay here for weeks longer so we could see more of you. You're real gentlemen." They treated us like kings. I believe that's typical southern hospitality. If not, they are one family in a million.

By the way, the older daughter's boyfriend is attending Carnegie Tech under the Army Specialized Training Program and he's taking the same subjects I majored in. Boy, what a lucky fellow to be able to go to school at army expense.

Every day new rumors that we'll be moving soon keep surfacing. Each day I become more anxious to leave here. I will have seen everything after Baton Rouge, and we can leave the next morning after I return, for all I care. When we move it doesn't mean that we'll leave the country any quicker. We could ship out from here, for that matter.

It's time for a shower and then hitting the hay.

Love to all of you, Hugh (Nothing like a good steak, eh.)

(If you have difficulty reading my handwriting, just send this letter to the decoding office in Washington. If they're stumped, return it to me, and I'll hire a stenographer.)

Friday 8:00 PM 11/19/43

Dear Mom,

Here I am again, recounting the adventurous episodes in the life of this Seabee: Hughie, the football fan. Yesiree, folks, I'm leaving tomorrow morning for New Orleans to see the game of games: LSU versus Tulane. I pity the guys who will be around me, because I intend to yell and jump around so much that anybody within a ten foot radius will be overpowered. I have a good mind to practice shouting tonight. When I arrive in Baton Rouge Sunday, I'll probably send a telegram home.

I had planned to see "Salute to the Marines"[1] with Wallace Beery[2] tonight, but instead I decided to rest up before the long trip tomorrow. Furthermore I had to phone Ann Linfield at 5:45 (the show begins at 6:00), purely on business, of course. She has been trying to secure some fencing equipment for us. Some of my friends are trying to promote a fencing program, and since I'm in the recreation department, I'm all for it. I'm trying to convince the higher ups that the battalion should have some fencing equipment. The problem is finding the stuff. So my chum, who is one of the promoters, asked the Linfields, that is, someone local, to purchase some foils for us. Unfortunately, neither Ann nor Mrs. Linfield could find any.

Today is payday. Now I'm rich with $10.00 which I'll probably spend during the weekend for transportation, eats and board.

Loafed again all day and continued reading *Dynasty of Death*. I'll really be busy beginning Monday when the physical fitness program will be in full swing. Monday night our company is planning to have a big party.

You really shouldn't have bought anything for my birthday. You know how uncertain the mails are now. If I do get the present, I'll be lucky. Thanks loads, anyway.

Oh, ho, if you think that after all the training I've been getting you will be able to put me to work when I get home, you're mistaken. KP or no KP, carpentry or no carpentry, you and Dad can continue doing the work you always did. I've already had my share. Seriously though, I've been exposed to a smattering of everything. It's the sort of experience that I can eventually make use of.

As far as my civilian clothes are concerned, Ronnie can take whatever he wants, including the gloves. Why pickle them? They'll probably be out of style when I get back. Let's hope not, anyway. Go ahead, Ronnie, wear anything you wish.

I've eaten everything you've sent me. Just this afternoon I finished the raisins. Yum yum.

I guess Ronnie will never make a student. So many boys aren't good students, but they're successful in life. Most of the popular fellows in my high school got poor marks, but they had brains just the same, and they'll probably go far. A student can't possibly get good grades by doing all his homework in study periods. To do homework thoughtfully and thoroughly to get good grades, you have to do it at home. However, if a person finds it hard to study, forcing him to do so won't do any good. A student has to apply himself of his own free will. I aspired to learn all I could in high school; the idea of learning thrilled me. To really learn and get good grades, a person should be inspired by and have a fervor for learning.

Some boys are in school strictly for social reasons. They feel that whatever they do must be practical. I think, in the long run, they may find happiness sooner than serious students, and in many respects become more successful. Ronnie is the social type. As yet, he hasn't bothered to think of his subjects other than that they are merely ordinary, and that he's obligated to learn them. Until now he's not a real student; however, he might become one in the future. Often individuals do better once they are in college. Becoming serious and appreciating the essence of learning, they apply themselves to studying.

I'm so happy that Dad has been able to find someone to help him. I felt a lump in my throat when I read that he will have much less to worry about and much less work to do himself.

Ronnie, you're a card. Your letter is a masterpiece worthy of Colonel Stoopnagle.[3] John F. wrote me that he sees you at the Y occasionally. By the way, "Phantom of the Opera"[4] comes here next week.

"From Memphis (I've been there) to Mobile, (I've been there) from Natchez (I've almost been there) to St. Joe, (I have not been there.) a woman's a two face, (You can say that again.) too, (But as we say here "Who cares about the face?") a worrisome thing (Are you telling me?) Ho,ho,ho,ho. Now how does the rest of the song[5] go?

Hmmmm. Your Tuesday's letter says: cold and pouring. All I have to say is ha, ha, heh, heh. Cut out the old modesty, Mom. Not only did your clothes look good, I know you were tops too. Boy oh boy, did your picture make a hit in Gulfport.

Boy, if I realized my letter to Aunt Anna would make such a hit, I'd really have put into it the old one two. It's swell to learn that the letter helped her get better. She's a swell aunt. I haven't heard from Aunt Pearl lately. After this weekend, I'm going to start writing everybody again.

How did it feel to receive a notice that you'll be getting ten bucks more each month? I hope you'll get another such notice in a couple of months. I'll do my best to make it happen.

Did you murder the spelling of "psychological." Wow. I hope your face is red with shame, but at least you admit you can't spell.

Now that you have extra help, how are you doing, Dad? Are you still kidding the gals in George's Luncheonette?[6] My present chief acts exactly like you, a dead ringer. He kids with me the way you used to. I enjoy his antics a lot. Whenever some fellow smokes a cigar (and not many do), I can't help getting near him to smell the smoke. Then I can easily picture you smoking your cigar in the living room. Doggone. You'd be surprised how it's the little things that come to mind, things that you and Mom and Ronnie did. But I'm hardened to homesickness; don't mind being away at all. Although I'm enjoying the responsibility, just so long as I know I have you folks to go back to, I'm content.

Methinks, it's time I knocked off. Bye now. Love to all of you. Hughie, (the guy who doesn't know which team to root for tomorrow. I think I'll root for both teams and get murdered.)

P.S. Stop me if you've heard this one. It's about the Pole who lived on the Russo, Polish border. Since the war began[7] he couldn't figure out whether he now lived in Germany or Russia. When informed that he resided in Germany, since Germany had taken over all of Poland and the border portion of Russia, he exclaimed, "Thank God, I couldn't stand another one of those Russian winters."

Yes, I had corn for dinner. Okay, okay, so it wasn't so hot.

Telegram 11/22/43

In Baton Rouge seeing sights and enjoying everything. Saw LSU-Tulane game in New Orleans. Will write particulars tomorrow. Love to you all.

Monday 11/22/43

Dear Folks,

I have seen so much and so much has happened in the past three days that I don't know where to begin.

I may as well start at 7:00 Saturday morning. By luck a truck picked us up at the camp gate and drove us to the bus station in Gulfport where we had breakfast (bacon and eggs). Three of us had left camp together, but before we reached New Orleans, we were four, having added a Seabee that we met on the bus. We had taken the super aluminum Greyhound to New Orleans, arriving at 11:30. After arranging for sleeping quarters at the USO, we revisited the French Quarter. In subsequent letters I'll be sending photos of various sections that I visited in the Quarter. I enjoyed this second tour of the Quarter as much as my first.

We ate in a strictly French restaurant called Toujages, a quiet, clean place that has no menu. You must eat whatever is being served that day, but it's good. The meal consists of several courses starting with pea soup, then some sort of French meat blend that looked like hamburg, and an assortment of vegetables. The meat was swell, but it contained hot green peppers and unwittingly I put a big piece in my mouth. Oh, oh mama, did I drink water, boy. After that I ate only a little piece at a time. Another and different meat and vegetable course soon followed, also hot but delicious. Plenty of good hard crusted French bread with plenty of butter was laid out before us. It felt good to sink my teeth into a hard crust for a change. For drinks French coffee was served. Of course, I wouldn't touch it, and just as well, because the others could taste the brandy in it. All this cost only eighty cents.

In the afternoon we went to the ball game, taking a street car that traveled the eight miles to the stadium. To give you an idea how large the city is, in all that distance we were still within the New Orleans city limits. However, few large buildings can be built there due to the base of silt underlying the surface. A few buildings rise fifteen or twenty stories, no more. So the city has to spread out. By the way, I was surprised to see many Jewish establishments here and there.

A true college spirit pervades the city. High school kids swarm onto the trolleys[1] dressed in the traditional green and white Tulane colors. The Tulane campus is beautiful with fine new buildings and a marvelous new stadium, one of the largest and newest in the country. Shaped like a bowl, and so large that it took my breath away, it is made of brick, cement and steel. Although 40,000 attended the game it can seat 70,000. The grounds around it are dotted with tropical trees and are gorgeous.

Servicemen paid only fifty-five cents to see the game for seats that normally go for $3.00. We had wonderful seats, quite far up, but on the fifty yard line. We could see everything clearly and hear everything distinctly. The band was enormous and quite good. The cheer leaders did an excellent job. It seemed to me that they worked even harder than the players. Pretty drum majorettes in extravagant uniforms welcomed the start of the game. You could feel a true college spirit. It was like a summer day back home, pleasant and warm, the temperature about 70. Although the sky was cloudless, the stadium is so situated that the sun didn't bother us.

Not much happened during the first half, with neither team making much headway. But in the third quarter Tulane scored twenty-one points and held their lead. It seemed that everything went against LSU during the second half. They fumbled often. As I mentioned earlier, Tulane won 27 to LSU's 0. With the spirit of the Tulane players and the crowd running high, the goal posts[2] were torn down. We servicemen were seated on the LSU side of the stadium, but, since I rather liked Tulane, I rooted for them. After all, what fun is there if you don't take sides? Since the program is far too large to send home, I'll keep it as a souvenir of my first college football game. Who would have thought that I'd see my first game in New Orleans? It was a damn swell game and I got one of the greatest kicks in my life out of watching it.

That evening we roamed the streets looking at store windows (The city was lit this time.) then taking in a show, "Sahara."[3] I'd have gone to the opera, but unfortunately none was playing. Before I forget, I must mention that we saw Wendell Willkie, who spoke in person between the game's halves. From the way he spoke, I gather that he'll run again. He said something to the effect that even though he knew we were a Democratic audience, and we probably wouldn't vote for him, he still likes us. Clap, clap, clap.

Next morning, Sunday, after a swell breakfast of oatmeal, etc., we split up. Two of us took a new Greyhound to Baton Rouge, eighty miles north, a two-and-one-half hour ride on a pleasant four lane highway. The road, which is flat without the slightest rise for mile after mile, is bordered by bayous, forest, fields of corn and grain, and oil wells.

Baton Rouge is a truly beautiful city. It contains the most beautiful buildings, both modern and old, that I've ever laid eyes on. Its trees are gorgeous. And the homes are something to rave about. I'd like to live there. We took in many points of interest, but, due to lack of time, we didn't see the LSU campus. I'll be sending you a few souvenirs of the place. I hope you got the telegram I sent you from there.

We visited the high rise capitol, taking the elevator to the top where we viewed the flat countryside for hundreds of miles. Sunday too was like a typical clear June day. We could see for miles up the Mississippi River. The city, with a population of about 50,000, spreads out from the east bank of the river.

Sailors are rarely seen here, but there are plenty of soldiers. The town is just jammed with girls. I pity the guy who dares to wink at one, especially if he's in a sailor uniform. He'd have a dozen girls on his arm in a flash.

We returned to New Orleans, where we caught the bus to Gulfport arriving late Sunday night. In all we traveled 320 miles, a six hour trip each way, in two days.

Today, back at the base, was uneventful. I worked in the physical fitness program, conducting calisthenics and refereeing games. What a gorgeous day. It's 75 with a nice breeze.

Finally our orders have arrived. No more liberties after Thursday, Thanksgiving day. The battalion will prepare for "departure from Gulfport" within seventy-two hours of Thursday, sometime next week, that is, to an unknown destination, possibly California. (Keep writing just the same.) We'll have been here ten weeks on Friday. Stay home evenings this week, especially Thursday night, and expect a phone call from Gulfport.

Tomorrow I'll write more about my trip. I have to cut this short. I got the package from Aunt Ida. Please notify her that I must delay writing everybody except you because I have so much to do now that we're leaving.

Love to you all, Hughie, the roving roamer

Tuesday 8:00 PM 11/23/43

Dear Mom,

Before I begin telling you more about my trip, here's my new address: Hugh Aaron S 1/c, Co Hdqrs, Plat 4, 113th Naval Const. Batt., c/o Fleet P.O., San Francisco, Cal. Don't forget to put "Naval" in front of "Const." It's now definite that we're going to California. We will leave Camp Holliday either Sunday or Monday. Keep writing.

I received your lovely birthday present last evening. It's wonderful of you. Thanks again, folks. I love all of you for it. I can use the refreshments you sent on the train ride to the West Coast. I also received your letters of the 18th and 19th and three home town newspapers. Thanks. I've already read the newspapers from first page to last.

Often I write as many as five or six letters an evening. I rather enjoy it. I still use the same pen you gave me at grammar school graduation. I never imagined I'd use it so much.

As you may surmise, there's no chance that I'll be getting home in the near future. Even on a ten day leave, I'd not go home, because it takes five days to travel each way and would cost a fortune.

I hear we're going to have a gala Thanksgiving dinner.

Enclosed is a card listing things that I could use. (When I signed myself the Bonbon King it wasn't meant as a hint.) But nothing is urgent. And please don't use your points to buy things for me. I don't have to have the things I listed. You needn't keep sending goodies if it's inconvenient, but boy, are they good, smack, smack.

The physical fitness program is slack now because of the indefiniteness of our remaining stay here. A man who sparred with Jack Sharkey[1] and who ran a gym in Chelsea is the boxing instructor. The program has five instructors.

I think Uncle Bill is a fool to marry. He should stay in the service because as a draftee he won't have as good an opportunity as he has now. He should learn to be patient. A man his age should be able to wait. Basic is the toughest training he'll ever go through, and, if he's inducted, he'll have to do it again.

I'm going to hit the hay now. Will write tomorrow.

As always, Hughie (California here I come, comin' in on the run)

Still in Gulfport Wednesday 11/24/43

Dear Dad,

I hope Mom's trouble is minor. Let me know how you come out, Mom.

And now to answer that letter of letters from the block I'm a chip off. Well, me blighty, yar sailor lankwitch is topside, whatever that means. You're on the ball, mess hall, and rillah rah. This is merely my attempt to sound salty. I fear it got mixed up with sugar or something. In all seriousness, your letter was, as usual, a humdinger. I'm glad to hear that my letter helped Aunt Anna. I'll be writing the folks again when I'm in California. I don't have much time now.

We expect to leave by early next week. Pullmans have been ordered; the trip will last four or five days. Now that I've seen everything worth seeing down here, I'm not sorry we're leaving.

I hope you'll save the souvenirs I sent you. I'd like to review them when I get home.

Bye 'til tomorrow. Love to you all, Hughie (Can't stand exercise anymore.)

Saturday 11/27/43

Dear Folks,

You may have to go without receiving a couple of letters next week. After I saw "Phantom of the Opera," I was so tired that I went to bed rather than write. And another night I went on liberty.

It was wonderful hearing your voices again. I could kiss Alexander Graham Bell[1] in his grave. Those few minutes on the phone were precious to me. They gave me a swell feeling. I can't describe it. I must call again when another important occasion arises. Money is no object. However, I phoned station to station, knowing that after receiving my letter, you'd be home. As you know, it's a lot cheaper that way. I called in the afternoon because at night the phones are so busy they're impossible to get to.

I have so many letters to answer, I don't know where to begin. Yesterday I received two from you, a letter from Ted Bagdikian who is now stationed at Camp Parks, Cal., a letter from Lenny's sister, a letter from John Fulgoni and a letter from Miss Rourke, a teacher at South High. So you see, the mails have been treating me well.

Sunday 11/28/43

Dear Mom,

Since I've been in the service, it seems I've developed an inclination to reminisce, to review unimportant incidents of the past and enjoy looking back on them even more than when they actually happened. Now that I'm about to leave the South, I can't help looking back on all that happened during my ten week stay here: that day we arrived amid a downpour, those weeks of drilling, the first time I fired a rifle, the march to the rifle range, Gulfport, Biloxi, basking on the beach at Cat Island, the first time I saw the Gulf of Mexico, the evenings spent with the Linfields, New Orleans, the ride up the Mississippi, Mobile, the football game, Baton Rouge, and a hundred little things that would fill many more pages. All seem so far away yet so vivid. I've seen plenty, learned plenty. I'll always look back on the days spent here as a time of happiness.

In spite of some disagreeable experiences, I can say, for the most part, it's been swell. Of course there were the usual disgusting sights, the drunks, the cheap women, and the filthy talk, but they were minimal and are easily forgotten. Certainly exposure to such things broadens a person's knowledge of men and life in general.

I was fortunate enough to have chosen good companions on my visits to the various cities. Each fellow was a prince. We always returned to camp with the desire to go out together again. I was never overly thrilled about going places alone. It's so much more fun to have someone to talk to, to make comments to on the various sights, and to receive a reaction.

Thursday night was my final liberty. The Linfields had invited my friend, who also visited them with me, and me to spend the evening with them for last good byes. It also gave me an opportunity to call you from their home. We spent the evening again listening to records, discussing every imaginable subject and eating pie. The evening reminded me so much of home. It's not often that a fellow can experience home life 2000 miles away from home. The average guy raises the devil and returns to camp feeling chipper. He misses his home so much that he does crazy things when in town. In going to the Linfields when I leave camp, I don't have to drown my loss with drink and women, as so many do.

We arrived at the Linfields at 6:30, rather early, when the girls had just arrived home from a Gulfport High football game, which it lost. Mary, the younger girl, a senior, went upstairs to dress for a dance that night. Apparently, Ann wasn't going. I had observed that every time I visited, Ann would stay home while her sister was always out on a date. I suspect that Ann has no desire to date. She's saving herself for that boyfriend in the army. There's loyalty for you.

At about 9:30 a rhythmical knock at the door, so typical of a young fellow's knock, interrupted the conversation. Mary, now all dressed up slick, looking darn pretty, flowers in her hair, opened the door and dashed out to the porch to meet her beau for the night. This was a different fellow than last time. He was a civy[1] and he wore a nice, new topcoat, and, as they walked to the car, we heard him remark that it was a new one. We all smiled when we overheard him make some modest remark about it. When she dashed out, in her excitement, she forgot to close the front door which opened onto the parlor where we were seated, so I got up and closed it. As I watched them, it occurred to me that I had just witnessed something that I had outgrown. I have never known what it was like to call on a girl, and now seeing it, I realized I had missed something wonderful, and that the opportunity was gone forever. I can't quite explain why I felt this way. You might even consider my reaction to this event, which seemed so singular and special to me, silly. Suddenly, I saw all the fun I had missed in high school by not dating. I saw as plain as day that all the fun I could have had from social contact was worth more than all my damn studying. Although there's only one year's difference in age between me and those kids, I felt so much older as I closed that door. I hope Ronnie will never make the same mistake that I made. I expect an "I told you so" from you, and I deserve it. For Ronnie's good, don't make him work so that he will have to sacrifice his leisure. Encourage him to go out and have fun, moderately and wisely, of course. I don't have to tell you people, do I?

I was unable to get in touch with you that night because of a six hour delay on calls to the Northeast. I should have expected it on Thanksgiving eve. Mrs. Linfield asked for your address. She'll probably tell you about "the bad boy" I've been. She also requested that we write her from California. As we were leaving, she offered to call you for me, but I wouldn't think of letting her. She asked in all sincerity that I return someday to visit her. She went so far as to suggest that, after debarking on the West Coast from overseas when the war will be over, to detour to Gulfport on my way home to Massachusetts. Maybe someday, after the war, I shall revisit all the places I've seen, and take advantage of her invitation, but I couldn't help saying that I doubted I'd every return to the South again.

Here's a woman who deserves much credit. Husbandless, living on the proceeds of her dead husband's insurance, she has to conserve every dime. Bringing up two daughters is quite a task, especially in this day and age when the South is full of servicemen. Near her home, though a residential district, a girl isn't safe on the streets at night because of attacks from servicemen. She's doing a wonderful job bringing up those kids.

The night of my last visit, Ann wanted to go to New Orleans on Friday, which meant skipping a period at college. She needed a note from her mother indicating that she was sick, or else she would suffer a reduction in her grade. But Mrs. Linfield refused to write a note that was a lie, and told Ann she could go to New Orleans if she wished, but she would have to take whatever punishment the school would impose. Ordinarily, Ann would take the train to New Orleans on the weekend at Mrs. Linfield's expense. But she preferred to leave Friday, because she'd be getting a free ride. But Mrs. Linfield would rather pay the $3.00 fare than lie and not have to pay the fare. This gives you an idea of the woman's character.

I received another letter from John Fulgoni even before I could answer his previous letter. As usual his letter was a riot with a cartoon drawing as its introduction. He's one in a million. Miss Rourke, from my high school, also sent a lovely letter informing me of what has happened to many of my high school friends. She gave me the address of Mr. Clason, my former chemistry teacher, now in the Seabees. It's a paradox. He has a bachelor of science degree from the University of Illinois, was a fine athlete, and is a brilliant chemistry teacher. He has also taught college. But he has only a S 2/c rating. Imagine! Surely he deserves a commission, but, because he wears glasses, he doesn't qualify. I'm going to write to him, although it will be rather awkward in view of my rank. What in the world are the Seabees doing to the brains of our nation? Yea gods.

Although I'm still in the physical fitness program, there's little to do because of the nearness to our departure date. Frankly, I don't think it will ever be the success it appeared to be at first. The majority of the men enlisted in this outfit to work, not play. Most are middle aged and can't stand any vigorous activity. They get tired within an hour from intense physical training. I've observed that at heart they are against the program, and, after all, the program was established mainly to please them. Furthermore, the program recently has centered around sports which holds no interest for me unless I'm a participant. Actually, I find umpiring, refereeing and coaching (softball, basketball and touch football) boring. So I'm doing my job without enthusiasm. This isn't good because enthusiasm is necessary to ensure success in anything. But I'll stick it out in the hope that my spirit will improve, and my position in the battalion as well. I don't much care what they have me do. I'm seeing things and enjoying it. What more could I ask for? You may remember that back home I became tired of almost every job I held. Maybe it's the same with me here. But what can I do? I'm willing to try anything and someday I hope I'll find something I like. I know I wish to keep busy. I hate sitting around doing nothing. I hope this darn war ends soon, because I'm anxious to be back in school. I do have some consolation in knowing that the correspondence course will arrive soon. It will give me a kind of experience that I can't get in the Seabees.

At your suggestion I saw "Phantom of the Opera." The music and sets were beautiful and enjoyable. Will you send me my zippered black leather brief case, the one I used to carry my school books. I'll need it for the correspondence course papers. Please save any papers in the brief case. I may need them in the future, perhaps in college. Also, send my slide rule.

I've accumulated quite a bundle of letters which I'll soon send home. I'm sure I'll enjoy rereading them someday. Maybe I'm just a sentimental fool. I dunno.

I appreciate the hours that Dad spends writing to me. Fortunately, I find the writing of letters flows with ease. I figure Dad is a temperamental writer too. Well, all the greatest artists are temperamental and are annoyed by interruptions. Dad has the making of a Poe Edgar Allen. Catch? Read this in a Southern dialect, and you'll know what I mean.

Mom, glad to hear that your trouble isn't too serious. There's always something to take your money, eh.

I think I could get around Boston pretty well on my own now. I have a lot more nerve than I used to. New Orleans can also be a confusing city. Even the natives lose their way there. I find my way easily by stopping at information centers.

After every meal and once in the afternoon, I'm still eating the marvelous birthday present you sent. The peanuts are all gone. I'm glad to hear that Ronnie is a saver. I'm not mercenary, but I do like to see the old dough pile up. It gives me a sense of security. I hope you folks are doing alright financially.

Thanksgiving dinner was really something, but it couldn't compare with yours. We had more than enough of turkey, dark and white meat, apple pie and ice cream, vegetables, sweet potatoes, and for each man a pack of cigarettes, a stick of gum and a bar of candy. Oh yes, stuffing too.

Doggone if I haven't written a volume. Before long I'll be competing with the *Encyclopedia Britannica*. I'll continue writing daily while en route. Mail will be sent even while we're travelling so you'll be hearing from me right along. I'll be using air mail stamps[2] to speed things. I'm almost certain we'll be going to Hueneme, (pronounced Waneemee) California, about thirty miles north of Los Angeles and near Hollywood. So long. You'd better wear your specs while reading this to avoid tiring your eyes. I hadn't figured I'd write this much.

Monday 11/29/43

Dear Ronnie,

We're making the final preparations for departure tonight. So far as I'm concerned we can leave this very minute; all my bags are packed. Thanks for Colonel Stoopnagle's unabashed fictionary. It should prove very helpful as a reference in the future.

My correspondence course arrived today. After looking it over, I'm more than pleased with it. A swell textbook is furnished with the course and the explanations seem clear. I'm afraid I've forgotten most of my trigonometry which I'll need to refer to. Once we're in California I'll try to borrow a trig book from a friend. Now that I have the course, I'll have plenty to keep me busy on the train. The package contains all eight lessons and none appear easy.

I admit,right now I'm flat broke. We'll be getting paid when we arrive in California. Travelling and eating in restaurants costs, but that's all I need money for anyway.

To settle the argument about equivalent rates in the army and navy, here they are.

Army	Navy	Pay
Private	Apprentice Seaman	$50.00/month
Private 1/c	Seaman 2/c	54.00
Corporal	Seaman 1/c	66.00
Sergeant	Petty Officer 3/c	78.00
Staff Sergeant	Petty Officer 2/c	96.00
First Sergeant	Petty Officer 1/c	114.00
Master Sergeant	Chief Petty Officer	126.00

Now you can argue intelligently with anybody. These are the hard facts.

The day was clear and fairly warm again. We're leaving a wonderful climate. I hear it rains a lot in California this time of year.

Travelling by Pullman will be a new experience for me. At least it will be much more comfortable than travelling by those darn coaches.

For old times sake, save the stub of the football game ticket that I'm sending, will you? And here's the bus ticket to go to Mobile. I'll soon send other bus tickets to New Orleans and Baton Rouge when I find them.

We'll probably leave in the evening. I'll write tomorrow.

[A Card] Tuesday PM 11/30/43

We are leaving on Pullmans about 4:00. I'm all dressed up waiting to go. Some way to spend a birthday.

En Route to California

Dear Folks,

Who would ever think that I'd ever spend a nineteenth birthday on a train heading north in Mississippi? Yesterday, right on schedule at 4:00 PM, we boarded a tourist Pullman and got under way immediately. I felt sort of sad as Gulfport faded away. I enjoyed myself so much there.

No doubt you'd like to follow my route, so I shall keep you informed of the cities we pass through. At 8:00 last night it was Hattiesburg, and at midnight we were in Jackson, both in Mississippi. They are quite modern with tall hotels. From the train I could see several tall business buildings in Jackson and the hotels Heidelburg and Robert E. Lee, towering over the city.

Last night was my first night in a Pullman. They are just like the ones you see in the movies, and they convert to coaches during the day. I'm going to enjoy this trip because everything is so pleasant and convenient. The Pullman's have double windows, they're heated, and have beautiful large lavatories. All this keeps us comfortable and clean. On our previous trips we were filthy from the soot, but here we don't know we're on a train. Last night I slept like a top in a nice clean bed. With clean sheets and woolen blankets we had all the comforts of home. Two lights, a mirror and an attending porter make it traveling first class.

We had a marvelous breakfast in the dining car, filling me up to the brim. It would cost a fortune for a civilian to travel this way.

After passing through Vicksburg, we pulled into Shreveport early in the morning and stayed there four hours. Shreveport appears to be a modern city with tall business buildings, trackless trolleys, and enormous bridges. As you can see on the map, we're now on the other side of the Mississippi River which we crossed while we were sleeping. Forgive my penmanship which is poor due to the rocking of the train. I'll keep you posted by one or two letters a day en route.

12/3/43

Dear Folks,

Going into our second day crossing Texas. What a state! Passed through Mexico a distance back. Sights too interesting to describe now. Have already passed through Houston, San Antonio and Del Rio. Heading for El Paso.

Arizona Friday 12/3/43

Dear Folks,

Right now we're stopped in Dawson, Arizona, so I'll scribble a little and take advantage of the train's motionlessness. About 5:00 PM Wednesday we pulled into Houston, then early Thursday San Antonio. Between Houston and San Antonio there's a wealth of things to see such as oil wells, cotton fields, flat plains, sage brush and typical small western towns. At nine last night we pulled into El Paso. From San Antonio to El Paso all we saw was sage, sage and more sage. This is the real range, enormous beyond description. After I arrive in California I'll give you a more complete report. I'm so busy seeing things as the train travels across the land that I have no wish to write. From 9:00 last night to 7:00 this morning I slept while we crossed New Mexico, which, of course, I didn't see. From now on we'll probably see only desert in Arizona and California where we'll be tomorrow morning. This part of the country is nothing like the East.

Chow's ready soon, so I'll close. I realize these letters are brief, but I can describe the trip much better after it's over. You can count on getting a very descriptive letter from California.

12/3/43

Hello Folks,

Pulled out of Tucson, Arizona, after a brief stop. A swell looking city. You should see the mountains out here. Valleys are full of cactus.

California, Saturday 8:30 PM 12/4/43

Dear Folks,

I could write a volume on what I've seen the past five days. No doubt I'll be talking about the journey in future letters for a week or more. Before I begin, I must mention the letters and card I received a few moments ago. Your three wonderful birthday cards touched me more deeply than any presents I've ever received on any birthday ever. I love you all so much. It's so glorious to have folks like you. With the cards there were also your letters of the 26th and 27th and a surprise letter from [Aunt] Pearl.

I know you're anxious to hear everything, so I'll delay replying to your letters until tomorrow.

The journey's vital statistics are as follows: Distance, 2500 miles; Time spent traveling, 92 1/2 hours; States covered, Mississippi, Louisiana, Texas and Texas and Texas (What a state), New Mexico, Arizona, California; Mode of travel, Pullman; Comfort, very nice; What seen? Well, that's what I'm about to describe.

The trip began at 5:00 PM in Gulfport under the usual clear skies. For an hour we rode straight north through Hattiesburg, arriving in Jackson about midnight. Both cities were typical of other southern cities I've visited: business buildings, tall hotels, clean and well paved streets. The sky was cloudy in Jackson, the first real overcast I had seen in eleven weeks. After sleeping from midnight until morning, we awoke at 8:00 in Shreveport, Louisiana. I had to go to bed late because I was on duty watch from 10:00 to 12:00. Shreveport with a population of about 300,000 was much larger than I expected. I was also surprised at the tallness of the buildings. I recall that the Shreveport Fire Station #3 threw several magazines on the train for our entertainment.

I found that I could sleep quite well in spite of the shifting of the train. We then headed west, crossing into Texas at Timpson and continuing through Nacodoches, Lufkin and Babill, arriving in Houston at 5:00 PM. The countryside between Shreveport and Houston is heavily wooded with pines and appears infertile. I was surprised to learn that this part of Texas is lumber country. The small towns I just listed are lumber towns built around sawmills. I was also amazed to see such beautiful schools in the towns.

The men were dressed western style, wearing ten gallon hats and high heeled boots. The downtown had only a few stores. But Houston is an enormous city with enormous buildings, busy streets, and a large railroad station. We stepped from the train in Houston to get some exercise, spending about an hour during which I bought a newspaper. I noticed that the price of meat was extremely low. I'm sending you clippings from the various newspapers I bought along the way.

From Houston we headed for San Antonio in the heart of the state, which I was unable to see because I was dead to the world. A beautiful highway, Route 90, leads out of Houston. The land was flat and extended as far as the eye could see. We passed several large oil fields where pumps and derricks were working. Miles and miles of the land are cultivated with corn and vegetables. I couldn't get over how flat the land is. About fifty miles west of Houston we came into cattle country where the land is drier. Here we saw ranches and cattle grazing. Sage brush, a plant common to the range, and mesquite began to appear.

It's Sunday morning and I'm standing by awaiting orders while I scribble. As I wrote earlier, I slept while passing through San Antonio, and Del Rio as well. I was also asleep when our eighteen car train crossed the highest railroad bridge in the world at the junction of the

Pecos and Rio Grande Rivers. We entered Mexico at that point in the early morning darkness. It's too bad that I missed the sight. When I awoke we were in the middle of nowhere, deep in the heart of open range country. So all that day we traveled from Shreveport, near the Texas border, to Del Rio. The southernmost point that we reached was Spofford, Texas.

California, Tuesday 9:30 PM 12/7/43

Here it is Tuesday morning. It seems I'll never finish this letter.

Our Pullmans were not the most modern type, but, I must say, they were comfortable and clean and equivalent to first class in civilian terms. All day Wednesday we traveled through the open Texas range, a semi-arid region where only sage brush and a little cactus can grow. It's not flat, but made up of oddly shaped hills, inclines, valleys and strange orange and gold rock formations. It's so different from any countryside that I've ever seen that I was fascinated. Everything, the hills and the broad expanse, are on a large scale. Since this part of Texas is hardly fertile, I don't see how cattle survive — but they do.

As we approached El Paso, we followed a mountain range. Most of the mountains were rocky and void of any vegetation. On the way to El Paso we stopped in both Alpine and Marfa and marched around the town for exercise. I imagine only a few hundred people live in such places. They are situated in the middle of the semi-arid range with a backdrop of large hills or a mountain.

After passing through Sierra Blanca, we arrived in El Paso on Thursday the 2nd at 9:00 PM. El Paso is also a modern city and well spread out. Neon signs light up the downtown where night spots appear all over the place. From El Paso we followed the Mexican border in New Mexico, passed through Hachita. I slept from El Paso through New Mexico to Douglas, Arizona. From there we could look across into old Mexico. Douglas is laid out on a flat section of land surrounded by mountains.

West of Douglas, the countryside is rather hilly. From Naco and north to Mescal and Tucson we traveled between mountain ranges along the bottom of a valley that was ten to fifty miles wide all the way to Phoenix. The mountains on both sides of the valley were just plain dirt and rocks with no vegetation. For miles and miles the floor of the valley was flat then suddenly became ridges and small rocky hills for more miles. The air is so clear that a mountain that's fifty miles distant seems no more than a mile away. Mountains fifteen or twenty miles off appear to be right close by. I can't describe how vast the scale is. You can see farther than you've ever seen before as the train climbs higher and higher. The land approaching Tucson is a flat cactus desert; then, as if from nowhere, Tucson appears against a backdrop of mountains.

We saw several army airfields and big bombers and pursuit planes taking off and landing and flying. Tucson was the most picturesque of all the cities we saw. The city is modern with well paved streets, underpasses, tall buildings and Spanish style homes. We debarked at the station to exercise and breathe the fresh Arizona air. The sky was deep blue, the air brilliantly clear. It was comfortably warm with a slight breeze. A native told us that this is typical of their winter weather. It rarely rains so it's quite dry. As we boarded the train the Navy Mothers' Organization handed us cookies and magazines.

From Tucson we headed north through more semi-arid desert, real cactus country, mountains still on both sides of our valley, to Phoenix. Some of the cactuses were fifteen feet tall. Just outside of Tucson there were large fields of cotton, yes, cotton. That it grew in Arizona was new to me. And bales of cotton had filled the freight yard. At Mesa, a little below Phoenix, we entered the most beautiful countryside I ever saw, owing to irrigation from dams in the mountains. It reminded me of the fertile region of Ohio and Indiana. I could see water running swiftly in man made ditches in the fields and even along the gutters of the streets. Gorgeous palm trees and other tropical trees line the streets.

The farms run for mile after mile across the flat valley, one of the richest in the nation. Here Pascal celery, iceberg lettuce, wheat and various other vegetables grow in enormous fields that extend across the valley from one mountain range to the other. This is also big sheep and cattle country. The animals grazed in large irrigated fields of grass. We passed several stock yards.

The homes were small but cute and had orange and lemon trees growing in their back yards. The fruit looked so good I felt like getting off and picking some. After pulling into Phoenix in mid-afternoon, we got off the train to exercise again. A nurses' organization gave us refreshments. Being the capital, Phoenix is larger than Tucson and also quite picturesque. We got only a glimpse of the downtown which was similar to Tucson's.

From Phoenix we headed south again into the desert, not sandy desert but sage desert. It was night and I was sleeping when we went through Yuma, Niland, California, and Indio and passed near the Salton Sea. When I awoke we were in the San Fernando valley, about sixty miles from Los Angeles. The San Bernardino mountains were on one side of the valley and the Santa Annas on the other side. It reminded me of the valley near Phoenix. Enormous groves of orange and lemon trees extended along both sides of the tracks. This is the home of California fruit and boy, is this place beautiful. I can't stop saying it. We went through San Bernardino, Pomona, and Pasadena before reaching Los Angeles.

The small towns are quite pretty. Little stucco cottages and Spanish style bungalows, with palm trees in front, border the streets. Most homes here appear to be small, quaint and made with stucco. The highways are beautiful.

The valley extends right into L.A. and on past to the north. We could see the center of the city from the train. There were only a couple of tall buildings because this is an earthquake area. The city sprawls. I think it's sixty miles from one end to the other. We stopped in L.A. for an hour to change engines and we saw several beautiful streamliners pass by. After getting under way we continued north through the valley, passing several airfields where I saw some swell looking P-38s.[1] We also passed by the Lockheed Vega plant you hear so much about. The plant runs for two miles under one roof. We could see men and women working outdoors on P-38s and medium bombers. The entire plant, including the enormous parking lots, were remarkably camouflaged. Everything was painted in a variety of colors. Fake trees, houses built on the roofs of buildings, netting covering certain structures, and several other devices made the plant undiscernible from the air. Even the highways and bridges nearby were camouflaged. I couldn't get over it.

We moved on into the hills, crossed the northern edge of the San Fernando valley, passed through a mountain tunnel and landed in Oxnard, sixty-one miles north of Hollywood. Three miles outside of Oxnard at Port Hueneme was Camp Rousseau, our final destination. We arrived there on Saturday at 1:30 PM. Was that a trip or was that a trip! I'll never forget it.

I hope I've covered the trip fairly well, but I know words could never do justice to what I saw. I'll be writing another letter to tell you more about it. So much is happening now. Enclosed are some souvenirs from previous trips and a Mississippi tax token I had forgotten to send.

Port Heuneme, California

Western Union telegram 8:57 PM December 6th
Arrived at Heuneme, California 1:30 Saturday (12/4). Only 60 miles
from Los Angeles. In Hollywood having swellest time in my life.
Love, Hughie

Tuesday PM 12/7/43

Dear Mom,

I have so many letters to write, so much to tell, a big wash to do,
and now I've been assigned guard duty, that I don't know where to
begin. Until I go on duty, I may as well write some more to you folks.

I know you must be wondering what kind of camp this is. Well,
it's the worst camp we've been in since Camp Peary. The lavatories are
bad: I must use my own hand mirror, the water is heavily chlorinated
and exceptionally hard, the stores are poor, and we live in Quonset
huts which is hardly convenient. However, surprisingly, I find that I'm
adjusting well to the inconveniences and making the best of it. As a
matter of fact, it doesn't really bother me that the camp isn't as nice as
Endicott or Holliday.

You should know that this is an embarkation center, and who
knows what that means? The weather is positively beautiful. It rarely
rains, so everyone in the camp says, and the skies are cloudless all day.
The nights and morning are very cold, but by 11:00 AM the air is warm
as a day in June and you can be comfortable even wearing a bathing
suit. Although the camp is right on the ocean, personnel aren't
allowed to approach the docks as we were at our other bases. The
camp is larger than Holliday, and possible larger than Endicott. Called
Camp Rousseau, it's located in a place called Port Hueneme,
pronounced Waneemee, just as Endicott is in Davisville. It's only three
miles from the center of Oxnard, a small city whose downtown is no
larger than Gulfport's. There's nothing of interest in Oxnard, so I
haven't stayed there.

The camp's best feature is its proximity to Los Angeles, (which
everyone calls L.A.) Hollywood, Beverly Hills, Santa Monica and
Ventura. Before receiving this letter, you will have learned that I was in
Hollywood. I'll tell you what happened with me there shortly. Oh yes,
you should know that there's a three hour difference in time between
here and the East Coast. After leaving Gulfport, which is on Central
Time, I turned my watch back one hour at El Paso in Mountain Time,
and back another hour when we reached California in Pacific Time.

After we arrived Saturday, our section was allowed Sunday afternoon liberty until 7:30 AM Monday. I took the 2:30 Greyhound from Oxnard to Hollywood, which is a part of L.A. and is six miles nearer camp than L.A. proper. That is, it's a northern suburb and serves as a sort of second downtown. We followed the shore route for the fifty-five miles to Hollywood, and I saw the Pacific Ocean for the first time. I was surprised to see how high the surf was, but I bet the swimming is wonderful, especially at the beach in Santa Monica, which is noted for its excellent swimming.

A CPO in the amphibious force just back from Rendova in the Solomons[1] sat beside me on the bus. He told me plenty about what had happened there. It was terrible. A native of L.A., he described many points of interest. We passed through wonderful Beverly Hills, where most movie actors and actresses have their homes. They're so extravagant as to be beyond description, built on hillsides, parts of a mountain range, steeper than even our Newton Hill. It's far more different than I expected, and more beautiful. Sections are like Westwood Hills in Worcester, only more elegant. I'm planning to visit them again more thoroughly.

Travel time from Oxnard to Hollywood is about 2 1/2 hours. This time we stopped for quite a while in Malibu, a movie actors' colony north of Santa Monica, which is southwest of Beverly Hills. In Malibu there's a road stand with a fancy interior; a picture of it is enclosed. I know all the names will confuse you as they did me at first. These are small cities you've heard about on the radio where the high muckamucks in filmdom live. One of them, Santa Barbara, is a very pretty city. Hollywood abuts Beverly Hills on the south and L.A. on the north.

The first place I visited in Hollywood was the Canteen[2] at the corner of Cahuenga and Sunset Boulevards. The Canteen's exterior looks like a barn, but inside it's far more elaborate. There's a swell dance floor and plenty of girls to dance with. Having a smile on their faces all the time, the hostesses, treat us like kings. At the bar, milk, sandwiches of your choice, and snacks are served free. Every hour the crowd changes; no one is allowed in while the entertainment is in progress. Although there's always a line, if you're there on the hour, you'll be admitted in two minutes regardless of how many are waiting. Some stay all day by getting back into the waiting line at the top of each hour.

After we dance for a while, a show begins. Pinky Tomlin, the radio singer, was the M.C. and he cracked some daring jokes and sang some popular songs. A famous Hollywood dancer appeared in a, ahem, scant Hawaiian gown and danced. Kay Francis[3] was in one corner and Olivia DeHavilland[4] in another corner signing autographs. I was unable to get Kay Francis's signature. As she walked about the Canteen, I was surprised to see how short she was. I spoke to Olivia DeHavilland (or should I refer to her as Olivia, eh, Dad), and she answered most pleasantly. As she signed her autograph for me, I asked her how much longer could she do this until she got writer's cramp. She laughed and said that she could take it, but I think, as I watched her expression, that she was rather bored. Dressed beautifully, with a remarkable hairdo, she is without a doubt a beautiful woman. Anyway, I hope you enjoy her autograph enclosed.

Time is getting short, and I must close. By the way, there were two swell dance bands at the Canteen. I'll tell about Sunday in my next letter. Love to you all, Hughie — running away with a movie star's heart, well at least her signature

Wednesday 12/8/43

Dear Dad,

By tomorrow, I ought to be pretty well caught up. I washed a big batch of clothes this morning and have arranged all my personal articles. Now I have time to devote to answering letters, which I've neglected to do along with the correspondence course due to the excitement. Both yesterday and today I'm on guard duty from five to eight in the evening and three to eight in the morning. Though I'm wearing gloves, pea jacket, sweatshirt, and undress blues, I freeze on the morning watch. It's not the temperature so much which hardly approaches freezing, but rather the penetrating dampness. By ten or eleven it's warm enough for swimming. I'm feeling more at home here, now that the helpless feeling I had upon first arriving in a strange place has disappeared.

I'll continue the account of my first visit to Hollywood. On leaving the Canteen two smartly dressed men handed us some tickets (My companion was a friend that lives near Pittsburgh) and asked whether we'd like to have dinner. I thought there was a catch, but my chum insisted on accepting the invitation so I went along. The men led us to a beautiful Buick and drove us a distance up Hollywood Boulevard to an attractive mansion where we were greeted by an elderly man. We were ushered up some stairs into a pretty room where there was a crowd of girls and tables set with dining utensils. I then realized that this was a church social or something similar, so I suggested to my friend that we leave and instead see the town. After all, I was anxious to see things. I gave some phony excuse, and I felt pretty rotten leaving just as soon as we arrived, but they were nice about it and asked us to return whenever we wished. I noticed that other servicemen were also arriving. This is merely an example of how well the people in Hollywood treat us. We're tops in their eyes. Movie and stage show admissions are half price. Servicemen are invited to attend radio programs and visit the film studios. People in cars stop to ask us where we're going. A serviceman could spend a week here without having to spend a cent; everything's geared to the serviceman, everything's free. It's a serviceman's paradise.

After leaving the mansion, we walked down Hollywood Boulevard to Grauman's Chinese Theater, where all the premieres are held, and the footprints of the big stars are encased in cement on the sidewalk. The earliest footprints were made in 1927 and continue to 1943. I didn't visit the theater, because I was anxious to become acquainted with the city first. It's swell to see all this, Sunset Boulevard, Hollywood Boulevard, Vine Street and many other famous streets which were all so brilliantly lighted by theater marquees, extravagant store windows, neon signs, and fancy night clubs and cafeterias. It has all the "glitter and swank of New York's Park Avenue." It's all so new and clean and modern. The streets are wide and well paved. Beautiful cars whiz up and down them. (You'd never know there was gas rationing here.) The theaters are stupendous. What marquees! I've never seen anything like it in my life.

I stood at Hollywood and Vine just as I said I would someday. Then I went to Western Union to send a night letter home. Soon it started to rain, although it's true that it rarely rains here. As a matter of fact, this was the first rain they've had in months. It's so rare that the newspaper announces the amount of rain that's fallen. As luck would have it, it had to rain the night I was in Hollywood. I sought cover in a USO, where I mailed several cards. My chum met a hostess there, a middle-aged woman, who had come from near where he lived. Giving us her address, she invited us to visit her on our next liberty. She showed us the town in her car. She also has a plane. We'll probably visit her the next time we're in town. She also suggested many places that we should see in future liberties and how to get to them.

I'm planning to visit the places she recommended, including a stage show, a musical and a ballet, (the Ballet Russe is here). I also wish to see the Hollywood Bowl, Wilshire Boulevard, and the Wilshire Bowl, several radio programs at NBC and CBS, Grauman's Chinese Theater, Beverly Hills, Santa Monica beach for a swim, and revisit the

Hollywood Canteen. But this is only a small portion of what there is to do and see here.

Since it was still raining when we left the USO, and it was too late to take in a stage show, we figured going to a movie would be a good way to keep dry. Our bus back to camp was to leave at 1:15 AM We went to the Warner, the nearest theater to the bus station. What a beauty of a theater with its gorgeous marquee, spectacular interior, usherettes dressed in gowns, and wonderful sound and projection. I enjoyed the picture, "Old Acquaintance,"[1] with Bette Davis[2] and Miriam Hopkins.[3]

Getting back to camp didn't go very smoothly. Because the 1:15 bus was so crowded, we were unable to board it. By sheer luck we made the 1:30 bus; however, it had to leave some sailors behind making them A.O.L.[4] After arriving in Oxnard we discovered that there were no buses to camp. I thought sure we'd then be A.O.L. ourselves until I spied a cab, and stopped it in the middle of the street. Several other sailors also trying to get to camp joined us. We yelled "Gate Four" as eight of us packed into the cab. Boy, what a stroke of luck: it cost us only twenty cents apiece. After getting no sleep Sunday night, I made up for it Monday night. Now when I go to Hollywood, having caught on to the transportation system, I'll know where to go and how to get there. The only trouble is, I'll not be getting any sleep when I visit Hollywood.

Yesterday I got the November 22 *Gazette*, and this morning a letter from ever faithful John Fulgoni. Your mail takes about a week to get here. Not too bad. That does it for today. Bye.

As always, man about town now, eh?

Thursday 12/9/43

Dear Mom,

I'll be writing for weeks it seems. Only this afternoon I mailed sixteen Christmas cards. For the first time I've been in the service, I'm flat broke. Those liberties in Baton Rouge and Hollywood were costly. The transportation and food are the most expensive. I'm surprised at how well I stretched my monthly $12.00, but I normally find it enough.

I'm still on guard duty and hate it, but being under orders I have no choice. I'll do anything they ask. There's no use in complaining, but many do.

I'm allowed liberty tonight, but rather than go to L.A. I've decided to get some sleep. Furthermore the weather is miserable: high winds, rain and hail. Believe it or not, we're having a thunderstorm, thundering and lightning all day, in December. Such storms are rare here, still I have a good mind to call the L.A. Chamber of Commerce and bawl them out for issuing false propaganda. It seems we've come here at a bad time; it's rained two days out of six.

I received your letter of the 30th. Thanks for your good wishes. I must mention again how lovely your cards were. I got a kick out of Ronnie's—entirely consistent with his letters. And your card, Mom, the letter to a son, is the king of birthday cards. It was so good I read it over and over quite a few times. And thanks, Dad, for your card. It did my heart good to see that famous left-hand signature of yours, "Dad."

Being on the west coast, I now realize I'm truly far from home. My first few days here were pretty tough. For the first time I got a little homesick. I wasn't that way in Gulfport, but everything out here seemed so strange that I longed to be home. Oh, I wasn't really carrying on; only I'd think of you folks more often than usual. The trip to Hollywood lifted my spirits which enabled me to get over my homesickness quickly. I feel much better now. Now I'm content and acclimatized to the scene. (Don't use that word "acclimatize." Remember seeing "White Cargo"[1] a year ago?)

I hear talk that overseas equipment will be provided us this week. That doesn't mean that we won't go East. Every battalion undergoes the same procedure. But you can never tell, anything can happen.

We aren't getting much milk in camp, but apparently the cities are getting plenty. The food is only fair and improving daily. There's plenty of ice cream. By the way, I have a map of the U.S. on which I've marked all the travels I've done.

The picture you sent is of John Grimik, the muscle man and the best built man in the world. I think Uncle Bill is making a big mistake quitting the service to get married, because he'll go through much worse than he's been through as a private. See what love will do to a guy. I guess you were right in thinking that it was best I wasn't accepted into V-12. I don't think I'd care for that kind of study.

I guess Ronnie will be a six-footer for sure with only one more inch to go. That letter from Dad is a humdinger. He really hits the spot. I even read excerpts to my chums who get as much a kick out of what he writes as I do. Listen, Dad, even though you write a great letter, you needn't go around bragging because Mom's and Ronnie's are darn good too.

Love to every one of you, Hughie, the sentinel

P.S. I failed to mention the effects of the difference in air pressure when we reach Tucson. We were so high that the decrease was noticeable, and my eardrums felt strange and sounds were subdued. But by the time we reached Phoenix, I had become accustomed to it.

12/10/43

Dear Ronnie,

I guess it's about time I received a letter from you, kid. Haven't heard from you in quite a while. How's school? Oh, yeah, that's a touchy subject. When I was in Hollywood, I sent many cards, and, in the excitement, I sent one to you unaddressed. Boy, did I feel dumb when it was returned today. So I'm sending it with this letter. The picture on it is interesting. Apparently other people make the same foolish mistake, as the Post Office has a stamp for it. This is the first time I've ever done anything like this.

Saturday 12/11/43

Dear Mom,

So you enjoyed "Old Acquaintance" as much as I did, I see. Please don't feel upset when letters don't arrive every day. I know how it is, because, when a day goes by without a letter from home, I feel the same way. But the time will come when letters will be arriving further apart. I may as well tell you now so you'll know what to expect in the next few months. We plan to embark from the U.S. within the next two or three months. It will probably be from here, but there's a possibility that we might ship East and embark from there. There's no indication as to where we are going. Guns have been issued. This afternoon I was given my own Remington .03-A3 high powered rifle. Since all battalions are issued guns, it doesn't necessarily mean combat. Combat groups normally get carbines, good for jungle fighting and close combat, and go to the South Pacific. The issuance of the Remington rifles puzzles us. I want to tell the truth but please don't worry.

Today a special muster was called—a calling together of the men— to announce the new V-12 drive. The navy is seeking more men to send to college with the exact qualifications I have. Five men are to be chosen from the battalion to enter the program. I satisfy every requirement except for vision: 18-20 minimum and positively no waivers. I even went so far as to get an application, but I was told it would be useless. So again, I'm licked before I start while I watch the other boys take the cake. You see, entering the V-12 program would also keep me in the country. Why, if I could pass the eye test, acceptance would be a snap, because applications are overseen by our superior officers who, because of my good record, would vouch for me and provide a good recommendation. Now, I'm forgetting the whole thing once again. However, after I've served overseas, my defects would be overlooked, so when I come back, provided the war isn't yet over, I should have a marvelous opportunity to qualify.

Tonight I had a most enjoyable experience. Your letter mentioned that you heard Kay Kyser[1] from Camp Parks, which is near Frisco. I was unable to listen to him because we aren't allowed radios — nor diaries either. Well tonight I attended a radio program. Did you listen to "Pabst Blue Ribbon Town" on Saturday evening? Well I saw the entire program. It began at 4:45 PM and officially went on the air at 5:00, ending at 5:30, but it continued until 6:00 for the live audience. It's broadcast to the East from 8:00 to 8:30 your time. I really enjoyed every minute from a swell seat five rows from the stage. The stars were Groucho Marx;[2] Ken Nyles, the announcer; Fay Mackenzie, the singer; Bill Days, a tenor; Robert Armbrewster's orchestra; and Frances Gifford, a new star from MGM, the guest. Groucho was a riot throughout; he's quite an adlibber. Do you know the difference between a sailor and a Seabee? Well, when a sailor goes out with a girl, he looks for a park bench, but when a Seabee goes out with one, he builds the bench under her.

Fay Mackenzie, a really beautiful girl with a beautiful popular voice, was dressed in a tempting gown. She sang several popular songs, one of them being "Put Your Arms Around Me Honey." Bill Days is a swell looking singer with a marvelous tenor voice. I enjoyed each of the several pieces that he sang. Frances Gifford is positively gorgeous, just how I would expect a movie star to look. She's very tall and has a good figure. The fellows went crazy over her. But I didn't think much of her personality; maybe she was nervous. I think she has played in a Mickey Rooney[3] picture. Ken Nyles, the announcer, a nice looking man, tall but not too young, was quite versatile. Of course, you've heard of Armbrewster's orchestra; it's always excellent.

After the program went off the air, the cast really went to town. Groucho cracked a number of spicy jokes; Kay Mackenzie sang a few suggestive songs and tried to tempt the men in the audience. Anyway, it was good fun. All the musicians in the orchestra were middle-aged and looked Jewish. The producer of the show, definitely Jewish, was introduced. He had produced the Charlie McCarthy[4] Show[5] for five years. Everyone on the stage was dressed in sport coats of different styles and colors, and they wore loud socks. Groucho, wearing no makeup at all, wore a sport blouse buttoned to the neck and sleek summer pants. His glasses are rimless, and he looks as Jewish as can be.

There were CBS microphones all over the stage. Just after they went off the air, Groucho received a telegram that read, "Good, keep up the fine work. You are making our sales increase. Schlitz Beer." Boy, when he read that it was from Schlitz, I almost died laughing. You see, his program was so lousy, that everybody was buying Shlitz instead of Pabst. (An explanation, in case you didn't catch on).

I'm sending you the ticket to the show which I got by luck. Forty men were chosen out of a hat, and I was lucky enough not to have duty that day.

I'll probably see plenty more stars before I leave the west coast. Fellows coming in from liberty every night tell about seeing Mickey Rooney and Hedy Lamarr,[6] and that deadpan girl singer (You know whom)[7] at the Canteen. They have also seen the big bands, Harry James,[8] Glenn Miller[9] and Ted Powell[10] among others, at the Palladium[11] and the Brown Derby.[12] It cost servicemen little to visit these places.

Shall write again tomorrow, so until then, so long, Hughie - radio shark or the Seabee that builds benches

P.S. Personally, the only bench a Seabee would build for a girl, would be his own.

Sunday 12/12/43

Dear Mom,

After four days of thunder storms, at last the weather has cleared so now, I plan to go to Hollywood tomorrow. The mountains fifteen or twenty miles away to the east of the camp are snow capped, but here at sea level it's comfortably warm.

I think I'll buy a raincoat after all. But I can't afford it on my stipend, so please send me ten bucks. It's a swell raincoat, and I can use it after the war.

I got a Christmas card from Johnson Fulgoni, one of the most novel ones I've ever seen. When I saw it I died laughing. When I find an envelope that will fit it I'll send it to you. You'll get a great kick out of it, too. And after you've seen it and can find an envelope, would you return it because I get a great kick out of showing it to the fellows.

I return to guard duty at 4:00 this afternoon. I don't know when I'll no longer have to do this work. It's boring and breaks up my sleep. But I have to do it, like it or not. In a way, it doesn't matter because it gives me more time to myself, although I spend most of it catching up on my sleep. But I have to do it, like it or not. In a way, it doesn't matter because it gives me more time to myself, although I spend most of it catching up on my sleep.

12/13/43

Dear Folks,

I'm going to Hollywood tonight. I don't whether I'll have time to write so am sending this card.

We were issued packs, shelter halfs and bayonets etc. this afternoon. By the looks of this equipment, I don't think we'll see much combat. Such material appears to be for defensive purposes only. Hope so.

I'm planning on see much more tonight. Will tell you about it tomorrow.

Thursday 12/14/43

Dear Mom,

Here I am again after another liberty night in Hollywood. I left camp with another fellow, but early in the evening we got separated in the confusion, so I made all the rounds by myself and enjoyed every minute of it.

After arriving in Hollywood at 6:15 I searched for a restaurant and chose the beautiful Maxwell House. There I had a swell supper for about a dollar, enjoyed the modern beauty of the place, listening to the music and watching the civilians. There's nothing as elaborate as this place to be found in New England. I noticed on the back of the menu a list of Maxwell Houses in various major cities across the country. Among them in black and white was the one in Worcester with its Main Street address and even the mention that it's next to Filene's. Upon seeing this I enjoyed the food even more. I know you consider the one in Worcester nice, but it can't be compared to this one.

After supper I visited the Hollywood Canteen. The comedians Reilly and Heller, who star in a new picture just coming out, were the first on the bill. The latter is female and a fine singer. They put on a swell act and made the spiciest jokes I ever heard even in the presence of the girls. By the way, you might be interested in knowing that all the women serving the refreshments are mothers of movie stars.

You'd like this joke, Dad: Reilly says, "I hear they're drafting men from 40 to 60 now, eh fellas? Just think how much money the government will save on saltpeter, and that good old GI coffee."

After the comedy act, a magician appeared giving an excellent performance. You've probably heard of the National Barn Dance broadcast on the radio from Chicago Saturday evenings. Well, the whole troupe was here and entertained us.

I missed seeing John Garfield[1] for I had left to see the Judy Canova[2] radio show at the CBS studio for which I had secured free tickets. I can't describe how beautiful both the NBC and CBS buildings are. The show was held in the Lux Theater[3] from which Cecil B. Demille[4] broadcasts Monday nights. As I expected, I enjoyed the Judy Canova show to the utmost. And Judy Canova isn't bad looking. No kidding.

The Lux Theater is on Vine across the street from the CBS building. It's small, hardly modern but pleasant. About ten minutes before the show goes on the air the performers crack jokes, the stars are introduced and everybody is exceptionally informal. Even during the show they laugh at each other's jokes, make faces at each other, and giggle at anything out of the ordinary. You'd never know they were on the air. We are asked to laugh our hearts out, told when to clap, and when to stop, all of which is picked up by a microphone hanging down in the middle of the theater. Clapping is used to fill in the time gaps. I had a fine seat up front.

After the show I walked around, saw the Palladium and almost went in, but figured I didn't have enough time. It's a classy nightclub, but servicemen pay only fifty cents to get in. Some day I'm going there. I walked by Earl Carrol's[5] gorgeous theater and night club on Sunset Boulevard, also Ken Murray's[6] Theater, El Capitan, where there's a show I plan to see. I also want to visit the Florentine Gardens, another famous night club, before I leave the west coast. I also saw the Brown Derby, a famed night spot.

I was to meet a friend, John, in a Cadillac at midnight at the corner of Hollywood and Vine, but he didn't show up. later, when I met him on the bus, he explained that the car wasn't available to him. It belonged to his boss, and he didn't want to keep it out in the open at camp. Having gone out with him several times before, I didn't doubt his word. He was a construction engineer from Cleveland. His former boss, who owns two cars, now lives in Hollywood.

While standing on the corner waiting, I observed the passing scene. On one of the corners of the intersection is a beautiful restaurant called the Melody Lounge. On a second corner is a tall office building; on the third corner a department store and on the fourth corner an Owl Drug store which is a popular chain here. By the dozens Lincolns, Cadillacs, Buicks and Packards driven by beautiful blondes and handsomely dressed men pass by. You'd never know there was a war going on. I never saw so many peroxide blondes in all my life. They seem to be the vogue out here. The women, beautiful ones at that, far outnumber the men. They come here seeking jobs in the movies.

Since it was too late to take in a stage show and with plenty of time on my hands, I went to see "In Old Oklahoma"[7] with John Wayne[8] and Martha Scott. Just fair.

Having to wait until 4:00 AM for the bus back to camp, I just walked around after the movie. Though the city was dead after midnight, I met a couple of chums, and we went sightseeing in spite of the hour. I had a chocolate malted in one of those outdoor stands that serves you in a car, except that I didn't have a car. A few of us might get together sometime and hire a car if it doesn't cost too much.

After catching the 4:00 AM bus, the last one, I arrived in camp just as reveille blew. Doggone it, an entire night without sleep, the first time ever. I couldn't sleep on the bus because it was so crowded. Fortunately, I wasn't assigned duty this morning, enabling me to sleep for two hours which helped plenty. To my surprise, I wasn't the least bit tired today. As luck would have it, this afternoon we hiked four miles as a prelude to longer hikes in the future with pack, rifle, canteen, eating utensils, etc. But I didn't mind the hike. In fact, it's 7:15 now and I'm still wide awake. After being given a demonstration on how to make up our packs, I caught on right away. It was most interesting, and I'm sure it will come in handy.

I get paid tomorrow, but don't know how much. So you heard the Groucho Marx program, after all. Isn't that swell; you listen to it, and I see it.

Regarding my letter from Houston, the time should have been 9:30 AM. I slipped. We arrived in Houston about 5:00 PM The time doesn't change until El Paso. I'm surprised that you heard so promptly from Mrs. Linfield. I didn't realize that I was so high in her mind. I know you wrote a fine reply to her, Mom.

Well, I guess it's time to wind up another Jergen's Journal, so until tomorrow, lotions of love to you all.

Wednesday 12/15/43

Dear Mom,

I'm the commander's messenger for a couple of days with my hours 8:00 to 12:00 mornings and evenings. I'm getting only five dollars a day which doesn't give me much.

I've been so busy relating my experiences that I've forgotten to ask how you folks are. How's the little trouble you had coming along, Mom? Is Dad working as hard now that he has more help? How are you feeling, Dad? Do you sleep better in your own bed? I know Ronnie is well. He rarely gets sick.

Aunt Yetta's [Henrietta] letter received yesterday is pretty good. I laughed when she wrote, "Believe me, I did not know you had such a wonderful sense of humor." My, my, what my relatives have yet to learn. So far as I know, I'm no different now than I've ever been.

Talking about being different, I should tell you what happened to me in Hollywood. After walking into a restaurant, I seated myself and gave my order to the waitress. While waiting, I went to the men's lounge to wash, and, when I returned, the meal had been already set at my place. After taking my glasses off, which I often do when eating or doing close things, for it rests my eyes, I began eating. Soon the waitress placed a cup of coffee next to my plate and looked at me oddly. I reminded her that I had ordered milk not coffee. She exclaimed, "Why, you're not the fellow that was here before." Looking at her queerly, I asked, "Was the other guy in a sailor uniform?" She answered, "Yes." After I mentioned that I had asked her for some suggestions concerning the menu, she then remembered. "Well, I'm the very same fellow," I said, and I told her that she had a keen imagination. The woman eating next to me almost died laughing, for she knew I was the same fellow all along. The poor waitress didn't know what to make of it, and she continued serving me and was very nice. At times the craziest things seem to happen to me. I should have asked the waitress whether the other guy was better looking, then I'd really have put her on the spot.

I'm sure I can reveal how well equipped we are without disclosing a secret. There's no doubt that we're beautifully prepared for anything. I have a wonderful Remington .03-A3 Remington .30 caliber bolt action rifle, the best in the world. I know it inside out: how it works, and I can take it apart and reassemble it. Our pack is regulation army with haversack, eating utensils and mess kit, the newest type canteen, cartridge belt and other accessories. We have the latest type gas mask which is something. We've had instruction on how to use these at Peary and Holliday, and we expect more here. Yes, I also have a bayonet and scabbard, and I hope to never use it. Mosquito netting is also furnished. All the equipment is tested and brand new. As you can tell, it's mostly protective material which doesn't indicate which theater we'll be shipped to. As I've said, I don't think we'll be in the jungle, because then carbines would have been issued. However, from various incidents, I have a feeling that we may be heading for some part of the tropics. We'll probably be here for another month or two. Before we leave I'll send you a telegram a few days before I phone you. (It won't cost more than $5.00.) That won't necessarily mean that I'll be shipping out. I could well be going East.

No Christmas leaves are being granted. If we don't ship East, frankly, I don't expect to be home until after I return from across. Even if I had a ten day leave, I wouldn't go home. It would take five days to cross the country each way at a cost of over $100. Travel by air is far too expensive.

I'll hold up mailing this letter until the evening mail. It's two in the afternoon, a beautiful afternoon it is: warm and clear, just like spring.

Thursday 12/16/43

Dear Mom,

Zowie! Are you treating me swell, yowsah.[1] The package of nuts, raisins and candy arrived this afternoon and right now I'm the happiest guy on the base. Everything in the box is just what I like—only more so. I don't have to, er, open the cupboard shyly and sort of help myself. All I need do is take whatever I feel like taking and that sorta makes me feel good, one hundred percent enjoyment. After each meal and in the late afternoon I take some refreshment, just as I used to back home when I'd go out and buy a snack. Of course, I share some with the fellows. Whenever they receive a package of goodies they do the same. I'll bet you'd like to have a supply of refreshments on hand, eh, Ronnie?

In addition to the sacred parcel, both your letters of the seventh and the eighth and a masterpiece from Johnson Fulgoni arrived.

I laughed when I read that Dad didn't like your telling me that I didn't write enough while en route. Thanks, Dad, but I don't blame Mom in the least. I'd feel the same. Of course, now you understand why I wrote so little. However, whenever it seems that my letter frequency is getting slack, don't hesitate to remind me. Mom, I'm pleased that you like long letters, because to my surprise, I have a constant urge to write. You know, I actually enjoy it and look forward to that part of the day. I don't understand the change in myself; I used to hate to write.

I'm glad that you are trying to go out a little, Mom. It's a shame that you and Dad don't go places more often. Yesiree, go out and enjoy life, like me, ahem. Ah ha, I'm one up on you: I sent a card to the Linfields days ago.

Too bad that Joe is working out so poorly. The young fellow you hired was no good either, eh? All the good men are in the armed forces now, not meaning to brag. I hear you're having a cold wave, and with storms. I can't picture such a thing anymore. The weather is fine here, warm, mild as a day in Whittier's[2] poem. This is the climate. If you want snow, just drive to the mountains to ski. I can easily understand why people don't want to return to the East.

I made an error when I wrote Dawson, Arizona in my letter. I'm sorry. There is no such place. It should have been Douglas. I don't know what I was thinking.

I haven't written Uncle Bill for a long time. I'd like to attend his wedding. Getting real sharp wearing a tux, huh, Ronnie. Boy, what would I give to get out of my monkey suit with bell bottom pants. The damn uniform is the most inconvenient blankety-blank thing I ever wore.

Oh, oh, wouldn't it just be your luck that when you're out, company comes. Aunt Eva is rather pleasant to talk to, but you can talk to her anytime. Before I forget, tell Goldie[3] that I'm still working on securing the watch. About next week when the battalion is being issued purchasing passes, I should be able to buy one. I've already gone to the supply officer twice since I've been here. It's no bother; I enjoy helping out the Ringers.

Johnson Fulgoni has been writing on average a letter a week, and he says he plans to continue. He's sending me a pocket manual on Russia from the economics course he's taking at Holy Cross. He attends two or three courses a week. He deserves credit. His recent letter concluded with these words: "I write you every week and if you shipped out and I failed to hear from you, I shall continue to write my weekly billet-doux to you, as I realize many times it's impossible for you to write under those conditions. But I shall be only too glad to write you, as I certainly enjoy you as both 'nephew' and friend." I suppose you wonder what "nephew" is all about. I don't know exactly how it started. In an early letter he jokingly assumed a haughty air and signed himself as Uncle Johnson. Well, following up, I signed myself as nephew. We've kept it up ever since; I always address him as Uncle Johnson, and he addresses me as Nephew Hughie. Anyway, we both get a great kick out of it.

I'm still a personal messenger to the Commander and the Lieutenant Commander, but I expect to be off tomorrow. While I was in Lieutenant Commander Mather's office, as I overheard him mention the number 202 to the phone operator, I remarked that if 55 were added, he'd be calling my home. Immediately he asked where I came from. Coincidentally, he attended Worcester Tech. It popped into my mind to ask whether he had ever gone into the drugstore corner of Highland and West streets. Sure, he had, he said. The store was managed by one twin, while his brother managed another store elsewhere in the city. He was surprised when I told him that Sol, whom he knew, was my cousin. What a small world. Except for the Commander he's the most influential man in the battalion having been schooled in Worcester and knowing Sol. The Lieutenant Commander is a prince, too.

Let's see now, anything else to say? Nope, so I'll write tomorrow. Bye. As Always, Hughie — messenger extraordinary

P.S. Note change in address: Receiving Barracks instead of Camp Rousseau.

Friday 12/17/43

Dear Mom,

Today was quite instructive. We hiked six miles with full combat pack, canteen, rifle and gas mask, to a gas chamber. For the first time we ate from our mess kits, and a good meal it was. Having had instruction at Peary and Holliday, I had the mask drill down pat. This time to test our masks we entered a tear gas chamber without wearing the mask, but boy did we put them on plenty fast.

After returning from the hike to our hut I was surprised to find posters of scantily clad pretty girls all over the walls. The were the Varga[1] pictures from *Esquire.*[2] I was fortunate and the envy of all the fellows when they discovered that I had a near naked Betty Grable over my bunk. Our place looks like a harem now, and, uh, frankly I don't mind it at all. I learned that the fellow in charge of keeping out hut clean felt like decorating the place. We humorously refer to him as the "hut mother" and call the hut the "hut sut."[3]

A Jewish friend from New York has some salami coming, so I have that to look forward to. I have liberty tonight, but I'm not going out because of lack of funds. Oh, well, it's a good excuse for me to get more sleep which I can use.

I hear that before embarkation we'll be confined for ten days during which we'll have no liberties, nor allowed to send letters or telegrams or make telephone calls. So if there's a big lapse of time between letters, you'll know I'm in the confinement area. I suppose that queers my plans to call you or send a telegram. But if I do get to send a telegram I'll sign it Hugh if I'll be able to call you, and Hughie otherwise. However, if I send a telegram while en route, I'll not sign it at all. I doubt if I can mention that I'm on the move. Is everything clear? Hugh means I'll call, Hughie, I'm unable to, and no signature means I'm en route.

Saturday 12/18/43

Dear Mom,

After a week of beautiful weather the rain has returned with no sign of let up, so I've been secured to our hut. Before having rifle inspection late this morning for the first time, I spent half the morning stripping it down, cleaning its parts with gasoline, and oiling it. It's some job. I also began the correspondence course. I've been so busy that I had to request an extension of time.

We've been issued rain gear, but it can't be worn outside the base. If I buy a raincoat, I'll probably have to send it home, so I'll not buy one and just keep the money you may have sent me. Anyway I'm broke. I hope you didn't send more than I asked. I'm trying to keep my expenses on liberties to a minimum which is especially tough to do on the West Coast. Once I'm across, with no place to spend money, and a 20% pay increase for overseas duty, I'll be able to save plenty. Rerates look more distant now. I hear no one will get a second rerate for months to come. Before I forget, I want you to record my rifle number in case I forget it or lose my wallet. It's 3 929 572.

This is another of those days when you stay in barracks and do nothing worth talking about. By the way my service number is 802 14 66. It's the most important number I'll ever have in my life.

A CPO friend who hails from these parts told me about a girl in Ventura whose father he had worked for. I had once mentioned to him that for a guy to really see Hollywood, he should have a native show him around. He wants me to meet the above girl who is 19 years old, a student, wealthy, beautiful, has a car and a beautiful home, and so forth. Reputedly she's wild and happy-go-lucky. Frankly I'm not in her class and scared stiff to make her acquaintance. Anyway, he insists, so I agreed to meet her sometime. In a way, I hope it falls through, that he forgets it. I wouldn't even mention it if I had something more important to say.

So again, I fail to write anything interesting. I've got to get "on the ball" alright. Actually, these letters are a diary, more or less, of what happens to me daily. You know how some days are dull while others have their high points.

I'm doing a swell job on the nuts and raisins.

Sunday 12/19/43

Dear Mom,

I've done nothing all day but write letters and do math.

I don't understand why Uncle Hy[1] is always smashing up his car. Dad has been driving for many more years and has never had such trouble. Hy must be a nervous driver. The letter I received from Aunt Ida didn't give me Cousin Bob's address except to say that he was in Utah. I doubt whether she wants me to write him. She's disappointed that he's not in the ground crew.

What a shame about Joe Ducharme. Remember the exact same thing happened to my favorite teacher, Mr. Lazotte? Why do such good people have to die like that—a brain tumor? Joe was a swell fellow, just like Mr. Lazotte. It's just like Grandpa said while he was dying, you're lucky to have lived as long as you have when all the young fellows are dying on the fighting fronts.

In reference to the bonds, I didn't sign up for any until August and that wouldn't go into effect until October so by the first week in January you should receive the first $25.00 bond for October through December. Since I have no dependents nor MAQ (Maintenance at Quarters) you know what my allotment is. I receive no receipt when a bond is issued. However, the government has a record of the withdrawal. You know about my insurance.

Today is real dead. I better get back to my math. It feels swell to be studying again. Although it's been a while, much comes back to me. As ever, Hughie, a math shark again

Monday 12/20/43

Dear Mom,

My duties today are so insignificant as not to deserve mention. I hadn't realized you'd get such a kick out of Olivia's signature. If the opportunity presents itself, I'll try to get signatures from more stars. I'm progressing nicely with the correspondence course, and really enjoying it.

I might go to Hollywood or L.A. on liberty Wednesday evening. last time I travelled by the inland route and entered the city by way of Cahuenga Boulevard, a street where, to my surprise, I saw four beautiful upholstering shops. They appeared to be small businesses like yours, Dad. The buildings were designed specifically for the businesses with swell display windows that show swell looking tufted jobs. I imagine these shops are cleaning up. Everybody here spends so freely that they seem to have plenty of money.

When I was home on ten day leave, I visited the Katz's on Garden Street to learn how my friend Lester was doing in the army. Mrs. Katz mentioned that she had friends in L.A. who would like to see someone from Worcester. So the other day I wrote her and asked for their address. I'd like to know more about this part of the country. By meeting people from here I can learn a lot. The majority of the Jews here are affiliated in some way with the movie industry or entertainment world and are well-to-do.

I must ask you to send me a mirror with a hole or holder so that I can hang it from a nail. The mirror I have is swell but inconvenient in the lavatories here (There are no mirrors on the base) for there's no shelf on which to place it. To hang a mirror is much handier. Don't buy anything too small. Something as large as a shaving mirror would do, but stronger.

                                                    Tuesday 12/21/43

Dear Dad and Ronnie,

Although today is the shortest day of the year, you'd never know it here. It's absolutely clear and pleasantly warm. The California winter is really something.

This afternoon along with your letter and the pocketbook on Russia from John Fulgoni, an enormous Christmas package from the Gallants arrived containing refreshments.

How did you make out with the bike, Ronnie, and what became of the car Dad was considering? Say, when you heard Groucho Marx that evening, I'll bet you missed "Abie's Irish Rose."[1] Do you still follow the program? I can imagine what you listen to on the radio at the office. I know as a fact that many people must go without a radio in their homes because of the unavailability of tubes.

Well, Dad, or should I say Matey, thanks again for writing. I know how busy you must be. Why in the devil doesn't Ronnie go out a little with some boys and girls. He should join school social functions. Don't let him make the same mistakes I made.

Well, well, well, so you're having below zero weather, eh. Now isn't that too bad. I guess a little cold won't hurt you once in a while, ha,. Of course, out here, we, ah, are basking in the sun and enjoying its glorious California warmth, uh huh. Boy am I enjoying rubbing it in, heh, heh. Can't stop laughing.

Tomorrow I'll have liberty, but I won't go to Hollywood this time. I also have Saturday, Sunday, and Christmas weekend off, so I'll probably go to Hollywood then, but I've made no firm plans. I think I'll also get New Year's off. What's tough is that I'm broke and may have to break into the watch money until I get paid on the fifth.

If you wish to send letters airmail, go ahead. Such letters arrive sooner, sometimes by two or three days, especially now that the Christmas rush is over.

Love to you both and you too, Mom, Hughie—the jerk who missed Albuquerque

Oxnard 7:30 PM 12/22/43

Dear Mom,

I'll probably visit Ventura this evening, but plan to return to camp early as we have rifle range early in the morning. This weekend, I plan to look up a woman who invited my friend and me to her home sometime. Before leaving this part of the country, I'm also going to try to meet some Jewish people. I have liberty only New Year's Eve, so I won't be able to see the Rose Bowl game or the Tournament of Roses Parade in Pasadena.

Believe it or not, I played baseball all day under navy orders. We had nothing else to do while waiting our turn at the range. It was funny to see us marching in military column to the drill field where, dressed in fighting coveralls, helmets and leggings, bats on our shoulders, and wearing baseball gloves, we played ball. Everyone got a great kick out of it. I was captain of one team, and, incidentally, the game was tied.

I'm afraid I'm all washed up with regard to the recreation department. Under the battalion's slack system, the work bored me, and the man in charge knew it, although I didn't complain. Anyway, I'm enjoying myself and I'm happy.

10:30 PM

Dear Folks,

I'm writing this from Ventura, a small city about twelve miles from Oxnard. It's a very pretty city with modern stores, clean wide streets and elaborate drugstores. And, yes, I had a swell chocolate malted just a few minutes ago.

California cities are very attractive, and, you know, I'd like to live here someday.

It's near 10:30 now and I'll be heading back to camp. Good night. I saw the 1782 Bienventura mission today. And by the way, the USO here is a beauty.

[Author's Note: To give the reader an idea of what the other side of the correspondence was like, below is a letter from Hughie's mother— exactly as typewritten, unsigned.]

12/22/43

Dear Hugh,

Did not receive any letter today, but did not expect any as three arrived yesterday, one taking six days coming.

I'm enclosing in this letter a money order of $10 for the last money order I sent you was for the raincoat tho when I sent it, it was for spending money. What I wrote you yesterday did not mean that I thought you were spending too much but I felt that you were keeping yourself too short in reserve funds. I want you to have as many good times as you possibly can, can in everything possible.

About your bike, the first Sunday I had the ad in we did not get a bite as it was buried in the automobile column, the next Sunday I put it in the articles for sale and had quite a few that called at the house to see it. Most every one wanted a 26 bike or the amount asked $45 was too much. The best offer was for $30 possibly 35. Shall advertise again in the spring think we can get our price. When you come home Dad hopes that he will have a car that you can drive when you have to go any where. and that you will not want to ride the bike.

Mrs. Mann [a neighbor] told me she received a lovely Christmas card from you, she wanted to know if you had received her birthday card. Let me know and I shall inform her if so.

Nothing more to write about to-day (this morning) so am going to send this letter out this morning airmail for I am anxious for you to get it quickly.

Love from all of us, Mother

12/23/43

Dear Mom,

I enjoyed myself immensely last night even though I didn't do anything out of the ordinary. The city was something new, I had a chocolate malted, and everything ran smoothly.

Today the gods were good so far as mail is concerned. This afternoon your letter of the 14th, and a very informative letter from Aunt Sadie arrived, while this evening I received a lovely Christmas card from the Gallants and your December 20th letter. Yesiree, that's getting mail from home in only 2 1/2 days. It came airmail, the first one addressed to Port Hueneme. I'd sure appreciate it if you'd keep them coming that way, if you can, Mom. Thanks for the swell kiss, too.

I'm happy that at last you got all those letters that were held up. It happens with me occasionally, too.

When I'm on guard duty I dress warmly, but in spite of how many clothes I wear, the California nights are penetrating. I wear my woolen sweater often, then when the sun comes out, it gets so hot that I can't stand it, especially when on guard duty as we're not allowed to take anything off. By now I know my blood is terribly thin, and since we are probably going to a hot climate, I don't mind.

I laughed that it took you forty minutes to read my letters. Gee, I hadn't realized I wrote so much. I probably had put several hours into writing them, but they seemed like only a few minutes.

Tomorrow we'll try to qualify firing our own .03-AS high powered rifles using live ammunition. Just think, a bullet from that rifle can penetrate fifteen inches of wood or one quarter inch of steel from 600 yards. It's muzzle velocity is about 27,000 feet per second. Although, as you know, the gun has quite a kick, we've been taught to hold it so it wouldn't bother us. The past few weeks I've been mostly drilling and on messenger duty.

Both Grandma and Sadie each sent me $2.00 which helped only a little. It cost $1.60 for bus fare to Hollywood and at least eighty cents for a meal. Such incidentals as writing material, soap, bleach and Christmas cards etc. add up. So transportation costs are high, and you know how expensive good food is. I know you want no excuses but that you want me to spend so that I may see things. We received a second issue of rain gear, so I won't need to buy a raincoat for across. That ten bucks you sent for the raincoat will come in handy over the holidays.

It seems every guy in the battalion owes somebody some sum of money but I owe nobody anything. I'm glad I don't make a habit of borrowing.

How'd you like me to have some portrait photos made? They're available right in camp. A photography expert in the battalion told me they're very good and reasonable—sell for standard prices. If you'd like me to do this, how many would you wish? They cost from $1.60 to $2.00 each, depending on size and quantity.

It appears that the song "I'm Dreaming of a White Christmas"[1] is popular again. I hear it played all the time in Hollywood. Boy, I miss the snow. When you tell me that Ronnie has gone skating, ye gods, do I wish I could go. Ronnie may have my skates if he wishes, though, no doubt, he has already used them.

You ask, doesn't it feel odd to awake with the stars still shining. I'm used to it now. Never before in my life, until the service, have I seen the night between 2:00 and 5:00 AM. I go to sleep and awake with the stars. It's light about 7:45 and dark about 7:00. I've spent a good part of my awake time in the Seabees under the stars.

I'm sure my eyes haven't improved although they're no worse than before. I don't mind going without glasses, but I wear them in camp, and I wear my new pair on liberties. (By the way, I've made an appointment to see a dentist. I don't have a problem, but I'd as soon have a checkup before leaving the country). There's a woman in L.A., a Mrs. Corbett, who can absolutely cure my eye ailment. She's wealthy and has enabled hundreds of boys with eyes that were once worse (3/20) than mine to qualify for the air corps. She takes care of Mary Pickford's[2] eyes, and presently Ambassador Davies's[3] wife is under her care. She also has restored Aldous Huxley's[4] (He's a famous author) eyesight. She has written nationally distributed books on the subject. As a matter of fact, a year ago, some eye doctors hauled her into court, and she won her case by offering absolute proof. I learned about her from a wealthy Seabee friend who lived in Hollywood. His eyes, which are as bad as mine, have been improved to 20/20. At present she has eighty-six instructors practicing her system around the country. The theory is based on muscular control of the eyeball to cure nearsightedness. After the war I'm going to take advantage of her treatment. Recently *Collier's*,[5] had quite a write up about her.

I'm proud of you people for the way you're willing to accept and rigidly face the fact that I'm surely leaving the country. Please don't have high hopes that I'll be coming East. You folks are just wonderful. I'm still at the correspondence course, but I find that with my duties here a bit more strenuous than at Holliday, I have less time to give to it.

The rifle firing training I'm getting is good so that I'm quite adept at handling my piece. I've fired several hundred rounds already. Since most of our liberties are at night, we wear only our blues here; my whites are at the bottom of my sea bag. We also have to wear our pea coats and boy, are they warm.

I'll hit the hay now. We are expecting an alert (practice) sometime tonight. Thanks again for the kiss, and here it is back again. Love to every one of you, Hughie

PS: My, you use pretty lipstick.

Friday, Christmas Eve 12/24/43

Dear Mom,

I spent the day at the rifle range firing my own gun for the first time, 30 rounds from 200 and 300 yards, and did fairly well, although far from expert. Frankly, I'm not a very good marksman. Boy, my rifle is something. It's wonderful but it packs quite a kick. What power! My shoulder is sore, and several fellows that had their lips close to the stock have cut and swollen lips. But this is the kind of rifle you want.

Here it's Christmas Eve and I'm sitting writing in the hut wearing only my underwear. It was so hot walking back from the range that I was drenched with sweat, despite having on only coveralls, pack and equipment. I'd swear it's summer again, hardly like a 25th of December. I'll be going to L.A. tomorrow at 8:00 AM and will return to camp Monday morning.

Say, how in the world were you able to secure fluorescent lights? I thought they were scarce. Going high class, eh. How are the tires on the car, Dad? Truck still pretty good? Do the heaters keep each section of the shop warm?

Sunday December 26, 1943

Dear Folks,

Right now I'm in the Hollywood Guild Canteen in a beautiful residential district on North Crescent Boulevard. This being a Jewish section, the B'nai Brith is established here. Hollywood is so jammed with servicemen that you can hardly walk through the streets.

After leaving camp yesterday at 8:00, I got into Oxnard by the skin of my teeth, and took the 8:15 Greyhound, again by the skin of my teeth, bound for L.A. The buses are so jammed with servicemen that civilians are refused passage. When I arrived in Hollywood, still early mind you, there were no beds or rooms available, but fortunately, again by the skin of my teeth, I found a bed at the Y where mattresses and bedding were laid on the floor of the handball courts. So last night I slept for the first time in a handball court, and very well, at that. After taking a good shower, I feel, now at high noon, swell.

I spent most of yesterday morning searching for quarters, but the afternoon was pleasant. The people whom we had met previously at the USO had us for Christmas dinner. They aren't wealthy. (The father works at Lockheed and is well-educated.) Mr. and Mrs. Myles live in a bungalow and have a daughter about Ronnie's age and an eight year old son. The dinner was swell, consisting of turkey, both dark and light meat, stuffing, potatoes, cranberries, vegetables, fruit cocktail and hot mince pie. There was plenty of everything and it was darn good. It's the first home-cooked meal I've had since I was home on leave. We talked all afternoon, and I beat Mr. Myles, after a good tussle, in a game of checkers. Mr. Myles had picked us up in Hollywood, and later drove us back there in his '39 Chevy. The Myleses are fine people and they treated us like kings.

Last evening the stage shows and broadcast were so jammed that we couldn't get in. So we went to Grauman's Chinese and saw "The Gang's All Here,"[1] a musical with Alice Faye[2] and Phil Baker.[3] It was entertaining and colorful. The theater is something gorgeous. I've never been in one larger or more elaborate. Decorated in a Chinese style, it's larger than the Palace.[4] The doorman is more than seven feet tall. Then my chum from Pennsylvania and I went to the Hollywood Theater and took in a double feature: "Princess O'Rourke"[5] with Olivia DeHavilland and "Guadalcanal Diary."[6] I enjoyed both.

The best way to see Hollywood and L.A. is to drive around to the various studios and the homes of the stars. Of course, since I'm not so fortunate as to have a car and the buses are somewhat uncertain, I did my best on foot.

I have tickets to the 2:30 matinee of Ken Murray's "Blackouts of 1944"[7] stage show, which has been running for two years and is considered to be entertaining by all. I also have tickets to the Fitch Band Wagon.[8] Although I'm not due back in camp until 7:30 tomorrow morning, I must leave here at 6:30 this evening to be sure I get back. As a result I'll be unable to take in several good available shows tonight.

Monday 12/27/43

Dear Mom,

Here's that night club hawk back again, minus a hangover and ready to tell about everything that happened in Hollywood. Boy, am I glad I don't do silly things in that silly town, so here I go with a clear conscience.

Although yesterday's letter outlined things pretty well, here are a few more details. As you know, my transportation to Hollywood was rather uncertain, but I got there. I had that lovely turkey dinner with the Myles family. Mrs. Myles is in her early thirties and very attractive, and her husband is a college man, learned and very intelligent with loads of personality. His pet subject is math, so I felt right at home. You should see his slide rules. Since two other families in the neighborhood had servicemen for dinner, all the families got together, and we just talked about everything. Mr. Myles had given his son a checkers game for Christmas, so he asked me to GIVE (ha,ha) him a game. We carried on a concentrated battle amidst the clamor of women and servicemen talking. Halfway through the game I was losing badly which made Mr. Myles overconfident. Slyly, I managed to get ahead and sew him up good. He had two kings and two men on the board while I had three kings and one man at game's end. He couldn't move. (You should see me patting myself on the back.) Now that my confidence is renewed, I'm ready to take you on anytime, Dad. I can't wait to get back to beat you. By the way, Ronnie, I've played a few games of chess with the fellows, but we never found time to finish them. To get back to the subject, Mr. Myles offered to let me sleep in his home Saturday night, but not wishing to impose on his family further I refused. Anyway, I like handball courts. Just think, I slept in a handball court, an ambition fulfilled. Since I've already written what I'd done that night, if you've forgotten just refer to my last letter, see.

Next morning I filled myself to the brim with a lovely breakfast of hot cakes, bacon, wonderful chocolate doughnuts and milk. The restaurant was beautiful and the meal cost only seventy cents. You can't imagine how expensive decent food is here. Any meal under a dollar is either lousy or skimpy. I must admit, that so far everything I've eaten has been swell. I feel that since I'm out to enjoy myself, and I like good food, yum, yum, I buy good food.

Oh, yes, I shouldn't forget that Saturday night I went to Sardi's. Did you ever listen to "Breakfast at Sardi's"[1] every morning on CBS? Well this is the same restaurant and what a beauty. The service was so poor, I got up and walked out. I waited much too long as it was.

Although I had tickets Sunday morning for a few radio shows, I didn't have time to attend them so I bought a $1.10 reserved seat at the El Capitan theater. After a swell lunch (veal) I went to the matinee at the Melody Lounge, corner of Hollywood and Vine. The lunch cost $1.13, but it was worth it. Well, that show, "Blackouts of 1944" with Ken Murray, the star, and Marie Wilson,[2] the costar (I've seen her in movies) was something. My friend Al, who has seen plenty of shows in New York and Pittsburgh, said it was the best one he's ever seen. I enjoyed every minute of its 2 1/2 hours immensely. Running for over two years, it was a comedy and variety show. I think I saw the 789th performance. Every act was swell. There were many beautiful chorus girls and it was quite spicy, but in a high class way. By the way, Daisy,[3] the dog from the Blondie pictures,[4] put on a wonderful act. After Ken Murray asked us to raise our hands, we saw that half the audience, which was of a reputable class, was seeing the show for the second time. Mr. Myles had also recommended it. That was one enjoyable afternoon. I have some souvenirs of the show including a booklet which I'm sending home. It was my first real stage show. If I remember, tomorrow I'll tell you one of the jokes from it. (Spent about $7.00 or $8.00 over Christmas.)

Before leaving Hollywood at 6:15, I visited the Canteen. As I approached, I saw Bette Davis driving on the boulevard from the Canteen. Pat O'Brien,[5] who was driving in a station wagon with his son, waved to us. We didn't have time to wait for the show and got back to camp at 8:00 last night and had a good night's sleep.

With seventeen fellows from the battalion, I'll be attending aircraft identification school. We learn the names of the enemy's and the United Nations' planes and how to identify them. It's much more interesting than I expected. Already I've learned ten planes. We are in school from 8:00 AM to 4:00 PM with time out for chow. One to three tests a day are given; I got 100% on my first one. Boy, does it sharpen your observation and memory. I should know most planes pretty well after I'm home. The course lasts a week.

This afternoon I received Christmas cards from Miss Rourke (my home room teacher) and Mr. Aldrin (the assistant principal) and your airmail letter of the 22nd.

I expect TO LEAVE THE COUNTRY BEFORE FEBRUARY 1ST, POSSIBLY BEFORE THE MIDDLE OF JANUARY. Definite preparations for leaving are in progress. I hear that our ship is being loaded, a three to six week process.

Dear Folks,

Don't worry, there's no danger of my missing a bus. I make sure I'll never be AOL (Away Over Leave). Glad to hear the folks in Boston enjoy my letters. Gee, maybe I am changing. What do you think? I smiled at your mention that Dad's not drinking coffee before bedtime so he can sleep. Yep, that's Dad all over. But now I like him this way. Isn't Mr. Barbour of "One Man's Family"[6] the same?

Hey now, I'm not hinting when I tell you I'm broke. If I want money, don't worry, I'll ask for it. Frankly, I don't like to withdraw money from the "boodle" there unless I have to. I'm not bashful. You've got me wrong.

Doggone decent of you, Dad, to let me use your car when I get home. Hughie, get out of the buggy, heh, heh. [A reference to a joke Dad tells about a family's argument over riding in a buggy that the father intends to buy.] Hey, are you ever going to get a car?

Yeah, I received a lovely birthday card from Mrs. Mann. I thought I had mentioned it.

The phys ed program has fallen through. Most of the men don't like that form of recreation. They accepted the program half heartedly and after all, without their cooperation, it's even useless to try to persuade them. They wish to build, not play.

I'm still in fine spirits and kicking.

Tuesday 12/28/43

Dear Mom,

I spent the day in aircraft identification school and rather enjoyed it. I like that we have to use our brains. The course teaches us to think fast. From the picture of a plane that's flashed on the screen for only a split second, we have to be able to tell what it is. We had two tests today.

Last night an alert sounded at 11:30 while we were sleeping. Everyone had to put on his fighting clothes, gas masks, packs, rifles, helmets, etc. and form in platoons then march a couple of miles in the darkness and form a battle line. Did we freeze! There was a cold dampness that goes right to your bones. The test is designed to get us used to such emergencies. I expect another one tonight. Since we didn't return to our beds until 2:30, we didn't get much sleep.

It's becoming more certain that our departure is drawing near. We're having our booster tetanus shots this week. It's now confirmed that our ship is being loaded. I plan to call you New Year's eve or soon after before I'll be confined. If I call, it will be about 11:00 PM to make sure that I'll get through. I realize I'll be waking you up early in the morning but I understand that calls to the East go through fastest at that hour.

I knew that you would enjoy "Holy Matrimony" which I saw at Holliday. I had read the synopsis of "Happy Land"[1] and I figured you'd eventually see it. I'll see it when I get back, and I will be back, mark my words.

Here's a return kiss to your letter of the 18th. Wish I could do it personally.

Wednesday 12/29/43

Dear Mom,

Changed my mind again. Have decided to buy a raincoat. I hear that there's much rain where we are going, and we'll have liberties. Of course, this may be far from the truth, and the men suspect we're headed for the Far East. Nobody really knows, not even the Commander himself.

I'm in Ventura on liberty this evening. Had a swell supper and will probably take in a show—or something. I don't know what I'll do New Year's eve; I think I'll go out.

It seems that you and Dad have been going to Boston quite often lately. I've been trying to maintain a steady correspondence with the Boston people, so they do have a pretty good idea of what I'm doing. I never realized my letters would be such hits. I guess they don't receive many good letters, so, even though mine are lousy, they consider them good.

Send some blotters, will you. I know you've got plenty, and I can · use them.

I'll try to send a longer letter tomorrow.

Love to you all, Hughie, the night hawk

Jan. 1st. 1944

Dear Dad,

Each of your letters is always better than the preceding one, to such an extent that by the time six more months will pass, you should be better than William Allen White[1] of the *Emporia Gazette.*[2]

Thanks Dad — thank-you with all my heart — for your demonstration of affection so beautifully expressed in your last letter. It did me good to read the letter. Not that I wasn't already feeling mentally or physically alright. It's one of those letters that just gives a son the needed uplift, that buoyant sensation, that is often lacking in navy life. Yes, with such a letter and such sentiments supporting him, a son cannot weather this war with just a flimsy, carefree attitude. He has something valuable to come back to, a debt that he can at least attempt to repay.

Your saying that you miss me is somewhat lightened in my heart by knowing that you have mother's and Ronnie's companionship. It seems that people within a family, having feelings for each other, can also sympathize with each other's predicament, softening those feelings even more. I must depend on keeping occupied, enjoying myself on liberties, and the ever dependable writing and receiving of letters to alleviate the burden of absentee affection. Being able to take it with a forced smile and resolute attitude, I've been hardened against homesickness. Yet, on occasion, I see things that remind me of you back home, of Mother and Ronnie, and it makes me more determined to do my job and get back there. I can't wait for that day when the war will be over and I can return. When I entered the service, I held no doctrine; as a matter of fact, I had no views about the war and my role in it.

The longer I'm away from home, the more able I am to steel myself against not being near you, yet the happier I become knowing that each day is that much nearer to returning. I feel this pretty well sums up what I feel about home. It is hard to put my emotions into words; I'm unable to express myself as I wish.

As you wrote, you'll expect a man when you see me again. These months, possibly years, are a transition period in a boy's life. He changes in many respects, with one exception: the love and devotion he has for those dearest to him. The changes I've noticed in myself are superficial. You will notice any deeper changes in me, but I'm incapable of recognizing them.

When I was home on leave, I was still the same boy that left a month earlier. I had only experienced boot camp and hadn't seen or heard anything that would change me. Even now, I really haven't learned the ropes, although I'm wiser to many things. Liberties in various cities, and the association with many men during the past few months have taught me things that I never dreamed were possible. So I have a pretty good idea how to act in public, and how to be tactful. I'm now aware when I make a mistake and say or do the wrong thing that I used to be blind to.

No, Dad, don't expect an outwardly changed son. I still have the same childish traits that I often see in myself. I don't want the war to make my attitude rigid, bitter and old. It hasn't so far as it has to so many others. I hope it makes me more sensible, appreciative and understanding. You folks and only you can tell how I change, not me. I hope I'll be what you expect when I come back.

The chances of not shipping out this month are slim. Our ship is being loaded and preparations are in full swing. I hope what you hope.

I am very sorry about your uncle's death. I didn't know him. Did I ever meet him? I can't remember.

Well, well, well, am I surprised that Aunt Annie liked my letters. Gee, if they're that good, I must continue. Frankly, I don't see anything wonderful about my letters. I think your letters beat mine by a mile, and Ronnie's humor is unsurpassable. Johnson Fulgoni is the guy who can write. Anna should receive one of his letters.

Doggone, I'm glad that I could make you feel proud with the people in Boston. You're getting like Mom and me, Dad: carrying pictures and showing them around. By the way, you have the negative to the picture you want enlarged. It was taken by the Gallants on my ten day leave. You'll find it around the house somewhere.

I got a month's extension in the correspondence course, so I figure I'll have time to catch up. My messenger's position at the Commander's was only temporary. I'll be going to camouflage school next week for a week. My assignments are not conditioned on my new rating.

I made eighty cents last night: I sold a trip ticket to L.A. that had been given to me.

Ronnie: Thanks for your letter. With so many girls around are you taking advantage of the situation? At Peary we were taught how to use the machete. At the time, it was kept a secret. Now it's no longer a secret. Since we weren't issued one, I'll be spared having to use it. We hear the Japs are scared stiff of machetes.

We just had a wonderful New Year's Day dinner: Vegetable soup, as much turkey as you wanted, delicious bread stuffing, lettuce, canned corn, diced carrots, pineapple, spinach pie, ice cream, fruit cake and a drink. Some feed, eh, and every bit of it good.

Enough for today. If I go on I won't have much to write about tomorrow.

Sunday 1/2/44

Dear Ronnie,

It's another one of those uneventful days, the sort of day when Mother would suggest that we bang our heads against the wall for excitement. When I awoke at 7:00 it was pouring, but now it's clear. Pancakes for breakfast easily made up for the dreary morning.

Say, did I ever tell you about the mock warfare incident on Cat Island? I was on guard duty about one half mile into the woods. One company was to "invade" the island, and another company oppose them, neither of which were supposed to have anything to do with our company. In other words, our company was not involved in the mock war. My orders, which were directly from the Commander, were to allow no one to pass beyond my post and to prevent anyone from going deeper into the woods. I and two other guards, each one about one hundred yards on either side of me, thus formed a no trespassing line.

The invading party landed at the wrong place, and meeting no opposition, was able to penetrate the woods to our posts. Meanwhile we three sentries could see the men approaching. When they reached an opening about one hundred feet ahead, we, naturally, halted them. However, the invaders, suspecting that this was a ruse by the opposition, continued to advance. Again we challenged them, and advised them that it wasn't a trap, that we were in earnest and they couldn't pass. Still, they chose to ignore our warning. We estimated there were at least fifty men spread along a two hundred foot line.

The three of us, who by now had joined each other, clicked off our safeties in such a manner that some of the oncoming men could hear. Of course, our Enfields were loaded with harmless blanks. One of the invaders spoke: he wanted to know why we turned our safeties off. We replied that our orders were to shoot anyone who defied us. Of course, you must realize we were bluffing. The spokesman then said, in a rather quavering voice, that he knew we had no bullets. I answered, "Oh, no?", pointed my gun in the air and fired a blank. The entire gang dashed back a couple of hundred feet through the woods in terror, yelling at the top of their lungs that we were nothing but murderers and willing to shoot to kill. Actually, they were scared stiff.

Soon a CPO came forward, and I explained the situation. After the men retreated the way they had come and disappeared, the three of us burst out laughing. If only I could bluff like that in a poker game, if only I played poker.

Bet basketball is now in full swing in Worcester and that South High is beating everyone. The Rose Bowl game here in Pasadena was poorly attended and it wasn't a good game. So I didn't miss much by not going.

I must shave quite often now to keep myself presentable: at least once every three days and sometimes more often. I learned that I can take my electric razor when we ship out. I don't know whether I'll be able to use it, but it takes up little room. How often do you shave? Every six months? Every three months?

I've thrown around enough baloney for one letter. I'll be back again tomorrow, possibly from Hollywood.

Hollywood 1/3/44

Dear Mom,

It's three in the morning, just after seeing the midnight show. I came to Hollywood alone this evening with no plans, but ready to do anything that would entertain his highness, the night hawk.

No sooner had I dashed into the NBC building from the bus when an attendant insisted that I accept a ticket for the Lady Esther Screen Guild show[1] which was to start in twenty minutes. No sooner did I say thank you, than I was gasping for breath in studio A at CBS. The program concerned the MGM picture, "North Star,"[2] and the actors that appeared in the picture performed. They were Jane Withers,[3] Walter Huston,[4] Anne Baxter[5] and a new star whose first name was Farley.[6] I don't remember his last name.

Jane, who was dressed to kill, is far from good looking, but she was pleasant and a good actress. Anne Baxter (Remember her in

"Assignment to Brittany") is quite beautiful, slender and short. Walter Huston has gray hair, is tall, and looks quite distinguished. I enjoyed the entire half hour, especially in such a modern studio setting.

I then had a full and enjoyable supper at a nearby eating place. Since I expect to return here later on in the week, I decided to spend the rest of the evening at the Hollywood Canteen again.

I had a swell time and you'll never guess what stars I saw. As a matter of fact, I got a few autographs. Since this morning I don't have much time to spend on this letter, I'll taunt you by withholding their names. Tomorrow I'll give you all the details and send the autographs of these actors and actresses whom you've all seen on the screen.

From midnight on, Hollywood was quiet so I went to a late show before taking the bus to camp. Now it's about time to catch it, so so long until you tune in to the same station tomorrow.

Wednesday Jan. 5, 1944

Dear Mom,

I'm well rested again and raring to write. Yesterday morning, in spite of no sleep the previous night, I felt unusually wide awake. However, about three in the afternoon while in school, I sprawled out for a little relaxation in the back of the classroom during recess. Inadvertently I fell into the depths of an ecstatic, impenetrable slumber only to wake up after a half hour in the middle of a classroom discussion. I was the most surprised boy in the world. Feinting ignorance at having fallen asleep, I participated in the discussion though I didn't know a darn thing. After class, one of my mates told me that I had snored but that nobody could locate who was doing it and the instructor hadn't heard it, so he left me alone. I was so embarrassed. I didn't mean to fall asleep, and I didn't want to miss anything. Anyway, one of my mates filled me in.

Today I returned to camouflage school wide awake and attentive all day. Yesterday was the first time falling asleep like that has ever happened to me. Friday is the last day of the course. Only twelve from the battalion are taking it. It's especially worthwhile for overseas service. I found it interesting, mostly due to the conscientious and worthy instructors we had.

I know you're anxious to learn what happened in the Canteen Monday night. To introduce the 1 1/2 hour show, Walter Wolf King was MC, and an excellent one at that. I was especially fortunate to be close enough to the stage to be able to reach out and touch the performers.

A young dancing star, a fellow about my age, performed a remarkable dancing act. He has been seen in many motion pictures and night clubs, but as luck would have it, I forget his name. Later that evening, after meeting him on Hollywood Boulevard, I told him how much I admired his act. He thanked me.

Then Dorothy Peterson[1] was introduced. You've seen her in several motion pictures with me, her most recent "This is the Army,"[2] I think. Remember, she was the mother of the flyer that sang—in the picture's audience sobbing as her son sang the flying sequence on the stage. She always takes the part of the mother. I asked her for her autograph. I liked her a lot. She looks, talks, and acts just like she does on the screen.

Finally, the main feature of the evening, Shirley Temple,[3] appeared. She is something beautiful; I was stunned by her beauty. Her features still retained some of the features of her earlier years, but this only added to her youthful beauty. She had long, streaming, curly hair, she stood about your height, Mom, and she had a shapely, well proportioned figure. Her voice was deeper than it used to be, but easy flowing. She had a cheerful personality which appeared as genuine as can be. Although you'd take her for only eighteen or nineteen, she talked like a young woman, not in the least like a child. She didn't perform, only talked. I was unable to get her autograph, as she left immediately after her appearance.

Do you remember Jimmie Dunn,[4] who years ago acted on the stage and screen? He cracked some witty jokes and gave us all a swell time. I could have listened to him all evening. Then, to my surprise, one of the most popular new actresses in Hollywood, appeared: Gloria DeHaven,[5] the new MGM[6] star, a fascinatingly beautiful girl. She's about nineteen years old.

Do you remember "Best Foot Forward?"[7] Well, three girls besides Jane Withers were featured in that picture. One of them was Gloria DeHaven, the gorgeous creature who danced and sang. Her figure is like a model's, and her face is beautiful, with the biggest blue eyes I've ever seen. Although her hair was reddish in the picture, it was blonde in the Canteen, and almost fooled me. She sang about five songs and has a really swell voice. She also has what is known as Oomph,[8] which made all the fellows drool. She has a uniquely friendly way about her. You will receive her autograph.

I was surprised to see how short all the actresses were. Anne Baxter is shorter than you, Mom, and Gloria DeHaven is about your height.

Les Brown's famous orchestra[9] played 'til midnight. I know you people don't know much about orchestras but take it from me, this one ranks among the best. Without a doubt, it's the best orchestra I've ever heard in person, although Robert Armbrewster's and the Screen Guild orchestras are excellent.

I got to talking to one of the bus boys, (He's about 26) who told me quite a bit about Hollywood and the movies. The bus boys at the Canteen are men from the entertainment world. In fact, this fellow was a supporting actor at MGM, his last picture being "The North Star," and he expects to reach the top. A college boy, he had served eight months in the army and was discharged because of some illness. I found talking to him interesting. That's all that happened at the Canteen where I spent a most enjoyable night, indeed.

So at last the grippe epidemic caught up with you. I'm at least consoled to know that you are on the road to recovery. I feel a whole lot better reading "am feeling much better." I hope Dad and Ronnie come through without catching it.

I note that I somewhat confuse you in postponing or cutting short many of my letters. Usually I have to do that when I'm on liberty and have limited time. Also often I'm called for muster. The reason why I might not mention a subject for a day or two after it occurred is that I wait for new developments or a more important subject takes precedence. Occasionally I mention something that's of only minor importance, or I don't know much about, or I don't have much to say on it. Yes, I'm aware that I've been in the service six months and still don't know what my job is. That's the Seabees, thoroughly confused. I'll probably not know what they want me to do until I'm across, but I'm not the least bit worried.

I don't always tell what I do for two reasons: it's trivial or it's something I shouldn't mention. I've spent many days standing by, doing nothing but remaining in barracks writing and reading before being called for guard duty or clean up detail or drill. The CPOs figure out things for us to do. As I've said, I've spent the past two weeks in school. Ordinarily I tell you the important things that happen, but you must realize I can't tell everything. Mind you, I'm not treated as an individual, but as a member of a group. Liberties are the high points in my life, therefore, the subject I write most about.

I have more money than I need. You really shouldn't send me $5.00 of Ronnie's money. I won't accept it, mind you. I don't like taking money from home savings. My pleasures here and now are not worth as much as an education after the war. When I'm across I'm going to send more money home to make up for the money I "borrowed" from the home fund. Please, send no money unless I ask for it. Don't worry I'm not bashful; I'm not afraid to ask if I have to. Please remember that I have my own little budget and if I should go beyond it, well, I'll have to suffer. It hurts me to see money come from home.

The dentist that examined my teeth said they're perfect and made some fine comments about them.

The lavatories here have hot and cold showers and clean indoor flush toilets. But the clothes washing and face washing facilities (no bowls, only faucets) are poor. Now that I'm used to them I get along pretty well.

I've been unable to go surf bathing because I work days and the nights are too cool—we even need to wear gloves. On days off I'm too busy seeing the sights.

I hear the battalion has $50,000 worth of airmail stamps for overseas use, and I intend to make use of them. Did I say that Mrs. Myles was in her twenties? Guess she couldn't be; I meant to say she looked it.

There are no really good dramatic plays in Hollywood. That's why I haven't gone to any.

Just this minute a happy fellow walked in to say he was accepted for V-12. Today five fellows were accepted from the battalion. This fellow said the test was a snap. I'm sure I would have passed it. Well, you can't have everything you want.

I'm having my jumper cut down so that it needn't be folded at the bottom. The navy is advocating doing it. It will now be much easier to put on and take off. The base tailor is charging thirty-five cents.

A smile of happiness crossed my face as I read that my letters shorten your day. You can't realize what your letters mean to me. I live for them. More than once, when I've read them in the hut, I've burst out with joy at what swell folks you are. I can't ask for any better than you.

It's a wonder that my pen point hasn't worn out. It has acquired a sentimental value. It's been with me wherever I've gone, and movie stars have used it.

Yesterday we practiced camouflage on the beach. That's the closest I've been to the Pacific. The surf is 12 or 14 feet high, dwarfing a man, when the tide comes in. I've never seen such combers in my life. The color of the Pacific is different from the Atlantic, though I can't describe how.

I have liberty again tomorrow evening, but I think it wiser not to visit Hollywood again this week. Once a week is enough.

USO, Oxnard, Thursday Jan. 6, 1944

Dear Mom,

Today I had the final test in camouflage. Actually, I don't care for the subject, but I figure it's worthwhile knowing. I don't yet have my grade.

I'm in Oxnard tonight to buy a few incidentals and will return to camp early. Now that I have my jumper back from the tailor I'm pleased with it; no more struggling like a mad man to take it off.

The opening paragraph of your New Year's Day letter mentions listening to "La Traviata"[1] on the radio. How I miss the radio. I'd give anything to listen to music. Instead I must tolerate my own lousy whistling and humming. I hadn't realized I'd miss it so. It's got so I even like swing, and I can't keep still when listening to the bands in Hollywood.

My going to aircraft ID and camouflage schools doesn't necessarily mean that I'll have a job in those fields, even though only a selected few are sent to those schools. We take such courses as a precautionary measure, in case there's a need to apply such knowledge. There are also many other schools, such as chemical warfare, water purification, communications, machine gunnery, 20 mm, B.A.R.,[2] and several others. It's good that some men in the battalion are familiar with these subjects in case it's needed.

The older men find the inconveniences of life here hard. They feel it, and as a consequence, the sick bay is plenty busy treating their ailments. Several have to be discharged. After what I've gone through, I guess I'm even immune to pneumonia. You'd go nuts if I did at home what I do here, but what you don't know won't hurt you. I can't kick, and I feel swell.

After I'm shipped across, I'll tell you where I am by printing it lightly in pencil at the bottom of the envelope inside. The battalion censor—a fellow I know—never examines the envelope. It looks like we'll be going to a fairly large base.

Doggone, so you bought a car at last, eh Dad. I'm as thrilled about it as you are. Now I have even more reason to get this war over with.

Next week may be my last liberty week, so I'll surely go to L.A. and Hollywood. I may call you. Contrary to what I expected a week ago, I may see February 1st in this country after all.

Dear Dad, (from the kin)

I've just read Encyclopedia Aaron, edited and written by the best father in the world, and offering everything that a son could desire. Between you and Mom and Ronnie I'm receiving enough pleasure to forgo liberties. I should demand a special leave so I can go home to shake your hand and thank you to the nth degree. Doggone, fella, if you continue writing the way you do, I'll have to go AWOL, over the hill, and skidoo home.

I'm guilty of many offenses, I know, the greatest, as you guessed, is that I'm a chocolate malted addict. Malteds are very nourishing, you know, and they add to my ration of milk. To me a malted milk is what champagne is to the king of England.

I should get to the main subject of this epistle. (Ask Ronnie what the word means. He knows.) Ordinarily, I'd begin with a "wow" and commence talking about the new car right away. But you know it's improper to rush a subject.

I don't remember what the '39 Ford deluxe model looks like. Of course, that's of little importance, just so long as the car is presentable. I'm as happy as you that after all these years at last you got a car. Congratulations. I hope you enjoy it plenty. From what you tell me, I'm sure it was a good buy. I know the Callahans from whom you bought the car, their boy Andy, in the army, and his sister. They impress me as being fine people. It's a lucky break that you found a garage, too. It looks like everything about the deal has gone your way. And it's a good idea to put it under the business's name.

Are they still fussy about cars driving on Sundays with B and C cards?[1] I can already picture you driving the car with a gleeful grin from ear to ear in the knowledge that at last you have a car of your own strictly for pleasure. Doggone, it's just dandy.

Dad, I know mother was only kidding when she said that you wouldn't let me use the car. She's only ribbing you. And Dad, listen, I could kiss you for being willing to share it with me when I get home, but you don't have to. Remember, I always like walking. How could I take advantage of your offer? It's much too generous. Were I home now, I'd expect to be treated no differently than always. And I'd expect that you'd let me use it on only those occasions that you deemed important. Of course, I'm saying this 3500 miles away, but I'm sure I'd say the same thing were I 35 feet away. Thanks again, Dad.

The weather that we're having here in California is considered unusually poor, but I think it's glorious. In spite of the warmth, I haven't seen any insects or flies, nor have I been bitten by a single mosquito.

The correspondence course will continue while I'm overseas; in fact, it was designed specifically for overseas duty by the International Correspondence Corp. and sponsored and paid for by the government. A civilian would have to pay at least $100 for the course. And provision is being made for continuation of the course after the war. I wish I could put more time into it.

I bought something today that I've been wanting for a long time and will need in college: a really good log-log trig slide rule. If you object, please don't hesitate to say so, for I welcome your advice now that I'm more open to heed it. The slide rule computes logarithms, chemical equations, exponents and higher mathematics functions. Every engineering and math student in college is required to have one. I'll find it useful and a time saver in my analytic geometry course. A precision instrument, it normally costs twelve or fifteen dollars. The boys at Tech buy them through the school for twelve dollars.

I bought the slide rule from a fellow in my hut; he's a great gambler and needs money badly. I've known him since I joined the battalion. He's well liked and honest, but he's a poker player. Since he needs money and has no use for the slide rule in the service, he decided to sell it. Before committing myself, I showed the rule to several college grads and engineers in the battalion to get their opinions. Everyone said the rule was accurate (from a test they knew), in good condition, and a good buy. The price is $8.00, and I can pay for it in installments so I won't feel it. I gave him three dollars and will pay the balance on pay day. If the other fellows had heard of it first, I think they would have grabbed it. What do you think?

My glasses don't affect my marksmanship, whatever. As a matter of fact, our best marksmen wear glasses. I like shooting; it's fun. After the war, I'll buy the rifle that was issued to me and I'll probably go in for hunting. Since I hold the rifle properly, I never bruise my lip.

Our boys haven't had enough swimming instruction. If we're under fire while on the high seas or on barges during an attack (predicaments which I doubt we'll ever be in), we'll drown like rats, God forbid. I've told our officers, but they just ignore me. That's the CBs for you.

My neck is no thicker, and I haven't added any muscle. This is an easy life compared to the workouts I used to have at home in the gym. The sailor suit doesn't fit tight because I gained weight, but because it is cut to fit tight. I don't know what I weigh now.

Now I pass by Hollywood and Vine without a second thought. Finding my way around Hollywood has become second nature. One of our CPOs was saying that most kids would give anything to see the stars and visit the places we've seen, and take a ride down Hollywood Boulevard. To them it would be like a dream, but it means nothing to me anymore. As ever, Hugh — the chocolate malted fiend

Saturday 1/8/44

Dear Mom,

I bought the raincoat today — size 40. It fits me just right and allows for underclothes. Now I can't wait for rain so I can try it out.

I've bought everything I'll need: toothpaste, tooth brushes, shoe laces, pencils, oil for my rifle and other incidentals.

I think I'll call you next week regardless of when I'm confined. At least, I'll be able to say goodbye instead of doing it through a letter, even if I may not leave for weeks. Gee, it would be swell to hear your voices again.

Sunday 6:30 PM Jan 9, 1944

Dear Mom,

I always look forward to Sunday to catch up on my letter writing; yet, when it finally does come, I lose all ambition to write and instead sleep and talk and read. One thing I've learned to do in the navy that I could never do before is fall asleep practically at will. I can nap for an hour or two any time that I don't have duties to perform or personal chores to do. During my nightly guard duty days, sleep was a big problem, but, now that I'm working days, my normal procedure is to take a hot shower and retire at 9:00 or 9:30 and awake at 6:00. Right now, having had no appreciable exercise for a couple of months, I'm in poor physical condition. Of course the main thing is to feel well, which I do.

Liberties are the highlight of navy life. While I don't crave for them as so many do, I must admit that I look forward to a night off. Transportation, especially getting back to camp, is the biggest obstacle to enjoying liberty. However, when I leave camp or arrive at my destination, I arrange to guarantee my passage back. I'm surprised how easy it has been to get acquainted with the area. Usually my first visit to a place is devoted strictly to reconnaissance, so on subsequent trips I can find my way around. I used to be bewildered on my first liberty to a strange city, but no longer now that I'm seasoned to handle each situation confidently.

I feel swell knowing that Dad's car is a reality. The price of cars here is stupendous. I see lots with cars whose prices, smeared on windshields, are higher than when the cars were new. Most of the cars we see here are high-priced and belong to celebrities, aircraft engineers, or motion picture actors.

By now, Uncle Bill must be a married man. Did you attend his wedding? I suppose I'll know in a couple of days from one of your letters.

I laughed when I learned that the museum called. I guess they figured I was 4-F. Johnson had mentioned that the models were poor. I never imagined they'd hope to find a 19 year old boy. They must be hard up. Were I home I doubt if I'd want to pose again.

With liberty coming up Tuesday, I may visit L.A. again. I'm anxious to see Harry James at the Palladium. Be back tomorrow.

Love to you, Dad and Ronnie, Hughie

PS: Corner of Hollywood and Vine one sailor said to a blonde passing by, "Your riggin looks pretty good. How are ya manned?"

Monday 1/10/44

Dear Folks,

Tomorrow I begin chemical warfare school for one week. After attending various schools, I'll surely be a jack of all trades but master of none. But at least I'll know some things that could be useful in the future.

Nope, I'm not in confinement yet. I don't know what to think. I understand that we were scheduled to leave a week or so ago, but for some reason the plans were changed. Our overseas supplies are supposed to be ready for loading, yet some men, including the Lieutenant Commander from Massachusetts, have been granted ten day leaves. There's talk, although it's hard to believe, that there will be another embarkation leave for all. It sounds more like scuttlebutt and the wishful thinking of some Seabee from the East.

I was surprised at the low price Dad paid for the car. It's a sure bargain, especially with all the equipment included. By the time I return home for good, Ronnie will be driving around like a king. Doggone, you're a lucky fella.

A new motion picture, "The Fighting Seabees,"[1] with John Wayne and Susan Hayward[2] is being released this week. The world premiere will be held here on the 14th. I'm sure Ronnie would enjoy it.

I heard from Lenny's sister that he's stationed at Quonset and that he'll soon attend a school in Illinois. How some boys get breaks! And Lenny has been third class for months.

I can't do anything in the way of a rerate. They just don't want to hand rerates out. Since there's no sense in brooding about it, I just forget it and let whatever happens happen. What else is there to do? I'm past the stage of disgust. Those days were foolish when I took such things to heart. Now, I let disappointments roll off as if they didn't exist. You'd be a damn fool were you to take such things seriously in this outfit.

I had elaborate plans to go to L.A. on liberty tomorrow evening, but I don't think I will. I'd rather save the money for the weekend. I could have some marvelous times if I could only dance. I avoid parties and even girls for fear of embarrassing myself and the girls. Dancing is the central activity at all social gatherings, the medium through which acquaintances are made and the only way to have real fun. I could have dates, but there's no sense in burdening a girl with a fellow who can't dance. After all, dancing is the principal entertainment at a party, and I can't expect a girl to go out with a guy like me. To be a success, you have to know how to dance. Truthfully, although there are plenty of opportunities, I don't even want to make a girl's acquaintance for that reason. The girls treat us like kings. But I'm not as bothered as I'd ordinarily be, because I'll be shipping out any day. Let me tell you I'm one sorry boy that I never learned to dance, because I've had to pass up many good times. And who is to blame? Yup, that jerk, Hughie Aaron. Ah well, I guess I must learn life the hard way. I can't complain though, because I have enjoyed the sights.

Happy birthday, Ronnie. I remember the good old days when I was fifteen. Yep, just call me grandpaw now. I only wish I was in a position to send you a small present.

PS: After we ship out, I expect we'll stay awhile in Hawaii. I have good reasons for thinking this. Let's wait and see how reliable my expectations are.

Tuesday Jan. 11, 1944

Dear Mom,

I've hardly mentioned the wonderful goodies that arrived three days ago. You seem to know just what I crave: raisins that I used to raid the cupboard for, cashews that I couldn't keep away from at Sol's drugstore, cookies that Dad used to taunt me with during the evening snack, and candy, the all time favorite. Thanks plenty.

I was swamped with today's mail. During the noon hour and this evening at supper time I devoured its contents. I learned that you hadn't heard from me for four days. That's really tough.

So Uncle Bill has taken the fatal step. I hope you were able to attend the ceremony.

You've been mentioning that I should take some photos so often, that I may as well break down and tell you that I have. I had intended to surprise you with them. Last night I slicked up a bit and had the base photography studio (a private concession and the work is done in L.A.) take some before I went on liberty. Their size is eight by twelve, not too large, and about as large as my colored graduation picture. I bought three, the minimum number. One will be sepia which they call gold tone. I'll have the proofs Friday—one serious pose and one smiling, (Some service, eh?) and I'll have the portraits ten days later. And I'll have them sent directly to you because I may not be here in two weeks. See, you spoiled my surprise.

I went on liberty Thursday for one reason alone which I cannot disclose. Yes, I can, since this letter won't reach you until after Ronnie's birthday. I went to every card, stationery, and drug store in Oxnard looking for a decent card for Ronnie. There simply wasn't one that was good enough, so during the weekend I asked a friend who was going to Hollywood to buy a nice card for a good price. I told him what sort of card to look for. Well, he forgot. So last night after taking the pictures, I went to Ventura (and bought a 9:30 return trip ticket) expressly for the purpose of finding a proper card. After searching a while I found one that was fairly decent, although not entirely satisfactory. I had no choice but to buy it. Forgetting my pen, I went to the USO to find one where I hurriedly addressed the envelope, but being anxious to catch the bus back to Oxnard, forgot to sign the card. Anyway, Ronnie, I'm signing it here and now: Hughie. I hope the card reaches you in time.

I hadn't figured I'd have so much trouble finding a card. It's a fine howdyado when YOU send me five dollars for YOUR birthday. Things are sorta mixed up, uh. What a country. Ya gotta fight to find a decent birthday card yet.

My pen is going on the bum. It no longer writes nearly as nicely as it used to, and it doesn't hold much ink anymore. This has suddenly happened. I think the damp, corrosive air here has spoiled it.

The mirror you sent is perfect. Nothing could be better for shaving. I can't leave it hanging near my bunk, as all the fellows use it. I received the blotters too.

Thursday Jan 13, 1944

Dear Mom,

I'm writing in pencil today because the pen finally went on the fritz. I'll get a new point when I visit L.A. this weekend.

Today we had chemical warfare field practice. Quite interesting. We had to put on our gas masks while there was tear gas in the chamber. Tear gas is no fun. I cried for a good ten minutes. Then we were taken to a field where vials of real war gases were exploded. Wearing masks, we had to recognize their odor as we walked through such gases as mustard, Lewisite, chloropicun and phosgene, all extremely deadly. The purpose of this exercise was to learn not to fear these gases, but to respect them. Furthermore their concentration was not sufficient to harm us, and we were told not to linger in their wake. I consider myself fortunate that I've gained such practical knowledge of gases.

I had gone out alone to Hollywood that night, because for once I wanted to do things my way. When you're with another fellow you also have to do things his way although you might prefer not to. However, I do enjoy the company of a companion. Another reason I like to go out alone is so I can visit a Jewish USO. I hope to visit one this weekend.

Yes, I know that there are no more men being accepted in the Seabees. You mean Uncle Bill would like to join the Seabees? Tell him he'd have no opportunity in the Seabees, and the training is tough, even tougher than at [Camp] Sibert. If a man doesn't have a trade, don't join. But the regular navy is okay.

Every day new equipment comes in for loading. It's rumored that our ship is about to arrive. Lately the meals have been better than usual. Guess we're being fattened up for something. It's also rumored that we'll have liberty at our next base.

Money doesn't last long around here. You are probably thinking that I'm making excuses. No, I'm not, but I'd like you to know what I buy, the way I used to back home. Maybe you don't want to know what I spend money on, but I prefer that you do. I still like to tell you everything that happens.

Friday Jan. 14, 1944

Dear Folks,

Today I finished the chemical warfare course with a mark of 100% on the final exam. The marks I've received in the schools I've attended these past three weeks have been pretty good: Camouflage, 96% and 100%; chemical warfare, 100%. However, I found the courses quite easy, grasping everything quite well due to my experience of studying in school. Although the courses will have no effect on my getting a rerate, they will help when I am considered for one. The marks are entered in my service record.

Today I received the proofs of the pictures. I hope you like the smiling one, the one I chose. [The photograph appears on the front cover of this book.] Although I didn't care for the serious one, I asked the photographer for his advice on which to chose. After explaining how to select a picture, what features to notice, he recommended the smiling one. Anyway, my graduation picture is serious, so something different is in order. When the photographer clicked the picture, I was unaware that he was doing it, making it a more realistic shot. The smile isn't forced because I was laughing at something the photographer had said.

I recall my French teacher at school who despised laughing pictures because, he said, he could never figure out what the joke was. Well, you know there was a joke in this picture. The picture will be ready in ten days and sent directly to you.

I have tickets to go to L.A. tomorrow afternoon. I plan to go alone so I can get around easier and see more. Today is a big day on the base. The camp theater will be jammed for the premiere of "The Fighting Seabees." I'm not bothering to see it, as I can imagine what the jam will be like; I'd rather wait for a time when the crowds will be less.

Saturday Jan. 15, 1944

Dear Mom,

First, I must mention that I'm writing this letter with a new pen point that I secured in L.A. I've had a most enjoyable afternoon and evening thus far while on liberty.

I departed Hueneme at 12:00 and secured immediate transportation to Hollywood. From there I took a bus to Wilshire Boulevard and found a bed at the Naval Aid Auxiliary Shore Station where I'm writing this letter. I must tell you about this place.

It's something wonderful, like being in your own home. It's a modern house designed specifically for servicemen. Each room has about six beds, soft ones at that, and a lavatory with a toilet and showers. The hostesses treat you like I don't know what: you're waited on hand and foot. The atmosphere is amazingly homey; there's a living room with comfortable overstuffed modern furniture and a crackling fire in the fireplace. The biggest surprise is finding girls everywhere to talk to or dance with. And to top it off, besides a bed, we get towel, soap and a swell breakfast, all for only fifty cents. I regret not having found this place sooner.

After signing up for a bunk, I took a long walk down Wilshire Boulevard to downtown Los Angeles. The day was gorgeous, like a June day. I passed by the famous Ambassador Club where Freddie Martin[1] is playing, the swanky Brown Derby, and several beautiful buildings, department stores, hotels and parks. I enjoyed seeing all these places so much.

After getting into L.A., I headed for Pershing Square at Broadway and 6th and 6th and Main, the city's busiest spot. I walked all over downtown, visited a few USOs, had a few milk shakes, and had my pen point replaced. I tried to send a birthday telegram to Ronnie in the lobby of the famous Biltmore Hotel, but no go. They wouldn't even take a congratulatory night letter. And I counted so much on sending it. Sorry.

After browsing through downtown for a few hours, I caught the trolley to Pasadena, about thirteen miles southeast of L.A. It's regarded as a most beautiful place; Cal Tech[2] is there and the Rose Bowl[3] and it's where the Tournament of Roses parade[4] is held. I was fortunate enough to sit beside a fellow on the trolley who was a Pasadena native. From his description of the town, I knew my way around pretty well by the time I got there.

He recommended a cafeteria where I had a marvelous and inexpensive meal. My waitress, noticing the CB on my arm and having a husband in the Seabees, treated me like a king. I also had a pleasant partner who sat across the table from me, a woman about sixty, and we talked about many things.

After a hearty meal, I walked along Colorado Ave., the main drag. By the way, Seabees are practically extinct in Pasadena. The stores were eye popping. I couldn't take my eyes off one especially ultra modern store. There were many gorgeous homes and the swanky, famous Huntington Hotel.

During the walk I noticed an elaborate building with a sign that read: "Ice Skating." Apparently the arena was about to open for the evening, for I observed boys and girls, kids my own age, and adults, entering the place in a big way. Since I'm a lover of skating, I needed no urging to investigate. I was amazed to find such a swell place inside. It had soda fountains, music to skate by, and a place to rent skates and check your shoes. The rink, all of it indoors, was enormous. Well, being in my glory, I had one swell time.

No, I didn't fall once. I got a kick out of speeding around the rink to music. Skating periods were devoted to couples only, then to girls only, and to men only and an intermediate period for all. It was fun. Despite not having skated since last winter, I did darn well on the ice. There I was, skating, wearing only my navy blues, no coat or hat, and warm as toast. It was wonderful. Gee, Ronnie, would you love it. The ice was swell too, not a crack and like glass. Of course, I wanted to get the maximum amount of skating in, so when the "couples on the rink only" sign went up, I found a partner to skate with. Yes, I actually asked a girl to go pairs with me, and she enjoyed it a lot. She was about my age, and came from Alberta, Canada. I enjoyed her company.

Not wanting to stay too late, I left after two hours, intending to go to a dance at the Civic Auditorium (picture enclosed). Since I had quite some distance to go to return to my temporary home, I took the trolley back to L.A. and transferred to the Wilshire bus to here, where it's now 12:30 AM. You know, while skating, all I had to do was close my eyes and use a little imagination and there I was, skating at Elm Park.[5] It's odd that just a few hours earlier I saw men in trunks playing tennis at the Ambassador Hotel courts, and men in bathing suits, sunning themselves in General D. MacArthur park[6] and boys and girls canoeing.

I have the address of a Jewish USO which I plan to visit tomorrow. On the bus back from Pasadena I sat beside a Mrs. Kaplowitz from New York, wife of a rabbi who died two years ago. She told me her life history and invited me to her home for the night, but I had already made arrangements for lodging, so I refused.

I received your long letter earlier today. It's a beaut, Mom. So glad to hear that the car is a success. At last you're capitalists: two cars and a radio too. Boy, I wish I were there in Boston to see Dad tipsy and feeling good. I'll never forget the New Year's[7] party at 396 Chandler Street. Yup, Dad, I heard everything that night. As I recall, you were quite the singer.

I sent a card from L.A. to Uncle Bill and Libby and I couldn't resist sending a humorous one. I'll write them as soon as I return to camp.

I'm pretty stiff (no, not intoxicated) from skating. A good night's sleep will fix that. Good morning.

Love to you all, Hughie

P.S. I'm surprised at how well I get around on the transportation system. I haven't made any mistakes yet. X fingers are crossed.

Sunday Jan. 16, 1944

Dear Dad,

I'm doing a fairly good job of celebrating Ronnie's birthday today. I have just seen the most beautiful homes in the nation. Man oh man do I wish you and Mom could see them. Here's a try at describing them.

My good luck began first thing this morning. After I awoke at 8:30, I took a good shower then went to the breakfast room, where I had corn flakes and milk, bacon and eggs, tomato juice and a cold glass of milk. For a while after breakfast, which didn't cost me a plug nickel, I read the paper.

Westwood, the most beautiful residential district in the nation, was first on my list to tour. While waiting for the bus on Wilshire Blvd., a young woman in a coupe stopped, yelled "Westwood" and there I was in only seconds speeding to my destination. She was a psychology student at UCLA. During the fifteen or so miles we traveled she told me all about Westwood, where to go, and what to see. This is one of the newest sections in the area, its earliest streets laid out in only 1926, and most homes not more than ten years old. The place looks like a fairy village. There were stores of the most unique modern design that I've ever seen.

I visited the University of California campus, a place well worth seeing. My description wouldn't do justice to the beauty of the landscape and buildings. After roaming around the campus for a while, I took a walk down Sunset Boulevard to view the homes. A man in the first car that came along picked me up and drove me about five miles down Sunset so that I was able to see everything. After the driver dropped me off, I began walking back to Westwood intending to visit BelAir. No sooner did I take a few steps than a woman in a Packard stopped and took me to the gates of BelAir where multimillionaires and movie people have built the most elaborate homes anywhere. Servicemen are extinct in this locale so I was in my glory. The area resembles Westwood Hills in Worcester, only it's twenty times the size, and the homes make the ones in Worcester look like pikers. So I began a walking journey among the estates, enjoying the beautiful grounds and million dollar houses. A $50,000 home here is considered cheap. The area is hilly so I had to take frequent rests.

The first house I stopped at belonged to a wealthy lawyer. I entered into conversation with the gardener who was washing a car in the driveway. He was most pleasant and invited me into the house for a drink. He told me all about the other homes, particularly who they belonged to etc. The lawyer's home, of colonial design and faced with stone, was only three years old. I was fascinated with it, the expensive cars in the garage and the expensive shrubs. Walking farther, I stopped at the summit of a hill where there was another beautiful home. I hailed the gardener, who was burning leaves. He allowed me to wander through the grounds. I stopped by the swimming pool and gazed in one direction across the countryside for miles and miles clear to the ocean. Facing another direction, I could have cried at the beauty of the snow-capped peaks in the distance. What a spectacle. After gazing for a while in wonderment at the scene, I talked to the gardener for a time. Soon the master of the house joined us, and we entered into a discussion on whether California was a better place to live than Massachusetts. The owner, Mr. Judge, was mighty interested in where I came from and where I stayed last night. About 55 or 60, he was very pleasant. Then Mrs. Judge with her two sons, one seven, the other ten, and her beautiful daughter, Ronnie's age, joined us. She's the type of person who pretends to be serious as she insults you and pokes fun at you. I enjoyed her, especially her easy flowing voice. All were dressed to kill, and they waved goodbye as the pulled their car out of the three car garage and drove away. Yes, that was Arlene Judge.[1] Remember her?

On the way back to Westwood I met a man about Dad's age taking his dog and five year old son for a walk. The dog, a beaut, took a liking to me and Ray Whitten, the son, cute as could be, wouldn't let go of me. With Mr. Whitten as guide we talked and walked for a distance. He pointed out Atwater Kent's[2] mansion, Gene Raymond[3] and Jeanette MacDonald's[4] home, and his own done in Spanish style and worth a good $75,000. He was most pleasant.

Imagine, a wall around one of the houses alone was worth $12,000. I'll never see anything like all this again, let me tell you. I could go on for another twenty-five pages just describing the homes I saw. They are designed in a variety of styles: Colonial, Spanish, Mediterranean and French.

Since it was dinner time, I headed back to Westwood, getting another ride as soon as I stepped into the street. There I had an excellent meal in a novel restaurant called Tips. As soon as the waitress spied the CB on my arm, the service was terrific. I never saw so many girls in one place and so many as beautiful as in the village of Westwood. Most were students at UCLA.[5]

No sooner did I leave the restaurant, than three Jewish boys my age offered me a ride, asking where I'd like to go. After telling them that I was sightseeing, they drove me around in their convertible

Mercury coupe.[6] We ended up at the Beverly Hills Hotel, a swanky hotel resort. There's also a USO in Beverly Hills where I secured a pass to see a stage show, "Yours for Fun" tonight. At this moment I'm waiting to be picked up by a party who wants some servicemen to join them for supper.

After arriving at the hotel about 3:00, I planned to go swimming in the swell pool, but all the bathing suits were taken. Since I had a supper date for five, I figured I'd visit the B'nai Brith Canteen in Hollywood for a while. After getting a ride to the Canteen, I found it closed. Had I mentioned that the average home in BelAir costs between $100,000 and $200,000?

It's about 8:00 PM Monday and I'm back in camp. I'll continue where I left off. The hotel where I had begun this letter is one of the swankiest in Southern California. All the swells and nobility from foreign countries stay there. It's an enormous place set amidst beautiful grounds. Cadillacs and custom built cars line its driveway. Gorgeously dressed women flit about. Some class. I guess I'm seeing all kinds of life, alright.

Well, after finding the B'nai Brith closed, I went another three miles beyond to Hollywood. Seeing me thumbing, a man in a custom built Lincoln convertible coupe picked me up. He was friendly and talkative and told me that, as a hobby, he owns a big cattle ranch north of Oxnard. When I finally asked what business he was in, he replied he was in the movie business. When I smiled, a puzzled look crossed his face. I said, "If it were me, I'd just as soon stick with the cattle business." He said, "Are you telling me that you'd prefer that when, after all, it was the movies that made buying the cattle ranch possible?" I told him I had visited BelAir that morning, and he said, "Yes, I had an estate there, sold it at the beginning of the war to cut expenses." I then asked him what he did in the movies and he replied, "Direct." "Maybe I know who you are," I said. "What's your name?" "Garnett, Tay Garnett,"[7] he answered. Yes, I told him, I had seen his name on the screen several times. He said he did two pictures last year, the last one being "Bataan."[8] Remember that one, folks? He just completed a picture,[9] whose name I forget, that will be released this month. After asking me where I was headed, he let me off right where I wanted on Hollywood Boulevard. As I got out of the car, and we shook hands, people stopped to gape at the car. It just goes to show you, you're liable to run into anybody out here.

I then went to the Hollywood Canteen to see what was doing. Kay Aldrich[10] (You must have seen her in pictures) served me a glass of milk. There were also a few other actresses that I've seen in pictures.

After meeting and talking with a few chums, I left to be back at the Beverly Hills Hotel at 5:00. After promptly sticking out my thumb, I got a ride to the hotel that took only ten minutes flat, far faster than any bus. At 5:00 a Cadillac picked me up at the hotel and drove me to the American Legion hall in another section of Beverly Hills. Another dozen servicemen arrived there in other cars. We had an excellent feed; then about 7:00 the girls began to arrive. We were forty servicemen in all with twice as many girls for dancing. Since I had a pass for "Sons o' Fun" at 8:15 I had to leave before the fun began. After getting my bearings, I worked my way to Wilshire Boulevard, where in about three seconds I got a ride with a couple about your age. Everybody who picks me up likes to ask questions and is especially impressed when I tell them that I'm a sailor from Massachusetts. They took me to La Brea and Wilshire, where I hopped a Hollywood Boulevard bus that was waiting at the corner. I got off at the Music Box theater where the show was. By the way, on the bus we passed the famous Arthur Murray's[11] dance studio and Slapsies Maxies, Maxie Rosenbloom's[12] night club where Phil Harris[13] has his orchestra. The place used to be called the Wilshire Bowl.

Well, I saw the funniest show of my life. Billie House and Eddie Gas, of Broadway fame, were the stars. The show was similar to Hellzapoppin;[14] in fact both men starred in that show too. The performers came into the audience and raised the devil, especially with the women. Then the chorus girls came and danced with the men in the audience. I thought I'd split my sides. No kidding. I'll send the program with a later letter when I haven't so much to write.

After leaving the show at 11:00, I looked for a place to sleep and where call service was available. Luckily, I located a USO, where I slept until 3:30 then caught the 4:00 o'clock bus back to camp. Sleeping all the way in, I arrived here at 6:00.

What a weekend and what fun. I don't think I've ever had a better time. I travelled at least one hundred miles through Hollywood, L.A., Pasadena, and Westwood without spending a cent. The uniform works wonders. I'll never forget what I've seen on this liberty. It pays to travel alone. I couldn't get rides if I had a companion, but alone I'm able to ride as I please in other people's cars. Sometimes, as I'd be crossing a street at a red light, people in cars would stop to ask if I was going their way. I also enjoyed the little travelling I did in buses. The city buses here are beautiful, with mohair upholstered seats, aluminum railings and seat frames and quiet motors.

Saturday and Sunday were like summer. The paper said that it was 72 degrees, although I thought it seemed warmer. In the afternoon my blues were too warm to wear. People were swimming as if it were summer; yet cars drove by with skis on their roofs, heading for the mountains less than an hour away.

Everyone dresses in sport clothes, sport shirts and summer suits. Women go shopping in slacks. Someday I'd like to live here. No kidding. The place can't be beat. Ride an hour and you can ski or skate; ride in another direction, and you can swim. Everything is so new and modern and clean. I repeat, it can't be beat. And there is gobs of money here, let me tell you. The people spend money as if it were water. They aren't four flushers. They have the mesuma.[15] Industry is enormous. This is the center of the aircraft industry. I bet in twenty years Los Angeles will be one of the world's top ranking cities. It's a center for everything.

Tuesday Jan. 18, 1944

Dear Mom,

Last night I had a good night's sleep to make up for the hours lost the night before. I'm back on guard duty for a while from noon to 5:00 and midnight to 3:00. I believe it's temporary. Yesterday we had hand grenade practice. Live ones were fired; it was the first time I've ever seen or heard them explode. They make quite a concussion which doesn't kill, but, of course, the fragments are lethal.

The issuance of more supplies, such as sun helmets and goggles, suggest that we're going to a hot climate. We've also been issued shorts, similar to gym shorts, in which to work, and a pair of Marine trousers to wear around the base. The trousers are similar to civilian ones; at last I have pockets. An enormous amount of construction equipment—about 80 trucks, jeeps, graders, bulldozers, etc.—have arrived. We've received radios, movie cameras, sports equipment, hundreds of cases of beer and liquor. I think our advance base will be either Burma, India or New Guinea, and we'll probably stay in Australia for a short time. The word is we'll be on the high seas for six weeks. Well, I'll find out pretty soon.

I hear the Republic picture "The Fighting Seabees" with John Wayne and Susan Hayward is lousy. They say it's pure fantasy.[1] We're depicted as supermen.

From your description the new car must be a nice looking job. Take some photos. How do you manage the situation? I think it's tougher back there than here. Here people drive as if there were no rationing, and the cars are so big, they consume a lot of gas.

This is supposed to be southern California's poorest season. From what I see, it's more like our best season back East. The rainy season isn't what you'd expect. It's called the rainy season when it rains once a week or once every two weeks. In their good season it never rains.

Thanks for trying to buy me a slide rule. Trying to surprise me, eh? You should see the beaut I bought. It's far better than the cheaper ones. The fellows have agreed to teach me how to use the slide rule, and I'm also sending away to the manufacturer for an instruction book.

I hear that we'll have laundry service at our base. Sixteen washing machines are included in our equipment. It seems certain that we'll spend some time at Pearl Harbor[2] for more conditioning.

I'd feel better if Dad did something about his leg. I suppose it's goof that business is slow so he can at least rest more. Don't let it go, Dad. What harm would it do to see other doctors?

1/19/44

Dear Mom,

Yesterday I had guard duty and today we went on a short hike with full pack.

Right now I have only $5.00 to my name. Here comes a request: how about $10.00. Frankly, I've run short because of the pictures, an expense I hadn't counted on. But I insist that you take the money for the pictures from my savings. I want them to be a present.

Thursday Jan 20, 1944

Dear Mom,

Now that I have a raincoat it just won't rain. Yesterday was 88 degrees, just missing the all-time high by two degrees. All week has been warm.

The Seabees seem to be getting more and more publicity. The magazines are full of articles about us. Why are they building us up so? Most of it is a pack of lies.

As I anticipated, Ronnie will be driving by the time I get home. He should go to driving school. It's cheaper in the long run.

1/21/44

Dear Dad,

Your weekly letter was received this afternoon with eager anticipation. I've come to expect them, but don't feel obligated. Mother's letters are primarily informative. Without them I'd be a sad boy. Your letters are like an added attraction, the frosting on the cake without which the cake would be mediocre, while mother's are the cake. Ronnie's letters are like the vanilla that lends a special flavor to the cake. Between all your letters, I get to enjoy a pretty good dessert. You may not appreciate this crazy talk, but it's the best way to describe how I feel.

Your last letter has created within me an overwhelming desire to get behind the wheel of the new car. Although, come to think of it, after riding around in custom built Lincolns and Cadillacs, driving your car may seem pretty dull. Aw, don't mind me, I'm just ribbing you.

Glancing at the righthand corner of your letter, what do I see, but the statement "Today, Ronnie is going on 16." Tell me, Dad, when did I turn 25? I wouldn't stand for that stuff, Dad's exaggerations, Ronnie. Stay 15 as long as you can.

Thanks a million to all of you.

Saturday 1/22/44

Dear Folks,

Last night, having a notion to see a movie on the base for the first time, I went to see, well, what movie do you think it was? "Higher and Higher,"[1] with that so-called heat wave, Frank Sinatra.[2] Evidently he's not so popular with the fellows who, every time Sinatra made an appearance, began clamoring and giving him the raspberry. Jealousy, yup, jealousy, that's all it is. What the heck, ya can't blame a guy for trying to make some dough just because he can drive a few dames dizzy. I tried to figure out what he's got, but I'll be darned if I can. I can imagine the theaters jammed to the gills with the fairer sex. The picture was fairly entertaining in spite of Sinatra.

Got your David Breger card of the 17th, preceded by your manna from heaven with the letter of the 19th. What a surprise! You folks are too good to me. Truly, the money was a lifesaver. I was wondering what I was going to use for money on my special liberty next week. I do have some money, but preferred not to use it for pleasure as I may need it later. Meanwhile, I paid for the balance owed on the slide rule. From the money you sent, I now consider the slide rule a gift from you. I wish I were home to kiss you all for it. So much money is nothing to sneeze at.

Now that you've classified me as a "birdling" or whatever you call it, I will say that I've not only learned to fly, but also where to fly. (I get around fairly well). You've used a very good metaphor, Mom, I must say.

You speak of the various forms of entertainment that you recommend I take in. Let's consider the nightclubs. These require drinking, a girl, and dancing. So far I don't indulge in any of these, and never hope to with respect to the first item. I do admit that I plan to visit a nightclub before I leave California.

Secondly, there are the shows. So far, I've seen the best two stage shows offered here. But there is no Broadway, so plays are rare. I would surely go to a play if there were one. Thirdly—as for opera, there is none. You'd have to go to Frisco to find an opera. Then—. good lectures. Listen, I know more about venereal disease now than most people. I'm fed up with lectures. Why should I want to attend one on liberty? Seriously though, I have no interest in deep subjects and lectures on them.

Then your last suggestion—dancing, and I note that you underline it—will have to take its course. I have much too limited time to spend it learning how to dance. However, I hope, in time I'll learn.

I expect that we'll be having more military training for all of next week. We are only marking time waiting for our boat to be loaded. It's now confirmed, as I suspected, we were originally supposed to leave on the fifth of this month. Now we'll be here to see next month.

Monday the V-12 boys leave the battalion to go home for three weeks then back East. They'll enter school March 1st. One of the fellows in Headquarters company requested MIT, where he plans to study mechanical engineering. What gripes me is that he's had no-where near the amount of math I've had. And if he's officer material, I'll eat my hat. Just as I always figured: it's not what you know but who you know that matters.

Next Wednesday night I'll look up a Jewish family in Hollywood. I'm curious to see what they're like. I suppose I have a lot of nerve barging in on them.

Lately during leisure hours I've been dressing pretty comfy. Actually, I'm leading a life of leisure. Lately, I've been adding some oil, something like Brilliantine, to my hair as recommended by one of the barbers. Yes, I have a private barber, a fellow who cuts hair only for a select few. He has been doing it for ten years, does a swell job. No more GI haircuts for me.

Sunday evening 1/23/44

Dear Mom,

This rainy day I've had a very entertaining Sunday in camp. I answered Mrs. Linfield's letter, which I owed her. She had already sent me two letters. Can you image, they've had snow in Gulfport?

You probably recall in my Gulfport letters mentioning the senior in high school several times. She was the more or less "come hither," or "hep cat"[1] type of girl. Now, according to Mrs. Linfield a profound change has come over her daughter, and she claims I'm responsible for it. Mrs. Linfield writes that her marks are now excellent. You see, I had had several long talks with the kid concerning studying habits, and I guess they took. Actually, I thought I was getting nowhere, and she had thought of me as grampaw, even called me that. Gosh, I wish I could do the same thing for Ronnie. It seems that Mrs. Linfield, anticipating that I'll return to Gulfport someday, guarantees me a permanent invitation to visit. There's true Southern hospitality for ya.

Say, I received a typewritten letter via Airmail on George E. Duffy Inc. stationery. And who do you think wrote it? Yep, Mr. Riccius. He knows I'm not stationed far from Santa Barbara, a city north of here. He suggested I look up a friend of his there. Listen to this description: he's seven feet tall, he's the head the Santa Barbara art museum, and his name is Major Buel Hammet. I think I'll pay him a visit.

It's good to hear that business is hunky dory.[2] Sometimes I wish Dad had his business here. He could clean up.

This afternoon I attended a classical music record concert at the base theater. The program is enclosed. I enjoyed it very much and plan to listen to the one next week. This evening I saw an excellent musical extravaganza in Technicolor: "Broadway Rhythm"[3] with George Murphy,[4] Ginny Simms,[5] Lena Horne, Charles Winninger,[6] Ben Blue,[7] Gloria DeHaven, (You have her autograph) and Tommy Dorsey's[8] orchestra. It was wonderful entertainment with spectacular sets and good music. Try to see it, and take a look at that Gloria De Haven.[9]

I can hear taps, so it's time for bed. Good night.

Monday 1/24/44

Dear Mom,

We went on a short hike today, nothing important. Evidently we're only marking time while awaiting the personnel ship.

For the life of me, I can't settle down enough to study my math course. I don't understand it. All I want to do is go on liberty and see things. I guess knowing that once across no more fun, I've been catering to my whims.

Got a letter from Miss Rourke. She tells me what has happened to most of my school chums. I was surprised to learn how many were overseas. I consider myself fortunate.

L.A. has two new plays: "Junior Miss"[1] and "Abie's Irish Rose." I hope to see at least one of them next week.

Just now I said goodbye to one of the V-12 boys. He's going home first then transferring to the regular navy for college training. I can't help envying him. Although I have so-called "peace of mind" now, I get low whenever V-12 is mentioned.

Wednesday 1/26/44

Dear Mom,

Well, well, it seems things aren't all roses between [Aunt] Libby and [Aunt] Sadie. For the life of me, I can't figure out their behavior, because they always seemed to get along well. And I don't understand [Aunt] Ida's attitude in the affair. It reminds me of children having pet squabbles. Here's Ida and the Bloom family wisecracking about Sadie and probably vice versa. Maybe I've begun to see things on a grander scale. The way the relatives in Boston carry on over the smallest things is degrading to their intelligence. For instance, Sadie recommends the Hotel Edison and Libby, in turn, ignores her. Can you see the sense in such goings on? Then they argue over who is going to take care of Uncle Bill with the grippe. What difference does it make, so long as he gets better? I'm afraid the marriage is starting off on the wrong foot with respect to the rest of the family. Everyone treats Bill, and fights over him, as if he were a baby.

When I get home I hope to be treated exactly as I was treated before I left. I don't ever want to be catered to or petted. Those days are over for me. I'm sure that with Dad's manly outlook toward the need to be responsible for oneself, and your partial agreement, I'll be treated as I've always been. Not that I was babied before. But I know that after a fellow comes back home, his folks' enthusiasm is apt to lead to fussing over him. That's what the squabble over Bill seems to be all about.

Speaking of returning home, I've learned what often happens on such occasions. A fellow in my hut (a teacher at Northwestern) went home over the weekend to find his brother, just returned from the South Pacific. Upon seeing his wife for the first time in two years, the brother heard his wife say the shocking words, "I don't love you anymore." This is typical of thousands of such cases. And I have heard of other similar instances. The brother was stunned, and turned to his wife's parents for help, but they could offer him no consolation. Only two months before going across, he had married the girl.

You may know that this area is the wildest, most uncontrollable, morally indecent part of our country. Every day the fellows return from liberty with tales of having gone out with the wife of some soldier in Africa, or a sailor in the Pacific. Although many of the tales may be exaggerations, I know, as a fact, that most are true. Just last week the vice squad found an eighteen year old kid from our company in a hotel sleeping with a soldier's wife. That's typical of what goes on here and what husbands come back will be faced with. When the kid was questioned, he said that the woman picked him up. It was the same in Gulfport. Not that every married couple would have such an unfortunate experience; however, it would seem that a certain amount of estrangement is bound to develop when the relationship between a husband and wife is based only on letters. I don't think there's a married man here who doesn't go out with other women while away from home, and I'm willing to bet that their wives are just as bad. Yes, there's an old saying that separation makes the heart grow fonder, but that's true for only a limited time; then the heart begins to forget. After the war, the divorce courts are going to be plenty busy. Frankly, I feel that anyone marrying before entering the service is making a big mistake. I hope, for Bill's sake, that his marriage will be successful. I think it will be because he has a fine girl; still, you can never tell.

I say all this for something to write about. It has struck me as sad, as for months I've watched the behavior of certain men in our outfit develop. I know of two divorces by California couples since we've been in California. They involve men in my own company.

I don't believe such a separation can develop between parents and sons. Their relationship has had a longer time for ties to breed. I think that as a result all parties have a more solid appreciation of the other. Even now, looking back on my ten day leave, I can find fault with my actions. Of course, I don't expect them to be perfect. But I had figured then on showing my appreciation for you folks by doing everything you asked. But, did I? Like fun I did. I can't explain why I didn't follow my original plan. So I've learned it's foolish to make all sorts of statements of appreciation and promises. I recall I was only interested in going to shows and visiting the Y. Yes, I remember the letter of appreciation I wrote at Peary, and I was sincere when I wrote it. Now Dad wrote something similar when he promised me use of his car, and I don't doubt, in the least, his sincerity. But I don't expect such favors when I get back. I'm sure you folks will feel different when I finally do arrive home. I'm not saying this because I feel you're not true to your statements, but rather because it's simply human nature not to grant me privileges. It's as I said, absence makes us more appreciative: I promise to do everything you folks want, and you promise to let me use the car. Well, I didn't keep my part of the bargain, because it's natural not to, and I don't expect you to keep your part.

Now that I'm away I can look at the past as if I were watching a motion picture, pick out its flaws and good features. I can see what I failed to see, and I'll go back with sincere intentions of repairing or touching up faults that were committed in the past. I say only intentions, because not all intentions are realized. This is what I mean: I imagine that I'll return home with every intention of helping you folks all I can while I'm going to college, because, after all, you'll be boarding me. Then one night Dad will ask me to come down to the shop and help with some deliveries or finish a chair. Meanwhile, there will be a good show at the Palace or I will have met a blonde I'd like to go skating with that night. Two to one, in spite of my appreciative intentions, I'll hem and haw until I get my way. That's Hughie for you. Then again, some night Dad will need the car. Do you mean to tell me he'd be willing to give it up? Oh, I'll try to persuade him, but I'll know deep down he is more right than I. See what I mean? When we deal with the real thing, it's altogether different.

However, when I do get home, I feel I'll be able to think things through a little better and be more sensible in considering my intentions. Anyway, we'll both see whether I'll be more considerate or not.

Now that I've revealed my thoughts on appreciation and human nature, I'm sure that you are thoroughly confused. I've had my say, and of course, you're free to object to anything I've said in a future letter.

Gee, I've been writing for over an hour. It's after 3:00 PM already, and I must dress for tonight. Yep, I gotta shower, shine my shoes, and slick up for a hectic night.

Be back tomorrow.

1/27/44

Dear Mom,

The old mail has been piling in during the past two days, the most I've received in a long time.

When I go to Oxnard I'll buy a CB sticker for Dad's car. As a matter of fact, I'll have a friend, who is going into town this afternoon, buy one.

I sort of took it for granted that you'd read the letters I've received and sent home. I'm sure I'll find them just as entertaining in the future as you find them now. When you mentioned Johnson's description of Carmen, I was reminded of the night that I read that passage to the Linfields. All of us being in a jovial mood, the passage set us all in stitches.

The schools I've attended here give me no added prestige. All sorts of fellows go to such schools; it's something for us to do. The Seabees will never change.

From the fact that Ted Bagdikian, who's often on KP, has been made S 1/c, you can see the rating doesn't amount to much.

I haven't been able to do any swimming, nor have I done any instructing since Gulfport, and I don't ever expect to do it again. The recreation department is set against a swimming program. The most important thing I do in camp is write letters. We spend many days just laying around, cleaning our personal articles or going on some senseless maneuver. It's very lax and demoralizing, but, as I've said, I have "peace of mind" and a carefree attitude.

Since you wrote about a subject that the radio dares not mention, underwear, this is to inform you that I have eight sets. I believe the more often you change your underwear the better your body feels.

Gee, Ronnie is lucky to have bought a swell set of skis. Good going Ronnie. How does it feel to buy things on your own? I hope it snows a foot this week. Man, the way you folks are buying things, I'm beginning to think you're millionaires. Well, it's about time that you enjoyed life. It only shows how much of a burden I was to you people. If the service hadn't come along, I'd probably still be on your necks so I'm glad I'm in the service now.

Of course, how you spend money is none of my business. I have no right to preach, but by all means take into account a rainy day. Try to gradually accumulate some savings. No doubt, you're doing it. In the next twenty years, I'll guarantee another depression will strike. Anticipating adds fifty percent to your present happiness. There's nothing like financial security. That's a major reason why I don't wish to receive money from home. This week you sent me $30.00. That's much too much, and frankly, I must tell you that it makes me ill at ease. I can remember when $30.00 would support the four of us for a week. No, I don't like your sending all this money, please believe me.

Friday 1/28/44

Dear Mom,

I can seriously say that I'm the busiest man in camp. Doing what? Why, doing absolutely nothing, of course. So this writer has very little to discuss. And since I have nothing of a serious nature to write, I must resort to that ever so entertaining but boring vein of humor from one such as me: genuine corn.

This night I attended the Shell show, a program done on the base with Ronnie Briar, the singer; a clever pianist, a very oomphuous dancer, a woman magician, and Johnny O'Brien, the best harmonicist I've ever heard. I'm sure you've heard O'Brien play the role of a hick harmonicist on the Bing Crosby[1] program,[2] Kate Smith's show, and perhaps in the movies.

The show was a corker—and a scorcher too. A woman ventriloquist put us all in stitches. Yep, when her small dummy remarked that he had dreamt he was playing poker last night, and she asked how he made out, and he answered that when he awoke he was reaching for the pot, we just applauded for more. And for a strictly stag audience—now, Mom and Ronnie don't read this, only Dad— Johnny O'Brien remarked, "Speaking of Lana Turner[3]—a lot of meat for two points, eh?"[4] No, my face isn't red. After all, I gotta be a full fledged Seabee. But seriously, I enjoyed the show plenty.

Day before yesterday we had some deliciously prepared coconut cream pie just oozing with tastiness. Usually when such morsels are served, the gluttons among us put aside their disguises and watch for those individuals who might dislike coconut cream pie. One such glutton sat opposite me. (I'm not one of the gluttons, but rather a professional connoisseur of good food. I don't have to rely on nuts who don't like pie. Instead, with my political drag, I go directly to the bakery and help myself.) As I was saying, one such glutton sat opposite me and next to a chum of mine. Apparently this so-called glutton had finished his meal and was merely sitting by expecting my chum to give up his pie. After several remarks such as, "Oh, you shouldn't eat that pie; it's lousy, but I'll gladly take it off your hands," he became increasingly confident. Yes, his mate appeared to be weakening as the glutton eagerly anticipated the pie's oozy lusciousness entering his aperture. Finally his mate, my chum, asked, "Do you really want it?" Then, making one big sacrifice, he lifted it from his tray, and daintily hurled it into the glutton's face. He flung it with such agility, that you'd swear he had been a former Max Sennet[5] comedy actor. So now we call the glutton "Pie Face."

Enough of this. I'll be back tomorrow.

Loads of love to all of you, Hughie—corny

Saturday 1/29/44

Dear Mom,

This Monday I'm going to Hollywood, and Westwood again if I have time. I'd like to see "Junior Miss" which is in town and take in several more radio programs. I intend to sleep at the Screen Guild USO. It may be my last long liberty in L.A. and Hollywood. It doesn't take much for me to enjoy the sights here, as I haven't seen anything quite like it before. I fear that when I get home the surroundings will seem rather humdrum.

I'm much surprised to hear that back East drivers don't pick up servicemen. After all, Worcester isn't a serviceman's town; people there see far fewer of us than they do here. If only people knew how much a lift means to a serviceman. Boy, it's swell when people put themselves out to show you around. I suspect many back East forget that their sons or brothers or husbands in the service might be asking somebody for a lift. Many servicemen have stopped to pick me up, and, if I had a car, I'd do the same. The reputation of a locality depends on how well it treats the boys, as they will write how good or bad a community's people are. For instance, Gulfport, where the boys are shoved around, has a bad reputation, although I was fortunate that I met some fine people. During peacetime Gulfport depended on the resort trade, but its bad treatment of the boys will do it little good after the war.

Oh, I don't eat all the sweets I get due to the invasion of my mates who must have a taste of the goodies from Massachusetts. And speaking of Massachusetts, you should hear how they make fun of my speech. When I say "car," "Harvard," "laugh" or "bath," or anything with a broad "a," I'm immediately corrected. They get a great kick out of the way I speak. Even when I say "Boston," they mimic me. We don't realize how different we speak until we are with a group from the Middle or Pacific West. I never dreamed that others pronounce so many words differently. Believe it or not, sometimes my mates can't make out what I'm saying. Take the word palm, for instance. They pronounce the l and say "polm." It's quite funny. When they correct me, I laugh like anything.

Learned today that my conduct rating is 4.0, a perfect score, and my proficiency rating is 3.8 which is above average. I'll speak up about a rerate as soon as the opportunity presents itself.

You're wrong this time, referring to California, when you say everybody's grass appears greener than your own. You can't beat it out here. The two months I've been here is considered the worst time of the year, and I still think it's tops. Listen, I've talked to people who have come here from the East and other parts of the country, and they wouldn't return to where they came from for a million. Many have lived here for years without ever getting sick of the place. But, don't worry, Mom, it still isn't home where I want to live. I'm perfectly satisfied with good old New England while I'm young and healthy. But this is an ideal spot in which to live out one's old age, if a person is lucky enough to live that long. Nosiree, I'm going home and live with you folks. Hang California.

The B'nai Brith bond drive sounds pretty impressive. The news about the bad way the Japs are treating prisoners[1] is bound to have a profound effect on the purchase of bonds by the public. Here the subject has made headlines for the past two days, especially in the Hearst papers[2] which are building it up super.

Swell, Dad; I'm glad you finally decided to see about your leg.[3] Here's wishing you plenty of luck. Anxious to hear how you come out.

Since I've been in the service I've become an ardent reader of the *Reader's Digest*.[4] You see, the *Reader's Digest* is very convenient when I visit the toilet, and during the brief rest periods between drill and mealtime. *Coronet*[5] is also a pretty good magazine; I'm now reading this month's issue.

I have been debating whether I should send the slide rule home or not before leaving the country. What do you think? It's all paid for. Maybe I should send it. It will come in handy when I go to college, and I should preserve it.

I wrote Aunt Pearl today, kidding her about her 41st birthday two weeks ago. Lately, I've been too lazy to write anyone except home.

Nuff said. So long until Sunday.

Sun. 1/30/44

Dear Mom,

This afternoon I plan to hear another concert and perhaps see a show afterwards. The card, enclosed, has a picture of the place in which I stayed the last weekend off.

Do you think it wise for Dad to have his leg operated on and stiffened? I suppose then he won't have any more trouble with it. I see plenty of men walking around with one leg stiff. One of my teachers in high school had one leg stiff, and he got around as well as anybody. It didn't look so bad. What will you do, Dad? Why suffer as you have been?

Mom, you're getting to be quite a Cleopatra.[1] In your new clothes and with your hair done, I bet you're tops. No kidding. Even the movie stars don't have hair as nice as yours. For instance, Betty Grable looks like a hag in real life, and that's the truth. Although I've never seen her, it's what the fellows tell me.[2] Say, how about taking a picture sometime when you're all prettied up? Come to think of it, to heck with the prettying up process. Take a picture as you are in the kitchen. You're beautiful just the same. Now don't blush, Mom.

Hey there, don't think of not writing every day yet. Here's why. We may embark for another port in this country, or we may go to Hawaii, which is considered no different than the mainland. Keep up the writing every day, please.

It may be months before we reach our advanced base. More training is expected at another base, and we may be there for months. I hear plans have been changed again, including our personnel code number. Now, no definite embarkation date is in sight. We may leave tomorrow, the day after, or maybe we'll hang around for another six months. Understand? Keep writing.

Enclosed is the program for the Symphonic Hour concert. I much enjoyed Scheherazade[3] and the Beethoven[4] 6th Symphony.

(I)   Tuesday Feb. 1, 1944
[The following names were listed on Hughie's Hollywood Guild and Canteen stationery on which the letter below appeared.

Two of the officers were Mrs. Abraham Lehr,[1] President, Miss Mary Pickford, 1st Vice President. Some of the directors were Mr. Earl Carrol, Mrs. John Considine Jr.,[2] Miss Dolores Del Rio,[3] Mrs. William Dieterle,[4] Mrs. Douglas Fairbanks, Jr.,[5] Mrs. John Ford,[6] Miss Janet Gaynor,[7] Mrs. Frank Lloyd,[8] Miss Myrna Loy,[9] Mrs. Jon Mercer,[10] Miss Una Merkel,[11] Miss Merle Oberon,[12] Mrs. Edward G. Robinson,[13] Miss Rosalind Russell,[14] Mrs. George Seaton,[15] Mrs. Spencer Tracy,[16] Mr. Monty Wooley.

[The Canteen was located at 1284 North Crescent Heights Boulevard. The Author]

(II)
Dear Folks,

This is my second day in L.A. and Hollywood. I didn't write yesterday because I've been busy seeing shows, and last night I was too tired.

Although I thought this would be my last visit here, it looks like I'll have another chance.

Right from the start I had good luck when a sailor drove me all the way from Oxnard to Hollywood. Immediately on arriving, I went to the Hollywood Guild Canteen, but it was rather crowded so I decided to stay at the same place I had slept a few weeks ago: The Naval Aid Shore Station, which, as I've written, is the nearest thing to home I could ever find. My thumb being in pretty good condition, a man in a Lincoln Zephyr picked me up on Sunset Boulevard and brought me to the NBC studios. It turned out that the driver was a singer, the one who had the accident with Kay Francis in "Little Women[1]." After giving me his telephone number, he asked that I call him some evening and he'll arrange for me to go to some parties that are frequented by the movie stars. Might take him up on that sometime. I secured a ticket to the "Blondie" show at NBC for 4:30, aired on the East Coast at 7:30. I also secured a ticket to the Lux Radio Theater for 6:00 PM in which Ronald Coleman[2] and Greer Garson[3] are playing in "Random Harvest."[4] Those were my preparations for the afternoon.

I took a bus to the Shore Station on Wilshire Boulevard, secured a bed, and headed for downtown L.A., transportation supplied by a salesman who drove me there. Then I went to Keufel & Esser to buy a very complete and easy to understand handbook for the slide rule for 50 cents.

A USO being nearby, I inquired about a ticket to a stage play and was handed a pass to the former Broadway stage play "Junior Miss" now running at the Biltmore theater in L.A.

Then I headed back to Hollywood by street car, had an excellent dinner and proceeded to see the programs that I had arranged for that morning.

My time is rather short and I'm quite a distance outside L.A. and the bus terminal. Even though it's only 11:30 and some time before the bus leaves, it takes quite a while to get to the city. I'll finish the letter this evening to tell about all that I saw.

(III)   Tuesday Feb 1, 1944
Dear Mom,

I'm back in camp now and it's 8:00 PM Since I have the rest of the evening to write this letter, I can go into more detail than I did in this morning's letter from Hollywood.

To review the story, you recall that I got a free ride to Hollywood, went to the Guild Canteen and got a ride to the radio studio by a singer (By the way, his name is Wally) who was hurt in a motion picture. Some night I'll give him a ring, but I'll make sure I have a chum with me. After the episode with that photographer[1] back home I take no chances.

After making the arrangements for an afternoon and evening of entertainment, I had a very good dinner at the Maxwell House. During the time between shows I went sightseeing around the city aboard a trolley or bus or in a car. For instance, after checking in at the Shore Station, I got a ride as soon as I stepped off the curb to downtown L.A.

It's just like having your own chauffeur and saying "downtown James," or "Hollywood James," or "home James." Then for a nickel or a dime, I'd take another route to Hollywood by bus or street car or subway. As a matter of fact, I doubt if I missed seeing any part of L.A. at all. I know how to get around quite well, know exactly what bus to take, though the city is larger than Boston. I'm amazed at myself.

To get back to the entertainment, at 4:30 I saw, in person, Arthur Lake and Penny Singleton with Hanley Stafford[2] on the "Blondie" broadcast. I could imagine you folks sitting home listening to the very same program I was witnessing. Remember the days when I used to drop homework to listen to "Blondie," then resume doing it after the program? I never dreamed I'd see the program in person. See, miracles can happen. Arthur Lake is a riot; his coming out before curtain call gave us all a laugh. Remember, this was the program concerning the idol made in New York? Ken Nyles, the announcer, appeared and cracked jokes with the audience for about ten minutes before the broadcast. He has a marvelous personality. I really got a kick out of one thing he did: he stepped off the stage onto the main floor and talked to individuals in the audience. Being in the middle of the third row from the stage, I was difficult to get at so was saved the embarrassment of being paired with a strange girl. (It might be fun, eh?)

Arthur Lake (Dagwood) looks exactly as he looks in the movies, dopey. However, he appears quite intelligent when his face becomes serious. He was dressed in the familiar bow tie and sport suit. Penny Singleton (Blondie) is fairly tall for a woman, has blonde hair, and loads of personality. She wore a red dress, but her face was so sunburned she resembled a blood corpuscle. Alexander,[3] played by a clever looking eight year old kid, was not the same kid that appeared in the movies. He looks Jewish. The baby is played by a full grown, and pretty, too, woman. She was dressed in childish clothing to provide the right effect.

As they act, they don't go through any motions, for the sound man[4] takes care of that, but their facial expressions are quite effective.

You probably know the original tune for the Blondie show which is played by a five or seven piece orchestra, whose leader looks Jewish. The familiar guitar tune is played by a man sitting on a stool beside a microphone. C-AM-EL-S is sung by the men in the orchestra. It was most enjoyable.

From the "Blondie" show I went to the Lux Radio Theater on Vine Street where I was admitted at 5:30, fortunately, since the line was terrific. I was lucky enough to have secured a ticket because several celebrities and press agents were handing out passes.

The show began at 6:00—9:00 your time, the familiar hour. I remember when at 9:30 you tried to get me to go to bed, I'd manage somehow to time my undressing so that I could hear the Lux Theater before it ended at ten. Well, there I was watching "Random Harvest" with its original stars. I had to pinch myself to prove that it was reality. Yes, I could picture you curled up on the sofa laying aside a magazine in order to listen to the show. And probably at 9:45 Dad would arrive from the shop, his face red from the cold, to sit down in his chair and continue reading the paper that he hadn't finished reading before dinner. And you would forget the program to discuss what he had done that night. I could picture it all while I was at the other end of the antenna in Hollywood.

Cecil B. DeMille, bald and unimpressive, appeared and gave his usual spiel; then the orchestra played the familiar score. You can only see the orchestra in the background through a partially curtained pane of glass. Before the program began, DeMille introduced the viewing audience, in a speech cluttered with ers and ahs, to what was to come. The entire program was very formal, even the interview after the performance during which the stars could speak informally. Everything must go according to the script.

Greer Garson looks exactly as she looks in technicolor pictures: tall, thin with impressive features, beautiful red hair and a girlish figure. While keeping her eye on the script only half the time, her acting was superb, especially her expressions and the motions she made. For your information she wore a tight fitting, rather loud, black and gold dress, it's length the same as a women's business suit.

In spite of his gray hair and aging features, Ronald Coleman is handsome. Only a little taller than I, he wore horned rimmed glasses to read the script. Holding himself straight as a die, he's most impressive looking. He wore an extremely well fitting business suit. Like Greer Garson, he got into the mood and took his acting quite seriously. His acting was something truly remarkable.

You can imagine how much I enjoyed the show. It was the nearest thing I've seen to a full fledged play up to now.

After the show was over at 7:00, I went to the Biltmore Theater in downtown L.A. to see "Junior Miss," curtain time 8:30. The trip from Hollywood normally takes an hour, but I arrived in L.A. before 8:00. Since I wasn't hungry after having had a large dinner earlier, I had a snack. Just as doors opened at 8:05 I entered the theater and took my seat in the middle. You know, theaters where plays are held are small.

Now it's 9:00 PM and bedtime. I'll continue where I left off tomorrow.

Love to you, Dad and Ronnie, Hughie, the playgoer

Wednesday Feb. 2, 1944

Dear Mom,

I have most of the morning off, a beautiful warm morning it is, so I may as well continue yesterday's letter. This will probably be interrupted during the course of the day and completed in the evening.

I forgot to describe Hanley Stafford. He's Baby Snooks's[1] pop too. He appears as I pictured him, short, heavily built, with a serious and intelligent, not handsome but impressive looking face. I'd take him to be in his middle fifties.

My last letter left off with the play "Junior Miss." Not being familiar with the stage, I didn't know the actors and actresses. From the applause they received, I gathered that they were famous. When I arrive home I'll bring the program, which is too big to send, along with my many other souvenirs from various entertainment spots.

The show has been ranking at the top on Broadway for a few years. It concerns a family with a daughter about my age and one about Ronnie's age. In other words it's about a family like us were Ronnie and I girls instead of boys. I got many laughs from the older girl's troubles with boyfriends, and the younger one's who was almost ready to go out with boys. The pop, having had troubles with his boss over his alleged relations with a pretty secretary, is fired. This, along with his domestic problems with his daughters, supplied us with laughs galore. Soon a long lost uncle appears about whom the younger daughter makes up a story that he was just released from the pen.[2] This causes hilarious complications. Pop uses "hell" and "damn" before the children which gives the play a kick. The elder daughter's beaus are a riot. She goes out with a different type boy, from the timid to wolf, every evening.

I've never enjoyed a show more. Now I know why Dad says that plays beat movies. It was wonderful, and I'm going to make it a point to see more plays in the future. If I get a chance I'd like to see "Abie's Irish Rose," which is here. Next week "The Corn is Green"[3] with Ethyl Barrymore[4] is coming.

So this marks another high point in my life, my first play. Since I've been in the service I'm seeing plenty of firsts. Isn't it wonderful? When I return I hope to be less ignorant of what entertainment is available. I've yet to see an opera to polish off my list of firsts.

I got out of the show about 11:30, caught a bus to Wilshire Boulevard at Pershing Square, and had an excellent eight hours of sleep in a nice soft bed. After showering in the morning, I topped it off with cereal, juice, and a ham and egg breakfast. Then being in L.A., I headed for Hollywood, a feat which I easily accomplished in only a few minutes of thumbing.

When I began liberty, it was raining so the raincoat sure came in handy. After the weather cleared in the afternoon, the thermometer rose to eighty degrees, but there was a comfortable breeze so it didn't seem hot. Next morning I checked raincoat and rubbers [galoshes] in Hollywood.

Oh, yes, I failed to mention that after dinner Monday afternoon, I had a few hours to kill and saw "Happy Land" at Grauman's Chinese theater. All around me people were sniffling. I enjoyed the show, because it hit home.

Speaking of motion pictures, "The Song of Bernadette"[5] had its premiere here Christmas day and has been running ever since.

With little to do on Tuesday morning, I rode around a bit then took the 2:35 bus back to Oxnard, a very pleasant ride in a new Pacific Greyhound.

That about sums up my thirty-six hour liberty, another well spent. If we remain here for another two weeks, I'll have one more weekend off.

While I was away, quite a bit of mail arrived, three from you, one from ever faithful John Fulgoni, one from [Cousin] Lil, and a V-Mail[6] from [Cousin] Charlie.

Johnson expects to leave Worcester before March 1st in order to better himself. Before leaving, he wants to meet you folks. He'll call you some evening. He's one swell guy. I'm sure you'll like him. It's the quickest and best friendship I've ever made. He's always asking whether he can do anything for me.

The V-Mail from Charlie was dated 22 Nov. 1943 and postmarked December 10th in New York. He describes how miserable and filthy it is in Sicily, but, when he wrote, he was in a fine camp, apparently not in Sicily.

Lil writes that [Cousin] Ed is at Camp Shelby in Mississippi. I was nearby when I visited Mobile.

Mrs. Gallant writes that she found the negative of the picture you wanted and will send it to you. Say, haven't you got enough pictures of me already?

I have an idea that you are boring people with my letters. When I write friends and relatives, I don't tell them all the things I tell you. I usually give them only a general outline of my experiences.

How are the skis Ronnie? Boy, I hope it snows for you. Today is Groundhog Day;[7] this will decide it. I hear you are having a mild winter. Here we're having a comfortable summer.

So you're getting high class with fluorescent lights all over the shop, even in the office.

Although the food has always been good, lately it has been even better. For instance, instead of sliced bread we now have rolls. Dessert is pie more often than in the past, small things of that sort.

There's a new rumor that the supply ship originally attached to us has now been reassigned to another battalion. It appears that we won't leave the States as soon as previously thought. They see our assignment has been changed. I don't know what to expect, but I'm not worrying about it. I never dreamed that we;we'd be here as long as we have.

I plan to see "The Desert Song"[8] with Irene Dunne[9] and Dennis Morgan[10] this evening.

Dad, do you know what mother said about you? She insulted you by writing that last Sunday, when you tried to write me your mind was blank. That struck me as funny.

I hadn't realized that the navy had published so much literature on post war conditions. Very interesting. I'll follow it up when the time comes.

Today I'm going to try to exercise in the gym, get myself back into condition.

Regarding my personal appearance, I'm merely continuing your policy. To look presentable, I shave every two days now. On liberty I see to it that my uniform is well-pressed and just so. I must have a shower every evening. It's become a ritual habit.

I'll be back tomorrow.

Thursday Feb 3, 1944

Dear Folks,

Today is very dreary with heavy clouds and occasional showers. We swabbed the decks and washed our canvas cots this morning as part of a general house cleaning. Battalion pictures were taken while I was on liberty. For your sakes, it's too bad I missed it.

Last night, instead of running the scheduled movie, "The Desert Song," "A Guy Named Joe"[1] with Spencer Tracy and Irene Dunne was shown. I enjoyed it very much. Its plot had both light and serious episodes. I'm sure Mom would like it, and possibly Dad and Ronnie. Tonight I'm planning to see "Madame Curie."[2]

I'm presently writing this during dinner and must drop it until this evening.

Now it's early evening right after supper time. Because of the rain I'm postponing seeing a show until tomorrow. Yesterday I launched myself on a conditioning program at the gym. I saw that my waistline had become soft and flabby. After working out for thirty minutes, I was disappointed to find myself in poor physical shape. I couldn't chin myself more than five times and I was lost when I tried to do sit-ups. And to think I used to do one hundred sit-ups as if it were nothing. After exercising enough to get up a good sweat, I limped to the shower room and from there limped to the barracks. Although I worked out for only a short time, and took it easy, I was sore from neck to foot.

Again this afternoon I visited the gym and limbered up for 3/4 of an hour. And again I'm sore all over. As I work into it gradually, I expect to be sore for about a week. And if I keep at it, I'll be in top shape again in a month.

But chances of doing so appear slim. From fairly reliable sources, it's rumored that we'll be secured near the middle of the month and ship out before its end. This could be accurate, and I wouldn't be surprised if it turned out to be.

I found your letter commenting on mine concerning war marriages, very interesting. To reply to your question regarding whether there are any fellows from Worcester in my company, there are none; however, there are some in other companies, and I talk with them.

Ronnie's letter is really something. Did you read it? On reading it in chow line, I burst out laughing while everyone looked at me as if I were odd. Yes, Ronnie, I saw Cass Daly[3] in "Riding High."[4] Ah ha, my dear parents, I see your son is poking fun at your arguments at the dinner table. Yes, yes, that's a good American spirit. A very good letter, Ronnie. If you could write compositions like that, you'd be sure to get an A in English. Let's hear more. Oh, I don't mean for you to deprive yourself of fun. If Mom insists that you write when you don't feel like it, just don't. I know how it is about writing letters. I never cared to write when I was in school, either. How many times did I use "write"?

I'll be back tomorrow.

Love, Hughie (Right!)

Postcard, Friday 2/4/44

Dear Folks,

In Ventura this evening with my chum from PA just to get out of camp.Had an excellent supper in a local restaurant and went to a movie.

Tomorrow we have a dress parade, our farewell to the camp. I'll tell more in tomorrow's letter.

9:00 PM Saturday Feb 5, 1944

Dear Mom,

I didn't get into camp until midnight so I'm a bit dazed after less than five hours sleep last night. Consequently, this letter will be a bit short,but I'll write a nice long letter tomorrow.

Friday afternoon I flatly told Mr. Tretter that I felt I deserved a rerate. In so many words, he told me that I should expect to leave the service as a S 1/c. He asked, "What can you do?" and I was at a loss for an answer. Having always been a student, I have no construction experience. He recognizes whatever gift of intelligence I might have, so he says, but that's of no use to the battalion, so I must suffer. My only salvation was the recreation program, but that's out after the Gulfport experience. After he told me all this, how can he expect me to work like a dog? Since he's no longer any help, I may request a mast[1] and speak to the Commander. At least I can tell him my story. I'll have to put some thought into this. If I try and fail, what harm can it do?

When I awoke the other morning, one of the fellows told me that I had talked in my sleep. While I was turning over he said I uttered, "Scolley Square"[2] and he swears he's not kidding. What do you make of that? Have I ever been there? I don't remember. But I got a good laugh over it.

At Mrs. Myles suggestion, when I was in Hollywood last Christmas, I looked up some friends of hers in Ventura last night. They have invited me to their home next Tuesday evening. I'll save this subject for a more detailed report tomorrow.

Saw "Madame Curie" at the 5:30 show this evening. Excellent. After reading the book while in my Junior year, I appreciated the picture, especially after seeing Greer Garson in person. I enjoyed the picture at the utmost.

I'll be back tomorrow to relieve your anxiousness to hear about the above subjects.

Oh, yes, I plan to listen to another concert tomorrow afternoon.

P.S. The white slip of paper enclosed is part of my pass to "Yours for Fun" that I saw several weeks ago in Hollywood.

Sunday 2/6/44

Dear Folks,

What a gorgeous day. The temperature reached nigh on ninety degrees, but I'm not perspiring. The air is so clear and refreshing that I had to spend mostly all day basking in the sun. Again I'm accumulating a tan. The crispness is due to the fact that the winds have blown across thousands of miles of ocean, while in New England it's less clear because the winds come from across land. Because there's so little dust here, clothes stay cleaner longer. Coal is virtually unheard of, and heat is derived from natural gas and an abundant supply of oil. At least that's the geological explanation.

Your lovely and touching Valentine's card came. The verse is wonderful.

First, the rerate matter: the unfortunate outcome of my experience in the recreation deal, has left me without a future in the battalion. Even today, the recreation program is a farce and unsuccessful. As Mr. Tretter says, since I have no trade, I don't qualify for a petty officer's rating. In the regular navy I'd be given an opportunity to go to school, but not in the Seabees, in which, if you don't have a trade, you're out of luck. Mr. Tretter made me understand that there are men with degrees, geologists, lower in rank than I. He's absolutely correct; there's nothing I can do in the Seabees. He also said that he knows I don't belong here, but that nothing can be done about it. So I plan to go to the Commander and tell him I want to transfer out of the battalion. If nothing else, at least he'll hear my story. And it may work to my advantage. Of course, I realize it's impossible to get a transfer. Certainly I can't make things any worse for myself. Now I have no incentive, nothing to try for. I won't get experience by digging ditches.

However, I'm not taking my fate too seriously. I won't let whatever I'm told to do, even if it's digging ditches, make me feel bad. After all, as you have said, this is merely an interim period in my life, and after the war is over what I've done will mean nothing.

A farewell party is planned for the 15th, which probably means we'll be in confinement. I expect to be secured at any time. I'm no longer excited about embarkation. We've been expecting it for such a long time that it's significance has faded away.

While in Ventura the other night I phoned Mr. Harry L. Smith, a mechanical drawing teacher in the local high school. Some time ago

Mrs. Myles had written him that he should expect my call, which I've only gotten around to doing. After I called, I met Mrs. Smith at the USO and found her a pleasant woman, indeed. I imagine the Smiths are in their thirties; they have two sons, the oldest being six. Since I couldn't visit their home that night, they invited me for Tuesday night. Of course, I've accepted the invitation.

I'll be interested in hearing what they have to say, because both are natives of the West Coast. I enjoy meeting so many different people. I'm sure I've already learned a little from the few contacts I made. The Smiths invited me to go to the mountains with them this weekend, which unfortunately I didn't have off. Mr. Smith is an excellent skier, and, since he's on the ski patrol, he was able to get enough gas for the trip. With an entire ski club going, I can imagine the fun I'd have had. Furthermore, since it is a hundred mile trip inland to the mountains, I'd have seen a lot of beautiful scenery. Just as well. I'd probably break my neck on skis now. Gosh, Ronnie, you'd be in your glory to have such an opportunity. I'll write more about these people after Tuesday night.

Now that I've seen about all there is to see in Hollywood and L.A., I plan to head north for a change and spend next weekend in Santa Barbara, a beautiful city about forty miles up the coast. I'll most likely look up Mr. Riccius's friend who lives there.

I have Dad's letter of a week ago before me. I've gotta admit that his quip about being a "sight seaing man" is pretty good. Imagine, folks, he admits spending from two to four hours on a letter. Tch, tch, so I insulted him by describing his letters as only being "the frosting." Say, Mom, will you give him a bit of the cake? Dad, Mom says she will give you a piece of the cake. So now you've got the cake. Hey, does Dad read your letters? I recall, Mom, you wrote that he doesn't always let you read his. I'd demand that he do so, if I were you.

I see, Dad, that in your recent letter you are delving into the realm of philosophy which I find very interesting. I'm happy to learn that you have faith in me. I'm pleased to know that while being on my own I've lived up to your expectations so far, and you can be assured that I'm determined to continue. I don't know what I'd do without you folks. I simply tolerate this crazy outfit; I'm trying to get it over with and get back to you people. As time passes, I become increasingly anxious to have your letters. One would expect the opposite, that with the passage of time my anxiousness would decrease, but the reverse has happened.

I haven't had guard duty for weeks. For the past two weeks we've been lying around doing nothing. They say it's the lull before the storm, that we're merely resting and made at ease before embarking. It seems like a good excuse for doing nothing anyway.

Oh, oh, I take back my letter about spending and saving. I'm sorry I ever mentioned that I was an expense for you. Ya just can't argue with a woman. They beat you every time. Won't I ever learn?

Monday 2/7/44

Dear Mom,

Happy birthday Mom, and God bless you. I sent a card today, but fear that you'll get it too late. Last week, after a long search for a decent card, I had no success. Not until the last minute did I discover one that expressed what I wanted to say. I'm not finished yet, as I'm waiting for something to arrive at the ship's store that I want to send you. The store ran out of the "thing." Now, I want to hear nothing from you concerning what I'll be sending.

At last you received the photos. Now I can relax and not have to deal with your reminders about them. Whew, I'm glad the matter of the pictures is over with. Seriously, I'm so glad that you liked them. But, listen, at the rate you're exhibiting them, I won't be able to face anyone when I get back. Goodness, Mom, people aren't always interested in other people's sons in the navy, and the same words apply to you, Dad. People have their own to think of. I have the idea that you may be tiring others by continuously talking about that jerk in the navy. I appreciate your enthusiasm, but please try to realize that you may be boring others. Remember how I dislike how Aunt Ida carried on about Cousin Bob, quoting this letter or that? I hope you're not doing the same thing. I understand how you feel, as I feel the same way about you folks. Although I don't know what you are saying, from your letters I gather I'm a frequent topic. I feel swell to know that, like licking the whole world, but you might be giving the impression that I'm an angel. Now don't be mad at what I've just written. I know you do what you think is best. In a way, I'm sorry I ever mentioned this.

If you think you're proud of me, you should know how much I display your pictures. Mom, do you know that you don't look your age. Seeing your picture, anyone would take you for thirty-five or younger. For this reason I can't remember how old you really are. By the way, I think the photographic equipment here is newer than the equipment used on my grad pictures. Hollywood lighting, as it's called, is used here—much different than the lighting used back East.

It's too bad about Frank F.[1] His main trouble was that he ran around (I learned this from his mother) and paid less attention to his studies, so, of course, when it came to a showdown, he didn't know his stuff.

What a swell kiss, Mom. And I'm giving you one back. Sorry, no lipstick. When I get back it will be tough having to wear a collar again. I'll probably act like a dude for the first month or so.

I expect some pretty good training this week. About thirty of us have been chosen to attend scouting and patrolling school. Today is my first day. We had lectures all day, and the rest of the week we'll take hikes, do field maneuvers such as crawling on our stomachs, and get plenty of exercise. This will loosen me up, put me in better condition. The course is a good one. In today's lecture I learned how to read a compass, make accurate azimuth readings, and read maps, signs, and symbols. I also learned how to compute my bearings by a watch and how to make magnetic declination readings. I feel fortunate to know such things. They will be very useful to know in the future. The course ends Friday.

Tomorrow evening I plan to visit the Smiths in Ventura. Most likely I'll not be able to write tomorrow as I have little time to spare on liberty nights.

[Amid drawings of musical note symbols.]
Happy Birthday to you, Happy Birthday to you.
Happy Birthday dear Mom,
Happy Birthday to you.

Love, Hughie

Wednesday 2/9/44

Dear Mom,

As expected, time was so limited yesterday that I was unable to write. It was a pretty tough day. It was cloudy during the morning and rain was due before afternoon. All the members of the scouting and patrolling school hiked four miles to the military training area where we listened to lectures outdoors on finding direction, then ate chow from our mess kits. Then the rain came down in sheets. The wind blew like a hurricane from the ocean across the sand. We figured that we'd be sent back to our barracks, but no, the Marine instructor wanted us to be tough. By the way, all the Marine instructors are veterans of Guady (canal) or some part of the South Pacific campaign. So we had maneuvers amid the sheets of rain, running around as our rifles got soaked and our bodies grew cold from the penetrating wet. The ponchos (a waterproof cloak) thrown over our shoulders protected our packs. But it offered little protection to our lower body and our feet were just floating in our shoes. Finally, after the weather cleared, we headed back to camp, a torturous hike when you're soaked. As soon as I arrived at camp, I read your letter of the 5th, dashed to shave and shower, put on my blues, and went on my way to Ventura.

After getting there about 7:00 PM, I called the Smiths and arrived at their home a few minutes later. As I may have mentioned, he teaches mechanical drawing at the Ventura high school. Ventura has a population of about 13,000. Its main industry is oil, followed by fruit growing. Mr. Smith, of course, is a college man, a native of California, extremely pleasant, and about my height. The Smiths have two boys, one 4 1/2 and the other about 8. They live in a cute stucco cottage (which they own) on a hill overlooking the entire city to the ocean. The view from their front window would entrance any artist.

After we talked awhile, Mr. Smith, being a ski enthusiast and a member of the ski patrol, asked me to join him in attending a ski club meeting where some movies were to be shown. Mrs. Smith is also a ski enthusiast. You see, they go in big for that stuff, because they are natives of northern California. By the way, Mr. Smith neither smokes nor drinks coffee or tea and was interested in weight lifting at one time. He was also in the army in the last war.[1] He's much quieter than I am and very easygoing.

So we went downtown in his '42 Desoto to the meeting where he introduced me to several couples, a few young fellows, some civilians, some soldiers and several naval officers. The president of the club, a native of France, is a former skiing champion of the world. I found both the people and the movie interesting. After we returned home, we discussed all matters of world importance until midnight; then Mr. Smith drove me to the bus station.

Before I left, Mr. Smith invited me to ski with them at Big Pines in the San Bernardino mountains. It's about 150 miles southeast of here. To get there we must pass through the Mohave Desert. I'll be able to see more of the state and beautiful scenery. I'll let him know Saturday afternoon if I can go; meanwhile, he's getting me skis and shoes. I want to go badly, but I couldn't commit myself, with my leaving the country as indefinite as it is. Don't worry, if I go, I'll be careful not to break these skis.[2] Mrs. Smith asked me to sleep over Saturday night, but I'm not sure I should accept, for I feel it would be an imposition. If things go according to schedule, I'll go to Santa Barbara Saturday afternoon, look up Mr. Riccius's friend, that night either sleep in a Ventura USO or at the Smiths, then the following day go skiing. I'm thrilled about the idea and can't wait for Saturday afternoon.

Observe my new stationery. It's the new battalion stationery and cost twelve cents a pad. Mom, why don't you try a chiropractor for your arthritis? "Lifeboat"[3] is now playing at Grauman's Chinese. By the way, the Academy Awards will be presented soon at the same theater. I haven't had time to see any shows this week due to my schooling. Dad, what did you think of my suggestion to have your leg operated on?

I'll be sending personal papers and souvenirs home, and my slide rule too.

So you think you put on weight. Listen, Mom, I bet I beat you. You've been telling me how my pictures show that I've put on weight. I hadn't noticed it until today. This afternoon a fellow told me that I look much heavier than when he first saw me six months ago. He says that my physique shows more. Who knows, who cares? But I guess I'm really heavier. It takes someone else to point it out. Well, folks, I'll be Mr. Five by Five when I get home. Come to think of it, my clothes, especially my blues, fit me tighter than they used to.

This afternoon I told a fellow Worcesterite about the new USO there. He almost fell through the floor. He used to work at Morgan Construction and knows George K.[4] well.

Aunt Annie's letter is swell, but she has difficulty deciphering my penmanship. Don't blame her. Wish you'd stop bragging about me so much, Dad. Makes me feel funny, but boy I love you folks for it.

As ever, Hughie (Jughead)

Thursday 2/10/44

Dear Mom,

Training is pretty tough this week. My feet are blistered, my body is aching and my face is suntanned. After the past month of inactivity and lying around, I feel the exercise more than usual. However, I'm glad, because it will toughen me up. At day's end I take a shower, dress comfortably and write home and read a bit. I'm too tired to go to a show or write to anyone else. I'm getting plenty of sleep. By the time the training is over, I should be well into the rehardening process.

Yesterday, a beautiful sunny day, we were assigned field problems: hiking and locating positions by compass. Today, another glorious day, we learned map reading, layout and symbols on military scales. It's interesting and well worth knowing. I'm happy to be one of the few receiving this training. Now that I've attended four different schools on various aspects of warfare, I feel confident that I'll be able to handle myself in any emergency. Not everyone has been given such an opportunity.

Although I planned to see "Lifeboat" tonight, I don't have the time for I must study for the exam on scouting tomorrow. "His Butler's Sister"[1] which you mention in your letter played in Hollywood several weeks ago but hasn't come to the camp yet. I'll try to see it before we leave. We still expect to secure Monday, but nothing is definite.

The base gym has just purchased some weight lifting apparatus. Now I feel right at home. Just as we are about to leave, we get weights. Can you beat that?

Jesse[2] is lucky to be in the country for such a long time. Those are the guys who will be shipped across now.

After the massage I had, my skin cleared for about two weeks then gradually returned to its original bad state. However, my complexion changes often. When the pictures were taken, my face was quite clear. Now that I'm getting a lot of sun, it's breaking out again. The masseur wants to put a mud pack on my face. I'd have to spend a buck for the material at a drugstore, but I don't want to spend that much just to rid myself of a few pimples. I believe my complexion is clearer than when I was home.

Mom, you have jumped to some wrong conclusions about me. I've always observed the shape, appearance and dress of man, woman, or beast, but I never vented my views until I began writing letters and described people whom I see and meet. Maybe you didn't know as much about me as you thought. My dear young lady, I confess I admire genuine pulchritude when I see it. I bet when I was home you didn't think I was human. Well, I was whether you knew it or not.

To tell the truth, Mom, I'm even surprising myself these days.

Boy of boy, Ronnie, do I wish you could be with me this weekend. You have the skis up north while I have the snow down south — sounds crazy.

A new order has been issued requiring that we have fifteen minutes of physical training every morning. It's a good idea; I'm all for it. Today, being our first day of training, I feel better already.

Very soon, some Waves will be assigned to the base. The new commander will be a vice admiral instead of a captain, the rank of its present commander. After the war it's planned that this will be a recuperation center.

Our Marine instructor had been stationed on British Samoa in the South Pacific for some time. He told us a lot about the area. Very interesting.

I keep up with the news pretty well, as I buy a paper every morning. I must say we're doing quite well in the Pacific.[3]

The majority of the men I'm in contact with are anti-Roosevelt and anti-Russian. Some who have lived here on the West Coast feel Europe is none of our affair. There was a discussion about Jews today during dinner hour. No one knew that I'm Jewish. Until today I never realized how much anti-semitism existed. Of course, I kept my mouth shut. The men believe that Jews control all the capital and moneyed interests in the nation. It's the one point they all agree on. Pure Father Coughlin propaganda.[4] I listened to many un-democratic remarks. If these beliefs are typical of all Americans, then we are great suckers for propaganda. When talking about world events and expressing prejudices, they sound like a group of grammar school kids. Their discussions are so ridiculous, I never enter into them. And the more intelligent men stay out also.

Russia is discussed at length. The men fear that nation, expecting that it will dictate the peace and control Europe. They hate communism, don't understand it, or know what it's all about. In my opinion, they hate the word, not the theory or its significance. I've heard several college fellows praise Lindberg[5] and express isolationist views.[6] I'm sure people on the West Coast are inclined toward conservatism due to the area's distance from Europe. Occasionally, I've had some friendly political discussions. I'm considered a radical, but I like that. After all, every idea is radical before becoming conservative. Democracy was once a radical idea. People here aren't as concerned with politics as people back East. They are more interested in enjoying themselves.

The men consider Japan the greater threat. They despise the Japanese more than Easterners do. After all, this has been a Japanese section of the country. They did business with the Japanese. The Japanese controlled the fruit markets and owned thousands of acres of orchards. Our campsite once belonged to a Japanese farmer. But, after the war, the Japanese will return and carry on as before. People forget easily, and plenty of appeals for the ante status quo will be made. Now, Mexicans, are being imported to pick fruit from the orchards. Cheap labor. Many cities here have Japanese names.

Forgive this abrupt ending. I'll write tomorrow.

As ever, Hughie (Jughead Jr. Grade) (Jughead refers to a seaman.)

Saturday Feb 12, 1944

Dear Mom,

I didn't write yesterday because after scouting class I was busy all evening washing and getting ready for the weekend.

I departed for Ventura (fifteen cents fare) at noon, phoned Mrs. Smith to tell her that I accepted their invitation, and hitched to Santa Barbara. Two navy lieutenants in a Jeep picked me up. Santa Barbara is about 30 miles north of Ventura, 40 miles north of Oxnard and 100 miles north of L.A. When I phoned Mr. Hammet, Mr. Riccius's friend, his wife answered. She promised to relay Mr. Riccius's greeting to her husband. She invited me to visit, but, since there were no buses to take me the four miles from downtown to their home, I was unable to make a personal visit.

The city is very picturesque, with Spanish style the prevalent architecture, even for the shops. There's a considerable half breed Mexican population here, although it's also a popular place for wealthy people, especially old folk. On the whole, Santa Barbara is considered to be a swanky place. The stores are most attractive, and many are owned by Jewish people; I've found this to be the case in every city that I've visited.

The museum is interesting, but not as large as Worcester's. The courthouse is a marvel, built in a Spanish motif with murals on its walls and articles of historic interest on exhibit here and there in its chambers. The courtroom is unlike any I've ever seen: beautiful.

Palms are everywhere, lining the streets, adding tropical color. Today is like a typical summer day and the sky is bluer than I've ever seen.

I'll return to Ventura by the 7:20 PM Greyhound and stay at the Smiths for the night.

Yesterday, I completed the scouting course, thank God. Although it was tough conditioning, I feel better for it. I'm sure our move and confinement are approaching. The Skipper has hinted that next week is the week.

I'll tend to both your letters after my jaunt to the mountains on Monday, if not sooner. Keep writing, whatever happens.

Love to you all, Hughie (the Massachusetts traveler)

Feb. 14, 1944

Dear Mom,

Everything swell after a wonderful weekend. You will get a whopper of a letter tomorrow.

Monday 2/14/44

Dear Mom,

I know you're anxious to hear how I made out yesterday, but before I tell you, I'd like to answer your letter. I've done nothing all day but tend to personal duties. Tonight, in either this letter or another, I'll discuss Dad's masterpiece and teach Ronnie how to ski.

Everyone in the battalion is excited about the rumor, not yet confirmed, that we will be secured Thursday. The final packing of our miscellaneous equipment has begun in preparation for transport to San Pedro, California for shipping out. Some believe that we'll leave Hueneme by train for one of three destinations: San Francisco, San Pedro, or back East. I think the first location is the most plausible, and the last would be too good to be true. Then there's always the possibility we'll embark right here at Hueneme.

Now for your letters. Your detailed description of what transpired in Boston is perfect. I can readily see that Dad managed to have everybody take a ride in the new car. To tell the truth, Dad, I'm as proud of the thing as you are. I've done my share of bragging about your excellent buy.

Ah, ha, canned salmon again, that dish of the gods. Yes, I had salmon Friday, but fresh fish salmon. Some of the fish we get is probably shark meat, because I've never tasted anything like it before. In spite of its strangeness most of it is pretty good.

Flash—your letter of Feb. 8th, arrived today, about to be commented on. To answer your question: Why don't I thumb my way back to Oxnard? There are too many competitors, and I'd be wasting too much time. Thumbing back is uncertain and could take up to two hours. Returning late to base is a serious offense, which the Commander himself handles. By returning by bus, I'm able to enjoy myself right up to the end of my liberty.

Yup, the raincoat is fine, no leaks; yet, how can it leak when, as they say in Hollywood, it never rains. The rain I've seen is purely a figment of my imagination.

Now that I shave more often, the electric razor is proving useful. Despite the frequently variable voltage here, the razor sounds and performs beautifully.

I've heard so much about (but have never met) Mrs. Ringer's sister, Betty, in the course of my life, that I gather she's quite a gal.

Well, well, well, never did I realize the profound effect that the pictures would have upon you. Listen, let's forget them for a while. Write about something else. I'll be getting a big head before you know it. Still, Mom, I'm tickled pink that they make you feel better. I've had a few other photos taken in the course of my travels here, and I'll try to get them to you. More about that later.

"Good looking, well built, and lovable," just the precise description that I've made of Ronnie to so many people I've met. I'd have given a million to have him along yesterday.

Flash #2—card of Feb. 9th received today. Bulletin: was not very explicit in my letter from Ventura due to lack of time. Please pardon.

Hurry, hurry, hurry. How deep did it snow that day? I'm praying for a foot.

This sounds good to me: "Business good and Dad goes down nights very little."[1] That's an achievement, to be able to carry on a busy business without putting in overtime. That's it for you, Mom. Just hang in for the rest of the letter, while I address Dad and Ronnie.

Flash #3—Dear Dad, (Manager and thinks he's boss)

Receiving your seven page letter the minute I took off on liberty was indeed an excellent way to begin a weekend. Here's a page by page commentary. Page 1: which was devoted to the mug in the picture, very interesting, but, uh, well it made me darn happy. Page 2: Let's see, you were writing at 9:30 Saturday night. Don't tell me you missed "Can You Top This One?"[2] Say, Mom, I think Dad is secretly a song fan. He mentioned Frank Sinatra and seems to know a bit about the jerk. Watch out. He'll be singing "Shoo, Shoo, Baby,"[3] the most popular jive tune on the West Coast now. Page 3: devoted to the weather. Good, I always enjoy hearing about the kind of weather you're having. It's good that it's so mild, easy on the driving and the coal. Page 4: Your advice and philosophy impress me. I can only say with reference to this page that you are doggone swell folks. Pages 5, 6, 7: Fifteen miles to the gallon isn't bad for driving in cold weather, especially with the low octane gas you get now. Dad, I wish you wouldn't feel so guilty about not being able to write as often as you wish. What you're doing now is tops with me. I, jughead Hughie, personally excuse you if you write less often.

Again your letter hit the jackpot. Dad, I only wish you could be with me to see the sights I see. When the war is over you must make it a point to visit the West Coast. It's far more spectacular than anything you've seen. While in Santa Barbara, I saw a most interesting upholstering shop. It was centrally located in a modern one story store off the main drag. Its surroundings were nice: palm trees along the street and quaint shrubs. Its windows extended clear down to the sidewalk, giving the viewer the impression of gazing into a warm home. The display window was divided into different types of rooms fully furnished with lamps, end tables and other pieces of furniture; beautiful rugs covered the floor. It looked just like someone's living room. Yes, you see similar windows in furniture stores back East, but not so quaint and realistic. They were clever displays. From the looks of it, this was the only upholsterer in that city of millionaires. I think the shop was downstairs. The display sells. Even a blind person knows that.

Okay, Dad, hang in with mother while I instruct Ronnie on the art of skiing — and falling, and only hurting one's backside.

Flash #4: I'll begin where I left off in Santa Barbara Saturday afternoon. After writing home, I skidoodled over to the bus station to learn that I could only buy a ticket for the 7:20 bus at 7:20, so I roamed a bit more, then had an excellent supper at a cafeteria before returning to the terminal at 7:00. Since the 7:20 bus was overcrowded, I waited another hour for the 8:20. When it arrived, the civilians, (Some had been waiting two or three hours), were told that they couldn't buy tickets. I felt so sorry for some of them who seemed pleasant. I was lucky since those going to Ventura were allowed to board the bus. You see, the bus travels from Frisco to San Diego, a distance of about 1,000 miles. Having only 30 miles to go, I didn't mind standing during the 30 minute run. But as fate would have it, the Super Greyhound had a flat in Carpenteria, a small town about 15 miles south of Santa Barbara. Nine-thirty, then 10:30 passed, and I became impatient. The repair men couldn't get the jack under the bus. In the meantime, while waiting in the bus, I got into an interesting general discussion with the other servicemen about the war. Most interesting, however, was my talk with a California native, a young woman school teacher, who knew Mr. Smith in Ventura, in whose home I was to sleep that night. After telling her that I was thinking of hitch hiking rather than waiting all night for the bus to get under way, I was surprised when she suggested that she would like to join me if I did. So, in the 10:30 darkness I flagged down a car; but, before I had a chance to call her, three soldiers were seated beside me and the car sped on without her. Poor girl. She probably didn't reach Ventura until early morning. The people who stopped were two well-dressed men. The car was a beaut. I grew a bit wary when one of the fellows asked if we drank. The response was an agreeable "yes." To their astonishment, the liquor-thirsty soldiers were handed Cokes. Boy, did I get a kick out of that.

As soon as I arrived in Ventura, I called Mr. Smith, who had almost given up hope of my arriving at his home that night. On taking a shortcut to his house, I had to pass through a cemetery, and in the darkness I missed the path. After running into five or six gravestones and probably knocking over a few, I finally extricated myself from the burial ground without waking the dead. What a dreary place it is at night. Never again! By 11:30 I arrived at the Smith's house atop the hill, to find Mr. Smith in good humor, oddly enough, and in pajamas. Quickly I washed in the very beautiful bathroom (nicer than Cousin Lil's) and slept between clean white sheets, quilt and all, for the first time in five months.

After a sound sleep I arose wide awake at 6:15 Sunday morning (I've learned to sleep anywhere) and had a scrumptious breakfast of all the hot cakes I could eat, crispy bacon, fruit, bananas and cereal with cream and milk. By 7:00 Mr. Smith and I joined six others who were waiting for us downtown. Besides the blues I was wearing, I brought woolen gloves, two pair of GI socks, and my pea jacket. We took two cars, Mr. Smith's, a '42 Desoto with fluid drive, and a '40 Pontiac owned by a fellow called Frenchy. Frenchy is Swiss and the 1930 international ski champion. About forty, he runs an auto body repair establishment. There was a couple in their thirties, very pleasant and seemingly devoted to each other. There was also a Barbara Atwood, about 19 or 20, wife of a corporal stationed in North Africa. Why in the devil I meet only wives, I'll never know. The other members of the party were Wally, a lad about 17, and Werny, also Swiss, and a machinist. Mr. Smith, Wally, Werny and I were in the Desoto which rode like a cloud. The two girls and Frenchy and the husband of one of the girls were in the Pontiac. We drove for about three hours at forty to fifty miles per hour, so you can easily figure out the distance. Time never passed so fast in my life. It seemed more like three minutes rather than three hours. We traveled past orchards, up mountains, through valleys and desert, snow and more snow. It was such pleasure to take in everything while riding in the front seat of such a fine car in which shifting isn't necessary. Passing through acres and acres of orange and lemon orchards during the first part of the trip was fascinating. The experience was new to me. In the distance, dense, black smoke could be seen, and upon reaching it we could hardly see twenty yards ahead of us. The smoke had come from smudge burners that were burning oil in the groves, creating a dense smoke to prevent the frost from damaging the fruit. There were burners along the road too.

I'm incapable of describing the valleys and mountains except to say that they are enormous. The Mohave, a semi-arid desert, had cacti and various desert plants scattered about. It's blistering hot there in the summer but comfortable this time of the year. After crossing the desert, we came to more mountains on the other side, only they were steeper and higher than the mountains we encountered before entering the desert. We went constantly up for about twenty miles, the final eleven miles close to vertically. Even though we had sandwiches, rabbit, and cake for lunch, we stopped at a small roadside stand to have a bite.

We finally reached Big Pines about 11:00. Immediately I put on my boots (Mr. Smith secured the right size and a pair of 6 foot 4 inch skis that were better than the ones I have at home) and removed my jumper, replacing it with my navy turtle neck sweater. Tucking my trousers into my boots, I wrapped them tightly to my ankles with a rubber band made especially for that purpose. After donning this regalia, I looked more like a full fledged skier. In fact, no one in a million years could tell I was a sailor. We hiked a half mile up the mountain to the ski runs. The snow was two to three feet deep, and in some places deeper. There were three inches of soft snow on top of a crust making it perfect for skiing.

When I first got on the skis, I admit I was comically awkward. Although I couldn't maintain my balance, once I got going, Barbara managed to get me down the run a little way. I showed off some beautiful stunts while falling. She was determined to teach me so we went to a shorter, easier run. Being awfully rusty, I forgot everything I knew last year.

Since the party broke up into partners, I spent the day with Barbara and found we had some things in common. Being a pretty good skier, she eventually took off to a steeper run, while I practiced by myself. After about an hour I got the knack of it, and was able to turn, stop and keep my balance perfectly. Before this I stopped by falling, usually on my face doggonit, and she'd get a great kick out of it. Well, soon I went to the steep run and announced to Barbara that I was ready to go down. She giggled, expecting to see me do something funny, but I felt confident and insisted that she go first. Well, off she went and immediately after I dug my poles into the snow and headed down lickety-split. After passing her like greased lightning, I reached the bottom, sliding to a perfect stop like a veteran. You see, the incline is still steep where I stopped. To tell the truth, I felt proud of myself but tried not to show it. Well, when she reached me at the end of the run, she looked at me queerly and asked why I had been kidding her all morning when all along I was a good skier. I had a heck of a job convincing her that I really wasn't any good, and that only after practicing for the past hour was I able to get the knack of it. I had the same thing happen years ago in swimming: I caught on all of a sudden.

As I kept skiing, I gained more confidence, went higher and higher, and came down faster and faster, and boy, did I come. I don't mean to brag, but I did darn good, let me tell you. I could turn corners without a second thought, and slide to a stop merely by shifting my weight, even at top speed.

Before long I suggested that we go the entire length of the run, a half mile down the mountain. Was that girl surprised! I went first, and, yea gods, did I travel. I weaved in and out of the trees at a good 20 or 25 mph, and probably faster down the straight run. Soon a curve came up, but I was going too fast to make it and headed for a cliff on the edge of the run. Preparing for a jump, I settled down to a crouch and successfully made it, but fouled up at the bottom where I met an unexpected dip in the terrain. After rolling over in the snow like a ball, I picked myself up quickly, went back to the run, and continued speeding the rest of the way down. When I got to the bottom, she wasn't there, and after waiting five minutes, still no Barbara. So I trekked back up the half mile to the top, sort of worried, thinking she may have fallen. There she was, all smiles, at the top, while I stood panting to beat the band, ready to raise the devil. No, she hadn't followed me. She simply wanted to see if I could do it. After all, she said, why do a run where we'd have to hike up a half mile. We then went to a shorter but faster run where there was a tow line. The tow line is wonderful. You ride up on your skis from the bottom. All you do is grab a rope and up you go.

At about 3:30 when I suggested skiing to the bottom again immediately after dinner, Barbara exclaimed, "What, you haven't eaten yet?" For several hours I was so excited using that run that I forgot to eat. Glancing at my watch, I was surprised to see how late it was. I had been enjoying myself so much. So between runs I'd grab an apple, an orange or a sandwich. At 4:30 I was still going strong, skiing down the run and taking the tow up again. But I could tell that Barbara was growing weary, and I had a great time ribbing her about being weak etc. Before long she had too little energy to even go up the run. It seemed that the others were also getting tired, so the whole gang went down to the car. As I was going down the long run to reach the car, I went over the same cliff again and did a beautiful somersault at the bottom. Did I get a ribbing. So help me, I've gotta go back sometime and make that curve.

I should mention the trees, enormous pines, firs and oaks, two to four feet in diameter. The area is heavily wooded, and wild animals are abundant. In fact, I saw two deer.

After we changed back to our traveling clothes, I my sailor clothes, we had sandwiches. Before starting back about 5:30, we took pictures of the whole gang. [See photograph section below.] By the way, a plate camera was used.

Because of gas rationing there were few cars at Big Pines, but there was enough of a crowd to make it fun. Everybody was so friendly; you'd talk to absolute strangers as if you had known them all your life. The girls outnumbered the fellows, and were better skiers too. The few soldiers there skied on their rear ends most of the time. I got a great kick out of watching them. Practically everyone there was a native Californian, a very unusual thing to find in California.

We arrived in Ventura about 9:00. Having time to pay attention to my body on the way back, I began to feel the results of eight hours of skiing. I had no bruises, but oh, my muscles! On getting out of the car, I could hardly move. After having a supper prepared by Mrs. Smith and talking a while, I arrived in camp at midnight.

What a time! I can say that I enjoyed myself on this liberty more than any other thus far. It was my last liberty in this country and I doubt that I'll ever forget it. Boy oh boy, I'm a confirmed skier now and can't wait to get home to ski next winter. When home I plan to visit the famous runs in New Hampshire.

Oh, yes, several pictures were taken without my knowing it and I'll try to get them. I was informed that there is one of me herringboning up the mountain. I must have looked funny.

So, Ronnie, you never figured I'd be going skiing in sunny California, eh. It only goes to show you what God's country California is.

I'll probably write again today, this evening that is, so stand by.

Love to you, Mom, you, Dad, and you, Ronnie, Hughie (somersault artist)

Tues. Feb 15, 1944

Dear Mom,

It's now been five months since I was home, and I'm still in the country. I never dreamed I'd be here this long, but the day of departure is drawing near. Some say it will be this week, others say next week, and still others say we'll ship out without being secured at all. Of course, no one knows the truth. Since our departure is more or less certain, I plan to call you next liberty. You understand, of course, that I may never get a "next liberty."

I want you to continue writing but won't go into the reason for such a request right now.

I can understand perfectly how you look at my failure in the recreation job. I must admit that you are exactly correct. I didn't handle the matter wisely at all. I'm learning fast, though. In every job that I've had, including the one at Sol's drugstore and at the laboratory,[1] I can't deny that I was at fault, either partially or entirely, and, in a way, I've learned how to successfully hold a job.

Mr. Tretter has been a sad disappointment. The personnel dislike him and I've lost faith in him. He doesn't know how to handle men. On thinking it over, I've decided against going to see the Commander. My reasons are too complicated to explain.

What do you mean you'd like to move to California? Can't take it where you are? Shame. Now, just a minute, don't even kid about coming here or I might take it seriously. It costs to live here, and if you don't have the money, you shouldn't come.

I thought it odd that Ronnie's poor grades don't bother you. I'm glad that you look at it that way. Ronnie will be a success, mark my words. I am too moody and serious to be a carefree fellow, but travelling is considerably changing my point of view. Ronnie has what I lack, and don't I know it. But differences in character give the world variety.

"Lost Angel"[2] played here yesterday; didn't see it. Most likely I won't have time to see movies, now that preparations for leaving have begun.

In addition to all that I've written about the weekend, I could write more. For instance, Big Pines, about 7,000 feet, is the highest I've ever been. My ears popped both ascending and descending, and I couldn't hear well. For one to hear normally again, swallowing or yawning does the trick. In fact, when I took out my pen to write an address, I found it covered with ink. It had actually leaked because of the altitude.

Enclosed are pictures of platoons 2 and 4 of Headquarters Company taken the day I was on liberty. Mr. Tretter is the third CPO on the right. I paid only ten cents for each. They're poor pictures, so I didn't buy the larger ones.

Until tomorrow, adieu. Toujours amour à Mom, Ronnie et Dad, Hughie (jughead on skis)

Wednesday 2/16/44

Dear Mom,

As usual, I did nothing in the line of duty today, so I stocked up on various necessary articles such as socks, underwear, shoestrings, soap, toothbrushes, V-mail, and stationery. Now I'm all set to go.

The weather has been consistently clear and warm. Thursday evening we are to have a farewell party, which leads me to believe that, after it, we'll be immediately secured.

I forgot to mention that due to the rare atmosphere and the sun's reflection off the snow, we all got sunburnt Sunday. When I awoke Monday morning I looked quite brown. And I'm still sore all over from the exercise.

I took a trip down to the docks Tuesday afternoon to watch the Liberty ships and LSTs[1] being loaded. It's a busy place, operating 24 hours around the clock. Five ships are loaded at a time. Our destination's code name is Edur 28. Note that it spells "rude" backwards. The codes are interesting. For instance the code for the 126th battalion is Bifi. I was fascinated watching the loading. I also saw Charlie Chaplin's[2] yacht, now in government service, in the harbor.

Yesterday, I dug ditches to install a pipe main, merely a sample of what is to come. I don't mind it, though; at least I'm doing something useful. Those who have had experience in their field are up for rerates before we leave. I'm out of luck.

Good gosh, I'm actually running out of things to talk about. Expect to write tomorrow.

Thursday Feb. 17, 1944

Dear Folks,

At last it's happened. We are secured this minute, and this may be my last, or one of my last, letters for a long time. A farewell party is scheduled for tonight. My sea bag is packed and ready to go this very evening. I'll try to phone you early in the morning, although I have my doubts whether I can. I was due for a liberty this evening, but now of course that's out. Here is my new address.

> Hugh Aaron S 1/c
> Co. Hdqrs. Plat 4
> 113th Naval Const. Batt.
> c/o Fleet Post Office
> San Francisco, Calif.

It looks like we'll be going to the South Pacific for sure. I expect that we'll go by train to the port where the ship is and immediately board her.

The men are berserk with happiness. Everyone is anxious to go overseas. But I'll bet they won't feel that way in a month or so. The band is playing, and everyone is trying to drink as much beer as they can.

Mom's letters, along with Ronnie's humorous masterpiece, arrived this morning. Well, Ronnie, old top, I beat you to the punch skiing. A friend, Burnstein, who just got back from New York this morning, told me you had snow. Have a swell time skiing, fella, and thanks loads for your dandy letter.

Goodbye, Mom, Dad and Ronnie. I'll write whenever I can.

Love, with all my heart, to all of you, Hughie

Friday Feb. 18, 1944

Dear Mom,

I'm as surprised as you that I'm able to write this letter. So far no letter writing restrictions have been imposed. When I'm across, you understand, of course, that I'll be unable to write every day, not because I wish not to, but because of battalion restrictions.

Last night at the party, which is not worth describing, the Commander gave us a few leads, such as we're going to the South Pacific aboard a large, fast ship, large enough to accommodate several other units besides our thousand man plus battalion. We'll land first at a large, established base to become acclimatized to tropical conditions. By the time we return to the States, we'll be confirmed "Shellbacks," the name given to men who have crossed the equator.

My bags have been packed, labelled "Ships Hold" and loaded into a freight car. Only a miracle will stop us from leaving now. I'm not sad about it, since I've known for the past five months that this would happen. I consider myself fortunate for having been in the country as long as I have. Actually, I look forward to the voyage and the experience with eager anticipation. Any other attitude would be childish and make me miserable.

So again, more firsts. First time aboard a ship, first time on the high seas, first time out of the country. By being across, I'll be that much nearer returning home. Get the thing over with and get back; that's all I want.

Action. I doubt that we'll see much of that, most likely none at all. But if a showdown comes, I have confidence in myself, for I've been given good training, and I've taken seriously everything I've been taught.

Services for the faiths will be held Sunday. Most likely we'll depart that evening or the following day. The procedure will be train to ship.

I'm taking only the barest essentials: two toothbrushes, a flashlight, toilet articles, electric razor, my Blue Jacket Navy Manual, a pocket book on Russia, a small book of Dickens's[1] *Christmas Carol*[2] which some guy gave me, and a Jewish book of prayer, (The books are for reading aboard ship), a few cakes of soap for both face and washing clothes, glasses, scout knife, four sets of underwear, four pairs of socks, two sets of dungarees, two towels, sewing kit, a limited amount of writing supplies, rifle, full infantry pack, canteen, and helmet. And oh, yes, I managed to tuck in my correspondence course. All this fits into my bedding bag, hand bag and pack. The rest of my clothes are on their way home.

This letter may be held up at the post office. I'm awaiting your letter this morning. Love to you all, Hughie (future Shellback)

Saturday Feb. 19, 1944

Dear Mom,

Being secured to base means doing nothing all day, so I read, walk around the base and write letters to you. Before I went to bed last night, I intended to wake up at 2:00 or 3:00 and call home. Instead, I awoke at 4:45 which is 7:45 back home, too late to find Ronnie at home, while you folks would have most likely left for the store. Tonight I'll go to bed earlier to wake up earlier. I can't call in the PM because the phones are jammed.

I saw two enjoyable pictures last night: "Rationing"[1] with Wallace Beery and Marjorie Main[2] and "The Miracle of Morgan's Creek"[3] with Betty Hutton[4] and Eddie Bracken.[5] No doubt you'll laugh like anything when you see "Rationing" at the Palace. It's very funny. The second picture, also very good, is the craziest picture I ever saw. It was so funny, I almost died laughing. It's very daring in spots and full of witty remarks. It's sort of a continuation of "The Great McGinty"[6] with Brian Donlevy[7] and Akim Tamiroff. If I told more, I'd spoil it for you. You must see it. It will probably come to the Capitol[8] theater.

It's 9:00 in the morning, and I'll delay finishing this until after the 11:00 o'clock morning mail.

The mail arrived, including Dad's humdinger which I'll discuss in another letter, keeping me busy reading the rest of the morning. I'm writing in the library, listening to the sound of rain beating on the tin roof. Yep, it's raining today for the first time in weeks. What a coincidence that Ronnie was skiing the same day as I was. While Ronnie was breaking his neck on Newton Hill,[9] I was speeding towards the San Bernardino mountains.

By the way, if you get around to it, would you send me some saltwater soap once I'm established across? Can't find it out here.

Good to hear that your arthritis has eased, but I feel uneasy about Dad's ailment.

Tonight I plan to see "None Shall Escape"[10] with Marsha Hunt.[11]

Further comment on the picture of Dad is due. Have patience. I want to spend some time pondering Dad as "Superman."

Love to each of you, Hughie (son of "Muscleman")

Sunday Feb. 20, 1944

Dear Folks,

This is really the last letter you will receive from me for weeks, possibly months. My next letter will come from either Hawaii, New Caledonia or Australia. When calling you at 3:45 AM, I didn't realize that today would be the day. By 1:30 AM tomorrow, I'll be on a train, presumably heading for San Pedro, Calif. to board a big ship. It's rumored that the ship is the USS *West Point*,[1] a former American luxury liner.

Tonight I'll get only 2 3/4 hours of sleep. But last night, retiring at 8:00, waking at 2:30 AM, talking to you at 3:45, returning to bed at 4:00, then waking at 7:30, I slept nine hours.

I'm all packed this very minute. It should be quite a sight to see us board with full infantry pack and rifle slung over the shoulder, a duffel bag and gas mask under the left arm, and personal bag under the right arm.

Unfortunately this is the sort of day that the Chamber of Commerce would deny existed. It's pouring cats and dogs. As we were talking on the phone, I could hear the rain beating against the side of the building.

I had difficulty in hearing you because 25 or so other fellows were in the room talking. You see, the base has no phone booths. I'm surprised I heard as well as I did.

I feel much better after hearing all three of your voices. You folks are really something to come back to.

You may be amused to learn what transpired while I was holding the line and hearing nothing. I heard the New York station ask Dad if he would accept the call collect. Then there was a silence, and I said, "Hello," but there was no response. After I waited a few minutes, some operators came on the line and deluged me with questions. My operator asked whether I was done talking and I explained, impatiently, that no one had answered. She then reprimanded the operator in Ventura for cutting me off. When two women get to arguing you can never tell what will happen. Anyway, I finally got through, and that's what counts.

I'm leaving the country in perfect health and in good spirits. To my amazement, I'm not in the least nervous or sentimental. I expect to return in the same condition.

I'd like to get this letter off early. When you receive it, I'll be on the high seas. Don't worry about anything. I wish I could express myself more forcibly than just:

Love to the best mother, father and brother in the world, Hughie (the Salt)

OVERSEAS IN THE PACIFIC THEATER

En Route to Islands Unknown

Censored V-Mail 2/26/44

Dear Mom,

I'm writing this aboard ship. It's just about sundown after a hot day spent lying around in this ——. We are —— expecting to see that ————. Everyone is browned by the sun and looks as if we had spent a week in Miami.

I must confess that I was stricken with seasickness the first day at sea, but I've made an admirable recovery. I imagine that it will soon feel unnatural to stand on something not rolling.

I feel swell and manage to enjoy myself, especially since the sea has always attracted me. To be truthful, I've already seen enough ocean on this voyage so far to last a lifetime.

All my future mail will be censored. Frankly, I'm having a devil of a time avoiding saying anything I shouldn't. I'll probably be unable to go into my usual lengthy descriptions and factual accounts, and will have to confine myself to less interesting stuff. At any rate, I guess I can get away with saying blank blank and this minute, even without restrictions, if I wanted to, I couldn't tell you where I am. My writing isn't very clear due to the rolling of the vessel, but will try to do better in future V-Mail letters. I believe V-Mail will be faster for both of us.

V-Mail 3/9/44

Dear Folks,

I'm still aboard ship en route to an unknown destination. Oddly enough, time has passed swiftly. The Pacific is a big place, let me tell you. I've already seen enough ocean to last a lifetime. However, during the voyage, which is nearing its end, the weather has been pleasant. Only an occasional squall interrupts the calmness of the sea. I'm fascinated by the flying fish that shoot away from our bow. We've seen them since before crossing the equator.

I've been fairly comfortable, spending most of the time on deck reading and talking to friends. By coincidence I met a fellow from Worcester in the ship's crew. He lived on June street. We had a swell time discussing our hometown and some friends we had in common. He hadn't been home in over a year, while, by comparison, I was fresh from Worcester.

The heat here doesn't bother me. I'm feeling tops. Be assured that everything will be fine. I'll write at the first opportunity.

V-Mail 3/12/44

Dear Mom,

This morning I received your first letter, the V-Mail of 2/26, (What wonderful service) since I left the States. As a result, I've been sitting on a cloud. Please continue using V-Mail. Not only is it fast, but also it's a pleasure to read, especially your typing. The next best alternative is air mail, and Free Mail is extremely slow.

Since we've crossed the international date line, I'm now one day ahead of you. We're limited to one letter a day, which I'll take advantage of. Although I'm not allowed to tell you where I am, I will be allowed to give you more information in several weeks. Although we're still aboard ship, it's not the one we were originally on. We're in the tropics, south of the equator, amidst a humid, uncomfortable climate. The nights and the mornings are comfortable, but oh, the heat in those afternoons. I take salt tablets, which keep me stimulated, so the heat doesn't bother me. The food is good and water is plentiful. Really, I feel swell in spite of the inconveniences. Sincerely, you may feel at ease concerning my welfare. Everything is hunky dory.

I must have reread your letter at least a dozen times by now and can't wait for others to arrive.

Finschafen, Papua New Guinea

March 17, 1944

Dear Folks,

We're at our destination at last. I'm still limited as to what I can say about this place or the voyage, but eventually I'll be able to disclose quite a bit. My last letter from the States was accurate, so you know something about the trip.

Our first day here was quite hectic, but after 24 hours I was settled down enough to do some washing and scribble this. The old heat is unceasing but, fortunately, it affects me little. As a matter of fact, I feel tip top and rarin' to go. To my surprise, I've been assigned a job, yes, back in recreation. I'm responsible for maintaining and distributing all athletic gear and associated equipment. I'm optimistic about the whole deal.

Continue writing via V-Mail or air mail. Because of its personal touch, an occasional air mail letter would be appreciated. I'll write both ways; let me know which is faster.

V-Mail Wednesday March 22, 1944

Dear Folks,

Due to the failure of the mail having been sent out, my letters have been few and far between. From now on I'll try to write daily. I must admit that I can't say as much as I used to or like, but you may look forward to vivid descriptions just the same.

I'm in the midst of the tropics somewhere in New Guinea. It isn;t half bad. The food comes from Australia, and it's good too. The water is excellent and iced. There's fresh water swimming in a stream, ocean bathing and fishing. More about such pleasures in another letter.

We made two stops en route: at Noumea, New Caledonia, and at Milne Bay, New Guinea. We changed ships at Milne Bay.

I expected it to be much worse here than it is. By taking an Atabrine pill every day, we keep malaria pretty well under control.

I received your last letter at Milne Bay. Since my arrival here, I've received no letters. Expect some soon.

Sat - Sun March 26, 1944

Dear Mom,

I received my first letters from the States two days ago. They were the best letters I've ever got. You can't realize what they meant to me. I began answering them the very day they arrived, but I've been so busy with no time off that I've not had a chance to write more until now.

No doubt you are wondering what I'm doing, but before I tell you about this place and the trip, I'll give you an idea of what this is all about. As you know, while en route I was assigned to recreation. I spent three days taking inventory, driving a jeep to round up the necessary equipment, and helping to establish a recreational facility. You may be surprised to learn that we have over $12,000 worth of recreational equipment, including such outdoor recreation material as baseballs, volleyballs, badminton games, etc., and a motion picture projector, ice cream machines, radios, phonographs and more than a thousand popular and classical records, a juke box, and innumerable smaller items. It was a good job, but I was offered a better deal.

It began aboard ship when I met a new fellow who had just joined our battalion. He is Albert Malter, Jewish, in his late twenties, a communications engineering graduate from Columbia. Prior to his induction he worked for Pan American Airways. Having a residence in Beverly Hills, a ranch in Idaho, and three cars, he's quite wealthy. He's in charge of battalion and regimental communications, an influential and powerful position. A first class petty officer now, he's about to become a C.P.O. After taking a liking to me and learning that I wasn't doing much and learning less, he asked me to join his commuications group, when the time would be ripe. I jumped at the chance. When I accepted the job in recreation, I knew I wouldn't stick with it, because this deal was brewing.

So through Malter's efforts I've been transferred to communications, namely radio and telephone. Dad, you'll be interested to learn that I'm striking for an electrician's mate rating. After I acquire some general knowledge in the field, the officer in charge of communications will recommend me. Malter, who has given me many text books on the subject, feels that I'll catch on fast.

I'm starting in the telephone section. The communications section is a crack organization. The day before yesterday I went into the field to help the fellows install a line. I work on the ground and learn to do connections. The fellows are a swell bunch who are eager to teach me. Yesterday, I learned how to install a telephone. Already I've learned a few tricks of the trade. Yesterday afternoon, I worked with Al Malter in the radio department, where I expect eventually to remain. So far, I'm crazy about the work. I'm learning and it's thrilling being outdoors most of the time and traveling around the base.

So you see, I've had a break at last. I'm learning something and I have the opportunity to be conscientious. I must say, things are turning out for the best.

Beyond being happy with my job, I'm also pleased with our base. It's enormous and very busy. I'd be happy to stay here for the duration. We live in tents, five to a tent, with plywood floors, in this climate a very pleasant and suitable abode. The weather is like our hot days of August. Not only am I acclimatized to the heat and humidity, I actually thrive in it. Going shirtless all day, I'm all brown. But we must wear long trousers for protection against insects, snakes and mosquitoes.

Under the circumstances, the food is excellent. We have fresh meats (liver, lamb, rabbit, mutton, etc.), mostly canned vegetables, sometimes fresh, all the butter, spices and sugar we desire, good potatoes, fruit such as apples and pears, cold juices such as lemonade, tomato, pineapple and grapefruit, ices, ice cream which is not yet in full production, cold wheat cereals, hot oatmeal, and powdered milk only, which tastes pretty good, and contains a nutritive value equivalent to fresh milk.

Our food is far superior to that of the army which lives on C rations and dehydrated food. They envy us and often come to our mess hall. The Aussies[1] think that we are living like kings, and, since they are an amiable lot, we often invite them over to eat with us. They, and the local natives, love American cigarettes. Yesterday, I watched a blond (peroxide) native walking down the road, his head held high, aloof to the world, puffing on a cigarette, while following him another was devouring his. They are like little boys, but they are good bargainers. For example, they'll climb a tree and retrieve a coconut for a cigarette. They like knives, and would do anything to have a Jeep. Their relationship with our American Negroes is comical. The natives, who are jealous of most of the Negroes (We call them Jigs[2]) who drive our trucks, ignore them and keep their women out of sight.

Speaking of coconuts, I've partaken of them often, both the meat and the milk, and am now tired of them. I've also discovered that both meat and milk are excellent laxatives. They cleaned me out pronto. Our encampment is set beneath a canopy of coconut palms.

After some conniving and a mile of red tape, I've sent you a cable which I understand hasn't yet gone out.

The trip across had both its interesting and monotonous moments. Although the ship was a beauty, our accommodations weren't the best, but I weathered it quite well. I can't say too much about the vessel due to restrictions. You already know more about her than a civilian should know. It would be impossible to tell you here all that has happened, but, as I write more letters, I'll reveal more about the voyage and what it's like living here in New Guinea.

Malaria is well controlled here; actually, we have fewer mosquitoes than you do in the summer. Snakes are plentiful, but they avoid our camp. Only a few are poisonous. The rats, which are as big as rabbits and hop like them, confine themselves to the jungle and appear only when the bulldozers are clearing an area. I understand that Frank Buck[3] had caught his biggest python in this neighborhood, but they too avoid the camp.

I take salt tablets daily as well as Atabrine after supper to prevent us from contracting malaria. We wear the familiar tropical helmet, although, being mostly under the palms, I'm usually bareheaded.

The swimming is wonderful, both in the surf and the streams. Oh yes, bathing suits. What are they? In the streams we usually swim beneath a falls, some 12 to 15 feet deep. The ocean bathing is similar to Cat Island in the Gulf of Mexico.

I listen to the will-o-the-wisps, the parrots squawking in the palms, and the sounds of a variety of multi-colored birds. We have no lions or tigers. Bananas and pineapples grow wild. And you may be surprised to learn that sugar cane originated in New Guinea.

On the whole, I'm quite well fixed, healthy and happy. After seeing other outfits, I can now say that I'm glad I'm in the Seabees. We get the best food and have the best equipment. Anyway, the navy has it all over the army. You may be assured that things have turned out for the best. I've become so accustomed to being here that often I forget that I'm not in the States. The radio broadcasts give me a big lift. Everything is calm. Danger is rare.

March 27, '44

Dear Folks,

I have so much to write about that I don't know where to begin. Since I can't get airmail stamps for a while, I must use this meager V-Mail.

The island is peculiar in several ways, one being that you must drive on the left hand side of the road. At first I found it hard to get used to, but I expect that by the time I'm back in the States I'll be mixed up again.

We had steak this evening for supper. The battalion has a laundry equipped with the latest washing machines, and it's free.

Yesterday, I witnessed a spectacle that people rarely see in a lifetime. I attended a native festival in which the natives dressed in costumes danced their rituals to drums, and a wild boar was sacrificed. I'll give you a more detailed description later. Don't worry, I won't forget.

There are plenty of Jap souvenirs here, but I don't go in much for that stuff. However, I'll be sure to bring something home for Ronnie.

March 31st, 1944

Dear Folks,

A year ago tomorrow I took my test for V-12. I thought that day would shape my future. A year ago tomorrow I hadn't the faintest inkling that New Guinea would be my destination. Life is truly quite an experience.

I haven't written since last Sunday. Why? Because I'm busier than I ever imagined I could be. I work day and night, although I get plenty of sleep, but have little time for myself. I'm helping with the procurement of replacement radio parts, setting up a transceiver, and installing a whip antenna. You may readily guess that I find it interesting. I like my work.

Yesterday and today I hit the jackpot: five letters came, including yours written just before I left the States, a card from Aunt Pearl, and your V-Mail of March 7.

The letters I received from the three of you were the acme of all your letters. All were true masterpieces. You can't imagine how much I laughed, and how happy reading Ronnie's made me. Dad's letter is something. I shall keep it in my writing tablet always. Yours, Mom touched on everything that I've been wanting to say to you. Such letters appear only in books. These three letters will never leave my folder.

First, Ronnie's letter. So I got the jump on you skiing. After my living here in this tropical climate for over a month, that day seems so distant and unreal. I'm glad that your letter reminded me of that experience. I'm so busy that homesickness is the least of my worries. You gave a marvelous description of your escapade on Newton Hill. Say, how about it, spring should be approaching back home. Autumn is due here, the start of the rainy season, but we've had comparatively little rain so far.

You wrote about listening to Groucho Marx. Ah, yes, it seems an age since I witnessed his program. Time is passing swiftly. You asked if I could grow a beard. To tell the truth, yes. Many have excellent growths, some well trimmed, some shabby and in every shape and form imaginable. Most, myself included, are clean shaven for comfort's sake. We perspire so much that a beard becomes uncomfortable. Using my electric razor, I can keep myself shaven, as if I were in the States. Keep those letters comin'.

Now for you, Dad. What can I write after reading your wonderful letter? Its sentiment is so deeply and sincerely expressed that I'm at a loss of what to say. I want to thank you with all my heart. No gift or reward could surpass the sentiments you feel.

I got a kick when I read that mother was dead to the world when the phone rang. Number two phone call will happen, mark my words. Keep in mind, however, that it won't be tomorrow, or the next day, but the day will come. What is time when there's so much to look forward to? I have much patience. There's a new world for me to return to.

The picture ("Gay 90s")[1] is really super-duper. Hey listen, you have to pry into that old trunk. You have me clamoring for more such pictures. Yesiree, my Dad was a he-man when he was young, alright, alright. Please keep me informed concerning the "Episode of the Trunk in the Shed." The big question is: will the trunk be opened, and is there really a body in it? Bet this twists up the censor. Don't worry, Mr. Censor, this isn't code. This letter is similar to a telegraph message. I wonder how many actually read this thing.

Now I'll turn to Mother. I should say that your letter of the 21st is your best. Maybe, it's because you hit the nail on the head. You need say no more. I can only say, what wonderful parents you are. Hey now, don't get so keyed up when I'm on the phone. Bet you thought you were talking to President Roosevelt himself. I'm deeply honored. Seriously, Mom, I feel the same way.

Regarding our embarkation, it rained cats and dogs that night. We probably didn't ship out of Port Hueneme because the ship was too large to enter its harbor.

I'm no longer under Mr. Tretter and rarely see him. I now report to a Chief Electrician's Mate and a Chief Warrant Officer. Both are swell men to work for.

So glad you liked the Seabee service pin. It gives me a thrill to learn, after I had sent it, it's what you've wanted.

Yes, we missed Hawaii by a long shot. But I'm in a safe area. It's not considered a combat zone. No one can remember when the last bombings occurred.

It's amazing how much more organized our outfit has become. The Seabees really can do the job when they want to. When on our own, we're a good outfit to belong to.

In the platoon pictures I sent you, many were absent. The size of platoons vary. Mine has only twenty men, but the standard complement is thirty.

Say listen, your joke about the woman peering through binoculars looking for the equator as she crosses it, came originally from me. Mr. Aldrin, our assistant principal told it. Anyway, I laughed all the more knowing that you forgot where it came from. Expecting a tavern or a Howard Johnson's, I was disappointed when we crossed the equator. There wasn't even a gate.

The more I hear about the college training programs, the better I feel about being where I am. For overseas duty (and everyone will be over sooner or later) I can ask for nothing better. I might add that the chow is even better than it was a week ago. It's excellent—delicious deserts, fresh bread, fine cold drinks, and suitable meats. This past week our living quarters were improved. A tent roof is placed above a framework with a plywood floor that sets off the ground. It's comfortable and roomy with plenty of places to hang incidentals (mirrors etc.). We have nice cots, towels and laundry service. I built a swell desk with shelves (pretty good, if I do say so myself) and covered the top with a sheet of glass that I picked up. For the evening we have a Coleman lantern that shines as bright as an electric light bulb. Soon, I understand, electricity will be installed. At present, I share this quaint and well protected abode with only one other man, a Mr. Baldner (Baldy for short), who is a former professor of languages at Northwestern. We get along swell (he being in his 30s) and enjoy our spacious living, while others sleep five or six to a tent. We rigged a few chairs from canvas and wood, and I must say they are comfortable. Baldy is now sitting in his favorite chair, cleaning his array of pipes and contemplating the building of a pipe stand.

By the time we're done making improvements, we'll have so many gadgets hooked up that it will be just like home sweet home. The place already has a homey atmosphere. I never had a writing desk as good as this one back home, no kidding.

We listen to a radio station that plays popular records over loud speakers that have been installed around the area. I often hear Australia, but never the States. Boy, it's swell. It doesn't seem that we're overseas. Heard Harry Von Zell[2] the other night. We also hear recordings, usually a week or less old, of the most popular programs back home.

Your last V-Mail mentioned "Song of Russia."[3] Got to see it. The battalion has two 35 millimeter projectors, the latest type, remarkable pieces of machinery, with a throw equal to that of a regulation theater. After the projectors are set up next week, we'll be booking all the latest pictures. And you should see our FM radio transceiver that transmits as well as receives.

Of course, in the process of getting settled, I've neglected my studying, but I'm anxious to start. Presently I'm learning radio.

Good going, Ronnie, No D warnings.[4]

Taps is blowing. Time for bed. We sleep under mosquito netting at all times. Early in the morning we need blankets. Whew, I'm all talked out and ready to hit the sack.

Hugh Aaron 802-14-66

3/31/44

Dear Mom,

Hit the old jackpot again today. Listen to this: your letters of Feb. 17 through 19, V-Mails of March 4th and 10th, a letter from Aunt Sadie, another from a school chum, and one from Aunt Henrietta with $3.00 enclosed. Can you beat that? I'm a happy boy after receiving all those letters, eating good chow, and spending the evening writing to you which I love to do. I'm now more comfortable and contented than when I was in the States.

I happened to be reading your letter of Feb. 17 while having a good beef supper (chicken tomorrow) in the chow hall. Enclosed was a clipping concerning "special assignment." When I read the clipping to the fellows, they had a good laugh over it.

I have more money than I know what to do with. The Red Cross furnishes us free toilet soap, shaving cream, toothpaste and toothbrushes, and cigarettes (for those who smoke). We are able to buy beer (Pabst Blue Ribbon) and Coke, but, since I don't care for either, I don't spend anything. However, I plan to accumulate $100 for emergency and keep it inthe battalion safe. It was swell of Henrietta to send me money, but, frankly, it's not worth a dime to me here.

Oh, oh, from your letter I see you still hope that I'll go into the upholstering business after the war. While in college, I'd like to help Dad again. Possibly sales (the outside end), knowing how much he prefers to stay in the shop. What do you think, Dad?

I informed Mr. Smith of my whereabouts. He requested that I do that. Remember? He brought me skiing.

I failed to mention that while aboard ship I got a short clip, similar to a German cut. I did it for comfort, but now it's fully grown and wavy. I won't have my hair cut short again, because it offers protection against the sun, and I'm now accustomed to the heat.

I quote your letter: "Like yourself, (Ronnie) is in a rut --." No longer. That's all changed with me now. I got out of that rut down in Gulfport. I have to make a confession. I never wrote you that I dated a girl in Gulfport. Yes, I dated Ann Linfield. I phoned her, and we met at a USO and talked awhile. Although I intended to take her to a show, I found nothing decent in town. If I had known how to dance I could have had a swell time. But now that I'm way out here such days of pleasure are over for me. I'm content with what I have.

V-Mail 4/2/44

Dear Mom,

On the whole, today was quite pleasant. I spent the morning constructing some stairs for our "castle" and cleaning it up. Had an excellent dinner of creamed chicken, mashed potatoes,string beans, peas, ice cream, fresh buns and lemonade. After dinner, I had a swell time surf bathing with two mates. The water is quite warm and crystal clear. The surf is fair, not as high as on the west coast because of the protection offered by the coral reefs a distance out. I learned surfing, a new sport popular on the west coast and Hawaii. We ride the crest of a wave, sometimes 100 feet or more. Boy oh boy, what fun! We're now planning to build surfboards and ride the waves on them.

Saw some Jap weapons and books and maps this evening. Quite interesting. I hope to secure some Jap invasion money and coins to bring home with me.

P.S. Believe it or not, I've started reading *Gone With the Wind*.[1]

V-Mail 4/3/44

Dear Dad,

Since it rained practically all day, I did very little. Had a little trouble with a Jeep this morning. After taking the Jeep to a stream to wash, I drove it into the stream as we always do. But this time the bottom was sandy, and it got stuck. I put her in four wheel drive, but no go. Result: we had to be towed out by a winch. I then went farther down the road in search of a better spot. Instead, we ended up on the beach, so backed the contraption into the ocean and had a pretty good time washing it.

I'm quite involved with reading *Gone With The Wind*. I find it excellent entertainment and can't let the book alone. I expect to resume the correspondence course as soon as my job settles down. I'm still doing a lot of running around.

The mud here is even worse than the Mississippi stuff. It's slimy, sticky, disastrously slippery, and deep. I say disastrous because many a man has taken a spill in the cursed slime.

Good night. Will be back tomorrow.

V-Mail 4/4/44

Dear Folks,

Observe today's date: all fours. The main purpose of this letter is a request. Send me a good face cloth, a bottle of vitamin B complex pills, and a bottle of Vitamin A pills. These will be instrumental in keeping me in good condition. Our food is not rich in vitamins.

I'm quite surprised to hear about Mr. Edinburg.[1] How is his son doing?[2] Do you mean to say that Joe Ducharme died? [from the brain tumor mentioned earlier] Already, I can see that things are changing and will be changed more by the time I return.

First issue of our newspaper, *The Scarifier*, came out today. I'll try to send it home. How about sending a *Gazette* once in a while? Even one a month old is better than nothing.

I'm still waiting for your letter informing me that you've received my first letter from overseas.

V-Mail 4/5/44

[A drawing of a tent amid palm trees under which are the words in fancy script:]

EASTER GREETINGS
From Somewhere in New Guinea

This drawing is a marvelous representation of the sort of tent I'm living in right now. As in the drawing, our tents are situated under palm trees.

4/5/44

Dear Mom,

The fellows are raving about a big 3 1/2 hour army show performed last night. The talent came fresh from the States, consisting of actors from Club Matinee and Ben Bernie's orchestra. Sorry I missed it, but I expect to see many shows in the future. Frankly, my only desire is to write and read during my spare time. After my relatively "wild" life in Hollywood, I want to settle down and take it easy. I find reading a tremendous lift, especially when such fine literature is on hand at the Red Cross.

I'm filling out an application to join the Veterans of Foreign Wars. It's a federal institution[1] and has been fighting for servicemen's benefits. I feel it's well to join.

Just heard an announcement regarding a Passover[2] supper on April 7 at 7:00 PM. Most assuredly I'm going.

Enclosed are three Jap coins, invasion money. It's only made of aluminum, but quite interesting. It's said that the Japs figured that Australia and America were right over the hill. When they were being hacked down, they clutched the money with all their might and main. I have quite a bit of it so will send more home in the future. Many of the fellows are making bracelets for their wives and girl friends, but, not being adept at such things, I'm sure the unadulterated money will suffice.

My job is going well, although not everything about it is settled yet. I'll gradually acquaint myself with what has to be done.

On the average, letters arrive twice each week and already I can't wait to receive more. I'm a glutton for letters. This week twelve in two days aren't enough.

To tell the truth, I'm running out of material, so am anxious for your questions to replenish my supply of gossip.

Love to you, Dad and Ronnie, Hughie (the coin collector)

V-Mail 4/6/44

Dear Mom,

Quite a tragedy, the death of the Sherman boy.[1]

Just returned from visiting the various army and navy bases to find replacement parts for our radios. Such stuff is hard to find out here.

I'm going to review my French with George Chast,[2] a former professor of French and Spanish. It would be well to keep up with my languages.

I awoke this morning to find coffee rolls on our desk. A baker friend[3] leaves them occasionally. In return I do him a few favors.

I'm writing this letter earler than usual, 5:30. Now it's time for chow, and you know me: I gotta eat. Be back tomorrow.

By the way, at Hueneme, we were secured for only four days. It's a coincidence that I called you the very day that we left the base.

How's your throat, Mom? Speaking of colds, I don't know what a cold is. Rain, wind, drafts, etc. have no effect on me. Living in the fresh air and sunshine keeps me pretty well tuned up.

Mom, I'd call your letter of March 4 BEAUTIFUL. It's a letter I'll never forget and always treasure. I've put aside certain letters written by each of you that express what's in your hearts, and those I read and reread. I only wish I could express myself as well.

Your most recent letters have been V-Mail. Fine. Airmail provides a slight personal touch, so use that too. Remember never use regular mail.

Wish Harold Greenberg[4] luck. Let me know what branch of the army he gets into. Haven't heard from Johnson since I've been over. Wrote him a brief V-Mail note. Please tell Sadie and all the relatives to use V-Mail or airmail.

Last Sunday was quite a day. I watched a real native festival sponsored by the British and Australians. There were some British women on a raised platform watching the proceedings. First women I've seen on the island. Going through a weird set of rituals, the natives danced and banged their drums. Their faces were painted and their bodies adorned with long green grass and cockatoo feathers and what not. They ran in circles all afternoon chanting.

These natives looked unclean, and they are probably diseased. They wear a short scarf across their loins and their women (their slaves) wear just as little, with a child on one breast and a pig on the other. They mar all their features, cut off the edges of their ears and insert earrings in the portion that remains. Most of the men wear a steel band around their biceps. The British keep them happy by giving them gifts of sugar and salt.

I witnessed two wild boars being sacrificed. I watched from the time they tied the wriggling bodies to long poles, then knocked them senseless in the snouts with a big hammer, to the time of the final barbecue. Sometimes they are known to cook the boars alive. They are unsanitary in the butchering; when cutting up (dexterously) the carcass, they throw the meat on the ground. But the native butcher certainly knows his stuff. It's the first time I ever saw the entrails of an animal.

I was a member of a party that accompanied a naval officer from our battalion to the festival. Because the officer was present, an Australian major general showed us around the native encampment. It's a sight I'll probably never have the opportunity to see again.

Tomorrow being Sunday, I'll write more. And tomorrow I plan to spend most of the day making gadgets for our little "castle." So until tomorrow, adios and Love to the three of you, Hughie, the desk builder

Easter Sunday eve April 9, 1944
(This letter could go on forever.)

Dear Dad,

Today is that day when everyone dresses chic, in a zoot suit[1] and new hat, and struts down the main avenue showing off the apparel. But for me, this day, this year, means just the opposite and has proved to be one of the most spectacular days of my life.

I went on what might best be called a "photographic excursion." We were a party of nine that left camp at 8:00 AM. Transportation: one Jeep and one weapons carrier. Destination: S------. Purpose: to photograph subjects of interest, both still pictures and movies, and boy, we did.

Our preparations and supplies were as follows: a big box of ham (not kosher,[2] I know) and cheese sandwiches, two carbines and two forty-five automatic pistols, the radio transmitter and receiver to maintain contact with our base, two still cameras and one motion picture camera, chains (skid) on all four wheels of both vehicles, and an extra five gallon can of gasoline, and oh, yes, cigarettes and knives for trading with the natives.

So after everything was satisfactorally prepared, we set out, four in the Jeep and five in the weapons carrier. After seeing our special pass issued by Base Headquarters, the guard at the entrance to the trail to S------ admitted us.

Before continuing, I want to mention the conditions imposed upon us as a result of the weather. It has been raining on and off for the past three days. Now out here the rain doesn't sink into the ground the way it does back home, due to an underlying coral formation. Instead a quagmire of sucking, slimy mud forms, coating the dirt road surface. The trail we had to travel was only wide enough for one vehicle to pass. Furthermore we had to ascend a mountain range from sea level to 2600 feet where S---- is located.

Getting back to the story, we encountered our first problem when a steep incline coated with slippery mud confronted us. The Jeep, blessed thing, admirably made it wearing skid chains and in four wheel drive. We found we had to use both drives for the entire trip. But the weapons carrier, after churning chunks of mud as it crept up the incline, fell against an embankment and became stuck. After the weapons carrier's several attempts to extricate itself failed, we backed the Jeep up to it, hooked a chain on to it from the Jeep's winch, and let her rip. As the wheels of the weapons carrier spun to beat the band, while the Jeep churned, the weapons carrier gradually crawled out of the ditch and both vehicles worked their way on up to the summit. This was only a sample of the trouble that was to come.

The tropical sun beat down so, that, when we stopped, the jungle seemed to seethe. It was virtually steaming. Flecks of mud, thrown off by the wheels, mixed with perspiration, covered our faces. We all looked far from handsome.

Our company consisted of Al Malter, the radio man; a chief petty officer, a corpsman (first aid man); the chief in charge of communications and myself, who operated the radio at intervals. So, you see, we were capable men.

We wound through the jungle at a snail's pace, twisting, turning, bogging down, slewing and churning. Man oh man, what a ride. As the Jeep passed over unavoidable holes a foot or more deep, it was thrown into the air and came down with the full force of its weight. (I sat in the back seat with the transmitter). No doubt, you've seen cartoons of Jeeps virtually flying over bumps and holes. Well, believe it or not, we were similarly in the air three quarters of the time. And oh, Papa, my rear end. I won't sit down for a week. Take it back: two weeks.

Occasionally we ran into a corduroy road consisting of logs laid close together across its width. They form a good foundation in the mud. You can imagine what it's like to race a car across logs. Let me tell you, I wish it were only my imagination, but my backside reminds me that it was reality. Riding over the corduroy road, while easier for the wheels of the vehicles to grip the road surface, was rougher even than the dirt road on which the oozing mud often allowed the wheels to sink in gradually.

But, of course, we only ran into intermittent intervals of corduroy. By the way, this was the first corduroy road I've ever seen. The entire trail is probably, and will remain, one of the most interesting and important undertakings of the New Guinea campaign. Of course, the war has progressed forward and the S---- trail no longer has its former significance. It was the site of the most decisive battles in New Guinea. Japanese ambushes and machine gun nests lay in wait for the Aussies, as they pushed forward. At certain points, knolls, bridges, and gulches, there were raging battles. We stopped often to examine the battle remains, ingenious fox holes where the Japs were dug in, dugouts and machine gun emplacements. The Japs lived like filthy pigs, evidenced by the holes. Wonderful records have been kept of the whole campaign that we had read about in the newspapers, not so long ago. Clearly painted signs had been erected at each point where an action took place so that we actually felt like tourists.

Onward we pushed toward our mission, only stopping for brief rests. (Not so much for us but for our weary engines). We took pictures along the route, stills of the whole gang in tropical dress sitting in our conveyances, and action shots showing the difficulties we had to endure as we wound up the desolate trail. Boy, will these be spectacular to see when I get home.

Soon we reached an army listening post supported by a handful of men. Having not seen the States for 2 1/2 years, they were happy to see us and very pleasant. During their combing the countryside for snipers months before, they had collected many articles of interest such as Jap scabards and rifles. To top it off, having a supply of Jap ammunition, they took pot shots with their Jap weapons. I will say that the Jap rifle was well-constructed and fired accurately. I also fired one of the Aussie rifles and found that it kicked like a mule, worse than my own rifle.

Because the four wheel drive weapons carrier is as big as a one ton truck and was retarding our progress by constantly getting stuck, we were compelled to leave it behind at the post. The Jeep, however, was designed to hold four men comfortably, but nine men, no. Since everyone was determined to continue on, each man found a spot: one sat on the hood, one squeezed in between the two front seats, and the other three sat with their buttoxes emplaced at the gunwhales in the rear, their feet dangling in the air. "Three Men on a Horse"[3] or "Nine

Men on a Jeep," both seem like a miracle to perform, but "we dood it,"⁴ and how we dood it.

The jungle appears nothing short of fantastic to a boy like me who hails from the gentle slopes of New England. The trees, mahogany, ebony, and teak, with huge, gnarled trunks covered with mysterious thick vines hanging down from the limbs like boa constrictors, tower over everything. Below these were all types of palm trees growing at random, including wild banana and pineapple trees (the first time I've ever seen them in their habitat) that thrived in the wilderness among the weeds which were eight or more feet high. I have never seen such a variety of vegetation in all my life, so dense that the eye could only penetrate a few feet into the jungle on both sides of the road. There was also an enormous variety of species of beautiful flowers, gorgeous butterflies and birds. I'm not sorry to say that we saw no animals.

On and off, on and off, our crowd stumbled from the Jeep as time after time she sank into the quagmire. Less weight on board actually gave it more traction when she sank into the mud. I say in all truthfullness that we passed through mud up to the hubcaps, up to the seats, and up to the hood. That Jeep is a miracle machine. It can't be stopped. Water can't stop it, mud can't stop it, and man can't stop it. Wouldn't you call that a miracle?

Finally we reached a native village. Since it's almost time to go to bed, I'll continue tomorrow and leave you in suspense. So solly. Excuse pleese. Love to the three of you, Hughie (the explorer)

4/10/44

Dear Mom,

(Do not read before letter of the 9th.)

Before continuing yesterday's account of my journey, I'll answer your letter of Feb. 25th which just arrived.

I wrapped the slide rule in wood so that it wouldn't break. Cardboard would never have done. What do you think of the rule?

Has Ronnie started with girls yet?

I see you still don't understand how I managed to make the phone call to you. Here it is: I went to sleep at 8:00 PM, awoke of my own accord about 2:30 or 3:00, got dressed, walked to the other end of the base where the telephone hut was situated, called after waiting an hour, walked back to my barracks and went to bed again and slept until 7:30. Understand now? Good!

On occasion a *Gazette* would be swell. You are allowed to send newspapers to me and packages within a certain size without my request. I'll get more information on this for you. Remember you are allowed to do what I say. Pay no attention to what others say. Various overseas areas have different policies. Now for the story.

Remember, we stopped at a native village. As we drove the Jeep right into its center, the women scampered into their thatched shelters as the men and children crowded around us. They were all smiles. Our tall, six-foot-three-inch, chief warrant officer requested to see Number One Man. Of course, Number One Man refers to the chief of the tribe. Since a few of the natives understood him, Number One Man, wearing the familiar "towel" around his waist and a hat that looked like a Pullman porter's cap that distinguished him from the rest, stepped forward. He spoke English fairly well so we told him "We want to make picture." While this conversation went on, we gave the kids cigarettes which they smoked like veterans. Number One Man was given a package of Twenty Grands, the cheapest cigarettes the battalion had. One youngster, about eight years old, taking a liking to me and smiling whenever I'd look at him, clung to the side of my trousers so as not to lose me. The natives are very human. Number One Man carries a definite air of responsibility about himself and the older men looked quite distinguished. The features of the children are clean cut; none are ugly. As a matter of fact, I found myself liking them, for they acted just like American children.

One kid kept asking for "masses, masses," until I finally caught on that he wanted matches for his cigarettes. Soon we asked that the Marys (women) come out of the huts so that we could take pictures. Women are the men's slaves. When we offered the women cigarettes, the men wouldn't allow them to take any. The women constantly stood in the background, holding their babies. One girl, no older than fourteen or fifteen, had a child. The women were quite modest, covering their breasts, which is unusual for the natives here. Evidently the missionaries[1] had influenced this tribe.

After we took many still and motion pictures of all of us with the natives, [See photograph below] we turned on our radio receiver. The natives mumbled among themselves as the voice from the box aroused their curiosity. Contacting our base operator, we told him that Number One Man would speak. After we put him on, he began a spiel in his own language. The fellow at the other end answered that, "It sounded good, damn good, but what the hell did he say?" When the natives heard "good" emanate from the speaker, they burst out laughing and were delighted that the "voice in the box" liked what Number One Man had said. And the kids, dancing up and down with glee, got a great kick out of it.

One of our boys offered a jackknife for a comb that one of the natives had in his hair. After that transaction, the other natives came towards him clamoring "Me got comb too." But we had no more knives and had a devil of a time convincing them. These natives are far more intelligent than I had thought they were.

Then all nine of us continued on our way, encountering more ditches and viewing more battle sites. At some of the sites, the trees were blown to bits by machine gun bullets and mortar fire, at others the land was just laid waste. Signs saying "At this point (so many) Japs were killed in ambush," or that "Company (so and so) encountered heavy opposition," and a battle raged. Along the way tops of trees had been blown off, shrapnel visibly embedded in their trunks and limbs. Quite a sight.

After running into ditches that seemed impossible to cross, I learned that the Jeep was amphibious. At times the mud was so deep that it came up onto our seats. When we approached a ditch, we dashed into it head on at high speed and gathered enough momentum to push us through the mud with minimal skidding. Many's the time I bounced into the air and bounded right back down onto my seat with a thud. At each encounter with a hole, I tensed myself, gritted my teeth and with a wild yelp, "Whoopee," was able to make the ditch without getting hurt. As a matter of fact, I had the time of my life. All of us were laughing at our silly expressions. I wish I could describe some of them and remember the crazy remarks. You would die laughing. By then, we were covered with mud, but what the hell, we didn't care.

By the way, we had eaten dinner back at the army outpost, with one bottle of Pabst Blue Ribbon beer for each person. I drank water. Each man brought a full canteen of water, because the mountain streams couldn't be trusted.

Soon we reached a point where the Jeep could go no farther so we continued on foot, carrying cameras and guns and leaving the transmitter behind. While on the foot trail, we saw more fox holes and ambush locations, examining them closely. The Japs dug right under trees, covering their holes with twigs and branches so that the holes couldn't be distinguished from the tree trunks. Remarkable, truly remarkable. We found live Jap mortar shells with their detonators still untouched. Not wishing to invite disaster, we left them alone. I give the Japs credit for knowing how to dig in. After walking beside chasms thousands of feet deep along a mile or so of trail on which the mud almost sucked off our high shoes at each step, we finally reached S----.

Having once been a German mission, the place was now in ruins and desolate. This had been a Japanese stronghold. The few buildings that were left standing were riddled through with bullets; every wall was like a sieve such that the buildings seemed ready to crumble. Three hundred Japs died here.

We found a shed that was used as an Aussie arsenal, still full of live ammunition, unfired hand grenades and live shells, but we kept away from that stuff. Inside a schoolhouse the children's desks were torn apart. S—— sets on a bare hill 2600 feet high. The view made me gasp. Everything was so vast. Jungle, jungle everywhere. On entering the blacksmith shop, we found tools that were made in London. We located a kitchen and other utility structures. All the furniture was made of mahogany and teak. We visited every building, searching for things of interest. I found a Jap gas mask and scabard case.

We took many pictures among the ruins. We photographed the enormous bomb craters sprinkled throughout the area, and a bomb that hadn't yet gone off. Wait 'til you see those pictures, boy oh boy. We found an old cemetery in which German words and names were inscribed on beautiful marble slabs, some dated 1902 and 1908. One grave was marked by a wooden cross dated 1936. There was also a church, or what was left of it, in which only the pulpit remained standing. The natives had made it out of teak and decorated it with beautiful red and blue carvings of various figures. As four natives with packs passed by, I got them to pose beside the pulpit and I snapped their picture.

We spent several hours, our curiosity keen, exploring the remains and not altering them. I'll send you a page from the German primer that I found in the ruined school house that had been used as a barricade.

Heading back on the treacherous trail, we met the same old bumps and ditches, and arrived at our base at 6:00, filthy and weary. A good hot shower did wonders for me. I was able to write yesterday's letter before going to bed early that night.

Next Sunday I expect to go on another trip, this time in a different direction. Can't wait to get going.

I'm having as much fun sightseeing here as I did back in Hollywood, no kidding. I'm see a lot, including many things that I can't tell you about. I'll fill in S—— when I get home.

Gone with the Wind has captivated me so that I can't leave it alone. I'm going to read it after I write.

Love to all of you, Hughie (the trailblazer)

[S—— is the German missionary village known as Satelberg.]

V-Mail 4/14/44

Dear Mom,

The technical work is just beginning now that most of the communications equipment has been set up. I have been designated the general utility man, learning and doing many things while striking for a rate. I'm very much satisfied with what I'm doing.

I spend most of my leisure time reading which I do enjoy. I have no desire to go to the swell movies that are shown here because after work I'm too tired. I like being tired; I sleep like a top and feel fine.

My working hours aren't bad: 8:00 AM to 11:30 and 1:30 PM to 5:00. After work I shower, change clothes, eat at 5:30 then for the rest of the evening settle down reading and writing and talking. I'm truly leading as settled and contented a life as I had back home.

Monday 8:00 PM 4/17/44

Dear Folks,

I haven't written for several days for lackof subject matter. Each day I expect that a letter will come, but no, nothing. So I've lost patience, and, in spite of no letters, I must write.

In the near future, yes in the very near future, you'll not receive any letters from me. We will be so desperately busy that none of us, especially those in communications, will have time to write. Take my word for it though, everything is fine, fine and dandy, It's just that we have a raft of work. The lapse will be brief though, and I shall be writing again, describing and philosophizing with you.

Lately I've taken to some entertainment. Last night I saw "It Began with Eve"[1] with Deanna Durbin and Charles Laughton[2] plus an entertaining companion feature. I enjoyed it tremendously, more than usual, as this is the first show I've seen in more than two months. We have a swell outdoor amphitheater equipped with two thirty-five millimeter projectors. The pictures are clear and the sound excellent. Since a good friend[3] is the operator, I was able to watch the show from the projection booth. He explained how the intricate machines work—very interesting.

The operator, about twenty-three years old, as clean-cut a young fellow as I've ever met, is one of my best friends. We've been companions for about five months now, frequently journeying to Hollywood together. He hails from Evans City, Pa, near Pittsburgh. Having no father, he supports a mother, a sister about my age, and a brother. I may have mentioned him before. He is madly in love with a girl back home, and, believe it or not, reads me her letters and seeks my opinions. Quite odd, considering how inexperienced I am when it comes to the opposite sex.

Henry Wolf, the Jewish fellow from Philly, is still one of my finest companions. Lately, we have been having evening chats. After I return home I have dozens of invitations from across the nation. Friends from Hollywood and California always remind me, "When you come out here, we're glad to have you." But after I'm home, I won't want to travel for many, many years. I've had my share of seeing the world already, and I have yet more to see before this is over.

I took my electric razor apart the other day, oiled it with 3-in-One, checked the brushes, and oiled the heads. Thanks to Dad, I know how to care for it; it runs like a charm. Although I should shave every other day now, out here I let it go to once every three or four days.

I was quite thrilled Saturday night and Sunday afternoon to hear San Francisco over the high frequency receiver headphones. Richard Crooks⁴ sang. I listened to a symphonic program, and I just missed Bob Hope. Quite a thrill. We get Tokyo, Berlin and South America quite well.

I'm still engrossed in *GWTW*. Considering that I read only an hour or two a day, it will take some time to finish it. I've begun French lessons under the guidance of a most diligent and patient teacher: George Chast, another Jewish fellow.

I've not been able to exercise and keep myself in as top physical condition as I had anticipated. The reason: lack of time. However, in the coming months I should have less to do, so I'll be able to devote some time each day to exercising. Still, I feel better than when I was home.

The fellows often get to talking about home, about life in the States, as if the past were a dream, only a vision. And my mind wanders sentimentally back to past instances which, at the time, seemed so insignificant. Yet, I confess, I enjoy, inexplicably, my present experience. Its uncertainty thrills me. Yet the anticipation of returning someday and seeing Mom all powdered and dressed up just for me, of Dad cracking witty jokes, and Ronnie whistling down the walk as he comes to dinner, the anticipation of witnessing these things again is something that, how should I say it, urges me on. The struggle seems so enormous out here, with no end in sight, yet we all dream of that momentous day. For me that day will be long in coming. It will cover an enormous span of my life, a greater fraction than for most, since I haven't lived very long. When we come here and fight and build, we forget the significance of our cause and, instead, think only of home. That's what we're fighting for, not the principles that the demagogues so exuberantly shout. Home represents everything for us, including what they are trying to say.

By no means am I alone thinking such thoughts. Everyone here thinks alike on this subject. Some ask, "what is home?" We've all heard high sounding and sentimental definitions, but recently I heard a mate define it better than anyone. Home is not a house with furniture, or a familiar landscape. Home is where your friends are, where those you love, those nearest you, those who have a personal interest in your welfare and safety, even mere acquaintances, are. Without these people the place in which you live cannot be home. Isn't that true? The proof is evident when you move from one locality to another. How miserable and desolate you feel when you leave your old friends and have few new ones. It's even worse when you leave your loved ones.

I've been rambling heedless of the fact that you may not understand what on earth I'm saying. I'm sure you will, but only those having the experience can truly know the feelings I describe.

I'll make every sincere attempt to write you as often as possible, and after I've completed my task I'll be writing as loyally as before. Keep your chins up.

Tuesday April 25, 1944

Dear Mom,

Many days have passed since I last wrote, and from my last letter you know why. In spite of being tremendously busy, I've been given some personal time. After a week without letters, seven blessed ones arrived yesterday from home. I'm now overflowing with enthusiasm; I just have to write. However, expect lapses in my letters in the near future. Please believe me, I'll have good reason for not writing.

I'll answer your letters in chronological order.

Realizing that you don't like V-Mail I shall use air mail as much as possible. I prefer air mail myself. Never use regular mail.

The supper you served Anna, James,[1] and Harry[2] on Saturday night March 4th had me salivating. Let's see, I was in New Caledonia that day.

I received the money from Yetta, you know, but truthfully, I have more than I'll ever need.

Now two in our family have visited New Orleans recently. Most likely Ed[3] vividly described the place. I had passed by Armands, but didn't eat there because of its stupendous prices. I wish I could have afforded it, but I ate in an equally famous, though less expensive, French restaurant.

I've received letters asking for my photo. All I can say is "It's out of my hands," and I'm glad. It's your problem now. Folks, you asked for it. I'm so glad your pleased with it, though.

Your letter of March 21st.

While you write of a blizzard, and I'm settled in hot New Guinea, it seems that you are in another world. Lucky boy, Bob, getting a twenty day furlough. Speaking of furloughs, I'm optimistic about the future. Here's the story. The war in the Pacific is progressing well, and from what I see and hear, we'll be home sooner than we expected. Understand, of course, that this is merely my opinion. There is still much to be done, but mark my words, plenty will be happening. I have no idea when and how. Furthermore the Seabee units are being rotated better than any others. Our stays here are shorter than others'. You'll get that second telephone call yet.

My letter that was mailed from New Caledonia was written on the high seas a week earlier. I could picture your reaction when you received it. While writing this I'm listening to a radio broadcasting popular tunes: "Night and Day,"[4] "A Pretty Girl Is Like a Melody,"[5] "Let's Get Lost,"[6] etc. Makes me darn near homesick. How I love to listen to the radio out here.

My first letter was censored so much because I wasn't sure what I was allowed to write. Your letters are not censored.

I've answered Dad's letter of March 23rd by a previous letter.

Letter of March 28th.

So glad to hear that you've recovered from your brief illness. That's what I like to hear. It seems you folks have been visiting the relatives in Boston often the past month. Again, I see, Dad is bringing Lil and Eva[7] with you. Tell Bobbie to look up Al Barios,[8] if he can. No doubt, he's in the Middle West training to be a pilot. I'll write [Uncle] Bill at the first opportunity.

I can't remember the name of the sailor from the crew aboard ship. We were supposed to meet before I debarked, but in the rush we never got together to exchange addresses. No need to continue writing my serial number after my name.

Letter of March 31st.

See, didn't I tell you that the navy is best? Bill can now vouch for that. After learning about other outfits, I'll take the navy and the Seabees any time. I consider myself lucky to be in the Seabees. We do a better job than any of them and command the most respect.

Keep telling me about the movies you see. I'd like to know about the latest pictures. I'll probably have a chance to see them a month or so later.

Letter of April 1st.

To answer your question, "Is there anything you want?" my answer is, some Neatsfoot oil, leather preserver or saddle soap so that I can keep my shoes and other things made of leather from mildewing. The dampness is terrible here. I wrap my blues in cellophane, keep my shoes polished, whether I wear them or not, and continually air out my bedding and other clothes. In addition to my white navy blankets I have a new army blanket that's softer and finer than the one back home. I use the army blanket in my pack. The navy blankets are beautiful. I'll be taking these home with me plus a pile more clothes than I had in the States. I also have a hammock. We work in army summer suntans, the same worn in the States. They are comfortable, cool and dressy.

Letter of April 5th.

Now you know I'm in New Guinea. I'm at an enormous advance base. There are no training bases overseas. We don't expect to remain here very long. Yes, there's much fighting still going on in New Guinea, but I'm seeing none of it.

The area is controlled by the British so that the natives speak a form of pidgin English, not French. We're called Americanas. When I say I'm enjoying myself, I'm not kidding. It's not gay[9] and glamorous like Hollywood, but I find everything that's happening thrilling. I haven't deceived nor will I deceive you. I tell you nothing but the truth, although I can't tell all. I'm not allowed to write about many things, but when I say everything is fine, it's entirely true.

I'm not affected by the climate and my health is excellent. What more could I ask for? I'm contented with my job and this outfit. I live only for the day that I can come back to you. After I'm home I can tell you more. Of course, you must know that war isn't fun. Being used to all sorts of conditions, I'm easily satisfied.

I've not heard from Johnson Fulgoni for some time, so I sent a letter to his home in Medford.[10] In fact, you are the only folks I've heard from, but I'm satisfied. You are all that counts.

I'm enclosing some pictures that were taken on my trip to S----. I'll comment on them once I'm home. For military reasons I'm unable to send other pictures that I've taken. They show signs, etc.

The rainy season has begun; it rains almost daily, and right now it's pouring, but it doesn't bother me. It makes the flowers grow. I intend to subscribe to the overseas edition of *Time* magazine. It's excellent. How about sending me an occasional *Gazette*? Yesterday, I received the Kiwanis[11] paper which I enjoy, although it's quite condensed. The other fellows from Worcester receive it too.

That about answers your seven letters. Don't be afraid to inquire about things that interest you. It will give me more to write about. I can say quite a lot despite the restrictions. I prefer that you don't know where I am. I got a real scare aboard ship when it was reported over the radio that the Japs had sunk us. You may have heard it and worried needlessly. Fortunately, the false news never reached the States. Now you know why it's best that you not know where I am. Believe in me; I can take pretty good care of myself now.

I'm listening to "No Love, No Nothin'"[12] over the radio. I hear it's a top tune back home. Good night all.

P.S. Frankie Swoonatra is singing now.

Wednesday April 26, 1944

Dear Mom,

Your letter written the day after Passover arrived today. I can remember that very evening here. It was unique, as you know from an earlier letter. It would have been fun to be with you and see everybody again.

Before I left the States, I saw "Broadway Rhythm" alone. Gloria DeHaven's okay, huh. I enjoyed the picture.

The rain has stopped, and now it's beautiful but hot. I'm incessantly busy, though I'm getting plenty of sleep. I'm determined to get a rating in a month or two.

Fortunately, we hear the news. I know what's going on in the world and out here. Surprisingly, things are reported weeks after we've learned about them. Rumors, which travel fast, often turn out to be true.

Life is humdrum which leaves me with little to write. I anxiously await your comments on the photos.

My plans for what I will do after I'm permanently home are developing. I think of such things more often now because I'm nearer home in terms of time than I've been in eight and one half months. My lust for learning continues strong, and college is certain. I'll not be happy otherwise.

From what I see, education is all important, even in military life. I'm optimistic about the future for all of us. That feeling makes me a contented boy no matter what I have to face here. I fully realize now that this experience has done me good. If many of my flaws are still the same, at least I recognize them now.

I've planned my homecoming to the extent that I've taken into consideration how I'll travel and with whom. Frisco will probably be my home port. Isn't it strange that, having just arrived here, I think of returning? Time is virtually slipping under my heels. A month seems like a week. At this rate, I should be home in less than twelve weeks. I hope time will continue to pass as it has. A year no longer seems a long time anymore. For the present, that's the way I want it.

I can say little about our activities here for obvious reasons. Don't expect much information from me for quite a while. Don't try to guess where I am. It will only confuse you all the more. Watch for my key words "All is well" and remain free of worry. I'll never stoop to deceiving you.

Since you've mentioned that I'm due a letter from Dad, my anticipation is aroused. Come on, letter.

Love to you, Dad and Ronnie, Hughie (the jungle jolly jerk)

May 2, 1945

Dear Mom,

It's seems like an age since I last wrote you, and I suppose it is, but for a very important reason which I can't reveal. Please accept this excuse, and I will explain in weeks or months to come.

I've received scores of letters from you: today four, the latest dated April 13. You receive my mail sooner than I receive yours.

I've had a few mishaps lately. I've lost my treasured pen, not that it was valuable, but I liked it. Luckily I had brought a spare one with me from California. I had kept the old one for years. I'd appreciate your sending me a cheap pen as a spare. Another loss: my right eyeglass cracked while lifting a cot. I can still see quite well, but I prefer to send it home to be replaced as soon as possible—and that isn't too soon. When I retrieved my spare glasses from its case, lo and behold I found the left lens cracked. I can get along with it fairly well. As a matter of fact, I don't wear glasses most of the time because of the heat, and I get along fine.

In spite of this bad luck, I still consider myself lucky. My health is perfect; I feel swell, and the work is pleasant.

According to your April 3rd letter, I see that you heard over the radio that we see movies before you do. Not true. I haven't seen any less than two or three months old.

Referring to your April 6th letter, secure a good map of the S.W. Pacific and locate Milne Bay where we put in. Don't worry, I take my Atabrine[1] daily. How in the world did Dad rate a B[2] gas card?

I'm not allowed to tell you what our battalion is doing, but I can tell you about my personal duties and no more. Have patience.

Burton Chase[3] is making quite a name for himself as a crap shooting fighting Marine. Let him make $900 his way; I'll do better the honest way. I don't care for gambling, even when I hear of the big stakes being won.

Most of my letters are uncut because I keep posted on what I can and cannot say.

Your letter of April 11.

I haven't heard from Johnson and don't know why. He had insisted that we correspond while I was overseas.

My regular job isn't difficult, and we are kept busy which I like. Currently I'm gradually learning things, and, after we get settled, I'll be learning more rapidly. But God only knows when we'll be settled. I'm still working under Al Malter.

[Cousin] Bobby has really been having a gala time alright, alright. I had enough night life and entertainment in Hollywood. I'm not crazy about such things. If I know Bob, he's going nuts over it. Too bad he couldn't have been in my place in Hollywood. A person that drinks etc. can really enjoy that town.

I've had many opportunities to send home a recording of my voice, but, since you don't have a phonograph, I ignored them. I'm sorry now, for your sake, that I didn't.

Send airmail stamps if you wish, but make sure you enclose them in waxed paper, as the tropical climate makes them stick together. I can't buy all the stamps I need here.

As much as I like candy and cakes, I must caution you not to send them. If they don't get crushed en route, the tropics will ruin them by the time they arrive. Furthermore, I can get along very well without goodies.

Don't worry about how much money I have. I spend less than thirty cents a week. For most, smokes are the biggest expense, but not an expense for me. I may buy an additional set of underwear or some soap and toothpaste.

I need a lot of clothes here, because, due to so much sweating, I must change daily. I have six work trousers (two army suntans), and five army and navy shirts which I wear only in the evening. I find taking a salt tablet daily helps.

I had to laugh when you ask how the natives dress. You should ask, what don't they wear? The pictures will provide you the answer.

Letter of April 13.

I think it would be better to let Ronnie go to camp rather than stay at home. Let him learn to be on his own. He should try for junior counselor.

I hadn't realized that Mrs. Rome[4] is so concerned over my welfare. Do you suggest that I write her? I fear I'll then get a letter from Harriet[5] and that I don't want. Say, do you ever hear from Mrs. Lynn?[6] How is Harold Greenberg?

After learning that my cable, which cost me forty cents, didn't go through, I got my money back.

I saw the picture "Rationing" back in the States.

One of your recent letters mentioned that you heard the Seabees were being merged into the army. Now I'm glad to be overseas. I wouldn't want to be in the army for anything. After I told the fellows about it, they have no wish to return, for fear of being transferred. All of us are happy to be in the Seabees.

As you may have suspected from my many doubtful statements and inconsistencies, something is up. Nothing to worry about, though, because it will be better, believe me. Just wait.

I've now covered your four letters. Frankly, I thought you'd have more questions. I guess my letters are doing a pretty good job anticipating your questions.

There's been quite a bit of war news about New Guinea lately. Everything is coming along quite well. Although we aren't in on it, we are affected by it.

I went swimming in a stream the other day and had a swell time. It was welcome relief from the hot day.

The nights are becoming cooler, and it's now raining more often than when we arrived. At the beginning we worked seven days a week, and, as we got more settled, we were given Sundays off.

I'll do my best to write tomorrow, but I don't know for sure whether I will then or a month from now. I mean it when I say don't worry as everything is ALRIGHT.

P.S. Will you send me a subscription to *Time*?

V-Mail 5/3/44

Dear Mom,

Things are back to a dull routine, and I have plenty of time to myself.

I have decided to send my glasses home one pair at a time to be fixed. If I had a prescription it could be done here, but even then it would take an age.

Sorry to disappoint you with such a short letter, but there isn't much to talk about today.

May 4, 1944

Dear Mom,

Good old Mass. was well represented today with letters from Anna, Yetta, and home. I get mail almost daily, and rarely less than three at a time. There's no telling when a ship or plane will come in with the mail, but lately it seems to be coming in amazingly regularly.

After your letter of the 17th, so chock full of news, here comes your Seabee Aaron's daily comment. I can't get over how frequently you visit Boston, more often than when I was at home.

I don't wear glasses virtually all the time now. I can't stand them since I sweat so much.

[Uncle] Bill deserves to be a PH M 1/c due to his good education. He's sure to rise fast in the ranks. Men with experience are advanced, even in boot. I'm glad he likes the navy after being in the army. I like it too.

Henrietta is under the impression that I'm allowed to send only one letter a day. Okay, I'll go along, but you may inform my relatives that I can send as many as I wish. She is asking me to send answers to her questions to you for relaying to her. I can understand why you told her that; however, I now have the time to write as much as I want. See what you started. Watch saying those untruths, for I may write something not consistent with what you say. So tell the truth or say nothing. Don't ever exaggerate. Yep, I'm scolding you.

I wrote to Uncle Louie, or rather [Cousin] Evelyn,[1] a long time ago, but received no answer. How is Louie?

Is your new hat describable? Women's hats fascinate me; they stimulate my imagination. When it comes to hats, I bet the native women here beat you women back home.

By any chance is Burton Chase considered Worcester's boy wonder? He reminds me of Al Malter, who, after finding an old school desk in a German mission in the jungle, sent it to his girlfriend in Frisco. By the way, he has asked me to write her, so I did. God only knows what her reply will be.

I had to laugh over your concern when I went bathing directly after eating. Just like a mother. Don't worry, Mom. I waited a good two hours. Don't you realize that I've been on my own for almost eleven months? You're a card. Hey, Dad, tell her how you were at my age, what you did. Thanks to your upbringing, I do things in moderation and sensibly.

You don't understand why I'm enjoying *Gone with the Wind*, eh? Well, it's not strictly a love story. It has its historical and philosophical aspects which, no doubt, you ignored. Then again, maybe I like a story with a love element. Have you considered that possibility?

Instead of my customary afternoon snack or a frappe, I now have coconut juice or water, but I'm sick of the former so I elect the latter most often. Yes, we have fresh butter three times daily. Yesterday we had fresh tomatoes, and we always have fresh potatoes and meat.

Again, I remind you to expect a lapse in my letter writing.

Lenny is a lucky boy. He really got a break.

It's now raining daily; the rainy season has begun. The morning was beautiful which got me thinking about summer in New England. Since Dad always wanted a cottage by a lake, I think he ought to investigate now. There should be plenty on the market while there's strict gas rationing.

5/6/44

Dear Folks,

I've come to the conclusion that I realize I don't know my own mind, and that I'm unsure of myself. No doubt, it's the culmination of months of unconscious thought concerning prior doubts that I had refused to accept.

This surfaced after a most enlightening discussion last night. We were four: a Cal Tech graduate geologist,[1] a University of Cincinnati graduate civil engineer, and a former language professor from Northwestern University [Baldner], and myself. During the course of the evening we discussed every phase of education.

I enjoyed listening to the talk and making comments. Of vital interest to me was the discussion on fraternities and advice as to what I should do in college. I inquired whether they would advise me to follow my inclination toward theoretical science. I explained my interest in chemical engineering, especially the subjects related to it which motivated me to consider it. I explained that I thought I'd enroll in a college and first get a feel for what course I should follow, whether chemical engineering or just plain business.

I'm now seriously thinking about the possibility of a liberal arts college. An engineering school education would be confined to technical subjects, while I'd have no opportunity to study psychology, history or literature etc. which I find equally interesting. A liberal arts school would enable me to study a wide variety of subjects, including science.

If I were to attend a liberal arts college, I'd chose one out of town. Clark[2] doesn't impress me. It doesn't rank among the best.

Furthermore, it might be better for me to leave home. I'll certainly be well off financially, with the government possibly paying my tuition. And as for living expenses, their cost would be well worth the independence I would have. I would prefer a small, high ranking eastern college, perhaps spending my first two years there, then branching out to a large university, perhaps on the West Coast, Berkeley for instance, in order to specialize in a scientific field. The University of California is a state college with a low tuition, and, having a notable faculty, it ranks at the top in world science.

My geologist friend suggests that I start off in an engineering school. Then were I to change my mind, I could use the credits gained there in a liberal arts college while the reverse wouldn't hold. In that case, Worcester Tech[3] would be fine, and, if I found that engineering wasn't for me, I'd still be able to transfer what I learned there to a liberal arts school.

Don't think for a moment that I've written off the idea of joining Dad; however, I'd only do so after I finished college.

Now you know that my mind is no longer running in the narrow channels of my pre-induction days. My intellectual friends have had a profound effect on my thinking. Nothing is definite. I'm just turning things over in my mind. I may yet change my mind a dozen times or more. I anxiously await your comments. But don't think that my idea of going to school out West is absurd. Unimagined things have already happened to me. Anything I may do educationwise would seem tame by comparison.

I had once made up my mind not to go to a coeducational school. Now I'd consider it—with a certain anxiety. It would be good to be exposed to the female element. Good lord, at the rate I'm going, I won't even know what a woman is.

----------------------------------[4]

In one of your recent letters you wrote of reading "C/O Postmaster" in *Liberty*[5] [magazine]. Coincidentally, I ran across a condensation of the book by Corporal St. George in the March issue of *Omnibook*.[6] It struck home and I laughed my head off. I'm now indulging myself with the April issues of *Coronet* and *Reader's Digest*.

Hollandia, Dutch New Guinea

[The censors deleted large sections of this letter.]

Sunday Mothers Day May 14, 1944

Dear Folks,

There have been many changes during the past week and a half. I'll explain why I couldn't write for some time.

We have moved: another ocean voyage. So that you wouldn't worry, I had written previously that I was busy, and you should expect a lapse in our correspondence. We were busy alright: breaking camp. I'm now permitted to tell you where I have been located. We were at ------[1] New Guinea in the ------ corner, almost opposite ------. I'm still in New Guinea, but of course, at a different location. ------ was an enormous base and outside the combat area. You can now ask any questions about the place that you wish.

After being all packed, with gear and equipment loaded aboard ship, and with only a heavy infantry pack on our backs, orders were changed, and our departure was postponed for a week — or less — until further orders. Every type of conceivable shelter, from pup tents to jungle hammocks, had to be set up. Many slept on the ground, using a door for a roof. I immediately procured some cots and a six man pyramidal tent from a neighboring unit. Of course, it cost a little: and each of us chipped in the two dollar per person fee. So, as a result of quick thinking, we lived comfortably. I'm writing on stationery that I just procured from the Red Cross, thus the Red Cross letterhead emblem.

We were scheduled to embark on Sunday. After a hectic week of downpouring rain and more rain that created mud all over the place and kept our feet continually damp, we departed on Friday. The voyage wasn't half bad, although, by civilian standards, it was, should I say, inconvenient.

At our new destination, which is virtually virgin territory, we lived on the ground for some time. However, I was able to share a tent and cots with the rest of our communications men. Most of the fellows sleep in any suitable place they can find. It will be weeks before we can live like human beings again. A kingdom for a mattress. Tell me, what are things? Did you know that the ground is no worse than a feather pillow, and that a bare cot is as good as a Beauty Rest mattress? We feasted on K rations for a while, but now we're eating cooked food. Believe it or not, we had steak last night. The Seabees can do wonders; no wonder the Army Engineers marvel at us.

Not having my shaving equipment which is still packed in my bag aboard ship, I have quite a beard. At present the ship is only partially unloaded. We get our water from springs and bathe in the ocean or the clear streams. I keep quite clean, bathing daily. If you could only see me now, tanned and sporting a swell beard. In spite of the rough living and hardship, I feel just wonderful. No rheumatism or creaking bones yet, so guess everything is hunky-dory. So long as there's plenty of water, chow and some kind of shelter over my head, I'm happy. We'll be sitting pretty again in a month when a chow hall, showers, and tents will have been completed. We eat out of mess kits, straddling them on our knees while sitting on the nice, comfortable ground. Camp life is fun. I think I'm gaining weight. Take three salt tablets and Atabrine daily.

The countryside is quite pleasant, raw, and unsettled, but we're doing our part to change it. It rains almost daily, but today was cloudless. Jap souvenirs are plentiful. I'll be sending two pieces of Jap invasion money.

Having not received any letters for an age due to our move, I anxiously await yours. We have a pile of work to do in the next few weeks. I'll write as soon as I can.

P.S. Happy Mother's Day, Mom.

May 15, 1944

Dear Mom,

Only yesterday I wished for letters, and today my wish was granted: two letters, April 21, 22, arrived from home.

It seemed odd to read of movies in your letter. Everything that contributes to enjoyment seems to be in another world. Inconvenience is our way of life to such an extent that we joke about our hardship. But I'm a lucky boy. I haven't fired a shot yet, and won't have to. By the way, throughout Pesach[1] I ate bread, but last week I made up for it. Yesterday, we had the first bread in a week. Now that we're getting settled our chow will improve as the days pass.

Last night a wonderful thing happened. After setting up the high frequency receiver, we heard Frisco as clear as a bell. This was the first music and first news we've heard in an age. The news bulletins were the same ones you heard that evening, and the music was both popular and classical. Listening to the James Melton[2] program was heaven.

Here are the facts on our time difference. There's a 21 hour difference between East Coast time and Pacific time. In other words, we are always 21 hours ahead of you.

To top it off, we heard a program especially directed to the boys called Home Town News. If you don't know it already, for your information, the house at Whalom Park[3] near Fitchburg[4] will be torn down. Yep, that's what I heard announced. I recall your mentioning Whalom often. You used to go there when you were young, didn't you, Mom?

Being so busy, I almost forgot the vitamin pills, but I'm happy they are on their way. One needs a tonic in this infernal heat. I requested Vitamin A for my eyes. We don't have street lights, of course, and I find it hard to see at night. I don't wear glasses at all now and get along fine, although I admit I miss some things. Since neither my eyes nor my head aches, I suppose it's all right. I'll send a glasses frame home so that you can have lenses made for the same size frame.

Doggone, it sounds like you're pickling the new car. I wish I were home now. I'd pay for its upkeep, just so I could use it. It would save me transportation time when I'm in college.

I'm curious to know how much I've saved all told towards a college fund. How long will this war have to last for me to save one thousand dollars? It's just my idle curiosity.

I feel bad about Dad's leg troubling him. Don't worry. I think we could work something out when I get home. In spite of my wish to go to school out of state, I'd gladly attend school locally and work with Dad. I'm sure that with a conscientious helper, which I'd certainly be, he could take it much easier.

Remember, however, that I don't expect to be the same kid that went away. I hope you don't still think of me as that impractical, self-willed kid. I've learned a little.

Saturday May 20, 1944

Dear Dad,

Everyone is busy with more work than he can normally handle. At any rate, the time flies by. This week seemed like only a day.

The mail is arriving better, which certainly makes me feel good, despite the deluge of work. I received your old letter (March 20) yesterday, but such confusion is to be expected.

Now that I've experienced some camp life, I have definite ideas on the handiest things to have. One is a canteen which is indispensable for drinking and washing. I drink three or four canteens a day here. Another handy thing is our steel helmet, not that we use it on our heads, but rather as a wash basin and bucket for rinsing out odd clothes. Without these two items I'd be lost.

By the way, I could use a few good combs. They don't last long here in the heat. And I could sure use a metal watch strap. I've already gone through two since I've been overseas. Perspiration and dampness rots them quickly. Please find a strap for a thick wrist, as most straps are too small for mine.

Haven't been paid for more than a month, so you may expect quite a money order home next payday. I don't spend a dollar a month.

Lately the weather has been cloudless clear. This so-called tropical rainy season isn't as bad as we figured. I like the country here much better than down in Finschafen. It's hillier but less muddy.

I hope you can take it easier, but I suppose the spring boom with the business is on.

Sorry, I don't have time to write more, but I'll make up for it after I'm more settled.

May 22, 1944

Dear Mom,

I'm still a busy little bee, taking time off only for chow and sleeping. For obvious reasons no one works after dark. Uncle Sam's mail has been slow lately. Your morale tinglers will be arriving soon, I know.

Of course the first phase in establishing a base is rough. I do line work and continually work in the sun and fresh air. You'd be surprised how much I've picked up by watching the men work. I can do splices already.

With a floor under my bunk, I'm now living more comfortably. Having retrieved my books from the library, I'm also resuming the reading of *GWTW* after a month's lapse.

Received a letter from Lenny's sister in which she said that he's stationed in San Diego. I haven't heard from Johnson. Will you look up his address in Medford on the back of one of his letters?[1]

The weather here has been exceptionally clear. Indeed, we could do for more rain.

Remember the blackouts we used to have back home? Boy, was I surprised to see Noumea, New Caledonia lit up like New York, and Milne Bay lit like Paris, oo la la and all that stuff. When we got to Finschafen, we were surprised to see lights everywhere. We actually dare the Japs to come.

Our landing here was interesting. As usual, it was pouring. How could it be otherwise? So most of us took off our clothes and had the first fresh water shower since Finschafen. (We had only sticky salt water showers aboard ship.)

Food being a problem, we dove into our K rations and gobbled down the dog biscuits and stuff (or whatever it is) with relish—and I don't mean pickled relish. That problem dispensed with, the next one was to learn how to straddle that ever famous slit trench, known in army lingo as a latrine. I, being used to the comforts of the world, including appropriate reading matter and a closed door, was certainly in a tizzy.

As for roofs over our heads, there were two varieties. One was the sky, oh so high, and the other was a pup tent so small that when going in or out, one had to rub one's nose in the dirt, and when lying down one's feet stuck out beyond the opening, and would eventually be tripped over by someone searching for a place to urinate.

In the morning, when you're looking for water to wash the cobwebs from your sleepy brain, (that is if you were lucky enough to get any sleep that night), you finally find water, only to have some fiend say "Uh, uh, don't touch. For drinking only"; so instead you drink it and forget the face wash.

Hey, darkness is slipping in fast, so gotta quit. Will write again at first opportunity.

Love to the three of you, Hughie (that camper extra odd in ary)

May 25, 26, 1944

Dear Mom,

Uncle Sam continues playing me dirty: still no mail, but *tempus fugit*[1] and I can wait.

Having built a swell new desk and chair, I'm living almost normally again. I'm getting to be quite a carpenter if I do say so myself, harrumph. Business is good; there's plenty to do. We're now eating fresh vegetables and fruit, although the variety is somewhat limited. We expect the chow to improve as soon as more facilities are built.

I'm feeling swell, and I get more than enough sleep, but due to the constant heat I think I've lost weight. I don't mind the heat and I keep myself powdered and clean to prevent chafing.

Of late, for some mysterious reason, I've acquired the name of Muscles. Whenever a heavy box has to be lifted, the fellows say "Let Muscles take one end and three men take the other." I haven't worn a shirt since I've been at this base. Mosquitoes are few, far less than at home in the summer. But I still take Atabrine and salt tablets, and will continue to do so as long as we're overseas.

And now for another episode in the life of a typical Seabee. Let me discuss reveille. At 5:45 AM some mustachioed jerk blares that detestable call with unsurpassable gusto. But unlike in the army, we react by turning over in our beds, moaning some, and the more ambitious among us yell back, "Knock it off," or "To hell with reveille," and fall back into a snoring coma. Thus, I awake at 6:30, but sleep through to 8:00 when work is supposed to begin, unless I have hunger pangs. In that case, I lumber, still dazed, out of my cot, dash a helmet full of water on my face, and rush down to the chow hall. "Life can be beautiful."[2]

Another request: please send the Schick razor. The head on the Remington is going. Much more delicate than the Schick, the dampness has eroded the head although the motor is still fine. I do have another less efficient head to use on it until the Schick arrives. I shave once every three days. Electricity is being installed in our tents. We're now living even more comfortably than at Finschaven.

Enclosed are four Jap postcards. The scenes are typical of this kind of country.

May 28, 1944

Dear Folks,

The jackpot again—thirteen letters today: six from home, one from Beverly Ringer,[1] one each from (Aunt) Sadie, Mrs. Linfield, (Aunt) Ida, two from the Gallants and a cordial note from the YMCA. I expect to be writing replies for the next two weeks. Lucky boy that I am, before the deluge arrived, with a desk, chair and electric lights in our cozy tent.

Before beginning with my everlasting chain of comments, here' s my news. I can now reveal that we crossed the Pacific on the *West Point* (formerly the *America*), the largest U.S. luxury liner afloat. And please folks, don't think that I used the swimming pool (It was full of cargo) or that the voyage was as enchanting as any Mediterranean cruise. Yesiree, that's one voyage, notable mostly for heat, sweat, filth and inconvenience, that I'll never forget. But I, uh, liked the flying fish. The best feature about being on the *West Point* was that it was the fastest ship in the merchant fleet.

Now we're back to our usual comforts: good sleeping conditions, excellent chow (fresh meat, fresh fruit and vegetables, cake and wonderful bread) and a contented state of mind.

I received some of your old letters via regular mail. Two and one half months coming is a long time. It's good that you're using air mail and V-Mail recently. Keep at it. Do you know that I wasn't supposed to know that we were to cross on the *West Point*, nor were you? However, somehow I learned about it prior to embarkation.

Regarding the excursion to S-----, the name of the place, and where the pictures were taken, is Satelburg. Yes, I was sweating when the picture of me standing beside the cross was taken. I had just climbed a steep hill. But the heat bothers me little, and the nights are pleasantly cool and practically void of mosquitoes.

Mr. (Al) Malter is no longer with the battalion. Having had malaria before coming to the tropics, he succumbed to it; it finally got the best of him. He's now in Australia waiting to be shipped back to the States. Too bad. He was a loyal and influential friend. I intend to correspond with him.

My former bunkmate at Finschafen (Baldner, the language professor) is now a transportation dispatcher.

Good going Ronnie; glad to see that you joined Young Judea. Don't be a flunky as I was when a member of AZA.[2] Get in there and do something.

The girls must be pretty hard up to request the address of a boy overseas after only viewing his Hollywood style portrait. My, my, this younger generation! I await Miss Chase's[3] letter with interest.

Since Bill finds very little to do in the navy, I hope it's perfectly legal and not an example of what we call in the navy goldbricking.[4]

With so many people going to beach resorts and taking vacations, I can only interpret this as nonchalance and an utter disregard for the war and the boys over here. Civilians will never appreciate how fortunate they are to be alive in a country such as ours.

Finschafen's eternal mud had a profoundly adverse effect on our shoes. The mud was caked so thick on them, you couldn't find the leather. Having several pairs of G.I. shoes, I was able to change often, while one pair dried. But here the mud situation is not nearly as bad. At work we wear the army suntans that you see in my picture. I haven't worn a shirt in three weeks.

I can't wait for my savings to hit the $1,000 mark. I feel more secure about having an education already.

Dad's usual morale builder of May 6th arrived. So happy that the pictures pleased you. Don't expect me to look like that boy in California. This is New Guinea, where sweat and dirt are as common as water. I haven't sent any souvenirs home because they can be dangerous to handle. I do have a swell Jap ammunition box made of cedar in which I keep personal articles, and a coat hanger on which are Japanese engravings, which I use. I'm not interested in Jap weapons, only things I can use, but of course, I'll certainly keep any spectacular things I might find.

Now that electricity is installed, you can expect more letters. My evenings are free.

Just got through reading Ronnie's letter to my bunkmates and all had a good laugh. Love to all of you, Hughie (in housekeeping again)

P.S. Mrs. Linfield sends you her best regards from Gulfport.

Memorial Day Tues. May 30, 1944

Dear Folks,

If only you could see the gleam in my eyes and feel my spine tingle with happiness when nine letters rolled in today. In addition to Johnson's long awaited letter giving reasons for his delay, there were letters from Dad, Mom, a swell letter from Sadie, a V-Mail from the Chase girl, a card from a school chum now in the army, and a letter from the correspondence school. Quite an assortment.

Dad's letter as usual fulfilled all my expectations. Not wishing to take lightly your imagining that I'm sitting sipping lemonade while basking in the cool ocean breeze, I'm seriously considering making it come true, but I'll need a man Friday[1] and a bottle of Pepsi Cola to do it right. Also after telling me that I should at least match the Chase boy's gift—a scarce automobile tire—to his parents, I've made a mental note to send you Hirohito's[2] chair to put in the shop window once I arrive in Tokyo.[3]

I'm amazed that I remember the gear locations of the great variety of trucks that I've now driven. Bowing my head in shame, I must admit that often I make the vehicle go in the wrong direction (even sideways) when I'm distracted.

I'd like to hear of your line experience,[4] Dad. Here, of course, line work is more hazardous, and things are done in a temporary manner. Since Malter's departure, the work isn't as exciting, and I'm not learning as much as before. As a result, my chance for advancement is reduced. But I can't kick, for I realize I'm lucky to have something worthwhile to do. I'm content. What I do is less important than keeping busy. I'm involved in strictly telephone work, which isn't very technical or complicated.

This afternoon I built an addition to my already comfortable quarters, a handy plywood cabinet for clothes and personal articles.

Chow is nothing short of excellent. For dinner I gorged myself on mince pie.

The correspondence school has written requesting that I send in my lessons. I'm ashamed to say that I've neglected the course, and, since the school is willing to forgive me, I'm surely going to buckle down and get on with it.

Oddly enough, there seem to be no blackouts near or in the war zone. Only after an air raid warning are "lights out" required. I have more Jap invasion coins than I need, and have given many away. I'm surprised that more people back home haven't seen them. Haven't the other boys in the South Pacific sent them home? I was amused, when Johnson Fulgoni wrote that Ronnie retrieved a Jap coin from his pocket to convince a friend that I am truly in New Guinea. By the way, I'm not 7,000 miles away from home as you think. Rather, it's more like 10,000 miles.

Although the trip to Satelburg was a most enjoyable one, it was done in the line of duty. We retraced our tracks on a test run to the mission the following day, got the Jeep stuck in the mud and had to walk back through the jungle in Stygian[5] darkness amid sheets of rain, arriving back in camp sopping wet. On our return trip, the dud bomb was no longer there. Instead, there was a large crater. A native, saying, "Big boom yesterday," and gesticulating wildly, thereby explained that the dud had decided to go off less than twenty-four hours after we were there. Should I become a fatalist?

For your information, both powdered and canned milk taken cold taste just like fresh milk and have similar nutritive value. I'll be sure to acknowledge your packages on arrival. I can't kick about the way the mail is coming in.

You may recall that Henry Wolf had gone with me to Providence and New Orleans. I like him plenty. He works in heavy equipment. Most of the well educated men in the outfit are seamen because they are misplaced here. We'll be having our first movies at this base tomorrow evening. After being with the Seabees overseas, I now know why so many boys want to transfer to this outfit. We're a good outfit to be in.

The natives here appear to be more civilized than the natives in Finschaven. But they're to be pitied. Most of their villages have been blown to bits. The Japs treated them cruelly, raping the women and killing the men. They greet Americans with a salute, and speak little English. For reasons that I haven't figured out, they build their thatched houses on stilts in the bay.

While our climate is decidedly tropical, it's hotter but less humid than in Finschaven. There's always an ocean breeze, and it's always comfortable in the shade. The days are gorgeous, and the mornings are glistening after a usual nightly shower. The nights are cool; the hottest time of day is at 11:00 in the morning, while the afternoons are less hot. The land is hilly, even mountainous, very pleasant, and the soil is rich. Finschaven is now in the midst of its rainy season, raining continually, but not here. We left that part of New Guinea just in time. The Americans have New Guinea well in hand. Every place I've seen here was captured from the Japs, thus all the Jap souvenirs. The weapons we carried to Satelburg were for protection against snakes, wild boars, and Japs that might still be hiding in the jungle. We usually carry weapons whenever we go into the jungle.

You've often asked what we're building. I can't say anything about our vast projects, or reveal what my mates do.

Your letters rarely arrive in chronological order, so that I can't reply to them chronologically.

I have a pile of letters a mile high to answer and the answering campaign begins this evening.

V-Mail 6/1/44

Dear Mom,

Nothing new is happening. Things are progressing at an even pace. Daily conditions are better; life becomes more pleasant.

Malter's leaving has left me up in the air. The only way to advance is to have a higher authority go to bat for you and now that authority is gone. Instead I have been demoted with no opportunity to learn more. The excuse is that seamen cannot be given a responsible position. So I was offered the job at the switchboard, a position which I obstinately refused. I want to be active during the day and not sit around pushing plugs in and out. Furthermore, the work hours allow little sleep. I'm aiming to find something different and better. My hopes are high. Again, I say, my job is secondary, so I'm content.

V-Mail 6/2/44

Dear Mom,

I'm beginning to lead a more settled existence with more time to read and write. And I'm making fine progress in the correspondence course and expect to submit my next lesson soon.

Received a letter from Uncle Bill today. Very funny. He writes like Johnson, a pleasure to read.

Another request: Send air mail stamps but make sure their sticky side is lined with wax paper. Can't find air mail stamps here.

My love to the three of you, Hughie (in his castle)

P.S. Have finished *Gone with the Wind*. Wonderful story, even better than the picture.[1]

V-Mail Saturday 6/3/44

Dear Mom,

At present there's little to write about.

From what I hear, and from my distant observation, I figure that you and Dad are sorely in need of a vacation. Why don't you folks go away for a couple of weeks during the summer slow season? It can be done. Where there is a will, there's a way. To tell the truth, it would make me feel a whole lot better. Why, you could go away singly, while the other takes care of the business. You did it while Dad was in the hospital, and he did it when you were too. Just pretend that each of you is going to the hospital, so that a vacation looks more like a necessity. Think this over. Let me see both of you get away. I want a direct answer to this letter. Remember, you'll be doing me a favor.

Sunday evening 6/4/44

Dear Mom,

Heard some swell programs on the short wave last night: The Frank Morgan[1] program and several big time bands. What a feeling I had when the theme song of the Morgan show, "You and I,"[2] was played. For a while it made me homesick as a dog. Most of the latest songs are already strange to me.

I had a good laugh out of the Australian programs. They play mostly American tunes, have the same plugs, and the same silly stories. But it's funny to hear a sophisticated voice with a British accent announce that "Uncle Pappy's pancakes, hip, hip, are rally good," and then an unearthly tune is played, introducing the sketch that is to follow. I don't believe any nation can compare with us in showmanship and radio programs. The Australian news announcer speaks in a matter-of-fact manner, with no inflection whatever in his voice. He seems so uninterested in what he's saying that I wouldn't be surprised if he'd be yawning before his broadcast was done.

I went swimming this morning in the coolest, clearest stream I've ever seen. It was heavenly. I plan to visit the secluded spot often.

You'll recall that I wrote that my chances for advancement in communications are practically nil. I've arranged for a transfer to surveying, where I'll be a helper and learn something new. Eventually I should be able to qualify for the drafting room. It's too bad that things turned out the way they did in communications. That group was a swell bunch of fellows, and I was learning a lot. But pushing plugs in and out wasn't learning. I'll keep going from one field to another until I find an opportunity to learn enough to make a rate. The communications chief asked me to stay on, but there's no push to the man. Furthermore, in surveying and drafting I'll be getting into a mathematically oriented field.

In a week, I would say, our living conditions will be superior to those we had in the States. Our enormous chow hall is almost completed, swell showers and wash stands have been installed, and morale is at its highest ever. Wish me luck in my upcoming venture, folks, because I plan to work like the devil.

June 6, 1944

Dear Mom,

I've made a bungled mess of my ambitions in the service, of my lust to get ahead. Feeling I had no chance for advancement in the job of telephone operator that was offered, I asked to be dropped from communications. Now, a transfer to the surveying and drafting department according to a prior arrangement is off, because the department has been closed and its personnel assigned to other details. However, the closing is temporary. In the meantime I've been assigned to guard duty indefinitely. I have only myself to blame. I'm now right back where I started a year ago.

I've tried so many jobs in which I found that no matter how hard I work, I can't get a rerate. I'm thoroughly disgusted and have given up hope once and for all of getting beyond S 1/c. Yet, I'll try again to join the survey crew once it's renewed, but I won't expect a rerate. So there it is. I've got it off my chest.

I lack stick-to-it-iveness. By God, when I get the next job that is a job, I'll stick to it come hell or high water. Getting tired of one job after another, I had the same experience in civilian life. I think I've learned by now. Too bad I have to learn the hard way. In spite of it all, I can always take supreme comfort in what the future *appears* to have in store for me.

Your letters are wonderful, and the seven I received yesterday most certainly lessened my sense of disappointment. Yesiree, all of them were humdingers.

The opinion my friends and relatives have in common suggests that I'm best suited for the journalism field. Frankly, journalism is very enticing, but I realize as would any lame-brained critic, that my letters are quite amateurish, and nothing exceptional. I confess, however, that I like to write, especially when I'm in the mood, either when happy or disappointed. You may remember the days when I would sit at the kitchen table strewn with dictionary and library books, trying to write a mere composition or a simple letter. No more, no more dictionary to consult, only my (blank) mind to draw on from a supply of seemingly fluent sentences. I find that once I'm started, it takes a while for the blood to clot. I'm able to ramble on for quite a while by thinking of the next sentence while still in the preceding one. It's fun to write. It offers me an outlet for my feelings, desires, and moods. I've found letter writing to be "manna from heaven."

You wonder whether the battalion is still in training. No, Mom, that ended the day we left the States. Projects, and more projects, are being assigned to us. Now we're working—and accomplishing the impossible. We are now a <u>construction</u> battalion <u>constructing.</u> The Linfields' cousin, Grantley Vaughn, is still in the company and attached to malaria control.

I don't think the city of Worcester is very considerate of the local employees in establishing the new school hours.[1] Actually, it doesn't help the war effort.

Does Dad plan to replace the teeth that he plans to have pulled, with plates? Speaking of teeth, mine are doing fine—not an ache or a cavity.

You are mistaken in thinking that we are suffering in this climate. Once you're used to it, it's not half bad and can even be agreeable. Only excessive activity is debilitating. Take it easy, and you feel swell. That's the way to endure living in the tropics.

The pictures of Satelburg are all that I can get, since I don't own the negatives, and the lab has a limited supply of print paper. Please take good care of those I sent home, and we can have a good laugh over them when I get there. I fear that I'm being over publicized with your displaying photos of me. How you folks do carry on—but I like it.

Remember your trip to Ayer, and the depot there? It poured the afternoon I boarded the train after induction at Camp Devens. I'll never forget the depot or Ayer.

Well, well, well, so my present got through to you after all. I could have cried with happiness when I read the passage describing your seeing the present. I'd give all the $675 I've saved to see your face then. And listen, buy a box of good cigars for Dad from my money for Father's Day. This is a request. Even though Dad doesn't believe a heck of a lot in "these commercial holidays," I'm sure he'll lower himself to accept a gift from his "backwoodsman son." Smoke the cigars in good health, Dad. I'm sending a money order for $53.00. Three dollars are for Dad's gift.

Boy oh boy, Harold Greenberg really has it tough.[2] By comparison I'm in heaven. The army engineers marvel at and envy us. Harold shouldn't let the world know how bad conditions are with him. It's bad business, apt to worry his friends and relatives. If he thinks he has it hard where he is, he should be with the army engineers here. They live like rats.

Thanks for the subscription to *Time*. I'm crazy about the magazine, since news from other sources is so limited.

Nope, I don't eat toothpaste. It doesn't agree with the digestive tract, or else I'd use it as a substitute for candy. Yeah, I used to sell Pycope at the drugstore. It's a good dentifrice — nothing more than flavored salt.

Never believe what "somebody had said." The statement that the temperature rises to 135 degrees is a gross exaggeration. Of course, in the States on a hot summer day you could fry an egg on the sidewalk. But here, although the sun is hot, the temperature never rises above 90 degrees (or goes below 70). But the humidity is uncomfortable. Of course, it's winter here too.

Malter requested that I write to his girlfriend, because he lacked the time and had no writing ability. We never sent the desk that we took from the mission to the States, because he became ill. How we brought it back from the mission with eight fellows in the Jeep is still hazy in my mind.

After I finished reading *GWTW*, two other fellows began reading it and are now deeply involved in it. It's a very thrilling and human story, and I confess, the love element was interesting.

Seems that Uncle Bill is getting a taste of the same stuff I got, guard duty etc. He won't have it for long; his chance will come.

At last, I'll answer your often asked question concerning our sanitation. I never meant to slide by it. The toilets consist of large screened-in outhouses which are cleaned and burned out daily. As a result of this daily practice, there's hardly any odor, and it's hardly agony to go to the "head" (navy slang for toilet). Our food and serving facilities are also kept clean and subject to a doctor's regular inspection. One time, due to neglecting such things, we contracted dysentery, so now our sanitation practices are closely watched.

I'm all talked out. Don't feel bad about how things have turned out for me. I feel better already. After all, this war won't last forever.

Wednesday June 7, 1944

Dear Mom,

I got a load off my chest in yesterday's letter, and I'm feeling much better. Today things are beginning to look brighter. Surveying is being reformed, and I've been requested to join the crew, so in a few days I can kiss guard duty good-bye.

I had a talk with the chief draftsman this afternoon. He's all for getting me into the drafting room after I've spent a while with the surveying party. Knowledge of the field work would make the work inside much easier. I've already got a book on the subject, a book which the department recommends, and I've started studying it.

Although all this sounds swell, I still have no hope for advancement. Here's why. Only men with prior experience who weren't fortunate enough to have rates are getting ratings. I should have observed this before. Furthermore, the college grads aren't getting rerates due to their lack of experience. I have neither experience nor an advanced education. Actually, all my thinking and working for a rerate have been in vain, especially when you consider how many men are more deserving of a rate than I. As I've said so often while in the States, this is no outfit for someone like me to advance in. I can see that now with greater clarity. Oddly enough, I'm not disappointed, and I feel that my new job will keep me happy. Even if I'm not satisfied, even if it turns out to be the toughest assignment in the world, I'll STICK TO IT. I'm sick and tired of myself, of my knocking around.

I hope yesterday's letter didn't get you down. I feel so much better today.

Our laundry isn't set up yet, but wash stands have been constructed, and hot water is available when the laundry begins working. I'm all caught up with my washing. I feel as you do after a Sunday wash: relieved and sort of tired.

Lately we've been getting some rain, nothing excessive.

If you've been following the news about New Guinea the past few weeks, you could guess where I am. Once or twice you've come mighty close. Examine the papers that came out about the time we got here.

V-Mail 6/9/44

Dear Mom,

As yet I haven't been transferred to my new job, but it's a sure thing and I'm waiting patiently.

I've just been going over my clothes and found a couple of gabardine army pants, pairs and pairs of socks and underwear that I haven't worn. My mates comment on how well I take care of my clothes. I never figured the ones I wear would last so long. Nothing has worn out. I'll have plenty of work pants etc. when I get home.

V-Mail Saturday 6/10/44

Dear Mom,

It's already the end of the week, and it seems that it just began. The sun is shining, the birds are singing and all that, a beautiful day. My watch just struck 4:00 in the afternoon, and I just finished a snack of luscious raisin filled hermit cookies that the bakery was so kind to donate. (Remember our 3:30 to 4:00 o'clock snacks, Dad?) I worked on the math this afternoon and have only one more question to answer before mailing the lesson. I'm boning up on surveying and drafting and enjoying it. By doing a certain amount of homework daily, I feel as if I'm back in school again.

Our new chow hall is about to open. What a humdinger it is. It has aluminum serving counters (like a cafeteria), ice cold water, and boys serving in whites. Spotlessly clean, it's better than in the States. I suspect we have the best chow hall in New Guinea.

Everyone is very happy about the European invasion.[1] I am looking forward to an invasion of the Philippines before fall—just a premonition.

V-Mail Sunday 6/11/44

Dear Mom,

I've been writing short V-Mail letters lately for lack of anything to write about.

Tonight I'm mailing my first completed math test and will start the next one tomorrow. I'm enjoying the course more than I thought I would.

I report tomorrow morning to the surveying department. Am I happy!

I aired all my clothes in the sun today. I found them still fresh and clean smelling when I unpacked them. Shows I took pains. After I sewed up holes in some clothes, washed my toilet containers, combs, and other articles, my personal gear is now in good shape. I plan to keep everything spicker and spanner than ever.

Just heard the Jack Benny[1] program[2] over the radio in the tent next door.

Tuesday 6/13/44

Dear Mom,

I'm working now, back on a real job in the surveying department. Since I'm beginning from the beginning, I'll probably be chosen to do the dirtiest duties, but eventually I should rise in position. I'm finding it most interesting. As part of a surveying party, I record figures, make computations on a slide rule and read elevations. Fortunately, I had done enough reading on the subject to understand what I'm doing. I've learned how to work a transit (not entirely, of course) and from it compute elevations. This requires calculating quickly by means of a slide rule, but I'm somewhat slow because of my lack of practice. However, since I understand what I'm doing, speed will come.

I like doing the math, especially operating the slide rule and doing mental arithmetic. I'm also always outdoors in the sunshine. I enjoy the work. What I'm doing applies only to this project. On another project with another surveying party I'll be doing something entirely different, depending on the project's requirements. So I'll be learning not only surveying, but also map drawing and drafting.

I must say, that although I'm not getting much of a rate in this outfit, I am getting plenty of valuable experience doing all kinds of work. Having learned how to hammer a nail straight, I've been able to make sturdy furniture, thereby making my living quarters more comfortable. I've learned how to string telephone lines from poles and make splices. I've learned how to operate a telephone switchboard (a cinch), and now I'm learning about surveying, drafting and topography.

Our new chow hall is officially open, and it's a pleasure to eat now. As comforts go in New Guinea, our camp is at the acme.

Now after a day's work I'm quite tired at the end of the day. It's 8:00 PM so I'll hit the sack, rise at 6:00, and will have plenty of sleep.

No mail has arrived since the last batch a week ago.

My love to you all, Hughie (surveyor extraordinary)

Wed. 6/14/44

Dear Mom,

Still on the job running around the countryside and getting plenty of conditioning. I just realized I haven't described the terrain here very well.

It's mountainous, rather steep low hills, heavily wooded to their summits, foothills to the mountains inland. There's a large variety of plants and trees: enormous 100 to 200 foot tall mahogany and teak trees with diameters of four feet and more, coconut palms, sago palms, wild fruit and vines everywhere. And there's a myriad of other plant life. The timber must be worth a fortune, but it would be a hard task to haul it down the mountainsides. The mahogany and teak trees dwarf the trees in New England. Their wood is extremely dense. Most of the native furniture that is made from this wood and beautifully carved, would be priceless back home.

Coconut palms are growing everywhere but most are concentrated in groves along the beaches. Bamboo, which grows like an enormous bush, sometimes towers up to thirty feet. The natives make starch and flour from the sago palm by cutting into its thick trunk and reaming out its white pulpy core. They then dilute the white pulp with water and after straining it through palm leaves the liquid contains only the starch. I saw the natives performing this process while in the jungle today.

There's plenty to eat in the jungle, and we take advantage of it. The *pièce de résistance* of the tropics is papaya, which grows on a tree. Shaped like a squash, it's a big melon with a yellow-orange smooth skin when ripe. It tastes like peaches and cream. It's so delicious that, whenever I'm in the woods I manage to find a papaya or two for a snack.

My second most favorite fruit is wild pineapple. The fields are full of them. They're not ripe when red, and almost ready to eat when green. But when they've turned yellow, they taste like no pineapple I've ever eaten. Their flavor easily surpasses that of any U.S. pineapple. We gobble them up one right after the other. I had two today for a snack.

Bananas are plentiful. We pick them green and let them ripen, but they aren't as tasty as the cultivated ones from Central America. There are also all kinds of berries, many of them edible and tasty, but, not being familiar with which ones are safe, we leave them alone. There are many abandoned native gardens still growing yams, squash, green beans, cabbage and other common vegetables. After spending a day in the jungle, I'm not hungry come meal time. I'm getting plenty of fresh fruit and vegetables for sure. This is the food the natives subsist on. I think it's darn good stuff.

Much of the terrain is similar to New England's, dotted with grassy fields and fragrant with flowers. Much, but not all, the grass grows taller than a man. We find thatched native huts and Jap dugouts here and there on the hillsides. Many of the rock formations are enormous, hundreds of feet high in which there are often large caverns and small caves. This coastal area is much healthier than the interior where it rains daily, and the jungle is much denser and steaming hot with swamps and mosquitoes galore. Being a coastal unit we don't have to bother going into the interior.

Of course, parts of the coastal jungle are also so dense that you can't see more than ten feet in front of you, and in some places sunlight barely penetrates.

The natives here like to wear clothes and are more civilized than those at Finschaven. Speaking little English, they always salute a white man, probably the result of Jap training. The women are homely. Only today I observed a native family walking through the woods. The man of the family wore a loincloth that resembled Jockey underwear, and the woman, with breasts that hung to her waist, wore a grass skirt. The children, heavily laden with the family's goods, followed behind. Only the father carried nothing, while the woman was loaded to the gills with food that hung from a strap wound around her head.

I've just returned from supper, which reminds me: I must mention our bread. It's delicious, fresh daily, and better than any store bought bread I've tasted.

There's a movie tonight, "Presenting Lily Mars,"[1] with Judy Garland, But I prefer to stay in the tent and do some writing. I figure I'll see plenty of movies when I get home.

That's that for tonight. Some mail should be arriving very soon.

My love to all of you, Hughie (strictly a vegetarian now)

Thursday 6/15/44

Dear Mom,

Letters and more letters are arriving today and tomorrow. Among them was a letter from Al Malter's girlfriend. I can't locate Malter, though I know he's somewhere in Australia.

I'm enjoying my job, despite the fact that it's not easy work. I'm contented once more. I'm not kicking. Mostly all the men I work with are graduate civil engineers.

Regarding your mention of the difficulty I had with Miss Phillips, my English teacher, such memories are no longer a part of my life. How petty and trivial she seems now. Many things that I took seriously in school now seem small and nonsense. This is such a big world, which I now know only too well.

My, my, how my letters seem to have affected my relatives. It's magical. Yetta wants to send me cookies, candy, and the *Reader's Digest*. Why all the rumpus? My letters are quite ordinary. The letters I've received from home and from friends are far superior to mine.

With reference to your letter concerning mine of 5/18 on a college education, I see you still consider me a romanticist and a dreamer. Nosiree, folks, too many practical things have happened to make me a full-blooded dreamer. Everything's plausible. Nothing is impossible.

I think about my education often, and I realize I don't know my own mind yet. However, I plan to follow your advice so you can have peace of mind. I'll go to an Eastern college and take up chemical engineering. The more I think about it, the better it sounds. Money can be made in engineering, a very practical profession. It's a new field.

Although I'm sick of being away from home, I've also come to like travel and being in other places. It's new to me. I don't expect to spend the rest of my life in the East. Some day I want to go West, but I won't go before everything at home is secure. I fear that opportunity in Worcester will be limited—and too controlled. The West is so different, so progressive, and the opportunity unlimited.

I know I can't ever repay you folks. My ambition in life is to make us, all of us, live as comfortably as possible, more comfortably than ever before. I'm determined to make life easier and more secure for you and Dad. I don't look upon this as an obligation, but rather as an achievement necessary for my personal happiness. I won't be happy until I'm certain that you folks are happy.

But remember, there are always men who are motivated, not by the mighty dollar, but by their own personal measure of happiness. Many a man could make a fortune by using his abilities, yet he's happy doing what he likes for less pay. I realize that to make a good living is essential, and that I'll do, if I have my way. Yet, I'll not fail to remember that money isn't the be all, and that a man's ambition isn't always directed towards financial achievement.

As you ask, why discuss this now? So let's drop the matter until another day. I'll probably have a different view in a month or two. Let's both of us be procrastinators.

Friday June 16, 1944

Dear Mom,

Every time I write this salutation, the song of the same title comes to my mind. Remember "Dear Mom" sung by Kate Smith?

I'm getting a kick out of reading the *Gazettes*. I've clipped the news about what's happening where I am. Much of it is true, but much is also exaggerated or altered. So you can rely on the papers for some of the truth, but not all the truth. I pass on the papers to other

Worcester boys who pass them on to still others. Everyone is clamoring to hear news from their home towns.

I hadn't been able to keep up with the latest songs or ballgame scores, but now I'm getting them in the *Gazettes*. Even the guys in my tent from Illinois, North Carolina, Texas, Minnesota, and New Jersey listen attentively as I read aloud things in the local paper that may interest them.

A loudspeaker system has been installed around the camp. Now we can hear re-broadcasts of baseball games and hit tunes.

The enclosed clipping reminds me of the day in Los Angeles when I saw "Junior Miss," my first play. That day seems so long ago.

Enclosed also is a battered etching that I found in the hills. Ronnie might show it to Johnson Fulgoni.

Oh, yeah, got a haircut this afternoon. Now I'm all slicked up to go out on liberty which in New Guinea language means "bed."

My love to the three of you, Hughie (Jungle jolly is the word)

V-Mail 6/17/44

Dear Mom,

Everything is humdrum and routine. Lately we've been hearing the news from the radio over the loud speaker system. It's a tough war in progress in Europe.[1] Personally, I feel this war in the Pacific is entirely independent of the one in Europe. A quick victory in Europe will affect us little here. However, I fear that in Europe we'll have a tough fight on our hands, tougher than the American public anticipates, although not the American strategists.

The same goes for the Philippines. Many think that we'll bypass them, but so far as I can tell, all strategy points toward a Philippine invasion. Japan can't afford to lose the Philippines, and I predict that it's there we'll have the showdown fight.

Needless to say, our outfit is doing wonders, and that as a result we may see the Philippines. Still, there are many good arguments against our going there. I've stopped thinking about what the future will bring. But I'm certain that our past good luck will continue.

V-Mail 6/18/44

Dear Mom,

The days have been gorgeous. Everyone is working at a back breaking pace and taking no days off. Even today, Sunday, religious services were held in the evening.

With everything routine again, I'm short on subject matter to write about. From the stack of *Gazettes*, each day I manage to read one from first page to last. We have movies every other night, but I rarely go because I'd rather study or read. Only on movie night when everyone in the tent goes to the show can I get anything done. When everyone is home, we shoot the baloney all night.

I've been writing quite a lot lately, writing to everyone. I don't understand this mania of mine. I guess I do it to fill up the nights. I'm done with work at 4:30, retire at 9:30—five hours of leisure time. My routine after work is to shower, change clothes, have chow, then write or read until my eyelids begin to droop, brush my teeth, hit the sack, awaken at 5:30 or 6:00, have breakfast and report to work at 7:00. Our noon hour break is from 11:00 to 1:30, the hottest time of the day.

Tuesday 6/20/44

Dear Mom,

At the end of a good day's work my weariness disappeared when four letters piled in.

I expected you to become impatient during my lapse of letter writing while en route in early May. Now you know that the reasons were purely military in nature and far from my intention.

I was amused by your mention of the art student's comment on my modeling work at the museum school. Many of the girl students there expressed a wish to go out with me. You might say they were "wolfesses." When I ignored their advances, they kidded me along. I realized perfectly well at the time that they were only having fun with my so-called bashfulness. Also during that period I had little time to fool around with girls. I worked at the museum, for monetary, not social reasons. It was strictly a business proposition. Even though my attitude has changed regarding the feminine sex, I still wouldn't behave differently.

If I were as bashful as the art student claimed, do you think I would have posed in the semi-nude before teen-age girls? Johnson has written that the caliber of models is now very poor.[1] When I return, I'm sure I'll be in no condition to model again. It will take a good year to regain any semblance of the physique I had. Furthermore I'd want more hours and more pay. I prefer to help Dad if he'll let me.

Thanks for the airmail stamps. I also use them to send letters to the other folks. I write others about once a month or every two months.

Those letters that seemed so optimistic regarding my coming home have no foundation at all but merely express the hope of most of us. The battalion has been doing such a brilliant job that everybody is optimistic.

Uncle Bill will find that most Navy regulations are nonsensical. The regular navy is even worse than the Seabees. Actually, while overseas, we Seabees are probably the most free men in the service.

I hear that Ronnie is handsomer than ever. When in the devil will he start to go out? Do something, Mom. Don't treat him as you did me; let him go. I hope that by now Ronnie knows the whole story. When I left home I needed to learn a lot more. Don't neglect telling him the way it is, especially after the way youth is going berserk today. You folks didn't tell me a heck of a lot. Those so-called books of enlightenment weren't sufficient. The service has taught me much, but it presents life in a poor light. Only as a result of a proper upbringing, have I understood the right way and clung to decency.

Ronnie will find his association with other boys, yes, Jewish boys too, embarrassing if he doesn't know the facts. Boys his age think they know everything and make up marvelous tales. I know. I encountered such episodes continually, and had to clear up in my mind what was true from what was false. Ronnie's lack of association with girls is not good, but it would be worse if he begins such an association without knowing the score and a girl takes advantage of him. A certain type of girl will, you know. You'd be surprised how the high school angels and mothers' darlings change color outside their homes. I suppose I'm raving foolishly and without foundation. However I have been concerned about Ronnie's social life.

My love to the three of you, Hughie (with advice to the lovelorn)

6/21/44

Dear Mom,

Received two packages today: one containing the vitamin pills and peanuts which were stale, a fate to be expected after two months en route. The second package containing candy and saddle soap, which is precious here, is most welcome.

The men in our tent compete with one another over getting the most mail. Although the fellow from New Jersey is hard to beat, I've been a close runner-up. On the last mail call I was ahead.

This afternoon we did some surveying in the bay. At low tide you can walk out quite some distance on the coral reefs. The sea bottom, with every color imaginable, was beautiful. The purple, green, orange and yellow sea plants were spectacular. I saw a navy blue starfish and another aquamarine. Fish of all shapes, about the size of goldfish, looked as if they had been painted, some a brilliant blue, others bright scarlet. There were also two-toned fish with yellow upper parts and blue bottoms. The coral formations are beautiful, looking like artistic creations. Sponges are plentiful and I picked some.

The sand beaches are brilliantly white and the texture of the sand very fine, quite unlike our beaches back home. It was made from the coral. I don't particularly like the warmth of the ocean here. I went bathing yesterday, and it felt like taking a warm bath.

Since most natives left during the fighting, few natives were around when we arrived. Now they're returning, and I see more of them daily. Their villages have been shot up, but they don't complain. Yesterday, I watched a small kid, not more than five, paddling a dugout canoe like a veteran. He made it skim beautifully on the surface of the water. The kids are cute, and smart—and usually wear no clothes. Now the natives have learned to say OKAY.

V-Mail 6/22/44

Dear Mom,

The war progresses and each day[1] is that much nearer to returning home.

Tests for rerates are now being given. What test can I take? I don't know enough about a particular trade to get to first base on a test. That's what's tough about the Seabees: you aren't sent to school to learn a trade, and as a striker you don't learn much in the short time you're on the job, plus you only learn one phase of a trade, not enough to qualify you for a rate. Some kids my age are getting rates because they worked at a trade a year or two before they entered the service.

So I'm not taking a test or making any attempt to get a rate. I'm not in the least disgusted, or even disappointed. I know I'll never get ahead in my present job because of the limited number of men needed. Still I'm learning something. I'm taking it all in stride and biding my time.

6/23/44

Dear Mom,

Now that the ordeal of spring cleaning is over, I can picture you still groaning for a week after. You should visit the Y for a loosening up before tackling such a stupendous project. Good goin', Mom, I'm proud of ya.

Obviously Nason's[1] graduation would be boring. Why, even my graduation bored me. Graduations are for one purpose only: to please the proud parents. Sensible parents consider it so much nonsense. Formality, that's all it is. Formality: it's the way of the navy. If we spent less time involved in matters of form, and more producing, our efficiency would increase by twenty-five percent. When I'm a civilian again, I'll detest formalities, and so will everyone else that has been in the service.

And conventionalism is old-fashioned. The man in business who develops something new will succeed. The individual who does something original will get ahead. Of course, no one can deviate too far from convention. If he stays within safe limits, he'll get along fine.

I read in the *Gazette* that your temperature is surging into the nineties. That's warmer than here near the equator. Our average temperature rarely goes above eighty-five. In the early morning it's seventy, but the humidity is high, although it's offset by a cool breeze off the bay. The days are beautiful, raining only at night and not to excess. The thundershowers back home are far more torrential than the showers here. Only when working do we sweat, or while sitting in the sun, otherwise it's comfortable. The sun doesn't tan you as much as it does in the States. By now, after being out in the sun so much, I should be black. Instead I'm only a bronze brown, which, were I to wear my shirt, would disappear in a week. Odd isn't it? We don't have a monsoon season here, as they do in India and Burma. However, it's a different story farther into the interior of New Guinea.

I'm enjoying the vitamin pills. Already, I'm prepared to tackle a regiment of Japs. Tanks Mac.

Well, I'm really surprised that mention of my former whereabouts was excised. I was informed by a reliable source, the officer in charge of censorship regulations, that mentioning it was permissible. I presume the censor was unaware that referring to the place by name was allowed. Knowing who censored the letter, I'm sure that he wasn't sufficiently informed. So let me repeat what I wrote: "I am now permitted to tell you where I was located. I was at Finschaven, New Guinea, in the northeast corner of the island, almost opposite New Britain. I'm still in New Guinea at another location. Finschaven is an enormous base outside the combat area. I can answer any question you wish about that place."

Where I am now is not considered outside the combat area. However, Uncle Sam has this place well in hand. Refer to the newspapers concerning New Guinea during my last days in ------ and you'll know approximately where I am. The newspapers will tell you that it's safe here.

Hey, don't think that I've gone through superhuman hardship. I haven't. I've had only inconveniences, nothing comparable to what the boys on the front lines are going through. Listen, this war has been a picnic for our battalion thus far. I haven't so much as aimed my gun at a Jap yet, but I'd sure welcome the chance. The dead ones stink. I imagine the live ones do too.[2]

If things continue as they have been, I'll return a healthy boy. Yes, I know that the Seabees are being constantly lauded. I can readily understand why. This battalion is without a doubt a crack construction outfit. Our commander is a go-getter, and he makes sure his men are well fed, taken care of, happy and *working*. He's by no means a model officer, but I'm glad that he is at the head of our battalion. I'm all for him.

6/24/44

Dear Folks,

Today, unfortunately, I had to use my safety razor. The faithful Remington, the deserter, finally called it quits. I patiently await the arrival of the Schick you sent.

During the many months I've been Uncle Sam's servant, I've never described our daily routine of waiting in lines, chow lines, store lines and miscellaneous lines. The chow line occupies approximately 1/8 of our daytime hours, depending on when you hit the line, how hungry the boys are, and the efficiency of the KPs. In the morning there's never a line so a fella can walk right into the chow hall without waiting. The reason: most of the guys are too lazy to get up for chow during the wee hours. It's worth missing breakfast for an extra half hour of snoozing. That's the popular opinion.

Dinner (lunch) and supper lines, however, are always long. Because of this, there are always a few jerks who sneak into the head of the line offering the excuse that they must get back to work immediately. It's amazing how many men have to return to work immediately. Our Master at Arms, the official battalion policeman, received so many complaints, that he stationed a man at the head of the line to prevent such goings on. Still, many guys manage to finagle their way to the head of the line by presenting passes signed by some admiral or, possibly, the president himself.

Chow lines are interesting and enjoyable, because it's there we meet our friends and shoot the gab for a while. Many's the time a fellow gets so interested in the conversation that he fails to see the line's progress and a gap develops. Then loud hoots and hollers are heard, waking up the diligent conversationalist who then dashes ahead to quiet the hecklers. Lately, the length of the chow lines has been minimal due to a fairly fast serving system.

Other lines, such as those formed for securing money orders after payday, and for purchasing personal articles at the store, are more tolerable. Occasionally, however, one finds that he must wait in line to go to the toilet, a wait which can often be disastrous. I've been able to avoid the rush by establishing a very original hour to do my duty.

As a result of having to wait in all those detestable lines, I've come to the conclusion that once I'm home I'll never wait in line for a movie, or in a restaurant. Be back tomorrow.

6/25/44

Dear Mom,

Time is irreplaceable, and, as it passes, only memories remain. I find that the memories I cling to the most are the sweetest. Memories of embarrassing moments and the like slip away quickly. Yet, the memory itself is always sweeter than the actual occasion that gives rise to it.

A year ago today, I left school. At the time I found the process of graduating a torment. I was aggravated over having to endure what seemed to me so much nonsense. And I detested having to wear a tux. But today I look back on that day, not as sacred or even significant, but as amusing and wonderful stuff to think about, as something to picture occasionally and feel warm inside about.

Do you recall that day? It was just 4 1/2 years earlier to the day that you attended my graduation from Prep at the Clark University auditorium. Do you remember how I cursed having to rent a tux because gowns weren't chosen? I swam in the ill fitting jacket, although the pants weren't bad. Black shoes. Who wore black shoes? So we rented them, little imagining that I'd be wearing nothing but black shoes in the near future.

I was surprised to see that Grandma and Uncle Bill came to Worcester to witness the proceedings, that Grandma had the patience to sit through it after seeing three daughters and a son go through the same ordeal. And I give Bill credit. It must have taken considerable courage and willpower to have come. Graduation ceremonies will never change. Ask Grandma. The ritual is eternal.

I remember what the speaker, some history professor, looked like, but I'll be damned if I can remember his name. I remember that he spent at least 3/4 of the ceremony explaining that he had no intention of making a long speech. We had all we could do to suppress chuckling, as he became beautifully confused and had to stop to recapture what he had just said. Boy oh boy, we had one heck of a time trying to follow him.

Of course, we had student speakers, chosen for their brilliance, or perhaps their nerve, for how could they know whether or not their enemies might toss rotten tomatoes at them? At any rate, one speaker turned out to be an avid Communist, a reformer of democracy, who said he planned to vote for Roosevelt in 1944. Yes, I remember his name: Charles Parsley. Many of our normal students thought him odd, but he really wasn't. He was just a woozy character who didn't get around. That's all he was.

The female speaker, of course, was pleasing to everyone. She was quieter and rarely, unlike her fellow male speaker, went into tantrums. "Oh the sweet thing," that's what I heard a few say.

The victims, both visiting parents and students, especially the students, were definitely bored by the whole proceedings. Ah, yes, and how we were sweating. Perspiration trickled down the curve of my spine, down my arms and my legs so that a single move would have surely produced a shower.

It was a relief to stretch our legs when the time came to stand. I certainly wished that the band, lousy though it was, would strike up the Star Spangled Banner once or twice between speeches so that we could stand. But standing proved to be quite an ordeal. Remember? When the boys rose I thought the seats of our pants would tear off from the adhesive action of the newly varnished chairs which on that hot day seemed coated with fish glue. Glancing slyly behind me, I saw a beautiful imprint of my trousers on the chair seat and I was relieved to see that the seat of my pants wasn't there. Some of the other fellows weren't as fortunate. Their chairs rose with them, and an occasional clack of a falling chair resounded throughout the gym. Remember?

After graduation exercises were over, my first aim was to find you and get home, which I did. What a relief to get out of those togs and into comfortable clothes. Those were the good old days, yesiree.

6/26/44

Dear Mom,

The climax of the day was a feast on fruit. If someone were to have told me six months ago that I'd be eating lemons picked directly from the tree, sucking the sugar from sugar cane, or picking figs, I'd have called him crazy. That's what I did today. The lemons were far more bitter than the ones I'm used to, but oh, so much tastier. To suck on a sugar cane stalk is like drinking flavored sugar water. The land here is abundant with fruit.

I've always had a perception of the climate here that is nothing like the way it really is. I'm more than pleased with it, at least this part of the tropics.

Again looking back, a year ago today I was admitted to Worcester Tech. I wonder when I'll be able to take advantage of it. I see from the newspapers that more and more boys who I know are attending schools. Now I can honestly say that it's just as well that I didn't get into school. I'm sure I'll benefit from this quirk of fate.

I just listened to the news on "Home Front" by Robert Kincaid.[1] I get great pleasure from hearing what's new back home, such as the latest movies and best sellers. I see the Republican convention is getting hot. I think that Dewey,[2] if nominated, stands a darn good chance of getting elected. He's young, a capable governor, seems honest, and he's not a loud mouth. If the Democrats nominate a poor candidate, I'll vote Republican in the coming election. I believe Dewey would do a good job. However, I'm much in favor of Roosevelt for a fourth term. It's only natural that as a war president, he should also have a hand in making the peace. But he's tired and growing old. I wonder if he'll run.

I don't consider Wallace[3] a good candidate; although he has been effective cementing friendships with other nations, he's an idealist. Idealists may be fine, but look what happened to the last peace because of idealists. A down-to-earth man such as Roosevelt or even Dewey is the kind of man we need in making the peace.

Bricker[4] seems too much of a politician, but the California governor would be a powerful choice for the Republican's vice-president. I'd like to see Saltonstall[5] make the senate. I understand he has no competition. One must admit that the Republicans have strong candidates.

Tues. 6/27/44

Dear Mom,

Any improvement in penmanship that you see in this letter is due to my using the brand new pen I received today. It's a corker, sturdy looking, and blends beautifully with my white, ahem, teeth. Your choosing a small pen is excellent judgment. That's you, Mom, as dependable as Gibraltar,[1] with supreme taste. The comb couldn't be better. I don't carry a comb. Who has time to comb his hair? I need to keep a good, sturdy comb in my locker for use after a shower. By the way, finding that it massages my scalp, I use a hair brush now. I'm pleased with the watch strap. After coming here with a stock of three cloth straps, I found they last only three months in this climate. My present supply should last out my stay. I think my watch can use a cleaning. No wonder; it's gone through plenty.

I received three letters with the little green pen. I'll have a chat with you tomorrow, Dad, so I'm putting your letter aside. Only a letter directly to you, Mom, will do in response to yours.

I find the short passage in your letter commenting on my so-called improved penmanship velly velly amusing. Any improvement is purely ACCIDENTAL.

I see Ronnie has contracted my former craze for canoeing. Odd that he couldn't find someone to go with, especially in view of the male shortage. Hmm.

Ah, ha Port Moresby[2] is way old stuff in New Guinea. You should realize how far we've progressed on this island. No sooner do we take an area than it's built up enormously. Once there was nothing but jungle where we are. Now, our stupendous projects are remaking the land, as if by magic. Our stay at Finschafen, which was also considered an advanced base, was designed to acclimatize us to the area, a prelude to the real thing. We're strictly on our own where we are now.

As time passes, I have a sense that our battalion is accumulating prestige. Because of this, I expect that we're slated for a more difficult job in the near future, perhaps in only a couple of months. Of course, there's only one direction to go: north, the Philippines, some lesser known island, or China. Who knows? I'm betting that there's a bigger assignment for us somewhere.

Last night I saw my first movie at this base: "Coney Island"[3] with Betty Grable, George Montgomery[4] and Caesar Romero.[5] Since it has been so long since I've seen a movie, I enjoyed the Technicolor and the music more than usual.

This evening we'll be given some beer. I usually accept mine and give it to friends. It's about time to pick it up. Bye. I'll be with you tomorrow, Dad.

6/28/44

Dear Mom & Dad,

My past few letters have been a tale in retrospect, about things that took place one year ago, principally because during that brief period the monotonous course of my life was interrupted.

I've now been in the service one year to this very day. It has been one year since I raised my right hand. I call this day the first anniversary of ENLIGHTENMENT. Not until I left on the train from Boston, can I say that I was on my own and completely independent. That day began a test for us all. Did you as parents do a good job in bringing me up? And do I, your son, live up to the standards that you have set for me?

I can say, unflinchingly, in absolute truth, that both you and I have succeeded. My triumph is entirely dependent on yours so let me tell you what I've done.

When I set out on this venture, I confess I was unsure of myself, and I could see in your eyes a degree of faltering confidence in me. Both of you must have wondered what the culmination of the past eighteen years under your guidance would be like, and I also wondered whether I could live up to what you tried to give me. After reviewing each crisis of the past year, I can say that I'm proud of you both, proud as a son can be, for I found that I could cope with every situation that was unlike any I've ever had to face before. Not that I did the right thing in every instance, but, knowing right from wrong, I have a clear conscience, and I believe that the past year represents a job well done by all.

It's less my achievement and more your victory. My actions reflect on you. I've tried to make them shine brilliantly.

I long for the day I return. Inspired by an appreciation of your success in my upbringing, I can take supreme delight in this day. Thank you both, my parents.

Evening 6/28/44

Dear Dad,

Due to the recent excellent mail service my morale has improved 100%.

Since my latest photos are a hit, and everyone is "getting a kick out of the coins and bills," as you put it, I'm inclined to believe that you are getting a great kick out of showing them. You're worse than a kid and that's how I want you to be: eternally young.

It has been quite dull around here lately, too dull for comfort. As a rule, whenever things return to normalcy, off we go again somewhere else.

Dad, I read a paragraph in Aunt Sadie's letter that struck me square in the face. It concerned Cousin Bobby having written a will making his mother beneficiary. Dad, that's absolutely ridiculous. It's tactless. It's something that is designed to tear at a mother's heart while glorifying the son's role in a battle that he hasn't even participated in, or may never have to. Anyway, the worldly possessions of a lost son would automatically go to the nearest of kin. I don't wish to belittle Bobby especially, but I do blame those men who are instigating such a practice. Some of my friends are friendly with fighter pilots, and even they have never heard of such a practice. Boys who make wills should be taught a lesson by being exposed to combat conditions immediately. If a boy is worried about dying, and concerned about his parents' welfare after his death, why break two hearts by making a will? Why inflict worry on his loved ones?

Since being overseas, I haven't seen battle and I hope I never have to. Before embarking from Finschafen for this base, most, if not all of us, expected hot and heavy action. I admit the thought of dying did enter my mind. But it faded immediately. I felt confident and was determined to do my part. All of us felt that way. We had no thought of death and believed sincerely that we'd enjoy the spoils of victory. To consider dying and making a will seemed absolutely foolish. Of course, when we learned that we wouldn't see action, we were relieved. Any seasoned soldier will tell you that the anticipation of battle is harder to endure than being in the battle itself. So I experienced the first stage, that of anticipation along with everyone else. And not a man among us thought of making out a will. We're 10,000 miles nearer to the enemy than the boys at Bobby's airfield, and not one of us considered doing such a thing.

While I've hidden very little from you folks, I don't tell you everything to avoid causing you needless worry. Things that happen here that might alarm you seem insignificant to us.

Most of this letter is venting my wrath after reading the passage in Sadie's letter. I'll try to do better tomorrow when I'm not so mad.

6/29/44

Dear Mom,

Today's surveying project brought us far away from camp across the bay. We found a beautiful mile-long palm fringed beach. Only a handful of navy boys were stationed there. Of course, we had a job to do, but we weren't about to pass up doing some swimming in such a beautiful spot. I stayed in the warm water for over an hour; I enjoyed it so much. The surf, combers as high as ten feet, was great. What fun, boy oh boy. The spot was typical of those seen in magazine pictures of the South Seas.

Yes, I've often thought of the hospital care that is available to veterans. My prime concern now is government-financed education. Take notice of any information on the subject. We hear little of the government's postwar benefits.

Each day I see indications that we're not going to stay here very long. Bear in mind that this is merely my opinion, and not a statement of fact.

I plan to visit Henry Wolf, the boy from Philly, who lives in a tent about three minutes from here. We're both so busy, we rarely see each other.

Al Martin, the fellow with whom I spent most of my liberties in Hollywood, is in charge of the movie projector. He visited me the other night.

I've made some fine friends in this outfit. There are four or five of them I'd like to correspond with after the war. One of the men with whom I share a tent is a structural engineer, age 34, comes from central Illinois. He's quite a chap, a swell guy. In the evening we have many talks discussing all sorts of things. During the past two months he's given me advice on many battalion matters. In fact, he was instrumental in getting me my present job.

Mr. Baldner, my former bunkmate in Finschafen, lives elsewhere. We were separated when the tents were erected for the communications group to which I was then attached. Since then we never got to share a tent together, but I visit him occasionally.

It's 8:00, time to leave for Henry's tent. I'll be with you tomorrow.

6/30/44

Just to fill up a little spare time:

A CAT'S TALE

Even after two and one half years and a world away in the Pacific, I can remember him vividly enough to write this.

I found him in our back yard when, I guess, he was a kitten and a half. You would probably know more about the adolescent age of a cat than I. He was hungry. Anybody could tell. He had a lean body, not very large features for a male, and a gaunt, hollow face. At the time I was hunting grasshoppers, and, those I offered, he ate with relish. Perhaps you remember when grasshoppers and snakes were my constant passion.

I invited him, forcibly I admit, to the house, and we fed him a little milk and meat scraps. Of course, he carried out to a T the usual cat procedure before taking his meal. He had to familiarize himself with his surroundings, a trait common to his race. He moseyed under the sofa and beds, tried to pry into the closets, and peered into cracks to see whether he had missed anything important. Evidently he was satisfied. After the meal he looked no further and made himself at home by falling into an enviable slumber.

We put him out that night expecting never to see him again. Surprised were we when bright and early next morning, he was sitting at the back door already looking better. How could we refuse to take him in? All of us after a few minutes deliberation agreed to accept him as our steady boarder.

As a rule, the first thing a master does when he gets a new pet is to name it. We searched endlessly for a suitable name. My mother had little to offer on the subject because undoubtedly she had already used up all the names that ever suited her on her two sons. Finally, we unanimously decided to call him just plain Kitty, mainly because he answered to that name if pronounced with the proper accent, as my mother could do so well. When she called in a tinkly voice, "kitty, kitty, kitty," in quick succession, he always responded by coming to her.

Now Kitty wasn't especially handsome, nor for that matter was there anything particularly outstanding about him — his physical appearance, I mean. His size was unspectacular, his fur average in texture and neutral gray, but his face, one had to admit, was pleasing, not cross like so many other tom-cats I know. His face was fascinating to watch. Such emotions as anger, boredom, happiness, and supplication were clearly definable, requiring little or no imagination to recognize. Because of these human expressions, we came to respect him and treat him as an additional member of the family.

The four of us, Dad, Mother, my younger brother and I had distinctive relationships with our new pet, and they were often amusing. For instance, my father's was the most complex — that is complex to my father. He was not one to make a row over cats or dogs, as the rest of us were inclined to do. In fact, he contracted a downright dislike for them, because they annoyed him when carrying on transactions as a salesman of reupholstered furniture in the homes of pet-loving customers. (On the other hand, it never occurred to him that were it not for the damage cats did to his prospective customers' sofas and easy chairs, he would have had less business.) During our deliberation on accepting the cat, he was definitely against admitting him to our household. But seeing our concern over Kitty, he gave in and permitted him to live "out of his pocket," as he put it.

On occasional evenings after work, while Dad was sitting in his cigar perfumed chair, reading the evening paper, he would eye beyond its corner either my brother or myself gleefully ruffling up Kitty's fur. Down the paper would come followed by wild expostulations that we would surely come down with some dread disease, bubonic plague or something of that ilk. In the morning after stumbling out of bed, still dazed from sleep and spying the cat, Dad would assume an air of wrath and make false motions to kick him. The rest of us would be outraged at this performance, but we confess he never followed through with his kick, nor for that matter did we ever see him actually harm Kitty.

Indeed, one day I caught him red-handed slyly petting Kitty's fluffy mane and talking to him in a murmuring monotone, outdoing Kitty's own purring. Finding this exposé most embarrassing, he was so perplexed that he offered no explanation and pretended indifference.

I believe Kitty liked Mother the most, because she handled him so gently and tactfully. She never aggravated him, which my brother and I were wont to do. She was usually the one to feed him, and her tender caresses inevitably brought on ecstatic fits of purring. I'd say Mother had a special way with cats.

Although my brother and I treated Kitty much more roughly than we really should have, he seemed to forgive us after each ordeal was over.

After a few months, we took Kitty for granted, expecting his silent begging at mealtime, assuring ourselves of his presence with glances of approval at his relaxing by the stove on wintry evenings, opening the back door in the morning to watch him strut in, his fur coated with dew. All these things we got used to and accepted as part of our daily routine.

Of course, he had his problems. During the time when cats seem to go berserk, the so-called mating period, we nursed his cuts. He was quite a scrapper, for sure. But I observed that, although he had certain neighborhood admirers, before long he won the respect of all his enemies as well. I believe he was the only cat who could saunter through the field behind our house without some jealous rival pouncing on him or some barking dog causing him to arch his back in defense.

Often, I feared one morning we would not find Kitty at the door. It was during the week of Pearl Harbor, when that morning finally came. How I remember it! Instead, the phone rang. My mother answered and I heard the voice of a nearby neighbor boom through. At first, my mother's voice was high-pitched with delight then it simmered down to an almost imperceptible whisper. My heart gained a beat. I couldn't make out the conversation. Why was my heart pounding so? I knew something was wrong. The click of the receiver resounded in an odd and suspended silence as the words, "Kitty was just run over," surged through the thickening atmosphere. Impossible, my mind insisted. Never before had I suffered the loss of a loved one. And why should I feel this way about a mere cat? Yet my mind kept repeating, impossible, impossible.

Very shortly afterwards the neighbor brought Kitty to our house. A flicker of life remained in his limp, matted body. After my mother laid him gently on a pillow on the kitchen linoleum that was so familiar to him, she administered water through an eyedropper to his parched lips. But it was no use; he couldn't swallow. His eyes closed tightly then relaxed, as a tear trickled down his agonizing face.

Leaving Kitty in my mother's hands, I reported to school very low in spirit. But my thoughts remained with Kitty in the kitchen where he lay. During sixth period my mother called school to inform me that the Animal Rescue League took Kitty away. Nothing could save him, she said. Containing myself until I got home, I sat down to dinner without an appetite. Half way through the meal, a lump formed in my throat and gradually thickened until finally I exploded into a shower of tears. Feeling a deep release, I was experiencing my first tragic loss in life.

Next morning, by pre-arrangement the week before, a new linoleum was installed on the kitchen floor. Kitty, our loved and marvelous cat, and the linoleum so familiar to him, were both gone forever.

7/1/44

Dear Cousin Sol,

Hanging over the mantel in your living room is a portrait painting that everyone is drawn to by its warmth. Invariably, the viewer, full of admiration, comments on it. You nod approvingly. To you its significance is profound. Beyond the fact that the subject of the painting is dear to you and that you're sentimentally affected by it, you also appreciate every brush line put into it.

You perceive in this representation of your father, as a meditative interpreter of God and a learned old man, something symbolic. He symbolizes a great religion and its enormous history of trial. But everyone who gazes at the painting can't help sensing its eternal meaning. But you see beyond the abstraction of sensing. You are conscious of its positive significance, because you are proud of your father.

Were I to say to you of your father's death, "I'm sorry," or "I feel for you," or "I know how it is," or "It's all for the best," or "Chin up," I'd be speaking only superficial, banal phrases which only serve to probe your wound and are inadequate to ease your pain.

I know you loved your father as I love mine. How can I offer you true consolation? But take heart in knowing we all love, and will continue to love, the man, your father, in the painting.

Sat. 7/1/44

Dear Mom,

With mail from home coming regularly, happy days are here again. Yesterday was the first day I've had off since arriving at this base. I wrote a few letters, studied, and just lay around.

I hear that Dewey has been nominated. With him running, I expect a close election. We're hearing news of the European front daily.[1] It won't be long before the Pacific war will be making headlines again.

Sun. 7/2/44

I saw another show last night, "The Bride Came C.O.D"[1] with Cagney[2] and Bette Davis. Who said we get the latest pictures? That's what they tell the folks back home, but we don't get them.

Enclosed is a picture of almost everyone who was in communications in Finschafen. (See photograph below.) The beards, which were raised for such pictures, were ornamental. The men are now minus their beards. Notice the coconut palms in the background. The area was covered with them. The fellow kneeling third from right, name of Collins,[3] comes from Jefferson, Mass.[4]

The other pictures, which I couldn't send before because of the sign appearing in them, were taken at Satelberg. Al Malter is holding the lamp in one. (See photograph below.) By the way, I received a letter from him only yesterday. He is still in the -------- Guinea or Australia.

We have a Red Cross in the area, girls too. However, they confine their work to combat flyers and the like. When the base becomes more settled, a permanent Red Cross building will be erected. Usually such things happen when we're about to leave.

7/3/44

Dear Mom,

By now you folks must be getting a taste of the sort of weather that we've had to endure for almost five months. Impossible! Five months overseas already. Seems more like five weeks. I can remember when to talk in terms of months seemed such a long time; yet, now two months are nothing. It's odd how one's concept of time changes so suddenly. It's similar with distance. A hundred miles is a short stretch. I predict that after the war people are going to do more traveling, because the boys coming home have no sense of distance. Where I am is probably as far away from home on earth as I could possibly get. My next escapade will have to be to the moon.

Do you realize that I've not really been homesick since being in the service? I had been a boy who never left home for a single day by himself; yet once I left I hardly missed its atmosphere of security.

Speaking of traveling, I've made rough plans to see Australia before returning home. Henry Wolf will join me to spend our leave in three cities: Brisbane, Sydney, and Melbourne. If I get there I want to see a lot of the place. Henry and I click together. We had swell times in New Orleans and you may recall that I was with Henry the day I called you from Union Station in Providence.

7/5/44

Dear Mom,

Thanks for the watch straps, but please no more. I can now go into the watch strap business. The newspapers are arriving steadily and furnish excellent material for my after dinner indisposition. Nothing like a good bathroom library.

Some of your statements lead me to believe that you underrate your letters. I want you to know, Mom, that they are tops, and can't be beat, and without them I wouldn't be worth a darn. Sure, your letters are factual. What else could they be? And some express sentiments and feelings that no one could express better. Whether they are about Aunt Suzie's cat or a trip to Boston, they put me in heaven. My Mom's letters can't be beat. Do you hear that? Now I want no more apologies from you concerning your letters.

Tell me folks, has my face in the snapshots that you've placed on open exhibition changed expression? After all the attention it has been getting it should have by now.

Ronnie, Ronnie, Ronnie, what's wrong with you, passing up a chance to see a double header? Boy, I'd give a million to see one right now. We listen to the games over the radio every afternoon, and with the Boston Red Sox too.

More than a year ago I more or less expected Grandma's marriage to fail. Too bad she had to learn that there can be no substitute for Grandpa.

I've always had the impression that I wasn't popular with my aunts. And they had good reason to feel that way due to my stubborn arrogance and tactless behavior. However, I'm glad that I'm now popular with them. I still don't understand the sudden change of heart, but I sure welcome the swell letters they've been sending me.

I think I'm gaining weight again. I suppose I'm eating more than I can sweat off.

You've persuaded me to retract my request for the Schick. You're right. I'll use the safety razor while overseas.

So you find the price of pineapples high. Not me. I just go out and pick 'em free. I had a delicious one yesterday. But our regular chow is also swell.

To answer your question regarding bathing, I go bathing in both the surf and in streams.

You should give Stanley the Jap postage stamp that I sent. We rarely run across foreign stamps, because all the foreigners have been evacuated. However, I'll keep my eyes open for some.

I'm not sure what Jap articles I'll bring home with me. From experience I believe in traveling light. I don't wish to bring home a mess of junk to clutter up the house. Some boys have Jap weapons. Not having a serious desire to scavenge for souvenirs, I'm not as lucky. Soon, I expect, you'll find the country full of them. It will be just like the last war was with German weapons.

I imagine Ronnie quit Young Judea for the same reasons I quit AZA, for which I don't blame myself. The members spent money foolishly and lavishly. They didn't talk about girls with respect. And those girls with whom I had contact were unimpressive. The organization was controlled by a clique.

I've been writing this letter on and off all day. Just returned from seeing a show, a Blondie picture. Had a box seat too, (that is, I was sitting on a box, Seabee style, since not all the seats have been installed at the theater). The picture was funny. Last night I saw Rosalind Russell[1] and Fred McMurray in "Take a Letter Darling."[2] I'm getting to be quite a movie fan again. The movies are months old, but it's my only recreation.

Don't worry folks, I'm off dud bombs for life. You'll never catch me near one.

I've seen few animals or snakes in our neighborhood. There are a few wild boars, and I've seen a baby kangaroo.[3] The snakes here don't bother us. It's as safe living on the land here as it is back home. I still haven't figured out why the natives build their villages over water. The hills drop right down to the sea. Maybe that's why.

You hit the nail on the head when you wrote that we'd move as soon as we regained a normal way of living. But I don't mind. It's thrilling to move and watch things grow from a wilderness. No doubt the wanderlust has captured me. I'd like to see more of this part of the world.

The Chase girl wrote a mostly introductory letter requesting that I give her info about myself. Frankly, I'm sick of writing about ME. I find it detestable. Anyway, I answered her because I welcome new correspondents. She might help me break out of my shell when I get home.

Taps just blue (I mean blew), and I must douse the glimmer. All the mail coming in sure does my heart good. Since I have tomorrow off, I'll take it easy an indulge in some "horizontal recreation," lying in the sack to you.

7/6/44

Dear Ronnie,

Your letter was a humdinger, kid. It brought many a welcome chuckle to this Seabee. Yousah, yousah, let's have more of them.

You might try various ways of persuading Dad to let you drive. Threaten to report him to the Gas Rationing board for pickling his car and accumulating gas coupons to sell. Another way would be to trick him into driving down Mill Street while you pester him so much that he puts you behind the wheel. That's what I did, and it worked. Trouble was, when I took off, I almost knocked the transmission haywire.

Life has been dull here lately. No more Japs or rodents to hunt down. It has been raining in the late evening the past few days, causing the guys with leaky tent roofs to suffer. A corner of our tent leaks. The poor guy sleeping under it awakes in the morning swimming in a puddle.

Recently the water pressure in our showers had dropped so that after you got wet and soaped yourself the water would turn off. After this happened a few evenings we got madder and madder. Now it's fixed and back to normal.

The natives are often funny. They like to wear clothes and dress in the oddest ways. Some walk around with army canteens and such junk attached to their person while wearing parts of navy uniforms. Where they get this stuff is a mystery.

The other day I watched a native walking in a haughty fashion. He was so proud of his gay[1] new clothing. Yep, he acted as if he were king of them all, bossing everybody around. From his manner you'd think he could only talk to God. He was wearing a beautiful, dashingly gay set of full fledged American pajamas. My, my, monkeys and our natives are the cwaziest people.[2] Bye.

5:30 PM 7/8/44

Dear Mom,

I couldn't write yesterday because our party was on a job some distance from camp, and we slept over. After returning this evening, we expect to leave again for a couple of days so don't expect any letters for those days.

It was pretty tough out there for a while. Yesterday the heat was like an inferno, and today it poured, and we got drenched to the skin. Actually, we returned to camp to change our clothes. Although it was a bit rough I enjoyed it. Swimming in the surf made up for the inconveniences. Remember, when I was a Boy Scout and you were skeptical about letting me camp overnight? I'm doing it now, Mom, and enjoying it.

9:30 PM

I just left the theater (and now have a debutante's accent) after seeing "Stronger than Desire"[1] with Walter Pidgeon and Virginia Bruce.[2] Enjoyed it.

Tonight, after a day of rain the sky is crystal clear and the moon is gorgeous. It compares with any tropical moon shown in advertisements and the movies. It has a golden appearance as it hangs low above the horizon.

7/10/44

Dear Mom,

I just returned this evening after spending two days away from camp on a job. We slept beneath palm trees in jungle hammocks on a coral-fringed beach. The swimming was glorious. The water is so warm that I usually stay in for a half hour or more. Still it's invigorating, and you're not chilled after getting out.

Last night the woolen blankets came in handy, or we would have frozen during the night. However all was not rosy. Our work was hot and hard. But who cared, with a good swim waiting for us after work.

My watch has finally gone on the blink. It runs for a while, then stops. I find a watch almost indispensable. I believe if I send it home to be repaired, it will get there.

Yes, switching from one job to another has not been good. But I had hoped to get a rating at each change. When I saw that my chances were nil in Recreation and Communications, I saw no sense in staying with it. However, I don't expect to advance in my surveying job, but, at least, I have a good job which, since there's no night work involved, allows me to get a night's sleep. I vowed that I'd stick with this job no matter what. Although the work isn't easy, it's not bad. I'm continually outdoors, and often the work is pleasant. I don't plan to do surveying in civilian life. I'm not crazy about doing this for a life's work. I did like the work in Communications, until I was assigned to the switchboard. One thing is certain: I'm discovering what I don't want to do after I return.

The camp's conveniences have probably reached their peak. Of course, now it's time to leave. I hear that Saipan,[1] a very valuable base,[2] is now in our hands.

I'm sort of weary this evening. You know how swimming does that. After sleeping in a sagging hammock, my bunk looks mighty inviting.

7/11/44

Dear Mom,

Having been given the day off after yesterday's camping trip, I did little more than lie around reading and studying. No doubt, I do find it hard to concentrate due to the heat and the noise from the fellows. You know how much I like to study when it's quiet. Still, often when I had my mind fully on a subject, I could study despite a hubbub. I blame my inability to concentrate on not having studied for over a year. Nevertheless, I'm completing my lessons in spite of the difficulty.

I just learned that there's an experienced watchmaker with his own tools in the battalion. Rather than send the watch home, I plan to look him up.

Lately I've had spells of impatience with being in the service. I find it monotonous, and it seems that from now on it's all a waste of time. I'm tired of a life of always being the underdog. But I must dismiss such thoughts from my mind. As I say, they come up only occasionally. You needn't preach to me that this period is only temporary. Beneath it all, I know that.

Hundreds of opinions abound regarding when we'll see the States again. Some predict by this Christmas (which I consider ridiculous), others in two years. A battalion's average stay is about eighteen months. Since the war here will reach a climax some time within the next year, we'll probably remain here for the duration. It does no good to speculate, to be optimistic or pessimistic, but instead we should consider the cold facts. Logic tells us we have considerable time still ahead of us here.

Of course, the armed forces rarely act logically regarding troop rotation, so who knows when we might return? Frankly, I'd rather return for good after the war is over, than return and have to ship out again. So what we need is a hasty end to the war to be sure of our return.

Well, folks, I've been in the service over a year and haven't had a cup of coffee or tea, although it's served daily. I don't consider this any sillier than abstaining from smoking cigarettes. Anyway, I don't see what pleasure I'd get from any of the stuff. Instead, I've been relishing our delicious water and fruit juices. As you know, we have no milk. I do enjoy the cocoa, which is served often. I imagine that you and Dad figured I'd be drinking harder stuff. Nosiree. I should have bet on it, before I left.

7/13/44

Dear Mom,

The past few days have been comparatively easy. There's been little work, although the slowdown is only temporary, and at night I watch movies.

Last night, sentimental fool that I am, I saw an Andy Hardy picture[1] that we had seen long, long ago. The second time proved to be doubly enjoyable because it reminded me of the civilian heaven of the past.

A few days ago I talked shop with a couple of upholsterers who are in the battalion. Until that time I didn't know there were any. One of them specialized in car upholstery in Chicago, and the other owned a small upholstery business near Grand Rapids, Mich. I felt completely at home discussing such things as Cross tacks, BFM webbing, J.K, Birch & Co. and Andrew Dutton.[2] Oh, we had a grand time looking back, estimating how many times we banged our fingers with the magnet hammer and how many tacks we may have swallowed. Understand, though, that I didn't profess to be any kind of upholsterer. That I had a Dad in the business carried enough weight with them for us to have a jolly discussion.

My long, oh so long, years of association with Dad permitted me to express my views on brocatelles, mohairs (extinct now, eh) etc. After using Dad's line admirably, I was able to convince them that I was a veteran of the trade.

The businessman from Michigan sold out before enlisting in the Seabees and anticipates re-opening upon his return. Trying to persuade him to play sick and be discharged, I guaranteed him a job in Worcester, but alas, the poor man has already gone this far, so he's reconciled to going the rest of the way under the navy yoke. Poor soul.

I miss the ever so familiar fragrance of cigar smoke that I knew at home. Indeed, I've done my darndest to promote the purchase of cigars by our tent personnel. One of my mates, Ralph, cooperates and withholds smoking his cigar until I'm present. But cigars being in great demand, and the supply meager, about all Ralph can do is smoke one a week.

To me a cigar and Dad go together. That's why I like smelling cigar smoke. Of course, the idea that I'd ever smoke a cigar is ridiculous, but having been brought up in an atmosphere of cigar smoke certainly profoundly affects my desire to be in the presence of that intoxicating inhalant.[3]

With little more to say than "Bye 'til tomorrow,"[4] I close with Love to you, Dad and Ronnie, Hughie (Crazy? Could be.)

Thurs. night 7/13/44

Dear Mom,

Recall Dad's and your remembrance of places past when you'd say, and probably still do, "When I was a boy, I roamed those alleys," or "When I was a girl, I frequented that dance hall." I can picture in detail Dad's pointing out a familiar place in OLD Boston. Now, I don't mean only the Boston of the gay nineties[1] where he spent a phase of his boyhood. Behind his enthusiastic descriptions were deep feelings that cause him to revel in his old haunts such as Pie Alley,[2] with the many stories it elicited, Washington Street[3] and its crowds. That's what I mean: places mean plenty. They play significant roles in our thinking.

Obviously, through the years I've developed an attachment to dear old Worcester, especially after visiting so many other cities. But even something about those cities, places that were wonderful to see, seems vivid in my memory, and I'd like to seem them again.

Just returned from seeing a show: "Stardust"[4] with John Payne[5] and Linda Darnell.[6] Although its plot was simple, it was entertaining. The setting was sophisticated Hollywood, and there on the screen I saw again the sights of my California liberty days. Doggone, they looked good. I'm surprised because after a month or so I wasn't so enthused with Hollywood. I thought the place would mean little to me, but instead I was happy to see it again in the movie. How odd, that the memory of a place can be so sweet, can stir a melody within you, and can lift you to heights of glee.

During my travels, I've seen a lot of America, the good side that is. I've purposely ignored the banal and cheap side.

With someone else doing the thinking for us, there isn't much here to keep our minds active. Although back home my mind was occupied with little things, I also had to deal with big things, school, and it occupied most of my conversation. But out here we think of only the little things. The service offers nothing big to think about. That's why my letters seem to deal with minutia. I wouldn't be surprised if they often bore you. Unfortunately you're my unwilling victim of an occasional silly notion or a passing thought.

Having some time to spare this evening, I thought: what could be more entertaining than writing you about a momentary thought. Thus this letter.

7/14/44

Dear Mom,

It's Friday night. And surprise, I attended Jewish services. A Jewish chaplain, Chaplain Whittaker U.S.A. from Brooklyn, of course, (Where else?) arrived in our area. Considering the abnormal conditions here, he conducted the service well. The scene was picturesque: a small European chapel battered by myriad bullet holes, dimly lit by three Coleman lanterns. The chaplain was extremely friendly, inquisitive, and charming. I hope to attend more of his services. I also met a few boys there from Massachusetts.

Some mail arrived this afternoon, but woe is me, none from home. Johnson's letter, always welcome, was as jovial and vigorous as ever. Gad, his letters do something to me. His sense of humor is unmatched.

Yetta wrote a very sweet letter, patting me on the back for this and that, and reminding me to keep punching. Uncle Harry enclosed a well written typewritten note. As a talker he's marvelous at putting his thoughts across, likewise as a letter writer. He discussed my present transitional experience. I'd like to study the note some more, before sending it home for you to read.

I also received my first issue of *Time* magazine, which is about two weeks old but up to the minute so far as I'm concerned. Not only do I find its articles interesting, but I also enjoy its coverage of cultural subjects, cinema, literature, politics etc.

The war news of late appears encouraging, with Saipan taken, and attacks on Guam[1] renewed. I suppose things in Europe are going about as well as could be expected. For certain Germany is doomed. It's impossible to wage war on three fronts,[2] perhaps four including Yugoslavia. Two fronts were difficult to maintain during the last war. It's absurd that Germany could think that she can sustain armies on so many battlefields.

Along with Germany Japan is fighting a losing war, and she knows it. Both nations are searching for a means to lessen the penalties due them. They can only count on a last stand and their diplomatic skills to convince us that they aren't so bad after all.[3]

7/16/44

Dear Mom,

After just completing a long letter to Johnson this evening, I'm about to have writer's cramp. I just realized that were I to compile one week's worth of my daily letters to you, it's equivalent to six hours of writing.

Chow was pretty good this evening; ice cream was the highlight, our first taste of it in more than two months. In the future, we expect to have it more frequently.

I'm still with the surveying crew tramping the hillsides and enjoying it. I always did like walking. The most exciting thing around here is the anticipated birth of pups to the dog next door. Evidently the boys are planning to go into the pup business. Having built a home-made kennel they introduced a very passionate male as husband to their lively bitch.

The *Gazettes* are coming in so fast, I can't keep up with them. I was amused over the row the newspapers made over D-Day. The American people are certainly demonstrative. I don't think that running about or shouting wildly was appropriate that day.

It's so dull around here that in vain I'm trying to write something interesting.

7/17/44

Dear Mom,

My cabinet shelf is abundant with reading matter such as newspapers, *Time* magazine, *Omnibook*, a book on Russia that I'm now reading, and a to be read borrowed book on religious philosophy. After glancing through the book reviews in *Time*, I have the desire to get my hands on some best sellers. I had considered asking you to send me a book occasionally, but on second thought I decided that would be impractical, as I already have more baggage than I can carry.

From what I read, the latest information regarding postwar education for veterans is this: you're eligible for a free first year of college if under 25, the annual tuition allowance will be $500, and there will be a $50.00 per month bonus for living expenses. If your school performance is satisfactory you become eligible for three more years of free tuition. The legislation has now been passed, and it's time to work at securing the benefits. I've asked Johnson to investigate what the procedure is for applying. With such positive financing, I may alter my choice of college. I find MIT[1] very attractive, as I presume it also is to you. But we'll postpone a discussion on this matter until we can thrash it out back home.

If I remember correctly, the premium on my insurance policy is about due. I know that you'll take care of it. This is merely to let you know that I'm thinking about it.

I find it easy to picture mid-summer way up there in New England. Last March I found it difficult even to conceive of snow, and felt strange when you mentioned it. I suspect that you, having winter blood as thick as jelly, are suffering more than we are from the heat. My blood is now so thin that I fear its red coloring will disappear in another six months. If I happen to arrive home in the winter, I'll be certain to experience the most miserable winter of my life. Only last week a few of us were complaining of being cold on a rather cool day when the temperature reached the amazing low of 74 degrees Fahrenheit. In such a frigid, yes, arctic temperature, they shivered while taking showers. Discouraging, isn't it?

The more I read about Dewey the more I like him. He isn't the clever politico that Roosevelt is, and he is indebted to nobody. Roosevelt had to hand out favors in return for favors. But Dewey has asked nothing of anybody. By saying as little as possible, he seems to have broken with the conventional way a candidate gets elected.

I have the impression that the U.S. has not expediently handled the problem of recently captured areas. Italy appears to have strong Communist leanings, and so does France. The great reforms that can be expected after this is over may not be so democratic. In Germany, Italy and to some extent, in France, democracy has failed. Russia has a better opportunity to foster movements than does the U.S. and Britain. I like the spirit of American individual enterprise, but I also find myself admiring the Russian form of government that existed prior to the war.[2]

7/19/44

Dear Mom,

After the show last night we had cookies and ice cream, and this morning, helping me get over my hangover, two letters from home arrived. Your use of the poetic phrase "a song in my heart,"[1] strikes a sentimental note unsurpassed in any previous letter. I liked it, Mom.

Now that you've received the prescription for my glasses, I hope you'll have them made as quickly as possible. At this end, I'm seeing what I can do to have new lenses made on a hospital ship. I don't wear glasses except to see a show. It must be amusing for others to see me watching a motion picture between the cracks in my lenses. But I manage to maneuver around them without sacrificing the full benefit of seeing some curvaceous beauty on the screen.

What a break: an experienced watch maker is cleaning my watch. Fortunately, no parts were needed. The watchmaker commented on its fine seventeen jewel movement. Its purchase at Endicott has proved to be quite a buy. I could get $100 for it here, but nothing doing.

Dad, do you remember the good old days when silk floss (kapok) was plentiful for making pillows, or is it no longer extinct? If it's still hard to find, I can easily oblige by sending you some kapok in the raw. That's right, there are kapok trees, the size of maples, here. The kapok itself is found in green pods. So, Dad, for the mere price of postage, I'll send you all you want. Of course you'll have to process the pods, separate the seeds from the silk, that is.

I've also made another great discovery. There are rubber trees here.

7/20/44

Dear Mom,

Many things that I like to write about are really unimportant. I know you want to hear about me and what I'm doing but after a while there's nothing more about ME to write about and what I'm doing is merely daily routine. I could fill pages every day about this or that which has nothing to do with us at all. My story about the cat is an example. I've written things for myself because I enjoyed doing it, then tore them up fearing that you'd be bored reading them. What I'm getting at is to ask whether you'd like me to send some of this nonsense home to you or would it be disappointing and of little interest?

I try to make every letter interesting, but, frankly, I don't always write what I'd really like to write. And I'm afraid what I like to write won't please you, because it would only express thoughts and not be informative. Most parents, of course, like to know what their sons are doing. It rarely occurs to them that in the service their sons are doing less as individuals than when they were civilians. We spend much of our time just lying around, little food for letter writing. Knowing that you like descriptive letters full of information, I've hesitated to write a story I might like to tell or discuss a passing thought that I'm enthused about.

Lately, I've become interested in modern literature and would like to read more best sellers. I enjoy *Omnibook* because each month it offers condensed versions of the five best sellers. No doubt you know what's coming. Yep, a request to send me a subscription to *Omnibook*. For its size it's an expensive magazine, but I think it's worth it. How about it, huh?

Enclosed is Uncle Harry's note. Pretty good, don't you think? He suggested several things that I never considered. I felt guilty when he referred to my so-called suffering and responsibility for myself. I haven't suffered a bit, Mom, and the navy has to a great degree assumed responsibility for taking care of me. I replied to Harry this evening.

Tomorrow being my day off, I expect to go on a little excursion of my own around the bay. I plan to write a longer letter tomorrow if my plan materializes.

7/21/44

Dear Mom,

This evening, contrary to expectations, I have no great experience to tell about. A N.G. drizzle kept me confined to the tent all day reading. In place of the anticipated description of the trip I didn't make, I'll fulfill an old request of yours and introduce my bunkmates.

We are now seven in this tent, and I'll begin from right to left as you enter. The guy in the righthand corner comes from North Carolina. He's six feet tall, blond, a fine looking rebel, who has spent a year at the University of North Carolina. He is, reputedly, a dashing Casanova and receives oh so many letters from oh so many femmes. His greatest problem in life is writing a letter as passionate as the ones he receives. Currently, he drives a truck.

Bunking next to him is, Ralph, a middle-aged fellow from Illinois. My most intimate friend in the tent, he and I customarily dine together and talk about events over the chow table. He wakes me up in the morning, if the reveille call fails to. Ralph is reserved and clean cut, and a structural draftsman by trade. Not having had a college education, he's a self-made man who studied evenings while holding down a fine job in civilian life. Our officers have implicit faith in his judgment and constantly consult him. His ambition is to get more schooling then get married, before, as he puts it, he can no longer find the dividing line between his face and his scalp. Oddly enough he actually does structural drafting for the battalion, even though he's a structural draftsman. Catch?

Next is a guy from the land of lakes, Minnesota. No, his name isn't Olson and he's not Swedish. He is middle aged, unmarried, not a bad sort if you ignore his arrogance and silly prejudices. He likes to argue, and so do I, so I keep my mouth shut which makes both of us happy. Also a truck driver, his ambition is to return to his beloved Minnesota and meet some charming damsel.

In the far lefthand corner is a six foot tall, slim, red-headed, freckle-faced boy of nineteen. Pardon me while I wipe the sweat off my brow. Ding—that's what we call him—hails from Joisey. He's a pretty smart boy and has often been away from home. Right now he's homesick. A nice boy, he is also madly in love with some fair damsel to whom he writes letters after spending hours every night pondering what to say. As a civilian he worked for Armour Meat Packing, and his hobby was raising homing pigeons[1] and hell simultaneously. He services the battalion's bulldozers.

We'll skip over the next guy who comes from Worcester because he's a jerk anyway, and we know all about jerks.

The next bunkmate, another professed lady killer, is a boy about nineteen from South Carolina. His pappy—that's what he calls his father—is a mail carrier, so that's what he wants to be. His motto: "The mail must go through."

Lastly, is another boy my age from North Carolina, and of course, an avid admirer of females. He operates a bulldozer. We call bulldozer operators catskinners, so he's a catskinner. He used to work for the TVA and considers himself the black sheep of his family.

That's all of us in this tent. None are Texans, Californians or bums[2] from Brooklyn that have been my predominant bunkmates in the past. We are a pretty fine, harmonious bunch, always chipping in to do the cleaning of tent and grounds.

Our pet subject is fighting the Civil War all over again in which each man maintains that his state is the best. I'm branded a Bostonian Yankee, definitely not a Worcesterite, because they can't pronounce the name of the city anyway. A few are irked with and others are fascinated by my so-called accent. In vain I try to convince them that it's they who have the accent. I believe that Colonel Lemuel G. Stoopnagle, in his forthcoming book that he wrote to stop the draft that blows through the gap between his two bookends, explains the situation famously. The Colonel says, and I quote, "A Virginian says oot for out (I can vouch for that), a Brooklynite says berl for boil (moider for kill, too), a Bostonian (ahem) says Haavaad for Harvard (caa for automobile, too) and a Californian (the magnificent Californian) says dew for rain (Ain't it the truth)."

So long folksies until tomorrow and don't pick any sour apples as you're liable (I'll sue you) to fall down and hurt yourself.

Love to all of you, Hughie (Yep, I'm still sane.)

7/22/44

Dear Mom,

This morning the repair man just returned my watch all cleaned and in tip-top shape. Cost: one dollar. I call that a pretty good break. Also this morning my eyes were tested for glasses, but the examination was haphazard and incomplete. Our doctor had only a limited variety of corrective lenses. So my vision will be far from 20/20 with glasses. I expect to have the glasses in a month or so, but, knowing they won't be right, I'm afraid to wear them. The doctors aren't at all conscientious, and, furthermore, don't seem to give a damn. I prefer to wait for the glasses from home.

I received your letter today and the wholesale document written by the Aronovitz troupe.[1]

I see Cousin Nason could stand some military training. It might knock some respect for others into him, eh. I think he'll eventually outgrow his arrogance. If he doesn't somebody will do it for him. I can tell you, this outfit taught me something about arrogance. I saw a sign the other day that read, "Maybe the boss isn't always right, but he's always the boss."

Camp: I think it's an excellent idea that Ronnie should get away and meet new kids. So he doesn't know the other kids. He'll strike up acquaintances. You must realize how soon boys get to know each other and become friends. Hey, just a minute. I read your letter wrong. You say, it's a private camp. That's okay, I guess, but I still say he should have gone to a boy's Y camp.

The fun part about going to camp is in meeting other fellas. You know that as well as I. I admit that camp restrictions aren't always fun, but they are there for the kids' benefit. He'll certainly have fun if his chum goes with him. Two always have fun. Don't worry about him becoming homesick. If he does have a touch of it, it'll do him more good than harm. Bet he won't get homesick, though.

I remember only once having a touch of homesickness when I first arrived in California, but Hollywood fixed that up in short order. I often think of home and you folks, but rather than making me feel low, it exhilarates me. No kidding, I don't really know what homesickness is like. I've been surprised more than once at how well I've adapted to different environments.

The letter I wrote to the Chase girl was unimportant and hardly personal. Just the same, I avoid saying things that I don't want publicized. I try to write letters to friends and relatives that all can read without embarrassing me. What happens to my letters after they are dropped into the mail box matters little to me. My only love notes go to you, my dear, and I don't mind the world listening in. Of course, I know the personal matters I divulge to you will go no further. From now on, I'll address all letters to Muriel Chase as "Dear Muriel and All Relatives Who Are Curious. Come One, Come All."

Malter kept me off the switchboard against the wishes of his cohorts. When he left, they immediately put me on. I'm still surveying, learning, and enjoying the outdoors tremendously. I do plenty of walking, and you know I like that. It's a heck of a lot better than being cooped up in some telephone office. I don't think I could ever take a strictly white collar job. I like being outside, seeing sights and working in the fresh air. Remember how thrilled I used to be when I could make calls with Dad. That's because I enjoyed seeing various places and meeting people. You probably think that chemical engineering is white collar work. Not necessarily. It also offers plenty of opportunity to be outside, depending on the branch you're in. Of course, people who work outside don't have to think as much. All thinking jobs are done working inside. Since I like to think, I'd like to do some inside work. A proper blend of inside and outside work would be ideal.

Ronnie, I promise not to read more of your letters to my mates even though it will deprive them of many laughs. So stop blushing; you needn't be embarrassed any more. I'll just sit here rollicking with laughter over one of your letters while the other boys look on, their mouths watering, wondering what's so funny. Ronnie, it's awfully mean not to let them in on it.

Mom, your introduction to the letter of letters written by Aronovitz Incorporated was splendid. And Dad, I await that promised LONG letter. I have yet to settle down long enough to reply to Uncle Harry. I gotta think up some good way to rib him. Yea Gods, I went nuts when he mentioned delicatessen and stuff. How could he do this to me?

I'll be around tomorrow, so my dear pinup[2] gal, keep your chin up.

7/24/44

Dear Mom,

Believe this, Mom: I'm a damn fool, a glutton for punishment. I've taken a drastic step again. Yep, it's my doggone ambition working again. Let me explain.

I've been working in the surveying department, learning how to stake out grades, run a traverse, make contour maps, and set levels. I've done all this, read up about it, thought about it, and understood it. I feel confident that I know what I'm doing. When I'm a civilian again I'll be qualified to get a job as a rod man. Who knows? Such a skill may come in handy. Even during a depression a rod man makes a livable wage. When I was offered the job, I was elated and later found that I liked it. I don't work especially hard, and I'm outdoors, but the job had one drawback: I'd still have a white stripe[1] on my shoulder when I return home. I knew when I took the job that I'd never advance. The reason: experienced instrument surveyors are only third class petty officers, and my skills can't compare with theirs. So I decided to be satisfied and say to the devil with ambition. As you have said, "A rolling stone gathers no moss," so I vowed that I'd stick with it and gather some moss.

This evening I heard that there was an opening on a crane for an oiler, an apprentice job that can lead to becoming a crane operator. All Seabee battalions have several diesel shovels, cranes, and an assortment of heavy equipment, such as pile drivers etc. The man in charge of this equipment was also the same man who got me the surveying job, the Bulova wrist watch in Rhode Island, and the same man I often go to for advice and counsel. This evening, after I went to him again for more advice, he gave me the lowdown on the crane oiler's job. It's a greasy, dirty job and involves crawling through mud. An apprentice has to learn the machine inside and out: initially what bolts to turn, what gears control what, then, after a month, what levers to pull, how to judge turning and lifting, and, in general acquiring coordination in doing these things. It takes months of hard work.

In civilian life an oiler makes $1.50/ hour, a crane operator $2.00 and more. Sometimes the hours are pretty tough. By comparison my present job is a snap. Advancement? Yes, there's a chance if you make good. But what if I don't make good? My friend's answer: "Aaron, you WILL make good, if I have to stay with you day and night and teach you myself." There's a friend for you, a man willing to go to bat for me.

My friend got me the surveying job by telling the personnel department that I had no opportunity for advancement in communications. Now he's requesting that I leave surveying for the oiler's job because he needs me. So from all appearances, the transfer looks like none of my doing.

He purposely tried to discourage me by telling me the disadvantages of the job. He said it would be tough, but I'd be learning a trade. I told him I'm willing to take a chance since I have nothing to lose. I can always return to surveying. He said that if I found that the job wasn't to my liking he'd be willing to release me. I'm making arrangements with personnel for a transfer and taking the job.

So soon I'll be taking care of cranes and learning about their engines, a full fledged grease monkey. Some grease may do me some good. By God, I'll try. Let the mud come. Maybe I'll have a chevron after all by the time I get home. Mom, it's true that my ambition always gets the best of me. But this change may be it. I'll be working for someone who's 100% for me, who won't hesitate to point out my faults.

As a result of so many changes, will my prestige be compromised? I think it will be higher. The more I know, the more jobs I can handle,the more I become an all around man. It will look good on the books. I can splice wire, grade a field, lay out a building. I have a fair knowledge of many things that the Seabees require of their tradesmen.

Maybe, Mom and Dad, I'm making a mistake, maybe not. But the way I look at it, whatever I do can do no harm. By having many jobs in the service, I'm experimenting. I'm learning what it is to work at both easy and hard jobs. I welcome your opinion on this move. Of course, I've already made the decision, but I'm interested in knowing how you would have advised me.

We'll also see whether I'm mechanically inclined. I caught on to carpentry quite fast even though earlier I couldn't hammer a nail in straight. This will test me. Let's see what happens.

7/26/44

Dear Mom,

I read in a magazine that a fellow wrote he received a "heartfull" of letters. Over the past few days that's just what I've received from you: letters, newspapers and more letters.

Happy isn't the right word to describe my feelings when I read your letter from Old Orchard.[1] Actually I was more thrilled learning of your unique—at least to the domestic Aaron family—trip, than my own excursions back in the U.S. Before opening the letter I eyed the Old Orchard postmark with perplexity, then with excitement. I knew the letter would be about a new experience for you. Can you imagine it? My folks actually being someplace other than Massachusetts. If I remember correctly, the last time you left our native state was during another Fourth of July, way back when we visited Nashua, New Hampshire, and witnessed Darwin's theory of anthropology[2] for ourselves at Benson's Animal (or human) Farm. Not wanting to brag of course, I must remind you that, although you took a 275 mile trip, ya still don't come up to me. Why, I even put Eleanor[3] to shame. My close to 300 mile trip to Baton Rouge clinches my victory; you're 25 miles short. Again, I must say, that I let out a whoopee when I read that you went to Old Orchard, and I feel like talking about it now. I'm even worse than Dad was after his gall bladder operation. You see, officially, you are now a fellow traveler of mine, and a member of the traveler's union (Dues, three bucks a month).

Now I have documentary evidence proving that you were in Maine. And when you talk about it to others, as Dad did about his gall bladder operation, just say, "If you don't believe me, write Hughie. He'll tell you." Dad had gall stones for evidence and I have your postmark.

When I'm home again, I wonder if I'll ever want to go to Revere or Winthrop.[4] Our glorious palm fringed beaches put those to shame, but I guess, after some of your persuasion, I'd go just to be sociable, yes, even with a cigar maker's family[5] and a nutty upholsterer crowding me. (Don't believe a word in the above sentence. Just braggin', helps my morale). Anyway, I know it sure will be good to see the ocean again, the cold ocean, that is, to shiver me to the marrow. Dear, dear cold! Tell me, how does it feel? Cold, I mean. I suppose it's sort of swanky to eat in a hotel, but the tough part is the check. Take me, for instance, (on second thought, you better not) I eat chow in a nize comfortable chow hall, no tips required.

Surprised was I when Dad consented to extend his domain to Maine. It only goes to show ya what influences my Eleanor Roosevelt letters have on Dad. Bet he caught the traveling bug from me. Your cabin sounds super. I've got to try a cabin myself someday. In California they call them hostels, and every couple registers as Mr. & Mrs. Smith. (Catch?) Sad was I when I read that you couldn't stay longer. You're just like me. When liberty is up, boy you head back to camp or it's A.O.L. (away over leave). Oh sure, you didn't want to be A.O.L. from home. I appreciate your heartfelt sympathy. Yep, poor me sweltering down here sitting under a coconut palm on some coral beach with a mint julep in one hand and the other wrapped around a babe (I mean lady). Poor me.

The Ouija board (God only knows how to spell the contraption) is a complex gadget I suppose, whose intricate theories are far above me. I recall that the girls at school used to swear by its reliability. Not wishing to contradict (Aunt) Anna or some few thousand Sinatra fans,

I must say that the Ouija board misses the mark this time. Only a miracle will get me home in six months. I suppose their faith in the board is so great that they are now floating around dreamy eyed. Anyway, who in the world would want to leave this paradise for home? Just about every soldier, sailor and marine in the S.W.P., that's who. However it's a good question, because undoubtedly some jerk will want to return here. The say, "Thars gold in them thar hills."

I'm so happy that you enjoy the letters that I write to your sister, sister-in-law and Aunt Sadie. I beamed when I read "You have such a good sense," then became distraught when reading further "of humor." Pish, posh. I'd just as soon have good sense, but I realize I'm nuts.

(Aunt) Pearl's dog is Pearl's everlasting motivation to exist. I get a great kick out of her letters concerning "darling Jumbo." (Uncle) Walter[6] better watch out. Jumbo is keen competition. Last I heard Jumbo swallowed a rope and X-rays showed nothing. My patience is racked while waiting to see whether Jumbo will get sick from ropemonia (or pneumonia?).

Your 7/5 letter is a whopper. I gotta beat that right here and now, so here goes. Foist (my current New York accent, strictly Flatbush) this is to let you know that I have been receiving the air mail stamps you are sending pretty well. Second, I've concluded that Dad is ashamed of his once magnificent, miraculous, stupendous physique. Daddy don't wanna wear a bathing soot. This corroborates my belief that the old pot is creeping up on him (just like Willie in Moon Mullins).[7] Or is it that Dad's afraid his hairy chest will over-excite the femmes. This is meant to be a challenge, Dad, so be ready to talk fast. Why won't you put on a bathing suit and go into the water?

I'm still attached to survey crew waiting for my transfer. I can't help admitting that I rather enjoy the job. Still I prefer to work harder at a job in which I know advancement is possible. It will be fun to work on machinery for a change.

Can you beat that? You want me to enlighten Ronnie about things. What in the devil would you do if you didn't have an older son? When I get back maybe the kid will be almost seventeen and still ignorant. It's not right, Mom. Ronnie should have been informed years ago. The fact that he's embarrassed at the mention of the subject shows that he misunderstands. When discussing it, there's no reason to blush. Good lord, what would he do if he were introduced to a society of men only—like the service? He'd be constantly running around crimson faced. I strongly urge you to send for literature. Don't wait for me.

Yes, there are snakes here, but let's discuss them another time when I'm in a less jolly mood. We don't like them, and they definitely don't like us. In reply to your question why the natives have such tummies, I suggest you look at Dad's. Unless you stopped feeding him, he hasn't rickets or is suffering from malnutrition. Boy oh boy, am I tearing him apart in this letter. No kidding, the natives have bad eating habits, unbalanced diets, and, of course, their posture isn't the best. The natives here are, on the whole, healthier looking, than those you saw in the picture with me at Finschafen.

Before I forget, send me more stationery. It's scarce here and it has been a month or more since we've been able to buy some.

We do some work in the swamps along the coast, and we keep our bodies well covered to protect us against the mosquitoes. We also take Atabrine as further protection.

I look forward (wishful thinking) to your getting a new parlor suite. To tell the truth I was sort of doubtful whether it was worth returning home. I don't look forward to brushing the old freize chairs weekends.[8] I've had my share of rotten details. All kidding aside, I'd be glad to take over Ronnie's cleaning job at time and one half. Sunday is overtime, you know.

Say listen, I get plenty of mail as it is without worrying about a string of girls not writing me. Let the other guys get that "Dearest Honey" stuff. I mean it when I say the fellows are sick of the tiresome, mushy letters they receive. Would you believe that guys who have met a girl only once or twice get such letters? Any sensible letter—and those are the only kind I get even if I don't write sensible letters myself—is worth ten of the other kind.

I await snapshots of the Rolls Royce, and if you write "wish you were here" on the snap, I'll moider ya. Here's why: Today while working around the Fleet Post Office, I saw two civilian sedans (1942 Mercurys) behind the building. Thinking it was a mirage, I blinked, but sure enough they were pleasure cars. It being so long since I've seen one of the contraptions, I had to go up to one and touch it. Furthermore, having forgotten what one looked like, I wanted to refresh my memory. It sure was fun to peer in through the windows (real glass too) and see nice, shiny leather upholstery and a fancy, complicated-looking dashboard. I was sort of disappointed when I noticed that the steering wheel was on the righthand side. The car was probably an Australian make.

Confidentially, I've often wondered how a European makes love while driving. An American Don Juan steers with his left hand, and a

European with his right. Hardly practical for love making. Just ignore the above comments. It's the result of being influenced by Hollywood with a dash of Seabeeism.

The poem "Dear Mom," fits us two perfectly. Everything I've wanted to say is said there. And, understanding every word, you knew it also meant us. I'll save it and when I get back we'll re-read it together. Instead of "tears of longing" we can finish it with "It's you I love with tears of joy." I'm no poet. I wish I were. I write everything in prose, hardly comparable in expression to poetry. I'd like to thank the author for his poem. Little did he realize that he was writing for you and me as well as for his own mom.

P.S. I'm now a full-fledged member of the Veterans of Foreign Wars. Hereafter address me as Comrade Hughie.

V-Mail 7/27/44

Dear Mom,

Am remaining on the surveying crew for a while yet, as the number of shifts that the cranes work has been reduced, causing a decrease in the need for an oiler. However, when the position does open up, I'm assured to have A-1 priority. As I've said, I'm happy with my present position in surveying, if not its lack of opportunity for advancement. Although I'm still ambitious, I'm not as enthusiastic as I was a year ago. I don't go around moping the way I used to, because I know there will be opportunities for me. My existence is pleasant, and I'm willing to try anything that comes along, but I'm not willing to do nothing or chase after something.

Please excuse such a short letter. I'm feeling sort of lazy this evening. Beginning next week, we're getting Sundays off.

7/28/44

Dear Mom,

We hear so much about the havoc and destruction in Europe that we take pity on the populations there. We are like healthy people watching cripples, and we have no way of understanding their plight. Only a cripple can know what being a cripple is like.

Here the destruction is far less drastic. We have no big cities, only the torrid forests and small, unimportant villages. Yet, the local village in this area demonstrated for me on a small scale what war can do to someone's familiar back yard or field.

On the day that I first landed in this small, tattered village, I tried to reconstruct in my mind what it must have been like before the war.

I saw stuccoed mansions, and cute thatched homes. I saw green fields, running springs, flourishing flower gardens, small children walking down the country road lined with blossoming trees, that passed through the center of the village. I could see it all as if it were still there. It took little imagination, and the longer I remain here the more realistic the scene becomes.

The ruins left me with that picture. But now those remnants have disappeared.

What I saw that day of my arrival was actually a town that had undergone a terrific naval barrage. Every structure, cozy bungalow, and thatched cottage was gutted and torn by bomb fragments. While no doubt the Japanese had changed the town considerably from what it was, they made use of its buildings. One home became a dispensary, another a headquarters, another a brothel. The Japs made use of every house. But the Americans are different. We are accustomed to using automotive and mechanical devices when waging war and building things. Narrow country roads and pretty homes don't fit our requirements for creating a base. So we change everything.

On that first day, the church, a simple stucco chapel with a corrugated tin roof and mahogany pews, had been completely riddled with machine gun bullets such that the plaster was crumbling from so many holes. Sections of the tin roof were falling off and not a window was left. Today both the army and navy are using the chapel in the very same condition it was in when I first saw it. Suffering least from the bombardment, a few of the sturdiest stucco mansions with mahogany verandas and attractive shutters were still standing. Some had antique furniture inside.

When I first arrived the army converted one of the homes into a headquarters. An order was flashed: "Send a patrol into the hills to rescue two wounded Americans with two Jap prisoners." Orders such as this were common. The invasion was over, but the results were still ongoing.

As trucks and Jeeps ground sour rice into the earth, its stench clung to the air. Filth was everywhere. Rotting food manufactured flies by the second. A European car was a curiosity. A few cheaply made Jap trucks were the only things mechanized. With bullets and shells scattered helter skelter everywhere, souvenirs were plentiful. On the beach old European and Japanese vessels stood wrecked and desolate, their hulks combed over by us curious Americans.

The only unmarred remains were the crystal clear springs and gurgling brooks that crossed the town in a checkered pattern. These still flowed, somehow revealing the original quaint atmosphere that the village once had.

I found children's shoes scattered about, European footwear, European literature and children's primers, all evidence of a quiet, pleasing civilization of mothers and fathers, sons and daughters. In some dismembered front yards, roses still survived and picket fences still stood in defiance of the bombs and bullets.

Not far from the village, in a pretty green glen beneath low branching trees, there was a small burial ground overlooking the bay. During scarcely twenty-five years, no more than a dozen people were buried there. It wasn't hard to surmise that each grave had a yarn to tell. A man with a European name had died at the age of forty-two. A woman died at twenty-three. A child lived only two weeks, June to July 1939. The stones were carefully carved, awesomely spelling out human sentiments of devotion and love. They were unlike our burial stones. Small thatched canopies were constructed over the length of each grave and an inscription in glass was framed at the head. A small spring ran through this hollow to the ocean, as if to keep the dead cool in the tropical heat.

Everything has changed. The grand scale of Americans in action has dwarfed and crushed everything. The weaker structures were razed and enormous warehouses now occupy their sites. After tarpaulins were thrown over their roofs to cover the bullet holes, the mansions became offices. The once green lawns have been trampled into dust. A supply depot now stands next to the chapel. The streets have been widened, filled with the hustle and bustle of Jeeps and trucks that kick up swirling, choking dust. Telephone poles dotting the area support a criss-crossing network of wires. Even the once clear brooks have been made into drainage ditches. The beach is coated with oil slick from the big freighters that tie up to docks only one hundred feet from the shore.

I don't recognize the burial ground now. Stones have been stripped away, name plates torn off the graves, broken glass strewn everywhere. A blue mark on one grave serves as an elevation point for the surveyors. A chipped stone on another grave bears witness to some American boy souvenir hunting. A road now passes through this once green paradise, and dust and mud insult the sturdy graves. In war there's no respect for the dead.

Now beside the Stars and Stripes a European flag flies over this unrecognizable village. Will the original inhabitants ever return? I wonder. The hundreds of thousands of dollars spent excavating, building warehouses and ditches will leave a permanent scar on this place. To bring it back to its former luxuriousness would cost countless millions. The fields and brooks and burial ground are gone forever. The spirit that once pervaded this green valley can never be revived. Those poor people.

The Americanization of a village.

I guess this letter is quite impersonal, but perhaps it will help you visualize what it's like here, what I see.

7/30/44

Dear Mom,

I dropped a nickel in the slot, pushed the lever down and hooray, the jackpot: five letters from Mom yesterday. I was excited, floating in the clouds and looking forward to answering your every question. But today turned out to be another historic day in my life so I'll postpone answering your letters until tomorrow and tell you what has happened.

After breakfast Ralph Dix, one of my bunkmates, and I decided to hitchhike to the airstrip which is about twenty miles inland. The road there is good, if very dusty, and with so much truck and jeep traffic getting a ride was a cinch.

We first stopped at a Javanese village of thatched houses. Hardly marred by outside influences, it's located in a beautiful spot amid a grove of trees. The women were attractive, and the men and boys very jovial. I enjoyed watching the older women cooking food and performing their daily duties. This quaint village is near a large, clear lake, the largest (except for the Great Lakes) that I've ever seen. For a while we strolled along the sandy shore and soon found ourselves in front of a pretty house surrounded by a green lawn and coconut palms. Ralph and I suspected that it was a private area and verboten. Soon an M.P. approached and politely informed us that we were gazing at ------ [MacArthur's] front yard. After gulping twice, we shot the breeze with the M.P. for a while and learned more about the lake and the surrounding area. On our getting more acquainted, he invited us to go for a swim, but, since we were anxious to move on we turned him down.

Picking up another ride, on our way we saw three Jap prisoners in a corral. They were the first live Japs that I've seen. The Javanese look like Japs to a degree. They too are slant-eyed, but their complexion is darker, and I think they're handsomer.

Lasting several hours, the ride to the airstrip gave us the opportunity to see some beautiful scenery. We passed through heavily wooded towering mountains and rolling grassy hills and a beautiful level plain. I was amazed that the countryside reminded me of New England. I never imagined how much this part of the tropics resembles the eastern U.S. The difference is in the presence of palms, banana trees, and mahoganys, equivalent to our pines, corn and maples. The airstrip consists of an enormous level area that extends for 10,000 feet to the base of a mountain which dwarfs everything in sight.

At the outset we expected to miss Sunday dinner, even sacrificing ice cream for dessert, for the sake of seeing more of New Guinea. However, we struck up the acquaintance of an A-20 attack bomber crew chief who invited us to dinner at his camp. A swell fellow from Cleveland, he told us he was once a gunner. Before we ran into him, Ralph and I browsed around the airdrome examining the P-38s,[1] B-24s,[2] Billy Mitchells,[3] and a car load of other aircraft. I got a kick out of talking to the mechanics and watching the pilots climb out of their P-38s just after a flight.

Soon it dawned on us that we might be able to finagle a ride. It was while on the search that we met the fellow from Cleveland. After shooting the breeze for a while, we explained that we had come a long way to see the airstrip and planes. After he realized that we were the invincible Seabees, he immediately took to us and tried to arrange a flight. So the three of us went trotting around the field to one plane after another asking Joe or Mac or whoever was in charge to find out which plane was scheduled for a flight. Having no luck and tired of running around, our new friend from Cleveland went directly to the operations office and explained that we were his chums from the good old home town; he would sure consider it a favor if they would arrange for us to go up. His request immediately granted, operations chose one of the newer A-20 attack bombers, having twenty-five missions to its credit and 130 hours in the air.

After chow, for which we graciously thanked our sergeant friend from Cleveland, we were introduced to our pilot, a first lieutenant, a tall, fine looking, Southern boy.

· The pilot asked, addressing me, "Say, have you ever seen the cockpit of an A-20?" In two shakes of a lamb's tail, I was sitting in the pilot's seat being shown how to make the ship go up or down, release bombs, and fire the 50 caliber machine guns in the nose, etc. Even though the plane was still on the ground, what a thrill it was. Then I was invited into the middle gunner's turret which, to get into, took much squeezing and squirming and where I played gunner for a while.

Before boarding the plane, we tried on parachutes and were told how to operate its gadgets. After detailed instructions, Ralph, after noticing a brass ring, wondered aloud what it was for. "Oh, that's the thing you pull," said our pilot. Well, how soon after the jump do you pull? "Listen, Mac," said the pilot, "don't worry about that. Just pull hard and sit tight." Then the pilot showed us how to open the escape hatch in case of a crash in water. He also showed us how to use a microphone which wraps around your Adam's apple. I found talking through your larynx instead of your mouth quite a novelty. With his confident Southern drawl, the pilot reassured us, "Just safety precautions fellas, but I doubt if you'll need the chutes. This ship is quite a baby." So we decided not to wear the chutes but kept them ready beside us, just in case.

We climbed into the bomb compartment which had one small window on each side. Our pilot suggested that we keep the bottom hatch open so that we could look down and also get an excellent breeze. High altitude photos from a camera directly behind us are also taken through this hatch.

This being a "check up" flight, no one else was on board except the pilot, Ralph and me. The engines revved, dirt flew, and we taxied down the runway for takeoff. Gee, what a moment! It was my first time up, and in a bomber yet. Oh, yes, I should mention that the pilot gave us a bucket in case of air sickness, but we laughed at this.

After the control tower gave the signal, the roar of the engines became deafening, (Bombers aren't insulated like Stratoliners) the pilot gave 'er the gun. We saw objects whizzing past faster and faster, then becoming smaller. The plane felt as if it were skimming along the surface of smooth water. We were in the air.

We immediately opened the bottom hatch, knelt down on our knees on the cushions supplied us, and prepared to see sights galore. As we circled over the lake, and gained altitude, we could feel ourselves rising and the earth sinking, sinking lower and lower to eternity. Soon the trees became a tiny vast panorama. I looked at Ralph and screamed, "Boy oh boy, we're up. Yippee." It didn't do me much good to scream because the engine's roar drowned out everything. But who cared; we were heading skyward.

After a few minutes of being fascinated by everything, we noticed more A-20's floating on each side of us. Looking down, we saw the shadows of the three of us in V formation moving across the land, ours being the command ship. There they were, slowly rising, falling, gliding beside us. What a thrill!

We could feel ourselves gradually going higher. We passed over the lake which extended for miles and, beyond that, a vast, tremendous forest. Soon we were over the ocean, blue as can be, breaking on silvery beaches. Exotic. Beyond description. Up, up, we went faster and faster. Looking behind us from seaward, we could see for miles and miles into the interior of the island. Suddenly a billow of white flew by. We were in the clouds, and kept on still higher so that we were soon looking down on a white quilt in a myriad of patterns. It was all so peaceful. The blue ocean waves looked like miniature ripples, and the land Lilliputian⁴ in scale.

Then came the fireworks. I couldn't tell whether it was the plane, but I thought it was the land and the sea. The earth was revolving around us, swerving, twisting. Good lord, I wondered, was I mad? Then we zoomed, my ear drums popped, my heart rose to my throat, and my eyes bulged, as we hurtled earthward, ever earthward. We zoomed again in the reverse direction causing my ears to pop again, my heart drop to my feet; my eyes bore into my head as up, up we went with the earth racing away from us. Then there was calm, peace, and Ralph and I laughed at each other's shock.

"C'mon pilot, let's have more." Again we banked, dove and swung back up. It was like being on a super elevator. And it gave us a super sensation. We felt happy, wonderfully free.

As we flew up the coast we gazed down on muddy rivers, enormous swamps, endless forests and more silvery beaches. Once in a while we'd drop to a lower altitude so we could see the dense jungle growth in more detail. After our pilot took to maintaining a level course, our two neighbors resumed floating beside us, but in a different formation. Suddenly we peeled off, nosed earthward, producing the same extreme sensations, then leveled off above the trees and sped along the shore. The earth flew by in an unrecognizable mass. Our speed? A mere 310 mph. God, impossible, but there I was. Up again we went, the world a panorama, and we headed back to the strip.

Soon the drone ceased, replaced by a whistle as we glided earthward, getting closer and closer until with a slight jolt we touched earth. Good old *terra firma* again! After taxiing to our revetment, the pilot shut the engines down, and everything was silence. Yea gods, I'm deaf, I thought. Pop, pop went my ears. I could hear again. "Here's your old can, chief," I said. "There's nothing to clean up." Who ever heard of air sickness? Not I. For a minute after my feet hit the pavement I was wobbly, but I ignored it, being more interested in learning how long we were up, what our maximum altitude was and how far we flew. "Wal," the pilot said, "I guess we were up about 7,000 feet for an hour and ten minutes. I'm loggin' in that we flew 235 miles."

It was the fastest hour and ten minutes I ever spent. Ten minutes was more like it, but my watch read 2:30, a good hour plus since we took off.

I thought, "Something to write the folks about." So there you are folks, only five hours after the momentous occasion of riding high. Oh, yes, I should add that our A-20 was called "Miss Devil's Partner," and quite a devil of a partner she proved to be. From now on call me "parachuteless Huey, the guy who saw New Guinea through a bomb hatch."

Love to the three of you, Hughie (They couldn't get 'im down.)

Tuesday 8/1/44

Dear Mom, (fellow traveler)

Observe the freakish dates on six letters I received from you Saturday: June 24, July 7, 8, 13 & 18 from Boston. Here are my comments:

You may remember my request for a crane oiler's job, that it was granted and later turned down because of lack of work, so I remained on my surveying job. Today I was informed that the surveying department is over-complemented due to a decrease in the number of projects. Since I was its newest and youngest member, I was chosen for dismissal from the survey crew along with another fellow. As a result I have been transferred to work at the saw mill. I'm in such a state of confusion. They shift personnel around so much that a guy isn't absolutely sure what in the devil he is. At any rate, it's for sure that I'll be working at a saw mill, not the worst job in the world. I really don't care; it's a job.

I'm still angling for the oiler's job for some future date, but if the sawyer's job seems pretty good I might stick it out. I'm resolved to not give a damn anymore. I'm not so much disgusted as indifferent. There's no need for you to repeat to me that the war is temporary etc., because I realize all that which explains my present attitude of indifference. I suppose you are confused over my constant job changing. Bear in mind that this change is due to circumstances and not of my making. I'm powerless in such instances. I'll see how I like the new job, and, if I don't, I'll try to do some finagling. I'm not the least downhearted, and I'm curious to see what my new job will be like.

I guess I never made it clear that Tretter has been ousted from his commanding position. Here a man's true boss is not the company chief, but rather the man for whom he is directly working. I don't feel, for reasons I've already given, that my changing jobs has reduced my prestige.

I think you misinterpreted the letter that mentioned my enjoyment of writing. I never stated, or even hinted, that I'd like to go into journalism. Read that letter again. I said that I find it an easy task to write to you and my friends, and that the words flow easily. I like to write because it consoles me, and serves as an outlet for expressing myself. By no means do I consider myself a suitable candidate for a career in journalism.[1]

Got paid today and withdrew only $10.00. I want to leave $100 in the pot to use for transportation home when I reach the States.

Doggone, I'm sure happy that Dad got a good present from my birthday-Father's Day fund. Cigars are swell, but shoes, boy oh boy. Thanks Mom. I only wish I could be there to see the shoes. Perforated too! A regular sheik now, eh Dad. I suppose it's pretty tough having a birthday so near Father's Day. Since you're not sure that your birthday is July 10, why not be practical and change it to sometime in January or February, the months when great men are born? Look at Mom's and Ronnie's chests swell.

It's quite the novelty when a person hands out presents on her birthday instead of the customary reverse. Ref: Aunt Anna's gift to Ronnie on her birthday. I'm all for it. I'm debating who is the best dressed man in our family. Seems that Ronnie and Dad are really becoming dudes.

Tell Mary, the girl who sold vegetables in Ralph's market and is now the cashier in his NEW (didn't know that before) store, "Thank you." Remember, she had sent her regards. I take it you're still trading there.

The trick[2] that Rothstein played on you took plenty of nerve. It's labor's day now. Workers are sure taking advantage of the war. After the war I think they'll suffer for their actions. Take Rothstein, for instance. You'd as soon hire an upholsterer who's a veteran than retain him, wouldn't you, especially after the stunts he's pulled. After the war big business will act similarly. Independent workers are due for a letdown. Some independence during wartime is good, but going too far will only hurt later.

True, despite your many requests, I haven't tried to explain where I am. Your knowing does neither of us any good. You can logically surmise where I am from the facts I've revealed. If not, I prefer to leave you guessing.

The vitamin A pills are spoiled, although the B complex are in good shape. I'm unable always to keep them in a refrigerator because the cooks would rather not have outsiders in the kitchen. You can't blame them. Although several of the cooks are my friends, I don't wish to impose on them. In the future send only the B Complex. Forget the vitamin A, unless you can get it in tablet form which lasts longer than the capsule. I take two of the B Complex daily and feel excellent. I've had only one cold, lasting two days, since I've been across. I think my resistance is quite high.

Out here the recreation department is a farce. I'm glad I didn't stick with it.

It's about time that you sent for something on the facts of life for Ronnie. It's odd how boys think they know what's what. Guess I felt the same way myself. By chance, was it my prompting that led you to act on the subject?

I note that your latest letter was written from Aunt Pearl's house. Sounds as if you enjoyed your stay which makes me happy. Truly, you are now a member of my Wanderlust Club. Now you've been to Pelham, N.H. Bet it feels swell to have the Ford. What in the world do you use for gas?

Sure glad that YOU enjoy my letters addressed to my AUNTS. It's like this: you gotta keep up the civilian morale. Since I turned out to be a real crackpot, I feed 'em the old complements—and they like it. Furthermore, they use the same salve on me so it's my duty to return it. Most of what I write is just kidding, and they know it. I still enjoy Aunt Sadie's struggle of Sadie versus Excess Fat, and Aunt Pearl's great concern over her dog Jumbo, and family. All the relatives have been swell writing to me. It seems they can't do enough. I appreciate it.

The fellows are encountering the same spirit among their friends back home, and it makes us all feel swell.

Aunt Ida writes a demonstrative letter, even to the point of imprinting a kiss of lipstick on the paper. I'm not sure whether she is sincere or not, but she has been exceedingly pleasant. Aunt Anna's letters are always welcome, because hers seem the most genuine of all the demonstrative letters I receive. Even though I haven't been an intimate nephew, I feel we have a mutual understanding. I fear that Cousin Bobby is the loser for his uncaring attitude toward letter writing. Aunt Yetta and Uncle Harry have been a surprise. I never felt close to them, and I imagine I occasionally irked them when I used to reject their hospitality. Now they write consistently, and long letters too. In fact their letters are more numerous now than when we began corresponding.

Sadie, always swell, writes a wonderful Walter Winchell[3] column, even bringing me into her confidence sometimes. She's not demonstrative, which I prefer. I get a kick out of her letters. Grandma's letters, which are rare, are short, serious, to the point, yet loving. Despite her several shortcomings[4] I still think she's tops. She has always been wonderful to me. Lil writes an excellent letter, usually serious, but not overly so. Her sentences are meaty, flow easily. She's analytical and writes about mature subjects. Beverly Ringer[5] writes the sort of letter that befits her young age, perhaps even superior to what you'd expect. I find her description of the dances she goes to, her schooling and nursing, which is all she dwells on, interesting reading. She had an overwhelming curiosity about Hollywood and its people while I was there. Girls are inevitably fascinated by the place. I never receive letters from Uncle Louie or his family. That's okay, though; I still like him. I don't think that branch of the Aaron family goes in for this writing stuff. Lionel Gallant hasn't written since I've been overseas, but his folks write continually. Not having his address, I can't write him. I feel sort of bad that we haven't maintained a correspondence. Johson is a true gem and his letters are always a pleasure. They are the essence of wit and humor.

Malter's girlfriend[6] in Frisco writes and keeps asking that I write her. Her letters, which I always enjoy, are beautiful and intelligent. She asks me to write, because she can get more information from me than from Al who is very close-mouthed. From her last letter I learned that Malter was in Sidney, Australia. Even though Al has left, she encourages me to keep writing. That girl is sure in love with Malter. I expect he'll be in Frisco before I get home. Now I have at least one friend there.

The Linfields are slow to answer my letters, and I'm the same, but that's the way both of us prefer it. Mrs. Linfield's letters are always pleasant and informative.

Thought you might be interested in what I think of this or that guy. Let's compare notes.

I'll probably be around tomorrow. Adieu.

8/3/44

Dear Mom,

I'm now wholeheartedly involved in *A Tree Grows in Brooklyn*,[1] the current best seller. As a matter of fact, I'm enjoying it so much that

I find it tough to lie down and switch to letter writing. You must read the book. It seems so realistic that it reads like a biography. The bums the author describes are right from life. Even Dad would enjoy the book. The reading is easy. The story brings the reader into the stark reality of the early 1900s. Of course, my only familiarity with that period derives from Dad's propaganda about the gay nineties.

I've now participated in mostly every profession, trade, and gold-bricking detail that this battalion has to offer, from wielding a skillet to sticking picks (or whatever they call it) into floating logs and feeding them to a saw mill. I'm a jack of all trades, master of none, and whether I'm a jack is questionable. Still the battalion has enough faith in me to assign me jobs whether I know what I'm doing or not. At last, my so-called brawn is coming in handy. My present job requires bulging muscles slick with sweat. I work from 4:00 P.M. to 12:00 P.M., which I find to my surprise are pretty good working hours. My co-workers—15 in all—are a fine bunch of fellows who sympathize with one another and are forever looking forward to a breakdown, if only temporary, of the machinery. There are worse jobs in our unit so I'm not complaining, but I confess I have a few aces left to play which I plan to do.

I seem to have lost all ambition for studying. I suppose it's the environment. Somehow, I'll eventually drive myself back to it. Once I give it my undivided attention, there will be no stopping.

The war seems to be brightening for our side. The enemy is on the run on all fronts. There's a wave of optimism among us; yet I maintain that the worst is yet to come—in the Asiatic theater, that is. I suspect the climax will come in the autumn. Our grand strategy here is obviously clever, and the Japs are powerless to do anything about it. Winning the war is no longer in question. That was inevitable from the outset. Most important to us, we see home sweet home coming ever closer.

I'm still bragging about our plane ride last Sunday, that momentous day. Now others, inspired by my experience, are planning to visit the airstrip and finagle a ride by using their charms on the grease monkeys.

By the way, Worcester was represented on that A-20. Marked on an attachment to the earphones which allows you to speak to the pilot by pressing a button, were the words "Made in Worcester, Mass." This also reminds me that on the deck of the *West Point* there was a valve marked Rockwood Sprinkler, a Worcester firm.

The Aaron family, Ronnie, Dad, Mom, and Hughie, 1943

Mom (Gertrude Rose), August 1943

Dad (Barney), 1944

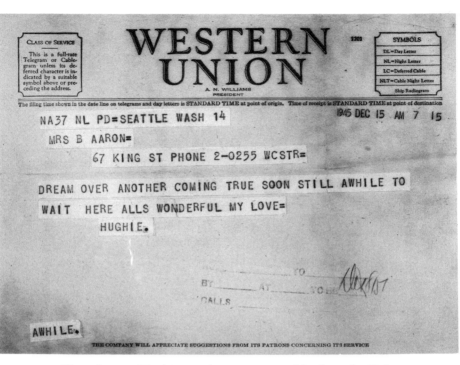

CLASS OF SERVICE

This is a full-rate Telegram or Cablegram unless its deferred character is indicated by a suitable symbol above or preceding the address.

WESTERN UNION

1201

A. N. WILLIAMS
PRESIDENT

SYMBOLS

DL=Day Letter
NL=Night Letter
LC=Deferred Cable
NLT=Cable Night Letter
Ship Radiogram

The filing time shown in the date line on telegrams and day letters is STANDARD TIME at point of origin. Time of receipt is STANDARD TIME at point of destination

NA37 NL PD=SEATTLE WASH 14   1945 DEC 15 AM 7 15

MRS B AARON=

67 KING ST PHONE 2-0255 WCSTR=

DREAM OVER ANOTHER COMING TRUE SOON STILL AWHILE TO

WAIT HERE ALLS WONDERFUL MY LOVE=

HUGHIE.

AWHILE.

THE COMPANY WILL APPRECIATE SUGGESTIONS FROM ITS PATRONS CONCERNING ITS SERVICE

The telegram Hughie sent home on arrival back in the U.S.

Hugh at age 70, Cushing, Maine, summer 1995

8/4/44

Dear Mom,

Four letters arrived today: yours, Sadie's, Mr. Riccius's and one from Lester Katz, who is now in England.

I see you have found merit in that primitive and obsolete form of locomotion: good old plain walking. Walking has always come naturally to me. It's my hobby. With time to ponder what's around you, and adjust your gait to your mood, you can see much more. Walking is more than simply exercise. I find it brings comfort to the mind. Bernarr MacFadden[1] may be nuts concerning many things, but as the greatest of all walking enthusiasts, he's right on that score. You should make a habit of walking a little each day. It will do you a world of good.

I recall a character[2] in *Return of the Native*, one of Thomas Hardy's[3] novels. Having known Paris and Berlin and many other large cities, he was a man of the world. After returning home to the desolate moors of England, he became a bush cutter. Although he found the work hard and aimless, he enjoyed it, much to the sorrow of his beautiful wife, Eustacia, who was intoxicated with thoughts of great cities, grand waltzes and handsome men.

Not unlike that character, I find that I actually enjoy the hard work I'm doing. As we work, moonlight is reflected off the sweat on our bodies, and I feel good. Of course, I appreciate the short rests. After work I'm weary, but glowing by the time my head hits the pillow. I can identify with the man in Hardy's book, ambitious, yet consoled by the simplest and severest of labors. They call it romanticism, and I like it.

I can sympathize with Eleanor writing "My Day."[4] I'm having a devil of a time trying to find something interesting to gab about. I bet she has a similar problem, although, were I paid, I imagine I could make up some nonsense to bore my public: Mom, Dad, and Ronnie.

I think you are treating my letter to Sadie too lightly. What I wrote was more than filling up space. Sadie had asked for some advice, and, although she may have asked in jest, I replied in earnest. Can you deny that I wrote the truth? You fail to realize that a son can learn from his childhood experiences. I honestly believe that children indulge in thought more than their parents. They are more sensitive to what their parents and others think about them than is commonly thought. While their capacity for deep thought hasn't been developed, children's emotions are extremely responsive. I feel like an old man when I think of my early days. I was reflective at thirteen, at ten, even

at four. My feelings and thoughts of those years are sufficient to qualify
me for offering some advice.

I honestly think that elders often get less from life than youths. I
really do. Elders are too engrossed in making a living. A young person
is still free to use his imagination. But an adult can stay young if he,
too, uses his imagination. You can tell by looking at him. I hope that I
can keep my imagination alive, that I can benefit others by what I've
learned. Mom, I really resent your laughing at my letter to Sadie.

It's odd how what seems important to us today is unimportant
tomorrow and vice versa.

This ends today's lesson. Now, class, let's turn to

Love to the three of you, Hughie

                                                              8/5/44

Dear Mom,

Today I find myself more than content, almost on the verge of
happiness. I'm feeling this way because I've just finished reading a
book with a happy ending, and then I read the marvelous war news.
For the first time, the end of all this is in sight.

I order you to read *A Tree Grows in Brooklyn*. I marvel at its
simplicity. For the past month I've been reading anything I can get my
hands on and enjoying it more than ever. I think I know why. Recently
I read a condensed version of *The Gay Illiterate*[1] by Louella Parsons,[2]
which I enjoyed simply because of its locale: California. For the same
reason I enjoyed *You Only Live Once*[3] by Grace Moore[4] and *Good
Night Sweet Prince*[5] by John Barrymore.[6] Much of the local color in
these books was familiar to me. No longer do I have to imagine what
California and the deep South look like. I can now reach into my store
of memories and see clearly what I once had to imagine. Don't you get
a kick out of reading a book about Boston or New England? I
remember liking *Time of Peace*[7] because I was familiar with its setting.
Being more familiar with a variety of environments, I can now receive
pleasure plus from many books. In a way, I'm glad that I'm in the war.
It has enabled me to see so much more than I ever anticipated. Yes,
one can travel and see very little, but not I.

Since I'm enjoying reading much more than studying, I'm
abandoning the latter. So I went to the library and selected several
books that I've always intended to read such as *Les Miserables*[8] by
Victor Hugo[9] for a starter. Now I have a request. I'd like to have a
complete volume of Shakespeare's plays. Often I've wanted to read
them, but in my busy civilian life never got around to it. Of course, use
my money, and find as complete a volume as you can.

Our enemy's destiny, route and defeat, is now more than certain. Not so long ago, although I wrote otherwise, I expected to be overseas for two years or more. Now I can honestly say that it will be more like one year. It's no longer the war but the peace that interests me. I'm all for the peace plans that Roosevelt has set forth. I'm sure that the Germans will react favorably to the absence of reparations and war guilt clauses while given loans and dealt with as an equal among nations. A powerful League of Nations will be established. The idea of an international police force is utterly stupid and contemptible. It will only breed more differences. Haven't we learned that to suppress a nationality or religion only embitters that population all the more, and once the pressure abates it goes berserk? It's better at the outset to prevent any chance of resentment arising.

I doubt if Japan will be treated the same as Germany. She'll probably be stripped of her strength and policed. China will be made secure and financed as a bulwark against any possible rise of Japanese nationalism. Education will be promoted in both Germany and Japan as the best solution to maintaining a successful peace. Many think that Russia will be a problem. I doubt it. I think she'll have to concede much and in return be given an ice-free port. Actually, Russia has already gone part of the way with us. She's had to adopt a form of capitalism to conduct the war. To erase it would be the Soviet's biggest mistake. We, ourselves, are tending socialistic. From opposite poles, Russia and the U.S. are moving towards a common goal. I wonder what will happen once their systems become the same. Not that I'm a Drew Pearson[10] predicting things to come, but I like to speculate on the future and see how it works out in time.

Sunday 8/6/44

Dear Folks,

My day off is now more than complete. Dad's treat, a humdinger from Mom, a letter from Lil, another from Lenny, ice cream tonight and a half day off tomorrow make this a pleasant weekend.

First honors go to the pictures of that magnificent, stupendous, marvelous vehicle, the pride of Dad, Esquire, the deluxe Aaron pleasure car. Just like the fella that shows a picture of his best girl to the boys, Dad says it doesn't do her justice so he'll have to take another (and more flattering) picture of her. Just think, when I get back home, I'll be able to rub my hand across the glistening hood of a real pleasure car. God, wouldn't that be heaven? Here ah am (Ah is spoken with a Southern accent now which ah contracted down Mississip) looking longingly at pictures of another world. Hi ya Mom. I see ya through the window, and you sure look pretty. Bet she says "Love is blind," but that's just pure modesty. And Dad looks wonderful. Even the blurred pictures are something to see. Tell me, Dad, how do you keep your youthful appearance and those wiggling biceps? Is that really Ronnie? Impossible! Not that tall handsome kid that's leaning on the running board. Sure enough, it is. He even makes the car look small.

For a few moments let's Dad and me settle down to a little gab session while the rest of you folks stand by for a few minutes. For some reason or other, Dad, you have a guilty conscience over not writing me as often as you'd like. That stuff has got to stop. I understand as sure as I'm in New Guinea that your time is filled up and that it's tough to drum up interesting subject matter. Sure I understand, and your occasional letters are equivalent to a dozen letters a week from somebody else. Keep doing it the way you have been, and I'll be one happy fellow. From reports concerning the old baloney that you flaunt, I know your heart's right here with this Sadsack.[1]

"Bachelor for a Week" or "Brief Ecstasy" sound like good titles for a book describing your week. There you were, poor you, all by your lonesome self while Mom was away enjoying life. Pretty tough, wasn't it? I'm practically in the same fix. I'm literally a bachelor with no folks to pamper me and all that. As one bachelor to another whadya say we go out together on a bit of a fling, or don't you dare? No? That's what I figured. Mom has you trained well, so you eat in restaurants by your lonely self, read the evening paper which collects a week high beside your chair, then go to bed at midnight. To hell with house cleaning. The week is complete after Mom returns remarking how filthy the house is and how disorderly the desk down at the shop is.

I have a few thoughts on politics. I feel Roosevelt is sure to get in again. Even the fellows here who are going to vote for Dewey agree. Remember, Dewey isn't necessarily the G.O.P.s choice but rather the public's. The navy has gone to great lengths to see that every eligible man votes. Charts defining districts and counties for all forty-eight states have been posted.

I figured Cousin Bob deserted his relatives. The kid's going in the wrong direction. He should stick by the folks nearest him. They are the only ones who will help him in a pinch. Some gal will probably get hold of him and calm him down. No one is too busy in the service not to write home at least four times a week.

I've put out of my mind the episode concerning Bob's sending a will home. When a fellow comes here, he knows he's going back. I'm returning as sure as shootin' and so is everybody else here. Wills, purely ridiculous.

Today a notice requesting more applications for V-12 appeared on the bulletin board. Those who pass the test will be sent back to the States. Lists of colleges were also posted. It appears that the government is trying to give the fellows overseas a chance. "No waivers will be considered," cuts me out good and proper, similar to the last time, so I just gaze at the notice and wish some other fellow good luck. Except for my vision, I have all the qualifications. Mother's clipping about the G.I. Bill of Rights[2] sounds wonderful. I'm going for that, come hell or high water. Everything seems to be turning out for the best.

My whimsical letter concerning A CAT'S TALE was only some reminiscing I felt like writing about when I had nothing else to say. By no means did I intend it to mean that I wanted a cat. Cats are okay, but not around the house. If ever we get a home of our own, a dog would sure be nice.

That winds up Dad's letter. Now for Mom's. Razor blades received, *Time* magazine arriving weekly, and the new pen is fine. It's only me, not the pen, that's the problem.

Now that Ronnie is an Izaak Walton,[3] I expect some super duper fish stories about the one that got away.

Don't you realize that fatness, or pleasant plumpness I prefer to call it, is a great asset? Venus De Milo[4] is no 110 pounds. I'd be disappointed if when I got home I found a skinny mother. That would never do. Stay the way you are; that's the way I like you. You bet.

Do you remember the guy whose name I underlined in the clipping I sent you? He's the fellow who picked me up on Sunset Boulevard that afternoon in his deluxe Lincoln Zephyr.

Saturday night, rather morning, after work at 12:30, I saw "My Friend Flicka."[5] Went to bed at 2:30 and awoke at 11:00 AM. I can't see the early show on this job.

Lil wrote from Old Orchard, and at last Lenny got to write. He has a pretty good deal in San Diego. Lucky boy.

Time mag is beside me tempting me to read the latest in national politics, and I'm pretty well talked out except for,

Love to the three of you, Hughie

8/8/44

Dear Dad,

The most important thing that has happened in the vicinity of my tent is the arrival of a barnyard hen. I'd also say that it is the most important thing that has happened in this part of New Guinea for some time. Nothing ever happens anymore.

Do you recall the two dogs living nearby that were supposed to be a mama and papa? Evidently there was no love between them, so they finally disposed of the male who refused to be a father. In his place a womanly acting hen has been placed in a pen beneath the dog's tent. She struts about with a characteristic superior air and constantly torments the dog living above her.

Currently the hen is a subject of controversy between the city boys and the country boys. The city boys claim she'll have no eggs because there's no rooster, while the country boys say a rooster isn't necessary for a hen to lay eggs. The argument remains to be settled. I've adopted the country boys' point of view. My Bostonian friends brand me a deserter, and a traitor. But I still insist that I expect to have a few of the hen's eggs rooster or no rooster.

This afternoon I found the business and finance section of *Time* quite interesting. Predicting that people are expected to spend a lot on luxury items after the war, the article claims that the future of the economy looks bright, indeed. So after the war is over, you should be able to clean up, rather than now when you and so many businessmen are struggling with goods and labor shortages. I'd bet that the re-upholstering business will slump while sales of new furniture will pick up. I think people with money would rather have new than fix up the old, and they'll prefer the expensive article over the cheap one. Unlike the head of a big business, a small businessman need not look way ahead, because he can easily adjust on short notice to the new demands of the market. I'd look forward to an era of custom built new furniture — more than ever before. I'm merely applying to your business the economists' view reported in Time.

I have often wondered whether you'd expand were your business to experience a great upswing. I recall that when you did have more business than you could handle, you were handicapped by labor and supply problems. But after the war, this wouldn't be the case. If then a similar situation were to arise, on an even larger scale, would you be ambitious and enlarge, or would you be satisfied to carry on the way you have been, making a living, perhaps saving a little, and taking pride in your small business? I'm really curious, Dad. Of course, I'd prefer that you took advantage of the inevitable coming boom. Here's a key statistic: there are 7,000,000 newlyweds in this country who haven't gone into housekeeping because they lack household fixtures and furniture due to their unavailability. Furthermore, there's going to be the biggest home building boom in U.S. history. All this spells furniture.

I also read that demobilization will be at 250,000 troops a month, a mere trickle. A greater percentage of combat troops will be released first. Men serving in the tropics will be favored over others for the sake of their health and morale. I also believe that the Seabees will be among the earliest to be demobilized. The reasons: there aren't enough camps to hold even a fraction of our total complement. Peary is being converted to regular navy use. So is Rousseau and Holliday is no longer a Seabee camp. Only Camp Parks near Frisco and Thomas (which adjoins Endicott) are all that remain, and both are very small. Secondly, Congress has discontinued appropriations for the Seabee battalions because our work is nearly done and the army engineers are taking over our remaining jobs. Thirdly, since our men are skilled laborers, we are not suitable for policing troops. And finally, our skills will be needed in the civilian economy to take on neglected major construction projects and to build homes. What little work needs to be done overseas will also be taken over by civilian contractors. All these reasons would suggest that we'll be released sooner than the other branches of the service.

From my point of view, the sooner the better, because I want to be one of the first to get a crack at the government's college program. I've already waited more than two years, and, when I get back, I don't want to waste more time.

8/10/44

Dear Mom,

Last night I saw "The Sullivans."[1] It was extremely touching, such that it quieted that usually hooting crowd to a mumble. I enjoyed every minute of it.

This morning I received Yetta's package of May 22nd in a somewhat mangled condition. Evidently, it has been cruising around the islands for quite a while as it had a "missent" stamp on it.

I expect to go on another little excursion Sunday, this time with a camera, my chum's, of course.

Although it's been hotter than usual, the weather has been very pleasant. I have yet to catch up on a pile of letter writing, but lately I've been in a dazed condition for hours after rising at 11:00 A.M.

I give us another two or three months here, then farther up we go. Although it's a guess, it's only logical. I may not know any more than the next fellow, but I know our battalion will soon be on the move again.

I received a letter from Malter's gal[2] in Frisco and already, I feel she's an old friend. She also writes as if she has known me all her life. The West Coasters are marvelous that way. From her last letter, I gather that some of my so-called "classics" (quote) are being exhibited among her friends, and she rereads the things rather than Eleanor's My Day column. So it seems I have a second Barney Aaron type plugger on the West Coast. It's fun to know that people do enjoy reading these darn things. Fun indeed. Having convinced you that I'm an artiste at bull throwing, I guess that explains it. Although I've considered joining Stoopnagle's liars club, I know I don't stand a chance against Herr Goebbels.[3]

I keep pretty well up on the daily news. It's actually a pleasure to read it. Won't be long now. I see by the papers that the Seabees are as publicized as ever. At one time many of our boys didn't want to wear the CB emblem on their sleeve. But now just try to get them to take it off. Our overseas exploits have changed many attitudes.

About time to knock off for my reading session: *Les Miserables*. I'll try to muster up some more baloney tomorrow.

8/12/44

Dear Mom,

Not all the mail has been sorted yet, but I have yours of July 28th that I'll answer before going to work.

Your morale building "keep a stiff upper lip," and "make the best of it," stuff is really not necessary. I fully realize my position, sometimes seemingly unfortunate and other times fortunate. I see it sensibly and have accepted things with good grace. If I gripe in an occasional letter, I'm only unloading, being normal. Good griping is GI Joe's[1] universal vernacular. Remember that. My so-called moments of depression and tension are temporary, and fairly rare. Never fear, my dear. I have too much to look forward to, to be unhappy.

Patience! That I've lacked. During the past year, how I've needed it. I am now more tolerant with forces beyond me, and I have more patience than before. I truly believe that I've learned to wait. The service, which metes out plenty, teaches patience if nothing else. I still have the same old quirk of hating to be disturbed when reading, but instead of telling someone to shut up, I now go elsewhere to read undisturbed. What I used to do back home I can't do here.

Dad, it was pretty tough without Mom around, wasn't it? Yeah, it's the same with me. Still, I'm glad that Mother and Ronnie go away. They needed it; you needed it. All of you are entitled to a vacation.

During these times of stress you need it more than ever. Today we should live for more than subsistence; we should also live for pleasure. With money so plentiful we should all be able to live for pleasure. Now is the time to take advantage of these good conditions. I hope that next summer, whether I'm home or not, the whole family will take a vacation.

Looking back, I can see some of the flaws that account for my former lack of sociability. Ronnie seems to be following the same channel. It isn't good that a boy constantly work with his father. It destroys his ability to be independent, his sense of what his labor is worth, and in the main it breeds discontent within the family. You were probably unhappy that Ronnie left for a week or so. How can a boy respond normally to his natural impulses if he's under a yoke? By working for someone else, even if the boss were demanding, he would still be independent. Ronnie will certainly follow in my footsteps if he's constantly tied down to the shop. I agree, it may be his duty during wartime. That's still no reason to begrudge him time off during the summer. The biggest mistake you've made is to have me work for you. When I broke away, relieved from pressure, I felt free and independent.

Granted, you need Ronnie. Perhaps he shouldn't work elsewhere at this time because of his value to you. Okay, then treat him like the rest, neither favor him nor impose on him. Pay him on Saturday when you pay the others. Set his hours and let him go his own way after those hours. Give him an afternoon a week off. If he doesn't do things the way he says he will, then for that hour or so take it out of his pay. If he doesn't do what you want, he isn't worth the money. Make him understand that. Perhaps his situation is different from the way mine was. If it's the same, don't treat him as you did me. In other words use him and pay him like any other employee and give him time off for pleasure. He'll never meet people so long as all his time is yours. I want you to answer.

Mom, just as back home, I can study and read only to a point with noise. Some people can concentrate, others aren't made that way. I still like quiet and solitude when I study. I envy those who can do otherwise. That's me. Nothing has changed it.

Yup, this is the kid that doesn't drink tea or coffee YET, your same old Hughie, a little wiser perhaps, but hardly changed. What did Dad used to say about me? "What a tin can (or something) he turned out to be!" That's me.

Time arrived this morning. Truman[2] is a strong vice-presidential candidate. I think the Democrats have the election in the bag. I expect something big to happen in the S.W.P.A.,[3] signified by the presidential conference in Hawaii. I feel it in my bones.

8/13/44

Dear Mom,

Today, Sunday, in New Guinea was as near a summer Sunday back home as I've experienced. The sky was clear, a cool breeze blowing, and we performed our Sunday chore cleaning the tent. Everyone was listless, just lounging around. Some of us took pictures of each other in freakish positions, all wearing little more than shorts. This afternoon we heard the president speak, assuring us of a quick and ultimate victory in the S.W.P.A., to us already evident. Booming over the public address system, his voice had a soothing effect on the whole area. Tonight, after a speech by the captain of the entire naval base, we'll have a movie.

We've been promised entertainment plus for the duration: USO shows, including Bob Hope and other celebrities. The amphitheater that our battalion built is suitable for such performances. Our battalion's prestige appears to be great. I confess I feel proud that I'm in this particular outfit.

My job is going well. I like the work, and I do it with moderation. Although it's a laborer's job, it's pleasant, because of the gang I work with, and the freedom it allows. My hours are tops: 4:00 PM to 12:00 midnight. It's much easier working during the cool nighttime, and I can sleep until ten in the morning. Maybe I'll never get ahead on this job, but that's incidental.

We had a small tent discussion about cars (said with a Harvard accent) during which I exhibited the picture of Dad's vehicle. Everyone said it was a steal.

The routine is rather pleasant, affording me plenty of spare time. Unfortunately, I lack ambition, and spend most of my time reading. The climate is ideal for simply lying around.

So I expect to take some pictures. Some friends have offered to let me use their cameras, if I supply the film. Send me some 127 and 616 film, and I'll send you some pictures. Send tropical film (treated against humidity and heat), if you can get it. A roll of each will be sufficient.

The principal food and drink in my diet has been fruit juice: pineapple, tomato, orange and grapefruit. I imagine I take a half quart or more daily. Them's my cocktails minus the rum or whisky. I wonder if I'll even look at the stuff after I'm home. Ice cream for dessert this evening!

Dear Mom,

I've seen three movies the past three nights, a record-breaking attendance record for me. My job is coming along fine. I've received a box of cookies from [Aunt] Ida. That's all the news there is. There isn't any more, Dull, isn't it?

The weather—a universal subject— has been ideal. It rains about five hours a week, only in the evening. I'm now totally involved in *Les Miserables*, can't lay the book down. When I'm done with it, I plan to read *Jean Christophe*[1] then Tolstoy's[2] *War and Peace*.[3] Reading is my favorite pastime. With so much time, what better use could I put it to? Don't be surprised if I send some books home.

In the past week I received two packages and a letter, and I discovered that the letter is worth more than the two packages. The packages may be good, but the letter contains something a heck of a lot more valuable. All the fellows agree.

I'm eating plenty: peanuts, nuts, raisins, olives, pickles, lemon cocktails, fruit juice, chocolate and gum. These constitute my in between meal diet. I wonder if I'm gaining weight.

8/16/44

Dear Mom,

I'm now ready to go into business: the confectionery business. Another package arrived from Newton Avenue [Cousin Lil]. I'm everybody's pal, bent and sore from the deluge of back slaps. Everyone in our tent is now regally feasting. If I ever wondered whether it pays to be in the service, now I know that, at this rate, it does.

I gather the uh Hollywood trumped up photo of this guy, hasn't lost its ability to impress family and friends. Isn't it remarkable what a photo studio can do to the worst of us? I urge you to donate the photo to a New York art gallery, where it can be truly exhibited. For the love of Mike, Mom.

A few evenings ago I saw "New Wine"[1] concerning the life of Franz Schubert.[2] In the background his Unfinished Symphony[3] and "Ave Maria" are played throughout. After not hearing good music for so long, I appreciated hearing the Schubert pieces all the more. It was simply marvelous. I plan to take advantage of so many pleasures when I get back. What a blind fool I've been.

8/18/44

Dear Mom,

Yesterday I received the GI glasses from Australia, in a case, in perfect shape. Today, I received the glasses from Mr. Bloom,[1] in an envelope inside a cardboard box. The right lens is cracked, but it's hardly visible. I should think that Mr. Bloom would have used better judgment than to send the glasses the way he did. Under normal circumstances I could probably use them for years without the crack getting worse, but out here there's no telling how long the lens will last. The GI glasses are just plain lousy. I can't see nearly as well with them as I should. I'll only use them in a pinch, and in the meantime use Mr.Bloom's pair. I wear glasses only for reading and at shows. Tomorrow, I plan to send both pairs of my formerly broken glasses home. Have them repaired locally and send them back.

Heard from Johnson Fulgoni again. He sent me a swell picture of himself. Sure would like you to meet him.

I'm glad you enjoyed having my picture in the paper. I didn't. Here's how I look at it. Only my correspondents are interested in my being in the service. I have no wish for others who care nothing about me to know. Perhaps you get some satisfaction in advertising your son. I see no sense in it. The less people know about me, the better I like it. Parents are funny. I don't feel honored at being a former Tech Pharmacy employee, which was mentioned. Also mentioned was my career or something as a swimming instructor, which doesn't amount to a row of beans. In other words the article is a device designed to impress, just plain advertising of an ordinary fact: that a son is in the service. Mom, I've always disliked having my picture displayed. I've always disliked your bragging about your son in New Guinea, exhibiting my letters and so on. But I know you enjoy doing it. I understand that you feel proud, which makes me also feel proud. Still, inside of me, I hate it. Some people don't mind sharing their privacy, and the spreading of laurels, even if undue. Not I. Maybe you think I'm crazy. But these are my sentiments, and there's nothing I can do about them. The matter is unimportant, trivial, and best over and done with. Just a reminder that any sort of publicity isn't to my liking.

When I'm attending school, I don't plan to specialize. I'd rather grope about, investigate the opportunities, and see what I prefer. I've mentioned earlier that I'm not set on chemical engineering. I picked the field arbitrarily, because it seemed appealing, and it encompassed a wide variety of subjects. By not specializing, I'd have more time to find something I'm sure of. If I find that engineering is something I'd like, I think I'll have a conflict between exploring what's available and being practical.

I'm now more conscious of racial and religious prejudice than ever. My choice of what field to enter will have to take that into account. Since you feel that such prejudice could be a threat to my success in the chemical engineering field, what do you suggest I go into? The war may be a boon for a Jew to become a chemist, and then again it might not. Only the future will tell. I'll deal with it when the future is the present.

I'm enjoying my pleasant existence these days, especially sleeping 'til late in the morning. Ah, heaven it is. I always have something to nibble on, some delicacy to keep my stomach supplied. I'm still reading to beat the band, and writing little.

Ho hum, you poor, poor civilians.

Love to all three of you, Hughie

P.S. Fuzzy, wuzzy Ronnie, the guy with a two week growth. You should have seen me when I landed here.

8/19/44

Dear Mom,

An all out drive is being made for V-12 applicants. It appears that a quota has to be filled. Lionel Gallant is now a second class petty officer. He's a good kid. Received my corrected geometry lesson. Got a 93% grade and the instructor is very encouraging.

I have so much to do. I can't put down the books I'm reading, I must keep up with the correspondence course, I must and like to write letters, I read the popular magazines, I want to see movies and shows. All this I manage to cram into my free time. It's wonderful to be so busy over here; time passes quickly. Then I keep in close contact with my special friends: Henry Wolf, Al Martin and Stand Dichter (a new friend from New York). We have pleasant discussions daily, consult one another, dream of the future, and unload our troubles.

My daily routine is somewhat changed now that I work evenings. Let's begin at midnight when I quit work. At 12:05 I'm taking a shower, putting on clean clothes, and ready to skip down to the chow hall for a bit of a snack: cake, pie and sandwiches. At 12:45 I'm at the amphitheater; the picture is over at 2:00 A.M. (Shows are on Monday, Wednesday and Saturday evenings.) Thence to bed and awake at 10:00 A.M. On nights when there are no shows, I arise at 8:00 A.M., put on lounging clothes, sneakers, no shirt, shave, do my house cleaning, and I'm ready to settle down to a pleasant morning of reading, writing, studying, and talking. I receive frequent visits through the day from friends and, I visit them on occasional afternoons. This is entertaining and fun. At 3:30 P.M. I'm dressed in my old clothes and ready to go to work. Today, Saturday, for instance, is always a little better than the rest of the week. It's like Friday back home when I was in school. After work tonight I'll go to a show. The following day, Sunday, I have off and don't return to work until Monday at 4:00 P.M. You can see that I have plenty of time off, plenty of entertainment, and plenty to do during my free time. Not a bad routine, eh? The days are usually gorgeous. When I awake the earth is glistening in the sun and a light ocean breeze blows through our bright tent.

I understand that in order to receive the benefits of the government's financing of education, one must show that he is financially incapable of paying his own way. Actually I'll have enough money saved to send me through college. Once investigated, would I be considered well off? Doubt it, but there's always that possibility. What's the story on that, Dad?

8/23/44

Dear Mom,

As we brought our mission here to completion, a stage was carved from the wilderness and what happened on it profoundly boosted our morale. Let me explain.

Last May, after our party landed, we pushed the jungle aside with our bulldozers, and as if by magic, made roads in the red earth. The smell of freshly sliced soil filled the air; the roar of diesels drowned out the sounds of the jungle; trucks struggled along the fresh ways. Everywhere the enormous American process of civilizing the land — American magic — was evident.

There's a fork in the road about 300 yards from my tent site, probably the busiest junction in our area. At this junction a bulldozer created a huge bowl from what was once a densely wooded ravine. Grades were established, the earth was smoothed, and suddenly, after several days of construction, a beautiful amphitheater majestically appeared. Footlights were installed, a curtain improvised from colored duck cloth, a silver screen erected, and dressing rooms added. It is a real theatrical and movie stage, magnificent and fascinating to behold. From a distance, the place — a theater built by amateurs for professionals — lit up at night, looks ethereal.

From the stage a performer sees a bowl of earth cut into tiers by our dozers, and beyond them a terraced hill that melts into a one thousand foot mountain. Everyone wondered why we had built such a gorgeous stage and elaborate theater. Movies? Only a screen would be necessary for movies. Eventually, forgetting its true purpose, a place for shows, we thought of the stage as a monument to our accomplishments here. We impatiently looked forward to each semi-nightly movie, our few hours of reverie.

Soon a few performers – speechmakers: the captains and commanders – appeared on the stage. We were told of the wonders we had created, of the war's progress, of our purpose, and about home. They exalted us with their words. Everyone felt proud and admired the theater still more.

Then music came, the first to resound in the surrounding hills. Local bands and orchestras appeared but nothing professional. They played waltzes, hit tunes, symphonies, jazz rhythms, melodies; New Guinea had never heard it before. Our stage introduced it, and it made the men happy. The anticipation of an evening's entertainment after a day's work inspired us.

Yesterday an order was issued: all evening work would be halted. a grand show was due.

Last night the amphitheater was jammed as the throng extended to the rear most terraces. Every uniform imaginable filled every corner and cranny. Higher and higher, terrace upon terrace, was filled; it was a capacity audience.

A car, a civilian car, bearing a flag with two stars on its left fender, moved through the crowd. A bugle blew and everyone stood at attention as the admiral took the seat for "The Admiral and his Guests." Barely five minutes later a motorcycle, followed by two, three, four cars and some jeeps appeared at the junction and wended their way toward the stage. The air shook with yells, "There they are," laughs, roars, the sound of 6,000 strong. The band then struck up a popular tune which mingled with the noise of the crowd. After the actors went behind the stage, the roar quieted, becoming an excited murmur.

Soon a man walked out onto the stage and the loudspeakers blared: "Presenting Bob Hope and his troupe." The crowd became hysterical. Only the master's voice[1] itself could quiet the tumult.

Familiar to us all, his actions and words made everyone feel nearer home. Close your eyes and you're in your easy chair listening to the Pepsodent program.[2] His jokes were suggestive, funny, crazy, silly, senseless, sensible, and witty, and everyone understood. The war was forgotten.

A beautiful dancer, daringly clad, was presented amid catcalls and vociferous male squeals. She smiled and danced. Her name: Pattie Thomas. Everyone was having a good time.

Frances Langford[3] then came on and sang several songs. After each one there were screams of "More, more." Jerry Colonna,[4] crazy but a riot, put us in the aisles. Hope, fingering Colonna's mustache: "What a crop, what a jungle!" Colonna: "Careful, don't touch. Snipers." That sort of nonsense. Tony Romano with his guitar was tops. Lanny Ross[5] spoke and sang some. The former owner (and now Lieutenant Commander) of the Chicago Bears[6] was introduced. This was entertainment plus.

The entire cast sang "Thanks for the Memories"[7] signifying the end. After the Star Spangled Banner was played, the road streamed with boys dashing to escape the throng of which they had been a part. In ten minutes the theater was silent, resplendent in the glory of what had just passed. You see, the whole Hope cast marveled that such a grand theater could be carved out of this wilderness. They marveled at its beauty and the ingenuity that went into it. Little did any of us imagine that this stage would grace the greatest comedian of our time.

The men are still talking about the show and will probably be for months to come. Other shows are now expected. Knowing this is in store for us, everyone is feeling better. We've left Hollywood, but miraculously Hollywood seems to be following us. I certainly enjoyed yesterday.

It rather struck me as marvelous that but a few months ago there was only jungle here, and we carried loaded guns while walking about. That's Seabee magic. We are being rewarded for our hard labor at the beginning. The stage is manna from heaven for everyone.

Love to the three of you, Hughie

P.S. Show lasted 1 1/2 hours.

8/24/44

Dear Mom,

Your letter of the 14th has arrived in record time. The equator has gone north. You poor people way up there near the North Pole in Massachusetts must be sweltering while we bask in tropical frigidness. I've seen hotter days back home than down here. However, here the sun is terrific, its rays far more powerful than in the northern latitudes. The thermometer has never gone much beyond ninety-five degrees.

We aren't over the effects of the Bob Hope show yet. You may be interested to learn that draft boards are taking men depending on how they react in this test: after a copy of *Esquire* is handed the would-be draftee, the board observes which page he turns to—so says Bob Hope. Hope also claims to have more flying hours than Bing Crosby's stork.[1]

I understand we're due another show sometime this week. Tonight, a movie.

Still working at the same job, and I'm satisfied, though my security is questionable. There's a possibility that the saw mill will close down, leaving me jobless and eligible for unforeseen details.

The European news sounds great: Paris and Marseille taken yesterday. I expect important events in the Pacific soon. Everybody can see them coming. I can feel it.

8/25/44

Dear Mom and Fellow Travelers,

Today was good to me—two whoppa letters plus pictures.

Yea gods, it doesn't seem possible: Ronnie almost a full head over Dad. Oh, oh, I'm considering remaining in New Guinea for good. All the pastings I used to inflict on the young'n offer him a good excuse for retaliation. Have mercy kid, will you? Look, I'm nervous already. Truth is, I'm astounded. Hereafter, I'll refer to Ronnie, that big hunk of man, as my big brother. No more brat, young'n, kid brother, small fry, jerk *ad infinitum*.[1] The table is reversed. Tell 'im to go easy on me, will ya, Mom?

Boy, *Omnibook* coming is swell, and the stationery you're sending is sure to come in handy. Thanks my fran. And while you're in the sending mood, whenever convenient, waft a can of talcum powder and a small bottle of Vaseline hair oil my way.

Doggone, Mr. Durgin[2] [Dad's mentor and first boss] finally came up from Philadelphia to Worcester. Coincidentally, just last week Henry Wolf (He's from Philly) and I were talking about postwar friendship. I'll seriously consider visiting him after the war is over. He's a swell egg and we (as they say in England) get along famously. Such a visit would serve a dual purpose: at the same time Dad could also visit the great boss, Durgin. On the way to Philly I could also drop by to see friends in New York and later extend the trip to Pittsburgh, where I have another close friend.[3] Who is the comedian who always says, "Well, it's possible?" I'm much interested in Dad's reunion with his old boss and look forward to hearing all about it from the old time telegrapher ....

Am still reading to beat the band and enjoying it to the nth degree. *Time* arrives regularly. After managing to read between the biased presentations, I get plenty of info. It's a Republican magazine.

Yonny Yonson from Minnesota (accent on Minn) presents no trouble at all. Arguments are at a minimum.

I can't get over my family's wanderlust. They tell me it's contagious. Guess you caught it from me. Mohawk Trail⁴ here you come. If you do finally make the trail, it has taken a good six summers to make it.

Say, it's close to a year since I was last home. *Tempus fugit.*

Dad, my delicate piece of sugar, the guy who melts in lake and ocean. Shame, Dad. Water would do your leg good. I have yet to persuade you to join the Y to take advantage of the soothing effect of its pool, the hot showers, steam bath, ultra violet and massage. Such things take the mind off the regular routine and soothe the body. Exercise isn't necessary.

Much to the amusement of my snickering fellow listeners, I'm reading your comment on "Our New England Accent." I must laugh because I said the same thing as you a year ago. The fact is, we do talk differently. We don't speak the way radio announcers do. You must be exposed to other dialects, before you are aware of the difference. For example, note how an announcer pronounces car, bath, Boston, Harvard, talk, bottle, beetle, and a host of other words. Our A is broad, our O different and our T is stressed. We slur our Rs. Those speaking universal English come from Ohio and California and thereabouts. The minute I open my yap, I'm spotted as a New Englander. Of course, we don't realize how differently we speak. They make fun of Roosevelt. I read just the other day about a script writer from New England who appeared as a guest on the radio. After the show he was inundated with letters, correcting the way he pronounced certain words. Still, I like our accent—and it's definitely an accent. Do you still say aprom for apron, Mom? Don't be stubborn now.

Dad was very merciful: he neglected to write "wish you were here," of the picture of the super Ford.

Nothing much happening around town lately. Can smell another step coming. Nothing certain, only plausible. War news is tops. At this rate, Germany will be finished by the first of the year. Some predict sooner. "At this rate" are the key words. The rate may not continue. Rumania has succumbed to the Reds—a resourceful victory. I fear the making of the peace more than the war. The International Monetary Conference at Bretton Woods⁵ signifies harmony and considerate peace making. The German nation cannot be subdued, that's certain, and it won't be. Equality among nations should be stressed, and I think it will be. The task is enormous. Actually, an expedient peace plan will only lengthen the period between this war and another. It cannot stave off another war. I can't believe that it will.

8/25/44

Dear Ronnie (alias Don Juan),

A very personal question. Have you any hair on your chest yet? So the lad shaves. Heard the beard is pitch black. My, my, time marches on. Congratulations. Pay me a visit after you've grown a remarkable crop and are no longer embarrassed. Beards are in competition out here. The man sporting the best beard gets a free shaving mug, a set of clippers, shears, and associated paraphernalia. After using them he'll send them home to his wife who would slit his throat if he arrived home with the aforementioned crop.

Let's be serious for a few minutes. I'm glad to hear that you are beginning to think of the future. I've been waiting quite a while for the time you'd mention it.

Interior decoration is a marvelous field. The interior decorator must have personality, a good appearance, and a business mind. I think you have all three. However, most important he must be intrigued with the field. He must have good taste, artistic ability, and good judgment. The first of these are open for discussion, and the last I know you have. Of course, you wouldn't want to be just an interior decorator, but also an intelligent, conscientious, and educated interior decorator. You must go on to a school of higher learning, major in art and associated subjects. Begin now by investigating what schools are well suited to your chosen field.

You like doodling and drawing with a pencil, and you like music. In other words, you respond to the arts, show a definite leaning towards them.

Dad will tell you that the compensation in the field of interior decoration knows no bounds. You will cater to the wealthy who have money in good times and bad. It's a very attractive and highly regarded vocation. I think it would be wonderful for you to go into it.

Your high school curriculum will require another subject. Next semester elect art. Approach your adviser and find out from him what qualifications are necessary to apply to a school of interior decoration. Don't delay. You are now in your second year. Half your high school career is over.

I'm glad for both you and Dad that you find the field enticing. By the time you graduate college—and you must and will go, if I have to finance it—Dad will need your help. He needs it now, but I think with aid from you and me we can ease a good deal of the pressure on him. The day will come when Dad won't be as active. Because of his bad leg, his activity is already somewhat lessened. What will happen to the business? Entrust it to the hired help? It's possible but most likely not profitable. Although Dad would be in charge, the jobs he now performs are bound to be bungled by others. But the addition of an interior decorator to the staff of such a proud and well-established business would be an enormous boon. It would lead to its expansion, and open up untold possibilities. Here you are with an affinity for art, an interest in interior decoration, a knowledge of furniture, a possible future education in decoration, and a business that more than welcomes you to step into. The setup is inspiring and ideal.

You are aware that my ambitions run along other lines. I might add that I've been struggling in my mind with the alternatives of following my chosen calling or giving Dad a hand and going in with him. Having suggested that I join him in the past, he'd like me to take over either the outside or inside end of the business. I feel that he was disappointed that I'm not especially crazy about the upholstering business, although I know it's an admirable field. I rather think that in our discussions we didn't consider your future seriously. I didn't because you weren't considering it either, and your future was indefinite. We decided to wait until you came down to earth. Now I think you're solidly there and dependable and the possibility of your having a role is marvelous. You'll not only help yourself by taking up decoration, you'll also take a load off Dad's mind. It's gives him a more secure future. I've set a goal to make Dad's and Mom's future happy and positive. That should also be your aim. Of course, there are some limitations to this. They also want us to be happy, for our happiness is also theirs. With the arrangement I've just described, no one need sacrifice his goals, but if either one of has to do so, then we must and will.

Just to mention again the unbounded opportunities in your field, let me add that you need not limit yourself to Worcester. Although desirable, you don't have to join Dad in business. In big cities, in localities where construction is extensive, in Hollywood for instance, in all the population centers, the field is wide open for a host of decorators to thrive. I've mentioned in earlier letters that construction will occur on an enormous scale during the postwar era.

Here's wishing you all the luck in the world. I'm all for you. Go to it.

Love, Hughie

8/28/44

Dear Mom,

Today is simply gorgeous. The sky is a blue that it is capable of being only in the tropics. Because of an incessant sea breeze, it isn't terribly hot. I have before me a letter complaining of the stifling, humid, almost unbearable New England heat. I can picture you nodding, thinking that your son must endure such heat daily. Ah, but you're wrong. Please accept my sincerest feelings of pity.

It's Monday and I have both today and tomorrow off, compensation for having worked yesterday, an unusual event. This morning I finished Victor Hugo's *Les Miserables*, a very stirring and beautifully written story. While it's definitely a classic, it hardly fits our conception of what we call a best seller. I'm now planning to embark on Tolstoy's *War and Peace*, which is almost as long as Hugo's book of 1200 pages. Wishing to finish the book before we leave this place, I'm ready for a "California or bust" campaign.

Just a word about present conditions here. There's no opposition activity whatsoever, and there hasn't been since our initial landing. That's the truth.

My interest in politics is that of an onlooker 10,000 miles away. I learn only the varnished facts from which to form an opinion. Obviously my opinions are weakly based, but one must not treat politics as being a farce. When the destiny of our nation hinges on the decisions of corrupt politicos, our interest should increase rather than diminish. Truman is a politically sound, good candidate. Wallace's situation is unfortunate. He's a victim of fickle politics. He played the political game and lost. Politics is just that—a game. Wilson[1] lost too, you know. Politics, his prejudice against the Republican party, prevented him from gaining the support of the nation at a crucial moment. Let's hope that Roosevelt will share with the opposition party the glory of making peace agreements. It's mandatory.

I discussed fabrics recently with a new friend and co-worker who owns a fabric manufacturing company in New Jersey. What I don't know about fabrics. Oy.

In my reference to Chaplain Whittaker's "inquisitiveness" I meant that he was interested in our welfare, home, family etc. He amiably questioned us on all these points to make conversation and for our enjoyment.

Why you insist that your letters are uninteresting is beyond me. Here and now let me say that reporting you took a trolley from 47 Lincoln Street [the shop] to 67 King Street [home] is enough to set me in virtual raptures. If, when you reread your letters, you think they're bad, why then stop rereading them. After all, I also love your typographical errors. They build character in a letter. Only you can innocently produce a beautiful pattern from crossed out letters. Everything in your letters, mistakes, trivia, the whole works, is tops.

Dad and highballs mix perfectly. They make him feel happy. This brings to mind a certain New Year's Eve party [when Dad got high] at 396 Chandler Street [an earlier home]. Remember?

His other interests hardly restrain Ronnie's affinity for girls. That's good. I hope that he'll satisfy your wish to bring girls home. You always wanted a daughter. Undoubtedly, Ronnie will be the first to give you one. Let's hope that Ronnie will make up for your disappointment in me. I'm afraid I'm little changed on that score. I don't especially care to associate with girls. I find other interests more attractive and compelling. My eyes have been more or less opened to what makes the world go round, which has broadened my view of girls. Still my attitude toward them hasn't changed. There you are saying, "Wait, he'll change." Who cares?

Yes, I know that pilots go through hell. I've talked to many of them. They are subject to a terrific amount of mental fatigue which accounts for the reason why we lose so many. But it's not only in the air that the mind cracks. I've seen mental cases among the ground forces too. They are horrible to witness.

Our theater has made history again. I just returned from seeing Judith Anderson's[2] show. the cast: Helen McClure an MGM vocalist, Shirley Cornell a violinist in Dinah Shore's[3] program, Paul Parmelee a pianist (at 13 played in the Rochester Symphony, also with Jose Iturbi,[4] also with the Philadelphia Symphony), Lt. Robert Wallsten, who played opposite Judith Anderson on the New York stage, Judith Anderson, whom you know and who has acted before the queens and kings of Europe, and Ann Triola accordionist and cast comedienne.

It was a high class show, too good, I fear, for the audience. Miss Anderson was marvelous. Her speech, her air, her gait, her personality, all were perfectly charming. With Mr. Wallsten she performed a scene from *Macbeth*,[5] the like of which I shall probably never see again. I did so enjoy that show.

Just think, two years ago I was reading Shakespeare and discussing Judith Anderson in *Macbeth* in class. It seems impossible that I would soon watch her act from a front row seat.

That's what I want to see after I return: good acting, good plays. I want to hear good music. Informally, I'm getting it here, but I also want to see it with a full set in all its color. Unfortunately, the audience responded unenthusiastically to the show, but it showed respect. Everything about Miss Anderson commands respect. But how could she make herself master of an audience of ruffians?

There's a movie tonight. As you can see, I don't lack for entertainment.

The deadline for ending the war in Europe is set for October 31 and the Pacific campaign a year later. Of course, that deadline is flexible, but it will give you some idea how much longer I'll be here. Expect me to stay for quite a while and you won't be disappointed. What the hell, I'm getting $4.40 seats free. Who wants to go home?

8/30/44

Dear Mom,

Every morning I have a unique — and special — visitor. About two mornings ago I dreamt of a hen contentedly clucking. I couldn't imagine why such a dream. Gradually awakening, greeted by a musical downpour on the tent roof, I groaned then turned over to fall again into that delightful slumber that's so desirable on gloomy, sleepy mornings. In my half consciousness I continued to hear an occasional outburst of clucking. Annoyed, I summoned up my wits sufficiently to realize that the clucking hadn't come from my unconscious. After scanning the area nearby through drowsy eyes, I saw nothing. Still, the clucking persisted. After looking high and low throughout the tent trying to track down the sound, I eventually found it on an improvised shelf in an open cardboard box. There she was inside, an innocent, contented setting hen. Since she was apparently tame, I cautiously stroked her plumage, and she loved it. But soon, after chasing this she-devil around the tent, I evicted the proud beauty.

Again this morning my reverie was interrupted by the same contented clucking. And again I found our Esmeralda (my prodigy) in the very same place as before. Thank God she isn't a rooster, or mark my words, one of these days we'd be having rooster for dinner. Esmeralda belongs to a neighbor. We'll tolerate her meanderings, unless and until the old gal gets nasty.

We've been getting our share of rain lately, but it has been comfortably cool. Forgive the brevity of this letter. New Guinea is becoming a terribly dull place.

8/31/44

Dear Mom,

It was my second goodbye in nineteen years. My grip was ready. We were ready. You embraced me; we kissed. I watched you muster a smile. I felt torn because I was anxious both not to go and to go and see more and different things, maybe terrible things.

I said, "Be back in a year, Mom," and we broke. As Dad conducted me past the hall doorway, I had my last glimpse of you, of our living room, of the three of us together. The door shut.

The car was waiting at the street corner. I introduced Dad to the fellows. The delay was driving me crazy. Dad, forcing a grin, shook my hand. We mumbled something. The car door beckoned.

Already a year has gone by, and I feel anxious again. Imagining what it will be like, I'm impatient for my homecoming. I listen to every rumor, and falsely scoff at it. Rumors are cruel.

I follow the news diligently. Every day is more promising which uplifts me. Yet so much remains to be done.

I'm given to spasmodic moods, not the temperamental kind, but rather the kind that rises with hope and falls with anxiety. At one time—not so long ago at that—my return, that glorious day, seemed so remote that its anticipation was ridiculous. I was more patient then, resolute, and didn't give a damn.

I'm sorry that I couldn't keep my promise to return in a year. At the time I made it, I didn't believe it in my heart, but saying it made me feel better. Give me another year, and we'll both be surprised.

Love, Hughie

9/1/44

Dear Mom,

The most thrilling part of a trip is often in its preparation. Lately, you have been carousing quite freely around New England and probably preparing for your trips weeks in advance.

I can distinctly visualize what happens on a Sunday morning before you embark on a LENGTHY fifty mile trip to the big city, Boston —contrasted with my after supper scurrying before taking off for Hollywood sixty miles away.

Here's how it goes:

Come Sunday morn, for one reason or another, Dad is desperately tired and he manages, aided by a subtle assisting force (namely Mother), to rise and feel his way towards the bathroom to take a luscious hot bath (drawn by Mom) which he discovers has gotten cold, because he didn't get up early enough to take advantage of it while it was hot. Amid an explosion of curses, he stubbornly slams his foot down on the floor and relights the water heater. Meanwhile you're impatient to get breakfast going and over with.

You planned to leave at 8:00, but Dad is still waddling about the bathroom, and the coffee is pretty well boiled out. Eventually, our man of the family—he is indispensable because he does the driving—struts from the bathroom wide awake, prepared to scan the morning paper during his breakfast which he eats while paying no attention to its contents. Every so often he emits a wild outburst, "Gert, listen to this," to which you yell back asking that he speak louder or shut up while you're making the beds.

Our subject then wanders to his favorite chair in the living room in which he settles down, much to your disgust, to have a good and appreciated cigar hand made to order by Hymie, his favorite cigar maker. In the meantime you are in a wild hubbub yourself, dashing from the bathroom to your bureau, then to the closet to collect and lay out the clothes to be worn on this eventful day. As the perspiration pours off you, nonchalant Dad is enjoying enormously Bill Shirer's[1] report on the battle in France. By now you are all prettied up, your hair collected into an exciting coiffure, a mixture of sweat, powder, and rouge dexterously applied onto your appealingly round face, and your dress neatly in place. You are almost ready to go except for a few adjustments to your under paraphernalia and a swirl to and fro before a mirror to approve a job certainly and undoubtedly well done.

Our little woman is ready, and Dad has stalled long enough. Rising from his chair to avoid the start of fireworks, he proceeds to get dressed—slowly and precisely—in the suit you selected for him. He doesn't like the tie. He prefers the green one, but after wasting five more minutes hemming and hawing, he is compelled to submit to a stronger force—my Mom—and wear the tie that was chosen for him.

Ronnie is also being herded about. His method for stalling consists of "Naw, I don't wanna go," if he must wear such and such a trousers. Coming close to not going, he reluctantly submits to your selection. I, too, used to adopt the same procedure.

By some fantastic miracle, everyone is finally ready to go. It's at least 9:30 and, good lord, we'd better hurry. All dash to the car which Dad has either left on the street the previous Saturday night, or just brought up to the curb from the garage. From the middle floor above the apartment, we can hear Fatso [an unpleasant lady neighbor] screaming above the racket of our hasty clambering as we depart.

If the car hasn't a flat, there must surely be another excuse to cause a good fifteen minute stall. Oh, yes, the car needs gas and oil. Our guilty driver turns into a gas station and orders gas—Ethyl, twenty-one cents per and oil, number 20—and "Listen, check my water will ya fella, and while you're at it ya may as well look at my transmission—it's grinding—or maybe I need a ring job. Say, why in hell don't we call the whole trip off. I'm tired anyway. I slave six days and six nights a week. I'm tired."

So in the direction of Boston, under your supervision and amid your scowls, the Aaron brigade heads. The interior of the car is perfumed with the aroma of fresh, new clothes, of camphor and scent delicieux from our delightful lady. Everyone is calmed down by the soothing drone of the motor, and for the next hour and one half there are discussions from soup to Hughie.

Boston, the last stop, and, at whichever home we stop, wild and impressive exclamations pour forth from the host and hostess. "What a surprise. I didn't expect you." or "Hey folks, Barney and Gert are here. Ronnie, you darling little boy."

This is the pleasant portion of the grand voyage. The worst is over, the tide of hostility among the three of you has receded, and all settle down to an enjoyable day with the astounding Bostonians.

Love to the three of you, Hughie

9/2/44

Dear Mom,

Last Christmas—such a long time ago—was a day of varied experiences, from sleeping in a handball court to partaking of a turkey feast.

I had spent dinner hour and part of the afternoon with the Myles and Uplingers who did everything possible to please all four of us, a Marine, two Seabees and a soldier. To commemorate that day we took pictures, and now, nine months later, I've got my hands on them.

One of the photographs is of the whole party minus Mr. Myles, our distinguished, modest photographer. From left to right, they are: Al Martin, my bosom buddy, Mr. Uplinger, Mrs. Myles's daughter, Mr. Uplinger, Mrs. Myles (with whom I had loads of fun), a soldier guest holding Mrs. Uplinger's daughter, your Seabee, and a PFC Marine (his last liberty in the U.S.) who is holding Mrs. Myles's youngster. [See another photograph above, taken at the time.]

Since you've never seen Al's picture before, I should point out that the photo in which he is in a crouched position is nearer to his likeness. He is embarrassed by his awkwardness, blinded by the sun, and somewhat cramped. Al hails from a small town (Zelionople) near Pittsburgh. We visited Hollywood together several times and chummed around Gulfport. He is a fine boy, clean-cut, with high ideals and hopes to own and manage his own theater before he dies.

Having made good money as a motion picture projectionist, he has resumed that position in the battalion.

Al is easy to get along with, is somewhat nervous and has a subtle but responsive sense of humor. I like Al and he likes me. He seeks me for counsel in spite of being four or five years older than I. His greatest weakness is his love for a girl back home—Lorraine—about whom he often discusses his thoughts and confides his feelings, and reads me her most intimate letters, sometimes to my embarrassment. But Al is sensible, thoughtful, and devoted to his mother (His father died a drunkard), sisters, and brother. He is ambitious and works hard. I'll do all I can for this boy, if ever he asks for help. After the war I'd like to visit him and his new wife.

Mrs. Myles's personality was the most outstanding in the group. Jovial isn't enough to describe it. Both families are fine people—ref. my letter of December 27.

The picture enclosed was taken just off Hollywood Boulevard, between Hollywood and L.A. Observe the tie tucked into my jumper. Reason: just finished eating and my neckerchief always behaves as an unwelcome bib. I expect yet another picture from the West Coast with snow in the background.

That about completes my comments on these happenings, which now seem hardly real. Any further questions you might ask are welcome.

I'm still seesawing splinters (floating logs) on the swing shift, reading a lot, and chatting with my closer friends. Lately mail is scarce, which will probably result in a big batch arriving soon.

9/4/44

Dear Mom,

The war has gone well for us since I've been in the service. This month is the fifth anniversary of a world torn and gutted by war. For five years Europe has repeated its role as a battlefield, a cauldron of hatred and misery. For five years civilization has followed its natural bent. People have been distinguished and extinguished. Men and women have cried and died. Our greatest scientific achievements have been applied to advance the hatred between races, Orientals against Westerners, and one nation against another. Devotion to country has been revived, principles have been established and ignored, books have been written, watchwords shouted, intrigue has been rife, and politics has gone on as ever. Now our legions are pressing and routing the enemy to make way for the wheels of diplomacy and peacemaking. Hopefully, the peace will endure long enough for people to adhere to the call of civilization and form battalions to prepare for a more terrible future war. War is merely a grander, enlarged expression of man's inherent disposition. A natural function, beginning with the individual, it accumulates and becomes mass behavior. So it seems.

Having said all this, everything concerning myself seems insignificant, utterly unimportant. War belittles us, and, of course, the universe more so.

And now we have five years of war behind us, three of them having involved our personal lives. You are almost unaffected by it all, and I'm only partly affected. Indeed, we are fortunate people.

I'm eager to read the daily news, more so now than ever. The news is wonderful and terrible. I am selfishly concerned with how it affects me, and only vaguely concerned with how it affects the destiny of the world. That's our trouble. The big scene is so incomprehensible to us, that we can only understand our individual welfare. We discuss the war and the peace, become exasperated with all the opposing ideas, and go no further. We leave our fate in the hands of a few who will bungle or succeed. No matter, what happens is temporary, long enough to allow the world a breathing spell, a chance to heal its wounds and erase the scars. What the world needs is a good plastic surgeon. Throughout history mankind has been searching for such a surgeon.

I'm very much interested in the peace to come. Our leaders know what not to do to solve the peace, to make it lasting. But they must also know what to do, so that the next generations will know and also not forget what not to do.

I predict that we'll have a prolonged peace, enforced by expedient agreements satisfactory to all, but anyone is a fool to be oblivious to the certainty that another war will come.

Why this sudden philosophizing? I don't know. This is only a fraction of what has been going through my mind. I enjoy pondering our condition and expressing my opinions. Although I know your feelings towards me motivates you to read everything I write, I'm still honored that you listen to me. And if my thoughts bore you, thanks for tolerating me.

When I have a book in hand, I have little patience to write. I think about things in a disorderly, incoherent state of mind. I dash from one idea to another as my mood changes back and forth between depression and elation. It's odd, the way I think. I feel uncertain yet cocksure. I enjoy thinking a great deal. I'm anxious to apply my thoughts to some useful project, something constructive for all of us.

Love, Hughie

9/5/44

Dear Mom,

A lovely, long, and enjoyable letter arrived from you, the week's first. Prepare for some arguments.

I knew my letter relating the plane ride had portions cut out. As a matter of fact, the censor told me what he had cut out.

Let me clarify the Shakespeare situation. I want the book, because this is the most suitable time to read it, and once I'm home I'll be too busy; because I enjoy reading the plays and have always wanted to read the complete works; because I have plenty of time to read everything I receive — newspapers, magazines etc.; because it won't cost much, and I'd just as soon invest in such a book than see four or five shows in the States; because I've received every package sent to me (Boys that are members of the Book of the Month Club receive their books on the dot); because I can wait two or more months to receive it; because, after reading it, I can send it home, as I will do with other books rather than carry them with me; because I'm a silly boy. And I hope you'll buy an unabridged edition. Despite your arguments, I see you still intend to fulfill my request. My folks are tops. Thanks.

It isn't that I lack the ambition to study, rather, in this heat and hubbub, I find it difficult. I'm aware of my weakness in neglecting the correspondence course.

Civilian rumors are as absurd as rumors in the service. If by some miracle I were offered enrollment in V-12, I'd refuse it. With the war almost over, I'm anxious to become a civilian again and return to civilian schooling. To enroll in V-12, I'd have to enlist for six years — and the V-12 boys will not be released at the war's termination. My eyes have neither improved nor worsened for which I'm thankful; they had been getting progressively worse. I wear glasses only when reading and writing. I followed your suggestion to submit to a Navy eye examination. Remember, you thought an up-to-date examination would be wise. I had the examination on board a ship in the bay.

After I've finished the book I'm now reading, I'll get into *Song of Bernadette*. I meant to read the book last year when I was in high school.

We've been getting fresh eggs, and now a supply ship has arrived to replenish our larder with fresh foods. Due to the absence of supply ships, our food hasn't been very good lately.

I'm enthusiastic about Ronnie's ambitions. If things go well, that is if his ambition isn't curbed, he has a future made to order.

Yes, you are correct. The Seabees build and expand bases retrieved from the Japs, and, when their job is over, they are assigned to another project. So far as I'm concerned, my fate in the service, with respect to rank and the job I'm assigned, doesn't amount to a tinker's damn. The war is too near the end for me to be concerned with the present. I'm too absorbed with the future.

Charlie Goodness, who was mentioned in "Banx to the Yanks"[2] is an old Seabee buddy. When I left home on September 12 last year, Dad met him in the car that was waiting for me. Charlie and I figure on returning to Worcester together after shipping in to Frisco. He used to be a draftsman at Morgan's[3] and is now a cook.

The European news is stupendous. The end of the end is near.

9/7/44

Dear Mom,

In answer to your letters of Aug. 23 and 26:

I look at the volumes you've sent rather as a young kid does expecting something in his Christmas stocking. Shakespeare dry? Why Mom, his plays, language, the emotions he portrays, his human understanding are astoundingly stirring and clear. His stuff has always affected me. It's unfortunate that you aren't able to respond emotionally to his genius. The stories aren't so meaningful to me. The substance of the works lies in their wisdom and insight into human nature. From your description, the volumes sound complete. After I examine them, I'll let you know whether to buy a pocket edition. You're swell to buy them.

War and Peace doesn't let me alone. The story is marvelous, and its philosophy realistic. I hope to continue reading after I return. I never read so many books, so many classics, one after another, with such zest and enjoyment as I do now. It's as if I've discovered something new.

When I get back I think I'd like to join the Book of the Month Club.

I've been receiving the razor blades right along. Depending on how much I let my beard grow, I get from three to five shaves per blade. I try to shave twice weekly here, but were I home, I'd have to shave every other day, perhaps every day.

Since I sleep so late in the morning, I don't have breakfast, but I do have a midnight snack before the movie.

It seems that the William Shultzes, [newly married uncle] intoxicated with love, are living the life of luxury. Such free spending and exaggerated living can only be temporary, and I fear for them when they finally come down to earth. Few people, especially the young, are looking toward the future.

If *Earth and High Heaven*[1] is available in book form, send it along. It sounds excellent.

I don't care for the *Reader's Digest's* attitude. One of its recent articles concerning the Palestine question distorted the obvious truth. In a subsequent issue there was a feeble attempt to rectify their bias. However, it remains a cleverly biased magazine and has succeeded in deceiving the multitudes.

Still one article in particular, Eric Johnston's[2] speech in Moscow, in the August issue was extraordinary. He addressed the Russians eloquently, urging the adoption of measures "to bridge the gulf between the U.S. and Russia." It's a must for Dad to read.

I find *Coronet* boring because of its aimless point of view and insignificant articles. Although *Time* is Republican, I enjoy reading its news and views. It may be obviously biased, but it makes no attempt to hide that fact. Being a Democratic sympathizer, it's good that I'm exposed to the views of the opposition.

9/8/44

Dear Mom,

Your startling nights — burglars, mice, radios — remind me of ours when we first arrived here. Out of the darkness a sudden blast would shake the air, followed by distant bursts from the hills. Soon the whole world seemed to be emitting shells. Scanning the heavens, I could see endless streams of tiny comets reaching towards the faint drone of Jap aircraft. Below, as we muttered oaths under our breath, we dug our foxholes deeper. I would have welcomed mice or burglars or the sound of a radio then.

I feel sort of — how should I say it — paternal, having been partly responsible for hastening Ronnie's enlightenment. Any more questions on "Bringing Up Brother"?

How can you think of such a thing? You deprive yourself of a necessary vice just for the sake of getting thin, when, to me, a pleasingly plump and charming mother is a sacred vision to return to. Mom, I'd be disappointed if I went home to find a skinny and girlish mother.

Any references to me as a scholar directly insult my aspirations. A mediocre student, I despise being considered a scholar. And not having a competitive nature, which is so necessary in athletics, I'm no athlete. As you know, I never did compete. So what the devil am I? Just a crazy guy who likes to read a book now and then, and a guy who takes pride in acquiring a somewhat fit body. The heck with that scholar stuff.

Reason for this sudden outburst: it's the result of your "relatives — always thought of you with respect, knowing you are a good son and a scholar." Inwardly, I confess I feel flattered.

Secretary Forrestal[1] has made a very ----- statement. The navy will not ------------------- terminated. They will strive to get over ---------------- by July 1945. That statement I do not like.

I want to get home for more than the reasons of being with near ones and having a future. I want to get home and get out of the service ----------------. I now know that a military career is not suited to me. A serviceman's existence, in which all the world's complexities are eliminated by a system of orders, personal security, and monotonous stability, is very simple. I've witnessed, endured, and understood it. Because of its temporary nature, I've not bothered to ponder its effect on my personal life. Someday, I'll be freer to explain what I mean. Meanwhile, in spite of the circumstances, we are winning the war and that is our all important objective.

9/9/44

Dear Mom,

Our stray hen's (Esmeralda's) antics have broken the week's monotony. A few mornings ago she strutted into our tent cackling a little more than usual. Labor pains, we thought. After we let her wander among the shelves unmolested, she eventually found a comfortable spot for the great event. At first, she emitted a guttural mumbling, soon followed by a shrill shriek, then silence. After slowly regaining her composure, she began chatting softly and rose from her nesting place. There it was, a pullet egg, as fresh as they come. I wonder, is it better to have chicken a la carte for a single meal, or a fresh egg for breakfast every morning? Today she laid another egg in her converted "henhouse." All we need now is a rooster. Then we could go into the hen business as well as eggs.

I hear that the saw mill is due to shut down. God knows what they'll have me do next. What I do really isn't important. I'm just another cog in the wheel.

Everything here is extraordinarily normal. Even the war seems remote. Tomorrow, my day off, I'll jabber and bask in laziness. In this heat that's about all you feel like doing. Sloth is a tropical madness, and everyone catches it.

P.S. They say brevity is a good thing—justification for this measly note. Poor Ernie Pyle.[1]

9/12/44

Dear Mom,

The past few days I've received some very heartening letters: yours of August 30 and September 2, one from Mrs. Linfield in Gulfport, and one from Mr. Smith in Ventura.

I received the report (on education eligibility) from the Social Service Agency the same day your letter mentioning it arrived. It is certainly encouraging and answers many questions. I've read it to several interested boys in the battalion. From the report many have taken the number of the War Department pamphlet. Everyone is more than interested, and I'm anxious to read the pamphlet.

You know how long *GWTW*, which I read complete, is. I read all 1200 pages of *Les Miserables*. *War and Peace*, which I'm now reading, is over 1000 pages, and *Jean Chrisophe*, my next book, has over 1500 pages. And I read only the unabridged editions. I seem to choose only big but enjoyable books to get hooked on. I'm a slow reader, although faster than I used to be. I find myself pondering some thought the author expressed, or a description that lingers in my mind.

This letter is getting screwy. Pardon me while I straighten it out. When *Les Miserables* was written, people didn't rush about as they do today. They had plenty of time. I suppose that's why the author imposed so many soliloquies on the reader, so many lengthy and unrelated discussions, so many opinions and such detail. These would hardly suit a modern best seller. The reader would call such a book dry. Although I often found it difficult to plough through the author's tangential material, on the whole I enjoyed reading it. The story is excellent, the philosophy espoused, and the language superb. Knowing that you like reading the modern novel which is much more concise and frank, I'm surprised that you enjoy the classics as much as you do.

You'll enjoy reading *A Tree Grows in Brooklyn*. In a recent letter Johnson discussed Lillian Smith's *Strange Fruit*,[1] saying that it relayed no message, and its vulgarity merely agitated racial feelings. As you know, several states have banned it. Beverly Ringer writes that she's reading it now.

How I envy you your trip to the Berkshires. I look forward to a very thrilling letter.

You seem to dread both Ronnie's and my departure from Worcester some time in the future. I don't blame you. For the sake of our collective happiness I hope that we'll never have to leave. But, and there is a "but," we can never know what will happen. We'll discuss this subject in four years or so. I confess I like to travel, and that I'm attracted to the West. To confine myself to a future in Worcester would be folly. It would limit the range of opportunities available to me. Please realize that I intend to aim high, as do all youths. Perhaps I'm being foolish with this vague talk. I hope Ronnie will remain in Worcester, since he has an opportunity to establish himself with Dad. Opportunities in the field I'm interested in are available in the bigger industrial cities. Yet, who knows, I may live in Worcester until I die. I don't wish to be cruel, but I beg you not to expect me to stay.

Ted Bagdikian, my chum in boot camp and later at Hueneme, is now in New Guinea. We've exchanged letters. I enjoyed hearing from him.

The saw mill has been closed for repairs. Meanwhile, I'm temporarily doing carpenter work, which I like. It's similar to what I did at Gulfport. When the project is over, I'd like to get into the wordworking or metalsmith shop, where I can learn something, and where I won't be ousted as a result of a breakdown or over-complementing. The chance of getting the crane job is less likely than before, because fewer and fewer cranes are needed, as more and more projects are being completed. I've put in a request for shop work. Wish me luck.

I repeat, I've learned much in the Seabees. I'm satisfied with my present position as a battalion jack-of-all-trades, master of none. My health is excellent, I'm feeling fine, chow is better now, and I complain only when no letters arrive.

Mrs. Linfield, a fine woman, sends you her regards and will write you. Don't forget to send her a Christmas card this year. She insists that I visit her after the war. Ann Linfield, the older daughter, almost paid you a visit when she was up Springfield way this summer. Now Mrs. Linfield would like to visit Massachusetts and have me tour her around Boston.

Enclosed is a picture of last February's skiing party, minus Barbara who took the picture—ref. letter of Feb. 13. [See photograph above.] You'll find the names in their respective positions indicated on the back. Mr. Smith's intelligent face is not obvious. Having had the photo taken at the end of the day, we were exhausted from our boisterous laughing and energetic skiing. We picked up the other sailor on the mountain—and he and I struck up an acquaintance back at camp. We were the only two sailors at the run. The man on the extreme right is a veteran European skier, a former world champion, and president of the Mt. Lassen ski club. Don't mind my dreary mug; I was doggone tired. The man holding the pole, as good natured as they come, was a riot. The car—a '42 fluid drive Chrysler, belonged to Mr. Smith. Look at that snow, heavenly snow. Just think, less than fourteen days later I was sweltering on the equator. We all got sunburned that afternoon. The snack—rabbit sandwiches etc.—sure tasted elegant. The tropics were never like this. Tell Ronnie to show the photo to Johnson. He would enjoy it. At the time I had written him about the trip.

I should really finish this page—paper shortage, you know—but I'm quite talked out. I answered Mr. Riccius's excellent letter yesterday. I'm pleased with all my correspondents. I think I've chosen the most sincere and the finest people to write to. Evidently last June my letter scared Miss Chase away. No reply. What in the devil could I have said? As I used to say, "That's girls for ya."

I'll probably be around tomorrow. Bye.

Love to all three of you, Hughie (from snow to heat in 14 days)

9/14/44

Dear Mom,

Our darling Esmeralda—you remember Esmeralda the pet hen—is no more. It's a brief and sad story.

Dear Ezzy began making a habit of visiting our tent at regular daily intervals to lay a handsome pullet egg, which delighted all of us, especially at breakfast time. Ezzy was never nasty. She was careful not to aggravate us, and she provided an excellent post-reveille call, which is most necessary to really bring us sleepy-heads to a state of absolute consciousness. Her quaint, mechanical motions and innocent cluckings brought us no end of amusement. She gave us a feeling that one gets from a pet that has adopted its master.

The other day, Esmeralda, cockily and happily strutted into out tent to lay her habitual egg. One of our less desirable bedfellows was in a bad humor and gave vent to his mood by shooing Ezzy away. But Ezzy was determined to lay her egg, especially in her familiar spot in the lefthand corner of our shelf. She persisted on returning to her spot, when our cruel friend lost patience, grabbed her by the neck, and hurled her to the ground. All of us were spellbound, finding it hard to comprehend what had just happened.

Pity having taken hold of our souls, we rushed out of the tent to see how Ezzy was faring. There she was, stunned, silent, and bewildered, slowly beginning to rise and walk away. One wing was broken. It hung loose, hindering the use of her left foot. She returned to the tent in obvious pain, laid her egg on the floor, closed her eyes, suffering, that familiar behavior of animals that have been hurt. I tried strapping her wing to its original position with a string while she allowed me and emitted a painful but appreciative cluck.

Esmeralda had to be killed, so she was. I don't know who performed the act. I'm going to miss Ezzy's welcome visits, and especially her generous eggs.

I'm back at the saw mill as of this morning, the day shift, 7 AM to 4:00 PM with 1 1/2 hours off for lunch. The work is neither interesting nor instructive, but it's a job, and the hours are decent. Once jobs are plentiful, I'll make a bid for a shop job again.

9/15/44

Dear Mom,

Wars of old were fought by men in dashing uniforms. The uniforms they wore to balls were the same ones soiled by mud and dust on a battlefield. They were the very same uniforms that became saturated with the red dye of the wounded and killed.

Modern war is different. The army and the Marines wear their comfortable and practical drab greens on the field of battle. These are the uniforms that become caked with a blend of sweat and dust, not the polished, proud dress outfits worn on liberty—although these too can look pretty bad after a disgusting drunken brawl.

But the Seabees are different. First, we've never really made up our minds what exactly we are. An approximate definition would be that of a combination armed force and construction engineering outfit. Secondly, we wear every field uniform there is: army, navy and Marines. Were a stranger to enter our camp, he would be bewildered trying to figure out what in the devil kind of outfit we were. He would see a variety of headgear: Aussie hats, army fatigue hats, caps, sailor hats, and improvised hats in every crazy shape imaginable, and so our haircuts. Indeed, our endless variety in oh, such clashing colors which would never do, puts New York and Paris to shame. We'll only wear something that isn't conventional.

For a while, some of us preferred wearing the apparel that is God's gift. We dressed as scantily as possible, many of us only hiding behind mere tans. Now that's taboo, sadly, because we found it so comfortable. According to our uniforms, and by virtue of our confused state, we are certainly members of the U.S. armed forces—in a word, Seabees.

The boys are now complaining about the influx of other units and of the new civilized atmosphere taking hold. The roads are being widened, speed limit and no passing signs are appearing, and a bus stop has been established which reminds us more of the U.S., which we love, but New Guinea can never be the U.S. So we boys are unhappy with the new safety restrictions and traffic regulations which are enforced by S.P.'s. An information booth has now been constructed at an important junction—not for tourists, but for G.I.'s. Worse yet, you have to wear a bathing suit to go swimming. Showers, unlike earlier, are now enclosed. Why it's terrible—the loss of our glorious freedom.

Last night Henry Wolf and I swapped tales of home and the foibles of our darling parents. On comparing notes, we saw that our lives have been quite similar—except for the girl situation. We had quite a lively evening just raving on and on.

9/18/44

Dear Mom,

From the generous supply of stationery that I received from you this morning, I gather that you expect me either to remain in the service for the next quarter century, or write you gads of letters daily. I can certainly use it, though I might have to go into the stationery business.

Your lovely and anxiously awaited description of your Berkshire trek made me homesick, envious, but glad that you had such a pleasant day. We are now definitely the wandering Aarons, gypsies in the raw. Good lord, how I wish I were with you.

Writing? My calling writing? Should I laugh here? If by some miracle I turn out to be a ham author, I've already started. That's right. I'm now a member of the battalion's newspaper staff, and my first article has been submitted for tomorrow's copy. I do like to write but only for the pleasure it gives me. To be a professional and go commercial would take all my enthusiasm and the excitement out of what I want to say. Of course, I realize that you haven't taken such a prospect seriously.

And oh, speaking of writing, I've received a letter from a Miss Dorothy Jayne (get the spelling) Goldstein that happened to blow my way after traveling from Seattle to God knows where and back. There was a blanket of "missents" stamped all over the envelope. You can imagine how old the letter must be. This 17 year old five-foot-five-inch girl is sunburnt, unmarried, goes to school, and is called by the quaint monicker, Dolly. According to dear Dolly, Miss Mimi Chase considers her nearer my age, so Gramma Mimi suggested that, instead of herself, she write this babyish 20 year old, this child. Now here I have a girl who frequents Tatassit and Coes Pond[1] and is ever so anxious to boost a lad's morale. As with all girls, she begins her letter with, "Now to tell you something about cute little me ----." How little tact girls have nowadays.

Last Saturday, a movie shown under the auspices of the famed Special Services Division entertained us. The Division shows only pre-U.S. released pictures. This reserves them the right to announce over the P.A. system their offering like this: "World Premiere tonight. "Marriage is a Private Affair"[2] with tantalizing Lana (accent) Turner (sigh)." And so it was, a genuine world premiere in torrid New Guinea. The picture will be released in the U.S. October 15. The idea, as I see it, is to let the boys see the pictures first so they'll write the folks back home and tell them to see it too. Thus the motion picture companies are accomplishing a two fold purpose: impressing the public by giving the boys a first showing, and via New Guinea and the other fronts widening publicity for a picture.

As for the picture, Mom would like it, particularly the love and baby scenes. Dad would grunt and scoff all through the picture and threaten to walk out. And Ronnie would blush occasionally, be baffled by it, and leave dumbfounded. It's a well acted, but drawn out story of a frivolous wife who is uncertain of her capability to be a good wife and mother. I enjoyed it; you'd love it. Some of the, uh, love scenes made the boys uncomfortable in the early evening heat. Bored, I gazed at the stars above until I heard the final smacking of lips. Lana is enchanting; no sweater this time.[3]

When a community sing flashed on the screen, there was one song in which a boys' chorus and a girls' chorus appears. Our fair G.I. Seabee damsels, trying to imitate the sound of the female larynx, burst into a melodious chant as they sang in their manly high pitched voices. I laughed 'til my sides split. A late army newsreel also flashed, the first one I've seen in ages.

Last night, Sunday, I attended Rosh Hashanah services which were rather improvised and also condensed, because the Jewish chaplain had to conduct so many services. The congregation was exceptionally large. Henry Wolf and I went together.

Other than the fact that I'm acquiring a new coat of tan, now that I'm working during the day, things are still the same with this little Seabee. Goodness gracious, how times fly, though. I'm constantly startled (and perplexed) by its swiftness.

Rumors are at a new high. To remember them is ridiculous and to repeat them sheer madness. I'm still waiting to hear the one that predicts an invasion from another planet similar to Orson Welles's[4] extravaganza.[5]

To fill up the rest of the page is a problem, so my
Love to all three of you, Hughie

9/20/44

Dear Mom,

I just returned from watching Cagney's[1] glorification of George M. Cohan[2] in "Yankee Doodle Dandy."[3] All during it I proudly let it be known that Cohan was a native of my dear old state,[4] from doggone near[5] my dear old home town.[6]

The belated *Gazettes* bring me both high caliber enjoyment and the reverse. I read of an occasional school chum killed in action—chums who were revered by the school rabble as cute, clever, brilliant, athletic and a swell guy. From this I perceive that each of us is small. Every death is only proof that our personal affairs, our vain existence, are but the minutest part of a complex pattern. Each of us is but a single thread without which there could be no whole fabric. Ignore this. I'm being selfish, boring you.

How can I say it? You've probably had presentiments—someday I want to write, because, well, because I just like to. The fact that I may write either well or poorly doesn't matter to me. What matters is that I like it. If someone likes or not likes doing something, well and good. I do not profess to have talent, but I know I've found a magnificent and inspiring outlet. I find myself thinking up stories, and composing commentaries on what I hear and see. I hope that this isn't just a passing fancy. My desire isn't spontaneous, but rather a gradual development.

Some people's singing voices are obnoxious, unmelodious; nevertheless these people love singing. Although I whistle poorly, I still love doing it. I write with indifference to standards of excellence, but I love writing. Blinded by your affection for me, you read my inadequate letters, but you love it.

I've often thought I'm still the boy who retrieves his toy six shooter from the closet, after seeing a thrilling western. I'll wait and see.

My new hometown, hardly by choice, "blank," New Guinea, is as dull as Boston must have been in 1630. Nothing interesting happens anymore. It's a struggle to rise in the morning. At work I'm an automaton. I see a show, I write, I go to bed, I'm bored, I'm patient—that's the 24 hour routine.

Although politics and the peace terms are excellent food for discussion and a source for arguments, I suppress my tendency to say what I think. Despite this, occasionally I find myself embroiled in a stubborn, provokingly persuasive argument. It's a hard habit for me to break. "The most argumentative boy in the class,"[7] is undergoing a gradual process of becoming unargumentative. Yet, I can't keep the old thing down completely. I manage to justify an occasional burst.

My frequent use of I is beginning to bore me. I want only to hear your I's, Ronnie's I's about high school, and Dad's regular I's.

9/24/44

Dear Mom,

During the past three days several letters arrived: three from you, another from faithful Johnson, and one from Miss Rourke, my high school teacher. Now for the answers.

My letter referring to Ronnie's birthday being in August was making fun of his pretending to be sixteen then rather than in January to impress his newly found friends. I admit I did a poor job of putting it across.

Bob Hope made a crash landing before arriving here — got away unscathed.

I saw "Song of Russia" last night. The music was superb, but there wasn't enough of it. I'm going to do something about music when I return. I have no talent, but I have an appreciation, an inspiring appreciation.

Glad you enjoyed the books I recommended. If you'd like to know what best sellers to read, just ask me. I keep up on them fairly well. Progressive New Guinea, backward Worcester.

My flying jaunt WAS dangerous — sure it was. But Mom, you have never known what real dangers we've experienced. This is overseas. We're not here to play, but to deal with danger. Once danger was imminent, but, thank God, all danger has passed. Men fly every day. The chance that they'll crack up is no more than the chance that you could be hit by a careening auto. Both cases are mistakes. I'm not a fatalist, but I recognize the role of destiny. For your sake I'll not go up again; for your sake I'll not tell you many things.

I eagerly anticipate seeing a well dressed Mom. I can picture you in an exquisite dress so well. I'm glad that you're buying clothes. Someday you'll be buying many more. Ronnie's new name: elephant foot.

Read the article on vitamin pills with interest. I'll continue to take them — feel fine.

When you consider [Uncle] Joe's and Aunt Sadie's position, (prosperous but unhappy), it makes you appreciate your own. You know I've never had a great regard for money. Why? Because I've been well taken care of and dependent on yours. I tried to make every cent count on liberties, a dollar's worth of pleasure for fifty cents if possible. You folks have taught me that. Yet, I'm glad to say that I consider money as a necessary but insignificant item in my life. I can never be a money worshiper.

Grandma's case is amusing, a farce. One should laugh at her ways rather take them seriously. We are all petty. Of course, her pettiness is extreme. Still she doesn't do anyone any harm. I like her and love her.

If I knew that you carried on the way Aunt Ida carries on, I'd go crazy. I'm so proud of you for your sensible outlook. Ida craves attention. Now, she has an excellent excuse. Cousin Bob [Ida's son in the service] has yet to learn what to write and what not to write home. His bragging and letters lauding danger for the sake of making an impression are selfish. Why tell his mother that he's gone on missions? Tell her nothing until he returns. If something is bound to happen to you, there's nothing you can do to change it. If a bullet is headed your way, your fate is sealed. Nothing you can do will swerve it. Unfortunately, civilians fail to look at it that way. That's why I say, keep your parents ignorant. Eventually, we learn to take care of ourselves. I take care of myself pretty well, if I do say so. I'm not one to encourage danger. I fear it.

All film must be developed here to be censored.

Henry Wolf has introduced me to a very interesting fellow my age [Raymond Albrecht]. With more than a thousand men in the battalion, I can hardly know all of them. He is a German refugee,[1] came over in 1938, had formerly been a member of the Hitler[2] Youth,[3] speaks English fluently with an accent, craves to become a citizen, is a clean-cut, and thoughtful boy. He majored in the physical sciences at a New Jersey high school, and hopes to study physics at Columbia. His position is exactly like mine. Being German, he's experienced prejudice, his education has been interrupted, he's an atheist (I'm not), and he thinks as I do. He was not offered entrance into the V-12 program because of his German citizenship, and feels bad. Most of his friends from school are in V-12. From the *Gazette* I see that most of the Worcester boys enrolled in V-12 at WPI and Dartmouth were my schoolmates. We've discussed our common situation at length. We concluded that it's inevitable both of us will get a government subsidized education. We've also concluded that the Seabees is the best thing that has ever happened to us. It makes us feel good inside to know that we're doing a man's job, and recognized as men. One can hardly conceive of those V-12 boys being nothing but boys. We've played a tangible and direct role in this war. The college students have only indirectly contributed. Their connection to the war is peripheral. We've undergone hardship, observed a cross section of the U.S., lived with both the scum and the cream of mankind, and we've learned that we know nothing, yet more than we've ever known. We both thank fate for allowing us to witness all that we have. We can actually feel the broadening effect. Were we now offered V-12 on a silver platter, we'd refuse. Such thinking is sincere, not a justification of our failure to enter college. Both of us are happy that what has happened has happened.

By the way, his view of the opposite sex is similar to mine. We're both virgins and unkissed, although he's been infatuated—I've never been. We realize and repent our mistake and are resolved to play a wide field for a happier future. I'm glad that I've found someone to talk to on these subjects. His background is amazing and different. He talks a lot about Germany—to me—and the thoughts he had during the early years there. A very interesting friend.

The letter from Miss Rourke is particularly frank and to the point. Quote: "Somehow this new life has shaken you right off your smug self. You needed it. I like this new you so much. You are so alive." Hmm. I only wrote her a plain, ordinary, informative letter.

Mom, if you don't find enough I's and Me's in this letter—well I'll be an introvert just for today.

9/28/44

Dear Mom,

A very unusual phenomenon: it's raining smack in the middle of the day. With the consoling chorus of the downpour beating on the canvas roof, several of your letters before me, and four days of not having written, I surely feel like writing now.

First a word about letters. Why on earth should I want copies of my sheer nonsense? I'm hardly that much of an egoist. Possibly, very possibly, if I should recopy some of this, I'd tear up both the original and copy. Many are the times that I wished I could retrieve a letter that's en route. I can refer to former letters by simple deduction. For instance, ref. letter Dec 27: I know that I visited the Myles (although you had the pictures confused with the Smiths of Ventura) of Hollywood on Christmas day. A two day liberty, I returned to camp on a Monday, when I undoubtedly wrote you about the entire preceding experience. Simple deduction, Mom, simple deduction.

And since my letters have impressed a few blind relatives, I have less confidence, as a result, that I can measure up to their expectations. What a sad disappointment I'm turning out to be.

I'm looking forward to receiving the packages galore that you and others have sent during the past month.

Quotation, Mom: "I have two boys to be proud of." Hmm. When was it that you said you preferred girls? Huh, Mom?

Other boys have told me about the hurricane up your way. Evidently hurricanes don't occur here. There are no monsoon[1] or dry seasons. The weather is consistent and erratically mild. The rain is moderate, and dry spells don't last long; however, one can never tell what the weather will be the next hour.

A school strike! Can you beat that. I must say that it was brilliantly carried out. Beeber [the principal] made a damn fool of himself. His feint to use physical force was ridiculous. The instigators of the movement, both pupils and teachers, were impressively efficient. I kind of liked their performance. It demonstrates the spirit of youth and the power it can wield. Powers' [the school superintendent] irascible appearance has always reminded me of a shrewd politician. I say that Powers was far from being expedient. Was he afraid to address the masses? Although the demonstration will probably fail, and, although it isn't exactly right, I'm glad that it happened. Student government in Worcester's public schools has been exceptionally weak. The student counsels, controlled by the school committee, are a farce. Committees in other cities are far more liberal. The strike made quite an impression on the population. Why, even Beverly Ringer sent me the newspaper article in a separate envelope.

For some unfathomable reason I consider the incident amusing and trivial. So much that happens back home that once upon a time I'd take seriously, I now find amusing. Which brings me to another issue.

There's a very enlightening article in *Time* that explains how young veterans are doing under the government-sponsored education program. It describes the cliques that have inevitably developed among the veterans, and their proud, reserved, and mature attitude. It also states that students fresh from high school are ignoring the veterans, and there has been trouble in the fraternities. "To many (veterans) fraternity folderol seemed childish, fraternity members immature." Many of the frats are hostile toward the vets. "(The vets) feel they have learned a lot in the war --." Such required courses as

Hygiene and Health, Behavior of Modern Societies and Principles of Learning seem old stuff or a waste of time. That is precisely the attitude of us veterans, myself included. Not that I desire to flaunt my experience, or look down upon others for being unaware of things and events that happen on a grander scale, but I have noticed that I find myself unconsciously smiling at civilian antics that once seemed necessary and sometimes important.

I know my attitude in college will be different in '45 or '46 (most likely the latter) than it would have been in '43 or '44. I know it and feel it. I'll want to associate with veterans who "understand." Colleges will have to adapt to the veterans. The unswerving veterans cannot adapt to the colleges.

Sadie's entertaining letter arrived. Beverly wrote (sounds like a good kid).

So Cacklepuss Harriet is attending a business school. Hmm. Amazing isn't it? I mean how the stupid, tactless girls suddenly win respect by attending a business college or taking some worthy college course. But I'm prejudiced against the girl, and I realize it.

Have neglected writing because of my new working hours. I have less spare time and feel more tired after working under the hot sun rather than the refreshing moonlight.

[Below is a different version of Hughie's letter written on 7/1/44 to Cousin Sol upon the death of his father, an Orthodox rabbi. The reason for two versions at different times is a mystery.]

9/28/44

Dear Cousin Sol,

There's a painting hanging over the mantel in your living room, that everyone entering the room pauses to gaze at and study for its warmth. Invariably, the person comments on it. You nod approvingly. Everyone cannot help loving that portrait over the mantel.

To you, the painting's significance is profound. Beyond the fact that it is a portrait of one who was dear to you, beyond the fact that its luster is further enhanced by your sentimental attachment to it, you adore every brush stroke.

In that real representation of your father as a learned old man meditating on God, you perceive something symbolic. You see the portrait as a symbol of a great religion that has endured an enormous era of trial. That is why everyone pauses and gazes at it. They too sense its eternal meaning. But you comprehend beyond the abstract sensing. You are intimately aware, in a real sense, of its truth, of its positive significance. You are proud.

If I were to say to you of your father's death, "I'm sorry," or "I feel for you," or "I know how it is," or "It's all for the best," or "Chin up," such superficial and banal phrases would only irritate the wound of your loss and would hardly help erase the inevitable scar.

I know I love my father. You loveD yours. What right have I to offer consolation? I love but have never—in the strictest tense - loved. But all love, have loved and will love the man in that painting. Hughie

10/1/44

(Writing on my lap, excuse penmanship.
Use Code Book No. 3. Also consult FBI
in case of undecipherable clauses.)

Dear Mom,

Your letter of only nine days ago arrived today, another from Lenny, now a second class petty officer and enjoying himself in my old southern California haunts.

I finally finished *War and Peace* this afternoon. The author's philosophy and his understanding of human character are absolutely brilliant. The book defined in a more comprehensible form ideas that I've thought about and tried to write down, ideas that have been beyond me to express, but are now clearer. It has swayed my thinking in a new direction. Soon, I must read another book that will counter Tolstoy's ideas, which, at this point, I'm convinced are a fundamental answer and partial solution to many eternal questions. Actually, the book has indoctrinated me with biased views. Someday, when my thoughts are less confused (My ideas are unsettled), I'd like to read the book again.

Since I've been on the day shift, I have less time to myself. I feel bad that I'm unable to read as much and as often as a month ago. I'm going to try to get on the night shift when it resumes. This situation also accounts for my fewer letters. I feel terribly guilty and will try to write daily, or at least bi-daily.

I'm glad that you sent only one volume of Shakespeare. I wondered how I could carry three volumes with me if suddenly we pull out. When I get back home (How often I use that phrase), I'll accumulate books galore. I can feel it already—and I'll read every one through.

The other night I saw for the second time—the first time in civilian life—Saroyan's[1] "The Human Comedy."[2] I was deeply moved when I saw the picture the first time, but the second time I was astounded by its lack of genuiness, reality and depth. Actually its errors and propagandizing amused me. This offers an example of my new concept of life. I can now perceive more clearly the genuine from the imitation. Daily, I'm acquiring a different outlook.

Our censors are apt to do ridiculous things. They are constantly being censured which accounts for their fear of allowing even the obvious and known to go through. That they cut out a quotation from a news broadcast that I heard and wrote to you surely demonstrates their uncertainty.

In case you overlooked the article in "Banx to the Yanks" concerning the 113th, I'm sending it back. It's a neatly exaggerated piece. Believe about two thirds of the buildup and you'll have an idea of what we have done. At least it does accomplish its desired purpose—boosting civilian morale. My, do the boys exaggerate.

I've read several buildups about "Since You Went Away."[3] I hope to see it someday, yes, someday. Pictures out here are antiques. Shirley Temple is a knockout. I know that from my own detailed observation at the Canteen.

When I get back, my one desire is to have my own private study. Because it's a selfish desire, I wouldn't insist on it. However, if, by chance, we move and we find a place with such a room available, it would certainly be attractive to me.

Bow ties yet. What is this? Ronnie gone hep? It's good that you enjoy it. I wish he would go out with girls. It would be good for him and better for you. I hope that he'll make up for your disappointment in me. He's most certainly a handsome boy. His pictures show it. His personality is pleasing, and he should be attractive to girls.

Since you are "nice and plumB," (your own typographical error, one of hundreds that have occurred) I'd like a definition of plumb used in that sense. In other words you are absolutely perpendicular to the ground. My, my, that's amazing. Since when have we been walking horizontally on all fours?

10/2/44

Dear Mom,

I'm anticipating many a joyful evening reading the *Tragedies*[1] that arrived today. I couldn't have chosen a better edition myself. It's just what I wanted. Vitamin pills, inkograph pen and candy all came in good order. Boy, I'm happy about the book. Can't wait to sink my teeth into it.

There's a pile of unanswered letters before me, but, for some reason I can't bring myself to write. The book offers a greater attraction.

I've been chummier than usual with my close acquaintances, Wolf and Albrecht. I'm possessed by a desire for company and happy that I have such good companions to confide in. My lack of concentrated interests and an association with girls and family, have only encouraged a closer companionship with friends who share my feelings and ideals. As a civilian, except for family, I also lacked these things, but now, being older, obviously wiser and more mature, I miss their call. So daily, Wolf and Albrecht (the German refugee) and I talk frankly and often about intimate subjects.

Last night we delved into subjects concerning the intellect and the infinite, that were, no doubt, beyond our youthful conceptual abilities, but we enjoyed the inner revelations they stimulated. Such discussions may be a "waste of time" in view of the letters I must write and the books waiting to be read. Nevertheless, I persist in pining away my valuable time in seemingly unconstructive discussions. But our talks and my association with friends are so attractive, so relaxing and so enjoyable, that I ignore my better judgment and "waste time." I can't say that, having such entertaining, learned and sensible companions, my routine is unpleasant.

10/3/44

Dear Ronnie,

You are now a master raconteur (tale teller to you). Why, with a letter as superbly written as yours, how can I resist reading it to my friends tonight? Boy, that's one thing I just gotta do.

Now, I know all about the adolescent war in Worcester and believe me, I'm all for ya. You betcha and I wouldn't miss the outcome for the world. "Petty Powers[1] is a jerk. Give the little squirt the works." (With this as my motto, I'll be the New Guinea standard bearer on behalf of the Worcester students). I feel rather like one of your revolutionaries. I could feel your excitement and enthusiasm in every word that you wrote. I guess the strike has given Worcester its biggest publicity in a century, and it took you kids to do it.

Don't you know better than to use "damn" in your letter? Why in hell did you do such a thing? I'm surprised. My brother cursing already. Tch, tch, tch. The younger generation is just terrible.

Hear you're going in pretty big for swanky clothes. Who is she, Ronnie? Yep, when I get back, I'll probably find my brother as wild as they come, always wanting the car and dashing back and forth about the house just rarin' to get out.

We could stand a strike around here to liven things up. You fellows have seen more excitement in less than a week than I have in two months. The Seabees should move to Worcester. Time to knock off.

Love to you, Mom and Dad, Hughie

Mom:
P.S. The damp climate ruined the razor. In the States it was in perfect condition. I shaved only once or twice a week.

Sadie asked me what I wanted. I know she will derive pleasure in sending me something. It's a book—Walt Whitman's[2] *Leaves of Grass*.[3]

Friday 10/6/44

Dear Mom,
The mail has been dribbling in, one or two letters from you and other interested people.

I'm sorry that you are sending the other two volumes. The one I have will keep me busy for months. You can't read Shakespeare like a novel. I may return the additional books, after I receive them. If and when I accumulate enough wrapping paper, I'm going to send home my pea-coat, watchcap and gloves, etc. It means a lot to me when you send packages, and I understand what it means to you. Please, though, send no more candy or package unless I request it. I have plenty of candy and toilet articles (except for the items I've requested), and I'm over-supplied with stationery. I could become a wholesaler. I wouldn't mind having all the stuff, if only I had the room.

Send me [Aunt] Pearl's address and I'll apply a bit of charm to make her feel better. If it worked on [Aunt] Anna, it'll work on Pearl. See, you insisted on buying *Strange Fruit*, when I plan to borrow it from a chum. If you sent it to me, you'd be wasting your money. Hey, I should stop this ribbing. Doggone, I shouldn't complain to a Mom who is always showering gifts on her son.

Ronnie must be made to realize that math and classical Latin are not suited to his intellect. Continue some math, by all means; it will sharpen his reasoning powers, but he shouldn't follow a purely classical and technical course of study as I did. Economics would be excellent. I often thought it was the most useful subject I've ever studied. But it's a short course and quite incomplete. If he's reluctant to elect art, then he should see an adviser to find out what he needs to elect for his chosen vocation. If taking art is suggested, then he'll be convinced; if not he'll know he doesn't need it. If he doesn't have an adviser, then he should consult some teacher he respects, some teacher whom he feels understands him; for vocational guidance, I had such a teacher. Actually high school studies are superficial, and are only necessary as an introduction to knowledge and to become eligible for college. I'm not sure that art is a requirement in order to be accepted by a school of interior design. I only assumed it would be because of its relationship to decoration. Still, I suspect it is—learning about the blending of colors and training the eye to become conscious of what's beautiful and satisfying. Ronnie should find out. Don't let him delay. Get right to work on it. He must know what he's studying for, instead of wandering aimlessly through a maze of useless subjects.

No apology needed for Dad's and Ronnie's failure to write. I understand perfectly. I look upon your every letter as being from the three of you.

I saw something interesting yesterday: natives spearing fish. The spears are made of wood, sharply tipped and ornamented with colorful, meaningless carvings. Their dugout canoes are also generally adorned with attractive designs. A spear plunges into the water and invariably a fish floats to the surface. It's amazing.

Nothing has changed here; it's still the same humdrum inactivity. But the weeks continue to roar by, thank goodness. The daytime shift pretty well occupies most of my time. And the nights are filled with shows and relaxing conversation. Last night I saw Al Schact, the famous baseball comedian (never heard of him myself) who used to play big league baseball with Ty Cobb.[1] He lives and breathes baseball. After his humorous act, he and the crowd entered into a man-to-man discussion in which he exhibited unsurpassed knowledge of the game. Everyone enjoyed it, including myself, although I'm far from being a fan. But it helped that he was the closest link to the States that we've seen in over a month.

Will write again by Sunday.

10/9/44

Dear Mom,

Yesterday, a leisurely Sunday, I enjoyed a rare delicacy: chicken. And believe me, I became a confirmed gourmet by practicing your much enjoyed art of sucking on the carcass. Last night at supper I became bloated from eating ice cream and even took a few swallows of beer which I can take or leave, but I took to accommodate my ribbing friends. We're rationed five cold bottles a week. I usually give mine to some beer-thirsty drinker.

Sadie's latest letter, which arrived this noon, demands a "you name it" reply to her former request, "I want to send you a present." I think I mentioned in a previous letter to you exactly what I'd like. Please let her know. She threatens to send candy.

I've sadly neglected my writing. It's not that my desire has waned, but that I find my chums so alluring. I can't resist giving in to my nature to shoot the breeze so I jabber, jabber evenings on end.

Last night we talked about music, so at work today I've been singing, trying to recall the melody of Dance of the Hours.[1] I found it while wiping the sweaty salt off my brow. The saw engines (two with six cylinders) make such a racket that I hum, whistle, and sing to my heart's content without being heard. All an observer can see is a lunatic puckering his lips and beating time, happy that anyone is oblivious to sour melodies which to him are sweet.

As a direct result of my new associations, I've been thinking in a lighter vein. I'm still content, feeling positively regular. Can't recall when I had the last cold. Try to write every other day—please—so that I might see your silly typographical errors. Write.

P.S. Notice negative enclosed. I have no prints.
Surprised at Willkie's death.[2] Inevitability is cruel. Rather liked his recent policies.[3]

10/10/44

Dear Mom,

I habitually read both local and world news. Girls in my graduating class are getting married, and boys are becoming casualties —the majority, however, are in service college programs. I feel gratified, but not in an egotistical sense, that I'm here. At least I've triumphed. When I return, my conscience will be proud and I'll be more worldly.

I read the global news only half seriously. I see the world as an edifice of matchsticks. People seem to think that the final matchstick will cause the edifice to crumble. It doesn't occur to them that from the foundation up every matchstick would be responsible for such a catastrophe. To them the final matchstick consists of the leaders of nations. No. It's the entire mass of sticks governed by an infinity of laws that causes failure. The diplomats will try to solve problems that have a large number of causes, with a limited number of solutions. The real solution is beyond us. It's an ideal, a Utopia, unattainable. Whether this philosophy is valid or not, how can I help being amused by the human machinery now at work?

As I read about the Dumbarton Oaks peace conference,[1] the political campaign,[2] the credit given to our commanders,[3] the labor squabbles,[4] the P.A.C. machine[5] and military strategy,[6] I see how important the outcome of all these are to our generation. Looking farther, I can see how minor in importance their outcomes may be in terms of the eternal future (and past) in which a limitless number of unforeseen problems are bound to arise.

We keep playing our game, enhance our human self-esteem, argue, construct and destroy, and contradict ourselves to satisfy our sense of importance. I'm no exception. I, too, argue and discuss these matters. Humanity owes its cruel condition to its failure to realize its futility.

10/11/44

Dear Mom,

The temperature is getting hotter. Summer is approaching. The sun is hot, not the shady areas. It was overcast today and comfortably cool. I don't in the least mind the heat. By day the air is like an uncomfortable blanket over us, and, as the sun sinks, the blanket melts away leaving behind a pleasant warmth. Regardless of the temperature, we sweat. The humidity is constantly high.

Due to the uncomfortable, monotonous climate, we get little exercise except at work. Hang my physique, I wish only to relax both physically and mentally. I'll continue my physical training program after I return, and even then not as fanatically as before. In college, I think I'd like to try for swimming, shot put and discus. No football or baseball for me. I do want to participate in athletics, because it's an important part of one's education. I messed up on athletics in high school — silly boy.

I've written Sol a sentimental note on his father's death. [See letter of 9/28/44 above.] He's had tough luck lately.

Why won't Dad buy a house? Oh, not especially now, while property is expensive, but after the war. That should be our goal: our own home. Pay rent to the government or a private bank instead of a landlord. He should draw more wages from the business. The business can afford it. Good lord, it can surely support more than our basic necessities and a few pleasures.

Tell me, what is a "sking" trip? Oh, pardon me — the word is skiing. I'm thinking of writing a comprehensive dictionary on the translation of G.R.A.s [Mom: Gertrude Rose Aaron] words into simple English. It's amazing what I do find in your letters.

I love your "grandma at 20, cradle at 30" stuff. There are two types of girls: 1) beautiful and dumb and 2) just plain smart (beauty doesn't enter into the latter category). I can determine fairly well from her letter whether I like a girl. When a "cute little me" wants to know how "itsy bitsy cute little you wages war," it's high time to become your unappreciative son. If a correspondence isn't sensible and doesn't show logical thinking and some maturity, then it can't boost my morale. It's not genuine; it's a farce. I want my friends' letters to have a message, and not be an exhibition of the writer's egotistical self. I want letters that are entertaining and informative concerning the writer. I answer every letter that I receive.

I've had no contact with any of my former school chums except for Lenny, who is as ignorant of their fate as I am. A few days ago I was fingering through an old *Index* [the school yearbook] and indulging in some nostalgia. I just had to write someone who would have some information on the others. So I did, a young lady, and look forward to a reply. But I'm keeping my fingers crossed that it won't include that "cute little me" nonsense.

Although I haven't stopped being argumentative, I have discovered how to avoid having arguments. I excuse myself and walk out, or I commence an unrelated conversation. I can now see the futility of arguing.

I'm surprised at Ronnie's talkativeness. Once I thought it was merely a stage he was in. Maybe not. I've noticed that my own blabbing is rather spasmodic. Now I enjoy hours of silence, where once it would have been unendurable. In conversation I now prefer to listen—sometimes for hours—which I used to find difficult to do. I also find that I can write thoughts down more clearly than I can say them—something I could never have done once upon a time. Talkative people make me nervous. I walk away from such people once they get going. For some reason, rather than thinking out loud, I now prefer having interior thoughts.

10/13/44

Dear Mom,

Friday the thirteenth, superstitious people beware. But everything has gone well today. I'm still at the sawmill which is subject to being closed without notice. I'm indifferently satisfied with everything. Spirits up, health good, future bright—what more could I ask for?

I've taken a few pictures—comical poses—with my special chums. Sunday off here is like Sunday off in the States: reading, taking pictures, jabbering. Tomorrow our drooling inmates expect an all (wow) girl U.S.O. show to appear. Lately our movies have been curious antiques. I expect Buster Keaton[1] to show his mug[2] on the screen one of these nights.

I continue to thirst for music. It's an emotional escape, soothes the mind, appeals to our innate rhythm. I'm making a note of that. It's one thing I want to make up for later.

Read in the Kiwanis H.T.N. [Home Town News] that they will give a gallon of gas per day for thirty days to men on leave. I must keep that in mind — only God knows for how long.

How's business? Are you getting ahead? Same guy still working for you? Same yearly customers?

Say, is Dad's leg at all improved? Want a detailed report on your torturous dieting. Keeping yourself prettied up? You'd better. From all of Dad's most recent pictures of early summer, I think he looks wonderful. The past year has brought no change in him at all. I don't have a recent picture of you in full plumage. What d'ya say you accommodate your best boyfriend?

10/15/44

Dear Mom,

Last night the all (6) girl show came off and was received with our usual demonstrative cordiality. The usual vociferous hoots and howls rent the air, in response to the mere lifting of a dress to the thigh, the same ohs and ahs; and at the sight of an embrace, the same whoops of envy. Since the girls were neither amateurs nor polished professionals, their show lacked that special flick of the artist's touch, but they were girls, and boys always like girls. Each fellow, eyeing his choice among them, argued about which one he'd like to take out. Of course, he had to be satisfied with just arguing and lustful gazing.

There was also a pretty good excuse for a band manned by army boys with an army singer who had a well-trained, melodious voice. He received the sincerest ovation on curtain call after curtain call. On the way over I had seen him on the *West Point*. Which reminds me that I've never actually given you a detailed version of the voyage about which I can now reminisce.

When we boarded the vessel on Monday, February 21st, we were bewildered and stupefied by its monstrous size. None of us had ever been near such a thing. Encumbered by our heavy seabags, while being scrutinized amusedly by veteran sailors, we waddled up and through a seemingly endless maze of companionways to deck A, forward section. The bunks were five high with just enough space between them to allow us to exhale comfortably so that the bunk above wouldn't rise and fall with our breathing. We weren't discouraged by our uncomfortable quarters though. We were merely curious to see how sardines—and human beings—manage to retain their identity when packed in cans. Some of us sat bewildered wondering what to expect, others went about unpacking and still others began wandering about the ship. When word got around that WACs[1] and nurses were on board, everyone became alert and on the lookout for the freaks. We soon found out that these curiosities were living in the best of comfort, scared stiff at the approach of an enlisted man, and only available to the officers. Before the voyage was over we grew to despise them, probably because they wouldn't associate with us, probably because they were privileged, and probably because gold braid was their preferred attraction.

We gradually became acclimatized to the smoky, dingy enclosed A and Promenade decks, which were continually packed with men wandering about to satisfy their curiosity. We observed the still preserved staterooms on the upper decks, the elaborate designs, and artistic building of the foyers, and the impressively adorned main ballroom that had been converted into an infernally hot chow hall. All this made us aware of the vessel's former luxuriousness and wealthy patronage. Everyone was curious about the ship's history. Fantastic tales of her exploits at Singapore and of being under attack by enemy subs were rife. But it was true that Eleanor had christened her, the largest U.S. liner afloat, [the SS *America*] which was enough to make the Democrats on board happy anyway.

As expected, the first day, still in port, was one of confusion. We waited for hours in an endless and beginningless chow line, and when it didn't move, we hadn't the slightest idea where it would lead us. It went down one companionway and up another, through corridors, down, down into what seemed the very bowels of the ship. The moist thick heat below was unendurable. Food was carelessly slopped onto our mess gear. We ate standing up in what was once, as I mentioned, a gorgeous ballroom. Sweat poured onto our food which in turn we poured unappetizingly down our gullets as quickly as possible so we could leave once again to breathe fresh air.

So this was the routine—two meals a day in a suffocating dungeon.

At 1:00 o'clock on February 22nd we weighed anchor, and the massive hulk steamed out of the harbor. Crushing one another, we jammed the portholes and hatches for a last glimpse of our homeland for we didn't know how long. An odd silence, broken only by an occasional sentimental remark or an imprudent—and regretted—wisecrack, prevailed. It seemed that in only a matter of minutes the land became a distant and indistinct outline, and the vessel began to roll. It was the first time we had ever felt that roll.

Catalina island soon appeared. Dumbfounded, we stared at it. We were no longer in the U.S. It was unbelievable. Our longing began then.

The unfamiliar roll became only too familiar. As the vessel nosed down, our guts went down with it; but as the vessel commenced to rise our guts rose more slowly and lodged somewhere in the middle. We began developing headaches. When walking, we couldn't tell when or where our feet would strike the solid shifting floor. Even clutching anything nearby failed to steady us. Some crawled into their bunks, experimenting with positions that gave them only temporary relief. We heard that fresh air would make us feel better so everyone scrambled for the open, shifting deck. As the ship traveled at a brisk clip, the breeze was refreshing. With a wondering gaze, we stared at the blueness of the ocean and the aquamarine foam whipped up by the bow, as it cleaved the ocean. Soon, the sound of guttural vomiting began, and the ship's crew dashed all over the decks trying to carry out the navy's tradition of spotlessness. The "heads"[2] were certainly busy that night. The constant patter of running feet dashing to the toilets annoyed those in agony and not lucky enough to be able to vomit yet. At first, we had complained that two meals wouldn't be enough. We complained no longer. The smell of food was nauseating. I went one and one half days without eating. The plumper nurses wishing to reduce found their cure here.

On the second day, after sighting a flat-top on the horizon, we realized what fools we were for not bringing field glasses along. The one owner of field glasses, always surrounded by a curious crowd, was the envy of us all as, pointing here and there, he searched the horizon, commenting loudly on what he saw. We learned that many parts of the ship were restricted. Gruff guards were stationed to ward us off, making us feel like lonely, bewildered curs. Gradually, our boisterous equilibrium revived. Conversation began again, and those happy over recovering from their depressing misery began to sing. Eventually a throng accumulated, and all the services—the Seabees, army, air corps, Marines—vied with one another singing their service songs. Immediately, the spirits of all were uplifted. Bands of singers sang into the wind on various sections of the decks. One spectacular extrovert elected himself impromptu M.C. and directed us with impressive vitality. As darkness fell we went below happier, renewed.

In short order we grew accustomed to the established routine. The dread of visiting the restaurant inferno, the everlasting gazing at the technicolor blueness of the expanse, the contempt for the arms and legs sprawled over the decks, the shrill bugle calls, the harsh restrictions, the encumbering life belt, the gradually growing filth and the unkempt appearance of the restless men, the torrid sun, and brilliant, blinding sea, the painful sunburns, the rasping nerves, the privileged passengers, all began to tell in our countenances and actions. After a week we passed a climax. Anger and disgust evolved into indifference and lassitude.

Finally, our outfit was given a deck assignment: chipping paint on the fantail, a restricted zone. Given passes allowing us to enter the fantail at anytime (although none of us liked the idea of working), we soon began enjoying it, after the boatswain, our boss, arranged for us to have gallons of ice cream —at our own expense, of course—which, at several pints per person, we literally devoured. Even though our chow consisted of beans, beans and more beans, canned meat, canned meat, and more canned meat, we were hungry and ate heartily. However, it soon became evident that we were eating less and less, and sometimes not at all. Every afternoon it seems the ice cream was bloating our stomachs. Most took advantage of their passes and visited the fantail to escape the intolerable, stinking mob to sun themselves. Eventually, after wearing out our privilege, because we had used our passes too freely, we were again restricted to our old private province.

Everyone read anything he could lay his hands on. Books (pocket books) were issued, and we swapped them, until everyone was swapped out. The ship printed its own news bulletin. Our news-hungry mates followed around those who were able to secure one from an acquaintance in the ship's crew. Such lucky fellows promised a mate that he could have the bulletin next, which in turn he passed on to another and so on.

The barbers improvised a shop on one of the windy decks. You knew they were at work if suddenly you discovered a crop of hair blown between your legs. Closely shaven heads became a fad, then a curse, after the equatorial sun beat down on them.

I was fortunate enough to have brought a map with me. By the time we landed, it was no longer a map, but rather a shredded semblance of one. Everyone prophesied our position. A few geography wits were sufficiently convincing to be subject to frequent consultation. Although their guess was no better than the next fellow's, no one bothered to entertain that possibility.

We arose one morning, our skin clammy and sticky, greeted with an amazing rumor. The *West Point* had been sunk by Japs. It was that ever-present scuttlebutt starting again. Although nobody knew for sure where the report originated, it was thought it came from the ship's radio. We cracked sour jokes about our sinking, such as finding Davy Jones's locker a most interesting place. Never questioning the great importance of this ship, we were certain that we were rich booty for a Jap sub. As a matter of fact we had heard that the Japs had been searching for this tub for the last two years. Although never sure how many were on board, rumor had it between 10,000 and 15,000. A member of the crew told me the rumor had it about right. Some speculated, boy, what an experience it would be to have this ship under attack. Just think of the headlines. But no, there was no land in sight so we immediately retracted the idea.

Just before, and consistently after reaching the equator, flying fish were the latest curiosity. Because they are difficult to spot, only after three or four days were we sure that we actually saw the creatures. Once educated to look near the ship's prow, we could see them emerge in flocks from the ocean then glide in a glistening mass along the waves and eventually plunge with a plop into a crest. For days, the most our slow- sighted friends could see were the miniature circular plops. Soon, when they came to recognize a glistening mass taking form before their eyes, they went about bragging that at last they had witnessed the flight of fish. Eventually, the flying fish became a part of the monotonous blue expanse, eliciting no more of our attention than the once fascinating bluecaps.

The nights below decks became torture. Due to light regulations all hatches had to be closed. The air was putrid and exhausting. Many of us couldn't, or rather wouldn't, endure this below deck hell. We gathered up our ponchos (an oilcloth cape) and lifejacket (which was always at our side) and slinked above deck to curl into a gunwale or some obscure corner for a difficult but more endurable night's sleep. The night air was penetrating and chill, and it inevitably rained before sunrise. Our pillow was a lifejacket, our mattress a steel cranny, and our quilt a cold, stiff poncho. When the rain came, we curled up more tightly, refusing to go below. Soon the entire population below began looking toward the deck as a haven for resting, and soon it had to be stopped because such an aggregation of humans covering the decks would hinder any necessary emergency action. So the crew began rounding up the desolate deck sleepers to send them below. But an hour or so later they would only return to continue their rudely interrupted sleep. I had been awakened more than three times in one night, a most annoying score. Finally, I managed to find a spot that the crew hadn't discovered until the last night.

The night sounds were weird: the wind like a choir, moaning as it swirled around the mast, the deck rhythmically creaking, the soothing swish of the waves passing the prow, the crashing noises of the ocean, all topped off by a crescendo of blissful snoring. The heaving motion of the ship rocked us to sleep; the ocean sound was a lullaby singing to us. I enjoyed those heavenly moments preceding my awkward sleep.

The ship continued on its seemingly infinite course, weaving in and out, changing direction every few minutes as a precaution against subs. One morning the weaving was more marked. A sub was on our tail. Gad, what special people we must be—subs after us. The thrill of knowing, or supposing, that we were in the process of evading a sub tickled us.

Another afternoon a deafening boom resounded. The ship shivered and we with it. The effect was paralyzing. There was another burst, then another, producing a concussion of breathtaking gusts. The guns on the ship were being tested. I was weak with relief.

At last we noticed birds, floating debris passing by, and we saw ships more frequently. It was a glorious, sunny morning when we saw a blue, barely perceptible haze interrupting the horizon. Again our owner of the field glasses took first place in popularity. There, before us, was our first glimpse of foreign soil—New Caledonia. We were all intoxicated by the strange sight of actual land and the romantic, gigantic thrust of jagged mountains. Once again all portholes and hatches were crammed with men. Every small boat was an object for careful examination. The lighthouse on an island in the harbor greeted us with blinker signals, welcoming us to Noumea. Now the fellow who claimed to know something about code, pushed aside the field glass owner, and translated the signals into a meaningless jumble of letters. After this, the field glass owner resumed his former position of importance.

We lay up in the harbor for an entire day. The night was intriguing; lights were everywhere. The other ships in the harbor glittered brilliantly. Lights played upon the dancing ripples. We were impressed with the enormous size of this base. Perceptible only in the morning light, the harbor was a constant hustle and bustle of activity.

A blast vibrating the air, chains rumbling, told us we were on the move again. And again the portholes were busy with arms madly waving as we passed the ships at anchor. Once more the familiar rolling began, although *mal de mer*[3] was negligible. The Coral Sea was uneventful and unexciting. New Guinea was to receive us.

10/16/44

Dear Mom,

I've finished *Song of Bernadette*. A devoutly religious individual may glorify the story, an atheist ridicule it, a hypocrite made aware of his hypocrisy by it, but everyone is bound to be interested as he turns the pages. He'll certainly recognize its message of futility, of humanity's ignorance and its possibilities. I've read better, and better written books, but I can't deny that I enjoyed this one.

So now I'm tackling *Troilus and Cressida*,[1] so different from the modern novel, yet so entertaining.

I received a prompt reply from Dolly Goodstein of the Hudson Street Goodsteins. Her letter was sensible, entertaining, and typical. This Jewish girl enthusiastically writes that her brother, in his envied travels, has been blessed by the Pope and has seen the king of England. Here is a Jewess enthused about a religious contradiction. It doesn't quite add up. Puck[2] said it: "What fools these mortals be."[3]

It has been raining for three consecutive days — a rare phenomenon. We needed it.

I lead quite a narrow life — at least from a wanderer's point of view — from tent to work and back. For more than a month all I have seen is dust or mud and a narrow road. The tent has been my haven; my books my indulgence; my work, eating and sleeping, my existence. If this isn't security, what is? Independence is simplicity itself here. The dynamic tension of U.S. living is completely missing in our taken-for-granted security. No one should commit suicide here. As I become reconciled to being patient, my struggles diminish proportionately. I'm even weary of conversation. A change is due in the near future. Everyone wants it.

P.S. Send a padlock next package.

10/17/44

Dear Mom,

Today's mail: two letters from home, another from faithful, prolific Johnson, one from Ida informing me of [Cousin] Bob's whereabouts, and a package.

I'm sure I'd like your new black dress trimmed with "fusha." But what in the devil is "fusha?"[1] The natives here would probably know. They have words that sound somewhat like this "fusha" stuff. Since black slenderizes your lines — psychologically if not otherwise — I approve the color. You were undoubtedly a ravishing lady when you wore that other black dress at Eddie's wedding. The picture of you in that dress remains eternally in my memory.

Do you constantly wear your bridge now? I'm warning you, prepare to wear it for good, after I return.

It's difficult to convince my aunts that I want no packages. Refreshments are stale by the time they arrive. I can use only books, and then I have time for only a limited number. If they ask you what I like, tell them I'd like nothing, and, if they insist, tell them books. What books? Preferably the classics and best sellers.

It's good to hear that my money is coming in regularly. Having miserly, thrifty instincts, I silently gloat over it.

My friend, the former Hitler disciple, is more American than I am. He swears rarely — and that has been cultivated, he's intimately familiar with burlesque, he loves American girls (although he shyly abstains from their company), he smokes two cigars and one pipeful daily, and conducts himself with a typical carefree American demeanor. I was immediately attracted by his deep and coherent thinking and love for music. Being an atheist, he has no prejudice against Jews, especially one, like myself, who is inclined towards the same doctrine. Often, he has asked me what I thought of his being a German and once a prejudiced person. He loves sarcastic humor, of which I'm his favorite victim. Although Ray is a worthwhile friend, there has been a slight, but not serious, rift in our friendship. Having discussed everything imaginable, we've exhausted our subject matter and conversation has begun to wane.

I dislike using "I" continually, not because of you, but because I'm sick of it. If two years ago I was an introvert, I'm one more than ever now, although a more broadened one.

You must realize that we are all in danger from birth, and that chance deployed over countless possibilities decreases the imminency of danger striking any individual. Although I'm not a radical fatalist, I must respect the inevitability of the laws of fate. Never fear for my life in this unit; we are definitely non-combatant.

The number of men dying in the Pacific area is relatively small when compared with the enormous number waiting to die. The maintenance force alone is tremendous. Our inactivity, and the inactivity of the other forces here, are just a respite before the climax.

Your attitude towards your sister Sadie is childish and unwarranted. You shouldn't condemn her for flaunting the financial success of her marriage; this may be her only satisfaction and way of achieving mind's ease and happiness. Your own happiness is complete. What others say or do with regard to their own unhappiness has no bearing on yours. If more people were to be more tolerant of the vanity and pride of others, they would themselves acquire a more attractive and genuine personality.

Time for relaxation and a shower. For the sake of variety, while reading *Troilus and Cressida* I'm also reading short biographies of the great musical composers.

10/19/44

Dear Mom,

The mill is under repair. During the past few days I've been doing nothing, just standing by. However, my idle moments are well-filled. After Shakespeare had captivated me for two days, I had a sudden desire for music. Finally, I wangled a phonograph from the rec department and several records: Beethoven's *Fifth* and *Third Symphonies*, and the *Emperor Concerto*, Gershwin's "Rhapsody in Blue" and selections from "Porgy and Bess"[1] plus the *Concerto in F*, Strauss's[2] waltzes, Schubert's "Ave Maria" and "Serenade," pieces from Victor Herbert's[3] "Daughter of the Regiment"[4] with Lily Pons,[5] Andre Kostelanetz's[6] rendition of several semi-classical pieces, excerpts from "Pagliacci,"[7] Caruso[8] singing, some latest hit tunes from the States, and—let me think, what else?—oh, a mess of odd, well known other recordings. Listening for five to six hours a day for the past two days, I've been royally entertained. I almost forgot to include Mendelssohn's[9] "A Midsummer Night's Dream."[10]

Back home I was attracted to classical music, but here I crave it. Of course, I still enjoy popular music and good jazz. My taste is now more discriminating. Now, when I open *Time* magazine, I first turn to the section on books, then music, followed by science, and education. This spells out, in their order of importance as my unconscious sees them, my newly developed interests. These subjects appeal to my curiosity.

I read the news diligently, but I don't argue about the policies, strategies, politics or the fate of nations anymore. I don't see any sense in taking the news seriously. Why? Because—I must use a word I've used often lately—of the futility. What will and must happen, will and must happen. When reading of events and the commentaries on them,

I don't react with a tongue-in-cheek attitude, but rather with one of agnostic concern.

Our gorgeous weather is back, accompanied by a thickening heat. Have I ever described the heat here? No, I don't think so. Let's begin in the morning. At six the air is cool and still. While the rising sun's rays are subdued, it's pleasantly warm. By eight the heat begins, not exactly stifling, just thick, heavy. Even while you're sitting still, beads of sweat form on your chin and upper lip. If working, your body becomes covered with sweat, as if you just had a shower. The entire upper part of your trousers becomes drenched. Salty, stinging moisture drips from your eyelashes. As you continue working, your body becomes attuned to the heat and the perspiring decreases as the pores of your skin become clogged with salt. By now the heat is beating down on you like a hammer pounding. Your head throbs so you soak your hat in water, or bind a wet handkerchief across your forehead. You are constantly squinting your eyes.

Time for chow. Still bathed in sweat, you eat voraciously. Time to return to work. A breeze arises, arriving in cooling swells. Even while you work, the perspiration disappears, leaving a coating of salt behind. You begin to feel better, and your hair is blowing about. By the time work is done, your body has taken on a reddish brown hue. You return to camp and find final relief as you wash off the salt and grit in a cool, refreshing shower. Your head now feels clear. Your cooled body glows evenly and feels smooth. Smelling clean, you dress for the evening, and, if you stay quiet, you can remain cool. However, if you merely walk, or perform any slow action, your skin will become sticky, but you won't generate a flowing sweat. Sometimes, as you lie in bed, your entire body will exude quantities of perspiration. In a half hour you feel cool again. And by two in the morning you wrap yourself in a woolen blanket. Once you're used to this routine, that of the body's natural shower and the shower shower, you can enjoy the climate and the tropics.

Come down and see me some time.

10/20/44

Dear Mom,

In the two typewritten letters I received from you today, there is nary an uncorrected error. This is a rare thing with my hasty but ardent mother.

At Dad's suggestion, Lenny's sister sent her letter airmail. Her earlier letters were short, the much preferred V-Mail. One of my letters produces a shower of replies from both her and her mother. I dislike their dull answers, and my duller ones to theirs. So I don't write them often. On the other hand, I appreciate their kind and well-meant gestures.

I've fostered a contempt for army nurses and all service women. Gertrude Gordon[1] is probably no exception. My feelings are justified by what I've seen. I'm not so narrow as to classify individuals into a category, but none of these women have proven themselves worthy. After the war former service women will find themselves unpopular with veterans.

"Marriage Is a Private Affair"[2] did not arouse "my blood pressure." That it was a pre-released, advertised, show made it unique. The boys enjoyed the "I'm flat" scene[3] and predicted it would be too radical to pass the Hays office.[4]

I'm much interested in your reaction to *Strange Fruit.* You'll probably gasp at its frankness and abhor its substance. Everyone else seems to have.

Ma mere,[5] gypped is not spelled jipped. Webster, the dictionary man, should have lived long enough to read your marvelous versions.

Laments and praises have been bestowed on both Smith[6] and Willkie, as is typically the case with the lowest and the highest after death. The tyrannical Napoleon had his adherents who, after his death, presented overwhelming tribute. Hitler will, no doubt, be lauded for his political genius. The drunkard who dies in the gutter will be praised by his fellow drunkards. It's a quirk of our nature. The praise emanates from our heartfelt reverence for the dead, not because a person is who he is. A eulogy is a false, politic speech of the heart.

Too bad about [Cousin] Sol. Keep me informed. While he's recuperating, I'll write him.

If you thought that two cars would be as cheap to operate as one, well, you now know only too well, it's not true. When I get back, I wouldn't own a car on a bet. All the fellows want to buy a car. In accordance with my present plans, my thrift campaign won't wane.

10/22/44

Dear Mom,

I've finished reading the brief, and unsatisfying *Living Biographies of Composers[1]* from Bach[2] to Stravinsky,[3] who, by the way, I think is all wet. The book has aroused my desire to read a more complete biography of Beethoven and some other composers. Most of these composers are branded geniuses, but few were exceptional as youngsters (except Mozart).[4] They only bloomed into genius status after hard work, perseverance, and moments of inspiration. Their genius lay in their cultivated ability to translate their inspirations into a language sympathetic to and understood by those of us who are less gifted. Such genius can't be measured by intelligent quotients. Genius applies to one gifted in a specific field.

I've now begun reading *Jean-Christophe*, my own book. To my surprise and delight it's about a fictional composer. I'll send it on to you after I'm done with it. I find it so superbly written that I'm virtually tripping through it. So I'm reading two books at once, Shakespeare and Rolland and choose each according to my mood.

This is one of our glorious tropical Sundays after three days of overcast and rain. The earth is drenched and darker, the sky is technicolor blue, and the leaves are washed clean. A soothing breeze plays with our hair. It's the sort of day that lifts the heart.

The sound of locusts issues from the trees, then a silence, then they start again. Small, harmless lizards, resembling chameleons, only sleeker and more colorful, roam about. One just slinked by—a yellow body with horizontal black stripes and a tail of silvery French blue. I marvel at the movement of its tail, like that of a ballet dancer. Before one movement is complete, another begins. It's dainty, unreal, even mystical. Only drunkards curse the tropics.

Last night I saw Olsen and Johnson in "Crazy House."[5] I snickered a little at their slapstick and ridiculousness. Seeing familiar Hollywood spots—the Palace Theater, Hollywood Boulevard, Sunset Boulevard—our paradisiacal haunts of old, made all of us happier.

The boys are complaining that there isn't anything more to write about. They wrack their brains, gaze off into space, hoping to pull something out, then throw down their pens, and look for some excuse to rationalize their disloyalty to Mom or the girlfriend. It is difficult nowadays, very difficult, because we only continue to eat, sleep, work and be bored.

P.S. As for myself, I'm pretty well entertained with my own self-inflicted forms of enjoyment. I rather pity the "I don't know what to do" guys.

10/27/44

Dear Mom,

After a week or more without letters, two arrived full of sad and happy news. That's how I like 'em: newsy, gossipy with a female extravagance. Give my congratulations to Shirley and Ed.[1] Will cousins never cease? Not that I mind so many newcomers, but they are arriving at a rate to even give the prolific Chase family some pretty close competition.

Maguire's old store[2] should be preserved as a historical relic. Where in the devil will the rats live? And that platform behind the fountain![3] Good lord, whenever the gigantic Mrs. Mazur[4] waited on me, I felt like a peewee as she towered above me. Chandler Street won't be the same Chandler Street any longer.

I've neglected writing because of two things: my interest in the book I'm reading, and the simple, uneventful, void life I'm leading. I've attempted writing things more momentous than letters, things with inspiring thoughts, then rebelled and tore them up. I'm unable to satisfy the urge because of my depressed mood which stems from feelings that I have no aptitude for it, that I'm inexperienced and even insincere. I must wait and see—will my longing to write fade, or will my capacity to express myself improve?

From living with men, I've come to understand Dad better. There are men here who sleep with their glasses on, take a shower with a cigar in their mouth, and have the letter V cut into their coarse body hair. There are men here who drink like fish, frequent brothels, some a dozen times, men who love to tell us "younger fellows" about the good old days, their horse and buggy courting, big wages, about prohibition,[5] and the depression.[6] There are men here who are intellectuals who flaunt their philosophy, their books, science, college life and night clubbing. It makes up a brilliant cross section. And there are fellows like Dad, though a delightful rarity.

What I've learned about Dad and me I may forget after I'm home. The gist of it is that Dad and I take each other too seriously. Dad's stubbornness, his sense of being indispensable, and his righteousness had been a source of irritation because of a misunderstanding between us. However, his true nature is lovable. In spite of his exasperating attitude, I now find it amusing, and him likable. Dad's tops, every stubborn, headstrong fiber of him. I see Ronnie is also going through the same process that I went through under Dad's domination.

Life is cruel to [Cousin] Lil. I feel sorry for her. She has always been square with me and on various occasions tolerated my annoying temperament.[7] I wish I could help her.

What did I write about "Marriage Is a Private Affair" that so aroused you? From your reaction, I must have exaggerated what the movie was about. Look, for the last time: the picture was mediocre, although unique for out here; you enjoyed it, as I predicted you would, and that's that. I'm glad you liked Lana. I did too. And I'm glad you had some laughs. I did too.

Sadie has written that she can't figure out exactly what I do. She insists that she must know what kind of job I have in order to compare notes with other aunts who have nephews in the service. Not only is the preceding statement explaining her wish confusing, but also I'm confused because I've never been able to quite figure out what I am. As soon as I put my finger on it, oops, I have another job, and it slips away. Recently, for nigh on ten days, I stood by doing nothing—a very pleasant interlude, indeed. Now I'm working on the reconditioning and rebuilding of the sawmill which consists of some carpentry but mostly machine work, such as threading steel rods, chiseling out keyways and keys to fit shafts and pulleys. This gets me good and greasy and has caused me to bang up my fingers beautifully. But I am getting a great kick of being an all around person on this construction job.

[Two ink blots with the words "modern art" beside them appear on the letter paper.]

10/28/44

Dear Mom,

Our latest innovation is "WAC-ing." Several thousand WACs and nurses have invaded the place, and appear to be fulfilling a two-fold purpose, that for which they were trained, and for courting.

With new regulations in our camp prohibiting nudity, our showers are now screened in. The men are into slicking themselves up, and the question on everyone's lips is, "Have you gone WAC-ing lately?" The skipper encourages this overseas courting, the recreation department encourages it, and the transportation department does its best to supply courting vehicles.

The procedure is like this: a fellow visits the WAC camp nearby, and strikes up an acquaintance which eventually leads to a date. On show night several couples can be seen cooing on the hard theater benches. After the show the couples return to their truck or jeep or weapons' carrier, which has been made spic and span for the occasion, and follow the natural, inevitable course that occurs under an exotic tropical moon.

Next morning the lover reports to work, eyes shining, extremely talkative, and gay. Others, who until now hadn't entertained the thought of this unique way of courting, become interested. The lover then arranges for the victim to have a date with his Wac's friend. The number of men now courting each night is quite high. War? Who ever heard of the war?

We have our comedians; you find them everywhere. Have I told you about one comedian in particular? In case I haven't, I must tell you about such a fellow back at Camp Endicott. As I crept into my bunk, I stopped suddenly before I put my second leg under the covers. I watched a small, intelligent looking man in the bunk beside mine, creep into his bunk wearing his glasses and bury his head into the pillow with a sigh. Creeping out of my bunk, my curiosity aroused, I walked over to his, tapped him on the shoulder, and reminded him that he had his glasses on. "Oh those," he said innocently. "I need them to see my dreams more clearly." [Hughie forgot that he had related this episode in a letter from Camp Endicott.]

In the shower the other day, there was a fellow vigorously soaping and massaging his body, and singing loudly despite having a cigar between his lips. I piped up, "Need a light, Mike?" "Oh, no," he responded. "I just loving chewing on the damn thing whenever I take a shower." Then he went nonchalantly on with his lathering.

Yesterday a guy with a pipe in his mouth walked into the shower building. "Aw hell," he yelled, "forgot to leave my pipe in the tent. But damn it all, I'm not going to walk all the way back there." He strutted into the shower, pipe and all, and puffed away until, filled with water, the pipe went out.

I saw another guy take a shower wearing his glasses and his waterproof watch. Claiming that he likes to tell the time when he showers, he added that if he didn't wear his glasses in the shower they'd never get washed.

We are delivered by truck to the sawmill which is about two miles from camp. Every day one of my mates, who works only nights, accompanies our crew to the mill, which is situated on the edge of the bay. After arriving there, he removes his clothes, changes into a bathing suit and stands all day, hands on his hips, searching the bay. This has been going on for several months. One day I asked him what he found so interesting out there on the bay, why he so carefully scrutinized each ship that steamed in. "Well, I'll tell ya," he said. "My brother is on LST 93. Maybe there's a chance one of these days he'll pull into the bay." If such a virtue exists, there's patience for you. What a way to use one's empty days! Someday his ship is bound to come in, if he waits long enough.

There are many more amusing and interesting things that continually happen, but I quickly forget most of them. The presence of the WACs is producing many corking stories which I'll write about another time.

A good example of our 113th Seabee spirit occurred when an SP [Shore Patrol] stopped one of our weapons carriers in our very own camp area. He insisted that the vehicle had too many personnel aboard. The men, eyeing him with some hostility, got out of their vehicle, walked over to his jeep and proceeded to tip it over. Immediately the SP, scared silly, hopped into the Jeep and drove away. No one dares to boss around the boys who built the roads without some risk. If only I could remember more of them, the number of fascinating incidents is endless.

                                                              11/1/44

Dear Mom,

My indifference towards advancement in the service is partly pretense and partly sincere. I'd like the extra money. But I don't have much faith in government programs that are as unstable as politics itself.

In working at the sawmill, the job I <u>had</u>, I was content, worked hard, and was recognized for it. I couldn't be certain that I'd be recommended for something better, and expected nothing, but I hoped. The possibility of advancement wasn't my motivation. Rather, it was because I was content doing a man's job, and working outdoors during civilized hours. It turns out that I'll get nothing for my conscientious labor. Although I proved myself satisfactory to my boss, the impersonal higher-ups were unimpressed.

Last night I was stunned when I was assigned to detestable KP. After protesting to my superiors, who agreed that I was a good worker, I received no satisfaction. There's nothing I can do about it, and I see myself going backwards. Ironically, my progress in the service is futile.

I suppose there's a lesson to be learned for the future from my accumulated dislike of government service. I can't say that I don't care about my lack of progress, because I do care. I want to be out there working, not dawdling in a chow hall. Being in a helpless position, I feel contempt for my indifferent superiors. As a result, I enjoy my reading and writing all the more. They help me feel better despite my disappointment. No one need remind me that everything is temporary. I know that, thank God.

I'll be returning the books by mail when I'm done with them. Don't turn them in to the library. I'd like to keep them. Prepare yourself: I'll have plenty of books around after I get back.

The other night I saw a fairly recent picture, "Christmas Holiday"[1] with Deanna Durbin and Gene Kelly.[2] It's her debut as a serious actress. Although nobody else did, I enjoyed the picture. It's a typical Maugham[3] story and well acted. I didn't think that Kelly was suited for the part, but, in spite of this, he performed well.[4] Tonight we're having a semi-classical[5] USO show.

The unfortunate thing about most of our antique films is that many are botched and I've seen some of them before.

I'm sorry that my letter to Sol arrived amidst all his hardship. It was hardly appropriate. To tell the truth, I was dissatisfied with it, and after mailing it wished I could recall it. I don't know why.

I don't expect a room for myself when I get home. If I said it, I didn't mean it that way. Only if we moved and such a thing were possible, I'd be pleased.

With publication of the battalion paper constantly postponed, I've lost interest in it. The editor, somewhat of a writer in civilian life and capable, claims to be too busy with other matters. After he asked me to write something like a gossip column, simply to stay in his good graces, I didn't refuse, but I don't intend to write one. It's out of my line. I'd only submit articles on our work projects etc., nothing about personalities.

I'm sure you can understand my present predicament. Please realize that I'm not responsible for it. I don't especially mind it as I can see my situation far more clearly than I could a year ago. I just want to get it all over with, one war or the other. It all ends up in the same place: home.

Love to all three of you, Hughie (the KP kid)

11/3/44

Dear Mom,

In spite of my keen perception of the general situation, I cannot help feeling humiliated at the turn of events. Rerates were issued today and many of my friends received them. All around me people are advancing in grade. Knowing that I've worked hard, I ask myself why I'm less deserving than many. Feeling sad and downtrodden, I'm gradually getting over it. Nevertheless I can't blind myself to the present. I can't help feeling the weight of being rebuffed and disappointed. So finally I've decided to make one final appeal to the skipper, not for advancement but for a permanent position. After all, I've been removed from the last three jobs against my will and under my bosses' protest. If my appeal fails to bring results, I'll only be a little less happy. I will still have my books and the future for consolation. I'm not in such anguish as I would have been a year ago, merely temporarily disillusioned. You shouldn't feel bad. I'll get over it in a couple of days.

I saw the semi-classical stage show night before last. It was excellent. The talent—four concert and operatic singers (a baritone, a tenor, a soprano and a contralto)—was superb. They sang pieces by Victor Herbert and Gershwin, and pieces from "Showboat"[1] and "Carmen." The also sang popular songs from "Oklahoma!,"[2] "Carmen Jones,"[3] and several other Broadway musicals. The concert pianist (one of the three women) was good. She played selections such as "The Firefly"[4] and "Flight of the Bumble Bee."[5] Even the fans of swing participated in the wild ovation. The entire evening was most pleasant.

Oddly enough, I knew the scheduled date for the Philippine invasion[6] weeks before it came off. Much rumor often turns out to be truth.

Ugh. I pity Grace's son after spending three years over here, then having to return. I wouldn't care to repeat what I've gone through—the inconveniences in the crossing and getting settled.

We were encouraged to send home clothing that we didn't need. It gives me more room in the seabag for books which I wish to keep with me. You mention my identification bracelet. I hate wearing things on my wrists. A watch is quite enough.

No packages have arrived yet. It's too near Christmas to expect good service.

11/4/44

Dear Mom,

I feel relieved. The weight of my disappointment has lifted, and I'm actually feeling happy. I'm hinging my hope on an appeal to the skipper who is notorious for being a hard nut to crack. I've decided on submitting a written appeal, which I believe will serve to reinforce the impression of my sincerity. If it proves effective, it will be a moral victory in more than one way. It will also prove that I can write powerfully enough to affect a reader.

All my writing has been confined to letters, and then to only a few special people. I think of putting ideas in writing more often than I actually write. I have the ability to write easily and confidently, but I often lack the desire. Only when I write letters, do I express my free thoughts.

My love for music is in a confused state. Is listening an appreciation, or simply an emotional outlet? Is it entertainment or a profound and incomprehensible experience? I don't understand. My mind is free of thoughts, inactive, while listening. I want to understand what's happening. I must listen much more yet.

I'm still reading to beat the band. I love it more than I ever imagined I would. I'd be lost without books to depend on. After reading more than half of the 1900 pages in *Jean-Christophe*, I find I understood every word, every thought. Books such as this make our modern novels seem mediocre.

Time arrives regularly, but *Omnibook* has stopped coming. Will you find out what's wrong for me? The *Gazettes* arrive whenever they feel like it, their dates in a jumble, but that's okay. The local news needn't be in sequence. I enjoy reading it anyway.

11/7/44

Dear Mom,

Nothing new. There never is anymore. I'm feeling fine. Good health is especially a blessing over here. Tonight, I approach the skipper. He's a fine leader, but stubborn. I'll be surprised if I'm successful.

On the voyage over we were not in a convoy. Our ship was well armed and too fast for a sub to tail us. We sighted ships only as we neared port. At Milne Bay we changed to a freighter which was less crowded but no less inconvenient. Did I mention that during our voyage last May, the steel deck was our mattress? I slept wonderfully.

I was acquainted with the Goldstein boy. He's talkative and fanatical about girls, discusses them in an immoral way. I never liked him. Despite his reputation at Clark [University] he didn't impress me as being an intellectual or gifted. He's certainly not one to confide in.

Very few boys please me. They needn't be ideal, only thinkers, sensible and morally pure. I've met, at most, three boys who meet these qualifications, and I intend to keep them as friends.

As I've said, "Song of Bernadette" was fantastic. And the fantastic does exist in reality. I may doubt the story, but I don't insist that it's not true. The author is most convincing. I believe that there are many things beyond us, unbelievable things, because logic and our senses are limited.

So if I'll be coming home to a plump Mom, it's a plump Mom I want. Send a padlock as soon as possible. Although I've had nothing stolen, many have. During a move someone is apt to get the wrong bag and a padlock will help me identify my own more easily.

A couple of nights ago I saw "The Imposter"[1] with Jean Gabin.[2] The story, the acting and the message were weak. Most of the fellows liked it, but I didn't.

No doubt the October 23rd issue of *Time* won Dewey many votes. The magazine's Republicanism was most evident. Dewey has fallen drastically in my opinion. His campaign is weak, and his speeches aim to deceive. Roosevelt is more reserved and is conducting a dignified campaign. Dewey may be sincere in what he proposes, but rather than stressing that, he instead twists the facts about the New Deal[3] to his own benefit. It's easy enough to point out the present administration's failed attempts to solve problems, but when they were introduced, the public was all for them. However, the Democrats don't have convincing arguments either. Only the people's confidence in Roosevelt will pull him through. Even the Democratic political platform, which constantly refers to the blunders of the Hoover[4] administration, is an utter deception. The political arguments by both sides are ridiculous and best ignored, which I do.

11/8/44

Dear Mom,

Coincidentally, both your letter and one from my former teacher, Miss Rourke, which I received on the same day, touched on the same subject. You called me a man, my masculine nature more mature. And Miss Rourke wrote that she saw in me definite promise of "eventually becoming a man." Either I've changed, or neither of you realized the nature of my deeper thinking which distance seems to have dragged out of me. I find neither statement flattering, nor do they hurt my pride. I know neither of them is true. My words aren't necessarily a guide to my actions. I confess, since I'm distant from the world of my past, I'm more tolerant of it and emotionally aware of its charm. Perhaps I'll eventually learn enough and grow in my present environment to merit the opinion you express. I'm well-aware of the frequent changes in my thinking. I can't and don't analyze myself, nor can you analyze me based on my letters, which only appear to betray the writer's nature. Don't expect a radically changed son to return, one with a smoother nature, as the letters would seem to indicate. I would be a figment of your maternal imagination. Please don't.

Last night I went before the skipper. I was both pleased and displeased with the results. Commending me for my written appeal, he sputtered and laughed over it, but as he progressed down the page he became serious. Twice he said he liked what I had written which made me feel better, and satisfied with what I had done. So I proved myself capable of putting my thoughts across. After clipping both sheets of paper together, he laid it before him on his desk. I had the feeling that, before he tosses it away after I leave, he'll read it once more. He understood me perfectly, and I understood him. He knew when his excuses were ineffective. Throughout our talk, I assumed neither a demanding nor hostile attitude, but a rather appealing one. He's a clever talker, smooth, rational and pleasing. After talking to him, one invariably feels better whether one succeeds in getting what one wants or not. His informal way puts the listener at ease. Trying to reassure me, (but I doubted his sincerity), he promised to submit my name for a job in one of the shops where he said I could "learn a trade." He guaranteed nothing. Nevertheless, I felt better after seeing that my written appeal made an impression. He asked that I remain at my present job in KP until the end of the month.

I did have a problem. Last night, I was supposed to secure the written approval of my company commander before approaching the skipper. This is the required routine, but my company commander wasn't to be found. The skipper questioned me about my not having my company commander's approval. I had to tell him that he wasn't available. At this the skipper thundered a request that the commander report to him immediately. Of course, he knew that the commander, a young lieutenant fresh out of college and considered inexperienced by his fellow officers, was at a show. This commander is vain, self-pampered and has little concern for his men. I've never disliked him, but then I've had little to do with him. He soon stormed into the commander's tent, angered at not being able to see the end of "The Seventh Cross"[1] (which I sacrificed seeing for the sake of the mast I requested), angered that I had gone over his head, and angered that he was discovered at the show, when he should have been on duty to sign requests to see the skipper and grant approvals. His voice overflowed with contempt for me. Although I hadn't intended to aggravate him, circumstances made it unavoidable. No doubt, after last night his indifference toward me has turned into dislike, especially after the skipper supported me against his biting remarks. The skipper understood me while the company commander was too involved with himself and his predicament to do so.

When I left I knew I had the commander's sympathy, but the lieutenant's hostility. The skipper can, and I believe will, do more for me than the lieutenant, who commands a smaller group of men. However, I need the lieutenant for a recommendation in order to advance in rate. He'll be a difficult rock to move in the future.

11/9/44

Dear Mom,

There being nothing local to discuss, I may as well take you into my confidence and give you an idea of my ideas.

I correspond with approximately twenty individuals who reply faithfully. Claiming to like my letters, they make exclamatory remarks about them that flatter me and feed my vanity. Gulfport likes my style; Frisco displays them; Worcester lauds them; Boston calls it talent; New Guinea, insisting that my articles are worthy, says, send them to the States, and I: they stink.

What brings on my sudden outburst is Henrietta's recent letter that she wrote Sunday night after the entire Aronovitz clan had departed. She likes my letters. Her friends say "publish them," and she says "publish them." She states it's a unanimous recommendation. She suggests presenting some to a periodical. Have you been talking to her? This is absurd.

Frankly, I'm pleased with only a few of my letters, and then never entirely. Many are impressed with them. Of course, my ego is stirred by the compliments. I can even spot that occasional letter in reply to mine, feebly attempting to copy my unoriginal style. At last Tuesday's request mast, my carefully worded appeal was successful—a success that morally meant much to me. I ache to write when I'm in the mood, which is frequently.

But when I do write, I recognize my limited ability to express myself regardless of what others say. I have no confidence in myself, nothing sincerely tangible to inspire me. My inspiration is a formless mass, nothing specific that I can finger. I feel that the letters people have liked the most are forced and false.

In view of my ardor to write, I'll accept that it appeals to me. It follows then, as some have suggested, that I should do it professionally. But to write successfully and make a living at it, I must have self-confidence, talent, the ability to make discoveries, and sincerity. All these are necessary for successful authorship. I can find only the last item in myself. If I were to choose writing as a career (an unlikely possibility), I'd certainly confine myself to the classical, artistic branch of the trade. My inexperience and utter lack of belief in myself would disqualify me. And I could never stoop to writing cheap, rabble appealing, money-making trash. So, as a result of my idealism, the whole effort would be impractical and a failure. In order for me to produce a written work, to my mind it would have to be better than good, a most unlikely event.

So, liking to write, I must find an outlet for this permanent, I hope, lust. Therefore, I've found it in the realm of personal communications with friends, a few letter scraps here and there. Although writing letters satisfies me, the letters themselves don't. I wonder what I'll do once I'm home, and the outlet I now have ceases to exist.

You may have wondered why my sudden compulsion to read. While I enjoy reading, enjoyment is not my only reason for doing so. I also read to learn construction, how thoughts are expressed, how things and events are described, and about an author's style. I compare one author with another. I study an author's technique and try to apply it when I write. But when I compare my work with that of others, I'm ashamed. My own material can't compare.

When I return to school, I intend to follow the scientific course I've set for myself. I'll write only for my own amusement and personal satisfaction. If something ever comes of what I write, I'll not be sorry, but I'll never force it.

I'm not sure whether what I've just written, my writing professionally, has ever entered your mind. If not, I'm duly embarrassed at having made such a vain presumption. If it has, I'm glad for having dealt with such a possibility.

11/10/44

Dear Mom,

It seems that our battalion newspaper is being rejuvenated after all. It will be coming out bi-weekly under new management. I was appointed a sub-reporter, assigned to write gossip which I have refused. I was astonished to hear that the forthcoming issue will include an article on the sawmill as its main feature. And when I told the chief reporter, who told me this, that it was my article, he too was astonished.

The staff is composed of college grads, experienced newsmen and publishers who, unfortunately, had been thrown into this heartless outfit long ago. I'm the youngest and least experienced staff member. I have the impression that the management aims to create a model newspaper, one good enough to have excerpts of it reprinted in universal navy pamphlets.

I was rather disheartened when the chief said that the sawmill article is being revised—changed, cut. This made me mad. I insisted that if any changes must be made in any of my articles, that I wanted to be so informed and allowed to make them, or they'll never get another word out of me. The chief backed down, and made some

concessions. I don't blame the editors for revising the article, because
I too disliked it. I prefer that they toss it into the wastebasket, rather
than botch it up and distort what I submitted.

My next article will be on the amphitheater. It won't be forced
like the one on the sawmill, which I admit is a lousy article. I can enjoy
writing this one. So help me, if they cut it to pieces, they can write
their own articles. I'm as independent as hell, and they actually
respect me for it. Although I don't take my contribution to the paper
seriously, my innate pride causes me to revolt against any attempt at
distorting anything I scribble. I'd certainly like to work full time at the
paper, but no such luck: I'm only a kid.

P.S. Latest expression: Seabees now say, "I'm a duck, Wac, Wac,
Wac."

11/13/44

Dear Mom,

I've just turned the last page of *Jean-Christophe*. It is
indescribable, like a beautiful melody, the work of a genius. It has
affected me deeply. I caught the point of the story, but won't discuss it
here. Whatever flaws it has are hidden. It's about truth, love and life.
Before I die I shall read it again.

No other book that I've read, or know about, has told about the
eternal struggle of existence with more clarity and depth. When a
writer can put music into words, when he can write such last words as
"And the child answers: I am the day soon to be born," he has written
a great work.

The plot, the story itself, is spectacular. I was immediately taken
with it because of the recurrence of Jewish and religious problems.
Examples of both the foibles and worthiness of the Jews appear in its
pages. Listen to this: "The Jews have been true to their sacred mission,
which is, in the midst of other races, to be a foreign race, the race
which, from end to end of the world, is to link up the network of
human unity. They break down the intellectual barriers between the
nations, to give Divine Reason an open field."

The seemingly insignificant characters in the book are portrayed
as thoroughly as any principal character in a modern novel. Even the
ways of an upholsterer, one of the subsidiary characters in the story,
whose ways you and I know, are accurately presented.

This is a story of the river of life that empties into the
unfathomable depths of a vast, infinite sea. I am not waxing poetic to

impress. I felt what I'm saying. I felt both the sorrow and joy as if they were one and the same.

Of the meager number of books I've read so far, three stand out and will always remain with me. They are Lion Feutchwanger's[1] *Paris Gazette*,[2] Tolstoy's *War and Peace*, and Rolland's *Jean Christophe*. All three have a universal quality. Hugo's *Les Miserables* almost qualifies for this list of books that deal with the incarnation of the human soul, except that it lacks the sound of the modern trumpet.

One of my friends corresponds with a Worcester girl. He showed me one of her letters. A high school senior, she has girlish dreams of being an author. Indeed, the thought of becoming famous overwhelms her. Her work, which has appeared in her high school's paper and is highly prized by her teachers, is mediocre. However, she thinks she has talent. She included in her letter a few excerpts of her published writing. They showed neither originality nor style, but they reveal an aesthetic sense. She loves music (which remains to be seen) and attends concerts regularly. She loves art (which also remains to be seen) and wishes she could paint.

Good lord, am I like that—without ability and clarity of thought and only inspiration? This girl, I suspect, is going through a fanciful stage, which will inevitably lead to an appreciation for the arts, but not necessarily talented creativity. I may be of the same mettle, caught up in the same fancifulness, deceiving myself, having only the desire to write and nothing more. Desiring to achieve is but a small fraction of actual achievement. Many beautiful works have been written in the mind by those who lacked the desire to put them on paper. They had the ability; their desire was far less important.

Four letters arrived yesterday: two from home, one each from Johnson and Lenny. The career news you sent does not help. It tells me nothing. To some extent the article is discouraging, not so much for what it says, but because you sent it. You know that I'm uncertain and wavering. I know that you consider the field I've chosen impractical. While you sanction my pursuing it, your presentiments are not encouraging. While you feel I shouldn't, I feel I should try science. If I didn't I'd never forgive myself. It doesn't necessarily mean that after graduating college, I'll enter the scientific field. I may not. I'll at least discover whether I'm suited to follow a career in chemistry or physics. Even if I do well in college science, I still may not pursue a scientific career. I'd like to go to Worcester Tech or MIT,[3] explore, flounder about, and make up my mind then. I suppose I'm not being in the least practical letting the future decide for me. But that's the way I want it.

Ronnie's letter hit the mark. I start grinning from the D in Dear, and it's guaranteed that I'm laughing before I'm done. And if you think that I keep his humor to myself, you're entirely mistaken. I share it with my friends. Whether Ronnie is embarrassed by my doing so, he must understand that it is the price he must pay for being so funny.

Yes, I'm thinner. The tropics exacts its toll. I'm not aware of any maturing. I'm impatient to receive photos of you. Thanks for buying a Christmas card to send to Mrs. Linfield.

Dad, Uncle Lou and Uncle Hy have a great time arguing with one another. Two years ago I'd listen to them with my undivided attention. Now I would be amused. I haven't lost my argumentative nature. It's only that I now restrain it.

Johnson writes, "But honest, I enjoy hearing from you, whom I consider one of my best friends." And to think I knew him only a scant three months before I left. He is one of my best friends, too.

P.S. Better watch your step, Dad. Ronnie has duplicated your handwriting exceptionally well. I'd advise keeping all check books away from him.

11/16/44

Dear Mom,

In contrast to my letters of a week or so ago, this is a happy one. Today has been full of good news and wonderful gifts.

Both my glasses and the gorgeous watch strap arrived. Surprised doesn't describe my feelings. I gazed at the watch strap for a full five minutes before daring to put it on. And once I had it on, I tried to get everyone to ask me the time so I could show it off. What's wrong is, it's far too nice for out here, and I fear it cost too much. However, since I'm crazy about it, it didn't take long for me to dismiss those reservations. They come no better than my folks.

Other packages followed: talcum powder, hair oil and film. Everything perfect. Then *Strange Fruit* from Mrs. Ringer, then another package from Lil containing more talcum powder and hair oil with three excellent pocket books and some goodies. This is the second package from her in less than a month. Now my supply of toilet articles is sufficient to start my own "ship's store." It's wonderful of everybody. I really do enjoy the gifts.

Before I recovered from the unfamiliar gleam of the watch strap, there was more good news. The skipper summoned me to his office for an interview with a chief warrant officer. My appeal to him did the trick. A job finally became available. After asking me a few questions, the chief warrant officer seemed satisfied. My work at the sawmill, especially the machine work, impressed him. He asked how I'd like to train as a grease monkey and mechanic on a harbor dredge. I would, of course. The skipper pointed out that I'd be learning a trade, able to strike for a rerate, and have a secure position with no more switching from job to job —under the condition, of course, that my work would prove satisfactory—which I intend it to be. Many would give a lot to have this opportunity. The work, which isn't easy, probably involves more responsibility than the crane oiler's job that I was angling for several months ago. But I'm sure I'll like it. I want a real man's job, and that's what this is. Good-bye KP forever, I hope.

Several letters ago I mentioned the new importance of the battalion newspaper. According to the editor (to whom I give little credence), the skipper plans to advance those who do a good job. Yesterday I turned in my article on the amphitheater with a certain degree of doubt. I thought it was better than the sawmill article, which is the feature spread in the coming issue, but still not good enough. I was surprised to learn indirectly from an authentic source that it made a hit with the editor and would be the big splash replacing the sawmill article. Good lord, here I am competing with myself. I'm astonished that none of the other reporters had submitted big splash articles. Why, I could turn out an article a day, at least one a week anyway. Now, I'm formulating another article in my mind. Notice that the enclosed picture of the theater, snapped a few days after the Bob Hope show, was taken from the road above. The bay lies beyond the trees. Once this area was a wooded ravine. The entire place was inundated with a sea of men during the show.

Your long letter arrived. I don't condemn the service women for being aloof. On the contrary, I resent their familiarity. They are far from aloof. The nightly dating here is shameful. There's a war going on, I say, so each and every person should be doing his job, especially here. This is no place for courting and God knows what else. Everyone will be happier when we move to unsettled territory again.

Ronnie should join the navy and get out on his own. Then Dad would appreciate him more. Of course, because of his young age, that's impossible. What in the devil does Dad expect from the kid? He made a mistake with me, and I felt it. Because of the way he trained me I would have trouble working for someone else. Leave Ronnie alone; he means well; let him use his own initiative. I repeat, Ronnie is going through exactly what I went through. Dad means half what he says and is convinced it's true.

I maintain that it would be a good idea were Ronnie to get a part time job elsewhere. I see a number of them advertised in the local paper. Since Ronnie doesn't take to studying, he wouldn't be deprived on that score.

I have one hundred dollars on the books, twenty-five are on the way and another twenty-five are due me at the end of the month. I should have well over one thousand dollars by the time I get back.

I received a letter from Helen Lyon, Al Malter's girlfriend, in Frisco, asking me to continue writing and wishing that I could be there for her wedding. Al Malter is there awaiting a medical discharge. They're getting married in December.

Then I received a letter from Al in which he wrote, "First I want to say that above all, your friendship and companionship shall always be remembered. Helen has fallen in love with your letters, son, and we both love you very much (my comment: superficially speaking, of course). Always know that in years to come I shall always be by your side ready to help or assist in any way possible to add toward your happiness and future." You may recall that Al is a wealthy man. A very sweet letter.

11/19/44

Dear Mom,

I've been on the new job three days. Here's the lowdown. The dredge, which looks like a boat with decks below, portholes and companionways, and rocks like a boat, is about two hundred feet long. Now I can honestly say that I'm no longer strictly a land sailor, although I do live ashore at present, and eat only two meals aboard. I work in the engine room in which there are two steam, three cylinder, four cycle engines, a steam generator, and several small single cylinder steam engines. The latter are under my care, with others to come as I gain more experience. My job is to keep them clean and oiled at various intervals. I wipe them down, change their oil, take them apart at designated intervals and install gaskets when necessary. Before my daily six hour stint is over, my cheeks and body are covered with a blend of grease and healthy salty sweat. We work three men per shift: an operator and handy man (which I'm learning to become), a maintenance man, and an oiler (which I am now). During a twenty-four hour period, we work six hours and have eighteen hours off. I work the 6:00 AM to 12:00 M shift, thus I have more than enough leisure time.

Most important, I like the job. I'm learning satisfactorally and fast. If I wasn't mechanically inclined, I've suddenly become so. My performance on this job refutes the psychological analysis that said I wasn't.[1]

It's hot below in the engine room, damn hot, but the ventilation system is efficient enough to make it bearable. I don't have to attend to things every minute. Between tasks I go on deck, browse, go below again and sit in the ventilated portion of the room. Now, I'm officially a member of the black gang, and like it. I'm content. If I do well, and I think I will, it's my job for keeps. The skipper, who has visited the ship a few times while I've been on duty, observed my satisfaction with the new job.

I haven't written for several days, because I'm moving into a "bachelor apartment," a neat place. Building it has kept me from writing to you. The floors are plyboard, the walls screened in; it's high and dry, in the shade, near showers and the chow hall, has electricity and affords me privacy. Oh, it has about everything a bachelor could ask for. Now I can read and write without being disturbed by thoughtless mates. I'm free to do what I please such as lights out early, if I wish. No more card games to all hours, no more noise. Many of the boys who also seek such privacy have built similar apartments throughout the area beneath tents situated on a slope. Henry Wolf has one which is where I've been reading all day, because my tent was too noisy. My other chum, Ray Albrecht, just built one and so have dozens of other fellows built their quaint private apartments.

When I want company, I simply visit a chum, or, as most often happens, they drop by and visit me. Besides the cabinet that I've built with a hinged door, I'm also planning to build a comfortable easy chair with a small portable board to lay across its arms that will serve as my desk. That way, unlike with a desk, I can read, write and relax in solid comfort. There will be an inkstand extending from the right arm. When I get home, perhaps I should have one made to order, ahem. So not only has my job improved one hundred percent, but also my living quarters.

You know one thing I've learned is that you should take care of yourself because nobody really gives a damn about you. With such a policy I've kept myself well preserved, comfortable, and my ego intact. Once it was intimated that I tended to be hermit-like. Now I'm almost that. Except for my select chums, I live as much alone as possible under the conditions that exist here and I'm happy. I'll be eating Shakespeare by the volume now, and with no disturbances, breeze through novels.

With my new hermitage and new job, I have the best combination of living and working conditions that I've ever had since being in the service — the States included. I'm curious to see how long all this will continue.

11/22/44

Dear Mom,

I haven't written for several days, but now that I'm settled I can return to writing as usual. Today I put the finishing touches on my castle, a porch, and I've installed all the comforts of a home-made hermitage. The privacy seems so strange; without the usual clatter of my mates rising, I oversleep reveille.

The two Shakespeare volumes arrived in sad condition. Both were soaked, one almost ruined. I feel bad about it, because it's absolutely uncalled for. I take much pleasure in keeping books in an unsoiled condition. I treasure them to the point that I don't care to lend them out. The damage is no one's fault, but it annoys me when I think that I didn't want the books sent.

Yetta has sent me a book, *The Forest and the Fort*,[1] which arrived in excellent condition. She enjoyed it; I doubt that I shall. Narratives, especially historical ones, bore me. I've taken to the classics and philosophical works. She meant well; all is appreciated.

Letters are arriving in dribs and drabs. Birthday cards received and loved. Thanks folks. Maybe in my 21st I'll be back there. We left the States nine months ago today, the fastest nine months of my life, thank God. About this time in 1943 you answered my telephone call from Gulfport.

While you talk of snow, our torrid weather continues. I dread returning to the cold, but how I envy you.

If Captain Tronic was living in a converted garage, you can be sure the enlisted men were living in pup tents. I know too well the service's caste system. I detest it. It angers me when I hear an officer complain. Their complaints aren't justified. Not that I wish to be smug, but civilians can't appreciate the mental anguish that free, democratic men must experience at the hands of appointed superiors who are no better than they are and often inferior. I witness this inequality all the time; I feel it. The enlisted men endure their inferior status by appearing cordial and relaxed, and actually they are happier than their officers. I think, were I an officer, my conscience would torment me.

The navy, that is the sea-going personnel, live well, and the officers live in solid comfort. A naval officer is like a pampered kitten; his hands are soft, his complexion delicate. An army officer pampers himself, but he has little to do it with. When we first arrived here, the navy enlisted men lived better than the army officers. However, the army officers were living better than their enlisted men. You can't compare navy living conditions with those of the army. Civilians simply can't know what life is like in the two services and how they compare.

My new job is going well. I've learned my way around, and I feel more confident in what I'm doing. If I've never worked hard before, I've done so in the service—and I mean, work, the rough and tough sort. I'm ready for a physically relaxed college life, some good mental activity.

I expect to be in the service longer than I ever anticipated—well over two years. I hate having to waste all this time. I'll be getting a late start, more reason to cram and digest everything. Of course, it's silly to predict how I'll be, but I expect I'll be an introverted, unsociable student again. At this point, it would be a pleasure to fall back into my old rut.

11/23/44

This noontime in the chow line I was reminded of Thanksgiving back home as turkey and cranberry sauce was being heaped on my tray. How well I remember our past Thanksgiving dinners with the folks from Boston, and Grandpa Sam's nap after the meal, and further back, our dinners with Uncle Bill and Aunt Tiabe at their restaurant[1] in Fitchburg. I wonder when I'll be able to partake of our next great dinner, when I'll smell the aroma of the food from the moment I awake, and when Dad will be sitting at the lefthand corner of the folding table.

Many of the fellows are running about in their whites this evening, the first time they've worn them since Gulfport. It's the opening night of the men's swanky dance pavilion—Club Tropicana— the first nightclub in these parts. What next?

This week our theater has been host to three shows. The first was a series of wrestling matches. The staged matches were a riot, and our catcalling audience would put any in Brooklyn[2] to shame. The wrestlers growled and groaned, and bathed in sweat slithered all over one another as the hecklers, growing hoarse, screamed to goad them on. No doubt the excited, unthinking hecklers embarrassed the WACs in the audience. Such language!

A troupe of famous Broadwayites (unknown to me) put on a play last night. Although it was mediocre—one can't expect to have the finest here—everyone enjoyed it. It offered us a happy contrast with our New Guinea living. We saw men dressed in business suits, and a divan for the first time since leaving the States.

Tonight an amateurish comedy act bored me, but there were some good laughs. Lately, we've seen some more recent movies such as "An American Romance."[3] Last summer's pictures are being shown.

Off to the sack and a good night's sleep.

                                                                11/24/44

Dear Mom,

Now that I have absolute quiet, I sleep so gloriously soundly that reveille hasn't the faintest effect. I rise way late, dress as you've never seen, and wildly dash to work, usually forgetting to mail the letters I wrote the previous night. So here are two letters in one.

Because by habit we now follow the beaten paths that weave through the camp area, the rest of the area that we once trampled on is now sprouting grass and small tropical ferns. Their presence, especially their green fragrance, makes the place more pleasant. Why, this evening there's even a flower sticking out of my canteen.

During the past few months, there have been announcements concerning the new fathers in our outfit. Although they have no cigars to hand out, their beaming faces say it all. Soon, however, our men will want no more babies. They had better come now. If later, what consequences. Some of our men are frightened.

My job continues to go well. I'm learning about steam engines through practice. Before I leave the service, I should be thoroughly familiar with them. Whereas once I respected, even feared a little, their hammering motion, now the mechanical pounding and hissing is comfortably familiar. Engines are truly powerful things. I still respect their power, but in a more friendly way.

I visited our Club Tropicana this noon. It's quite cozy and romantic at night. Rumor has it that once you mention to a Wac you're a 113th man, she is so pleased that a date is certain.

I'm sorry that I neglected writing, very sorry. I have no excuse. I simply lacked ambition; I was in the grip of a mildly depressed mood some weeks back. I promise faithfully to renew my jabber.

I don't expect mail at every call. No letters? So what. I'm comforted knowing that some are on the way.

P.S. Had turkey aboard the dredge today.

11/27/44

Dear Mom,

Nothing new, nothing old;
Nothing gay, nothing bold;
Nothing seen, nothing done;
Yet the war is being won.
We know naught of the war,
Care naught of the peace;
It's love that we need
To put us at ease.
So time does pass,
Quite fast, at that.
Home, our goal:
Fast—how slow.

This describes our present situation. I scribbled spontaneously and that's what came out.

Whenever a unit becomes idle and manpower is overabundant, anxiety develops. We'd rather be building, escape from the gradual influx of --------, the laziness, the Americanization of our once free ways, and play a part in the conduct of the war. While at home progress is beneficial, out here it's the ruination of nature's virginity. Once the beaches were so clean; now they're covered with oil slick. Once the green foliage was bright and clean; now it's dulled with red dust. Once our area was like a countryside; now it's neither country nor urban, only civilized.

On our stage last night a navy band, consisting of members from other big name bands, played for about an hour. Since everyone said they were good, they must have been. I don't enjoy swing as much as I used to, so I was bored. Rather, I was amused, very much so. If I find it hard to be pleased with the entertainment offered, I take heart in knowing that a higher caliber form of entertainment is available, which, someday, I'll be able to witness.

Tonight, for two weeks, I work a pretty tough shift: 12:00 midnight to 6:00 AM

11/28/44

Dear Mom,

Strange Fruit being so short and easy to read, it didn't take me long to finish it. You wrote, "I was disgusted," Johnson wrote, "Smith [Lillian Smith, the author] was far short of her goal," and someone as young as Beverly Ringer would be confused, partly awakened, finding its message vague.

First, the author. Her style fits the story which she makes easy to understand in spite of her task of having to express a confusion of ideas. She knows her facts; she knows what she's writing about, and does it well, although hardly in the manner of a classic. No doubt she was inspired to write about her subject. Her ideas and feelings come across beautifully. She uses quaint and clever phrases, and she's exceptionally observant and sensual. She is not a poor writer.

Her story. I recall once how uneasy we all were when a group of us were sitting in a car as we headed back to Providence, and one of our members, a thoughtful, educated man suddenly remarked, "If every man were to be sued for mental rape,"—he laughed—"we'd all be in prison." Some of us giggled, some squirmed, and all of us felt uncomfortable. He spoke an undeniable truth which we chose to deny. This book, the reaction to it, and that incident are one and the same.

I'd like to meet that person who, once having started the book, laid it down unfinished. I'd brand any high moralist that did so a coward, and any low person, one who has a guilty conscience.

As there are all kinds of people, so there are all kinds of artists and writers. All are specialists who believe their specialty is best suited to them, either romanticism, realism or unrestrained naturalism. In each case the writer is deeply sincere in practicing the art of his specialty. Smith, Steinbeck, and numerous others express their inspiration in the realm of naked naturalism. This is their call to art. What they write can be as beautiful to some readers as any Tennyson[1] poem.

The real question is: should readers, the non-artists, be told the truth? People yearn for the truth; still, when it appears, their narrowness surfaces, and they deny it, reject it. Yet, they continue to yearn and read and digest and learn. Convention, an artificial construction from the word go, is a restraining force that restricts the mind's freedom. Freud,[2] the gospel of psychology, insists that such restraint is the cause of much unhappiness.

Here is a book that speaks the truth, bares the facts that we know to exist, hides nothing, uses four letter words because they are commonly used, yet, its readers hate (and love) to be told what they already know or suspect. People only pretend to seek the truth while continually running away from it.

Nothing in the book was new to me. To tell the truth, I've heard of things many times worse. I live among men who are ignorant and educated, clever and ridiculous, brilliant and stupid. Every man has some substance to him, some wisdom, something to give. So has the book.

The book can't initiate anything; it's just a matchstick in the edifice. The author attempts to solve no problem. The enigma of our nation and of the world is far greater than we are. While the author acknowledges this greatness, she doesn't show it enough, and misses a point here and there, but she's aware.

Religion condemns what's false and seeks to uphold the truth. And with this book the lay reader condemns what's true, calling it filthy. They want to see only a crystal pool, but if it were examined through a microscope it would reveal horrible and fantastic micro-organisms. I don't condemn this book, nor call it disgusting. It's art, the truth, only a sliver in a matchstick edifice, and something worthy.

How few of us are without hypocrisy. Let those who wish, express their views of the human story. Just because I dislike a picture, I refuse to ban or obliterate it. It still reveals a human truth.

End of lecture.

[Hughie's 20th birthday] 11/30/44

Dear Mom,

A year ago I breathed to the click of wheels on rails. Farewell South, hello West. It doesn't seem possible — a year already.

My watch is on the blink again. The repairman told me it would happen. The watch needed a new part which he didn't have. I sent it home this afternoon via air mail. Fix it immediately and send it right back. I feel as if I've lost one of my senses.

Lately, my job has been a racket. The dredge is under repair so I have nothing to do. I work only when the engines run. Fortunately, the breakdown has happened on my turn at the despicable graveyard shift: 12:00 M to 6:00 AM. For the past four days the routine has been easy and pleasant: report to work at midnight, eat a couple of steak sandwiches, at about 2:00 AM wend my way back to camp, hit the sack at 3:00, sleep 'til noon, eat chow, read and write letters all afternoon, take supper, watch a show, have a midnight snack then back to work again. You understand, of course, that once repairs are completed, it's back to work I go.

Don't be alarmed if within the next month, my letters suddenly cease coming. I may be busy, you know, busier than I've ever been. Nothing definite, just a premonition.

I received a nice birthday card from Grandma. It was very thoughtful of her. Nowadays birthdays are so easily forgotten.

Before long, I'll be returning some of the books I've already read. I'm beginning to accumulate a library. I'll keep the volume of Shakespeare, the one in the worst condition.

The mail has been slow for everybody. It's to be expected, though.

12/1/44

Dear Mom,

The birthday cards from Grandma and Sadie were perfectly timed. I had forgotten what day it was until they reminded me. Your letters arrived, a fortuitous present. I dislike this being twenty. Time is passing too quickly. I'm losing track of it. I would prefer that these past two years were outside of time, never happened, and that I could return home to my eighteenth birthday and begin again wiser. I've got to work fast once I get out. I mean, I have no hold on the passage of time. Once, in my ignorance, time held still; now its passage is frightening.

[Cousin] Sol is a sadist, always enhancing his own ego, having to continually prove himself right, and in a way offensive to his victims. I used to take him seriously. Now I laugh—and you should, too. My letter to him, written some time ago in a foolish condescending fit, hardly flattered the old boy, but it wasn't sarcastic either. I'd never admit being an "apron string"[1] boy, even if I were. Sol must suspect that I remained at home of my own free will. No one encouraged me to go out more than you. I chose to stay in; no one kept me in. I was more willful than you suspected. I usually did what I felt like doing, which wasn't much. Still, I say again that once I became involved in my studies, it was impossible to become active socially. If I can't apply myself to something with all my energy, I see no use in bothering with it. A social and intellectual life are in direct conflict. Some boys can be honor students, athletes, and handsome swains at the same time—at least, so they say. I cannot. More than likely my studies will possess me again.

I see nothing wrong with Nason's momentary infatuation, if, after it's all over, he has learned from it. It does a boy good to get that way. The letdown will be instructive. Nason is too spoiled to be thoughtful yet.

I don't get all the hullabaloo and ceremony over circumcision. It seems rather ridiculous to me, a silly custom—the ceremony,[2] I mean.

I'm pleased to see that you're getting involved in the social whirl, even if somewhat subdued. I hope you'll enjoy it. I never did like social organizations. They are petty, expensive, and sophisticated. But in your case, I approve, as if my opinion makes much difference.

Everyone here will be happy to learn that duck[3] [a heavy fabric] for the tents is in full production. Practically every tent roof in the area is leaking. They take terrific punishment from the torrential rains and penetrating sunshine.

Ronnie's letter did it again—a laughter sensation. No comment on his grades. He'll do alright. His drawing is good. The bookcase looks swell. Those shelves will be filled to overflowing, if I have my way. The sketch of the living room made me homesick. I rocked with laughter at Dad's chair, seemingly suspended in mid-air. Make it more oblique, Ronnie. That'll fix it. Let's have more of this kind of stuff—letters and drawings.

You guessed well, Mom. Very good. God what WAC specimens they take pictures of. Dating is forever popular here. I'm sure you know what I mean when I say that the WACs come in all conceivable and inconceivable varieties.

I have the impression that you are trying hard not to offend me, even apologizing for making suggestions. Never fear. Blast me all you want. In many instances, I've applied the wrong tactics while in the service. Don't hesitate to tell me so. There's no one here to censure me, so let loose whenever you wish. I'll not take offense, I guarantee. Dad knows his mistakes but won't admit them. I'm not like that, at least not to his extreme. I've had to admit my mistakes here. I've never forgotten that I lost my laboratory job because I refused to admit a mistake. But we all like Dad, despite his stubbornness. Without it he wouldn't be Dad.

I feel triumphant inside knowing that my most recent tactic has been expedient and successful. I'm most satisfied with my present position. I owe it to my own initiative—a rare occurrence with me.

Out here wearing things on the wrist is not wise. Perspiration always runs down your arm onto it. Until I received your elegant gift I used to hang my wristwatch from the buttonhole of my shirt collar, or from my trouser belt. A bracelet would never do while on my job, during which my hands are often submerged in oil and gasoline. I have enough sense not to tell Sadie. I'll send her a thank you letter and wear the bracelet when I visit her in Boston. As I've said, anybody wanting to send me a book should send me a classic or a best seller.

The book Yetta sent offers mental relief after what I've been reading. It's strictly narrative, requires no pondering, and flows along easily. It holds my interest all the way through. While Hervey Allen is not a great writer, compared with those I've been reading, he is a marvelous unraveler of tales.

Last week I saw Eugene O'Neill's[4] "The Hairy Ape,"[5] with William Bendix[6] and Susan Hayward.[7] It was quite good, much better than the run of pictures lately that insult our intelligence. The acting was excellent, the plot unique, and its significant message clever. I read in *Time* that "None but the Lonely Heart"[8] by Richard Llewelyn[9] with Cary Grant,[10] Ethel Barrymore, and Barry Fitzgerald,[11] is extraordinary. *Time* has a severe critic, so it must be good. The plot sounds intriguing.

Well, well, this is my longest letter in many a day. Every so often I find that I've missed discussing many things in past letters, and suddenly they all come together in a single letter.

P.S. Enclosed find money order.

12/1/44

Dear [Cousin] Lil,

I've never been able to forget it.

About sixteen years ago, after coming down with scarlet fever, while recovering from a mastoid operation, I was an invalid for several months.[1] I was truly at a low ebb. Only two things that happened then made me happy. One was when I heard the racket my father's Model T made on the drive outside, and he dashed into my lonely hospital room smelling of the cold outdoors. The other was receiving a vase of flowers, a purple vase I think. At dusk, as the nurse removed them from the room, I cried. Comforting me, she promised to return them in the morning. But when she did, the vase was different. They weren't the same flowers. Disappointed, I screamed, until she brought in the flowers in the purple vase. They were your flowers. You probably never realized what they meant to me.

Now, after sixteen years, you're giving again. Two packages containing exactly what I want, and like, arrived this past month. Whenever I receive a package, I feel somewhat awkward, because I'm incapable of showing my appreciation. I'm like the sincere beggar who can't do enough to repay his benefactor. I'm in a muddle, bungling my intentions.

Some give because it's patriotic—though it isn't necessarily—and others feel obliged to give; but for you, giving is a natural thing, a pleasure to do.

Frankly, I like to receive only when I know that the giver loves giving. Feeling this way, I enjoy your gifts. They celebrate my service career. But please, don't be so generous again. I'm beginning to feel embarrassed.

The books are perfect, the candy is perfect, and the toilet articles filled a sore gap. Everything was perfect. Thanks. You must be a mental telepathist. Everything was exactly what I wanted.

Hughie

12/3/44

Dear Mom,

There have been some changes proposed that will greatly alter my position in the service—I'm quite sure for the better. Nothing is definite, just a possibility, although a plausible one. Not only could this lead to an automatic advance in rate, but also the entrance into an entirely different and separate unit. I hope it goes through.

The arrival of an October *Gazette* stirred some memories of Fairbanks Street [Hughie's childhood neighborhood] of fifteen years ago. I see that Muriel Bergstrom[1] has received a scholarship to Clark. I read that right along classmates—both boys and girls—are doing alright for themselves in college. It's a paradox that in high school many of them were stupid.

From experience and from watching others, I'm now much less inclined to see marks as a measure of intelligence and knowledge. In high school, realizing that scholastic achievement can be mechanical and not derived from intelligence, I secretly had contempt for grades. But I wanted them, and often received good ones with an uneasy conscience. They were necessary to help shape my future. But I felt I didn't particularly deserve many of my marks. I didn't know what I should have known to have received them.

Now, having had practical experience in the service, I have less respect for marks. They can be so false. I refuse to consider them a factor in ensuring my ambitious future. So I've resolved to damn my past honors,[2] or any that may come, or any praise. I'm happy to remain on the safe side of the border. The subject's the thing; honest application's the thing, absorbing knowledge is the thing. Nothing else counts, regardless of the consequences.

Whether he knows it or not, Dad has espoused this doctrine. Ronnie corroborates it. He is not stupid. If I can keep this idea in mind, I'll be able to study much more freely. In other words my incentive will be the acquisition of knowledge, not meritorious standards.

12/4/44

Dear Mom,

Last night nobody swooned when Sinatra appeared in "Step Lively,"[1] but there was sarcasm and mimicking and at intervals, cries of "Oh, Frankie" from various sections of an amused audience. Some of the music was pleasant and catchy, but the lyrics were poor. The picture was one great farce, at points insulting to one's intelligence, but then that's what appeals the most. Its ridiculousness gave me a few good laughs and Gloria DeHaven wasn't distasteful to the eye. I'd like to see at least one really good picture.

The *Veterans of Foreign Wars* magazine that arrived today comprehensively discusses the Veterans Administration's educational program. It seems that it's in the bag for me. I'm assured of at least three years at government expense—one year plus the length of time in the service. With a $50.00 per month stipend, I should be able to save enough for a fourth year. All the money I have at present are savings and should be put to work. If Dad can use it for the business, it's his. It would surely be a worthwhile investment.

My staleness at studying will be a terrific handicap. I'll have to study doubly hard. It's no use studying here—the situation is against it. I'm afraid I've forgotten much. Going to college has become more of a challenge than an ambition. The future will be so interesting—a great test.

Nothing has been confirmed regarding my change of status. If I'm to be considered for advancement, I'll be competing with two others. I'm learning all I can, eating it up, watching every move that my boss makes. It's important that I know more and work harder than my competitors. I'm seeing to it. Last night, my boss, who is Dad's age, put me wise to a few things, little things that add up to bigger ones. My task is good experience for the future. The more I learn, the easier it is for him and the better for me. So we have a mutual agreement: he teaches, I learn.

12/5/44

Dear Mom,

I just returned from seeing "His Butler's Sister,"[1] which is probably ancient to you. The plot is meager but interesting. I left enthused over D. Durbin's (most assuredly operatic) voice. Despite a few scenes that were too long, it was well done. It was another of those pleasant evenings in which I'm happily entertained.

Again, I wish to remind you that shortly my letters will be less frequent. Soon I expect to be terribly busy. Meanwhile I'll write daily.

Send me airmail stamps. Although it's not official yet, I think my new job is definitely a permanent assignment.

Here I am sitting in solid N.G. comfort, tapping my nails, drawing caricatures with my pen that stubbornly refuses to produce words. Tonight there's nothing else for me to write about. It just one of those times when thoughts are impossible to summon. Forgive me for this, such a short letter.

12/7/44

Dear Mom,

I just returned from seeing "Mr. Skeffington."[1] Well done, very well done. The story, as with so many stories, demonstrates the ironic twists of fate. But in spite of its unoriginal theme, the characters, the setting and the situations were good. And the acting was superb. Claude Rains was clever, original, and dignified, while Bette Davis was at her best in a role that suited her. Despite an occasional scene that dragged, I enjoyed it very much.

It's been a long time since I've received five letters all at once, as I did today. There were two from you, one from faithful Johnson, Aunt Ida, and, believe it or not, from [Cousin] Evelyn Aaron.[2] Just when I'm at the point of weeding out those who fail to reply, new people are starting to write. Besides Evelyn, another teacher from school, an art teacher whom I knew only casually, has begun writing, and I hadn't studied art. Oh, I don't mind, but eventually I must weed out others. Someone suddenly mentions my name, and it reminds them they must write. The war effort, you know. Help the boys over there. Most people generally dislike writing, and I don't blame them. Only at rare ambitious moments are letters usually written.

If Mr. Mayo [a former teacher] is so interested in having me write him, it wouldn't be difficult for the old boy to send me his address. Ralph [Mayo] is a fine fellow, though. I'd like to drop him a line.

Funny thing—I requested that you send me a padlock, and now the store just secured a supply of them. The same thing happened with the stationery, hair oil and powder. The store was without these items for months. Just write that an item is on the way, and pop, it appears on the counter here.

From instinct, or from whatever compels me, I can't begin a letter at its climax. I take pleasure in leading up to one. It's a good way to keep you going to the end. If I revealed the big news first—what the devil—it wouldn't pay to include the rest of the nonsense.

There's no need to discuss my interview before the skipper some time ago. It's now past, and things have turned out well. However, to put you at ease, I'll explain some of what happened.

One night a week is reserved for making requests to the battalion commander. An application for making a request must first be approved by the company commander. My company commander was at a show on request night when he should have been in his office on duty to approve applications. After waiting several hours for him, I got mad. Since I didn't want to postpone my visit to the skipper for another week, (and luckily I didn't), I decided to see the skipper without the company commander's approval. The skipper, seeing that I had no prior approval and that the company commander wasn't on the job, sent for him at the show. I had hoped for the company commander's sake, not my own, that the skipper wouldn't notice that the company commander's signature was missing. You see, even if my C.O. had objected, I can still see the skipper over his objection, which, of course, is not a prudent thing to do. The C.O. was doggone mad, especially at me, perhaps because he missed seeing the end of a good picture, and for being caught off the job. He must have felt that I should have waited a week for him rather than see the commander without his consent. But in my judgment it seemed important to see the skipper that night. I was keyed up for it. I was even more determined after finding the C.O. not on the job. Why should I suffer another detestable week on KP because of his negligence?

It has turned out that I did exactly the right thing, because now you can see the wonderful results. My C.O has little if no jurisdiction over me. He can't hinder me. I have no intention of squaring myself with him, or kissing his ass, because he was negligent. I can't apologize to someone whom I don't respect. Furthermore, the apology is due me. He should apologize for not being on duty that night, doing his duty to his men. From now on I deal with the highest authority — the skipper.

[The censor had cut out the next few sentences. The letter continues as follows.]

---- stripping the engines down, --------. I now see how they go together. I enjoy stripping their works and reassembling them — much of it by myself. At the start, I didn't know a damn thing about it, but, before I was done, I could do it blindfolded. I removed the main bearings today, washed them down, and placed them back in the engine perfectly. My boss, who lets me work by myself, is anxious to teach me. He says I catch on fast. I use tools that I've never seen, and toss out terms such as wrist pin bearings, concentric connecting rods etc. that I've never heard before. I'm usually plastered in a comical way with grease — nothing that soap and water doesn't take off. I'm getting a great kick out of the whole experience.

I've made a few mistakes, nothing especially stupid, rather from ignorance, but I usually manage to discover them before anybody else does. Once in a while the boss catches me and laughs, I with him. For instance, he has sent me looking for a tool I've never heard of, and doesn't describe it clearly. I then return with some unearthly contraption, but, after I see what he wants the tool for, I use my bean, and try to figure out what it would look like. Now, I pretty well know what tools to use when I'm working by myself. During the past few weeks I've learned much. I don't yet know how to operate the engines, but I watch the operators closely in case something goes wrong. We shall see.

As I've said, there wasn't much of a chance that the *West Point* would be attacked. Its course was so serpentine that nothing could follow it, and its speed was far too fast for a tracking sub. The ship never stopped. The chance of an attack on it was one in a million. If only you could see the route we took. I've seen it on the chart. We went almost as far south as New Zealand.

You know, I think I say too much. Right away you jump to conclusions when I make a statement such as, "Good health is a blessing out here." After all, you know that the tropics are not the healthiest of climes. Without my going into detail, you should only heed the statement, "I feel swell, look healthy and tanned, and sleep gloriously soundly." If I return from the war as I am now, you'll find your son healthy if somewhat thinner. Be at ease. That's a mother for you, tch, tch. Never fear, my dear. This boy has learned to take care of himself (but not over confidently). Living right is the key to survival here, as it is anywhere, for that matter.

P.S. Gad, how atrocious my penmanship is tonight.

12/9/44

Dear Mom,

While nothing lavish, nor, for that matter, anything that I would have ever considered living in two years ago, my new home is a comfortable, even cozy, shelter from rain, mud, and people. I find it difficult to describe such simple, yet satisfying, quarters. To someone who has grown up surrounded by plastered walls, rugs, furniture, and everything else that makes a home civilized, my quarters would normally be appalling. One must live in the tropics for a time to realize that I'm really quite comfortably fixed. Because you haven't, there's no point in going into details about the place.

After you've been here long enough, you soon learn that if you want something, you must go after it, not illegally, but cleverly. I had no difficulty in finding materials to build this abode. In war, waste is rampant, but often the waste can be put to good use. Locate the waste, and you can find all the materials you need. Thus my small fraction of a home.

What a pleasure it will be to see your new living room. I wonder how new it will be when I finally do see it. I fear it won't be very new. Even were so much time to pass that the room begins to show scratches, cracks appear in the ceiling, the wallpaper grows dingy, plants mark the painted bookcases, even were time to drag as every moment adds an extra scratch and crack, and you'd be disappointed because the room's new luster has faded, and it's no longer new when I arrive, remember, Mom, that time passes frightfully fast for me, sweetly frightfully, and that as the room struggles to remain new as the months go by, those long months are but short moments for me. They are short, yes, I'm certain, because I'm comfortably unconcerned with the present. My present concern is only linked to the desire to see and learn.

Of course, the dredge works out in the bay, sometimes near docks, sometimes close to a beach, other times farther out. While the engines are running, I have a simple routine, but while the dredge isn't in operation I'm involved in repairing the engines, the most interesting part. Right now we're in the repairing phase, and I'm having fun doing it. I've always wondered what the insides of one thing or another look like; now I'm finding out. Nothing boring in that, is there? I like a job that has variety, that has something constantly new, something that I haven't seen before, something that challenges me. Ever since the battalion was formed, I've been a laborer. Being one is a monotonous ordeal. Actually, most jobs are. And I dislike monotonous ordeals. Only were I poverty-stricken, would I become an automaton, a lifetime user of my hands, a laborer. Meanwhile, I enjoy my laboring. I enjoy feeling what it's like, because I have no intention of making it permanent. I hope fate feels about it as I do. As soon as the job tends to become monotonous, I begin thinking and resort to my creative pleasures, my reading etc. I still stick to the job, waiting for the day when all will be final, finished. Now that my position is satisfying, I'm resigned.

After a day on the job, I'm quite tired, and for pleasure seek lighter entertainment—the movies. I've given up trying to complete the math course. Having no ambition to do so, I don't force myself. I have no desire to exercise or work out—my work leaves little strength for it—so I'm getting no thinner and becoming flabbier. I'm not concerned. It's next to impossible to keep in condition out here.

I'm having difficulty finding a camera. I had used Henry's but now he's gone.[1] I requested that you send two film sizes, 616 and 127, in case this happened. Unfortunately, you sent only one size, the size that fitted Henry's camera. My other friend's camera requires 616 film. Now I'm searching for a camera that uses 127 film. I may not be successful.

I would feel much better were I to have all three volumes of Shakespeare in good condition. One is in perfect condition and the other two, although the pages and binding were soaked, are legible. I shall be reading them for my enjoyment, but I'd like to have better ones—the comedies and histories and poems—on our bookshelf at home. Two dollars doesn't seem much, after I had spent so extravagantly back in the States. This way I wouldn't worry about the marred volumes I keep with me.

You may think it ridiculous that I take such pride in owning books. I confess I like seeing them in perfect condition, on hand, and ready to be consulted at any time. It's one of my pleasures. This should explain my demands here.

You may recall that I requested a dictionary for my tenth birthday. Even at that age I knew whether a book was good or bad. Although I knew you had bought me a poor dictionary, I still delighted in owning it. It was still in pretty good condition when I left home. I continue enjoy owning and preserving books.

You have been misinformed. *The Razor's Edge*[2] is months and months old. The Book-of-the-Month Club is late with it. I've read a review of it and understand that it's written in a unique manner, that it's almost not a novel.

I'm now prepared to send several books back home, but, alas, I can't find any wrapping paper. I'll hold them until some packages arrive.

By the way, this letter answers yours of 11/30. The mail is arriving regularly. I'm happy.

Taps blew some time ago—10:00—and I'm feeling drowsy.

12/12/44

Dear Folks,

I'm quite embarrassed. Not only does distance make the heart grow fonder, but evidently it also inflates the esteem one has for another. Such remarks as "Nothing seems too good for you," and similar words both flatter me and make me feel guilty. I appreciate the sincerity of your loving sentiments, but please, Mom, they, and the gifts you send, make me uncomfortable. I suspect I blush when reading your unwarranted praise. Oh, but I suppose that's a mother's love. My love is so undemonstrative.

My second and most recent story to appear in the battalion newspaper, which is still a farce as far as I'm concerned, dealt with the battalion's theater. Told with a human interest angle, it was more or less a brief history of the structure. I believe I got my point across, but, as I passed in the completed piece, I felt it wasn't so good after all. Nothing I write seems good. Before I'm halfway through a piece, I become disgusted. I'm not worried though.

Several of my lesser friends correspond with Worcester girls. For old time's sake, occasionally one of them reads me a letter. I'm not interested in who the girls are so I'm unable to tell you their names.

A word about education. Specializing is essential; a general education is a useless conglomeration of knowledge. Common sense is the best substitute for a general education. A course in a specialty serves as an inspiring stimulant.

I repeat: you have misinterpreted my innocent clause, "Good health is a blessing over here." For some nonsensical reason I included it in a letter.

Received a letter from Lil this afternoon.

SPECIAL TO RONNIE:

Dear Little Brother,

I received your amazing letter, which strangely was written in English. I found that I was quite capable of deciphering every word, but incapable of keeping a straight face. Thank you for the birthday greetings; I wish you the same, which you must keep until January 16th. The pictures of the bookcases were good, but not as good as the bookcases themselves. I congratulate you on your corkin, dandy school grades. Marks like these show that you are enjoying yourself, which I'm glad to see. I'm not paragraphing because I'm saving paper — the war effort. Replying to your horrible threat: "I'll stop writing," I say, "Wanna fight?" I get pretty well greased up on the new job, so I feel rough and tough enough to take you on, my little brother. Dad used to call you "the brat," and me, "the shloompa,"[1] but now he and Mom call me "dear son." What do they call you now? This man's navy does wonderful things for you. Through the mail you receive cake and candy deliciously flavored by the Pacific Ocean. Lucky boy am I. Do you still steal cake after dinner the way we used to? And are you making up for my absence in your raisin box raids? I hope you do; you have my permission. Dad will teach you how to play the stock market, if you wish. He's neither bull nor bear nor sheep. It's a life policy. Buy ten shares at fifty dollars, hold them for fifteen or twenty years, maybe thirty, and sell them for two dollars, or wait for them to rise by the next generation. I liked your jokes. All my friends from Iowa — the corn state — went into ecstasy over them. Send more on the cob, please do. My first name is Hugh, and how are h'you? The preceding statement is purely irrelevant, ridiculous, and whatever words an objecting lawyer uses. Okay, wise guy, you get off an elephant by jumping. I better not fill this page because of the paper shortage back there.

Your big brother, yes big, Hughie

12/14/44

Dear Mom,

Everything is fine now. I'm fine for no reason in particular — I'm just fine. Working is going along at a comfortable pace. Very odd, my present satisfaction with things, when there's still so much more ahead to make me ultra-satisfied.

This evening I saw "White Cliffs of Dover."[1] Beautifully done. Certainly you've seen it. Here is a motion picture classic. Not that its story is new. After all, it's the same old human story, but its import is great, truly great. It's a story about the greatest human incentive: hope. It makes me realize that my today's existence is worthwhile only because instinctive, sometimes cruel, hope goads me on. Hope and love, of no monetary value, are utterly free. Look at them. They can be so disappointing, so discouraging; yet after they are gone, vaporized, a miracle appears; new hope, new love rises in their place.

Such pondering is absurd. My short-lived life hardly gives time enough for me to see for myself the greatness of hope and love. And to scribble about it here is even sillier. In a week or so I'm bound to blush with shame over what I've written here.

In this fit of taking you into my confidence, I should add that religion is a parasite that breeds and nurses on hope and love. The ritual ceremony shrouds God's two greatest gifts — hope and love — in a mist. Religious worship makes excuses for bad human conduct. While reason produces agnostics and atheists, it's all beyond reason. However, in the case of hope and love, reason and instinct coincide refuting the agnostics, atheists and nihilists. All humans are God's subjects, his powerless clan, his amusing toilers. Hope and love always continue to be replaced by more hope and love. The supply is endless.

Our ego is capable of imagining great conceptions. Its force and momentum are unstoppable. Because of this I can learn tolerance.

You will pardon me, won't you?

Sunday 12/17/44

Dear Mom,

My day of rest and ease, a day on which I can comfortably unload a few gradually accumulated ideas.

My knowledge of the bustling surface of people's activities, of politics and paradox, of events, finance, and art is fairly thorough considering my tolerable remoteness from civilization. And I've been able to digest all such affairs as an immediate and unaffected observer. Unaffected by ambition, regard for the present, or romantic views of making a comfortable living, I read of world events from a neutral point of view. In other words, I feel a new quality within, an ability to come to conclusions with the least amount of bias.

The world is never stagnant. All the ages are interdependent. Neither the present, the past, nor the future can exist with one of them missing. There's always a force present, clearly visible at the peak of its momentum. From here that force appears most evident. It is the equitable distribution of wealth: Communism.

I'm not an ardent advocate of Communism, nor do I subscribe wholly to the gospel of democracy. Humanity is bypassing democracy as an intermediate step toward a more regulated, less dynamic, and more secure form of government. In its practical application Communism is becoming universal doctrine; attainment of its theoretical form is remote. Today, Communism is considered an ultra-radical form of government. In all truth, I'm for it. It's chiefly designed to lead towards an equitable distribution of wealth, according to a person's worth. There are too many forces at play, such as human egoism and fallibility, that prevent the realization of a utopian state. Communism, at least, offers a step towards that unattainable state. That's why I approve of it and would like to see its doctrine spread and eventually adopted.

I ask now, what will eventually supplant Communism after several generations and centuries? Communism, even were it to be achieved in its purest, idealistic form, is not the supreme solution. The future will not stop at Communism, just as it hasn't stopped at democracy. So as time passes, I expect to see Communism succeed. I don't expect to live long enough to see it fail. That will be left for some future generation to witness. I heartily believe that. A future generation will devise a form of government yet further advanced. Meanwhile Communism will suffice, and there will be wars per the customary order of human evolution.

Except with respect to pigmentation, whites are the same as blacks. The minds and bodies of both function alike. Both are attuned to the conventions of the times. Only their exteriors, a result of their ancestry, are different. Both races living in the same environment are without a doubt equally capable in science, art, religion, and murder. Spiritually both races have identical emotions, prejudices, and egotistical concerns. Both races have had to tolerate each other. The whites have tolerated the difference in pigmentation and a few other scant biological peculiarities, while the blacks have tolerated the whites' toleration.

On the surface, white man's thought is superior. The white man has accomplished more, perfected his art and science, more than men of any other color. The white man has created an enormous organization. His sense of superiority, ever present, is his master. And he despises, degrades, is insulted by, any foreign thing that threatens or encroaches on it. The color black is visible and foreign. Black men, with all their human foibles and ambitions, have entered into the civilized white orbit. Only love and hope are capable of eradicating the white man's superior attitude, leading to the blacks being welcomed into white society. Were love and hope to be universally practiced among whites, their sense of superiority would crumble, and all differences in color would become meaningless. When white men and women do not love black men and women, they object to their son or daughter marrying a black.

The rabbi [Levi Olan] deceived himself thinking that others would approve, when he made that apparently noble and democratic statement that he would not object were his daughter to marry a black. We are all prejudiced against a countless number of things. Our prejudices are beyond our ability to control, even though we recognize our folly in them. We seem unable to cure ourselves. They are the result of the ages. Something powerful is needed. Love is needed. Are there other powerful forces available?

The rabbi could not use the notorious four letter word, because, if he did, his lady listeners would desert him. Furthermore, his position prohibits him. Due to my dislike of vulgarity, I've never used it. I find it vulgar, because vulgar minds use it. However, were it not for its origin, I'd probably use it, and it would be included in the dictionary. Except for the article "the" that four letter word is used more often than any other by servicemen, either consciously or unconsciously, throughout a day's conversation. That's the truth. I've heard both educated and ignorant men use it in the same manner and just as often. To avoid the usage of such a word in unvarnished conversation in the text of a book, would be contrary to a book's truth.

I agree with Rabbi Olan[1] for the most part. I agree with him in view of his position in which he is restricted and often compelled to exaggerate, mollify and sentimentalize to make his point.

According to *Time*, by the way, as in Boston,[2] the U.S. Naval Academy has banned Lillian Smith's *Strange Fruit*, as well as (twentyish) Kathleen Winsor's *Forever Amber*.[3] And both books are banned in service libraries overseas.

I've been writing about every other day. Your letters are arriving regularly.

With six million men overseas, don't you think it would be quite impossible for all these men to receive their Christmas packages on December 24th? Sounds pretty difficult, doesn't it? Yeah, I guess so. So please, don't rack your brain trying to figure out why I got my Christmas packages weeks before Christmas. Consider that there's a big war on and ships must carry supplies and both shipping and warehouse space is sadly limited and six million boys expect to receive many more than six million packages and December 24th lasts only twenty-four hours, then you'll understand why I received my Christmas package early. This is the kind of statement Dad would make.

The job is going well, Mom. I'm still getting grease under my fingernails. Remember, I expect to be busy soon.

12/18/44

Dear Mom,

Tonight, I really haven't much to say. I'm just being faithful.

The same thing over and over for days on end is, according to the laws of chance, bound to break. I'm anticipating a new experience. Nobody knows what or when. We know that the war is gathering momentum and that individual units will be sucked into its vortex. All of us want to be one of those units. We're certain we will be. The end of uncertainty is a relief. Now, although the future is still speculation, at least it's something more than sickening repetition.

It's apparent that my present job is secure. If conditions continue as they have been, I expect to be on the dredge for a long time. A dredge, being a floating machine, is quite easily dragged from one place to another from ----------. I expect to go wherever it goes. Frankly, I hope so. It is an interesting way to spend a war.

Your son has been wavering lately. Everything is indecision and uncertainty. He doesn't know what he wants. His ambitions are becoming scattered, prominently so. It's this terrible distance. He hopes it is temporary, but fears it may not be. As a result of his indecision, he is too easily influenced. More than ever, he expects that his decision to go to college will be a beneficial, but, with respect to time, a costly experiment. He is prepared for it. Although expecting that he has yet a long time to serve, he's not discouraged. By God, these past two years and more have generated within him a sincere determination — but doubtful enthusiasm.

Truly, I'm like the blind man who says, "We shall see," and expects that he will see, literally.

12/21/44

Dear Mom,

Before long I expect that more people whom I've never seen, strangers, rather than friends and relatives will be writing to me.

Only rarely do I burst into fits of uproarious laughter over a letter, perhaps one of Ronnie's or Johnson's with its puns. Most amusing letters elicit a snicker or a weak smile. Today, I received a letter from one Sybil Hurwitz, blonde, pretty — so she immodestly confesses — a youthful seventeen and a hometowner. I just had to laugh and laugh, mostly at myself I suppose.

Last spring the "elderly" Chase girl ventured to write, and I politely replied. That ended that, and before long she palmed me off on Dolly, sweet seventeen. Since then, Dolly has written several exuberant letters, which I fear I answered perhaps tactlessly and a mite too frankly. The reason for the change in correspondents seemed to reside in the allegation that Mademoiselle Chase was too old for me and that Dolly would be more suitable. It occurs to me that maybe age does matter in conducting a correspondence with a girl, especially if her ulterior purpose is courtship and ultimately marriage. Still, I was puzzled. Wouldn't it also be fitting for a well-meaning woman, one twice my age, to correspond with me, let alone one only two or three years older? Apparently, the ages between twenty and twenty-five are years of marked intellectual development. Someone twenty-three or twenty-four would be intellectually vastly superior to a lowly twenty year old. Not being terribly concerned with correspondents whom I didn't know, I accepted Chase's rejection without giving it a thought and took on the less mature, but equally sensible — or nonsensical —

Dolly. This Dolly has done well, always answering my letters punctually.

Now, it seems from all appearances, I'm being palmed off again, or am I being being shared? Today a short, typical, pleasant introductory note arrived from one Miss Sybil of Cardinal Road. She writes this confusing statement: "I know a girl, who knows a girl, who knows the girl that used to write to you. But since the girl who knows the girl, who knows the girl that used to write to you is too old for you and since the girl—oh, I can't go through that again." Well, despite my morbid New Guinea conditioned sense of humor, I couldn't contain myself after reading that sentence—if that's what you'd call it. I rocked myself with laughter until I collapsed on the plyboard floor. Say, I'm even beginning to feel young once more, yes, sweet seventeen. If blonde Sybil will guarantee me more such childish and entertaining statements in the future, I should find it a pleasure to correspond with her.

In another year I'll be old enough to vote. For nigh on two years, responsible only to myself, I've been carousing about the U.S., the Pacific, and New Guinea. Frankly, I feel more cocksure of myself than ever and even though I lack an abundance of masculine hair on my chest, I also feel that I deserve the respect due a man. For what it's worth, I do shave three times a week. Now I have three girls, ages 22, 17, and 17 respectively, who apparently fail to recognize my manliness. The latter two, who have stuck by me, still consider me a kid just out of high school. I don't dislike being considered so, even if it somewhat wounds my vanity accumulated over the past year and a half plus. Maybe it will keep me young and in touch with the high schoolish frivolity that I had missed. All in all it's pleasant and lifts my morale.

The naivete of Ronnie's letters, of Dolly's and now Sybil's (I'm blind to my own naivete) gives me quite a lift in this life of disregard for oneself, hard labor, and seriousness. The letters are fun.

It's also possible, that if circumstances permit, and my studies occasionally go easily, I'll have in these girls two potential playmates, especially since months of letters have paved the way. And if their personalities and appearance prove charming, then I could have a delightful situation on my hands.

Whenever I'm reminded of their letters, I can't help beaming. I'm sure that this letter will make you smile at me, but that's alright. If you wish, you may also smile with me.

I'll bet both Dolly and Sybil are five feet ten.[1] I'll eat my hat if they're not.

After several weeks of working days, I'm back on the graveyard shift. Since I'm living in self-imposed solitude, and my home is in a choice, shady spot, I sleep well during the day. I went swimming yesterday and rode the surf in a home-made boat. The water is enervatingly warm, so after the swim I took a cold shower to cool off. But I enjoyed myself. The coral formations and fish are beautiful. And due to the cruel coral so are the minor cuts on the bottom of my feet.

The natives fish using hand-made grenades consisting of a tightly wrapped bag of dynamite which they toss into the water where it explodes, stunning the fish. I saw them toss several that sank minus an explosion. But the natives don't give up. They keep tossing their grenades until one explodes. With their blackened teeth they chew the wick into a soft pulp to make it burn faster. I expect one day a native will gnash himself to death as he chews on a heavily charged wick. The children are naked and can maneuver the biggest canoes like pros. They are the cutest kids you ever saw.

12/23/44

Dear Mom,

Last night the most elaborate show ever was performed here. The setting was an *Esquire* magazine cover. The characters consisted of four Conover models[1] including a Candy Jones, the 1945 pinup girl; wearing a tux and later tails (the first we've seen since Hollywood), an excellent tenor who sang Porter,[2] Gershwin and Kern;[3] Mr. Esquire; a few comedians, and a passable orchestra. Our audience, sweltering in the hot, humid evening, reacted sympathetically to the singer in his tux and tails. Everyone enjoyed the show, especially the exceptionally beautiful girls who wore all sorts of elaborate costumes, evening dresses, college dresses and everyday dresses. We were awed by their fast changes from one outfit to another.

Tonight is my last on the graveyard shift. Although I sleep like a top during the day, when I awake I'm covered in gooey sweat. The heat of the day does it. Some good news concerning the job: You may recall that I mentioned there were three men per shift assigned to the engine room: an oiler (normally rated as a third class petty officer according to our complement), a water tender (a second class petty officer), and an engineer (a first class petty officer). For the past one and one half months I've been an oiler, responsible for keeping the engines lubricated, and doing some mechanical work and all sorts of dirty jobs. Partly from necessity and partly because I've taken the initiative to learn all I could, my position has been elevated to that of water tender. For the past week since a vacancy occurred, I'm being broken in to the new job. I hadn't mentioned it earlier, to make sure that nothing would go wrong, that I wouldn't succeed at it. I didn't wish to be hasty. Now I've learned the fundamentals, and I'm on my own. I work the shift alone. The new job is cleaner, far easier, and it entails more responsibility than the old one. I am in a position to make the ship list, even sink, and blow up its boilers. I must know where every valve is on board, where every pipe goes, how much water we have, where to draw it from to prevent listing. It's my job to keep the bilges dry, maintain three horizontal and three vertical steam pumps, keep the constantly changing water levels in the boilers safe and consistent, and a dozen little things that I won't mention here. Last night, I was on a shift alone for the first time. Everything went well. My superiors, all petty officers, have confidence in me and constantly give me pointers, which I appreciate. So things are going well with my job on the dredge. Although I'm not looking for advancement, I deserve it and it's probably imminent. I'm the only person on board in a position of responsibility without a petty officer's rate.

I hope to send some books home in the next two weeks. I need the space. Due to the increased heat and my daytime slumbering, I'm not reading or writing as much as I was.

In spite of the lack of snow and cold, Christmas is quite evident here. The chow hall is decorated in a manner that's slightly better than my rooms in grammar school. Red and green stringers hang from the rafters, and an excuse for a Christmas tree, draped with crepe, stands at one end. I can't imagine where the tree, which resembles a pine or fir, was found. The Christmas people are supposed to do something extravagant, both with respect to quality and variety. On the 25th, our boys will have WACs joining them for dinner, the guests of their self-designated escorts.

Recalling last Christmas, I must laugh. Remember, I slept on the floor of a handball court in Hollywood. This year I have a nice soft, hot cot to sleep on. It's comfortable but not entirely satisfactory.

12/24/44

Dear Mom,

Tonight there's more to celebrate than Christmas eve. Everyone is jubilant. When I get home someday, ask me to tell you about this night. We've reached a kind of climax. Many of us, myself included, are unaffected, but many of my friends are wild with happiness.

I'm relieved to hear that you've received the watch. How I miss it. It's gone through a year of mainspring hell, believe me. Please don't spend money for another watch. So long as the sun shines, I can wait for the Bulova.[1]

To buy a watch here, from a mate that is, costs three times as much as in the States. My Bulova would sell for $75.00. Ronnie should not wear any of the navy clothing I sent home. When I hit the States, I'll most likely want my peacoat and sweater. Peacoats made a great hit with the girls down South. They snuggled in their warmth.

I see the Pincus[2] lad is in the same, or far worse, mental state that I was in most of the time while in the States. Soon one learns to stop griping and to let things go their way. Over and over things have gone from bad to worse to good. It's a process that I expect will repeat itself in the future. Complaining may make you feel better, but you come to realize it changes nothing. I expect to have many miserable, depressing, hard luck days, not in the too distant future at that.

Let's get one thing straight. I always write the truth, perhaps not always the whole truth, or I write nothing. The chow here had been good. Just before the invasion up north, and immediately afterwards, the chow worsened due to the increased demand for supplies. Fresh meat, fresh potatoes, butter, fruit, and vegetables were unheard of for a time. The food became pretty bad. But now our chow is back to normal. We are lavishly being served proper foods. There was no sense in telling you about this while it was happening when I knew why and that it would be only temporary. There's a war on, and war is no picnic. Don't expect me to be preserved in tweed trousers as I was. Should I gripe on your shoulder over every inconvenience? What's important is that I'm healthy, happy and strong. So long as I remain this way, let the war bring on its wrath. So long as I keep writing letters, don't ask, don't worry, and just know that all's hunky-dory.[2]

The most difficult thing for me is to do something someone else's way. I try to do things the best way. There's nothing like being your own boss. Four different experienced water tenders have shown me four different ways to do my job. I've since introduced a fifth way, my own, which I find produces satisfactory results. Nobody can tell the difference. I listen to instructions with some skepticism on the one hand, and seriousness on the other, and judge a suggestion on its merits. If no one found new ways to do things, progress would be at a standstill.

Tonight I watched a hot, professional jive band. For those who enjoy brassy swing, it was good. I didn't care for it. It sounded like noisy rhythm to me. Most of the boys went into ecstasy over it. In my opinion I could have walked out without missing a thing.

12/26/44

Dear Mom,

Before I comment on your letter of the 11th (with airmail stamps), I must talk about yesterday.

Many of us had a guilty conscience when, suddenly, we realized what we now have. We are guilty of deceiving you folks at home who read about our mighty struggle against nature's worst. Looking at our present comfort, we find consolation only from the past when things were tougher. Our good situation now is repayment for those early inconveniences.

Yesterday our chow hall was invaded by WACs, the dates of their battalion escorts. There was a gala celebration at Club Tropicana (the enlisted men's club) which did a land office business, as liquor flowed, coming from some mysterious source. The dinner menu ranged literally from soup to nuts. It would have been an expensive meal anywhere, and we gorged ourselves to the brim. Last night, a show topped off the day's festivities.

We are living well indeed, very well. At first we liked it, but now we are finding it troubling. We never objected to comforts while in the States. But out here, knowing there is so much to do and being done by others, not to be an active participant is demoralizing, disappointing and a deception. Something momentous has happened to the outfit, something unmentionable that has made us aware of all this ease. While no one craves to be exposed to trouble, no one shirks it. We are beginning to feel like shirkers. What we think, of course, means nothing. The battalion's destiny is beyond our control. We do hope, however, that our outfit will not lay dormant much longer as it has been for the past eight months.

Today I was given some duplicates of the Satelburg pictures of last March. Within the next two weeks I expect to have a camera.

"Jamie"[1] is playing tonight, and sadly I shall miss it. Tonight I begin the 6:00 to 12:00 swing shift. It's mostly a good shift, giving me days off, but a bad shift for seeing shows that begin at 7:00 or 8:00 PM.

What's this! Good lord, "The Cat's Tale" must be better than I realized.[2] I wrote it for your enjoyment, and fearing that you wouldn't enjoy it. I had nothing to write about at the time. I assumed nobody else would care for it. In high school I never could stand the stories the other students submitted, and I hardly ever read them. And everyone else felt the same. I wish it weren't published in the "Argus" [Ronnie's high school publication]. It won't amount to anything. Readers will ignore it, and I don't blame them. I wish you would keep everything I write between ourselves. Or at least if you do share it, spare me the embarrassment by telling me nothing.

Strange Fruit was not written for teen-age boys and girls. It was written for the sensible adult public. I can't find fault with a single word or action in the book. Those fellows to whom I have lent the book, consider it one of the finest of modern novels. I don't agree. The book doesn't compare with a *Jean Christophe*, which admittedly has a markedly different theme. I read the *Omnibook* condensed version of *Leave Her to Heaven*.[3] Johnson raved about it. You may recall reading Williams' *Time of Peace* at my instigation. I didn't enjoy *Leave Her to Heaven*. Either the condensation ruined the novel or recently my reading such classics as *War and Peace* and *Jean Christophe* has sharpened my critical appreciation.

Good! Glad to hear that you'll not send anything without my express request. I wish the relatives would do likewise. Soon I'll be asking for more books, but not until I finish reading the few I have on hand. I'm slowly plowing through *Troilus and Cressida*. With so many distractions about, I'm finding it hard to follow sentences in iambic pentameter. But soon I expect to get into the swing of it, because I've enjoyed what I've read so far.

This spring, or in late winter, you may hear from me through intermediaries. That's all I shall say for now.

Everything is hunky-dory ---.

P.S. Saw "I Love a Soldier"[4] (Goddard[5] & Tufts[6]), "Till We Meet Again"[7] (Milland[8] & Britton[9]).

12/27/44

Dear Mom,

It's about 10:00 AM, a gorgeous day. I'm only partially awake after a night's sound sleep and before that, a hot swing shift. Much to my amazement, the job is going remarkably well. I've been able to handle anything that's been asked of me. My cohorts in the boiler room (I work in the engine room) who depend on what I do to utilize oil and make steam efficiently, are pleased. Were this a civilian job, I'd be in a position to make or break a company by wasting oil and water. Although I'm sure the government doesn't in the least care, I do my best to conserve. Money and time are no object. Only results count. No doubt this is the best job I've had while in the service, and maybe will have in civilian life as well. The responsibility, the knowledge required of what you're doing, the good hours, the not laborious work, there being always much more to learn, all these make the job worthy of someone more experienced than myself. As yet my status is still uncertain. I don't know whether my attachment to the dredge is temporary or permanent. I've been told both. Someday, I hope to find out which applies. You may recall that many were confused about their status back in the States. The CB in Seabees has often been interpreted to stand for "confused bastards." I'm confused again, but I don't mind so long as I can report to work every day.

The watch repairers are robbers. Not only does it take only an hour to repair the watch, they also misinformed you concerning the movement. The watchmaker here really knows his stuff; I've watched him work on watches. He charged me the standard U.S. price of $5.00 for what had to be done. My watch does not have a Swiss movement. If it had, it could be fixed here. Only one part was worn out, and, were it available, it could have been installed in two shakes of a lamb's tail. On the other hand $7.00 isn't too much as wartime prices go, according to the magazines. I can believe that it takes four weeks to procure a few small cogs that are no doubt hard to find. So the magazines say. I'm glad to hear that you're going right to town getting it fixed. You're "on the ball." I ask only that the job be done well. The watch has plenty more hell to endure yet.

I've received nothing from either you or Sadie or Lenny's sister, but I'm a patient and confident lad. Few boys find their packages or letters are lost.

I'll be missing a raft of good motion pictures during the next two weeks. I was in a motion picture rut for a while, seeing them almost nightly. It will probably do me good to be un-entertained, cause me to appreciate the entertainment more.

No, I'm feeling like a true blue navy man as I fling navy terms about on the job, words such as aft, forward, port, starboard, wing tank, peak tank, avast ye landlubbers, heave to and all that rot. In keeping with tradition I now look forward to having a girl in every port. Already a blonde and a brunette are working on my morale, and then there's that luscious brunette, at 67 King Street, third floor left. [the family flat]

12/29/44

Dear Dad,

Every morning, since I've been on the swing shift, it's the same story. After nine hours of slumber, I debate, while still semi-conscious, whether I should get up or not. I do this for an hour, until the heat of approaching noon sun causes beads of sweat to form on my chin. Or maybe I hear someone scream "Mail." This morning "Mail" did the job.

From the thickness of the envelope I figured the letter was from you—one of your long and nostalgic letters. I read it—rather, I should say, devoured it—and I'm now sitting back in my home-made easy chair, feeling especially contented. I can't compete with you: my answer can't compare with your letter, but how I enjoy writing this.

At about this time in 1943 you wrote a letter that so impressed me I never included in my stacks to go home. During the past year I've read it over and over, more like a lover would read another's, or, as in our case, as a loving son would read his father's. Now, on its first anniversary, you have written another that will tide me over the next year, which I fear will present physical hardship—but not mental. Dad, you do wonders for me.

On the subject of what the war, this entire grand experience, has done for me, I can talk and talk with considerable understanding. I see the past laid bare, and the present with keen interest. I feel this insight has put me on an equal footing with my elders. And I now look forward to a personal renaissance in the future, one that is clear and broad, and an open field to the expression of my unmitigated ambition. I know that my flaws, including those that I recognize and have hopelessly tried to correct, will remain. Environment and experience don't change an individual's innate nature. The most satisfying, and surprising, result of my experience has been my relationship with men older than I. From all appearances they treat me as an equal, and, when they talk seriously to me, I cannot help but smile—a smile that puzzles many.

My present job has been most effective in reinforcing that equality. I learned the job more quickly and efficiently than I thought possible. While once everything I did was apt to go wrong, (and how well you know) now I hold the most responsible job on the vessel, and I'm not exaggerating. Were I to make one slip, one bad guess, much damage is liable to follow. I'm the youngest, least experienced, lowest-rated of the four men who are familiar with my work. Good lord, Dad, I'm doing a man's job. It's unlike anything I've ever done before—beyond going to war. I confess I feel damn good about it.

I'm relieved to know that you are prosperous, that your subsistence is comfortable. It's my greatest consolation. If it's within my power, I shall never be otherwise. And you know I have much more to tend to before it will be within my power, and I thank you for knowing that.

Contrary to the latest quip coined out here, I am not "nervous in the service." Civilianism is a more fitting description of our supposedly regulated routine. In many respects our lives are freer than a civilian's.

Indeed, I've never been freer. I have no boss, I work short hours, I have a large area in which to roam, and I have no financial or subsistence worries. Our freedom is only curbed by our environment, which has nothing to offer in the way of civilization's advantages and pleasures.

You flatter me by overestimating the value of my letters. Our relationship exaggerates their worth in your eyes. Their literary, cultural, or informative value can't compare with what professionals write. Although I write down my sincerest thoughts and describe what I see as accurately as I can, the letters are naive and amateurish. However, you must be taught a lesson. Go ahead with your ambitious intentions. I hope you will choose only those letters that reveal nothing personal. After you are satisfied and thoroughly disappointed, I shall have no mercy. I'll heckle and rib you as no bum from Brooklyn would dare. My dear parents fail to see that millions of other sons are simply amazing replicas of me. They have similar experiences; they learn similar things; they write similar letters, and they have the same motivation.

The battalion newspaper has appeared at last. My article has been so cut, added to—and I admit, improved—that the byline "by H. Aaron" (which I requested not be printed) is a farce. I'm ashamed of both myself and the editor. I'm not good at writing articles, that's for sure. I plan to write no more of them. In the article I originally submitted, I didn't show even a hint of ability or promise. I've always had reservations about it. I'm fortunate that I've never been enthusiastic about this writing spree.

Our base is now considered an antique. All souvenirs are gone, and what I did find I had to discard, because it was censorable. When we first arrived, tokens were plentiful. I still have a few remnants, some odd coins, which I'll send home for Ronnie. Someday, I expect once more to find souvenirs plentiful.

I've noticed that the natives are becoming extinct as our base began to show marked signs of civilization. They prefer to confine themselves to their villages. There are two kinds of natives here: those who are dark, short, and large-featured and those who are light brown, slant-eyed, and attractively-featured. Their tallest men are about my height [5 feet 7 inches]. The blacks have homely features and curly, bushy hair. And they are much cleaner and more intelligent than those at our previous base, although many have a scaly skin disease. Most speak intelligible pidgin English,[1] and they smile mechanically in response to our smiles. Their names are humorous.

Apparently the Japs trained them to salute, because when we first arrived, they always greeted us with a snappy, attentive salute. Of course, we jughead G.I.'s were thrilled with the practice. The natives appear to have been influenced by the European missionaries. They like to wear clothes, especially those that are white which, miraculously, they manage to keep clean. They also like wearing multi-colored clothes, pajamas for instance. All dress up in G.I. clothes, particularly our big clophopping shoes which they are apt to wear on the wrong feet, sun helmets, dungarees, and our navy skivvy shirts. Although they are shrewd, they are extremely honest. Some who have entered my tent to trade have made ridiculous demands. I give them candy gratis and show them picture postcards of the States which bewilder the youngsters but don't impress the elders. They conduct themselves in a meek, submissive manner; however, they don't hesitate to ask for something, and recently many have become as bold as our bold G.I. selves. You rarely see their women and girls, who seem to be their slaves. They usually remain in the villages. The women are generally decently clothed, but the youngsters go stark naked. They are as cute and mischievous and spry as our own. At the age of four or five, they handle canoes brilliantly. I often see them accompanying their fathers, who spend most of the day procuring food. The kids wave and giggle and sometimes make faces. The boys and the men aren't well-built, but they are wiry and amazingly strong. Relative to their bodies their feet are broad and large, like a duck's. On the whole, they lead a moderate, comfortable, harmonious, ideal life.

As a rule their villages are built on stilts over the water of lakes and bays. All are near the water. Their living quarters are thatched huts. They sleep on hard, bamboo shelves, whose surfaces are somewhat softened by layers of grass and vegetation. Their pastime is woodcarving. Their canoes and spears are beautifully carved and painted in bright colors.

Since the U.S. moved in, the natives have been having a heyday. Our ten in one rations made a hit with their dietitians. I do believe they can subsist on cigarettes alone. The kids are veteran smokers which hardly seems to have dulled their wits. They are positively clever.

The fathers are very fatherly, the mothers very motherly, and they don't hesitate to severely reprimand both their sons and their husbands. Their emotional and mental attitude towards family life is identical to ours.

The slant-eyed natives lead an almost civilized existence. Some of the women possess a strikingly oriental beauty. I've seen some of their men walking about in slacks and sportswear, all smiles, and happily greeting everyone.

The Japs raised havoc with the women, although I don't think they committed any atrocities. All I've been able to elicit from the natives concerning the past is, "Jap no good; Melican good."

This, I hope, will give you some idea of what the aborigines, or whatever you call them, are like. If you have any questions, send them along, and I'll do my best to answer them.

I wonder whether I should establish a travel and information agency here. I've tried to get around as much as possible, although not as much as I'd like. Traveling in the heat and dust, then the mud and rain, is most uncomfortable. With all this heat which makes one lazy, one must be a fanatic to muster enough ambition to sightsee.

Let's hear from you again soon, Dad. Meanwhile, Mom is handling the situation superbly. She gives me all the lowdown firsthand, far better than even Hedda Hopper[2] or the Associated Press.

From a proud son, Hughie

P.S. I'll send the rest of the set [of pictures] home in due time. All were taken, as you know, at our last base last spring.

12/31/44

Dear Folks,

Now I'm clear on the story of the "Cat's Tale." It serves Mom and Ronnie right. The situation is highly amusing, and it has given me such a good laugh that I won't bawl you out. Remember Mom, everything I write is between us, if for no other reason than to save me embarrassment.

I imagine I made plenty of grammatical errors in the story. I had taken no pains. That's why they have proofreaders and rewriters. Teachers are very conventional and they declare anything unconventional in a story wrong. At least I know that the story is well-done by sophomore high school standards.

I certainly enjoyed Ronnie's letter. I'm sending with this a few coins. Some Philippine money has drifted down here, but I haven't procured any. I'm not much of a souvenir hunter. While I was in Hollywood, I used to feel humiliated asking for autographs. I didn't want them for myself, but I knew you'd enjoy them. I take it if it comes my way, but I won't go to great lengths. Some of our boys are fanatics about it.

I smiled at your mention of the Rome[1] visit. I appreciate that, knowing how I feel about the cackling hen,[2] you rescued me.

By the way, my newly acquired female correspondents are holding up quite well. Usually by now they request an exchange of pictures. But nothing of the kind has been requested, for which I admire them. In a month or so I expect that, in response to their woman's insatiable curiosity, they'll break down.

My job is now down to a routine. Having devised a few short cuts, I do some things in ways that seem odd to my fellow water tenders, but I get the best results. Since my abilities are neither known nor recognized by my superiors, I expect no advancement. Nor do I intend to openly reveal my knowledge, knowledge that the higher ranking petty officers should have, because I wish to remain friends with everyone, and also because I'm not ambitious for a rate. A few petty officers have assigned me much more work beyond my regular duties in order to make it easier for themselves. Anxious to learn more than I'm even supposed to, I willingly accept it. Who knows, it may come in handy in a pinch.

New Year's day is slated to be another day of feasting: turkey etc. Here the new year rings in fifteen hours earlier than it does at home. On New Year's day of '44 I was trying to hitchhike to Hollywood, gave up, and successfully hitchhiked in the opposite direction to Ventura, where I didn't do much of anything. I never had the time to see this year go by. It just passed without notice.

After almost a year had passed, I wrote Mr. and Mrs. Myles of Hollywood. Apparently they were impressed. They sent a sweet, short note with holiday greetings, and a promise to write again "which doesn't necessitate an answer unless you desire. We do want to keep in touch with you." My vanity was touched upon reading, "We have thought of you so often during the past year, for you are outstanding in our memory, though we only knew you for a few hours." I was flattered when Mrs. Myles wrote, "Your very beautifully expressed letter proved once more to us that it would indeed be a privilege to know you as a friend." After reading all these undeserving compliments and flattery from this charming couple, I was sitting on top of the world. I recall Mr. Myles, who spoke perfect English with an impressive voice, seemed exceptionally bright. And Mrs. Myles overflowed with personality. I'll gladly answer their letters.

P.S. A pretty long one, too.

Three packages arrived yesterday: one from Yetta, consisting of canned foods, fruit cocktail, and sardines, etc., which are delicacies here. They arrived in perfect condition. Your dandy box would have been dandier, if it hadn't crossed the equator. The bakery products were spoiled, but the candy was good, and the baseball book, which was written by Al Schacht, who has lectured here on a USO tour, arrived in good shape. A baseball fan chum is devouring the book. Your sentiments were lovely, but it's too bad their expression wasn't more edible.

I received a package of what were once delicious cookies from Jordan Marsh,[3] but no return address. I presume it was from Ida. I feel terrible seeing the beautiful assortment of those once delicious cookies stinking with mildew and soggy from the equatorial humidity. I'll feed it to the rats. I don't know how I can impress on you folks that food doesn't last two minutes out here. That's why we have refrigerator ships. This isn't the Northern Hemisphere. Only canned food will successfully make the trip, and we get plenty of that here. Are you folks the victim of newspaper advertising propaganda? It seems so with everyone sending unasked-for packages. Explain this to the others. Show them this post script. It's a shame to torture me with the sight of all the spoiled goodies. Europe is cold. Food packages won't spoil there. It's never cold here. A package need only glimpse the equator to turn green with fear and mildew.

Again, I implore you, never send packages without my personal request. Please explain this to the others. It's rather difficult for me to do so. I might hurt their feelings and seem unappreciative of their well-meant intentions.

I'm chewing on some of the candy you sent—doggone good. Oh, I do feel sad when I think of that once delicious fruit cake.

1/1/45

Dear Mom,

I remember many New Years' eves when I minded babies for parents, and many that I can't remember because I slept. Despite a new base order that all lights be out by 10:00, we had a celebration. Although most lights were out, so were the boys.

Not being on duty last night, I returned from a show expecting to get some sleep. Every tent had accumulated a supply of beer. Becoming drunk, the boys threw bottles helter-skelter against rocks, splattering glass all about. Of course, I got no sleep. Instead, I cursed the loud fools, and they were fools, because once they were sober, they would have to clean up the debris. I heard the sound of a distant drone, like that of an airplane motor. As I listened, the sound grew louder, and new sounds joined in. As I rose, exasperated over not being able to sleep, the whole bay burst into a racket of fog horns, bells, and the echoes of hammers banging on the steel decks of happy men's ships. Nobody knows why all this happiness over the beginning of a new year — just a tradition of civilization, I suppose — because there isn't that much to be happy about. We have a long way to go yet.

I understand the night club was quite busy, and everyone had a rare time. The WACs are becoming more manly in appearance, much to our dislike.

That was New Year's in New Guinea, so different from what it must have been two years or even a year ago before we arrived. There's no war on this island now, not around here.

The arrival of 1945 was very liquid; a slow, warm, tropical rain fell. I wish the devil we could leave here and get to do real work again.

Christmas packages are arriving in abundance.

That's my Mom for you — worrying about it after I innocently mentioned that I overslept. I haven't been late for work yet, my dear, and, if I do oversleep, I only suffer the terrible consequences of missing breakfast — not being late for work. You see, I do have a delicious habit of oversleeping, a normal and routine function, which entails trading a meal for a few moments of slumber. I try to find out what the breakfast will be in advance, so I can be sure oversleeping is worth it. Rumor of a really good breakfast generally outweighs my will to sleep late.

Food aboard the dredge is better than the food at the mess hall. Since we are a small crew, our food is more easily procured and prepared.

Bob has written a most pleasing letter. After almost two years, I'm baffled as to why he decided to become aware of his cousin. More than likely it's due to a scarcity of girls in Italy, thereby giving him more time to write. He has quite a job, hasn't he?

I imagine I'll never have a job as easy as the one I now have: six hours a day, six days a week. Can you read this letter? I can hardly read it myself.

At long last I finished reading *Troilus and Cressida*. The plays aren't to be read like novels. Since all I know from *R & J*[1] is "Wherefore art thou Romeo?"[2] I plan to undertake that one next. I began reading L.C. Douglas'[3] *The Robe*[4] today.

For the past four or five days the sky has been unusually overcast — no rain. The sea breeze has been quelled, and the humidity has become thick. It's the kind of weather I don't like. The slightest exertion causes streams of perspiration to form.

1/3/44

Dear Ronnie,

I'd advise you to spend the five dollars enclosed. If you don't, if you add it to your gradually growing riches, I guarantee that in the not too distant future, I'll sponge it off you.

Now you're turning sixteen (or eighteen as Dad would exaggerate), old enough to hold down a job, and old enough to wreck the Ford before I get a whack at it. You're sixteen, never been kissed except by Mom, unless —, and it's about time that your manly five feet ten inches or more (or slightly less) be true to being a man in mind as well as stature.

At thirteen, you were a "man" [as a bar mitzvah boy]; at sixteen you suddenly discover that you are not yet a man in spite of your driver's license. When you reach the decrepit age of twenty, you'll be anxious to vote for Roosevelt.

I wish you a very happy sixteenth birthday [on January 16th] and please, don't follow in my footsteps when I was that age.

Your elder brother, Hughie

1/4/45

Dear Mom,

Between parents and their children, between a mother and son, there's an inexplicable attachment so profound that it is expressed in every innocent and ordinary action. Between them is a remarkable silent understanding far beyond gratitude. Words, inadequate though they are, do reach one that loves. Your words have often stirred in me dormant emotions. I have absorbed their meaning into my soul.

Your words are my greatest source of sustenance. Foolishly, blindly, I've often discouraged you to write. And I've written selfishly, coldly, tangentially. I haven't considered your maternal desire to compensate for the distance between us through words. I am ashamed of my complacency and misunderstanding.

So freely express your devotion and affection in letters and through gifts. I yearn for your every word, every particle of a word, every particle of your love. I embrace them.

Dear Mom, if I've hurt you, I've only hurt myself more. Please forgive me, a son never more devoutly devoted to his mother.

Your Hughie

1/6/45

Dear Mom,

From what I hear the status of the dredge is to be changed—and the crew along with it. I don't have the whole story yet, but if the change occurs, it will be to the crew's advantage. Although it's positively on the way, a formal notice has not been made. After the transfer, of course, I'll have a different address, and someday, a different rate. *Cela ne fait rien*—it makes no difference.

I received an enormous package, packed full of sweets and cakes from the loyal Gallants and have acknowledged it. I hardly expected such a profuse showering of letters, cards, and gifts after the few brief months that I had known them. It seems, oddly enough, that I had made more friends immediately before entering the service and while in the service than ever before. First, it was Lenny, then Johnson; down South it was the Linfields, who expect to see me at some future date; then, in the service, two fellows in particular—possibly a third—who have been constant and understanding companions.

At long last Sadie's wonderful package arrived. The bracelet is a beauty. Contrary to my usual dislike of wearing rings on my fingers and bracelets on my wrists, I intend to wear this one. Besides the bracelet she also sent books and candies. The big question now is, should I or should I not open a confectionery store? But business would be poor, because everyone else is loaded up with similar sweet meats and delicacies. I can't even give the stuff away. Too bad, Ronnie my boy, you aren't here.

The weather is getting damper and wetter. At least part, if not all, of every day is overcast. I go swimming rain or shine every third day on the average. Yesterday, I had quite a singular experience, at least for New Guinea. I talked to a woman for the first time in over ten months. Of course, she was a WAC, and as I was up close to her, I was amazed at the smooth texture of her skin. After continually seeing only the sun- tanned skin of men, a woman's seemed singularly smooth. The situation was amusing. The girl, having deserted her escort, put on an act of trying to make friends with my friend and me. She ended up by calling me an ungentlemanly snob from Boston (my so-called accent). I walked away happily grinning.

From all appearances these girls' passions are noticeably aroused. They like men and are actually taking on their masculine ways. For that matter, the men are also easily aroused by the sight of a woman, as is understandable. For us boys overseas the situation is difficult and wrong. The majority feel that women have no place over here. They are an unnecessary expense, a distraction, and often a luxury.

"Hellzapoppin" with a worthy Broadway cast was performed at our theater last night, and will do so for the next two evenings. I plan to see it Sunday. Everyone enjoyed seeing the fourteen girls and seven civilians march into our chow hall, go through the line, and sit with us. For the past few shows, the players have dined (an elaboration of eating GI food) with us. When one of our boys calls a slim blond showgirl "Hey Blondie," she just up and sits with the wolf, who can't help grinning from sideburn to sideburn, too enthused to say a doggone thing.

I may yet be a salty sailor of the fleet, folks. Let's wait and see what happens.

P.S. Enclosed are more pictures from Finschaven.

1/9/45

Dear Mom,

I had expected to work last Sunday night, but the fellows on the dredge, insisting that I go and see "Hellzapoppin," volunteered to work my shift for me. The deal was clinched after my boss approached me to deal with a practical physics problem which I solved in ten minutes. "Sure," he said, "go right ahead—good show."

So I went. I watched an hour and a half of light, typical vaudeville: the chorus girls, poor things, smiled obligingly—and forcibly—, showed their legs, and wiggled their rumps while sweat poured off their bodies. There were many lavish costumes, many new jokes, some corny, and excellent singing. Really, everyone had a good time. The "Hellzapoppin" show overseas is a condensation of the "Sons o' Fun" show I saw in Hollywood. The entire cast worked harder than I've worked in weeks.

This morning I finished reading L.C. Douglas's *The Robe*. The writing style was simple and easy to read, and the story would inspire any Christian to tears. Despite all its fantasy and contrivances of the imagination, it espouses quite a beautiful doctrine. However, I'm sure Grimm could write as fine a tale.

My new shift is from 12:00 noon to 6:00 PM—quite convenient for late morning sleeping and late evening show-going.

With no paper to wrap bundles, I can't send books home. I started reading *Romeo and Juliet*.

The climate and the uncertainty of my living quarters make it difficult for me to study the math. After having the course for over a year, I'm unable to apply myself to anything more than reading. I feel bad about it. Frankly, I freely submit to my whims.

I don't think my mind will get rusty. The problem that was presented to me a few days ago confused me at first. But in a few minutes little bits came back to me. What pleased me most was that I figured out the answer by reasoning alone, before consulting a given formula. Very encouraging.

I can't picture what sub-zero temperatures are like for the life of me. I had to smile when I read eight below. I much prefer this torrid warmth. Of course, living in the tropics has by now prejudiced me against cold.

[Cousin] Evelyn has written again suggesting that I read Freud's *Interpretation of Dreams,* if I so desire. If you see her before I reply, tell her that I so desire. How on Earth she ever got wind of Sigmund Freud, the gospel of psychology, I'll never know. Doubtless the book will prove interesting and beneficial. Freud goes quite deep. I'm amused to learn that Evelyn considers this lad a meditative and philosophical thinker—strictly a student. She had better get working on postwar prospects. Where did I read that there will be a postwar plurality of females?

This is all I have to say during these three days.

1/11/45

Dear Mom,

I was supposed to have written this last night, but instead I had unexpected company, and we jabbered 'til all hours. It's just as well because this tropical morning is gorgeous and breezy, the sort of morning well suited to letter writing.

Yesterday morning I began and finished reading James Hilton's[1] short *Goodbye Mr. Chips,*[2] an excellent way to begin the day and raise one's spirits. After my spirits' raising, I went to the library and took out Thomas Mann's[3] philosophical and latest book, *Joseph the Provider,*[4] which I'm now delving into and only half understanding. While at the library I found a sixty page pamphlet entitled "Personal Affairs of Naval Personnel and Aid for Their Dependents." While I don't expect to have dependents for a good many years, ahem, what interested me were the cut and dry passages on education and postwar benefits. I'm keeping the pamphlet.

Last night we saw "Home in Indiana"[5] and everyone left the theater feeling very happy. The film's color and freshness and heart-rending nostalgia put me in a glorious mood, a rare experience in New Guinea. That kind of picture should be shown more often here. They make us blissfully melancholy.

Evelyn has flabbergasted me with another letter that arrived yesterday. I don't know whether to feel flattered and honored or ashamed at my inability to keep up with her terrific pace. Although she never says much and frankly admits it, her letters are so friendly and frivolous and funny that I don't mind in the least receiving them.

I always enjoy hearing of your escapades in Boston. All the petty offenses and trivia that Sadie or Ida or Yetta harbor, somehow manage to crop up in their gossip. You're in Sadie's kitchen talking in subdued whispers about Grandma's latest run-in. I can picture it well. Then, based on kinship, you form an alliance and upon meeting your adversary one of you flares up while the other holds her piece — never do you attack jointly. Since nations have been following an identical procedure for centuries, I can't expect anything different from the lips of women who constantly fly apart.

Of course, Grandma is like a child. For that matter, you're all like children subtly slashing at one another and enjoying it for the sake of your own vanities and your irrepressible desire to be in the thick of things. I dare say you women would do a better job out here than we. To tell the truth, those gestures with their hidden meanings that are on display during any Boston visit, the secret talks, and the alliances against another, entertain me more than you can imagine. But I commend you, Mom, for your pacifism, and your use of better judgment in avoiding arguments. Ida reminds me of many people whom I've seen in Hollywood: the peroxide blonde hair, the uncommonly gracious manner, and lips that rise and fall faster than a P-38. But then allowances must be made: Ida has her problems. Bobby [Ida's son, Hughie's cousin] has a far more dangerous job [tail gunner on a bomber] than I'd wish to tackle; Hymie is hardly the model husband.

When I last saw you, you were quite happy. I intend to make you happier still. So just keep biting your lips, and suffer their insinuations which don't amount to a row of beans. After all, we have our own secret alliance to give us everlasting happiness and comfort.

P.S. One more word:
I imagine that on every visit you must endure open competition. For instance, Yetta would have her mercenary youngster bore everyone with his piano playing. But Yetta and Harry, glassy eyed with pride, somehow manage to guild the sour notes with silver. Most likely Ida carries on in exaggerated bereavement, but she has good reason to, for Bob proudly sports a citation that all agree he deserves. Meanwhile, my parents look on, witnessing all this raving over piano

playing and citations, and it's their turn, so in a dignified manner they read an excerpt from a very ordinary letter written by their son in the SWP. Well, well. That's all well and good. But your competitors see you and think "She's glassy-eyed with pride," "She thinks no one is better than her son," or something of that nature. Oh, I don't object. If you didn't think like that, I'd be one disappointed lad.

1/12/45

Dear Mom,

It's rather unfortunate that a week has lapsed between letters for no special reason. We aren't busy yet, but I expect to be soon, although later than I anticipated. The dredge is undergoing what you might call a rehabilitation.

It's also rather unfortunate that the censor cut out many references to the dredge in a previous letter. The censors are inconsistent. What gets by in one letter might not in another. They know nothing about dredges and when I say that ---------- power. Our newspaper, which we can send home, has more information on the dredge than I've dared to mention. Because they are being checked, the censors must be rigorous. You can't blame them for inconsistencies. I write such simple things that you aren't missing much by what's cut out. The blanks are easily filled in by using a little logic.

Send me a few rolls of V-122 film. I'll have a few more pictures for you soon. Cigarettes are plentiful. We can get almost anything we need at the ship's store, except film.

I just returned from seeing a USO show, one of the oldest — sixteen months — that came here from the Middle East. It lacked professional talent, but it gave me a few good laughs. I give the players credit, and try to enjoy their performances, because they really work hard. With a little more training some of them could be good. Most in this troupe hailed from the East Coast — one girl from Boston. They give the fellows what they want, but not what I want. It's strictly vaudeville, and sometimes a little less. Some jokes are better suited to risque burlesque, and our men love them.

I've been told that my name, along with others, has been submitted for advancement. It means nothing. My name has been submitted before. Although the fact remains that I'm eligible, it's highly improbable. I can happily say that all the name submitting, past and present, virtually guarantees no advancement.

Dear Mom,

We've had it pretty easy lately. Although the dredge is shut down a good part of the time, I must be on duty, whether it's operating or not so I spend the better part of the shift lolling about the deck reading and sun bathing. As a matter of fact, I've basked in the sun so much that my skin, unlike that of a below decks man, has become dark brown.

Yesterday a few Aussies,[1] barefoot, wrinkled, and weather beaten, with a thick accent and a thicker walk, came aboard. We fed them some of their own goat meat that we eat occasionally. From the quality of the meat we suspect that the goats have been climbing mountains for thirty years or more. These true blue seafarers were picturesque because they hailed from a ----------. Now ------- are almost a thing of the past. If only their jargon weren't so all fired confusing, I'd have probed them for a few of their exaggerated tales. One of them said that it took them three months to travel from Sidney.[2] But in direct contradiction and with a disapproving glare, the other "pshawed" him, saying that it took only sixteen days. Both agreed that their vessel had a speed of four knots forward and a good six knots backwards. After I saw the short bowlegged one, who was tattooed from neck to waist, swallow a tropical fish that we caught and cooked, bones and all, without blinking, I left the galley to continue my lolling in the sun.

Did I mention that I received a birthday card from Mrs. Mann [a neighbor] the last week in December? Say, if you can buy two or three Jockey shorts, send them to me. Underwear is scarce here.

I've been lax letter writing to everybody lately. I'm doing a fair amount of reading. Can't help it.

1/19/45

Dear Mom,

I know that in several of my preceding letters much in reference to the dredge has been cut out. It is difficult to know what I can say and what I can't. After all, the dredge is a vessel. But I know you are curious, and because you goaded me for information, I imagine I went too far. No doubt much that I write about this and that confuses you. Unfortunately, I can't clarify some things. To tell the truth, I'm slightly confused myself.

One thing is certain: I expect to be extremely busy. Letters may be scarce. Expect it.

Yesterday I received a letter from the new Mrs. Malter in Frisco. She and Al are married a whole month, and she insists "You must try it." Her letter pours forth personality. The salutation begins "Dearest" and the letter ends "Love." She writes as if she has known me all her life. I've found such friendliness, intimacy and warmth peculiar to most people on the West Coast.

Yesterday, I sent you the negatives, mostly ocean scenes. They will give you a pretty good idea what a native outrigger canoe looks like. In one picture, that mass I'm holding is actually a baby octopus. The stark naked youngster standing next to me had a wonderful time winding its tentacles around my hand. I didn't like it at first, but then didn't mind. That's an old sunken European barge. The planks have wooden pegs and hand made nails. I imagine it had been sunk during the original bombardment. The one of myself in the water, if taken in color, would have been quite beautiful. The water is crystal clear so that you can see colorful coral formations on the bottom. The photo doesn't do justice to it.

No one is getting much mail. Until recently we were receiving mail seven days a week. The weather is slightly wetter than it was a few months ago, although we are still getting our share of sunshine. Temperature remains the same.

Lil wrote me about her trip to New York. She's quite a concert and play-goer. I wish you were; but you will be. She thinks a writing career is intriguing. She, too! Where do all my correspondents get such an idea?

A couple of days ago I finished reading *Joseph the Provider*.

You wouldn't enjoy its complicated sentence structure, and its tangential philosophical portions. I found parts very difficult, although that may have been due to my poor background in the Bible. At least, now I have better than a vague idea of the Joseph story. Mann's style is classical modern, quite eloquent.

Reading a short biography of Disraeli[1] now.

1/21/45

Dear Mom,

It's a rainy, dreary, tropical Sunday, especially suited to reading or writing a letter. Imagine a warm, summer drizzle that weighs down your eyelids, and makes you lackadaisical, and you have it.

Months ago in our pioneering days, Sunday was a seventh day of work. We've had it off for a long time now. For most of us it means late sleeping, no breakfast, and fresh meat and ice cream for dinner. Even when I lose track of the days of the week, I can always tell it's Sunday. So long as Sunday is different from the rest of the days, the war seems a long way off. As soon as it becomes a tiring seventh day, we're playing a major role again. Either way, whether on or off, I become slightly nostalgic whenever it comes around: the *Boston Globe*, the best breakfast of the week, the best meals of the week, cleaning the house, the afternoon show, radio at night—"One Man's Family."[1]

But today, I work just the same—it's seven days a week now, you know. Of course, please realize that the shifts are only six hours long, easy compensation for a seventh day of work. Since we are presently not operating, my duties are simple and meager. It's little more than a matter of putting in the time.

The arid spell of the past week has been broken by a few letters from home. I take much consolation in knowing that Dad is taking care of himself. I'm very glad, Dad, to learn that you are doing something about your leg. Your leg has been an obstacle to my morale. I'm happy to strike it off.

I knew that the discussion concerning my female correspondents would make you laugh, Mom. I'm enjoying the situation. It's so light and amusing. We're all naive at heart, all guilty of ridiculous innocence.

I've not pondered college with any seriousness. My ideas are broad and unspecific, and I have left the future to decide the specifics. I haven't studied while in the service because I have sufficient confidence that when the need arises I'll be able to apply myself. I know that once I have the will to study, nothing, no outside influence, can distract me from doing it. I can sense the potential within myself. I want to do things now, such things as reading literature, developing social tact, and observing, which I won't be able to do once I'm studying. At the end of a hot day of labor, I'm not in a fit condition to study. I'm not able to absorb information as well as I should. But the capabilities of the mind do not wane. If the mind is active in other fields, at least it's active, enough to ensure a future of solid concentration. Mathematics or classical philosophy—both can maintain the mind's ripeness.

After submitting my first lesson in the math course, I received an excellent grade. I found the course astoundingly simple, yes, sometimes boring. Its repetition of my high school course secretly drove me to impatience. The course was too similar. I seek less repetition and something more difficult to concentrate on. College will offer this, not a correspondence course. I like to progress in my studies—swift and thorough.

When it comes time to return to school, I shall have had an excellent mental rest which will only reinforce my will to study. I fear I couldn't pass a college entrance examination under any circumstances. At the present time, why, any test, even one on which I received a good grade in high school, would seem formidable. But I know an exam won't be necessary. Here's where the laurels I earned in high school come into use. Remember I've been accepted by one college;[2] it's unlikely that I'd have to undergo a second acceptance procedure.

If I had to I could study now, but this is not the place for it. I still find the subjects I've already studied and new ones attractive — yes, more attractive than ever. I take my ambition for granted. I see a challenge, a marvelous challenge, delightfully confronting me now. I intend to meet it victoriously.

You know what my job is on board; you know what the rating should be for the job, but you don't know the politics of government service. I must insist that in spite of my eligibility according to my position for a higher rate, I shall never get one. The odds are against it. Recognizing this, I'm satisfied with my present situation. Believe me, the profit motive and healthy private enterprise are a blessing to both a nation and the individual. Civilian life is a haven for the ambitious, the sincere and the honest, but politics and governmental supervision are also essential.

Sunday PM

I appreciate your attempts to have my watch serviced. I can conveniently wait. Despite its resounding blare over the P.A. system, the bugle doesn't interrupt my sweet slumber. My chums drop in to wake me, and they are quite faithful.

You are an excellent reader between the lines. The Christmas Eve celebration was deserving. I feel fortunate that I wasn't one who was so elated. The reason for their elation derives from more than their reward. The aftermath of a disaster my be cause for joy as well as sadness.

What? You still have my civilian clothes? Preserve my navy clothing, but let Ronnie have my civilian ones. The prospect of spending many more months, perhaps another year or more, doesn't sadden me. The swift passage of time over here belittles it. Time is insignificant. A finale always seems near. Looking back, after it's over, I imagine it will have appeared torturous. But I'm oblivious to time from here to the end. After the end, time will be ecstatically real.

Thanks also for humoring me by purchasing the other two volumes of Shakespeare. Once I'm inspired I make great headway with the plays. I find that you can't just pick one up and enjoy it, unless you're in the mood, which is frequent.

I've acknowledged Sadie's gift. [Uncle] Harry once said to me: "To get along with people, make the other fellow think he's smarter than you. This will put him in your power." Excellent preaching. It's unfortunate that he doesn't practice what he professes.

Intend to write again tomorrow.

Love to my three loves, Hughie

1/22/45

Dear Mom,

Your letters have been arriving daily so I'm happy.

And now for you, my brother. I enjoyed your letter. You're a sophomore in high school now. That's when I read *Count Von Luckner, Sea Devil.*[1]

When you reach seventeen, I imagine the end of the war will be imminent. If we suffer reverses, and the war runs into 1946, you'll most likely be taken in by a national contagion of wanting to participate, if for no other reason than the novelty and glory of wearing a service uniform, not from any patriotic fervor or necessity. More for your sake rather than war's end, I hope that you'll never have to enter the service. Granted the training, living among a variety of men, and the entire experience are beneficial. But there are two things besides a regimented experience that are more worthwhile, more valuable and sacred: the preservation and happiness of our home and the earliest possible start in a career—for you, more than likely, business. If you go to college—and I hope you will—you'll be graduating at the same time as the veterans who will be out looking for jobs. You'll need a solid background, a headstart to compete with the veterans, for they will be a determined lot. It would be a catastrophe were you to neglect your education during the next four or five years. You would be swamped by those resolute souls returning from war, inspired to take advantage of an advanced education, seeking freedom through enterprise, and supported by veterans' rights.

To enlist before your time would have a stunning effect on Mom and Dad. I need not say more on this score.

The folks might think that I'm ridiculous to take your vague proposal seriously. After all, you have two more years before you'd be eligible for service, before your proposal deserves serious consideration. But the alarming thing that has happened to me was once seemingly impossible. Not to be deceived by fate is to expect to be deceived. Anything cosmic or ethereal can happen. Speaking epigrammatically: "The failure of deception lies in the expectation of deception."

When you jokingly commented on my atrocious penmanship, I was reminded of the many exasperated cries from aunts and uncles pleading with me to write more legibly. But once they decipher my scratchings, they confess that they enjoy the letters. I understand from one Dolly (of Hudson Street) that she consults with a group of girls to help her decipher my letters. A teacher at school with whom I'm corresponding has informed me that she had to labor over my last letter. My poor correspondents; I sympathize with them.

1/23/45

Dear Mom,

During the past year and one half I've never written a letter with any motive other than to please you. It has just occurred to me that my letters are actually a fairly accurate personal diary of my service experience. In my telling, I've left few stones unturned, and truly, when I finally return you will know everything worth knowing, and all your questions will have been answered.

I just finished reading *Disraeli* and have started *Tacitus*,[1] but I doubt whether I'll get a chance to finish it. I read in *Time* that Romain Rolland, the author of *Jean-Christophe*, died. I was amazed to find myself downhearted. When an artist, or a scientist, or perhaps a great politician, dies, it is a tragedy to me. I've always imagined they should have the special privilege of witnessing the everlasting success of their works, and to watch the evolutionary process of events. They are the most prominent contributors to our society. Regardless of the contrary and often beautiful doctrines they espouse, at least they are not spectators. My *post mortem*.

A few words of assurance. I've never felt better. With so much sleep and sunshine, how can I be otherwise? The majority of those who have found it difficult, have been sifted out and returned. Those with bone and sinus problems, and tropical diseases, have surfaced. The climate brings out those sorts of things. Many had no idea they were unfit until they came here. Come to the tropics and discover what ailments you have.

Those new developments mentioned earlier are definite and in the offing.

1/28/45

Dear Lil,

Nobody is particularly desolate here as the heat and routine persist, but nobody can deny that we are now suffering from an exasperating impatience. The pleasures bequeathed us — WACs, a nightclub, the movies, and shows — have actually lost their former luster and novelty, and only were we to be active again would they shine anew by contrast. Our insatiable thirst for participation has taken hold of our entire unit. Whether due to a healthy *esprit de corps* or a common natural urge, we've observed that even in the States we tired of a camp quickly. Ultimately and unconsciously, we've been goaded by the desire to end the war and go home.

In the meantime we have good reason to believe that this monotony will lift. We know that the war does not mean to exclude us from a role farther north.

I suspect we have witnessed a typical rise and imperceptible but certain decline of a base. Other bases have been reduced to mere relics. Possibly this too is fast, or at least slowly, on its way.

Most likely the natives will feel it. Now, they fish with home-made grenades made with gunpowder, and I expect that they'll have a devil of a time returning to the practice of spearing. Clophopper G.I. shoes will become scarce. Even though they often stumble about, as they wear them every way but the right way, they'll find that their feet have grown tender. And where do you imagine they'll find those classy pajamas? They like wearing pajamas, saving them for their Sunday best, or for whatever day is their equivalent. Come to think of it, I have no idea where the natives procured their pajamas. We never wear them. Truly, the local natives owe their principal subsistence to our generosity and their shrewd bargaining ability. I believe they receive their main source of nourishment from cigarettes. They smoke them with the artistry and impressiveness of a gangster in a movie.

I'm still a dredge man, constantly occupied munching on salt tablets, and perfecting a "blarsted" salty, cocky manner and gait. I now have a pretty good idea of what I'm doing. I've proudly graduated to the assistant thrice removed from the water tender and mechanic. With such a rate, whenever I assemble some newfangled piece of apparatus, I am allowed to have only one part left over instead of my usual two. A good part of the day my hands are greasy, very impressive you know, and I have a nice greasy rag to wipe them with. At least once daily I mistake this rag for a handkerchief which I keep in my other back pocket so that by day's end I've transferred the grease on my hands to my face. When I come up from the engine room all greased up like a pig, I'm very impressive looking. Glorious day, not only do I involuntarily look like a dredge man, but I'm also beginning to feel like one. When I came on board I didn't know starboard from up. "Where's so and so?" someone would ask. "Downstairs". I'd innocently reply. All heads would then turn to this despicable landlubber. I had just committed the gravest of errors. I should have said "Below." I soon adjusted my jargon to the elements. Using seafaring terms is now a cinch. "Where's so and so?" Now I reply, "Over the side."

Let me tell you that your letters are as much a pleasure to answer as to read. You touch on those subjects that I long to discuss.

Those of us who are interested are well-aware of the state of the nation, of events, literature, art, politics and science. We receive an abundance of books and periodicals. Such names that you mention as Grieg,[1] Williams' *Leave Her to Heaven*, and McInnes[2] are familiar to me. Music is the most difficult thing to send to us. What little we get is mostly popular and an occasional, much longed for, classical piece. My desire to hear good music is insatiable. Many of my friends are in similar straits. Our sweet imaginations fall far short of the charming real thing.

My aesthetic interest in music is a relatively new adventure—no more than a year or so. I don't claim to understand music. I'm resigned to satisfy myself with an emotional and un-analytic reaction. I justify this by telling myself that loving something is the essence of appreciation, while understanding it is cold, hard intellectualization. It's like seeing: it's rarely that two persons interpret what they see in the same way. A writer has one idea, a performer another, and a listener still another. All can be both different and equally plausible.

Unfortunately, I've never been to a concert. I have much making up to do. Your observations of such affairs are marvelous to read, especially for one caught up in a distasteful reality.

Romain Rolland—dead two weeks now at the age of 78—wrote about an artist. The artist was belligerent, but acclaimed by all, and in his old age had condensed his art into profound works. But a new generation rejected him. He played, understood and accepted its censures. He was satisfied. Let them talk.

It appears that you have witnessed something similar in the case of another artist doomed by a young public and its sham critics. One can draw a possible parallel in Fritz Kreisler.[3]

Reading, of course, is my mainstay. I found Thomas Mann's *Joseph the Provider* unique in that it is an expansion, when these days condensation is the fad. Out here, where time means so little, the book was a pleasure. Between books, I read a Shakespearean drama, and a Blondie, or Donald Duck in my ancient *Gazettes.*

I could ramble on forever about all the friends I've made both in and outside the service. It's character and personality that count. To describe a friend would be unfair to him. Bare facts fail to reveal why two people take each other into their confidence. I'd need more room than I have here to delve into personalities, and, since my penmanship gets worse the more I write, consider yourself fortunate that I'm not starting any detailed character sketches. Briefly though there's Henry, six feet two inches, Jewish, from Philly, amiable, practical, slightly more pious than unpious me, a born salesman, a remarkable judge of character, strictly not a student, made good money as the youthful (21) manager of the food department at a SunRay drugstore, loyal, my bosomest buddy, and a practical, but not a deep, thinker. We both shed tears while exchanging nostalgic memories of having hot pastrami, corned beef, and smoked lox at the homes of our relatives. Several weeks ago he was wounded, and we found parting very difficult.

There's Ray, born in Karlsruhe, Germany, once anti-semitic while a member of Hitler Youth for four years, came to the U.S. in '38, my age, worships Beethoven and lover of the finest music, expects to attend Columbia[4] after the war to study physics. Since we enjoy each other's company immensely, he has replaced Henry as my bosom buddy. He is a silent person, a much above average thinker, though a slightly above average student, an atheist, and hails now from Cliffside Park, N.J.

Then there's Al. Back in the States we were always together, but while overseas we eventually separated for no particular reason. Age 24, clean-cut, did well as a motion picture projectionist while a civilian, pessimistic, apt to worry, impulsive, excitable, madly in love with his girl back home which is near Pittsburgh, average intelligence, confides in me many of his innermost thoughts, and, although I never do so with him, we like each other very much.

These three are my most intimate friends. I have other friends much older than I: a college professor of French from California [Baldner], several lads from New York City, a geologist, [Albright] a civil engineer from Ohio, and many more with whom I've lived and been more than merely an acquaintance.

When I was down South, I met a lovely family [the Linfields], a widow and her two attractive daughters now in college. They still write. Two families on the West Coast [the Myleses and the Smiths], and a third that are newlyweds, write. The husband of my third West Coast correspondent [Malter] was a battalion chum (30 years old), who was sent home shortly after we arrived here. He's Jewish, a wealthy Los Angeles businessman, married to an Irish girl [Helen Lyon] who is an ardent correspondent.

I also carry on a unique relationship with an Italian fellow back home, a graduate of the Massachusetts School of Art [Johnson Fulgoni]. Our friendship began five months before I entered the service when I was a model in one the art museum classes which he attended. Due to an accident in his youth, he's a cripple, but a marvelous dancer and bowler in spite of his contorted leg. He writes faithfully. He hails from Medford, Mass., loves opera, and has a humorous, magnetic personality. Every night when I worked at the Y, he would walk home with me. His letters, full of puns and humor, are masterpieces of wit.

I can go on about my friends but this letter must end. If not yourself, the censors will lose patience. Briefly, and I hope clearly, you'll have some idea of the bulk of my friends. Because of them this experience has proven to be definitely worthwhile.

Regards to [Cousin] Sol, Nason, Isa and Mark [Sol's children]. Health to you all. Remember me to Aunt Eva. May Eddie and Charlie [Eva's sons] come back to her, as I expect I'll come back to my folks.

Hughie

1/29/45

Dear Mom,

By the time you receive this, your birthday [February 11] will be near or just past. In previous years, I regarded this day as an opportunity to express my tenderest love and devotion to you and it usually came in such forms as a set of good hosiery, or a pair of slippers that were too large, or a robe that made lint on the sofa which, as a consequence, I'd have to brush down on Sundays. Now, this year, I have only words.

I know you don't expect a gift, but if the arrangements I've made are followed successfully, you will have one. With respect to both my words and the gift, they express my sentiments poorly. But my words are the more valuable. If only I were a Byron,[1] my poem to you would be the loveliest that would ever be written.

I'd gladly relinquish a year, no, many years of my life, to have a glimpse of you and a kiss on this birthday. Although fate has painfully separated us, I've never felt closer than I do now. Your maternal comforting is with me always.

The day I shall see you again is bound to come. I constantly review it over and over and over and over. Your image appears angelic.

Mom, I'm dissatisfied with the weakness of my words. They are but a meager replica of my true sentiments. Bless you, Mom, bless you.

Hughie

1/30/45

Dear Mom,

TO MY MOTHER AT HOME

A sky so blue,
A sea of deeper hue
I never did see.

The sands so white,
The foam dazzling bright
Move and mingle so free.

A scape so green,
Patches of grass that gleam
All magic so charming to me.

A poem like this,
How insufficient, amiss,
Charm wanes,
My thoughts are with thee.

Hughie

We know why letters have been so scarce. Almost a week has passed without receiving letters. Yesterday was the first letter I had written in five days. Expect a longer lapse before the month is over. I expect to be really busy.

Everything is progressing at a safe, uneventful pace. I'm well and contented, suffering only from a lack of letters. Currently I'm reading the comparatively ancient *For Whom the Bell Tolls*,[1] after finishing *Romeo and Juliet* and faithfully following Donald Duck.

2/1/45

Dear Mom,

A raft of mail arrived making up for the empty days: three from you, a mimeographed thing from Ralph Mayo [a high school teacher], one each from Beverly Ringer [a contemporary] and [Aunt] Ida. I haven't written anyone besides you for well over a week.

The situation here is abnormal for reasons that you may imagine. I've got my work down to a simple, compact routine. It's a good job while I'm in the service.

Many rate advances were handed out today, some to friends, some to people for whom I have no use. It's not easy to see one of my co-workers advance when I'm doing a better job and catching on faster. This has happened to a co-worker in the engine room. Of course, by now, I'm used to seeing others who work right beside me pushed ahead. When my boss (who is a fair fellow) tells me that it's a shame that someone less deserving than I should get a break, laments over it, and tries to console me, I have to laugh out loud. I told him he should know better. Understand that there are three reasons, or a combination of any two or three, that cause a man to get ahead. First, he must not be stupid, and, second, he must not be lazy. And third, he must have the support of an influential person. In civilian life that person is not as important as in the service. In the service I have seen stupid and lazy men advanced. Immodestly, I claim not to be stupid, and in spite of my dislike of physical labor, I'm not lazy, so what I lack is that influential person. You must talk fast to convince such a person, which, as you know, I've done before with favorable results. However, to do so requires forfeiting a certain amount of independence, and bowing, which I find hard to do. You may expect me to return home with the same stripe on my shoulder that I had when I was last there.

As always, I enjoyed Ronnie's letter, which brought back to mind my letter of a year ago concerning skiing. Although I think Ronnie took the worst beating of the two of us, his letter was certainly the best. Keep it up big boy, and, when you wish to stop, try a tree. It worked for me. Even though I've been in the tropics for over a year, I'll never forget that to stop you must toe in—just toe in, Ronnie. Talking of that heavenly white stuff reminds me that I heard a recent newscast telling of the heavy snowfall in Mass. and Vt. and the entire northern U.S., including low temperatures as far south as Fla. Well, well, as much as I like skiing I must pause to chuckle. Gad, isn't that warm sea breeze wonderful? Have a pleasant winter, folks.

Mrs. Wolf has written me a second letter. Henry is no longer with the outfit, and in a month he'll phone you from Philadelphia. She is worried and fails to understand why her mail to him is being returned. I wrote to her before Henry left. After what I wrote, she should have no reason to worry, but mothers must be mothers. By the time she receives my reply, Henry should be back home shaking everyone's hands and talking about his overseas experience. Lucky boy, in more ways than one. When Henry left, and you may have surmised why he left, I lost my best friend in the battalion. We were bosom buddies. He, a tall, lanky six feet two inches and I, a short five feet seven inches, were a comical pair, as we walked down the sidewalks of Providence and New Orleans. Once I'm a civilian, he's one friend I intend to look up.

Since Henry left, Ray, the German lad, and I have become as close as brothers. He wakes me in the morning; I wake him; he calls for me to go to a show; I call for him to go to a show. Some think that I live in his "apartment" or that he lives in mine. Although he's entirely different from Henry, I shall miss him.

It's unfortunate that Ronnie is following in my footsteps socially. But he'll get along. It's not bashfulness, but rather a social inferiority complex. I'm also being self-analytical. I'm sure a remedy will develop by itself.

I've often wondered how I'll be socially after I return. I'm not worried, only curious. I don't care whether I'm distasteful to someone or not. If I'm bored, as I often was in the past, I don't intend to hide it. I wouldn't be surprised if some people will bore me more than ever.

When you write of youngsters such as Mazur attending pre-med, I become more aware of the years that will have elapsed before I finally return to school. When I was in high school, I was the same age as the other students and sometimes younger. I expect it will be difficult in class competing with younger students. Can you now understand why I say that college will be a challenge?

I figured you would bawl me out for sending Ronnie money. In the time I've been overseas I don't think I've spent $50.00. What I've given for gifts is my cigarette money for the cigarettes that I never smoke. *Comprenez vous?* (*Traduisez*, Ronald). I'm pleased that he got the money in time.

So our family no longer owns a bicycle. That's sad. I like a bike; it's far more invigorating than a car. Not long ago, Ronnie and I were fighting over who would ride the bike. Very sad indeed.

Concerning driving lessons Ronnie should make a deal with Dad: put $35.00 in escrow, while Dad coaches him. You, Mom, hold the money. If Ronnie burns out the clutch, Dad will have the $35.00 for repairs. If the clutch survives, Ronnie will gain $10.00, the cost of lessons elsewhere. Wait a minute folks while I prepare myself for your blows.

I don't regret not having had an experience similar to Weiner's.[1] It's odd that he should talk about it so freely. Dad shouldn't probe so. If he doesn't volunteer anything, forget it. I can imagine the jam session that must go on between the two men, with Dad acting like Clifton Fadiman.[2] Poor, poor Weiner. I bet he wishes he were back at Anzio.[3] In all seriousness, it would be tiresome to answer all the questions that the curious ask. It not easy to be beribboned.

I haven't heard from the Linfields since early last fall (by Northern Hemispheric standards). I'm surprised that our correspondence lasted as long as it did. We knew one another for scarcely two months, hardly long enough to warrant writing faithfully for an indefinite length of time. Fine folks, wonderful folks, the Linfields.

Send me some wrapping paper. If I had some I'd have returned some books. The paper on incoming packages is either worn too thin or torn. Forget about my *Omnibook* subscription. I've taken to reading only full length books. A condensation doesn't satisfy me anymore. When reading a novel, I'm interested in more than just plot. In fact I often find the plot superfluous. This was the case with *Joseph the Provider*.

Send three or four blades—preferably Gillettes—a month. I can't let my beard go longer than two days, or my face begins to feel itchy from perspiration. Very few of the men have beards now. It has taken most of a year to learn that in the tropics a clean shaven face is best.

This week the weather has been glorious—so much so that I was inspired to write a poem. The weather affects my thinking, not that dreary weather depresses me but that gorgeous weather lifts me. Then my thoughts are, of course, always of home, my folks, and our future.

2/2/45

Dear Mom.

I received a letter from Henry, who is in a Frisco naval hospital. He's due to travel East. I also received a Valentine's Day card from Ida. That's one thing about being over here: you receive cards for every conceivable holiday. I'm awaiting one for Washington's Birthday.

Grandma is getting old. She must be well into her sixties. Just think, for a woman her age having a man tagging after her—although possibly for her money—she's doing mighty well. As my grandmother she's always loved me, and as her grandson I've always loved her. Her faults, and her childish reactions to them, are amusing. Few people have been loved by so many fine people, as she has been loved. Who could be finer than Sam [her deceased husband]? Who are finer than her children (forgetting one)? Grandma has done well.

[Uncle] Hymie's dissolution is unfortunate. He has constantly needed someone—Ida, of course—to steer him on a solid path. I wonder if there's a rift between them. I wonder what the cause is, and more important, I wonder what the outcome will be. It's bad for Hymie, but it's worse for Bobbie [their son]. You must realize that Ida, also, has done well. It's her efforts that have principally sustained the morally weak Hymie. She has not been fortunate with her husband. I respect her for her strength. In spite of her falseness toward others, I believe she has been true to Hymie, and laid down the law. Is she giving up? Perhaps Hymie's predicament will blow over. I hope so.

I have a wonderful father, and you have a wonderful husband, haven't we?

Oh, ho, so the girls are inviting the boys now. And who might this young lady be, Ronnie? And what's this? You've had a dancing lesson? You're beginning to act like the Ronnie that I like—and that Mother likes. Get out there, Ronnie. Please Mother, if not yourself. Before long you'll find yourself pleasing both.

Oh, yes, it's "Arsenic and Old Lace"[1] tonight.

2/3/45

Dear Mom,

Last night I laughed more than I have for the entire twelve short months that I've been here. "Arsenic and Old Lace" was a riot. I was roundly entertained.

Tonight an excellent "Stars & Gripes" stage show is due, followed by "Frenchman's Creek."[1] Good shows lately, eh folks.

Mrs. Myles from Hollywood wrote a letter of four well-filled pages mind you, full of the stuff that I enjoy reading. The fact that she is a college graduate and has business training has, I believe, much to do with her letter writing proficiency and the development of her personality. She is a magnetic person, but I now see that her broad cultural interests are largely behind her attractiveness. It's a pleasure to correspond with such people. That she "loves" my letters and writes "Your gift is simply being wasted" feeds my male ego. Someday, I must visit the West Coast. I have two, yes three, sets of friends in L.A. and environs who deserve a visit.

This afternoon we were discussing private enterprise. That got me thinking about Dad and his business. It has been nine years since he has been the owner of the M.U. [Morris Upholstering] Co. He began with less than nothing, in debt; yet now you eat and dress well and live comfortably. Dad, with your important help, has done a remarkable thing. I'd like to write about it someday. I know you are proud of what you've done, and I'm prouder still.

2/4/45

Dear Mom,

The Christmas cards are catching up with us. The new U.S. mail slogan is "Better late than never." Should I take the cards as belated '44 greetings or extremely early '45 greetings? Thank Mrs. Stanley Mann [a neighbor] for hers.

I received a belated formal announcement of the Lyon/Malter marriage. She's a rare woman. Never to have met her, yet to know her so well and find her so friendly, is remarkable.

Last night's show was an ultra-risqué laugh riot. The chaplain must have been tearing his hair out. With respect to its lavish costumes and beautiful women, "Frenchman's Creek" was pleasing, but the story bored me. The combined stage show and movie lasted three and one half hours. I call it excellent. For the best and the latest in entertainment come to our theater in New Guinea. You folks overseas (an adaptation of last night's joke: so and so's brother was stationed overseas — in Wisconsin) should really visit and share our pleasant, if sometimes moist, evenings.

I might as well get all the entertainment I can now for, (should I say), obvious reasons.

Today being overcast, I couldn't sit on my porch, because it was too chilly. Can you beat that? The sea breeze gave me goose pimples so I had to go inside. Our respiratory and perspiratory systems will have their day of infamy the day we land in the U.S.

Chow has been fine. Aboard the dredge I average six eggs a week, and fresh meat twice daily. We had fried chicken last Sunday and chicken pie this Sunday, all supposedly as Mama used to make it — but they don't know my mother. There's a major distinction between our good cooking and your elegant cooking. Our notorious liquor connoisseurs would swap a quart of hard stuff for a glass of milk any day. I've heard it with my very own ears. Liquor is liquor, but milk, ah it's ambrosia, nectar, absinthe all combined.

2/6/45

Dear Mom,

For the next two weeks I have the tough shift, when I sleep, or try to sleep, during the heat of the day. It's 1:00 AM, a cool, tropical evening and the sea is calm. I'm just putting in time, seeing that things go right, and reading and writing. I must laugh when I think that as a civilian I had seen the early, early morning only a handful of times.

This morning I received a splendid surprise Christmas gift, a one year subscription to *Reader's Digest* signed, Helen and Al [Malter]. Belated though it may be, it was the smartest one I've received. Our relationship is reversed. They get married and for their wedding present they send me a gift. (The gift was sent about the time of their wedding.) They are wonderful people, eh, folks.

After many months of silence, the Linfields sent a Christmas card in which they promised that a long letter would follow. Both daughters are attending college, the older one studying art, and the younger pre-med. Mrs. Linfield never talks about herself. I can't decide whether she's unhappy or unhappy over a love affair her older daughter is having with a Texas college student. I think it odd that a girl has chosen medicine, especially the type of person the younger daughter appeared to be. She was frivolous, gay, very pretty—prettier than her older sister—unable to keep still or seated in one place for long. Either she has changed radically, or appearances are deceiving. I assumed that our correspondence had been worn out, and I'm happy that it has now been renewed. I encountered many fine people in my U.S. travels, eh, folks.

I was surprised to read in an early December *Gazette* about a girl and former schoolmate whom we both know. You may recall that while you were at Hammond hospital, the girl sharing your room had a beautiful, dark-haired visitor. Afterwards, whenever I met her swimming, on the street, or in her dad's theater she always asked for you. Again, during my ten day leave we saw her at the ration bureau. She now has a Hollywood contract.[1] I'd find it interesting to follow the careers of all my schoolmates. Many might well become something.

Tonight, or should I say this day's night, since tonight still seems part of yesterday, we plan to see "Casanova Brown."[2] Last night we watched Abbot and Costello[3] in "In Society,"[4] which was insulting to the intelligence, and strictly corny. If it weren't for its halfway decent music, I'd have walked out.

Speaking of music we are hearing some. After dinner and supper for one to two hours per siesta the P.A. system broadcasts popular and classical programs full blast from a local station called the "Jungle Network." It plays jive and opera, Tibbet[5] and Crosby, a broad variety of music. I may have said it before, but I must repeat that music is a great relief to my always hungry ears. The programs include recent—only a few days old—special G.I. shows with a host of stars and excellent talent, all without advertisements and unavailable to sponsors. Sunday I listened to Lily Pons and Andre Kostelanetz' orchestra. During the past few weeks I've heard The Family Hour,[6] the Jack Carson show,[7] the Frank Morgan show,[8] the Bob Hope show,[9] James Melton and Kate Smith, Rudy Vallee[10] and on and on. The shows are dubbed, for example, "Command Performance," and "G.I. Journal," etc. If they call this war, it's not what we expected. I wonder how much longer we'll be in a position to hear all this.

I have casual thoughts about home that bear no relationship to one another. I suppose Dad continues to deal with his old familiar customers. I suppose you still see Mrs. Lynn, Eva Lowe, Janet Greenberg, Mrs. Barker, Mrs. Tyler[11] and others. Does the Butcher girl still like Ronnie? Of course, you still shop at Whitman's. Do you visit Water Street[12] every Saturday night by car or truck? I can imagine your summer warmth and greenness, but it's difficult to picture snow covered streets.

It's now been almost two years since I've been home. As do all of us, I consider the period from now to September as a brief moment in the passage of time. We treat time, which is so intrinsically valuable, as the cheapest commodity. Its swift passage is sweet, but it will be less sweet once I'm back.

This, my folks, is nostalgia in the raw.

2/8/45

Dear Mom,

The other morning there was a sunrise the like of which we never see in the hills of central Mass. or on the New England coast. The night before last a star fell. Last night another one did. Whatever the state of mind is that leads one to watch the heavens, I have it. It's more than just the love of natural beauty; it may be boredom, or possibly ambition or homesickness. It also may be a form of insanity. Whatever it is I have it.

It's "Kismet"[1] tonight. By the end of the week we expect to have an ex-Broadway play.

The job doesn't amount to much these days while the dredge is merely standing by, not operating.

For Whom the Bell Tolls by Hemingway and John Donne[2] is now my most exciting preoccupation. The old boy either has a keen imagination (as you would say), or he has had extensive experiences. His description of bewildering sexual reactions compares with those of P.S. Buck[3] and M. Mitchell.[4] The story is a thorough expansion of a dashing four day experience. After flocking to buy the book, most people didn't like it. I wonder why. Although I'm not particularly crazy about it, I anxiously continue to read it.

Yesterday afternoon I borrowed *Vogue's First Reader*, an anthology of literary essays by contemporary writers. After reading the first two of the seventy in the book, I thought they were great.

I borrowed the book from a most interesting character with whom I've occasionally conversed ever since the battalion was formed. He's over six feet tall, forty years old, and he has been most vividly on my mind ever since I met him in a sailor's home on Wilshire Boulevard. From later conversations I've tried to learn more about his background. He's an etymologist, a Cornell graduate, class of 1930, now a second class petty officer, although he deserved to be a commissioned officer. He was a football player, evident at a glance, and his appearance wouldn't lead you to believe that he was a brilliant student. For the past fifteen years he has been a professional golfer earning more than $6,000 a year. His club, composed of the muckamucks of New York City, was the most exclusive in the U.S. Having a winter apartment in Manhattan, a summer provincial home, and spending the cold months in Florida, and owning three cars (mostly Packards, which he buys because of his connection with the Packard people) he lived what we would call extravagantly. His wife is the debutante daughter of the president of the sixth richest casualty insurance corporation in the world. This millionaire poppa detests his athletic, Springfield, Mass.-born son-in-law. My friend has two children in their early teens. I guess the poppa likes the children, because he boasted to the local draft board that his professional son-in-law is quite capable of being drafted as he, the poppa, will maintain the children throughout the duration. So the forlorn, reckless etymologist turned golf pro beats poppa-in-law to the punch and walks into the first door that he sees in the N.Y.C.P.O.[5] Building that suggests enlisting, thus the Seabees.

I've been conversing with the son-in-law more often than usual lately. He has limitations, prejudices, and he's an athletic fanatic. But he's far above the common lot here, and I'm out to learn all I can from him. He's also a very pleasant chap.

Oh yes, in a moment of sincere brotherhood he invited me to visit him at his club, and we made a postwar appointment. If I don't like golf, I may like polo or swimming in the indoor or outdoor pool, or tennis, or any number of things that he just kept on and on about. I needn't concern myself with transportation because his station wagon would pick me up wherever I am and take me where I wish to go. Look me up, he said. Reluctantly, I promised, but when he added that I'd have the opportunity to meet many debutantes there, I secretly decided I'd not follow through.

I don't think that people mingle on such intimate terms in civilian life as they do in the service. Revelations that would never be made under normal circumstances, are made here during fits of depression or while reminiscing and homesick. I'm in an ideal spot to study character and its origins. I pity the poor fellow who takes it upon himself to study mine.

2/12/45

Dear Mom,

We are having a mail famine again, and we know the reason why. Packages, *Gazettes* and Christmas cards manage to get through. They would; the padlock arrived.

All on board, myself included, are working eight-hour shifts, instead of the former six, and the night shifts have been eliminated. We are putting the dredge into shape in preparation for things to come.

The weekend brought us two stage plays—those that I mentioned earlier—produced and acted by "veterans of Broadway." "Personal Appearance"[1] was performed Saturday night and "Petticoat Fever"[2] Sunday night by the same stock company, one that may be worthy and all that, but which bored me. The plots were weak, and the acting fair, although excusable, considering the poor sound system and the muggy, hot weather. The latter play was set in arctic Labrador. The most difficult thing for the actors was to act cold, which they did admirably, in spite of the sweat glistening on their faces and the repulsive, hot parkas and overcoats that they wore. Instead of making the audience feel cooler by rubbing their hands, and wearing winter clothing against a backdrop of false icicles, we only felt hotter. It was sympathetic hotness, partly physical reaction and partly pity for the damsels dressed in Eskimo suits. If we enjoyed it, we were the only ones. The players, the poor players, certainly suffered. Furthermore, we've also seen better shows.

Ted Bagdikian—you may recall Ted from Monroe Ave. who was inducted and went through boot camp with me—is now here. The last time our paths crossed was back at Hueneme. Since I've been overseas, we've corresponded only twice. He went across about a month before I did and was fortunate enough to get around more: Australia and Port Moresby and Milne Bay for a short while. Well, Ted's unit, about one fifth the size of ours, has been assigned to maintaining this base. After learning the particulars of each other's whereabouts, we finally arranged to get together in our chow hall. His outfit, which isn't ashore yet, will be soon. We've now seen two shows together, including tonight's, and, as is typical with such reunions, talked ourselves right down to the dregs. Being a pianist, and a lover of classical music (preferring symphonies), he's right at home with my chum, Ray, who loves Beethoven. Despite my meager knowledge of music, although I appreciate it, it became the theme of our discussion, even overshadowing talk of home.

I was surprised to learn that Ted's father, now a minister, is a Harvard graduate of the class of '24, and his mother, also college bred, once taught at the American University in the Near East. He does have the necessary cultural background and proper parentage. While Ted's aspirations are fairly certain and high, he's a pleasure to talk to. If he has changed during the past year, I can't detect it. He now flaunts a black mustache.

On meeting an old friend, the past few days have been delightful and different. Since I'm a seasoned veteran here, I enjoyed acquainting him with our base, giving him all the facts, and finding him a good listener, I felt pretty good.

Now for some more serious thoughts that I've been brooding over for some time, notably the past few weeks. After reading a discussion of the Chicago Round Table,[3] I'm prompted to say what follows. I now have sincere doubts about my earlier choice of chemical engineering, or any related scientific field, as a career that will lead to success and happiness. That it's not practical, I've always been willing to partly admit. You and some publications have pointed out that the opportunity in the field would be limited due to prejudice,[4] corporate politics, and possibly one's lack of ability along those lines. I would not be satisfied to be a mediocre engineer or scientist, whereas to excel, which I would strive to do, would require the mind of a genius. In other words, as the aptitude test I once took maintained, I would have to be satisfied with a considerably lower position than I aspire to. Competition might well leave me in the dust. I know to learn I have to study hard. But my competitors may have natural gifts. I've seen this among my high school classmates. Furthermore, I hate being cooped up, hate routine. My laboratory job revealed this in me, just as my flitting from one job to another has. Research, while fascinating, pays little, requires working under confined conditions, and might not prove to be a suitable outlet for my insatiable ambition. And practical engineering, while it may pay well, is subject to corporate exploitation and prejudice, as I've said. On the other hand, theory as always interested me.

I have always enjoyed math, anything mathematical, its laws, its symmetry, and I've enjoyed physics and chemistry. My conclusion is to specialize in science. However, I've had my doubts from the beginning and have felt that the future would decide for me. I liked other subjects as well: economics, literature, languages, although these least of all. But math and literature are on an equal footing with me.

Not to specialize in college would be a sheer waste of time. We are a nation, a world of specialists. Specialization is the only reason I would go to college. An actively curious person can get a general education from life's experience. Generalization leads to confusion. One becomes a jack of all knowledge and master of nothing. So what does all my pro-ing and con-ing, which has been ongoing all through high school, add up to? It leads me to consider seriously other fields, particularly journalism and related subjects. I'll never give up mathematics. Somehow, I'll have to find a way to sandwich it into my courses of study.

My mind may not yet be made up, but at least now I have a solid alternative to consider. What do you think? Speak candidly. Spare me nothing in expressing your thoughts.

2/15/45

Dear Mom,

I realize my letters are now fewer and farther between. I'm not intentionally tapering off. It's only that I have less time and less to say. My excuse is a feeble one. I must be a proper host to Ted who has been visiting me nightly. But I feel guilty.

Squeezing some reading into those moments of waiting while on the job, I've managed to finish Hemingway and begin a book of delightful essays which I'm truly enjoying. And while I think of it, would you go to a bookstore and buy me Dante's[1] *Divine Comedy*?[2] I'm itching to get into it. You've never mentioned reading the classics. I suppose that's because *Collier's* and *The Saturday Evening Post* have victimized and spoiled you. My mother: her soap operas and her national magazines. My father: his cigars and his political, and supposedly, analytical reading matter. Tonight, I'm just a meandering gadabout, too lazy to hold to a subject, too lazy to bother paragraphing which reminds me of reading a Thoreau[3] (Ask Ronnie. He knows about Thoreau) essay entitled "Walking" during dinner hour this noon on the dredge in one of those pocket books that I keep

tucked away just for such idle moments. After going deep into the art
of perambulation, or as he calls it: sauntering, half way through he
had me reading philosophy and about the merits of Western culture.
No doubt he enjoyed writing his essay, which, with the cleverest
deception, finagled his ideas into my mind. Such writing isn't
practiced nowadays. It's now all to the point, unleisurely, lacking
freedom. The weather here is always the same day in and day out so
I'll not mention it again, unless I'm absolutely destitute of anything to
write about. Ted has been a frequent and pleasant companion during
the evening. I had exhausted all conversational material, until Ted
introduced some new subjects. Ray, who has taken to Ted, has joined
me in plowing him under with fantastic tales. Ray can't read music,
and Ted, who is doubtless a good musician, and rattles off the names
of musical pieces like a tobacco auctioneer, has won Raymond over
heart and soul. Tell me, has my penmanship grown worse? Do you
still have to call in an archaeologist knowledgeable in hieroglyphics?[4]
The famine persists. Famine? Whether it's mail or food, it's a famine
nevertheless. I'm conscious of increased confusion within myself.
Folks, I know now no more about what I want to do than I did when I
was in grammar school. Two years ago I thought I had narrowed my
choice down to one, but now it's two. There I hope it will remain. I'm
not worried yet about what I'll do; I'm only curious. The chow has
been good for the past several months. By good, I mean an
improvement over the past, but we're not feasting regally. The galley
cooks are perennial scapegoats. Everyone wants it the way Ma cooked
it. Apparently, the Mas never got together and followed the same
recipes. G.I. chow is a feeble attempt to blend all the Ma recipes into
one stew or chocolate cake—or Spam. Instead, the recipes taste like
nobody's. I've observed that many of the cooks are beginning to look
like barbers: bald. When we gripe, they refer us to the chaplain.[5] I
wondered whether the hair I found in my soup the other night fell in
from my orchestra conductor-like pate or from the balding dome of an
exasperated cook. In any case it was darn good soup. I wouldn't be a
cook for the world unless Mars were included. I've learned about
cooks from going swimming with one. I'm like his chaplain. It may be
months before I receive more letters. Continue to write as usual. Keep
sending razor blades and stamps. On second thought delay sending
The Divine Comedy until I ask for it. But have it ready. Reading matter
will be scarce in future months. Although I have no way of knowing
how you are, I'm wonderful at hoping for the best.

2/17/45

Dear Mom,

I don't know how things are at home, whether all of you are well or not. If I didn't know that the accumulation of many weeks of letters are somewhere, (and we have our suspicions where and why), this letter would be full of all sorts of questions.

I'm preparing myself for any eventuality, replenishing my stock of year old clothing, getting another accurate set of G.I. glasses, (duplicating Bloom's cracked ones), and having my teeth checked. Nothing had to be done to them. The dentist predicted that they would last a long time.

My days and nights repeat themselves, except, of course, the recent addition of Ted.

I've thoroughly reread the discussion of the G.I. Bill with the other fellows, and we're all pleased. I still contemplate doing one thing one minute and something else the next. Boiling it down, it's a struggle between art and science. A technical school is rigidly specialized with no language, history or literature. But a liberal arts school isn't specialized enough, unless I can find one where the exact sciences are highly regarded. After reading the G.I. Bill, I see no reason why I can't choose the best school. Why should I choose WPI,[1] when MIT would be available? Why choose Clark, when Harvard is an option? So I intend to choose the best, but, of course, my eligibility remains to be seen. Politics may offer me an edge against the competition. I wouldn't hesitate to use any influence, Mr. Riccius, for example. As soon as you can, find out what colleges are approved by the Veterans Administration.[2] I realize it's very early to get all the facts. At the proper time I will then be enlightened and able to make up my mind. By the way, I prefer not to refer to my high school record, or to the principal, if it's avoidable. I'm sure the college will establish my eligibility. If it were only a question of being accepted at WPI, I'd have no difficulty. You see, I don't regard WPI as a college.[3]

The news is constantly exhilarating.[4] (My use of that present participle[5] is a perfect choice.) It spells the imminent end of the war. I'd like to study the Big Three peace conference carefully to learn what's in it, not to criticize. Whether I agree with it or not doesn't matter. I believe that within the life span of my generation and the next, we'll be participants in another war, regardless of today's plans. The war may not be the same kind as ours.[6] My prediction of the future is based on my study of the past. If the future is in keeping with the past, and I have no reason to expect it to be otherwise, my prediction has a good foundation. It is possible, of course, that the future will be a freak. The policies of the great nations, their diplomatic, political, and nationalistic interests, are at play in the present conferences. But what guarantee is there that the welfare of the world comes before that of a single nation's? We can't know the motives of the diplomats, whether their nation is seeking its narrow interest or considering the broader interest of world prosperity. We will see as time passes; maybe we won't see until the next war.

2/19/45

Dear Mom,

Now, when I have no letters to answer, and I've written time after time on the general state of things, I must resort to nonsense, ideas about the past and present and memories, to let you know that all is well and my life is following its normal insane course.

To satisfy your hearthside curiosity it would be well to describe some event, perhaps that memorable day, when we sighted land after two weeks on nothing but a blue and dazzling expanse. Were I to use the conventional adjectives, similes, and metaphors that most writers use, I'd be reducing the experience to banality. Motion pictures portray the first sight of land with the romantic eloquence of spine-tingling and exhilarating crescendos, as a handsome hero stands, silhouetted against the sky, in the halyards of his frigate, pointing landward. What the picture and most authors neglect to show is the soul's lust for the land, it's slavish wish to take it in its palm and comb through its every crevice and chasm. I'm not capable of describing or somehow making you feel the magnificent lift that the soul experiences. That's best left for some undiscovered master, some wielder of words far superior to me.

Three times I've sighted land on the horizon, and not once did the thrill diminish. And three times plus one I've watched the land fade, each time with solemnity. As the ship moved away, our voices were hushed with a pathos and a shroud of melancholy enveloped us. I write "plus one." I separate the disappearing home horizon from the rest, because it is one that will someday reappear.

Look, what land do I have yet to sight for the first time? I know what land it is. I was nurtured on it, but never able to view it serenely from the vessel of time and distance. As I have seen a land horizon three times plus one, I see also the pure, clean horizon of the future. Before me I see a fresh birth, a renaissance of intent and action. But I was deprived of the chance to embark on the interminable and inconstant sea of life; instead, I embarked on a true ship on a blue ocean, a sea of constant yearning, remembering and hoping.

Does everyone forget what he yearned for, remembered and hoped? I think many will. I pray not I.

2/25/45

Dear Mom,

I had a tiny crumb, your letter of the 25th and one from Sadie, instead of the feast I expected. I'm so used not to getting mail that, when I peered into the box, the two letters that I sighted didn't register and I almost walked away without them. Your recent letter was a continuation of the ones I received weeks ago. They are so rare that I read and reread it all afternoon which put me in a life-loving mood.

Now you know that the 113th has a wide and worthy reputation after meeting and listening to FC 2/c Simkonis of the regular navy (or as we say, the common ordinary navy), aboard the USS *Walker* DD 517, broadcast our achievements. We hear of others raving about us too. I'm not as anxious as I was to leave the outfit for the dredge detachment. As battalions go, the 113th is an excellent unit. The man at the helm (Commander Nowell) — quick-tempered, loud speaking, enthusiastic, determined, and one who respects the commonweal — is largely responsible for its successes. When we were in boot camp and the advanced base depot and bored, he was unpopular. But once over here, his gusto was infectious. As we watched him watch us, it spread through the battalion. In his office, in the offices of his superiors, and sometimes in the field, he is reputedly a tyrant, but everyone knows he has good intentions. Since he is such a political and colorful character, and constantly on the go, our unit has borrowed his color and assumed his nature.

I wrote to Lenny some weeks ago. Like myself, he takes his time answering. He is aiming high and should be able to reach his goal. The boy has a friendly way about him which had attracted me at once. He is consistent and stable, remarkable assets that I shall never have. I like him, but our correspondence doesn't amount to much.

I haven't heard from Johnson for a long time. Quite a coincidence meeting Weiner. Weiner sounds like a fellow I'd like to meet.

Dad should buy an ultraviolet lamp while he's about it and maintain a tanned complexion all winter long. Those fellows who have returned home have observed how livid the complexions — the winter complexions, that is — of the civilians appear.

I suppose Henry Wolf has called you by now, as well as a few fellows from Jefferson and Holden.[1] No doubt "Pappy" Collins[2] has stopped in the store.

I have plenty of time over here to have regrets. Whenever I review my tour of the U.S., I really feel sad. I spent too much time being bewildered and doing conventional sightseeing. I regret not having attended concerts and not investigating what each city had to offer in the way of higher forms of entertainment. Instead, I just wandered aimlessly and tried to avoid crowds. If I had it to do over again, I'd do it differently. I discovered that you have to learn how to travel, and, this being my first venture, I learned too late. There'll be another time, though.

Last night, I saw the year old "Going My Way."[3] It was well-done, and how could I help not enjoy its universal appeal?[4] We'll be seeing "Since You Went Away"[5] Monday night. Often I've walked out of the theater, blustering and aggravated over Hollywood's sham and cheap productions. Rather than entertain, such pictures depress me, though those Hollywood classics that appear once in a blue moon do the trick and renew my respect for the industry.

Around midnight one night I stood at Hollywood and Vine simply observing the goings-on. Unlike in New York at that hour, the night-clubs were emptying, sleek Cadys noiselessly rolled by, containing shining blondes in rich furs and male escorts in tails and tuxedos. I had to return to camp early that morning in an ancient overcrowded Greyhound.[6] While watching all the sparkle and peroxide and elegance, I felt perplexed. Certainly I didn't expect civilians to feel penitent or to adopt voluntary martyrdom. Yet, I sensed that something was wrong. I found myself holding them in contempt. It wasn't from envy or selfishness. No, I think not. I've observed similar feelings in others as well and recently I've read about such feelings in books and magazines. It derives from the idea that the hearthside civilian, or the civilian who spends his time at the bar, has missed some deeper experience and doesn't know as much as we in the service do. Of course, whether this is valid or not remains to be seen. But I believe colleges will have to deal with it among returning veterans. I wonder whether parents and spouses will have to, too.

The book I'm reading is written by the entertainment elite. For instance, among its many subjects, music, literature, and the preparation of exquisite dishes are discussed. In a discussion of ships, the most expensive suites on the *Normandie*[7] are described. A discussion on food involves a palatable mush that puts caviar to shame. Such modern and nineteenth century women as Lady Astor,[8] Sara Bernhardt,[9] and Clare Boothe Luce[10] are presented as delightful playmates—that is, before they became bags. Two of the authors have a tug of war commenting on opera. The book, an informal, entertaining anthology of modern essays, is good stuff, fun.

Today is Sunday, my day off, when I sit and read, write and rest. We expect to have turkey for dinner to commemorate our first year overseas. Not until I've tasted that turkey melting on my palate, will I believe that it has been a year since I was on the pier in San Pedro harbor. Since we experienced no seasons, nor a personal purpose in living, the past year seems to have been something that happened outside time.

2/26/45
The 368th day nearer home

Dear Mom,

Have you seen "Since You Went Away?" You have? Yes, you must have. I've forgotten whether you've mentioned it in one of your letters.

The acting was so superb that I forgot it was acting, forgot that I was sitting on a hard bench. Along with everyone else I was moved, transported. I was reminded of our lives together these past eighteen years—or as far back as memory registers, say fourteen years.

I found two things in the film that struck me as highly significant. One was the presence of two cats on a nightly prowl watching humanity. The other was the use of eloquent, if worn out and often abused, words of love that I too have used in repeated letters, often when in inner turmoil. It was a sensitive picture, a grand success, and most meaningful to all members of a family.

I don't rave about the picture. After all, it was only acting. Some scenes were forced, others were too theatrical. To rave would be blasphemous to the sincerest human emotions. I must chuckle a little. I analyze like a disgusting pedant, always keeping my weather eye open for technicalities, and infinitesimal touches. Yes, I found them, some graceful, some trivial. I'm afraid it's my writer's eye cropping up.

Oh, by the way, my buttocks are sadly sore. Now for a good night's sleep and thoughts of home.

2/27/94

Dear Mom,

I'm both amused and amazed at the number of dogs, curs and foundling bitches that run loose around our camp and base area. All are mongrels—what else—and all are American. I say American because they have an American bark and chase after the opposite sex in a manner peculiar to Americans. They got here in some fangled way, most likely as stowaway mascots. Neither dogs nor any other animals are allowed on troopships.

I recall that one of our boys who had sneaked one aboard had a devil of a time finding food for her and disposing of her droppings. Unfortunately, she had no manners. Once the dogs landed on tropical soil they multiplied, divided, and multiplied again etc. So every once in a while during a climax at a show we hear a spine-tingling howl (causing us all to laugh) as a dog sights its mate. In fact, the dogs watch the show and heckle the performers more than we do. The illegitimate dogs of war.

The fellas proclaimed "Since You Went Away" a tear jerker, something the folks back home would like, not us. It's that feeling again: we know something the folks back home don't know. What you take seriously, we take with tongue-in-cheek and laugh at. I, too, participated.

There's a money order enclosed — fifty smackers. If you need it, take it.

3/2/45

Dear Mom,

March here already, blustery March, March 1945 — same as March 1944, nothing changed except nearer to home in time.

We've seen many fine pictures this week: on Saturday, it was "Going My Way"; Monday, "Since You Went Away"; Tuesday, "The Climax";[1] Wednesday, "Mrs. Parkington";[2] Friday, "None but the Lonely Heart." All good, some better than good. I'm being well entertained. Soon I won't be. How long have I been saying that? Soon is soon, no matter.

Of late, thinking has been my preoccupation and my companion. It has to do with the future. I have a plan, a flexible plan, that takes into account the best and the worst eventuality. Rather, I should say it's a purpose, more a philosophy. Yes, at last a philosophy. If I can adhere to it, maintain it, exploit it, live with it, by it, I'll enjoy life. It simplifies complexities. I feel good having a philosophy.

Here, there is only serenity. Serenity in nature, in our circumstances, in the sea. You should be a happy and unworrying mother. On the face of things everything is quiet, but the depths at our end of the line are slightly turbulent. They are small ripples washing on our shores from north of here.[3] All ripples wash from the north. Another year, two years maybe, no more, and it will be over,[4] then an interim period, temporary, a time for happy hunting.

Two or three incidents of the recent past have come to mind. When I think of them, I say to myself, "This is something that might interest the folks." When night comes and I sit down to write, pooph, there's no trace. It's forgotten, so help me, forgotten.

I'm not melancholy. Really, I'm not. I can't say what dictates my mood when writing a letter. A letter may be sad, or happy, thoughtful or nonsensical. Bear with me folks, bear with me.

3/4/45

Dear Mom,

After having chicken fricassee for Sunday dinner and receiving two letters from home, letters as rare as snow itself, I'm feeling pretty elated. Yesiree, both my stomach and my heart are happy, so I'm happy. It's annoying to receive late February letters right after receiving late January letters. I have no idea what went on in between. No doubt, after they arrive in a higgedly-piggedly fashion, I'll put them all in chronological order and reread them as they should be read. I'm most curious to learn how your birthday came off.

It's good to know that my letters are reaching you in good time. And I'm also consoled in learning that you are all hunky-dory. Regarding the shots I sent you of my quarters, I'm the one who lives on the lower deck. Not a penthouse, I realize, but that's my apartment. Although small, it's comfortable, convenient and private. The washing hanging on the line, maybe not snow white, but it's fresh and clean-smelling, is mine. The apartment has electricity, and a wash basin in the guise of a steel helmet which, observe, is hanging from a hook on the porch. I have running water by merely tipping a bucket which I replenish every few days. I have all the conveniences of home, you see.

Installing the electricity was an ordeal. Note in picture number eight the wire strung across its width. Tapping onto a neighboring line, I found that I was an excellent conductor, so before finishing the job, I secured a pair of gloves and taped the pliers and screw driver. The struggle was worth it. With an electric light bulb, a comfortable chair, and a book my evenings are luxurious.

Last night I finished *Vogue's* anthology.[1] It was entertaining to the nth degree. My next book will be *Music on My Beat*[2] by Howard Taubman, the N.Y. Time's critic. It will be light and informative, nothing more.

Do my colleagues' parents lament that their sons are in fighting zones, or do they brag about it? It's a mixture of both. They'd be better off if they didn't mention it. It's difficult to say the right thing to a parent or a wife. I'm fortunate. The poor devils up north are catching it. There's no place to compare notes, neither on Water Street[3] nor here. I must tell you that we'd like to be in action up north. There's no denying it.

My attitude is entirely unreasonable. I can appreciate the true worth of silence. Talk, talk, talk, lips incessantly flying apart, a son here, a brother there, a husband anywhere—it only makes things worse. Better not to talk or listen, just hope.

Ronnie, a junior already (an excuse for a senior)! Good lord, he'll be entering college when I will. What subjects do you like, Ronnie? What subjects, once you sink your teeth into, do you want to hold in your mouth to taste? That's the telltale sign if you like something. True, I often tired of my favorite subjects—math, and secretly, English. I always found Sunday a relief. But you need not be obsessed with a subject, only fascinated with it and have respect for it. A fellow who isn't cut out to study can find his reward in a craft or a business.

Well, Mom, I make many resolutions that may seem ridiculous and hasty. I don't mention them for fear of seeming naive. But there's one resolution that always remains vital and that is I intend to give school my undivided attention. No parties, dances, or fraternities. I'll seek pleasure at a theater, a concert, a gymnasium, and a pool. Nothing can deflect me from my goal. One infraction leads to another. A girl would be disastrous. She would sap my determination. I feel that time is short. In addition to the next four to six years, I must cram what I would have done these past two or three years. I shall be entering college very late.

When the war is over, and I'm home, I'm sure you will think my ideas unreasonable, because they are based on my being strictly independent. I'm aware that my previous paragraph is in direct contradiction to thoughts that I expressed not many months ago. It's part of the process of developing towards maturity.

Pause

I just returned from a scrumptious dinner, and I'm stuffed. It couldn't compare with yours though. But a few minutes ago I was given a new book to add to my collection, a six hundred page affair called *Morley's Variety*. Do you know Christopher Morley? He's a topnotch contemporary writer.

I don't believe for a moment that Al Malter was responsible for the R.D.[5] subscription. I know Al too well. His wife, Helen, is the giver.

The message on the card was in her writing. Al is too inconsiderate and businesslike. He's a terrific egomaniac.

This about winds up "Hughie's Variety" for Sunday. After I scan this, I suspect I'll find it unlikely that you'll know what on earth I'm talking about. Yes, it's very probable.

P.S. Dad states that R.D. is fascist. It's not; it's ultra-conservative. Fascism is absolute state control. R.D. is against state control, thus labor control as well.

3/6/45

Dear Mom,

A remarkable feast of letters today—six in all. I call it an event.

From reports, I see your birthday celebration was a riproaring success. Believe me, I'm happy for you, Mom, very happy. You have a friend of friends in Mrs. Ringer. Rather she's a devotee. One of her letters also arrived today. Her letter is grand, her commitment grander.

In pictures four and five I'm a blur. We aren't expert photographers. The other boys you see are merely acquaintances with whom I go swimming. However, my closest friend is in one of the pictures. I dragged him out of bed to take the picture. You can spot him by his annoyed demeanor. The forest in the background is not as dense as other forests I've seen. The jungle extends from the hills right down to the sea. The picture was taken in the protected portion of an enormous bay. The spot is a sheltered lagoon with a sharp coral bottom. Our camp faces the open sea.

When we first landed, we had to string wire through the forest you see. At the time there were some Japs about who fired on us. Some weeks later they were captured. We always carried either a sidearm or a carbine. But what we feared most was our own boys who fired into the jungle at random. It reminded me of my childhood days of cowboys and Indians.

The chow is fine, I repeat, fine. We have fresh meat twice a day, butter, an excellent variety of canned and some fresh vegetables. We are definitely well-fed. I've never deceived you. Only silence is deception. Fellows at other bases don't fare as well as we. The food is exceptionally tasty on the dredge where it is cooked for only a few. In my picture, I surely don't look hungry. Thinner maybe, due to the heat.

"My letters are not very satisfactory" etc. You've got a lot of nerve. It's for me to decide, not you. Your letters are the acme of letters. The others can't compare.

The best way to maintain one's health in the tropics is by means of both internal and external cleanliness. Liquor can be fatal. Showers provide the day's relief. Often we shower twice a day. It's essential to wear clean clothes daily. Dirty clothes irritate one's skin. We usually have an epidemic of heat rash. I've had a mild case but cleared it up myself. Some have been so covered with it that they couldn't work

----

We remove our clothes immediately after work. We can't wait. We wear mostly army garb, which is comfortable. Shirts are worn only at night; they would be quickly drenched with sweat during the day. But the officers must wear them, and they have my sympathy.

Lester Katz wrote. He's been in England for almost a year. During his leave he plans to study under army auspices at Oxford University.[1] The boys in Europe have that advantage over us here.

Mr. Riccius promptly answered my letter. He writes in an excellent, smooth-flowing style. His letters are always a pleasure to read. He mentioned seeing my name on the Jewish War Veterans Memorial. He wonders what the fellow named Zzizg does for a living. I often see Mr. Riccius' name in the paper, especially in connection with the music festival.[2] He loves art, all kinds.

Only today I was given a new mailing address:

> U.S.S.D. York Syme
> Navy 3115
> c/o Fleet P.O.
> San Francisco, Calif.

(D stands for dredge.)

Juliet[3] was only sixteen, but she was intelligent and serious, witty and determined. From the Commerce High School damsels I've received a joint letter. It was sheer nonsense. I imagine they were bubbling over with girlish glee as they wrote it. It's not the kind of letter I like to receive. I wonder whether these girls, who are about to graduate, are ready. If anything annoyed me when I was in school, it was the yappity-yapping and giggling of girls and their utter disregard for the subject matter under discussion. Only a few girls were reserved, tactful, and intelligent. Unfortunately, none of my intelligent female—Mrs. Linfield, Mrs. Myles, Helen Lyon—correspondents are young. Their letters are thoughtful and well written. I expect too much from high school kids. They mean well, but their interests are sadly limited. I'm unfair to expect more. You may well think: "What do you expect? Egg in your beer?"

At any rate, I smiled through it all. After not hearing from me in a while the blonde and the brunette were concerned and threatened to send me some fudge. Good lord, not that! Infamy! It would arrive as a liquid ooze.

This evening the mosquitoes are thick. We try to control them as follows: the mosquito control unit has issued us a freon aerosol bomb which releases a deadly (to mosquitoes), not ill-smelling gas into the atmosphere. We can see the mosquitoes drop as the vapor hangs in the still tent air. This keeps the pests away for about an hour. When the bombs are empty they can be refilled. They come in several sizes, some as small as a tin can.

A book lying on my plyboard cabinet has caught my eye, and since I've unraveled all my thoughts, I can't resist its charms any longer.

3/9 - 3/10/45

Dear Mom,

For several months I've been expecting to be "busy," but now it's confirmed that it's in the offing. The big question is what will happen to the dredge and its crew. As we devoted our days to putting her in shape, the dredge has been idle for many weeks. Lately, she has had to take plenty of gaff from both the crew and outsiders. Some insist that she should be commissioned and given a five gun salute, while others claim that she has already been commissioned. She has to be towed, you know, and this is a source of hilarity. My battalion friends ask me how many knots she'll do at low tide. Some say that when the time comes to move on, they pity whatever convoy she's attached to. Some ask me to explain which end is forward and which is aft. Well, of course, that depends on which end she's towed from. It's okay. Let them guffaw and poke fun at her. I tell the ribbers that our vessel will be up there dredging the harbor to enable their ship to dock. We are all staunch dredge men now, united against the mere landlubbers.

Letters, letters, letters, oh boy. Look at this: Jan. 27, 29, 31, Feb. 24, 26. Many of them include razor blades and stamps. Excellent. You may let up for a while on sending stamps, but I can always use more blades. I must shave more often now.

Ronnie's chastity is best revealed in his interpretation as obscene the lyrical "I Miss You, Dear."[1] In a few years, after he gets to know men, he will undoubtedly be shocked. He's done well in getting a good report card. The big boy is a ladies man sure enough. Who will bet that he marries first?[2]

I see you've elected art, Ronnie. Would you send me an outline of the subjects you have thus far, term by term? I'm glad that you are continuing math. Too bad you couldn't continue with a foreign language. At South [High School] only a senior could elect U.S. history. Not so there, eh. You now have two more years to go. They will be the two shortest years of your high school career—and the happiest. Now your class will manage its own proms and dances. By all means participate. Get in there: join clubs, committees, class politics. Don't repeat my mistakes. You have an aptitude for social activities. If Mom and Dad don't want you to follow in my dreary footsteps, they should encourage you. You needn't aim for the extraordinary grades that I so fanatically achieved. Average or slightly higher is good enough. Your social activity is also a part of your high school education.

From reading the newspaper I see that a "Teen Age Canteen" is going strong. The war has certainly made both the government and civilian adults youth conscious.

I find talk of skiing and skating sweetly nostalgic. Last night (It is now the eve of 3/10), this letter was interrupted by a friend who visited to engage in talk about winter sports mostly. He (a forestry graduate of University of Calif. at Berkeley, now an electrician) loves skating, frequents the dance floor, appreciates opera, the symphony, and Donald Duck. At times I find him naive, but we have similar interests and a mutual fondness. Like myself, he was a battalion man and is now assigned to the dredge. After we return, we plan to do Frisco together. He'll be a wonderful guide. I was amused to learn, in strictest confidence, that he brought a $25.00 pair of ice skates along. He removed them on the sly from a secret place to show them to me. Woe to him if anyone else gets wind of it. His rationale: he has them in case we go to Alaska. You must realize that nobody knew where we were going to end up in February, 1944. Which reminds me of the temperature here lately. I have been noting the readings on a friend's thermometer. In the early morning, the coolest part of the day, it reads 74 to 76, and we are shivering. By 8:00 AM it rises to 80, and we find that cool. In the sun the temperature has risen to 135 degrees. Imagine, a $25.00 pair of skates. After all, it is winter here.

I haven't seen Ted for well over a week. I understand he's now a third class petty officer. A week ago he was so disgusted with his outfit that he was ready to request a transfer. He should be in good humor now.

Infections and skin diseases are commonplace. Yet some go unscathed. Fortunately, I've had nothing worse than heat rash. Many have had to be sent home. Once in a temperate climate the skin problems clear up. Our medical department discourages us from giving information to the home folks on our general health and the prominent diseases circulating about. Except for malaria, I know of no diseases that are incurable. Since we are not given blood tests for purposes of morale, we have no way of knowing whether we are infected with malaria. The Atabrine we take keeps the disease dormant. If you have malaria, Atabrine lessens the intensity of the disease to an almost negligible degree. Nobody worries about having it.

I know as little about journalism as you do. I have no idea what the opportunities are for a writer. As far as I can tell, it's just as risky as a scientific career. However, I suspect a career in the sciences is more secure. I would abhor a career in economics; it's too utterly confining. Certainly most work is routine, but some work can be exciting, constantly opening up new vistas. A progressive writer leads an ever changing life. A scientist experiences changes in thinking. The changes consist of infinitesimal advances made through discovery, constant invention, and the solutions to physical problems. The writer adopts a philosophy and experiences events, travels the earth through time as he expresses his insights, offers revelations, and gains fame. I wish I didn't have to wait until I was home to make up my mind. Surely, however, I must wait.

Some people tend to be idealistic, especially composers, artists, and writers. They lead impractical lives, often in abject poverty. They rarely attain moderation. They are people of extremes. But they are happy whether poverty-stricken or wealthy. What's wrong with having high ideals and ambition? It's a curse, but also mental ecstasy never experienced by the mediocre or average person. Society gears itself to the average run of people, and all achievement is based on their practical good sense. That is, the vast majority of us do, particularly the most experienced. Were I to have no ambition, what would I become? Yes, Mom, I want to be more than just one of the flock. A good writer will be prosperous. So will a good engineer. Even a mediocre one in those fields can live comfortably. But one must begin at rock bottom. In which career could I go the highest? Do you understand my dilemma?

I grant you marriage is necessary. There's a time for it, but not too early. When two meet, when their paths cross, both helplessly succumb to dire forces beyond their control. I want to accomplish something before such an event occurs. It must not interrupt my course, but rather coincide with it. At the least, I must be progressing toward my horizon.

Damn ambition! That and chaos are so often partners. Either I outgrow it or suffer.

By the way, Dr. Sacks sent his wishes via Mr. Riccius. So did other friends, but I'm ashamed to say that for the life of me I can't recall them. Time is beginning to tell.

When we arrived cat-eyes were the craze. Not being handy at making things with my hands, I sat down and read books while my chums made bracelets. Hardly elegant, they are unique. Eventually they lose their luster and do an injustice to the wearer's wrist. If you wish, I'll try to get one for you. The shells thrive in the coral and stink like hell before being buried to allow the ants to eat the living matter. I have, by the way, a bracelet of local coins given to me by a mate in exchange for a beer. They sell for about $10.00. I'm unable to send it home because the coins would reveal our locality. As with a cat-eye bracelet, it's a dandy souvenir. I lack the American instinct for souvenir hunting. The boys are also making cat-eye earrings. I haven't the guts to try to make a set. Some of the things the boys make are quite beautiful. Remember, these are tradesmen.

I gather that your new upholsterer is satisfactory. I don't expect to recognize our living room. I remember on first entering the house in September 1943 that the kitchen seemed so small, as did all the other rooms. After working in limitless space and spacious rooms, I can understand the illusion. Not having rambunctious kids around — unless Dad continues to practice his usual antics with Ronnie — there's no reason why you shouldn't splurge on lighter, more attractive covers. Will slip covers invite moths?

Do you remember this fellow, Brierly? I don't recall whether you met him or not. He was most active in all class functions, including athletics. I corresponded with him until November 1943. He was madly in love with a girl who is in some photos taken at Coes Pond in June 1943. Why, I believe Brierly is also in one of them. I had the general impression, as did everyone else, that he had a charming personality and above average intelligence.

Lenny's sister (who is evidently growing up) wrote that Lenny's got it, and bad. Lenny's last letter intimated that he had revived his relationship with a girl with whom he had once been infatuated. Poor Lenny. After being spurned for some time, he's suddenly recognized by a damsel who now claims to long for him.

The Social Service Agency on Waverly Street sent me the latest report on new developments in the G.I. Bill. They still send me reports on a regular basis. I shall save them all.

To any onlooker, I am the laziest human being hereabouts on Sunday, tomorrow, my day of rest. To top off my sloth, at 8:30 PM (20:30 navy time) I'll be watching "The Conspirators."[3] It's gotten so that I look forward to Sundays with the same enthusiasm as Dad.

I heard some pretty decent music this afternoon. Brahms Lullaby[4] got me. I heard it sixteen years ago, when you used to sing it to me. Music to me is like one of your letters. My emotions are a slave to both.

Love, always love, to the three of you

3/13 - 3/14/45

Dear Mom,

Three, four, five letters have been arriving daily, mostly from you, others from Henry Wolf, Mr. Mayo, Miss Rourke, and the Gallants. Marvelous things, letters.

I've gathered all the photos and letters for commenting on your comments. Since we're having wet weather, and it's a cool evening, and the show tonight is lousy, it's a great time for letters. So I'll just ramble.

Picture #7—As I've written, I live in the lower space that's surrounded by mosquito netting. It's quite conventional, even ascetic, but comfortable and gloriously private. You see, the tents are built on steep slopes, providing plenty of room beneath them for another "apartment." The upper portion is the tent proper. The tent roofs are beginning to show wear from the sun and rain, and many are leaking like sieves. Since wind is rare, the rain usually falls vertically, so that the tents don't need sides. It's strictly an open air proposition.

Picture #8—Your son is sitting on his apartment's porch; above, are the second story tenants. I try to pay my rent by the tenth. This month I slipped up so the boys stopped me in the chow hall for payment, complaining that their taxes had increased. I promised to pay up immediately with an unsigned check, explaining that I wished to remain anonymous. Such conversation is typical—I mean it.

Picture #1—This fellow is a neighbor. He nurtures a black beard because his wife isn't here to keep after him. I took this during a moment of good will. A couple of afternoons later he saw me going swimming and asked to join me. Thus you have other pictures of him. By trade, he's a bricklayer, and hails from L.A. He's the father of two children, one of whom he has never seen.

Picture #2—These are my two swimming companions and some natives. The one wearing the sun helmet is middle-aged. The others are children.

You ingeniously dig deep and plot to discover what I've contrived to give you on your birthday. I planned to spend ten bucks and end up spending six. Well, that's my Mom, but another day will come, when I needn't share my secrets with anyone.

Ronnie, my boy, the general idea is to ski on your skis, nothing more. However, I remember a little more than a year ago mastering the horizontal technique. How's the foot?

Picture #12—These are the same natives who are in #2. I'm holding a young octopus by a string. The naked lad on the extreme left was having a fine time playing with it.

Picture #3—The fellow on my left is my closest chum, the German lad I told you about.

This letter has been ongoing for three days, and now it's late. Feeling helplessly drowsy, I must go to bed. I'll continue in my next letter.

P.S. Send the *Divine Comedy*[1] now.

3/17/45

Dear Mom,

It's a hot night, a miserable tropical evening, as a light rain splatters the earth. It's like being in an overcrowded room; under the hot electric light sticky perspiration shines on my chin. But I'm not miserable, not by a long shot. In fact my spirits are high. If it weren't raining, I'd have gone to a show.

A couple of nights ago I saw Boyer[1] and Fontaine[2] in the 1943 "Constant Nymph."[3] Now THERE is a picture. Breaking a rule, the original music was excellent. Since shortly before last December I've been reading about "A Song to Remember."[4] It's difficult to imagine Muni[5] as the effeminate Chopin,[6] but Oberon[7] would make a sleek version of George Sand.[8] So I gather the picture is not the real truth but rather the theatrical truth in order to make it more enjoyable. And then the music could make up for any deficiencies. I'm anxious to see it.

Here is more information on the photos.

Picture #14—This is not me. The improvised boat consists of two P-38 wing gas tanks.

Picture #13—The lens was speckled with water. I'm in an outrigger canoe. Notice the native wearing an army hat and a navy shirt. While we always shed our clothes, they wear them comfortably.

Picture #9—The starfish are multi-colored. Henry Wolf had left N.G.[9] before these pictures were taken. The fellow in the center is the

Angeleno, the one on the right an Indianapolis bookkeeper, now a battalion baker.

Picture #6—If your son looks gaunt to you, it's not valid. After fifteen months of searching, he recently found a scale and tipped it at 167+ lbs.[10] He is as surprised as, no doubt, you are.

That does the entire 14 photos. They were taken in December and January. The Angeleno wants copies of prints #s 9, 12, 13, 11, and 6. The other fellow wants #9. Have them made and let me know the cost.

Wolf has written again. He's in a Virginia hospital, not far from Camp Peary, our *alma mater*. When I saw him after the mishap, he was in the naval hospital here and gave me all the details. It was no clambake. His mother has written three times, inviting me to her home and encouraging me to maintain an active friendship with her son. Apparently, Henry glorifies his friends. It's for certain that he longs for them. His latest letter expressed disgust with his lot and a wish to be back here with us. He's been granted a seven day leave and some liberties, and he's due a thirty day leave soon. It's as I feared. Home can only be home at war's end, not before.

My short-lived acquaintance with Arell was a coincidence. After seeing him about for over a year, I met him in the chow hall only two days before he left. Before I could even ask, he offered to see my folks. He's like most of the fellows in the battalion: accommodating and friendly.

I see that my birthday gift to you was as I wanted it. Wear the robe in the best of health—and don't get lint on the sofa.

Mrs. Linfield's personality, a strictly feminine one, spilled over in her recent, nice letter. She made me feel good, for which I thanked her. Even though her use of words such as "sweetest" and "nicest" irks me like hell, I consider her tops among my women friends. I'm glad to hear that I'm my mother's child, but I'd be gladder to hear that I'm my mother's full grown son. Mrs. Linfield doesn't realize that I now have hair on my chest.

If a year ago someone presented me with the *Divine Comedy* I'd have dunked him in Coes Pond. I kick myself for the past, regret yesterday, tolerate today and tomorrow, and fervently anticipate the future. I'm pleased because I've adapted well to every environment in the past, and certainly will in the future. Although I'm reading the *Divine Comedy* for the present, I'm doing it more for the future.

I've decided that the conflict between my literary and scientific ambitions will be best resolved by a government-administered aptitude test that's offered before entering college. Whichever course I choose, I can always delve into the other for pleasure. I didn't intend to imply that I'd resort to dishonest politics to gain my ends. But a good word from a responsible person would give me an edge over someone of equal capacity. I have confidence in my worth. I feel that I qualify in all ways. Although I hate relying on my high school record, I suppose that's the way it has to be. If the best is available, I have no intention of settling for the mediocre.

Ronnie may talk of enlisting during a period when servicemen are envied. It makes him feel proud and manly. If the war lasts until he's eighteen, it's logical to enlist. I hope this won't be necessary. The war's pace is incredible,[11] such that Ronnie's talk may well remain talk and nothing more. He wouldn't like the service; I'd be unhappy if he did, and you'd suffer.

3/19/45

Dear Mom,

It's great to know that you can easily make out my handwriting, and greater still that you can read some of what I write with telepathic understanding. I'd rather write to you than to anyone for that reason, and many important others.

Recently, I've been honestly troubled over whether what one says or writes is sincere. Not only do I wonder about others, but I also wonder about myself. So when I write or talk, I do so half seriously. Of course, since I can't avoid writing and talking, I must tolerate this doubting. Now you know when you read my letters that in the yonder of my mind I have this uncertainty. So what I write about the present is sure, but not the future.

I expect Ronnie has adapted to my absence and, like breaking-in new shoes, enjoys family life. I expect we'll be competing to use the car. No doubt, of the two of us he'll be the greater Casanova,[1] and he may be hysterical in his demands. I'd encourage him to use the car, while I make my own grave.

I don't think that to have one of your employees living in the same apartment house as you is a good idea. Proximity leads to contempt, and confusion much like a modern painting results: an eye here, a nose there, never a pretty picture. You may tell Mr. Weiner that, though I haven't met him, I greet him as a neighbor with open arms, just so long as he can stand an occasional wrestling tournament on his ceiling.

Wear your new dress and spring coat in the bloom of health, Mom. How I'd like to arrive home in the spring, this spring, to see you wearing them.

I had made up my mind to end my correspondence with Dolly and Sybil. I found the recent letter disgusting. Today, in another letter, Dolly apologized. This letter was pleasant and sensible, the sort I don't mind receiving. It was so encouraging, and its tone so feminine, that I've changed my mind and shall continue writing her.

Earlier, the girls had me writhing when they informed me that a package was on the way. Then I was satisfied to learn that one of my predictions, based on my intuitive knowledge of women, came true. Finally, though the girl stood firm for some time, Dolly broke down and requested my picture—no doubt before she'd send any more packages. Ah, the eternal curiosity of a woman. How I enjoy it. But there's more. Her strategy is brilliant. She writes that a picture of herself is on the way, while I earlier had boasted to my companions that among my pictures on display there's not a girl in the lot, that I'm obligated to no one, and I'm as free as the wind. Some, the divorced, have admired me for this, while others, the happily wed, feel sorry for me. But boast I did, and never felt sad. Now that my record of no women in the photos is about to be seriously marred, funny thing, I'm not at all sad.

I wrote the last paragraph knowing that you would enjoy it. I went to a cackling hen's birthday party when I was sixteen. That was my forlorn debut, and so it was also for my companion, a redheaded beauty. As I wander through the past with the boys—each of us is taking turns reminiscing aloud—I wonder what became of that shy, pretty redhead. They wondered too.

3/20/45

Dear Mom,

I can hear in the far off mountains of the hinterland thunder playfully rumbling, and, when the lightning rents the darkness, I can make out the overcast. The entire camp had attended the show which is now over. When the first drops fell, all eyes turned heavenward, and we cursed; then the rain let up. That's service for you. We watched the show in peace. I'm here back in my nook writing, with no desire to do anything else, not even sleep. Since I've had few thoughts lately, you have been spared.

Now, after seeing my transfer on paper, I know that all my connections with the 113th are over, and that I'm a full-fledged member of Seabee Detachment 1082. Inform all you know, who write to me, of this. It will be months before I can notify everyone.

A few stray early January letters finally found their way here. After subsequent letters revealed fresher news, they lost their color. An early

November *Gazette* showed up, and I read all about Armistice Day[1] in Worcester.

Of the wonderful feelings I've experienced, the one I miss most is that which comes over me at the first burst of spring. Along about now —unless you're in the midst of a fierce blizzard—spring should be compromising winter. Along about now I curse the idle tropics. There's never a sign of rejuvenation out here.

3/23/45

Dear Mom,

My back appears mottled. My towel wipes off a thick layer of bronze tan. It's the result of our climate, full of sun and sweat-producing humidity. And where you are everything is so white: the snow, your skin, your wash. Only the crest of a wave is white here. The rest of it is deep blue.

Only this evening I read that twenty million people have died, not in battle, but at the hands of other people.[1] You should be happy that I'm over here. Every family should feel lucky that their sons are here. At least we're safe. Only a few of us (not I) know what a bullet wound is. Our stomachs are full, maybe not with the sort of food we were used to back home, but so what; our bodies are lean and solid; our minds are healthy, especially mine from the letter D in Dear. We are lucky, most lucky. With two letter A's in my name, I'm at the top of the list of lucky ones. My mind makes incoherent talk, unlike rational talk. I present you with unlike talk.

Nothing is happening here.

Some read, others think. As we talk of the U.S., we have no contempt for its minions, only disregard. We think that the public, anyone not over here, is having a pretty good time. We have solid proof. The letters from boys who have returned express none of the exuberance we expected. We figure that things aren't as they were before, as our boys remembered them. I don't think it will apply to me. I know that everything will be the same, even better with a new slipcover on the sofa and you wearing a new spring coat. Others are finding things have changed.

The ridiculous triangle is fast becoming a problem. The blonde, the more vivacious, more daring one and quicker on the draw than the other, now requests my photo, a disaster for sure. As I've written, the brunette has requested the same. She is more mature in thought, more down to earth. The correspondence will continue to straggle along until it becomes unnecessary, and there's not much I can do to stop it. When finally we meet in the flesh, what will I say? Hello, to one and hello, to the other? Then what should I do? Take 'em out? They'd be sure to expect it. Each separately, or both together? Doggoned if I know. I don't look forward to meeting these girls. To have a girl in Worcester is bad enough, to have two worse, but to have two who are friends is a catastrophe.

I'm not tired. Still it's late and the night says go to bed. But I'm not tired. The night wins. Good night and

Love to all three of you

3/24/45

Dear Mom,

I'd like to keep the letters flowing daily through next week, because it's certain that they will be abruptly halted for some time.

Worcester appears to be progressing. At last, it has ideas consistent with the beautiful auditorium. Hooray for the airport, a place for teen-agers to gather, a privately initiated "Worcester and the World" program, an art-music festival, and new galleries. Not bad for a conservative city, one that has been afraid to gamble. *Time* gave Worcester's "World" idea a brilliant writeup and praised the city and WTAG as well.

The movies have been good lately. Our masculine minds were impressed with "To Have and Have Not"[1] with Bogart[2] and that siren, Lauren Bacall.[3] It lingered in our thoughts long after it was over. She was the archetype of a woman on a fling. Tonight, I saw "Wilson"[4] which demonstrated that, while some pictures may stoop low, others try but fail to reach a height. This picture, while understandable to all who watched, was a dismal failure. Tomorrow evening it will be "I'll Be Seeing You."[5] I doubt if I'll have a chance to see "A Song to Remember."

Unlike last night, my eyelids are heavy, and I will sleep well knowing that this will be on its way. If slumber is peaceful, so must the mind and body be. Remember.

3/26/45

Dear Mom,

Things are about to happen creating a certain tension in the air. Having a fairly good idea of what our future holds, we are pleased. Although the chow is poorer, no one cares.

Since the dredge is no longer in operation and only waiting, my job as water tender no longer exists. For the past few weeks I've been getting plenty of electric shocks as an electrician's helper. I've also become well acquainted with the general principles of the trade. I'm now well qualified to relieve Dad of having to do any household repair work. It's worth knowing. As soon as the dredge resumes operation, I return to my original job.

I've mentioned that my boss, the electrician, is thirty years old, a graduate of the University of California. We have inspirational talks concerning what we should do when, when indeed, we arrive in Frisco (He prefers San Francisco). Like all Friscans he considered his city the pearl of the West Coast, and means to prove it to me. He wishes me to meet all his friends, including a thirty year accumulation of women. We'll visit the opera, the symphony, art galleries, his enormous college at Berkeley, and dine at the finest establishments. We'll go ice skating for which I have a mania comparable to his for dancing. I have his word that I'll enjoy myself.

A February 3rd letter that had gone astray caught up with me today.

I hadn't realized that Ronnie was so serious about joining the service. He has no idea how melancholy one becomes, how inconvenient things are. There's no glory, only thoughtless regimentation, the need for tolerance, time impatiently passing, accepting what's handed out without a word or a doubt, and loving without one's loved ones near. He, and others like him who are anxious to be available, will, after joining us, quickly abandon the swagger of their proud, glorified youth, and find themselves ground into the commonplace. They will be made to feel small, and helpless in the enormous dynamics of it all.

In war, one's individuality is threatened, and there's no way to meet it.

I disapprove, I do absolutely, your silly retyping of my letters. Is there anything I can do to stop it? When I hear of it, I feel ridiculous. So enjoy yourself; it's good typing practice but never let me hear of it again. I hate diaries. I derive pleasure from writing letters. It relieves me. My pen is free when writing a letter. But not were I to jot down I did this or that with no tangible purpose. I write letters for you NOW, not for myself or others later. Ink, paper, words are cheap commodities, but thoughts and their circumstances are priceless. My circumstances are now sad and timeless, full of memories an ocean away.

3/27/45

Dear Mom,

I just saw a cut and dried version of "Mexican Hayride,"[1] a USO show. The moon was so full and bright and the clouds the color of tarnished tinfoil, that I couldn't, for the life of me, concentrate on the show. When the moon is more spectacular than a show such as this, the show doesn't merit one's attention. I laughed, though not heartily, at the burlesque humor, and listened to the music of only a slightly more elevated caliber, and walked away at the finale feeling no different than before the show despite the show's intention that I shouldn't. Since there were girls, everyone was happy.

A few of our tropically bred dogs participated in the howling of the gallery. In one instance when the rambunctious, halfpint comedian[2] howled with all his worth at one of the chorus girls, there was a similar echo, not from the audience as would be typical, but from one of the dogs. If it was a male dog, we don't blame him.

I'm not sure that I'm enthusiastic about having a slim mother, still it's good that you're in top condition. All your vitamins sound like alphabet soup. I feel inadequate taking only a measly B-Complex. Imagine, you're casting away all the meat, vegetables, and scrumptious desserts for pills. Women, the amazing enigma! Enigma! hardly does them justice. The Buck Rogers[3] age must have arrived. Here's to curves (as I raise my canteen).

Is it tough for Ronnie at school? He doesn't like it? It's best that he takes what he likes and drops what he doesn't. If he doesn't plan what he'll do after graduation, if school is unimportant, then let him wait for the day of decision. If he hopes that the service will rescue him, he's a damn fool. He'll graduate high school with average grades; then what? Does he want college. The next two years will decide. How unfortunate for Ronnie that he must compare my worthless record with his. You have two unlike sons. But Ronnie is faring better. I believe he knows how to enjoy himself, how to be happy and satisfied. He doesn't want to do what I did, and I don't blame him. Impetuous youth must learn the hard way, which, I say, is good. Neither you nor I nor anyone can lay down his course. It's up to him. The only advice I dare give is he better get started.

This will be my last letter for a while. I'm very busy, you understand.

En Route to Parts Unknown

4/6/45

Dear Mom,

If from my penmanship I seem to be drunk, attribute it to the roll of the ship. We are several days at sea, and reconciled to all the inconveniences that at this stage of the game is old stuff for us.

You might call our voyage, as someone just did, a Coney Island[1] beach party. All over the deck, all over and under the equipment, spilling into every imaginable (and unimaginable) nook and cranny, is infantry gear and its somewhat grimy owners. Tiers of cots strung along the bulkheads fill the dank stifling holds, but we prefer the air and the sun, and yes, even the rain, as we strip down to take a freshwater shower though it is cold and cutting.

For the first few days I felt whoozy, and many felt sorrily worse. Our first meal on board, supper, went over the side in one form or another — either before or after digestion. The normal ones, gloating over their remarkable immunity, made the destitute souls only feel worse. To our bleary eyes, their smiles seemed cruel. Now everyone has recovered (I had only a mild case), as evidenced by the heated crap games, serious card games, solemn reading, industrious writing, laughing, singing, and reminiscing at dusk.

I've strung my jungle hammock across an aft mooring winch amid a nest of such hammocks. I sleep like a babe — that is after I trained the damn thing to respond to my maneuverings. During the night — once a night on the average — a groan, following a perplexing racket, rents the breezy dark silence; it's only a hammock giving way.

We hit a tropical squall the first day out. The rain pelted us like arrows, the wind screamed, and visibility was barely to the nearest ship in the convoy. Our gear was strewn about and soaked, but our bodies remained the same, and, when after an hour the sun broke through, tarpaulins went up as if by some magical command. So far our improvised shelters have been successful against a couple of recent nightly squalls.

We left the dock in such haste that we were unable to batten down all the equipment on deck. A pair of us built quarters with spectacular ingenuity across two pontoons. It consisted of cots set under a canopy made from a shelter half[2] and a pancho. After we got out to sea and mean swells, the pontoons began rocking, then separating. Scrambling to save their gear and their new home, the two fellows struggled to hold the pontoons together and prevent them from going over the side. Meanwhile, despite our seasickness and bloated faces, we laughed ourselves still sicker. So help me it was a veritable clown act.

On this voyage we have an exceptional menagerie on board. There are three bitches that dash wildly from one caress to another, six newborn pups that are mercilessly manhandled, a monkey that sits on its haunches screeching, a multi-colored bird in a cage that screams for its native haunts, a duck that waddles bewildered about the deck, and a few humans who behave like animals. You call Franklin Park[3] a zoo? Baloney.

We get news regularly. Sheets of it are printed daily. The invasion of Okinawa[4] gave us a premature thrill of optimism, because it's so near mainland Japan.[5] The appalling American, European offensive made me leap with glee. Oh, if it would only be finished over there. The end, so unreal until now, begins to be conceivable. The futility of a year ago was terrible.

The ocean is both to my port and starboard gaze. Every time I look at it and into it I'm reminded of wash day back home and the tub swirling with bluing water. The sea is yet bluer, iridescent. It's all so clean, chaste, untouched. Who can believe that all the world's waste empties into it. Methinks, I sort of like the sea.

Music is broadcast over the public address system to the breezy decks, mostly up-to-date popular tunes (I'll Walk Alone,[6] I Make Believe,[7] Tomorrow[8]). So we have resumed our usual self-imposed entertainment, as with half an ear cocked, we listen.

A twinge of nostalgia took hold of us during the hours that the land's outline grew misty. Altogether our stay at that spot wasn't unpleasant. Everything we left behind, we built or witnessed. I felt like brushing my hands against each other and saying "There, that's done."

The nights are getting cooler. We're unpacking our blankets. The days are still hot.

Our second year overseas has begun. May this be our next to last voyage. May this be that "once more," "one more job," then home.

4/19/45

Dear Folks,

Now at last, since I'm writing from one of the Philippine islands, I can reveal where I was: Hollandia.[1] This is merely a stopover on our way to a final destination. But with time for now being my own, I've scoured the countryside visiting villages. I'm making up for the boredom of doing and seeing nothing at the Hollandia location.

The past week has been as interesting as any of my Stateside liberties. The Filipinos put American hospitality to shame. They feed us, and talk freely and pleasantly. Their habits, houses, and customs approach our standards, making allowances, of course, for the climate, the former occupation,[2] and their incentives. Homes, which vary according to the owner's wealth, are built from bamboo and straw thatchwork. Pigs, chickens, and cows roam about the yards and under the houses which are built on stilts. Some even enter the house and make the damndest racket, at least to this city fella. The fields yield rice, tobacco, corn, tomatoes, sweet potatoes, sugar cane, and watermelons. I had my first watermelon in I don't know how long. I devoured it as if I hadn't had one in twenty years.

The people are short, well proportioned, quite handsome, clever, and seemingly thirsting for education. The young can speak English (they're taught it in school), the older ones Spanish, and in this locality all speak Tagalog (accent on the second syllable) which has a strain of Spanish running through it. I've caught onto a few easy and useful phrases, such as Saha na ghalim, meaning How are you? Baca is cow, mabuti is good, and magunda is pretty. The girls are especially pretty in an oriental way. They are small, shapely, of comely appearance and have long dark wavy hair. They lead a rigorous and honorable youthful life. Their parents marry them off to someone of the parent's choosing. The men court their women by serenading them which strikes me as being rather corny.

A girl smiles at you if she likes you. Since they like white boys, I felt like hell when I was smiled upon. If I would dare to visit her home once more, she'd be dubbed my girl. That's a neat way of getting hooked, so I remain clear. However, and I'm serious, I fear many hearts are due to be broken as the number of affairs is gathering momentum among my battalion friends.

The other day I rode across a stream on the back of a caribou (It resembles an ox). It beats the fun ride I had crossing the Mississippi at New Orleans. I felt silly as the devil and looked silly as the devil, but the caribou was dead serious as he expelled super-heated air from his nostrils. And his hard spine disagreed with mine.

The climate here is far more tolerable than that of the sub-equatorial New Guinea hot box. Although it's just as hot, it's drier and the nights are chillier. The natural growth is also less dense.

At this stop some mail has caught up with me—a couple from you, one from Johnson, Boston, and a portrait of my correspondent, Dolly. The kid's alright and the fellows think she's right pretty, but I can't whip up any enthusiasm for any girl either at home or abroad, by letter or in my presence. I'm too damn infatuated with a future of learning.

Not having any of your letters handy, I haven't answered them directly. No watch received yet, so I expect the worst. I'm awaiting news of your latest Boston adventure.

The chow is exceptional. Fresh vegetables, meats, and fruit juices are being served. Everything is just fine—both stomach and mind. A very long time to go yet.

5/1/45

Dear Folks,

For nigh on thirty days I have been on a ship living in my hammock over the winch,[1] bathing with a helmet and bucket full of fresh water, but eating three meals, two being fresh meat—not necessarily tasty. Well, it wasn't altogether unpleasant. We adjust to our environment with ease: give us two nights, and we refer to wherever we are as home.

I wrote my last letter while ashore on another island, one of many thousands hereabouts, so I understand. Now I'm on Luzon[2] where we will live until (such taken for granted anticipation) we finish our job. I think we have stopped moving west. It would be a waste of ink to say I hope so.

This is the nearest to civilization that I've been for fifteen months. Actually, I'm in civilization, a modern, ravaged civilization. I have walked on a smooth concrete sidewalk deteriorated from the neglect of a bloody occupation and nicked by shell fragments. The people live poorly, and temporarily, in filth, which is understandable in view of the war and the havoc, though actually part of it is due to the familiar squalor of their past, and the habits of a less cultured people (though no nation should talk). There are several towns about that are always interesting. They hold exuberant fiestas which are now in season. Having a personal cheering section, a queen is chosen by popular vote and a dab of politics. The G.I.'s seem to have control over every situation—from electing the queens to disposing of any shadow of a Jap.

I want you to know that everything, I swear, everything, is fine. I expect that your letters will arrive someday. I'm a patient lad. Knowing that they are on the way suffices. My next letter will be a long one. Now we're in the process of building our camp which offers poor facilities for procuring stationery, and getting our letters censored and mailed. (Most of my clothes etc. are still in transit).

Love, Hughie

Subic Bay, Luzon, Philippine Islands

Dear Mom,

Ever since I began making a dollar a week I managed to send you flowers on Mother's Day. I was always excited the day before. This year I'm disappointed. This letter alone, I know, is all you want, but it would have been so much nicer if I could have made some arrangement. We were three days out to sea when I had time to think and review the worn past, and since then the front door bell has been ringing in my thoughts.

Last month barely existed; it all happened so incredulously swiftly. It was a fascinating conglomeration of ocean spray, a new land, and a new people, and a reintroduction to a perceptibly American civilization.

The voyage lasted the entire month of April, which included a stop for a week or so at an island south of here [Mindoro]. The 113th is still there. Feeling sad about leaving the old outfit for good, I said goodbye to my friends. I have gone a long way with those boys — since August 1943.

During the one week I was on that island I made quite a few Filipino friends. When spoken to slowly they understood English perfectly, and speak well and intelligently themselves. Many discussions went on for hours. We talked about such subjects as the origin of the Negroes (They are curious about them), Philippine independence, (which they don't want because they fear a revolution), the United States (where all of them desperately wish to visit, make money, marry a beautiful American girl, and return), the Japanese occupation, about which they are explicit in their hatred towards the Japanese. Most of the men whom I met had been guerrillas operating in the hills and harassing the towns. Most of the women went with them, but apparently returned when we came. The Japs never seemed to concentrate a large force in a single area.

I arrived here on Luzon armed with a few greetings in Tagalog, a shrewdness equal to the Filipinos' own, and a general knowledge of their customs, many of which are Spanish in origin. Despite ceiling prices, inflation is rampant caused by scant supplies, and the black market runs wild. The exchange rate is one peso to fifty cents. The Filipinos want clothes, soap (a peso per bar), cigarettes (ten to twenty pesos per carton), and Atabrine, all hard to buy items, and dear. Money is plentiful; most have full pockets.

A Filipino wash woman takes care of my clothes as well as you used to. She gets them whiter than I've seen them in fifteen months, repairs them, even puts pleats in my trousers. About your age, the mother of eight children, her name is Orange. I like her personality, especially her maternal manner that makes me feel a little homesick.

These people have personality. They are happy and smiling; they are always singing and humming popular airs. The women's voices in particular are sweet and melodious. Every house seems to have a song book, many over four years old.

On our arrival, my reaction (I don't know about the others) to the colorful civilian dresses, lithe figures and girlish faces, struck me as most odd. The sight of girls walking the streets made me feel nearer home.

The houses, which are somewhat unfinished and not large, are constructed of bamboo and wood. One of my friends has waxed hardwood floors in his largest room. He has no furniture, just a few chairs. He and his family sleep on bamboo mats on the floor. But their clothes are spotless and they look clean, although I see no showers or toilet facilities.

One problem I've had has been to make it clear to some of my Filipino friends that I don't care to go stepping out. They insist on fixing me up. Last night when I visited Rosalio (age 24; his wife Purlita, age 18), he and his wife had invited an eighteen year old beauty to their house for me to meet. Unlike our custom, no introduction is expected. The man simply takes the initiative. They kept egging me on, psst-ing, while the damsel stood in the shadows examining me as would a vulture its prey, ready to pounce. I didn't know what the devil to do but play possum until finally the climax passed and everyone gave up. They couldn't figure out this new kind of American. I want to learn the language and customs, not waste my time in a courtship.

We expect to have many months of work here. With blistered hands from installing floors, I'm helping to build our camp. As to how little work I was doing while at Hollandia, my hands speak for themselves. Our camp is located in an area that used to be rice paddies. Everyone is as brown as the Filipinos themselves; I'm as dark as I was when we were on vacation at Winthrop some six or seven years ago. I go about in shorts with pockets sticking below my pants legs — one of my home made jobs.

Enclosed is a money order. I want you to spend five dollars of it. It comes from my little budget. I have no need for money here. Please use it and tell me what you bought. No excuses; take it and make me happy.

Love to all, Hughie

5/8/45

Dear Mom,

Your 4/21 V-Mail is the first letter I've received from home since I arrived. Those in between are somewhere and are bound to catch up. The dredge, which hasn't arrived yet, probably has a load of mail.

This morning we heard the official announcement of [the German] surrender.[1] A few let out a yell because it was the thing to do. Most just pondered the event and felt good inside. So far as I'm concerned the war is only half over.

Our small, permanent camp is just about completed. We are living comfortably and eating better than ever. As before, the dredge is a parasite unit, living off a large battalion. Our area is set apart from theirs, but we use their facilities, the chow hall, showers, toilets, store, etc.

My last letter included a $55.00 money order.

While the dredge is on its way to join us, I'm doing carpentry and electrical work at the camp, helping the man (now an electrician) from Frisco whom I mentioned in an earlier letter.

The climate here wonderfully agrees with me. It's not nearly as humid as it was three degrees below the equator, although it's just as hot by noon. The early evenings are balmy and the nights chilly. We sleep as never before. The days are replicas of warm summer days back home. The rainy season is about due. We'll have showers until August, then comes the incessant downpour.

I've been so fascinated with the country, the towns, and the people, that I'm dashing off to some Filipino's house almost nightly. My Tagalog vocabulary is increasing satisfactorally.

Since the people usually have fruit in their houses, I'm all the more motivated to visit them. I always accept their bananas, watermelons, and citrus fruits.

The monkeys and dogs, although somewhat decreased in number, are still with us. One of the monkeys ran off into the hills, and two sit about crying over one thing or another; the pups are growing bigger and more rambunctious; the three roosters croaked on board ship after fantastically leaping into the air and screeching. The remaining rooster wanders about the area suffering the buffets of the monkeys, the dogs, and our feet.

Tonight (Today is the 9th) I'm stepping out to visit friends. After tonight I expect to remain in camp to tackle the stack of mail that has accumulated.

This letter has been running for three days (now the 10th). Last night three of us were extended an invitation to attend what turned out to be a wake. A wake, however, is an event more for merriment than grief. Observing many Filipino customs that night, I learned more about the people in that brief time than ever before. They introduced me to some of their "ladies" (the unmarried) and on each introduction I felt that I was being pushed. So, it seems, that at Filipino wakes music, singing, eating, and matchmaking are quite typical. The dead man, who was in the room with us, was to be buried at 8:00 this morning.

Now that we're nearly settled, I intend to write more often. How about a photo of this new, slim, trim Mom?

5/13/45

Dear Mom,

On turning to my portfolio, I found the month of March still turned up. I couldn't help pondering the past month and a half when I wrote so few letters, so much had happened, saw so many new things, and when I had never been as conscious of the passage of time. Now I'm settled in a comfortable screened-in tent with wooden floors, electric lights and six harmonious friends. All seven of us had gotten together for an almost unattainable reason: want of quiet. We have no card sharks, crap shooters, drunkards, or lazy lummoxes, we hope, among our select hut personnel. I've built myself a neat little cabinet for my clothes which are delivered neatly creased and folded like you used to do them. Not that I wish to brag, but my chair is worthy of commendation. The M.U. [Morris Upholstering Co.] overseas branch has done its bit of handiwork. I can honestly say that, to date, I am now seated in the most comfortable chair that I've sat in for the past fifteen months. It conforms marvelously to my leg length, and buttocks width. An underslung canvas job, it resembles a combination Sleepy Hollow and beach chair. The arm and head rests are filled with kapok from an old life preserver. After finding a few 8 oz. carpet tacks and a strip of muslin I made use of my years of experience in upholstering (consisting mostly of ripping) [stripping upholstery]. While nobody else thinks so, I call it a masterpiece. Nevertheless, they are always anxious to relax in its enveloping luxuriousness.

This afternoon, if it doesn't rain, I'm going fishing in the bay with a Filipino friend. He has one of those outrigger sailboats called a banca. When we entered the bay, as we hung over the rail staring with curiosity at the new land, the natives drifted around the ship wanting to trade bolo knives, sleeping mats, bananas, liquor, and bamboo handiwork for cigarettes and G.I. clothes. They got the better of every deal, because they resold everything at an exorbitant profit. We didn't know that then. While I'm in the bay today, I can imagine how much fun it would be to dub as one of the natives (I'm dark enough), and do a wee bit of trading off a heavy cruiser, or a merchant ship. What a novelty it would be to have the tables turned.

The dredge is due in any day now, and my regular job as water tender will begin. Now that the camp is settled, I have time galore. Even after the dredge arrives, working a six hour shift will allow me plenty of leisure time.

The war's finale in Europe, so far as our units are concerned, affects us negligibly. Everything we construct on these islands seem to be permanent. There's no doubt anything that the dredge does will also be.

Although troops from Europe will soon be arriving, nobody expects to get home sooner. At least, no relief is expected with respect to construction units. Surely construction men will be much in demand in the U.S., but they are in greater demand out here. Many boys are intrigued with the opportunities the islands have to offer. Of course, none of us have witnessed the monsoon season yet. The land is rich and undeveloped, and labor is cheap. Quite a few subscribe to the idea that money is to be made outside the U.S., where competition is not as keen. After making their fortunes, they will retire to the U.S. or enter a less strenuous business. I think they have something worth thinking about.

Last night I visited the [Rosalio] Corum residence on Vista Street [in Olongopo]. I suppose the Corums may be called middle class out here, the average Filipino family. Their house, like all houses here, both of the poor and wealthy, is built of bamboo and thatch and mahogany, or a beautiful wood that resembles mahogany. Compared with other houses, the Corum's is a beauty. Before entering, we must remove our shoes so as not to scratch the hardwood floor in the main room. The other rooms have shiny bamboo flooring. I had mentioned that they have no furniture to speak of. The family sleeps on straw mats on the floor, with a head pillow and maybe a blanket.

I'm sure all have malaria. As long as we take Atabrine, we have no fear of an attack. If during the past fifteen months I haven't contracted malaria, it would be a miracle.

Last night the Corums served fried crab or shrimp or something of that order. I was crazy about it. Two of us from the unit had brought beer, pretzels and peanuts for them. They were crazy about these.

A few nights earlier the town put on a small festival parade to commemorate some warrior's death. The queens from the outlying districts (barrios), considered to be the finest of Filipino pulchritude, march becrowned and begowned to a slow moving locally concocted band. The music, which is different from what I'm used to hearing, was not unpleasant. The youngsters prance about like young bucks and sing and move their bodies in unison. The queens trail long trains that are supported by dainty maidens. Men carry torches above their heads to light up the procession and reveal the queen's glowing face. It's quite something. But, Mom, more about this in subsequent letters. I could go on *ad infinitum*.

Six of your letters are before me, so as I try to answer your questions, I'll browse and rant. The watch is probably carousing about some post office waiting for my forwarding address. Since this climate is not nearly as hard on metal, I think the electric razor will endure out here. I would like to have it, Mom. It's got so that I could shave more often than daily. I'm dreading using the safety razor just as Dad used to. Although my skin isn't tender, a sunburned skin smarts under a safety razor's sharp strokes.

You mustn't take my mild case of seasickness to heart. Seasickness is like taking a mental vacation: the sickness is one's only concern. I hardly saw Charlie Goodness in N.G. It was swell of his wife to call. Charlie and I were planning on going home together from Frisco, never expecting that one of us would depart from the battalion early.

It's great to hear that your amazing weight loss has made you feel better. Will I know my mother when I return? Today is Mother's Day, and by White House proclamation also a day of prayer. A prayer for victory and Mother are a fitting duet.

Aunt Eva's hospitalization is still a mystery to me. I'm awaiting earlier letters for more information. I prefer air mail; it's quicker; V-Mail is held up at the printing stations.

I haven't heard how the two Seders[1] came off. Ronnie's letter of March 11th poses a challenge. Better start oiling up the [boxing] gloves. Hey, wait a minute. How tall did you say you were? I'm all for your pursuing a career in interior decorating, boy. When the time comes, and you need money, and I have it (and I expect to) you're welcome to it.

A recent letter from Henry Wolf enlightened me on his telephone conversation with you. I presume there was much silence and stammering. I doubt whether it will be worth calling you when I land on the West Coast. I'll be unable to say a word.

My letters will be arriving more frequently, as I make up for the recent lapse.

5/14/45

Dear Mom,

My morale needs no lifting despite a call to report to work for 1:00 tomorrow morning. Finally, all your letters have caught up with me in one blessed batch. As a result my spirits are spilling over. I suppose today is nature's way of officially opening the rainy season. The land is soaked and covered with running water and our faces are chagrined, but not mine. No, my dear, because I feel suddenly and nonsensically elated; thoughts 10,000 miles away have done this to me.

The letters clear up inconsistencies and provide missing links, especially reports of losing two or three pounds now and then in your marvelous campaign. Now that you are making marked headway in regaining the comeliness of your pre-matrimonial days, of course, Dad's threats to find a curvaceous blonde and buy a sleek convertible roadster should have all but ceased. And soon, I expect you will be in a position to apply your art, so gallantly won, to taunt Dad. Today, however, the come-hither glance has lost its effectiveness even when accompanied by spirited curves. The reason: nowadays there are more glances and curves and fewer males. It's just like eating peanuts: you can't stop. I'll be watching you shed those pounds until the grand finale — the photograph of your remarkable achievement.

Now for your letters.

I've received all the pictures. What a stack. I shouldn't have asked for so many. I can get rid of those of myself pronto. My estranged correspondents request such "catastrophes to the imagination." Both friends Dolly and Sybil have lodged a request. In such cases I would never take the initiative. These girls are — oh how should I put it? — strictly not my type. They have no higher ambitions beyond high school, work for a brief time, then — my own guess work here — marriage. All well and good, to be sure, but a college-aspiring lass is so much more interesting. And then from the portrait alone of one Dolly, I can see by her lipstick coated lips and overall hairdo that this is the type girl I've avoided. From these observations I come to conclusions concerning her personality and character, which are of primary importance. Frankly, Mom, she is a typical Jewish girl who tends to be artificial rather than genuine and honest. It's their greatest fault. Trying to beautify themselves, they end up looking cheap like Astor's pet horse. They revel in promiscuity. I'm not blinded by some unattainable ideal; I know what I want and what's available.

The Goodsteins are encouraging me to write. It couldn't be for my "beautiful penmanship." They, too, confess they find deciphering it an ordeal. I'm glad others are interested in my letters. I enjoy writing about strange lands and people.

Just before I left Hollandia, I procured enough cat eyes to make a bracelet. One of these days I'll send the coin bracelet home. Perhaps I could send [Aunt] Anna a cat-eye bracelet for her birthday. When is it? There are plenty of souvenirs to be found here: straw and reed work, wood work etc. I'm keeping a weather eye open for something worthwhile to send home, rather than insignificant junk that will only clutter up the house.

So Sawyer's[2] made Dad an attractive proposition. He'd have no big worries, he'd have a secure and steady salary, a good thing as he grows older and becomes less active. Ronnie and I appreciate our parents — we do. During the past two years Ronnie has grown younger in his outlook compared to me. While I've been away, my perspective has come into perfect focus on you and Dad. I know the M.U. Company has unlimited possibilities. With its fine reputation, someone ambitious could bring it far. That's why I'm anxious for Ronnie to follow the course he's now prescribed for himself. I wouldn't hesitate to invest all I have in the future of the M.U. Company. I hope Ronnie will have big ideas, for big ideas make big money. The foundation is already there for him.

Back in Hollandia the fellows living in the tent above me would kid me about the rent. As it grew to be quite a joke the first of every month, I'd string along with them. Some of them would visit with me, shoot the breeze, and we'd have a good time talking nonsense.

Since I've been in the tropics, I've never witnessed the fantastic temperature of 160 degrees that you refer to. On a sunny day in Luzon the daily temperature ranges between 85 and 95 degrees. A rainy day like today is comfortably cool.

Since I've been overseas, the weather has been mild. Each time we moved, even in the States, we just missed bad weather. The weather in Hollandia was consistent year round.

For your information, a Floridian comes from Florida, an Angeleno from Los Angeles. As we say in Tagalog, iintindahan? Understand? And by the way, my Tagalog vocabulary is expanding nicely. But my Filipino friends have yet to set me straight on the grammar.

I have no dictionary to consult while in the service. As you know, I read a lot which has done wonders for my vocabulary.

Henry is not alone in being disgusted with Stateside duty. We hear similar reports from others. You see, after the freedom and laxity of duty overseas, the rigid discipline of a Stateside camp is in sharp contrast and seems silly. Then, the boys miss their service friends, all the girls are working, and there's the wartime regulations and rationing. It's understandable, natural and reasonable, that knowing it isn't over, that he'd rather actively participate, that Henry longs to be back with his friends and his unit. As I've said before, I prefer to remain here to the end. I can return to a U.S. at peace, a nation striving toward peacetime luxury.

Have I explained that officially and for good I'm detached from the 113th and assigned to the dredge unit?

Yesterday, having gone fishing Filipino style, I had an enjoyable afternoon, different from any before. Four of us, three Filipinos and myself, set out in a banca (a canoe with double outriggers, fitted with a sail) to search the inlets for signs of fish, a school or a fish leaping into the air. We must keep silent. Without removing the blade from the water, the paddling remains silent. We sight a school, say fifty feet away, and throw a grenade. An explosion follows, after which we speed towards it and dive into the water to scoop up the fish. One of us wore goggles and had a net, while the rest of us kept diving and searching the bottom for the white reflection of the dead fish. Our first catch must have consisted of half a hundred or more. The fish are no more than four to six inches long. I had a great time diving. We searched at one spot for a good half hour then returned later to find more that were killed by the concussion. The leader of our party made the grenade from Japanese dynamite and caps. Quite clever. The Flips[3] swim well under water, but I beat them at surface swimming. I'll describe the meal in my next letter.

The Filipino men are inclined to be slight of build, even the tall ones. They got a great kick out of my physique, quizzing me on how much boxing I've done. The kids call me by the names of comic strip characters and ask me to make a muscle, show my biceps. As we passed their friends in other boats, they referred to me as "the Filipino with the big body." The women stood gaping at me, so I left their presence as quickly as I could. These people respect the mind, and from the physical condition of their slight physiques, apparently they also respect the body.

They were so persistent that finally I consented to meet one of their chosen maidens. Of course, I made them understand that unlike other Americans, I would insist that everything be purely platonic. They agreed, saying that they realized I would prefer an American girl. So as not to insult them, I praised their womanhood and explained that I had no wish to marry until I had completed my education and settled myself in life. To this, though they were astonished, they nodded in understanding. "This is a good boy," they said, and they expressed admiration. By using such diplomacy, I get along well with these people.

In each letter to come I'll probably describe the people or the country as I see it. Others may express opposite views. I prefer to see the beauty and good in these people. I'm aware that I may overlook many of their more distasteful traits. But I know both their aspects quite well. I can write about the filth later.

Tomorrow expect another letter. I've been writing no others, only you.

5/16/45

Dear Mom,

This is the third day of overcast and off and on showers, creating mud and a miserable dampness in the air. Luckily the showers were suspended about movie time last night so we could watch Boyer[1] and Dunne[2] in "Together Again."[3] Sunday evening we watched "Music for Millions"[4] in which music of Chopin, Handel[5] and Beethoven, was scantily interjected, designed to appeal to a popular audience. Both the plot and the sharp interruptions in the music, especially Iturbi's playing, were most bothersome. But I had some good laughs over some ridiculous scenes in "Together Again," although other scenes of exaggerated adolescent rampages were slightly nauseating.

While it's raining, I remain in the tent sleeping or comfortably seated reading *Time* to catch up on all the news that I missed during the excitement of moving. I should be writing letters, but, for some stupid reason, I'm not up to it, yet fearing that my many correspondents will be irked over my neglect.

I heard about your wonderful spring snowstorm. I thought "That's New England for you. Snow in May." I love it there. There's one thing about New England: it's never monotonous. The weather itself prevents it.

"A Song to Remember" must be a romanticized version. Obviously Hollywood would do nothing else. You see, Chopin was highly effeminate, and George Sand was definitely not a lithe chicken.

By one means or another many of the fellows have managed to tell their friends precisely where we are. I'd just as soon keep it a mystery, not so much for security reasons as for your sake. Except to satisfy your curiosity it would do you no good to know. If by some freakish chance this spot were in danger, though I wouldn't be, you would needlessly worry. No, Mom, you must wait until I leave here, as with Finschaven and Hollandia.

Thousands of Japs were starving between Wewak[6] (taken yesterday) and Hollandia. In fact we often heard rumors that they resorted to cannibalism. The Australian troops still sent out patrols in the area. During the early part of the Dutch New Guinea campaign the newspapers reported these facts. But there was no more danger to those of us on the coast than at any Stateside camp. How would you have known that our unit was safe, while clashes were still being reported? Of course you wouldn't. You'd think the worst.

Just as I figured: the smattering of practical construction knowledge that I've learned has given you ideas. No doubt Dad is happy about it, and is so bold as to entertain the idea that all household complaints will fall to me and his Sundays will be free of fixing broken window cords, aerials and electrical fixtures. I see Sunday will have to be a day for extra diligent studying, allowing me no time for anything else.

Sorry, Mom, this lad will not return a dancer. I'm too anxious to get about and see things on liberty, nor do I intend to let up my pace of leisure reading. Extroverts aren't manufactured at will. Only chance will ever bring me to dance and step out, not intention. I'm too deeply in a rut to climb out of my own hook.

None of us can feel or talk about Chase's disaster[7] with reason, because it's all so unreasonable. The boy was no angel, and he's had it tough. I feel bad for both him and his parents, but more so for the mass of them, so many in all. I don't feel for Chase alone; I feel for the whole great tragedy.

Your round by round account of Ronnie's driving venture, including tantrums, arguments and all, gave me a few nostalgic chuckles. His graduation, the license diploma, must have been quite an event. Now make way for the battle royal. There are two vehicles in the family, and two licensed drivers, this lad a potential third. I'm used to getting around without a car. Where expenses are involved, I bow out. Ronnie and Dad will be the principal protagonists, I'm certain, and I'll bet Ronnie will be the victor. He won't find me much trouble after the novelty of my being home wears off.

I read the condensation of *Leave Her to Heaven*. Three or so years ago I enjoyed *Time of Peace* by the same author.[8] Now that my taste has radically changed, I think of *LH to H* as trash. I have no wish to read more such entertaining modern novels about absurd women. I'm searching for things constructive that challenge my mind, get me to thinking. I want to read so much that has been written in the past, that only the best of the present suits me. This may be only a temporary stage, I grant you. With so much fine material to read and enjoy, why bother reading about selfish, maniacal women? Heck, none can understand them anyway. On the other hand, I understand and fully appreciate Yetta's gesture [of sending the book].

It's very comforting indeed to know that everything's hunky-dory. That makes it the same for both ends.

Yesterday's climax consisted of the chase and capture of the rooster that had at last worn down the nerves of the 1082's inmates. Not only did the ---- -------- ---- (They called him other things too.) harass our habitual and much appreciated slumber, but he also had taken to sneaking into our tent and catnapping on a freshly sheeted bunk. Bullets and feathers flew, and so did the rooster, unscathed. A band of ten men or so armed with clubs and any handy object ran him down beneath tents and over rice paddy marshes. At last an erstwhile Frank Buck triumphantly took him alive and delivered him to a Filipino family that had a boy stricken with fever and nothing more than a meager supply of rice on hand. That's what I call catching a bird (and almost killing him) with two stones.

5/19/45

Dear Mom,

Letters that are only ten days old are merrily starting to come in. The latest were from Dad and Ronnie. Perhaps it's because they are rare that I enjoy them so. They fill in the gaps, adding a supreme completion to your letters. And yours Mom, they're part of my food, and often, believe me, more important. Oh, ho, I must stop being sentimental, this silly sentimentality that makes my face red, yet so often, from gratitude and a spontaneous awareness, I must, if awkwardly, get it out of my system. Dad's and Ronnie's letters deserve that extra special consideration of man to man jabber. Dad should expect that my next letter will be expressly for him.

Most of this week I've remained in camp during my leisure time and worked outdoors at all hours in downpours and sunshine near the towns. What am I doing? I'm not perfectly clear what it is. First, it's one job then another, never completing either. Since the dredge is still en route, we are doing construction work for the battalion. This being tossed around is confusing and slightly aggravating, but at least we have consolation in knowing that once the dredge arrives we return to our original jobs. In the meantime it's all a riot, and nobody is especially conscientious.

Yep, the bankroll sounds fine. It will be a good beginning, something to start with. I shall surely spend three years in the service, and now I can hardly call them years spent in vain. From these years I shall have saved a little money, qualified for an education, and gained practical experience. After all these assets are invested, what shall I buy? Did you say mink or ermine? Chinchilla is very nice. We'll wait and see.

There are plenty of fellows like [Cousin] Bob, and like myself as well. They think only of the present, rarely think of the future. It's one way to find happiness; avoid life's complexities. I've never had much to do with the happy-go-lucky ones. Their pace is too swift. Bob has a bit of his father in him. I have a bit of my father in me. The dissimilarities of the two brothers are reproduced almost identically in their sons.

Carrier pigeons are the solution. On my next voyage I'll send a pigeon home each day to ease your needless worry. It's now going on sixteen months. Aren't you used to the uncertainty of my whereabouts and the unreliability of receiving my letters by now? Of course, I understand. Have a little more patience when the normal course of my overseas living abruptly changes. By comparison to army and other navy units, our position is exceptionally stable. Give it more time before you begin worrying. How can I tell you not to worry? All I can say is have patience and postpone coming to conclusions.

In ordinary conversation or with someone less understanding than you, I'd never mention my objection to an innocent phrase. You offer an instance which, though not deliberate, must have an unconscious motive. You write "...for Charlie's sake, the poor kid away so long..." Your sympathy is understandable, but some would resent it. The breaks, the general acceptance of fate, is something new in my view of life. Such thinking exists with everyone here. Life is so hard and cold. Our outlook doesn't warrant sympathy. We dare not entertain the idea. I think I've put my finger on one result of the war: the changed philosophical attitude of the militarized civilian. That's what we are: militarized civilians. Charlie must be about thirty. Quite an old "kid." Kid, eh? Sure, you didn't mean it in the literal sense, nor even colloquially, I know. But it has negative implications.

In a recent issue of *Time*, I read of a discussion that Gertrude Stein[1] presided over and monopolized before a group of servicemen. She advised them not to be so serious, not to think so much, to laugh, be gay and smile. An objector rose stating that there's another war to be fought (in the Pacific). Misunderstanding, G. Stein reprimanded the G.I. for anticipating the next war, though she conceded that it is inevitable. She insisted that the G.I.'s in this war are different from their fathers in the last one. She accused the G.I. of perhaps feeling sorry for himself. He was exaggerating the situation and viewing it with ridiculous gravity. I believe G. Stein has something there. But so has the G.I. For ages, the common man hasn't been free to express his thoughts. Let him now express them either in the midst of muddle or order. The thoughts of the common man are visibly beginning to count in the fate of the world. Those who are fools and ignorant will never, with all their nonsense, determine the final path that humanity follows.

When I began this letter, I had no idea I'd fly off on such a tangent. It's a convenient way to blow off a little steam. Tell me if it scalds your hands.

5/21/45

Dear Mom,

Today was beautiful. I worked hard doing nothing important, and, this evening, I'm comfortably tired. We had turkey for supper and I ate a leg that approached the size of that of the local caribous that wander about. After supper I went to a show and saw one of those quaint, human pictures that Hollywood produces every once in a while. You must see "Roughly Speaking"[1] with Jack Carson and Rosalind Russell. I suppose I enjoyed it because it speaks of you and Dad and your fabulous era, the twenties and difficult thirties. Oh, it was colored up with a divorce and a few ridiculous hair-raising ventures, but I could see you and Dad in those clothes having your times, your struggles. My mind wandered off to South Station two years ago. As I watched, there was a blissful smile creasing my face much of the time.

Last night I met a Jewish lad my own age from Baltimore, now in a AA[2] army unit. With respect to education and general environment, his past is similar to mine with, of course, the obvious exceptions: girls, interests and ambitions. A good boy, the lad is morally clean and devoted to his proud parents. He has changed, but, when he returns, his parents won't know it. If they do recognize the change, there's no telling what his parents will do, what their reaction will be. But chances are they won't see it, not even a sign of what is on their son's conscience. He has had his first taste of life and its sensations which lead him to want more and more. It's apt to drive a fellow hog wild, especially when circumstances are so free and convenient. I know that my parents, and decent people like you, haven't experienced what I've experienced, seen what I've seen, heard what I've heard from my mates, yes, my very friends. None of this bothers me. I laugh and joke and agree, and I get along well. But I keep clean and clear. I keep myself on a sane, solid path with few cares, but, from my path, I catch glimpses of the gutter, and most remarkable, a gutter that has become an astounding path for most. In fact, after carefully examining the situation and the people involved, for them it ceases to be a gutter. Not that I approve (the gutter isn't for me), but I understand and easily tolerate what goes on. I've been raised according to convention and to practice restraint and taught a decent, civilized, way to live. I'm bound by it which doesn't make me unhappy. I've seen convention and restraint shed here to the point that their lack becomes quite conventional. Although not forgotten, morality is twisted. You can't imagine how tempting it is for a fellow to be changed by this easy, carefree attitude. You can't possibly understand until you witness it. It hasn't been difficult for me to resist its influence. But good lord, what it has done to some!

I'm tired and should get some sleep. Forgive this abrupt conclusion.

5/24-26/45

Dear Dad,

It's been quite a while since we've had one of our man to man ten thousand mile conversations. I needn't repeat telling you what your letters do to me. I miss your companionship (sometimes more fraternal than paternal) terribly, even the times when you bawl me out. After I return, Dad, we should go someplace together, spend a couple of weeks at some lake in Maine. I'm dead serious and stubborn as a mule. Perhaps, in view of your business obligations and all that, such a proposal seems ridiculous to you. Hang it; forget it; you can do it. Make me happy, Dad, and say that you will. Give me something to look forward to. I have another proposition to put before you a little later.

I'll lay off this for a few odd paragraphs to let you recover your wind. Not knowing fully the particulars of the Sawyer offer, I think it was fine of you to act as you did. I remember once—no, at least a dozen times—you said that you'd abandon your business in two shakes of a lamb's tale were a job with a steady salary offered you. At the time, I figured it was idle talk, but I suppose you were sincere. You've put your sweat, your very life into the business. One of us, Ronnie most likely, can make it flourish into something big. By God, if we don't show it now, in years to come we will appreciate what you've done.

The business needs big ideas. Ambition and ideas are capital. Sure, there's a risk, but good times are ahead.

There's some confusion—nothing unusual—in the unit. We hear that we must move nearer to our work in another part of the bay. This spot has been convenient, easy to get to town from, and near facilities. The laundry women come right into our tents to pick up and deliver our clothes, frequently during show time (after work). They find a quasi-nudist colony of immodest men. Nobody gives a darn. Most fellows have native friends in town to visit. Our lonesome fathers like families with children. The young unmarrieds carry on a free love campaign and completely support their illegal "wives." The girls are quite attractive, especially to our female-starved eyes.

When the Americans first arrived, the Flips (as we call them) were exuberant. Skinny as rails, they greeted us in rags and were willing to give us what little they had. Soon, after the generosity of the Americans became evident, their policy changed. They try to get whatever they can out of us. This is the procedure: Flip: "Veectoree Joe (Everybody's Joe to them), Japs burn my home, almost cut my throat (making a demonstrating sign), gotta cigarette, Joe?" And Joe, who by now is wised up, releases a torrent of profanity. As a result the Flips can now swear better than we do. They are shrewd bargainers. Bargaining between a Flip and an American sounds more like a hot session in Congress. The Flip can't understand or pretends not to, while the American raises his voice to a screech, which he believes, for some foolish reason, will make him more easily understood.

The Filipinos have done little to restore their land and cities. Despising manual labor, they thrive in the filth. Most of them, except for a few industrious persons, are poor workers. A large percentage of the young want to attend school and go on to college. The goal of many whom I've met is to get a good education; the goal of all is to visit the United States. But they have no illusions about getting there, merely idle hopes.

I'm becoming familiar with the language. When I make mistakes, my friends willingly correct me and provide me with the proper English translation. I get a great kick out of the youngsters; they are so friendly and happy and frolicsome. The adults too have a remarkable sense of humor. They definitely have an inferiority complex, especially in their relations with Americans. I get along with them so well because I speak casually and mingle freely. When with these Romans I do as they do.[1] When they are barefoot I go barefoot; what they eat so will I (within limits). I brings gifts of candy and cigarettes to my friends, for which they show their appreciation in so many little ways. They aren't sanitary by our standards. The average run of them is light fingered; a good number are pimps or act as such. Fourteen-year-olds have approached me pimping for their younger sisters.

In Manila (where I haven't been yet) one finds the more cultured and well educated Filipinos and nice homes. The religion is predominantly Roman Catholic, and there are some Protestants, mostly Methodists.

Merely as an experiment I quizzed my friends, the Corums, about what they knew of the Jews. They never heard of them. At least, I don't have anti-semitism to contend with. However, there are Jews in Manila, many of them German. (I'm sipping ice water as I write).

Thanks to my extraordinary training at the M.U. Company, my chair (that now so comfortably enfolds me) has become a model for others to copy. The neighbors come in and take measurements, as my mates luxuriate in the attention, leaving me high and dry.

It's true. I do feel prematurely old when I realize I'm now twenty-one. These past few years have come and gone so—like swift passing cars—that I can only remember the irresponsibility, the security, and the closed thoughts of my earlier time. At this point in my life, what I'd like most is to have a spot on earth where I can do as I please, rest, and take a breather from the bustle of it all. I'd like to own land—a secluded spot in some northern New England state where I can enjoy myself and the company of those whom I wish to bring there. I'm still young. Such a spot would be a comfort to me for the rest of my life. Perhaps you have long wanted such an arrangement. Mother likes jovial gatherings and the noise of crowded beaches. You, like me, like peace and the serenity of a lake. I know what camping is like. Good lord, I've had more than my share of it. That's how I'd like to begin, with some land. As years pass we could be saving to enable us to build a convenient and worthwhile place on the land. This isn't foolish talk, but something I've been hatching for quite a while. I believe it would be a wise investment. After I return I intend to bring this idea to reality before I finish school. I should laugh at my use of the word intend. So much can happen to change one's intentions. I'm wondering whether you'd like to be in on the deal.

For the past week or so the weather has been gorgeous but hot. Which reminds me that when one of the Filipinos overheard one of our boys remark that it was hotter than hell, he blurted, "These Americans have been everywhere, eh, Joe." After wearing nothing but shorts from sunrise until the afternoon wanes, I'm blacker than I've ever been. And I'm enjoying the near nudity. (At this very moment I'm taking a bite of a nice, delicious banana).

The chow is consistently good with fruit juices every morning, plenty of raw carrots, ice drinks, and fresh meat twice daily. I'm pleased and contented. Time is getting short as the months pass leading us down the royal road to home. Time is the pavement. I'll have been overseas eighteen months in July, and I don't expect many more months to go. If I end up spending two years out here, I won't be unhappy.

Let your letters come, Dad, even if the quantity detracts from their quality. Stay well, and keep the others well. Take it easy, keep young for me. My friends marvel at your youthful appearance.[2] I'm proud of it.

5/27/45

Dear Mom,

I had steak for dinner and chicken for supper; after devouring these, why shouldn't I be content? The dredge is here, but not yet operating. Meanwhile, we continue to work for the battalion. The situation is confusing and uncertain, a not unusual circumstance, and one not bothersome to me. I'm amazed at my indifference.

I've been keeping to camp evenings and catching up on the news, but I'm not writing. I'm simply too tuckered out at day's end to write.

Early last week I dropped by to see my friends in town. As always, we talked, I learned more of their language, and partook of their chow. We eat so well at camp; what a contrast with what they must eat. All their food, mostly rice, is from the black market. The children look half starved. I refuse to eat to no avail. Their insistence is so final that, were I to refuse, I'd fear insulting them. Nothing has been done to alleviate their poverty, nor are the people doing much to help themselves. I ask them what they need, and I try to get them what I can, such as soap, clothes and cigarettes. There's no immediate remedy. I hate the contrast of wealth and poverty, full and empty stomachs on the same street. After having a big supper at camp, I feel bad when I visit them.

Plenty are making money hand over fist. But money has lost much of its original value. If they would save for after the war, they could be wealthy. There are various examples of wealth and poverty, each for a different reason. "God helps those who help themselves," so goes the saying. From a leader's handy shove, they could become prosperous in these simple islands.

I had a brief talk with a Roman Catholic brother, after listening to him rile up his meager audience by means of forceful gesticulations and powerful Tagalog. His English was precise. Although he was ten years older than I, he remarked that I could teach him many things, that his education was far less than mine. I felt awkward, sensing what he meant. After I entered into a serious discussion with him, I discovered that he had an air of inferiority about himself.

I'm happy to say that your mail is arriving regularly. I received your March package of nuts, candy, and underwear. The nuts were as fresh and crisp as could be. They tasted elegant. Send more. The underwear is quite satisfactory. I really have too many clothes, even some from the original issue two years ago.

It would be fine for Bob and his folks were he to become a dentist. My cousin is a virtual stranger to me. I know nothing about the boy. From what I gather he's still jumping about and not knowing his own mind.

I patiently stand by awaiting reports on the slenderizing campaign. Whereas before, I was leery, now you've got me rooting. When you reach the mean low at last, I plan to celebrate (with ice water and bananas).

You must let up on flattering me, Mom. You haven't seen nor lived with me for going on two years. Since I'm your son, you must make allowances. My, how mothers fast become problems as their sons approach manhood.

I wish to make one thing clear. A girl's social standing or her family's or their financial status and their general environment doesn't necessarily shape her character or establish her worth. No, by no means. This Dolly does not appeal to me. Were I to love a girl, and she wore rags, I'd not hesitate for a second to marry her. Money, family background, all those conventional values, so-called values, count for little. What counts is that a girl be of solid, fine character whatever her background. I would marry her for herself, as she is, not for her past attachments. I don't know this Dolly's family. I know her brother, and I don't particularly like him. Frankly, I'm not anxious to meet either her or her brother.

A recent report states that in Russia there are five girls to every man, in Germany a yet more appalling ratio, in the U.S. a lower ratio, but a man shortage exists. No young lad of marriageable age need fear. He can be as independent as the devil and scan the crop.

I had never imagined that in this entire world, let alone the U.S., another person existed with the identical name as mine. Such a person does exist, hailing from a state bordering the Mississippi River. He receives letters from a sister living in Essex, Missouri. Surprisingly her name is Brown, Mrs. Helen Brown. The envelope is sadly blotched with imprints from rubber stamps, forwarding addresses and crazy scribbling. In ink, and clearly in Mrs. Brown's penmanship is written Hugh Aaron. Amazing.

P.S. Forget renewing the *Gazettes*. I don't have time to read them.
P.S. #2 I've renewed by subscription to *Time*.

5/29/45

Dear Mom,

The days have been beautiful. Mostly everyone complains that it's hotter here than in N.G., but I'd say it's about the same. Thus far the tropics have agreed with me. I've had none of the skin ailments, sunstroke, or heat rashes that so many others are susceptible to. There's no poison ivy here, and I doubt if I would catch it if there were. Knock on wood, I must be miraculously immune.

At Hollandia orchids grew wild. Here it's gardenias. Last night I visited "kaibegan ko," my friend Corum, to return a ladies umbrella that I had borrowed one rainy night. I left about ten with a gardenia in my button hole and an invitation to a fiesta tomorrow evening. One of the "dalaga" (dalago = unmarried girl, balae = married girl), of many who simply abound in the Corum house (bahai), had a gardenia in her jet black hair. (The hair styles are typically American, often upswept and with bangs.) Its fragrance intoxicated me. After I mentioned it, the flower was promptly tacked onto my shirt. Many's the evening I've had to tolerate flowers in my hair to please the young adolescents. Everyone, including myself, enjoys it. What a good natured lot all these people are.

I received a letter from Henry Wolf a short while ago. His hand is to be operated on. He's disgusted with the inefficiency and confusion at the hospital (at Lee Hall, Va.). His thirty days at home were glorious, but now he's restless. We plan to get together after the war, probably talk about old times and enjoy one another's company again.

Go ahead; send books. I should have time to read them soon. After the dredge resumes operation, I'll have plenty of time on my hands.

Your V-Mail of 5/14 and 5/28 arrived. Just two weeks.

I don't remember Lottie's son. I don't know very much about Lottie[1] and you know, I've never been clear how she is connected to Dad. Lottie and her husband—what's his name—Myron? have always been vague people to me, not in appearance, but in their association with us.

Sometime this week we move across the bay. It's continually pack, unpack, repack. I'm like you; I dread moving. I like to be settled at one spot and use it as a base of operations for traveling roundabout. When I return to the six hour shift I expect to do plenty of traveling.

In a few minutes I think I'll skip over to the theater and see J. Garfield[2] in "Air Force."[3]

"Magadang gabi po sa nyong lahat dian," which means, goodnight everybody.

Iniibit kita, lahat,
My love to you all, Hughie

5/31/45

(Having no lines to guide me, my handwriting will suddenly be atrocious.)

Dear Mom,

It's unusual for me to write at this hour: 6:30 AM. I know I won't finish this letter until tonight. I have what I guess you'd call a hangover from staying up late last night. This being a dreary, rainy morning (the first rainy day in a couple of weeks), you can imagine my state. By the way, there's a gallery of monkeys on the other side of the screen watching me while I'm doing this. They are free and run around berserk.

The fiesta was held last night in regal fashion, queen and all. The procession marched to a horrible, slow, tinny band— (As I predicted, I was called away to work, and now it's almost 7:00 PM). Well, as I was writing—tinny band, and to the squeals of the youngsters. Lit by Coleman lanterns, torches and the shining glow of the queen's and the maidens' smiles, it wended its way through the streets. The queen, whose history I soon learned about, was half American, though her beauty is mostly oriental. Her speech, with only a little more cultivation, would be worthy of any U.S. classical, professional performer's. Her train—a most elaborate gown with frills and uh, thrills too—consisted of the cutest girls I ever saw dressed in white, and sporting bows and flowers in their black hair. At principal points the procession stopped to perform a pretty, rhythmic, dainty dance in which every motion was significant. I watched as the guest of my friends, the Corums, who escorted me about. They were Rosalio, his wife Purlita, (only eighteen but with personality and charm), my girlfriend Lewanag (a sweet ten and never been kissed), Rosita (teen aged and pleasant), Theresa (early teens and positively brilliant), Louisa (my friend's girlfriend, sweet twelve and full of hell), two or three young lads who admire muscular men and like Americanos, and several more youngsters who attached themselves to us. You can see that I was chaperoned a la king.

Rosalio and I eventually deserted our excited admirers and the procession to wait for its return while in a store manned by a Mrs. Johnson (nicknamed Olineseman), fifty-five years old and the wife of a bloody Englishman for twenty-six years. She is Filipino; before he died in 1935, her husband was in charge of the once existing drydock. Her son Edgar (half English, of course), not yet in his teens, took to me like a duck to water. I'm just crazy about the youngsters here. I enjoy them so much. Meanwhile, I was introduced to two belles (sixteen and seventeen) who act older—and look it, too—than American girls their ages. Addressing me, they always say "Sir." Their manner and actions are refined. Were I to step out with one of them, a chaperon would be required. That is their custom. Not all are so chaste. There are those who parade around in slacks and wear war paint. One exceptionally beautiful girl, with an experienced swagger, continually stood too close to me. My friend whispered into my ear: "Watch her—hindi mabuti—no good." Indeed, a whore.

The dance began about 10:00 o'clock in a small yard surrounded by a hedge of sweet smelling bushes. The orchestra—a trombone, a guitar, and a fiddle—began playing "Alexander's Ragtime Band,"[1] then waltzes, jigs, and popular songs. From the cacophonous clamor I gathered that each musician figured he was playing solo. They never got together or in key, nor for that matter did they produce real music. But there was rhythm, if slow and often stagnant. Soon a selected speaker rose and said: "I am not good at thees making speeches. That ees why I am nervous now. I say it is wrong for the American and Filipino man to dance at the same time. Let American dance one song, then Filipino next. Tankyou." Among the gathering of about 200 people I heard a few mutters of dissent, but for the most part they agreed with him by acclamation.

The Americans danced with their dates; others in a typically informal American way, chose partners at random. Despite the bad music, I enjoyed the scene. With a remarkable swivel to their hips, the girls danced lightly and well. They made their own dresses in the current stylish American fashion. I didn't need to close my eyes to imagine that they could be American girls. They are so obliging and laugh so much. In general, we Americans dwarf them. However, some were as tall as you and others taller and a few even taller than my not--so-tall self.

The Filipino lads then took the (dirt) floor, and I saw that that is how it should be. The Americans should not encourage attachments as we are apt to do. Yet in the past many whites have settled here with Filipino wives. There are many half-breed Filipinos in circulation.

I was a straw boss today. I had my own detail of eight Filipinos working for me. The number one man (Usually they have several vice-bosses) was an old navy man (aged 44) who had spent several years working as a mess attendant aboard ships in the harbors of Boston and San Diego. Speaking in slightly more Americanized English than his "inferior" local countrymen, he recounted his experiences on Tremont Street in Boston, in Charlestown, Cambridge, Watertown, Quincy, Chinatown, and some ungodly hotel, etc., etc. Indeed he had been in America, and — oh, yes — he is the boss.

I immediately tried to win the hearts of my varied workers, most of whom hailed from localities as far as fifty miles away. The oldest, whom I dubbed "Tatai," (my father) was sixty, and I made him rest (pahina) often and long. The youngest was fifteen, a sprightly, obedient chap. At fifteen and sixty, doing the same job? Filipino progress maybe.

I said to Visini, the boss, "Draw me a shovel." "Sino?" (For whom?) he asked. "For me," I replied. He almost toppled over. But he returned with two shovels, one for himself, which he had no intention of using. Understand, bosses never work; they just supervise and enjoy watching the sweating brows of the others. So I entered into it and dug along with the others. "Ekow masaipag." (You are industrious.) Both the young and old kept asking, "What is your name? Why do you work with us? Our other bosses did not work. Why do you work?" I explained in a blend of English and Tagalog that with me even the boss must work. And as we worked, we talked of this and that, and exchanged translations of words. Soon I was "kaibegan"—friend. They offered to climb the palms to get coconuts for me; they invited me to their homes, to go to church with them this evening (the Church of Christ), and to meet their charming sisters and daughters. Meanwhile, boss Visini was muttering profanity at each shovelful I took. He couldn't stand by seeing his boss work and not he. I told him, "You need not work, Visini." "Alright, alright, I like to help," he said and got over it.

We were productive; yet, I didn't have to drive them as was the customary practice. As I sweated, they tried their best to beat me. I gave them periodic rests, which they appreciated. "Salamat," thank-you, they would exclaim. And so Visini came to me and remarked that they work well for me. "Psychology, Visini," I said, "psychology." "Siguro," sure, psychology, he returned.

Tomorrow, I won't be with them, and after I told them that, they said that they would be unhappy and that I must come back. Tomorrow, our unit expects to move across the bay.

I received two of your letters today—from the 19th and 25th. I'll comment next letter. I was cruel not to write as often as I might have. Everything was confusion and new and interesting. I'll do much better hereafter. When I stretched writing a letter over a span of days, it was because I had no time to finish it in one swoop; there wasn't enough time to say everything I wanted to say. Lately, I hope letters are coming in better. I've been trying to write at least every other day.

Now for the sack and sweet slumber. It's long after 7:00 and a thundershower is approaching after a beautiful day that had cleared this morning.

6/2/45

Dear Mom,

We're temporarily situated across the bay from where we were, living with another battalion. Unlike the landscape of flat rice paddies at the bottom of a valley where we were, this place is hilly. We expect to finish our job here in a couple of months then return to our original site.

The situation here isn't as convenient as at the other place, or as pleasant—yet. For the past month I've done everything from lugging fifty-five pound crates of dynamite to digging ditches. While the dredge was on its way here, the battalion assigned us good and proper to all the worst details. Now the dredge has arrived and preparing to operate, and we have been released from all battalion details. My water tending job is waiting.

I've taken it all in stride, enjoying the silly paradox, this grand vicious circle. I'm learning all points of view, including that of an idiot stick operator (pick and shovel). Not until my last day on the job was I put in charge of a Flip detail. It's all been interesting, and I can say that I've learned something new from each thing I've done.

I no longer envy my friends who have had the opportunity to go to school through the war. There's so much still before me. I recall your description of Natalie's[1] graduation; I'm aware of your obvious desire to see your son in the limelight. I prefer things the way they are. The less attention paid me the better.

Remember that I once used the terms "strictest independence," which was not intended to hurt you. It's only that I'd like to get away from home to go to school, away from those I know, but not too far. I'd like to be alone, even be a roomer somewhere. I'd like quiet without interruptions—like the raindrop that just fell on this paper a few lines above. Perhaps it sounds strange to you that I should write this when more than two years will have passed since I left home. Please do not take offense. A long time is yet to pass, and much can happen, ideas can change.

It's wonderful of Dad not to practice what he preaches this "commercial" Mother's Day. It was a success, wasn't it? I was afraid it might not be. Dad and Ronnie handled it well.

Since my mother is undergoing a great renaissance—a sleek figure, nicer clothes—she has stopped being totally practical, and that's fine. Practical gifts are a bore, for sure. Dad's a practical man. Why not kill two birds with one stone? Though I respect the value of money, hang how nonsensical it may be, I buy what I like in a conservative sort of way. In the many Mother's days and birthdays to come, I'll take a real fling and buy not something made of [good wearing] mohair but rather of delicate brocatelle. Now you're fit to wear a glamorous set of duds, trinkets, and what nots. You just leave the practical gifts to Dad. I'll do the rest.

All my pay records, health etc. were transferred to 1082, the new unit, including the money I have on the books (almost $150). Our unit is independent, but we live near and use the facilities of a large battalion. Occasionally, as happened last month, when the dredge is idle, we may be lent to another unit to do rush jobs.

Never fear, my dear, about the local maidens, or any others. This lad is too wrapt.

There's a show tonight, "Thunderhead, Son of Flicka."[2] If it doesn't rain, I expect to enjoy it. I see thunderheads approaching right now.

The sun's down; it's early evening, that part of the day I like most. Tomorrow, Sunday, we'll be setting up permanent tents. I've not had a day off for quite a while. When I work time goes quickly. August makes 18 months overseas. I hear wishful talk about going home more often now. I hope 1946 will see me home. 1945 has a pretty good chance of doing the job.

My love to my three

6/3/45

Dear Mom,

The erection of our tents is getting under way. I have my eye on a possible bachelor apartment. In the meantime I'm living in a tent with other fellows. The tents are 18 feet x 20 feet, normally housing seven men, but only five men at this base, because we have more tents than we need. Our tent has a quiet, harmonious group, but there's nothing like living alone. The tent has two electric lights with as many attachments as we wish. All tents are screened, with fine screen doors and, for the ambitious, a porch. For the tropics it's comfortable living.

Storm warnings are circulating. We are advised to batten down the hatches. A typhoon is due within a day. At present the air is still, and the sky overcast, although not yet threatening.

I enjoyed "Thunderhead" last night. The horses, the scenery, the color and the background music blended into a movie of beauty.

I already have a laundry girl from the local village. If you speak their language you're in. They get a great kick out of hearing an American speak Tagalog. So few Americans have bothered to learn the language, even the more common expressions.

The showers here run warm water. The water tanks are heated by the sun. All those months in New Guinea I got used to cold showers. Our skin is always clean. We perspire so much that our pores stay clear. I drink as many as eight house size glasses of water at a meal and take a salt tablet or two a day and salt my food heavily.

I give my ration of beer and cigarettes to some of my friends. If I wished I could sell them at an enormous profit. Beer costs us $15.00 for a two dozen case. There was a time when I could sell beer for a dollar a can. Cigarettes cost me fifty cents a carton. The Filipinos gladly pay five dollars. Although they offer to pay more, I sell beer and cigarettes to other friends at cost. I don't need the money that badly.

I don't have much to say this evening.

My love to all

6/7/45

Dear Mom,

For the second—and I hope the last—time in the Philippines, we have a floor under our bunks, wire mesh screen, and a permanent roof over our heads. Our tents are sturdily built, as fine as any we've ever lived in. It's quite a relief to have the rush of settling in over with.

Your letters are arriving regularly. I await the arrival of those much desired packages in about six months. If the razor fails to do the proper job, right back it will go. It has been so long coming that I've lost all claim to the Schick, but that's what I intend to use after I return. Out here it doesn't make much difference what I use. My skin is pretty tough. The problem with using a blade is I'm afraid my beard will break it. If I wished I could now raise quite a crop. But I have a soft beard and, after a shave, you'd never know I had one.

The laundry girl who services our tent is a cute fifteen and never been kissed. My wash woman across the bay is probably wondering why I deserted her. The girls at fifteen are more mature both mentally and physically than American girls their age—and also older. While they have less knowledge of the world, they have a greater capacity for living.

Yesterday, two amusing teen-age wenches invaded our tent to trade bananas. They drive a hard bargain, and I usually end up giving them something *gratis*. Yesterday, I gave them a mosquito net that our boys could sell for fifteen pesos, but I didn't have the heart to charge them, and I didn't need the extra net. Sometimes, I give them soap or a comb or cigarettes for their brothers or fathers. You can have plenty of fun with the girls, kid 'em along about their boyfriends, a subject that makes their faces turn kaleidoscopic colors. It's so amusing to watch them walking with a feminine gait and dainty motions, wearing American style dresses, yet absolutely barefooted. The dresses and bare feet don't seem to go together.

Most of the rooms in their houses are barren of furniture. There may be a bench against a wall, or a few uncomfortable dining or office chairs in a corner or a rickety old table. There's plenty of G.I. stuff to be found, maybe a cot, or a synthetic transparent protective gas cover which they use as a table cloth. Their stove consists of a stone fireplace located in an alcove. They sleep on mats on the floor.

I doubt that they would appreciate upholstered furniture. I invited one of the laundry women to sit in my famous comfortable chair, but, when she did, she couldn't relax. She kept her back stiff and upright, as if she were seated on a bench. After I suggested she lean back, she obliged me, but in two seconds she was on a bench again.

My campaign against coffee is still in force. I haven't touched my first drop, let alone Maxwell House's last drop.[1] When nothing else was available, and when I was mercilessly thirsty, I have indulged in a spot of iced tea. Once in a great while I'll down a half can of beer to slake my thirst and make my mates feel good. I'm always thirsty out here. You can't imagine how much we perspire. When I get back home, I'll have milk and nothing but milk and I'm not alone in making this resolution.

Again, I must remind you to forget that I'll be advanced. Few men in this world are fit to be leaders, even of small groups. Genuine leaders make it their business to know their men. The scarcity of leaders in the service is appalling, and it's to be expected. If you're in league with a genuine leader, that is the man over you is ambitious for his men as well as himself, you will advance. You see, I will never advance.

The censors didn't hack up my letter debunking Dolly and Jewish girls in general, but I did. I didn't want to say too much or I'd have to repent. I didn't imagine that my debunking would please you.

The cats-eye bracelet will be yours. I have the eyes but not yet the ambition to make them into a bracelet. But I'm determined to do it one of these days, before I return. Say, did Fibber McGee[2] ever get his closet cleaned up?[3]

I don't blame Ronnie for wanting to get out of taking gym. If he attends the Y regularly, that would be enough. The hasty exercises and regimentation in high school are a bore.

Of course, I'm now under a new skipper. I have been since November when I was transferred to this unit. I no longer have any connection whatsoever with the 113th. You are probably confused about this business. Were I civilian, so would I be. In the service nothing follows a predictable pattern, and change is common. *C'est la guerre.*[4]

Time gave "Dorian Gray"[5] a mediocre write up. They claim that Hollywood hacked up this wonderful story.

6/8/45

Dear Mom,

Again the rain has set in, and it depresses us. Your ten day old letter and news of Charlie's good fortune[1] has lifted my spirits. Only today, some of the older men told me that they are now eligible for civilianship. Men are now being returned for minor reasons. But we young fellows, we young, robust 'uns, are doomed to stay the duration and longer. Truthfully, I'd just as soon stick it out to the sweet end. Conditions couldn't be better. The fellows returning and being discharged rightly deserve it. While I haven't suffered in the least, the older men are war weary and show signs of their suffering. I'm perfectly willing to stay behind.

To warn you, when my great day does come, I, too, would ask for nothing more than some potato kugel.[2] It's our clan's universal delicacy. The others who have already returned have beaten me to the punch. And for supper I'd like—guess what—yep, a delicatessen feast like those we used to have on Saturday nights. And for breakfast whether Sunday or not, I'd like a fresh bagel and meunster cheese, with a couple of eggs sunnyside up etc. I must stop this. These are impossible dreams that I can't conceive of ever being realized. Yet, I really know that they aren't impossible.

I hope that Ronnie will take Mr. Ringer up on his offer. Keep at him. I tell you it's his inferiority complex. I've always liked Mr.Ringer. He has a way about him; he handles adult opponents admirably. When I was ooh so young, I always looked upon him as the adult of adults. I like the way he antagonizes and makes fools of others. That's a vicious statement, isn't it? You see, I like a fellow who's sure of himself when he speaks, and puts his best foot forward. Mr. Ringer has it. Another fellow who strikes me as having it, only in a more vulgar fashion and with less tact, is Harry Palais.[3]

During my cherished past I have heard you mention the inimitable Goldie's sister,[4] so well educated and all that. For the life of me I don't remember her.

We're mixing ice cream and my assistance is in demand.

6/9/45

Dear Mom,

The rain is still cutting strong, and the clouds are black, low hanging, and miserable. What's important is we're dry. The tents are a success.

Last night the ice cream was a deplorable failure. It was too rich. Others have produced excellent ice cream. We in our tent just don't have the knack. But we are determined to try again.

There are five in my tent. On my left is a fellow from the home state, Brockton if you please, now residing in New Hampshire. Thirty-one years old, he spent several years in the army in Panama, has seen much, has worked at numerous trades, but prefers to remain a millwright. At one time he was wild, but settled down with a nice girl, has a one year old child whom he has never seen. The man is a thinker, a pleasing talker, and tactfully frank. His way is odd, though attractive. His ambition is to own a New Hampshire farm, which his wife is now on the lookout for. I like him.

The fellow in his bunk to my right is my age and hails from Minnesota. Because of his naivete many underestimate his intelligence. Actually, he's quite clever. He's a wanderer, goes off for days at a time, and enjoys life. He has a keen and fantastic imagination. I get along with the lad well, and admire many of his ways. He's clean, but not neat, if you can understand such a combination. I'd call him a good bunkmate for our tent.

Next, is the man from Frisco who never hesitates to boast about his town. He's the fellow I wrote you about back in Hollandia. Just thirty-one, we dub him a bachelor. But he plans to be on the make, after he returns. As time goes by, he has become aware that his hair has been markedly reduced to a shallow, thin crop. On the plump side, he is conscious of the passage of the years. Although he's normally extremely good-natured, he occasionally blows his top, and takes a nip now and then, but he never gets drunk. He makes a likable bunkmate. I had worked for him on several electrical projects.

Lastly, we have a rebel from Florida who sports a white mop of hair that just won't stay back. He sees the world through a maize of fine blond hair. Talkative and fast moving, he's just what a typical Southerner isn't. When he's working, you'd think he was off to a fire, and he puffs as if was getting up enough wind to blow it out. Age thirty-seven, recently married, he was by trade an auto-body man. He never bothers anybody despite his exhortations and wild opinions. All of us get along with him.

So it's we five living intimately together and tolerating one another's company in pleasant harmony. Our tent personnel make up a quiet and intelligent group. All are satisfied. The only way to live harmoniously with others is to make concessions. With all of us doing so, everyone is happy.

I lost my chair in transit. Today I began making another, a better one, of course. Once it's built, I'll settle down to the easy state of my pre-Philippine days, and step out only when I'm bored.

My tiny laundry girl is washing the canvas for my new chair. Today, two more girls invaded our tent seeking to trade. They bring a bag full of life with them; everyone gets a portion of it. They have baskets full of fruit, mouths full of smiles, and happy voices. Earlier this afternoon my two Filipino friends, Junior, 13, and Penoy, 16, conducted a session in Tagalog with us. Penoy made up a list of useful phrases. On examination, I discovered that he was teaching me the words used to make love. I had some task setting him straight. In the meantime, my laundry girl (I'm chewing on a fresh pineapple) can't look me straight in the eye without blushing. Now I learn that Penoy and she are cousins. Why, why, I ask, am I always a matchmaker's victim? The pineapple is delicious.

It's now the end of an uneventful, dreary day, and tomorrow is Sunday. As yet, we don't know whether we will work. If we don't, and the weather is fair, I'd like to do some snooping about the countryside.

6/10/45

Dear Mom,

It's 9:10 PM by my watch. That's right, at last I have it and the klaks. It seem odd to have the time so handy. I'd pester someone else for it. In the morning I'd awake (usually after the constant prodding of one of my mates) with no idea whether I missed breakfast or not. And many's the time I missed breakfast after awaking too early then resumed slumber. What irks me the most is to get up and find breakfast over. If I knew the time, I'd have remained in bed. By the way, reveille hasn't the slightest effect on me while I'm sleeping.

I also received the package of wrapping paper. Eventually, I'll send home some of the books that I've read. I've given a couple to my Filipino friends. They had asked for a book by an "intelligent author." They should enjoy what I gave them.

Last night I saw a picture that you'd enjoy—and Dad too: "My Reputation"[1] with Barbara Stanwick[2] and George Brent.[3] It's a story about a recently widowed woman who seeks to overcome her loneliness and sudden helplessness.

The typhoon never struck, though the possibility still lingers. We're making fine progress building our tents, but lumber is a problem. Overseas, lumber is always at a premium.

Without screening on our tent yet, tonight the mosquitoes are having a grand feast on me. I'd best get under my netting and go to sleep.

P.S. *Gazettes* are stacked high and wide beside my bunk. So are *Omnibooks, Reader's Digests* and *Times* of weeks and months past. And I have letters to write. But this minute I'm a sad sack.

6/11/45

Dear Mom,

I don't have anything special to write about. There are no letters of yours to answer. And there's nothing cheerful about this dreary, wet day. But a ludicrous urge has taken hold of me: I feel like wagging my pen.

I'm trying to catch up on my reading, especially about world events. I know little concerning the progress of the San Francisco conference.[1] But soon, I expect to read with great interest about the antics. I ask myself whom will we be at war with once Germany is indefinitely kept in her place. I wonder, knowing that Russia would find war unprofitable, and she knows well it would be a threat to her system. We should no more be at war with Russia than we would be with Britain. Our systems discourage war with each other. Most likely there'll be a squabble among the small nations, and the big ones will take sides. Because another war appears unlikely and the militaristic nations remain subdued, the conference would seem very encouraging. But fate has an ingenious knack for balling things up. She can slyly find a way to promote disaster. The coming years should be momentous. I wonder if they will be.

On reading a review of Robert Frost's[2] "A Masque of Reason" in *Time*, I found a few lines that struck me as significant. Although they are intended to philosophize about things on a grand scale, they can also apply to a specific case.

> "Job and I together
> Found out the discipline man
> needed most
> Was to learn his submission
> to unreason;
> And that for man's own sake as
> well as mine,
> So he won't find it hard to take
> his orders
> From his inferiors in intelligence
> In peace and war—especially in war."

Another excerpt that quelled me:

> "God said:
> I've had you on my mind a thousand
> years
> To thank you someday for the way you
> helped me
> Establish once for all the principle
> There's no connection man can reason
> out
> Between his just deserts and what he gets."

This is a man who has hit it squarely.

Let me tell you about a bright, light talk I had this noon. Two Filipino girls, ages 14 and 16, came to our tent to trade fruit for clothing. They had been here twice before. The older one had an alluring figure, fine teeth, a charm about her. The younger one was vivacious, talkative, and extremely amusing. They are clever, tricky operators at trading, and they answered my questions with lies and evasions. But gradually with each successive visit they looked upon us more favorably. During their last visit, after I prodded them for the truth, they described their plight. With the price of food and clothing sky high, they trade what they get from us for those. One of them explained that she must lie, because the Americans make such proposals as "One carton of cigarettes for one night." She said it was essential that she put such Americans in their place. She pleaded, "There are not all bad girls among us," then added with a laugh, that my friend and I were different, unlike "thees Americans." At first she had thought that we were like the rest and so wouldn't answer our questions squarely.

These girls are so young and so wise. Americans have little respect for these people. I am coming to respect them more and more. There's much to be done for them, and they'd gather it in the way they now gather in precious food for their very existence. You know, I think I'm learning about people.

I prefer to remain a gullible fool and treat a person as my equal first, then raise or lower him in my esteem, as he reveals himself. Tolerance, I insist, is a great, great factor in the momentous years that are to come.

6/13/45

Dear Mom,

The past few days have been quite eventful. I saw a movie with you Monday. We saw it on a wet, windy night. The music sent both of us into raptures. At last, we saw "A Song to Remember" together.

But this evening I won't go into details about such enthusiastic stuff. One of my Filipino companions has been after me for weeks to visit his village, and I promised to do so tonight. He should be here soon to bring me there. I'll have much to write about tomorrow.

The patter of little feet is tripping across our roof. Yes, it's the monkeys having a devil of a time. I should devote a letter to describing their antics. Sometimes they're a riot.

Even if the navy never fed me, I wouldn't starve here. My cabinet shelf is full of pineapples and bananas, gifts from my female admirers.

This noon, some of these friends (only 16), neatly dressed and fresh looking, paid their respects, They sat and talked for a while, and in appreciation of my kindness and civility, presented me with the largest pineapple I've ever seen.

Early this evening, my laundry girl, who has made a proposal that creates an awkward situation and embarrassing complications, presented my friend and me with bananas—which I'm biting into this very minute. I'm told by intimates that this laundry girl suffers from an infatuation with me, and since my response has been negative, and my actions sheer cruelty (because I am the sorry victim) she has added the word "sawi" (hopeless) to my monicker. She is a fine girl, pretty and clean, a good wife for a nice Filipino boy.

My friend is here. I must go.

6/14/45

Dear Mom,

We had one of those tropical deluges the other night. Bundled up in foul weather gear, poncho and a visored hat to keep my glasses dry, I went to see "A Song," just the same. It was worth the inconvenience and then some. The music put me in a mood. It was the first fine music that I've heard in countless months. And Muni's superb acting was as powerful as the music. I see why you raved so. Both the picture and the music meant more than usual to me, because I could imagine that you were with me. There will come a time when we will really hear stuff together. You will come with me to concerts. Mind you, I can be a persuasive youngster. I won't go into a critical discussion on "A Song." It followed the typical romantic approach that the Hollywood people, mercenary souls that they are, love to do.

Last night, I visited the local village and met and talked with my new friends. They asked me to tell them a story; then, they in turn would tell one, a story about the Jap occupation. One fellow mentioned the word Jew, and I came to find out that he was confused about who the Jews are. I revealed to him that I was a Jew and from my meager store of knowledge, gave a brief outline of their history, their customs and culture. All were pleased with what I told them. When I left I said good night to solid friends.

To clear up any misconception you might have of the female affiliations that I must suffer, here it is in brief. Whenever the girls here, that is the good ones, are infatuated with a lad, they are reticent and shy and avert their glances. Neither party is allowed to put their best foot forward, and any friendliness must be sanctioned by the parents. It is understood that friendliness is a preliminary step towards marriage.

Well, these girls like Americans — with some reservations. If an American is good and treats them with respect, the girls immediately respond in kind. It's tough on a Filipino girl if she cares for an American. Usually, she realizes how futile it is, and has to live with only the figment of her infatuation. When an American leads her on, she is to be pitied. It's better to make it clear to her that although you like and respect her, it can go no further. I've adopted a policy of being suitably cool towards these girls, not offensively so, but I remain distant.

Once in a while we see an older man trading. I have one such friend who is in his middle forties. At times he reminds me that he has two unmarried daughters in their late teens. He insists on bringing me fried chicken and some nicknacks, next week.

I've found something for you, Mom, that you'd enjoy, although I doubt if they'd be comfortable. They are hand carved native wooden sandals, dress sandals at that. On the heels are carved and painted palms and native huts, called "bahai cubo." And for you, Dad, I've found some locally made cigars. I'm told they are mild. Try them anyway. I'll send them in a week or so.

At last the rain has let up, and the days are clear. The weather has been as whimsical as New England's. I never care whether it's rain or shine. It's cool when it rains, and it's pleasant to work when the sun shines. I dislike mud and I dislike dust. By working on the dredge I don't have to contend with either.

No, we don't have milk here. There is caribou milk which I dare not try. Of course, the animals here aren't tested for disease. I don't even care to eat the local restaurant food. Our own chow hasn't been so bad. Several days a week we have eggs for breakfast.

I'm still searching for something unique as a souvenir. I don't want the common run of stuff that everybody else has.

The evening is still young, but I've run dry for now. 'Til tomorrow.

6/15-6/16/45

Dear Mom,

I began this letter last night only to abandon it because of a sore right arm. Periodically, every six months or so we are given shots in the arm for unearthly diseases, and they usually knock the gaff right out of me for a day or so.

Today several men from the mother battalion are homeward bound as full-fledged civilians. After being discharged here, they're now on their own. You never saw a happier lot. Gradually, it's boiling down to only the young ones being left behind.

Between now and 1946, the full might of the extensive preparations taking place, much of it diverted from Europe to here, should be unleashed. It's more than probable; it's certain. Because I am witnessing and feeling this, I'm very optimistic that the war with Japan is coming to a conclusion. I think 1946 will be my year, the happiest year of my life. I hear that the commentators are spitting out the usual rash predictions, but what can they know?

I remember in Hollandia immediately before the Philippine campaign feeling the tension. Even before we saw the troops being loaded onto the LSTs, I had my suspicions. It's all so imminent now that I presume you in the States can probably guess what's going on.

Johnson has written as witty a piece of literature as you could hope to read. It's a shame that you have never met him. You simply bathe in his personality and come away refreshed.

Since I've been in the Philippines, I've had little inclination to write or even read. There are so many diversions. I'm never isolated here and usually in the thick of things. I waste more time intending to do things rather than doing them.

I realize my letters have been short. After a while I'll settle down to write without this fidgeting.

6/18/45

Dear Mom,

The better part of June has gone by, and in a week so will two years in the service. It all seems so unreal, a crazy mixture of nightmare and sweet dream. And now that the future is solidly ensured, I'm anticipating unknown things to crop up. So far, nothing has gone my way; so, why should I expect this natural phenomenon to change? I have a vague premonition that getting into college, let alone surviving it, will not be an easy task. I can see that my plans are fast becoming ridiculous. I should keep my options as broad and flexible as possible. I think the best thing to do is to stow away my wishes until the ideal conditions arise for me to uncover them. I'm on a merry sleigh ride—damn everything. I've set too rigid a goal, and I'd be scared stiff to abandon it. Whichever way I choose to go, I know I won't stand still. I must take chances. Dad has been too conservative; his path is too sane.

You may wonder with a snicker what brought this on. You might say that I've reached my periodic pinnacle, that I'm discharging lightning. It's merely a neat way of blowing my customary top. This outburst has been prompted by the plight of one of my Filipino friends. I'm momentarily aggravated with his lackadaisical manner, listlessness, and irresponsibility so common to, yes, characteristic, of these people. It's not only his ways that trouble me, but also the corruption and the dearth of fit leaders. I probably sound like Goodstein's brother who wants to remain in India to help improve the situation. In thirty years he'll have a dandy laugh re-reading his nonsensical tantrums. The impressionistic fool.

I don't take myself too seriously regarding such matters. It's only a passing glimpse of my thoughts, which take longer to read than think about.

In your letters of June 4 and 6, you mentioned that in trying to realize his career plans, Bob would be limited by the competition. This irritated me and has led me to spout off. I, too, fear that I might well have a hard time getting what I'm after due to stiff competition. I have no illusions. But I think it will be fun trying. So far as anti-semitism is concerned, I say what's good for Felix Franfurter[1] is also good for me.

My reason for remaining shy of Worcester Tech is that I don't want to be home. It's no reflection on you folks. Please don't think that it is. It's difficult for me to explain what I feel. Who knows, I might be more homesick fifty miles away from home than ten thousand. If I came scampering back, I wouldn't be ashamed. A fellow can go ahead faster and farther with no ties. Extraneous luggage, dear though it may be, is that much more to carry up the steep grade, that much more to hold one back.

You have me worked up to the point that I'll be pulling my hair out, if I don't receive your picture pronto. I'm all in a dither (just between ourselves) about this new, improved postwar model. It's odd that I hear no comments from Dad. Has he become senile that he's oblivious to the fascinating change? I very much doubt it.

Why, I hadn't realized that you too yearn for the serenity of cool waters and the moaning of pines. I thought you were strictly a card shark (or whatever you're playing nowadays), enjoying the company of women companions galore at a noisy beach. I'm thrilled that you approve of my proposal. If I have my way, it will become a reality. I'd like a summer camp in the worst way. I'll wait for Dad's reply, then work on it. At first, the land is enough. Remember, I now know how to build. Of course, land with something on it is better, but also more expensive. At this writing money is hardly an obstacle. A revelation, Mom: I'd like to build a place, myself, with my own hands.

Yesterday I took off to visit my old friends across the bay. Since I hadn't seen them in more than three weeks, they were about to give up hoping that I'd ever return. More friends than I knew I had greeted me with the familiar "Huey." I had a great time. Later in the afternoon, Robert (the man of the house) and I went for a walk through the neighboring barrios (borough to you). Having once been quite a prominent resident there, he knew everyone. He introduced me to many who were astonished that I could carry on a suitable conversation in their own language—Tagalog. I do enjoy speaking it. I listen to them speak with both ears fully cocked in order to catch every syllable and understand. I was also invited into numerous homes of fine, smiling people. They gaze at me and search my face with friendly smiles and expressions of hospitality.

The people in one house that we visited were outstanding. They impressed me as being go getters. One girl was at a sewing machine clicking away making quaint multi-colored dresses, while others were busy doing hand sewing. I sat on a box (I refused a chair that I forfeited to a lady) that I soon discovered was filled with crabs that were for sale. They enjoy my American clumsiness, (They walk lightly and move their hands with dexterity) and awkwardness, and fumbling with Tagalog. I laugh along with them.

Ah yes, there is always that special girl, whose stare freezes and melts into a blush on meeting your glance. This one, about eighteen, very intelligent, talked the way I like to hear a girl talk. She knew what she wanted to say and how to say it. As much as I'd enjoy the friendship of girls like her, I maintain a barrier which will save them much trouble.

My native companion is really flabbergasted by my attitude. He has quizzed my navy mates about my aloofness toward girls. I am an American freak. Realize, folks, that the life of these people is so simple that sex, marriage, and companionship are first and last in all their behavior. It governs their lives (in a very sensible way, at that) in every way.

More than once they've put the question to me: "Are all the people in America rich?" They think I'm rich because my wallet is always full, and I'm loose with my possessions. Their vision of America is like our vision of Utopia. I have given long talks to groups who egg me on because they want to learn. It's pitiful how little they know and how much they crave to know.

The other day a man (age 36), whom I didn't remember, entered my tent. He had overheard one of my discussions. As he introduced himself and his wife, he shook my hand earnestly. When I remarked offhandedly that we would have many more talks together, his eyes lit up. "Yes," he said in the manner of a servant, "I learn much by what you say." He addressed me as "Sir" (as so many do with all Americans) regarding which I at once explained that I was much younger than he and it was I who should say "Sir." His next statement still included the subservient "Sir."

On my way back to camp, I stopped off in another town, renowned for its night life. My boat wasn't due until 10:00 PM, so I nonchalantly waded into the reek and smoke of a cheap cabaret, hat askew on the back of my head, in keeping with the atmosphere. I watched everything with amusement, the dark corners, the faces of the stupid drunks, and the sober ones who were making damn fools of themselves, and the promiscuous dancers. I stood alone against a wall away from the crowd, just gazing. Soon a small boy who recognized me from camp shouldered me. Happy as could be, he begged me to dance with any girl of my choosing. He could and would get her for me. If I preferred not to dance (and I explained that I didn't), he offered to arrange for me to spend the night with one. I was his friend —any girl I'd like. He knew them all. I could hardly suppress bursting into laughter. Seeing me amused to the core, the poor lad was very much confused and maybe a little bit embarrassed.

Soon a slick looking Filipino youth summoned me to dance with a particular girl (as instructed evidently by the girl who was dissatisfied with her American). My watch conveniently read 9:45, and I slipped out, leaving him shrugging and confused. I want to see everything. I can work from the bottom out here. The top—well, that's waiting for me to see back home.

One of these weekends I expect to take off on a long trip. I'm anxious to wander about the island and see as much as I can, while I'm here. It won't be exactly a pleasure jaunt, because finding a place to eat and sleep is no picnic.

Henry Wolf has sent me a package, an enormous package, I should say, of expensive nuts. They were delicious. What a guy! I feel pleased with the friends I've made. I'm sorry that you know none of them.

6/23/45

Dear Mom,

I'm back on my regular job again: water tending, the night shift. After all the confusion and shifting from one job to another for the past three months, I find my old job very pleasant. I'll be working an eight instead of a regular six hour shift for a while. Wanderer's fever has taken hold of me. I have a strong urge to take off for a few days to see what I can see. Very shortly I expect to be able to do just that.

I have made new friends of an entirely different class and sect from those whom I had been mingling with. These are diehard Methodists, who, from what I gather, comprise the wealthy and the elite of the P.I. One friend in particular (I have only met the beautiful daughter) is from a family of great stature. Her father, the wealthiest man in town, is the general manager of a plantation. All the children aspire to go to college. They live fifty miles from the camp in an easily accessible location. Having an invitation in hand, I plan to drop by with six cans of beer. Although dancing, smoking, and drinking are prohibited, I hear that poppa has a weakness for non-intoxicating beer.

This all came about when I fell into deep discussion with a middle-aged man and his niece. Escorted by her uncle, the girl travels about selling popped rice in order to earn her school matriculation fee. Our discussion became so involved that uncle forgot all about his niece's matriculation fee and spent a good part of the afternoon in our tent talking. However, the niece didn't seem to mind the delay, nor did I. She was different in several ways from the usual run of girls in the province. First, her features were such that she would be acceptable in American society. She didn't have the characteristic pudgy nose and unbecoming nostrils. Her manner was even more surprising. She spoke without the typical timidity and suspicion, but rather was informal and inviting. She was quite different, quite pretty, offering some local boy a chance to marry into money.

So I've met another kind of people about whose customs, and trains of thought I am to learn. So far I've seen and talked with sluts, eaten with the poor, mingled with the middle, and now I'll get to know the well-off.

I hope that Ronnie's entry into the State Guard will suffice as a substitute for the glory (so called) of the service. A little military training wouldn't do anyone any harm. Having grown to despise it, once I'm free, I'll want no part of it. The guard will take up much of his time, often at inconvenient moments. It will be a burden. As I say, a smattering of military discipline won't hurt a soul. By the time the next war comes around, he'll have a better chance to secure a commission. As for myself, I've adopted a policy of playing a lone hand. No organizations for me, no chance of having my freedom restricted, no payments that don't bring returns.

Arthur Ringer appears to be taking quite an interest in Ronnie. Although you haven't intimated so, was he instrumental in Ronnie's joining the guard? Since I've been away, it seems that you have been much closer to the Ringers, seeing them more frequently. Am I right? If so, I'm glad. I know they are fine people.

And what has become of your other friends: the Greenbergs, the Lowes etc.?

The night before last I took time out from work to see "Hollywood Canteen."[1] It was good, solid entertainment, and somewhat nostalgic at that. The countless times I visited the Canteen, I always found some personality there. I remember the day I shipped out for boot camp two years ago, when we saw "Stage Door Canteen" together in Boston.

By the way, Dad, I learned that I can't send cigars to the States: revenue laws and all that. I'm in the market for some fine hand-carving work. Whatever I've seen costs a small fortune. With a little time and some finagling I expect to find something good.

P.S. Do you want more invasion money? I can make you rich with it.

6/24/45

Dear Dad,

I'm back again with another man to man session to fill the gap on the map. You know, Dad, you've done more toward filling the gap than you suspect, more perhaps than I know.

Yesterday, I wrote that I was back at my original job. After the dredge commences operation today, I should get into the swing of things. A degree of normalcy will prevail so that I'll be able to write, read, and travel without external pressures.

Next week, I plan to visit my friends in the hinterland. Since I've always had a yen for farming, or at least having contact with the soil, and since the people are landowners of comfortable means, I'm looking forward to going native. I intend to plant rice, plough the earth with the aid of water buffalo, and work in either the rain or sun-soaked fields. I had proposed this to Anita [See a photograph of her above], the family's daughter who visits my residence several times a week. With an amused smile she consented, guaranteeing her prominent father's consent, and no doubt suspecting a thread of insanity in our family. Her middle-aged uncle, Lucio, an agricultural inspector, plans to show me about and introduce me to households galore. This is just what I've been after: to meet the people in their natural environment, to live and work with them.

All this sounds very rosy, but there is a slight drawback, which lies in the beautiful person of Anita. She is most attractive, and no doubt irresistible to the lusty boys around here. At times, I feel she's much too alluring to have around. And she frightens me with her glances that should be for someone else. If I visit her family, an uncomfortable situation might arise, and I have no wish to make anyone unhappy. So I'll confine myself to absorbing the local color, hoping that everyone will stay happy.

The rainy season is beginning to show her true colors. Since it has arrived late this year, its tardiness had begun to dispel any idea that such a season existed. Now we have vigorous downpours nightly, and the days are mostly overcast. The earth hasn't yet softened to a familiar, despicable quagmire, but I insist, give it time. The worst days are yet to come.

I'm pleased that my camp proposal not only meets with your approval, but also holds the possibility of your participation. In both our lives, one in which the prime can be enjoyed, the other in which retirement should be enjoyed, a summer camp would be an ideal scheme. Unlike for so many, noise and cabarets and boisterous tomfoolery don't appeal to us. It will be a place where we can invite friends and relatives to visit, where we can live in quiet and make the best of our leisure, a spot for healthy physical activity and activity of the mind, for the restful enjoyment you need, and for the wholesome development of Ronnie's and my stature for a sound future. I'm certain such a venture would mean more in our lives than we now realize.

The drudgery of returning to the same place day in and day out, seeing the same scene, is unhealthy. So I see this as more than a luxury. It's practically a necessity in this day when luxuries are fast becoming necessities. I predict after this war the pace of living will be terrific. The wild twenties[1] will seem tame by comparison. Everything will be spontaneous and crushing. However, the government, not private enterprise, will try to extend a moderating hand. How effective it will be we cannot know.

The time to purchase a place is not now when the market is in season. We should search in the winter. As for me, I would take pride in building our own place. I have ample confidence in myself to do so, although it may cost me a few fingernails and the loss of a toe or two. All this may be slightly trumped up, but at least it lets you know how much I would look forward to having our own place.

Apparently you feel worse about the mattress episode than I do. After what I've slept on during the past year and one half, anything, just anything will do.

Mother, who has been making wild guesses as to my whereabouts, has missed. For that matter, I've never heard of the place she mentioned. Somehow, Henry Wolf found out. It's remarkable how information gets around. As soon as a fellow returns he has no compunctions about not adhering to security regulations.

I see that you are still confused concerning this unit's origins etc. Let me try to clear it up for you. Last November the dredge was assigned to the 113th and as a member of the battalion I was given a job on it. The original crew was from another battalion. I worked aboard the dredge until February while it was under the 113th's jurisdiction. During that period I was responsible both to the commanding officer of the dredge and the commander of the battalion. In short, until February I was still a member of the battalion. Then the dredge became independent of the 113th, a self-sustaining unit, and a permanent complement was composed and consigned to it. The names of those in the complement, which comprised the original crew and some members of the 113th including myself, were submitted through channels to higher offices for approval. By February, the approval came through and I and my papers were transferred to the newly formed dredge unit. Thus, I was no longer responsible to the 113th but rather to the dredge commander.

When we pulled out of Hollandia we were given a unit number, C.B. Detachment 1082. From February when I was transferred until the unit was assigned a number, our address stood as U.S.S.D. York Syme. Although we are an independent unit, we usually work in collaboration with a construction battalion. That's why we live with larger units. I hope this explanation makes it clear.

Red tape, the long lines of approvals, unforeseen obstacles, the uncertainty of war, tend to confuse the reasoning mind. There is so little logic in the service that the civilian mind, which runs along logical channels, cannot fully grasp our situation. There's little rhyme or reason to the things that happen to me and my associates. Yet, when the whole pattern presents itself, it oddly makes sense, and inefficiency proves to be efficient enough to win a war.

It's the middle of the afternoon of the twenty-fifth. Today, at 6:00 PM I begin working a six hour shift to midnight. Whatever our job ahead will be, I doubt if we'll be here long enough to complete it. Our eighteenth month commences next month, which legally, but not in actuality, should see us homeward bound. Most are optimistic—the typical American spirit. A few months beyond won't make much difference. A rotation plan has been formulated in which after the 18th of the month a certain percentage of each unit will go home. Others will follow in successive months. Replacements will be on hand to take over. You can easily understand that rather than come out again, I'd just as soon put in one long stretch of time. Of course, I have no choice. In three or four months we should know how we stand.

I impatiently look forward to our next chat. I'm as anxious to tell you about all I see, as you are anxious to hear it.

6/26/45

Dear Mom,

The rain is still sweeping in from the sea. It has been almost a week of downpour or threatening downpour. I'm surprised that my spirits aren't dampened by the weather. But everything seems to be progressing in such a peaceful, interesting way, that I can't be melancholy at the moment. If things were to continue so naturally until the time I return, I'd be perfectly satisfied. Once in a while I'm beset with a mania for excitement, for new scenes, and maybe some confusion. At least, here in the Philippines, I have an outlet: travel.

Henry Wolf sent a second package, a large box of assorted cookies. And he writes that there's a camera and film on the way too. Do I read your letter right? "A letter from Mrs. Linfield." I haven't heard from Gulfport for an age.

Our unit lives in tents set apart from those of the battalion personnel. All in these tents work aboard the dredge.

If I go away to school, I'd just as soon not live on campus in a dorm. I'd like to have my own room, be a roomer in a private home. We shall see. From the looks of things, I won't have a large variety of schools to choose from. Worcester Tech may prove to be my only alternative.

I manage to keep tabs on all the news. The shape of world peace negotiations[1] is far from encouraging. With the emphasis on power and national sovereignty, how can the forces for good neutralize the forces for evil indefinitely? I'm certain it's generally accepted that, by hook or crook, war will sneak up on future generations. Russia is proving herself to be not only a source of military wizardry, but also a diplomatic force, and as we shall see, an industrial one. All we, the people, can do is sit tight, close our eyes, and hope everything will come out just fine. I believe that for the public of the world, the making of a lasting peace is a greater, and more difficult ordeal than waging war which is a more tangible force. Now, we ordinary people are helpless; in war we had weapons.

6/30/45

Dear Mom,

I have a wonderful excuse for not writing the last few days, and what I did during them will surely make amends. I first visited my old friends then made new friends who live in one of the small towns that are scattered across the central Luzon plain [Pampanga]. The trip in itself was worthwhile.

I set out with an army duffel bag slung over my shoulder, containing toilet articles, flashlight, a change of clothes, and my week's ration of beer. In no time flat I hitched a boat ride across the bay, and was soon on a truck speeding inland. Along the way I saw signs of the tough time the invaders had. A damaged tank and some smashed enemy vehicles squatted along the wayside, the usual picturesque detritus in time of war.

To reach the hinterland, we must cross a mountain range. We had to follow a treacherous pass that twists and winds miraculously for miles between sheer cliffs. I have never seen such difficult terrain before. Where once towering forests stood, there were acres and acres of jutting, jagged stumps and bare tree trunks. Not a tree was unscathed. Tons and tons of bombs and shells must have been lopped into this pass. The landscape was hideous. Soon the truck stopped mounting and began coasting downward toward green, fertile country. A vast plain spread out before me to the horizon, a flat expanse with pretty trees spotted here and there, a momentary flash reflecting off some lazy stream. Green, green was everywhere. It reminded me of the Ohio and Indiana countryside that I had seen from the troop train a long time ago.

A good portion of the road crossing the plain was smooth two-lane concrete highway, with a few miserable stretches of pocked macadam. Some corn grew in the fields and tender sprouts of rice being carefully nurtured for their real planting in a month or so. Caribou wallowed ecstatically in sluggish, muddy brooks. Typical caribou carts with solid wooden wheels drawn by the lazy, powerful water buffalo plodded along the wayside. Cute little carts resembling jerryrickshaws, their sides and roofs covered with fancy decorations, pranced down the road to the jog of kempt ponies.

The first town appeared like a mirage in a desert. Made of concrete and stone, all the public buildings were in ruins. A lone, chipped statue stood symbolically in the main square. The streets were lined with flimsily constructed wood and bamboo structures, the usual run of Filipino "country homes." The main drag was infested with cabarets and restaurants. Into the open country once more, there were finer homes with yards containing banana, papaya, and mango trees, indicating the more prosperous farmers. Some were tropical mansions surrounded by elaborate stone and masonry walls that fenced in green lawns. At times I'd see a beautiful wall; my eye would follow a curving cement sidewalk to cement stairs then come to an abrupt stop. That's all that remained; the house was no longer there.

I went about eight kilometers beyond my destination, to a pretty good-size town. Inquiring of a Filipino in his own language, I found my error and headed back. While I was thumbing, the people in the residence nearby insisted that I come into the shade and sit down in their house. They would let me know when a vehicle approached.

I found the road that I missed and asked, "Saan ay bahai Lucio Reyes?"—Where is Lucio's home? An American is a veritable Pied Piper in a village not frequented by Americans. Children accumulate behind him and raise quite a rumpus shouting "Victoree Americano." The adults look up from their work and nod their heads hello, or say "Hello, Joe," or "Where are you going, Joe?" The women and girls rush to the open windows and gaze, smiling, the shyer ones from around the corners.

After trudging along with my boisterous escort, I found Lucio's house where he awaited me with open arms. When I entered the house, the children dispersed. As Filipino houses go, his was sturdier and neater. All the houses were set on stilts about four feet above the ground to keep the rain and barnyard animals out. Even so, an occasional rambunctious chicken has to be shooed out. All day long pigs, chickens, turkeys, dogs, cats, and ducks are squealing, grunting, clucking, barking, quacking and meowing in unison. Once I got used to it I stopped hearing them.

Lucio introduced me to his thirty year old wife who immediately began immodestly nursing the more recent of her two daughters. Like Lucio, she spoke English fluently. Anita, the beauteous adolescent, interrupted her busy housework with a hasty nod of recognition and went about preparing the preliminaries for our dinner. After I washed and cooled off, Lucio took me to the local primary school where I met the principal who was Lucio's compadre. (As compadre he was godfather to one of Lucio's children.) A graduate of Union College of Manila, class of 1940, he was fascinating to talk to. He in turn introduced me to the rest of the faculty, two young men and a young lady. They were to hold graduation exercises that day, and on Thursday, tomorrow, they would be rehearsing a play and some folk dances to be performed on the weekend. Alihandro (spelled Alijandro) Quiboloy, Lucio's campadre and the principal, and new friend, explained the ritual. At last, Lucio dragged me off to dinner.

When we arrived the table was all set. Each course was served on a separate dish. I was given eating utensils; they ate with their hands. First, the men eat while the women serve. Don't think that the women are subservient. No, man and wife operate on an equal basis. I saw no noticeable domination of one over the other. It's just that the children present eating problems for the women. You know how children squeal and make a fuss at the table. They thought I ate peculiarly. They were amused that I put everything on one plate and drank water, all the water I could consume while eating.

For this dinner I had two fresh eggs sunny side up, a glass of fresh milk, shrimp, a delicious fish stuffed with raisins, called milk fish, rice, and home-made bread. Everything was elegant. Need I mention how the sight of fresh milk affected me? My first taste of it since I've been over. It was caribou milk and tastes exactly like cow's milk. I had no fear because they had sterilized it for me. This was my first home cooked meal since December 1943.

The stove is merely an open hearth fueled by wood. I was overwhelmed by my hosts' generosity. Mrs. Reyes most pleasantly said, "You can't imagine how we prayed for you boys to come, and anything we can do, anything, can never repay what you have done for us." That afternoon I listened to the frankly told atrocity stories by those who witnessed them. I'll save these stories for another letter. Many of them are depressing and heart-rending. For the first time I learned about the reaction of the Japanese themselves to their own cruelties.

I'll stop here until my next letter. Before I close, I must mention that I wore civilian clothes for almost two days. I had on stylish gabardine slacks, and a polo shirt most of the time. The novelty drove me mad with excitement. I had a wonderful time, let me tell you. I talked incessantly as they listened with news-starved ears. They continually egged me on. Our discussions were deep, and on such subjects as government, Negroes, the Jews, and Christians. These people comprise the plain intelligentsia of the islands. They have good minds and knowledge. Unfortunately, they have run across few Americans who will discuss things with them, as I have. My ways surprised them.

Before I left, Alejandro said, "Let me be frank Hugh. You have entirely changed my concept of the Jews. My first impression came as a student when I read about Shylock[1] in the *Merchant of Venice*.[2] You are different, more decent than many of your American comrades. I like your race now." I swelled a little inside, and silently thanked you and Dad. I felt fine.

My love, Hughie

7/3-7/4/45

Dear Mom,

The Fourth of July and a holiday for everyone. My stomach is bursting from eating barbecued meat, hot dogs, and all the stuff that goes with it. The battalion (the 102nd) went on a wild spree and C.B.D. had access to everything including eight bottles of (Rupert's) beer per man—and some are beginning to feel it.

I didn't intend that so many days would elapse between letters, but no sooner had I returned from one trip than off I went on another. This one was distant (about 200 miles), and packed with new sights, people, and experiences. I went to the city. Regulations prohibit me from saying much. You can imagine how much destruction I saw. A friend escorted me about the city, pointing out what this and that building was, what happened here and there. I ate and slept at his ramshackle house. All these people brimmed over with hospitality and gratitude. It affected me to the core.

I wish I could describe the sights I've seen. There's no need to write a letter that would be torn to ribbons. It would be a tale that begins with a description of once gorgeous structures reduced to rubble and ends with a story told through tear-glossed eyes by a once proud mother, my hostess. I listened to more stories and saw more faces fiery with anger. Everywhere I went these good people couldn't do enough for me. While I listened and saw, I thought of you, safe and well back there. How comforting it was.

Of all the remarkable things that I saw last week, the grandest of them all was right here in the tent. Your pictures arrived. They brightened me—just what I needed to alleviate my weariness from a rough trip. Any picture of you folks would refresh me. They weren't just any pictures. I gasped when I saw you. You are absolutely ravishing, younger, yes, much younger than two years ago. The fellows remarked, with not a word from me, how lucky I was to have such a young mother. I couldn't talk; I just beamed. And Dad! Dad, they wouldn't believe me when I told them your age. You look wonderful. Am I happy, happy. This Ronnie, he's not the kid I saw when I left. I'm appalled at the remarkable change. I tell you he's a prototype of a tall, dark, handsome man. All three of you together—my folks—a great picture. They came at the right time, the booster I needed. I'm fit for anything now.

I have five letters from the sixteenth through the twenty-fifth. Thanks for writing, Ronnie. I got the usual great kick out of your letter. Well, boy, you wanted it, and you got it. If it's military training and drilling that you want, they can feed it to you good and proper. Oh, it's not really so bad, but it gets monotonous after a while. We gloat over the fact that we haven't had any military training for eighteen months. Nevertheless, remnants of that training surface when someone says jokingly, "Hureep for your left, left, right, left." A couple of weeks ago it dawned on me that I had completely forgotten the manual of arms. Tch, tch, sad eh? Like hell. If you find in your sleep that your reflexes pulsate to a left, right, left, don't be alarmed. And, folks, if, when eating, Ronnie raises his spoon in a mechanical, squared fashion, think nothing of it. It's all part of the process. Now you wear a uniform. Not nearly so tight and ridiculous as mine. That's a break. I can't wait to shed my monkey suit. One consolation in being over here is that we never have to wear our uniform. Sometimes, for that reason, I'd rather be here. I see the shots have knocked you for a loop. You'll get used to them. For the past two years my arm has been a pin cushion. The plague that I could catch hasn't been discovered. Our veins run serum, not blood. It's all part of the great process. The first rifle I fired was an Enfield, and my shoulder was sore for weeks. I'm sure that the bullet remained stationary while I, and that ton of wood and metal, bounded backwards. That's what it felt like. Before I fired, my heart was pounding to beat the band. After I fired, it stopped. You'll see,

Dad, I feel that I deserted you on Father's Day. And now again on your birthday that's about due, I planned to send you sweet-smelling Philippinas cigars, and those dirty dogs, the revenuers, said no. Anyway, Dad, a happy birthday to you. My thoughts constantly flash back to our times together. One of the great things I look forward to returning to is our companionship, renewed with even longer and better times. You're more than a father; you're an inspiration. What a great family the four of us are. We must always stick together.

I haven't sent the package yet due to my own shameful neglect. Instead of sending the books home, I've decided to contribute them to a good cause. My friends in the hinterland are trying to form a library and are thirsty for good literature. Whatever books I've read I'm donating to them.

Great! Only I wish you were spending more than a week at the lake. If you like the place, try to line it up for a longer period next summer. If you see a place that's worthwhile buying, I have money. Everything sounds just fine. Learn to enjoy life, for God's sake and mine. Need I say how much I wish I were with you?

I haven't written the relatives since leaving Hollandia. What few letters I've written others have been forced.

Having your latest image in my mind, Mom, I'm feeling homesick once more.

P.S. Send envelopes. I have plenty of paper.

7/5/45

Dear Mom,

This week I've been in the service two years. My ideas have changed, and, I imagine so have my physical features, but fundamentally I'm the same. After two years, I can now say that I have no regrets. So far, I'm satisfied with the outcome, with being here, doing what I'm doing, and benefiting from what I've learned. I can't say that it's been tough, because there has never been a time that I was taxed beyond my physical and mental endurance. I feel fortunate. I appreciate what I've been through. After I return I won't feel particularly proud of the part I've played, merely satisfied: my curiosity, my conscience, discovering that I can deal with both sensible and ridiculous eventualities. I shall feel a tranquil contentment.

This month is normally the rainiest of the year, and it's upholding its reputation. For days, a wind-driven deluge has been upon us. The days are cool, fine for sleeping, and the nights penetrating. Reconciled to the countless days of rain and the miserable, heavily moisture-laden heaven, I remain happy. But weather like this can break the spirit of most men.

I'm glad that I got a good deal of traveling in before this wretched week began. Having contemplated many more tours, when weather and opportunity agree, off I shall go again.

I hadn't completed the account of my first trip, but since my most recent one overshadows it, I'll cut it short. I ate well every meal, mostly chicken, fresh fruit, vegetables, and milk. Our discussions and my revelations brought these intelligent, sluggish, ambitious people around to thinking my way. I both praised and reprimanded. They could deny nothing that I told them. Once I gained their confidence, they spoke frankly which opened up new avenues for discussion. I enjoyed the experience immensely. I learned more about people and, to be sure, about myself.

It may startle you to learn that what had won their respect and confidence was, not so much my frank talk and innocent behavior, but what I didn't do. Unlike most Americans—in their mind, all Americans—I didn't ask for women. I was of a species they hadn't yet encountered. This concerns more than my simply not desiring their women. My feelings are no different from those of other Americans. It concerns the attitude of one race towards another. They received my respect and were elevated. I practiced restraint, that which is proper in dealing with others. So, as a result, I have new special, genuine friends who now feed my vanity, and among whom I can express my ideals and reign as someone who is staunch and good.

Merely as a project it would be interesting and worthy to instill some drive and initiative into these people. It would depend on how much of it I have myself and how much time I have. Having won them over, I'm in a position of power and influence. They are not yet used to thinking independently. They have no original ideas. They yearn for the suggestions of others. As young as I am, I'm able to hold their attention; they listen with ardent concern. More than anything they need initiative, even a healthy arrogance. It would bring them wealth, prestige and a cooperative society. I maintain that they have the stuff, the intellect with which to start.

I have a general impression that those Americans who were formerly here, that is before the war, were not altogether good. They were after the mighty dollar. Exploitation is definitely apparent. After all, pursuit of the material is to be expected. These people will always have to combat it.

I go off on one of my rampages about social and political matters without paying heed to what interests you. I guess much of this is quite irrelevant to you. But I know you bear with me, and encourage me to tell you everything. So I take good advantage of your commitment to me.

Lately, rather ever since I crossed the equator the second time, I've been deplorably lazy. My neglect of reading and writing has been shameful. At last, it seems, the tropics are having their effect.

Now another summer has arrived for you. I don't know any other season. Enjoy yourselves. Rest up. It's very important.

My love to all of you, Hughie

7/6/45

Dear Mom,

Last week I was a civilian for about thirty-six hours. I looked and honestly felt like one. Having two free days, I visited my Filipino friends. At their insistence, I circulated in pressed gabardine slacks and polo shirt. The sensation was great.

Under the careful scrutiny of the people, I wandered through the village observing everything. I watched them make nipa thatchwork, and sift and grind rice. My companions pointed out various spots where a few died, and where the survivors and heroes of Bataan abandoned a position during a retreat,[1] and where the guerrillas engaged in a skirmish. Many wrecks and remnants of vehicles that were used in the 1942 retreat were strewn about.

That night I slept well under a net on a hard bed. When I awoke about 7:00, I found soap, towel and a basin of water laid out for me. After having a hearty breakfast, my host and I commandeered a two man banca (canoe) and headed down a sluggish stream toward the sea a good many miles away. We stopped at a pond, an expanse of about ninety acres broken by islands of reeds and swamp growth, in which fish are cultivated. The small beds in which the fish breed were plainly visible. The cultivation of fish originated with the ancient Japanese who migrated to these islands. My curiosity concerning fish breeding and also farming led to so much time spent in discussion that we decided to return to the village rather than go on.

If I have a free upcoming weekend, I plan to return to the village. Since I don't want to impose on any one family, I plan to accept the hospitality of several others that have invited me. All this is quite a relief after having spent the past fifteen months in isolated drudgery.

7/7/45

Dear Mom,

I won't be able to write for the next few days. I'm off on another sojourn with the village inhabitants. This is becoming a habit, I know, but I find being with them great relaxation. It's easy to believe that I visit the village to see the beauteous Anita, but frankly, and to my astonishment, that's not so. After a few visits I expect that the novelty will wear off, their cordiality will become less lavish, and my interest will abate.

Tonight I plan to see my first show in two weeks: "Can't Help Singing,"[1] Deanna Durbin. Cake and ice cream will be served after the show to boost our morale. Speaking of morale, while we ate dinner in the chow hall a hot, melodious swing band entertained us. Many suspect that with this outlay of ice cream and music, the navy is seeking to entice peacetime prospects. See how the navy aims to please. Why quit?

Your most recent letter is only two days old. I was surprised to receive a letter from Hollywood, the Myleses, today. It was a pleasure to read—fine people the Myleses. I'd like very much to return to Los Angeles and visit a couple of families that I know there.

It struck me as funny your writing that the girls at the museum used to kid the shirt off me. Remember, I didn't wear a shirt.[2]

I just returned from the show—fair entertainment. Although it rained, it's hardly a bother anymore. We go with an armful of rain gear in anticipation.

It's late and I'm tired after a very easy day. Good night and love to my three, Hughie

7/11/45

Dear Mom,

I got back last night from three days of vacationing in the country. It was restful,—the important thing—new and interesting. It was enough to tide over my spirits until I get home. The food—fresh eggs, green vegetables, milk, seafood—the freedom, and the nonchalance I could assume, were a relief from camp life. So I enjoyed myself. I talked a lot to satisfy their hungry ears. One fellow who writes, made me read his stuff. The Reverend thirsted for news of the world. The girls wanted to know all about American girls, a subject I was ill versed in. On afternoon strolls my companion identified the plants and trees for me, and had me meet and watch the farmers in action. I watched clay pottery being made. Everyone put in his oar telling me more stories of the Jap occupation. Even while I loafed, the days were full.

Whenever you cite cases concerning fellows who are less fortunate than I, I can only conclude that you're trying to make me feel better. I'm truly glad that you feel that I'm fortunate. I'm satisfied with both past and present. There's nothing that I should become reconciled to. I'm glad about the way things are panning out. Believe me when I say that. I needn't be reminded anymore.

Since we have a tendency towards adopting a tranquil, placid way of life, I've never been more certain than now that we must secure a place for rest. I'm enthusiastically looking forward to it.

I'm sorry that my letter is so short. I promise to do better tomorrow.

7/13/45

Dear Mom,

Friday the thirteenth and all's well—so far. Yesterday, I received the books and razor in perfect condition. Today I sent out the wooden shoes (bahay cubo) and a coin bracelet. They are interesting, that's all. Letters fewer than ten days old arrive regularly. My correspondence has declined sharply since I've become an ultra-procrastinator. The girls back home should be permanently discouraged. I can't say that I blame them. The relatives have abandoned any correspondence long ago. Sadie is the only faithful one.

After I return home, I'll still have letters to write. Several here have asked me to correspond. I'm already corresponding with one friend in the city.

Again, I'm embroiled in a silly predicament. Anita has been partly responsible for making my visits to the country pleasant by cooking meals for me, making my bed, and seeing that I'm comfortable. I have been so involved in political discussions and other ranting with the men, that I've had no eye for girls. Out of the clear sky, Anita broadcasts that I'm mad at her, that I'm a woman hater, and so on. Well, I was flabbergasted. And when I tried to straighten the girl out, I only made things worse. It's an amazing paradox that I've made more female enemies by having nothing to do with them than if I were a vicious attacker. Once and for all, I give up and have resolved to keep girls out of my sight. Next time I return to the country I plan to live in a different house.

I'm showing off your new pictures, and the comments are positively flattering. My civilian friends are most curious. They marvel at the youthfulness of my parents. Ronnie has made a great hit with the girls. I beam like a father with his new born babe.

7/15/45

Dear Mom,

Today is just like many a summer Sunday that you're having back home: hot and humid, with a mean sun beating down. The farmers are having good reason to worry. Half the rainiest month has gone by with little rain. I suspect once the torrent is let loose it will really make up for it.

Now that the dredge is in steady operation, I have less time to carouse. My wanderlust has now become an essential part of me, and will, I expect, remain so for years to come. I'd like to browse around, see more of what there is to see. I'll have time later to settle down but there's never enough time to see things.

My plans are piling up from one moment to the next, and my ideas remain the same. For now, they make me feel better. But they have the best chance of being forgotten in the future. In the service our minds are most relieved when we plan what we'll do with the freedom awaiting us. I suppose it's wild fantasy. Our conversations sound like those of grammar school kids deciding their futures. Yet, they embody all our spirit and incentive. What will happen afterwards when the forces of reality stand in the way of the realization of our plans? That's when the fun will begin. Oh, boy!

I know my recent letters have been deplorably brief. They don't satisfy me either. I wonder what's gotten into me. It's the same with reading. My power of concentration and my patience are nil. It's sad. I'm dead set against wasting time, but I do a handsome job of it.

7/17/45

Dear Mom,

The rain is here again, and for the farmers' sake, I hope to stay. So long as it rains and so long working the seven day week continues, I expect to have to endure another bout of Hollandia-style boredom. I have plenty of books — indeed too many — to keep myself occupied.

The electric razor has proven very satisfactory. It does a clean job; I use it every other day now. When I first arrived overseas I shaved once every two weeks. Only when I shave do I stop to think that maybe I have changed. At least my beard is thicker. I often wonder whether I'll seem strange to you. Most here who have bothered to do some thinking have changed their outlook. Hair lines have crept back on some and new lines have emerged on older faces. In the younger ones, voices are stronger and deeper and babyish expressions are fainter. But the greatest change is in our outlook.

A good portion of our young men have gone the wrong way. I never realized what I was into until I abandoned my enthusiasm. The correct attitude is "Do your job, and no more." It's an attitude that I can easily assume with a clear conscience. But while all this energy of pent up enthusiasm remains unused, its fury boils inside. How to use it is a problem.

In life outside the service, there's room to wriggle around in, to vent it, to fight it out. In the situation here, you're rarely hoisted by the seat of your pants into a void for action. Here, as no place else, you are aware of the rotten forces marshalled against you. When I can wriggle a bit, I'll make noise — not for some cause — for myself. You can't help others while you're powerless. You've got to have ego and guts. Once you're up there, then actions count. If you're not weak from success, then good will come of it. Few of us actually become bastions of any sort. Humanity is a gaudy farce.

Why such an outburst? A mood, that's all. Actually, I've restrained myself. If I were to let myself go, I'd be frightened.

I'm reading a book on the Philippines that has caught my interest —as well as any book can nowadays. To know these people is one thing, to understand them a challenge. Maybe this book will help.

Your letters are doing fine.

7/18/45

Dear Mom,

For several days storm warnings have been blaring over the radio. High wind and penetrating rain have been sweeping in from the southwest. What a beautiful spot this is, smack in the least resistant path of the storms that originate in the mean South China Sea. We've been lucky so far, too lucky. Meanwhile, during time off we cling to our tents and absorb what warmth and protection they can offer as the beating rain almost drowns out our conversation. But about bedtime, the beating rain is comforting as it sings us to sleep. The temperature is low enough to allow wearing a shirt comfortably. During lulls in the evening, the air is balmy and breezy, soft to our hair. I almost like the rain.

You know how dull things can be around camp. Every morning a hen with a chirping brood passes by on her tour of scavenging. The monkeys, that have now accumulated a host of mates, dash about in all directions mimicking us; or are we mimicking them? They make extremely silly faces, eliciting smiles from our extremely silly faces.

While everything is wet, the Filipinos remain indoors. As far as the women are concerned, this tent is taboo. No one sees me lament when I'm accused of being the cause. Instead, the boys now visit the tents where the girls congregate to trade and sell. It's a fact that the boys like the girls and vice versa, even though neither can venture beyond a conversational distance.

One of my distinguished friends in the town I visit in the country was, prior to the war, elected vice-mayor, which is a sort of honorary do-nothing office. You should know that, while in his twenties, he was Chief of Police, a role that enabled him to participate in a few shady deals. The two political parties of that time had succeeded in cutting each other's throat, and were sucking the blood when election time came. So my friend's brilliant party members loaded the ballot boxes with fake votes—for the opposition, mind you. Came the count, then recount, then how to account for the fake votes, my friend, of course, remained Chief of Police. Rocking with laughter over his reminiscence of twenty-five years ago, he suddenly stopped short when he got no rise out of me. Well, the other party pulled a few stunts, too. As for the vice-mayorship business, he now boasts that he was drafted for mayor this time, well almost. He's not going to do any real campaigning. Too much bother.

During the occupation things weren't particularly rosy for him. The Japs commandeered his comparatively spacious house and when he returned, he found bare walls, insect weakened floors, and patched ceilings. He had once sported a distinguished and authoritative pot belly, like Uncle Willie's, or on the order of Dad's latest addition. Now his balloon has shrivelled flat and his once jet black hair has turned to a handsome silvery white. He knows everybody, though maybe everybody doesn't know him. Indeed, everybody seems to be his relative, which comes in pretty handy. Here, anyone with lots of relatives is secure for life. Sponging is such a respectable practice that any accomplished sponger need not have the slightest qualms of guilt. Aunts, uncles, police chiefs, any official, will hang about the family for a couple of decades then, tiring of the worn atmosphere, will move on for a change, or better yet, an improvement. I've heard of no one being thrown out of a house.

This former vice-mayor and about-to-be-mayor is none other than Mr. Santos whom I call "Dad," because the girls do. An old aunt living at one of the houses I've stayed in can't speak a word of English. Yet, she holds long conversations with me in her native Pampango, not a word of which do I understand. I obligingly nod my head in agreement with everything she says, and stop nodding only during time out when from her lips a salivary wad of tobacco juice wings its way out the window. From a giggling and charming interpreter I learned that Auntie has been fascinated with my blue eyes and wants me for her son. After I expediently consented, she stomped about expostulating that, when I return to America, I'll forget my mother in the Philippines. She won't come to America with me because, she says, "I'm old and ugly."

Love to you wonderful three, Hughie

7/20/45

Dear Mom,

At last my wanderlust is sufficiently quelled that my old desire to read and write is happily returning. In fact, I've finished two books:

Alexander Woolcott's *Long, Long Ago*,[1] and George Stewart's *Ordeal by Hunger*,[2] a ghastly story of the ill-fated Donner party. And to relieve the labor of wading through the *Philippine History* I tuck in a less monotonous chapter or so of Howard Fast's (and Lillian Hurowitz's) *Freedom Road*.[3] Eventually the relatives will feel the effects of my renaissance by receiving a letter of some sort. I haven't the nerve to renew my long expired correspondence with those prodigious townmates, Sybil and Dolly. Anyway, I'm now spared the ordeal of having to meet them.

What's news here? Nothing in particular, except that I'm two days older than when I last wrote. And the days, weeks, and months are magically disappearing into nothingness. They come but I don't see them go. Only after they're stacked up, do I realize that they once existed. Not long ago I awoke to the alarming fact that time is irretrievable, and I'm becoming more and more conscious of it. While it makes no sense to rush, so help me I find myself doing it in defiance of the sluggish tropics. Although these past years aren't wasted, they aren't doing all that I'd like them to do for me. After all, a patch of pride insists that I have something to do with molding my own fate, but lordy, how it has been injured of late. In many ways you can have fun taking things in stride. I'm sure it leads to a more contented life. However, many of us are content only when not contented, a paradox which probably explains the comparative infrequency of my gripes. When I look back, I find that I used to be much more proficient at the G.I. perfected art of griping. The reason for the change: I'm more content with my growing discontent.

Since we arrived at the new campsite, I've been using my knee as a writing desk. As difficult to read as my penmanship is under ideal conditions, my knee has reduced it to a horrible scribble. I rarely dare to reread my own letters. It's too much of a task for a fellow just back from a shift. Now I've procured — let's be frank: stole — a right size piece of plyboard to spread across the arms of my exquisite chair. The penmanship in this letter may or may not be an improvement. I won't attempt to look back to find out.

After considering your excursion to Benson's [Wild Animal Farm], I doubt whether I would have cared to be along. My reason runs deeper than you may suppose. It's beyond the sorry fact that my way of life has been infringed upon by barnyard freaks and jungle creatures. If I were home that weekend, I'm sure you'd find me running off to a refreshing swimming hole, and at night to a concert in Boston. I want to see dynamic and vigorous things, things that will hold my undivided attention. This may seem a contradiction to my oft repeated desire for serenity. It really isn't. Both activities have something in common: they enchant the emotions. A trip to Benson's now seems to me to be the most unexciting thing I could do. I remember that once the very idea enthralled me. See, you may look forward to having something to contend with after I get back.

Everything is so handy for you back there, that your inquisitiveness is blunted. Here, the people are intensely curious about the world and their country. Their information is limited to sports and hearsay. Word about politics, religion, culture, and human events is vague and incomplete. When suddenly I find myself holding the floor in discussions, I stop surprised at my monopoly only to have my friends goad me on. "We want to learn more," they say. Whatever I say I do so with candor and sincerity. I make no bones about a subject, even delicate ones. I am willing to discuss anything that they wish me to discuss. They have expressed their appreciation of this, often to the point of embarrassing me. I'm not timid, but I hate to be waited upon as they do me.

I have won their good graces by refraining from doing one thing which I discovered one night while visiting the Quiboloy brothers, both high school teachers who had also invited me to talk with them the previous afternoon. We sat on the verandah, (in extravagant reed chairs, by the way) our faces dim in the light of burning bottle of kerosene. About midway through our conversation that lasted for six hours, they mentioned having had American guests, sailors, at their home a few months earlier. They seemed hardly pleased, so I asked what was wrong. They said that the Americans had only girls on their minds; that's all they would talk about. I laughed heartily, less at what they said than at how they said it. Having made a point of avoiding the subject, I've won the respect of the men. After assuring them that the subject was taboo with me, I reminded them that it's normal for the subject of girls to insinuate itself into most men's conversations. They agreed and we let it go at that. As you have seen, my policy hasn't worked so well with the girls themselves. My only enemies are among the fairer sex. I've considered making love to them all, but I know that would be a quick way to get run out of town. On my very next day off, I know I'll want to scurry back to these people for more exciting conversation and relief from camp routine.

Since I'm the only American in this particular borough, I can sport civilian clothes unmolested.

My bunk is beckoning. I should retire early in order to rise early enough for breakfast. I've been discouraged lately after arising at nine, ten or even eleven. I can't remember when I last heard reveille call. Maybe I should enlist and begin over again.

[Hughie was asked to contribute his comments to a Symposium entitled "Is War Indispensable to Peace?" that appeared in the August, 1945 issue, Vol. II, No. 1 of *The Y.P.C.A. Journal*, published monthly by the Young Peoples Christian Association, Sta. Catalina, Lubao, Pampanga, Philippines. "Given free to members of the association, and non-members may request copies from the Editor."

This issue comprised 39 typed pages with headings hand-drawn in beautiful script. The editor was Alejandro T. Quiboloy, contributing editors were Rev. R. P. Songco, and Constantino T. Quiboloy, and the associate editors were Ernesto I. Songco and Ruth Carol. On the back page, page 40, appears the following advertisement:

CHARITY SCHOOL

A school for destitute and orphan children under the auspices and management of the YOUNG PEOPLE'S CHRISTIAN ASSOCIATION.

Admitted pupils are given free quarters, subsistence, books, clothing, etc.

WE NEED YOUR HELP!
SEND YOUR CONTRIBUTION TO:
The Principal
CHARITY SCHOOL
c/o Y.P.C.A., Lubao, Pamp., Philippines

Contributors to the Symposium were Mr. Abelardo Albis, Principal of the Lubao Institute, a private school; Rev. Roberto Songco, District Superintendent, Philippine Methodist Church; Miss Rosario Valenzuela, high school student; Mr. Conrado Sadsad, common day laborer; and Mr. Hugh Aaron, Petty Officer, USN, of Boston, Massachusetts.]

[Hughie's contribution appeared as follows:

"From the ages we can readily observe that war is the ultimate destiny of humanity. After all, as mere mortals, our own weaknesses seem to contradict any possibility of lasting peace. It is probable that peace is just an interval for humanity to catch its breath to prepare for another war. Or we can say that wars are a necessary evil in order to maintain only the shortest interval of peace. In any case, both war and peace have their varying effects upon mankind, and that we call progress. The aftermath of any war or peace introduces new things into the world, both harmful and beneficial. So what can a suitable conclusion be: war and peace, one depending on the other, ensure progress, and while progress is such a motivating force, maybe the greatest, the conditions encouraging it are inevitable.

"It is an enormous pattern beginning at the beginning of time. There is never one cause, but an infinite number of causes. Finite man searches the infinite with his finite thoughts. We waste our time deliberating over things beyond utter comprehension. There is another dimension we cannot discern. Wars will be until man ceases to be human; war is the working of mankind—mankind in action, mankind caught with his pants down."]

7/22/45

Dear Mom,

Yesterday the mail did surprisingly well—a letter from Sadie (with the real low-down), some reminiscing from Lil, one from effervescent Johnson, and a book from Ida. All, save Johnson, haven't heard from me since long before they last saw winter.

I'll bet you'll poke into every bay and lagoon of the Philippines to find me. As a bored high school junior back in that ancient, lovely era: 1942, I read about this spot, illustrious then for its role in hit-and-run raids and the evacuation. It was all so exciting to me. I recall that my heart quickened at the very thought, so absurd then, of ever seeing such a distant and strange place. As soon as the land became a blue haze on the horizon last April, we had nothing else on our minds. To us lowly unknowing ones, looking no farther back than our ship's wake, the choice scuttlebutt culled from a maze of channels advanced by the cook, the steward, the engineer *ad infinitum* was that our destination would be brighter, cooler, rampant with women roaming about, and anything else we might desire. That prospect of being where I now am stimulated the rebirth of those feelings of three years ago. My first weeks here were novel and exciting. I simply wanted to get out there and see. After the lid came off, the pressure relieved, what appeared romantic (and still would be to a civilian) was drained of its allure. I saw, talked, and listened, not enough perhaps, but it will do with my limited freedom such as it is. Many things that I've only half observed would, if I had any grain of consideration for your dreary lives, be unique and enlightening in the telling. My point is that after a few months have passed things are only hastily observed. Often, I fall into a dreamy state and only half see things so that my reports are poor. Keep asking me questions to make me perk up.

Most amazing, I discovered that in the era before shipping over[1] most of the men I know and knew until they departed here, had visited a harlot in every major city of at least half the forty-eight states and made no attempt to see their relatives. With the exception that their prime purpose was to visit their relatives (of whom they have no lack), the Filipinos are like the wandering Americans. Having been there, they know every province and city, are familiar with every hovel and palace. Their homes are merely a headquarters for their travel operations. Traveling and sponging is the current craze in the Philippines.

Tragedy and humiliation are the cohorts of squalor and poverty. The once well-to-do, from the upper classes to the men who made good by honest labor, are destitute today. The loyal resisters were pursued and hunted down everywhere. Everything they had was confiscated. They are surviving today by hook or crook under a system-less government. The officers of towns and villages, even the mayors, sell what they can to the G.I.'s. So do the people of all classes, including the tenant farmers, until the planting season sends them back to the fields. The literate folk who have been my hosts are just eating, nothing more. They are the cogs waiting to be oiled and shorn of rust. In the meantime they must do anything they can to earn an extra peso to tide them over.

When I was last in the city, my friend Antonio muttered dejectedly as I was leaving, "This is probably the poorest house that you've slept in." Sure it was. No sense denying what he knows to be true. I reminded him, however, that at the same time I found it the richest. Here was hospitality the like of which I had never experienced before. Here the men and women in his house had created a mansion. They had convinced me that it was. The warmth and honesty of his family made it so. At one time they had owned a fine home. I told him that aside from the holes in my mosquito netting, their ramshackle affair was just dandy.

In one house I slept on a hardwood floor (The Japs had removed the beds) that put a Beautyrest to shame. My hosts had the courtesy not to wake me. I was ashamed that I slept so late. Maybe these Americans like sleeping on floors. No doubt such a question crossed their minds. They haven't questioned my sanity yet. Throw out the mattress, Mom. I like sleeping on floors.

Love to you wonderful three, Hughie

7/24/45

Dear Mom,

I think I returned from my trip to the city on the second of the month. Having to report to work at 6:00 PM, I just made it to the minute. A swift glance at the bulletin board informed me of my advancement, which I had known was in the works the past two weeks. Then I went to work below and thought about the fresh and vivid exciting experiences I just had. Thought of the rerate never crossed my mind. When finally I did think of it, I chuckled. I felt no thrill, no inner surge of delight, no feeling of pride. Since regarding advancement, I just didn't give a damn, and haven't for so long, I thought I'd simply change the rank that appears beside my name, let it go at that, saying nothing. I consider it a token, given similarly to dozens of others at the same time. Beside the names of a few who truly deserve the rerate, were the names of men who have done little. Save for saving face, I find it hard to feel pride when my advancement seems so insignificant, as I turn toward broader ideas and ambitions. I see it pleased you. You enjoy talking about it to your friends. Then truly that is a reward greater than the incident itself.

My commanding officer had given me an oral test. The test would have been more suitable to a college whose fame rests on its football team and whose stupid, chickenbrained lummox of a fullback was up before its examining board.

We've lately had two full days of sunshine, a much appreciated respite from the rain. However, the worst of the rainy season is yet to come. So far we've been struck by nothing ferocious. There was a high gale a couple of days ago, and at times winds of hurricane force swept into the bay toward the mountains. Small whale boats foundered and canvas roofs were ripped off some tents. Next day, the head of the bay was strewn with grounded landing craft, pontoon barges, and timber. Standing on the aft end of the dredge, I watched a rogues gallery of objects scoot by. At the time it seemed pretty funny.

Yesterday, for the first time in a month, I dropped by to visit my civilian friends across the bay. As always, they were gracious. The men and their wives, the girls and boys, the youngsters yelling and yapping, were comforting to see and hear. Time and time again I protest against female entanglement, but alas, it's like the U.S. trying to completely ignore Europe. This one, Rosalina, possessed a rare thing: a white complexion. She is no doubt an interesting creature. Like few others, she can talk plain, sensible talk. Giggles and yes-ing are at a minimum.

Robert, my Filipino companion, his face wreathed in smiles as he reminded me of her heritage, brought me to her house. After the ice had melted and conversation begun, we sat on the porch when two weird, bepainted female creatures waddled by. After Rosalina gave them a typical hostile female once over, she inquired whether I knew those girls. Robert shook his head, saying "Those girls do business." "Oh, they're just office workers," I quipped stupidly. "Oh no. They do business. Bad, you know." I had hardly given the harlots a glance and only upon hearing the word "bad" did it occur to me what a "do business" girl was. I found the expression so comical that I burst into a hearty laughter. Such talk between men and women here is candid. Not used to such talk with women about, I felt uneasy. So I laugh it off, but each time, even though I know the subject is common, I'm still surprised.

This week the shift is convenient: 6:00 AM to noon. If I'm free this weekend, I'll be off on another countrified escapade. One ambition yet to be realized is to go into the fields and plant rice. The planting is done to guitar or harmonica music, as both men and women rhythmically sink the sprouts into the muck. The women are more agile and much faster than the men. I'd like to do it too.

7/26/45

Dear Mom,

Not more than an hour ago, I was splashing about in a paradisiacal, lucid, tropical stream. Great stuff—makes me feel like wading home. The freedom of going nude, forgetting the heat, relaxes body and mind and is a relief. Since I struck these islands, I've acquired a pleasant, carefree attitude. I wander about like a vagabond and feel like a million. I no longer take the job or the service more seriously than I have to. What a triumph it is to learn not to worry.

Pass on my thanks to George [Kalajian,[1] a neighbor near Dad's shop]. I'll enjoy the candy he sent, but somebody else will get the better portion. Once upon a time George thought he had converted me to communism. He certainly tried hard. Now, more than ever, I'm an individualist. Poor George.

We have a few men in the outfit who have a sense of humor. One or two of them announce clever witticisms over the PA system. I had mentioned that a good number of our men practice free marriage, even support families. Without a doubt they will eventually abandon these abject girls. Most of the girls have an inkling of what to expect, but for them only the present matters. So they assume the role of married women, a jealous lot at that, while the men let them rant about their temporary home lives. The girls frequently visit their "husbands" in our tents, which can be quite embarrassing to the "husband." Meanwhile, the other fellows take advantage of this opportunity to exploit their difficult situation. For instance, the PA system might blare, "Jack So and So, your wife is waiting for you at the tent with the groceries." It's certainly true that a good many of these freak romances could be branded as adulterous. A fair number of the "husbands" are married men. But it's also true that they expect the same behavior from their wives back in the States.

So, another gander at the human side of life, eh. Amidst the immorality, there's humor and decency too. It's a quaint mixture of blameless circumstances. Living with all kinds of men, I have no choice but to resign myself to approve their behavior. It's all simply one big, insane, hilarious experience. A war can't be won any other way. I guess people must be human.

7/31/45

Dear Mom,

Again, taking off to the country for three days, I relaxed amid the freedom and hospitality of the country folk. I don't stay with one family, but rather divide my time among several. We also congregate at various homes for discussions. I have stayed with the Reyeses, the Quiboloys, the Sangcos and the Santoses, all friends of mine and one another. I might have dinner at the Reyeses', supper at the Quiboloy's etc. One night we'll have discussions at the Sangco's, another night at the Santoses' villa.

They haven't placed me on a pedestal yet, but mighty near it. I've happily made a hit with all of them which I attribute to my straightforward approach. The men listen to me reverentially, which I sincerely try to discourage. Time after time I insist that I rarely practice what I preach. I feel very much at home with them, and they know it.

As for the girls, of whom every family seems to have a goodly share, they listen with fascination to my discussions with their fathers. They ask me to help them with their lessons, and, above all, they want to know all about the romanticized U.S. Sometimes we have long discussions, occasionally on delicate subjects. They love music, especially American ballads. (By the way, would you send me song sheets of songs on the Hit Parade[1] or whatever nonsense is being sung nowadays?) The Sangcos have an organ, and Sunday night their eldest daughter, Virginia, played a piece from Schubert's Unfinished Symphony,[2] the Bach-Gounod Ave Maria[3] and the wedding march from Lohengrin.[4]

The other night in a discussion with the girls the subject of dancing arose. The girls, the home type that is, don't indulge. There I was, an abstainer myself, now considering its merits, its necessity as a wholesome social outlet. I told them that dances are held back at camp. They asked if I went, and I said that I did. Then they asked with whom, and I said, myself. They asked why I went, and I said for the ice cream and cake, and they laughed heartily. Although convention restrains them, they still have an innate desire to dance.

My relationship with them is strictly platonic. I know how they think and anticipate their reactions pretty well. They are intrigued by the dashing American, by the very high bridge of his nose. I'm aware of what they say to one another because, as with all girls, they talk about one another to me. After slitting a few throats, they are satisfied that they've well disposed of their opponents. And as with all girls, for whom mirrors are an obsession, they make sure their jet black hair is just so. Whenever I swiftly scour the room and my glance meets a few eyes, smiles cross their faces. However, they fully realize the futility of becoming involved with an American. The infatuation and desire must remain silent, dormant. Ironically, the more timid a girl is, the more she's infatuated. An American is perfectly safe if he sticks to a "ne touche pas"[5] policy.

This recent vacation was in the main similar to the others, except that I was introduced to some new varieties of fruit. The villagers' insistence that I keep returning put me rather on the spot. They expect me to be a second "I shall return" MacArthur. They read about MacArthur's returning on the leaflets that were dropped prior to the invasion. Having taken pictures of this visit, I'm now faced with the problem of having the film developed. Somehow I'll manage.

Anita, who is apparently my favorite, was miserably ill with a cold, and absolutely refused to talk to me because her voice was unpleasant. After learning that she had a fever, I demanded that she be given aspirin. These people have no idea how to deal with sickness. A few weeks ago when Lucio had an eye infection, I made him apply a hot solution of some Boric Acid that I found in the house. His eye quickly got better.

During the three days I spent in the village, your pictures were on exhibition. They were fondled and marveled at by everyone whose gaze fell on your happy faces. The villagers positively couldn't get over the youthfulness of my parents and the handsomeness of my brother. Why, some even thought you were almost young enough to be newlyweds. You three reinforced my prestige threefold. Now that's the honest truth. I was bursting with pride.

When they look at pictures they examine every detail—your clothes, ornaments, shoes, the crease in your pants, your hairdo. The girls went completely daffy over Ronnie. So help me, I wouldn't stand a chance against him. Mothers and middle-aged women looked at you in awe. They branded Dad a middle-aged executive type. Mind you, I did no prompting.

I'm sure, Mom, Ronnie's new experience, so utterly different for him, won't do him any harm. A little grime, a few pounds lost, associating with a few wise acres, are all part of learning self-reliance—provided he keeps on the straight and narrow. Soon he will learn to make what is inconvenient less so. The first thing he should learn is how to spend money. Now and then a splurge that pays dividends won't hurt. His reversing telephone calls is wrong. It's his business to pay, his task to manage that thirty cents per day. He'll learn to leave the chow hall full regardless of how little food is served, or how poor it is. He can't be choosy about what he eats; he need only know what benefit he can derive from it.

Most important he should keep his body well rested, and free of tension. The two things necessary to maintaining this condition are sleep and cleanliness in both body and clothes. To learn how to sleep anytime, anywhere, is a great thing. I've succeeded at it. The eyes, the head, the entire body needs rest. Bodily cleanliness means, whenever possible, taking at least one shower a day. If it's not possible, then use a bucket or helmet, and make sure that water cleanses every portion of the body. This is impossible only when the boys are in battle. Clean clothes means frequent changes. As soon as they become grimy, change them. I wear two (sometimes three) pairs of trousers a week, three to five sets of underwear, two shirts (sometimes one), and three to five pairs of socks. In wet weather I make a complete change daily. To avoid your running out of clothes, more frequent washing is necessary. If washing isn't possible, then beg, borrow or steal more clothes. There should be at least a part of the waking day when you feel clean and refreshed. This is essential to ease the mind as well as the body. I've seen men that relax their personal habits, especially on board ship, become a miserable, wretched lot.

Frankly, it took me a while to realize the value of such seemingly minor things. Ronnie will learn these things too. I hope so. Above all, he shouldn't be over-enthusiastic, or anxious to do things, because nobody cares whether he will become tired or not. The only one that cares about you is you yourself.

8/1/45

Dear Mom,

I hoped that this weekend would see the war end. It wasn't an altogether absurd possibility. Damn them to hell. Unfortunately, the [Japanese] leaders, driven by a frantic and futile determination, are willing to let their own people be massacred and their cities laid waste. They are guided by a bent and twisted logic. To ignore our ultimatum means sheer disaster; yet, they persist. Apparently they cling to a flimsy hope for negotiations. They remind me of the stubborn fellow, who in the throes of losing an argument, can't bring himself to back down. Or as with Germany, they need more proof of our might. Whatever their reason, their decision makes me angry, and, for the first time, I wish that none of them will be spared. I can't help believing that wars, like people, die, when the forces of nature and chance are good and ready to let them die.

Last week was a gala one for seeing movies. I saw two notable mysteries, one with Gene Tierney,[1] and the other with—well, she was an eyeful anyway. I can't remember the names of the stars or pictures lately. I know during the most recent picture, despite the beauty that adorned the screen, my eyes were more often drawn to the eastern sky, as I watched a bewitching moonrise that gave an exotic cast to the land and the sea. The clouds, massed behind a magnificent golden sphere, were radiant with green, yellow and pink tints. The maneuver was serene and fleeting. Oh yes, her name was Ella Raines,[2] but her powers weren't as captivating as the moon's that night. The tropics can be so lurid and infectious at the same time, so completely magical and inspiring.

Here's eighty dollars, a tidy sum, to use if you need it. I still have a little over a hundred on the books.

8/3/45

Dear Mom,

When your letters arrive in only eight days, I feel that you are just around the corner. On examining yours of the twenty-fifth I find not a single error. I suggest that hereafter you type without your glasses, as you did that time.

I continue visiting my civilian friends, keeping your warnings in mind. You must understand that no matter where I go and with whatever family I stay, there will be girls. The plurality is evident, and every family has its share. This fact has amazed me.

The very situation that I've gone out of my way to avoid with the girl I like most, has, I recently learned, added to her misery and made me feel like a cad. Of all the native girls whom I've met, one, Anita, has impressed me as the finest of the lot. I've been cool toward her to the point of ridiculousness. Unable to reach any conclusion from her actions, I've had no idea what she felt. Only a short while ago did I become aware that she was keeping an eye on me. Her attempts to please only embarrassed me. When I departed her house and visited another last weekend, I was told that she was hurt. You see every home has girls.

This last visit really prompted me to think over the situation. After being in the country three days, I had spent only the last fifteen minutes seeing her. She had a cold and a slight fever. Ashamed of her wretched appearance (which wasn't as wretched as she supposed), she covered her face, refusing to speak and beginning to sob. Like a helpless child, I didn't know what to make of it and walked into another room to organize my thoughts. Immediately after, I left, very much confused. How strong her feelings are for me, whether she has or hasn't any at all, whether I'm responsible or not responsible for her odd carryings-on, I have no idea, but she has aroused my pity.

Not until this very afternoon, when her uncle paid me a visit, did I realize their dire financial predicament. Let me tell you about this family. The father, Domingo Santos, is stern with his three daughters (one is married) and three or four sons. They also take care of a stranded orphan boy victimized by the war. Mr. Santos was the general manager of a vast hacienda, making a wonderful living, and living in a fine house. His children were brought up under better than average conditions. But due to his old fashioned, stern methods his children feared him. Without question, he is lord and master of his household.

Somehow, I've won his respect. Although he listens to what I say, he argues and rants, but in the end he succumbs to my way of thinking. The question of education arose. He said he planned to send only his oldest daughter, Dolores, to school, while the younger one, my favorite, Anita, would remain at home to do the chores. Although mild and restrained, I blew my top, expostulating that it was necessary that his second daughter be educated as well, if he expects her to be on an equal level with American girls. I hadn't known until then that he couldn't afford the tuition fee ($25 entrance fee, $3.50 monthly thereafter) for both daughters. At any rate, that very afternoon, he registered both daughters.

After I left, Anita burst into tears. She had only one dress that was fit to wear to school and was too ashamed to go. Pacifying her, her uncle finally persuaded her to go.

The Japs had confiscated everything they had, commandeered their home, stripped it. Mind you, I didn't know their predicament. They were too proud to tell me their troubles. They gave but never asked for anything. A brother is contributing the measly $3.50 a month from his poor earnings. I intend to offer what I can to help. Now what would you do? Ignore the situation, or help? Help, of course.

So, do this for me. Buy a nice dress, suitable for a tropical climate, for a slender girl about five feet two, age seventeen, about a size sixteen, I guess. At the same time buy enough cloth to make a couple of dresses. The girls, having their own Singers,[1] are handy at dressmaking. Buy something nice, and above all use my funds. If I have my way, that girl is going to school. If my actions fan a flame, I'm willing to take the heat. Since the folks associate me with her, I would seem to be responsible for her present course. I may as well make her happy, as my term here is fast coming to a close.

No doubt you have some inkling that I care for the girl, partly from pity, partly for her companionship. I suppose I do. She knows as well as I do how hopeless an American and Filipino combination would be in the U.S. She knows the attractiveness of American girls, and she knows that I don't look at girls, including her, while other Americans use them only to satisfy their desire. Americans are not strangers to her. Many, among them officers, have offered her their affection. For that reason I doubt that she's infatuated with me. But I do know that she's very unhappy. I have no concept of what the symptoms of an infatuation are. But I hold her in high esteem, and shall continue to do so. Because I respect her so, and pity her, I want very much to make her content.

So please send the stuff as soon as possible. I can't say when we'll leave here. Most likely your package will arrive before then.

P.S. Sent a money order to you today.

8/6/45

Dear Mom,

A very short stay in the country this weekend—only a day, Sunday and a morning, Monday. The poor farmers are constantly watching the clouds. Rain when there should be rain—and lots of it—is nowhere to be seen. Rather, I should use the past tense, because just before I left this morning a shower was pelting the land in tropical fashion. At this time of the year the country is usually inundated. So far, the streams are slight, when they should be swollen and overflowing the land. I understand that the present dry phenomenon is rare, even in a lifetime.

Next time I visit the country folk, I'd like to get in some fishing. If I had a shotgun, I'd most likely be after ducks. Marshes being common roundabouts, it's quite the sport here.

During my visits my principal diet consists of lobsters, crabs and shrimp. (Mother would have a good time.) My hosts heap rice, the very bread of the P.I., before me. In all my twenty years I've never eaten so much rice in so many varieties and colors.

While visiting the village this time, I came to a definite conclusion, which is quite a relief. It is that "I don't understand wimmin," and the farther I keep away from them, the better off I will be, the more I can accomplish. They are the most confusing and confused creatures I ever did meet. Now this all may sound naive, but there's a lot of sense in abstinence. I can talk with women for hours and get no place, learn nothing. I've come to the point of almost being insulting, and their retort goes something like "There he goes again." Every time I'm around girls I feel I'm wasting time.

Speaking of time, I continually find myself counting the minutes and figuring out to what constructive purpose I can put them. This is strange in that my sense of time fleeting is mostly subconscious and eventually works its way to my conscious mind. Why in the devil I'm so in a hurry, so impatient all the time, is beyond me.

There isn't much happening around camp to speak of. There was a dance Saturday night, I hear, with an excellent swing band and plenty of girls and ice cream. The boys don't have much reason to complain anymore. Conditions and their morale couldn't be better.

The country folk are trying to persuade me to remain in the P.I.'s at least until Christmas. God, I hope not. But if the navy insists that we do, I'm looking forward to a pleasant December 25th. When these people celebrate, like Americans, they celebrate.

The books Lil sent, while once they were enough to hold my interest, now bore me. *Freedom Road* has an excellent message, is written simply and well, but it has lost its appeal for me. There are so many good old and so few good new books to read.

Here at camp I constantly exhibit your pictures whenever a victim approaches. It does my heart good to show them off. Swapping yarns and showing pictures from the past is a great pastime among us. We have a resumé of every character we know tucked away in our hearts to be released at the sight of a dear face. Some are prepared to do so at the mere sight of an attractive leg. The legs of their girlfriends? Well, that's an important thing.

These days the dredge is doing its job slowly and spasmodically. Low tide prevents us from operating around the clock. More and more I assume the attitude that it's something to keep us busy until we leave. Fortunately, neither job nor our way of life is unpleasant, a good way to spend a stalemate.

It's Tuesday morning. The rain that began last night has let up. The poor farmers. After the rain had washed the atmosphere, the east was brilliant orange. I'll peruse my books this morning, go to work this noon, and this evening see a show, if I haven't already seen it. I may as well begin the day.

P.S. Make two prints of each negative. Return negatives and one set of prints. The negatives were lent to me; they are mostly pictures of the dredge and Hollandia.

8/8-8/9/45

Dear Mom,

Over the radio and from everyone's lips is excited talk of the new atomic bomb.[1] Appalling and fantastic as it sounds, its grim and optimistic truth causes a futile sinking sensation within me. When man can cause such immense devastation with such a small mass in such a short time, surely anyone can realize with half a thought its significance for the future, the untold horrors of another war.[2]

Last night I saw the light and amusing "Molly and Me"[3] with Monty Wooley and Gracie Fields. It rained some, enough to send one flock away, and the flock that remained performed the acrobatics of putting on their rain gear. By the time the show was over, the sky was star spangled, and this morning is sunshiny. I can see waves of heat shimmering off the mountains across the bay. Today will be hot. We don't find a hot day distasteful, the way you dread a scorcher back home. Every day is so hot, always the same, and has been for the past eighteen months, that any remark about it would be unusual. "Gosh it's hot," is a rare observation here.

Yesterday Dante's *Divine Comedy* and candy arrived in excellent condition. I'm anxious to sink my teeth into this book, try to get what I can from it. Currently, I'm reading two books, one of them being J. Marquand's[4] satirical *The Late George Apley.*[5]

What little sweet tooth I had seems to have disappeared. Since I no longer care for candy, please send no more. Thanks, anyway, for the recent package. It will be disposed of quickly enough.

This morning the news broadcast announced Russia's declaration of war on Japan.[6] I think, Mom, that I shall be home sometime in 1946 for good. Between the bomb, whether it's exaggerated or not, and Russia's new turn, Japan is not only doomed, but proximity of its doom is impending. I wonder what the diplomatic wheels were that led to all this.[7] I can hardly wait for the end. At last, home seems near. A year ago, home may as well have been on another planet.[8]

8/11/45

Dear Mom,

When I awoke this morning, the sunrise made heaven into hell and the bay was rose colored. This is supposed to signify that a typhoon is lurking about, but, then, every morning greets us with a dazzling show.

For a change I expect to remain in camp for the weekend. If I hadn't become so magnetically drawn to my present friends, most likely I'd be carousing in all directions to see more of the island. The roads, other than the national highways, heading toward points I have yet to explore, are now miserably dusty. If by chance I have three days to myself, I'd like to visit the summer capital [Baguio]. It will be a long, tiresome trip, rewarded, I expect, by the sight of ruins, but still worth the trouble.

I envy the boys now in Europe in many ways. The educational program there gets my saliva going. I wish I had the opportunity to brush up on my studies. Yet, if they are as lax over there as they are here letting us roam, I'd soon become a continental tourist. Of course, there are boundaries in Europe and a soldier's freedom is necessarily limited.

A week after it arrived, my watch went on the blink. Same trouble. I'd swear it was never fixed. True, it lay about for a couple of weeks in a watch repairer's tent at an adjoining naval unit. So I took it into town to a Filipino establishment, and now it's running smoothly. When I couldn't use the watch, I was never late for work or chow. By glancing at the sun or observing the light of the day, I was usually within a half hour of the correct time. Now that I'm wearing the watch again, I must remind myself to consult it.

I'd like to do a little reading before the tent roof heats up. If you'll pardon me -------

8/12/45

Dear Mom,

A rough day today! Yesterday afternoon we were issued an order to work today, Sunday, crazy indeed with the war about over. A few, ignorant of the order, took off, while the rest of us had to work that much harder. For me, it meant ten hot hours, no time and one half, but some consolation in knowing that I would be allowed extra time off to make up for it. Now I'm solidly tired, perfect for the complete enjoyment of my favorite pastime.

I was at a show when the announcement of Japan's peace proposal blared over the PA system. Fortunately, the picture was almost over, or it would have been just as well to shut it off. There was a tremendous clamor; no one could be held down. A surge, I guess you'd call it exultation, tingled through me. I felt like diving into the bay and swimming home. Sporadic firing echoed throughout the area. Beer was issued to all. A good many became blissfully pie-eyed. "What the hell, let 'em fire it all off; we don't need the damn stuff anymore." It's three days later now, and we have a ninety percent feeling that it's in the bag. Waiting for the diplomatic formalities to go their rounds, we listen closely to every spot announcement. All agree that the combination atomic bomb/Russian entry brought the Japs to their inevitable decision. That, of course, will be for history to confirm.

The initial wave of thoughts that swept across my mind was a hurriedly confused jumble of home and my folks. It was sweet to think of in the comfort of the war's end. When you know it's only an insignificant matter of waiting, a boat ride, and maybe a little more waiting, you don't dream dreams, you dream a real past, present, and future consummated in one single moment. That's the moment of our reunion, sweeter now than ever. What a pleasure it is when realities are no longer grim.

I suspect many months will pass before I depart from these islands. I don't care. It's like saving dessert for the last: it's there and near and wonderfully accessible.

[The following is taken from the Wednesday, 15 August 1945 *Daily News Bulletin*, Vol. 3, No. 99, issued by the 113th United States Naval Construction Battalion. At the top of the editor's copy are the handwritten words "Happy Day of Days." Cecil Keesling, Co. A-2, was editor.]

JAPAN ACCEPTS ALLIED TERMS

A RADIO BROADCAST OVER THE UNITED STATES ARMED FORCES FAR EASTERN NETWORK AND RECEIVED

AT 0807 LOCAL TIME SAID THAT "PRESIDENT TRUMAN HAS JUST ANNOUNCED THAT JAPAN HAS ACCEPTED THE ALLIED TERMS OF UNCONDITIONAL SURRENDER."

No further official details were released regarding the Japanese note of acceptance at press time. A spokesman at No. 10 Downing Street in London, speaking from Prime Minister Attlee's headquarters, said "PEACE ONCE AGAIN HAS COME TO THE WORLD." This was followed by the playing of the national anthems of the four great powers engaged in the struggle against Axis aggression, the United States, Great Britain, Union of Socialist Republics, and China.

From Japan's front yard on the forwardmost island held by U.S. troops--Okinawa--their local radio announced that battle-weary troops were taking the news of the end of the war quietly and pondering what peace means to them personally. The most noticeable thing on this little piece of land 325 miles from the Japanese homeland, said the broadcaster, "was the sudden exit from danger. Only a moment ago the men were under the strain and tension that grips the lives of all men at the front. That tension has gone. This is their first moment of relaxation."

EVENTS LEADING TO JAPANESE SURRENDER

At 0800 this morning it appeared to be anybody's guess as to whether Japan had or had not decided to surrender. Seven minutes later the world received the news for which it had been tensely and expectantly waiting.

Late Monday night, Washington time--mid-afternoon Tuesday in Tokio--the world got pretty excited when the Tokio Radio broadcast word that Japan had definitely decided to throw in the sponge. But after the enemy broadcast continued, it got more and more confusing as time wore on.

Here, in brief, is what happened. Late Monday night the enemy radio broadcast this statement: "It is learned that an Imperial message accepting the Potsdam proclamation will be forthcoming soon."

Then in Washington Tuesday morning presidential Secretary Charles Ross said that the Swiss Foreign Office in Bern had informed the United States that a reply in code had been received from Japan. Ross told newsmen that at least it looked as if we were nearing the end of our long vigil.

A little after noon Washington got an urgent message from Switzerland saying that Japanese officials there decoded the message only to find that it was not a surrender reply.

Here's what the message from the Swiss Foreign Office said: "Japanese legation reports that coded cables it received this morning do not contain the answer awaited by the whole world." This note changed the situation considerably.

And to make things still more confusing, a few minutes earlier the Japanese radio again went on the air to announce that the Japanese reply was now on its way to Switzerland. (by George Chast, C-5)

IT IS NOT YET V-J DAY

WHITE HOUSE AIDES EMPHASIZED THAT IT WILL BE SEVERAL DAYS BEFORE V-J DAY. THESE AIDES STRESSED THE FACT THAT JAPAN ACTUALLY WILL NOT HAVE SURRENDERED UNTIL RESPONSIBLE JAPANESE LEADERS HAVE SIGNED THE DOTTED LINE, PROBABLY AT AN AMERICAN BASE ABOARD AN AMERICAN WARSHIP.

8/15/45

Dear Mom,

After a few days of anxiety, and a small shadow of doubt, at last it's over for good and for all. The relief is tremendous. Never had I realized what a burden our estrangement and the months of war, with nothing to look forward to, had been. I suddenly feel light in body and head. So it's over, and I can talk about a future that's real. No more daydreaming or thoughts of doubtful purpose. Now, I look no further than college. I prefer to see the next few years as if my life will abruptly end with them. I aim to enjoy them in my own conservative (if you wish) way.

No doubt I'll revolt in a fashion typical of most fellows my age. Being used to a minimum of control here (I broke away from the control of the military in subtle ways), I'm quite aware that I may be difficult to control. I'll listen to your advice, but only a portion of it will stop, before it passes out my other ear. The past two years have fostered within me solid convictions, dislikes and desires which will, I suspect, determine my course. Being home and under your influence will keep me within civilized bounds, so you needn't fear any radical digression. Although you'll find that I'll do what I please, since you made me what I am, my actions will be no threat. I know you're curious to see how I've turned out. Soon you will see. My letters have provided superficial hints. I only hope you will be pleased. I've tried my best to ensure a favorable conclusion. I know you both will always remain the same, a consistency that gives me solace. I know what marvelous goods I'll be getting.

This morning everyone was raucous and happy, and woke me up from a late slumber with a confounded second celebration. No work today, the contributor to our hilarity. This afternoon I shall cross the bay to visit in town and return before supper then later see a movie, "The Clock."[1]

8/16/45

Dear Mom,

I know at least one fellow who's elated over the navy point system. He's counting on returning and reviving his auto-body business. Fellows like me don't stand a chance under the system. Those of us in the Seabees hope that the arrival of civilian labor will hasten our ultimate dismemberment. Perhaps my desire to enter college will help me. As of now, I haven't the vaguest idea what course to follow. Responsible friends have given me their recommendations, but nothing convinces me. The lines I write here reveal my anxiety and impatience.

I say I can wait a while, because the road from here only leads up a rainbow, but at other times I feel like a rearing steed, raring to go. So many older friends say, "If only I had it to do over again." I'm conscious that everything lies before me with much to do and limitless choices to be made, such that I must tame my enthusiasm. No doubt, I'll be as big a fool as everyone else. My, what fun it will be trying not to be one.

I finished *The Late George Apley* this afternoon. A well done satire, it produced plenty of snickers. You should read it. I find the

History of the Philippines hard wading. Compared with literary works, history, especially statistical history, is boring. I've abandoned *Leave Her to Heaven*. Freud's (and Evelyn's) *Interpretations of Dreams* never arrived. Perhaps it was never sent. After a month's flood of letters from the Aaron branch of the family, there's been a sudden cessation of such amity. Evelyn's letters were amusing. Anna stopped writing well over a year ago. I always liked her, and at times regretted that she has remained my spinster aunt. In view of their distractions, my relatives have done their duty, and well at that. When the happy day of reunion arrives, and they spring from the leash to kiss and slobber over me, don't expect me to respond with equally affectionate demonstrations. I know my shyness at returning affection to my estranged relatives has always irritated you. I hope you will now understand. Affection or affectation, both are rituals that I've abhorred.

Sadie's letter revealed what you two proud folks have been broadcasting about me. I wish I could contain, in some way, the circulation of these letters beyond my own home. Besides telling me about myself, she gives me advice and remedies. Although I wish my letters would remain between us, I realize that it and you are impossible. It's a natural manifestation of your love and pride, and I can only love you all the more for it.

One of these fine days censorship may be lifted. It's merely a premonition. If and when it is, you may be surprised that I won't have much more than usual to tell you. With rare exceptions, I've already said everything worthwhile saying. What I've left out is past, and doesn't deserve to be recalled, though, I suppose, there's no harm in it.

We've had very little rain, and the days have been hot. It was amazing, indeed, to sit through a week of shows with nary a sprinkle. Meanwhile the farmers are either cursing or praying to the heavens. Instead of growing the usual rice, corn flourishes. The corn crops are extra large, but are not for human consumption. While not a famine, an acute food shortage is anticipated.

We are working neither hard nor consistently aboard the dredge. We are anxious for the Australians, who had leased the contraption to us, to take her over and back to Darwin.[1] Our hope, of course, may be groundless. All agree that the Australians are welcome to her every rivet. As a matter of fact, we will gladly throw in our rifles and G.I. gear to boot, or perhaps a jeep for further inducement. I remember when Jeeps were a dime a dozen. Bootlegging jeeps used to be an enviable profession. All elements sanctioned the practice, except the military police.

Now for a little indulgence in what is fast becoming my vice: solid sleep. I have become a master of the art under any and all conditions, and, believe me, it is an art, and an achievement.

Night prevails and I shall not. My sad cotton mattress and pillow that forever disperses feathers, beckons in a sinister fashion. In this moment of weariness and drooping eyelids it is too much.

8/17/45

Dear Mom,

Your 8/4 letter reeks of a sweet, unfamiliar fragrance. Whether it is yours, or contracted from a strange neighboring letter while en route, it is still nice to have around. Your letter brings up a few points that deserve my clarification.

Because of my lack of clairvoyance or because I have little else to write about at times, I've mentioned one or another girl of my acquaintance. The girls play a major role in every local household, and any guest could not avoid them. It's too bad that you cling to the impression that I gave you some two years ago during that critical adolescent period, (Not over until 26, I hear) which I now belie, that I have a warped abhorrence of women. At that time, it was a practical attitude, and I was in a deep rut. Now that rut is smoothed over, and I wander freely on an open plain unscathed. Suddenly, I've become human (a ridiculous observation), or have I simply cleaved through my old wall of introversion? Presently, thanks to your guidance and my conscience, my moral fabric is ultra-conventional. I am capable of resisting the eloquent charms of the female sex for purely practical reasons. Being neither susceptible to nor infatuated with any girl, I merely admire women and enjoy their comradeship. My actions are governed by 1) a respect for womanhood, 2) my personal ambition and aspirations, and 3) my code of consideration for those involved. If I am flattered and flustered by the attention paid me, I don't deny it, nor do I succumb to it. Though I protest loudly and often, I'm justified in terms of logic, but hardly sensually. I have a foggy conception of what's in store for me so I accept present events passively and you needn't be "worried." This is not a manifestation of my so-called belated and inevitable fling that everyone so positively predicted.

The fate of the Lowes is tragic.[1] Their son will never amount to much. There was something about Mrs. Lowe [Mom's former neighbor] that I liked. I can vividly recall the days when we used to visit them on the [Ellis] estate. I remember Aunt Gertie was a character.

What has become of the Lynns [another former neighbor]? Do you call them?

Yea gods, don't send, and advise everyone else not to send me Christmas gifts. What clothes I have are more than I need and a burden.

I read that in Detroit men have resorted to wearing women's panties. If Dad and Ronnie were to stoop to that I'd never forget or forgive. Keep yours well locked.

I'm occupied with Dante lately. He's not easy to master. Once I accustom myself to such lofty literature, the going should be easier. Meanwhile, I'm still interested and learning. It takes diligence and concentration to which my mind is ill-adapted. Although the heat and the work are tolerable, they're tiresome, and lend nothing to one's thinking capacity. But my will is still strong and is sure to prevail over this tropical languor.

A dark light lingers, the end of an overcast, humid day. Tonight another show—the G.I.'s salvation.

8/21/45

Dear Mom,

I've just spent another weekend of relaxation in the country. A good part of the ride for the thirty-five miles or so to my destination is dusty and bouncy. The trip takes me through a mountain range via a treacherous pass that tapers off into hillocks then a vast fertile plain. What a relief it is to reach my destination, where I can plunge into the gushing water of a cool artesian well. Refreshed, wearing a change of clothes, I'm ready for whatever my host has planned. Most of the time it's a discussion of world events, or an introduction to one of his eminent friends. If I had a shotgun, it would be duck hunting. Next visit, I plan to bring a fishing rod and indulge in my forgotten boyhood pastime.

I mustn't neglect to mention the olive-skinned daughters who manage to wangle my assistance in doing their homework. Assuming the manner of a stern teacher, I find my biggest task is keeping the girls apart, and preventing their sly glances at each other's paper.

The war's finale has infected these people with unbounded joy. They wonder why I'm not on my way home by now.

We are losing a fair percentage of our boys under the new navy point system. There's no doubt that we young fellows are destined to become the residue. Based on my age and lack of dependents, I'm far from having the number of points required to make me eligible to leave. The system is fair. During the past year I've seen several close friends off. First Malter, then Wolf, now my friend from Frisco returning with a back ailment. By the end of the week only three will be left in our tent.

When I read of Barios and Chase entering the throes of matrimony, I sense the years silently slipping away. It seems as if only last year we were romping around the grammar school yard together. I gather that Chase's marriage to a Gentile girl was a shock to our caste, even a disgrace. Where love is concerned, you know very well that a sensible course is rarely followed. It may be tragic that the survival of our race's posterity is lessened, but I can't accept a difference in religion as a cause for people not to come together. You don't choose the person you fall in love with. The force is stronger than you. These days where the intermingling of all sorts of people is so common, there's no guarantee that a person will marry his own kind.

I've never considered another person's convictions and beliefs ridiculous. I reserve for myself some leeway, a certain tolerance which enables me to say that I might be wrong, and the other person might be right. If one's religious spirit is conducted in a beneficial way, it little matters what or who the god is. If love can conquer bigotry and intolerance, I'm all for its consequences. I concede, however, that marrying one's own kind is safer and more likely to assure a harmonious union but—and there is a "but"—as we see exceptions fast becoming the rule.

The past couple of torrential days have answered the farmers' prayers. This week my shift runs from midnight to daybreak. The rainy weather makes the day comfortable for sleeping. Not only does the rain cool the air, it makes a rhapsody on the roof that sings you to sleep. I've just seen a gaudy leg show, "Diamond Horseshoe,"[1] and wait for the call to work.

8/22/45

Dear Mom,

Thanks to a third day of downpour I got some sleep that has enabled me to write with a clear brain. This morning I read Eddie's account of his journey to Berchtesgaden.[1] I thought it was great. He has an easy style, and tells an interesting tale with a fine dash of humor. Lil's letter is also pleasant. She writes the way she talks, and I've always found her talk pleasing and fluent.

As I read about other places, I compare notes with life in these islands. The tropical languor of the place affects the people enormously and the environment they create for themselves. Contrasted with the cleanliness of frigid air and the clarity of light blue eyes, the dark complexions of the people and the thick heat seem far less attractive.

I wish you'd stop sending books. I have more on my cabinet shelf than I have time to read. How can I convince you and others not to send packages, especially now when moving is imminent, unless I specifically request one?

As I stepped into the tent the other day, a fragrant aroma wafted in. It was from the flowers on a bush growing next to our door. Also behind the tent there's another strange, colorful shrub. When I enter a Filipino household, I notice there's always a vase full of aromatic flowers on the table. The girls adorn their jet black hair with sweet-smelling sampeguitas, the national flower, whose fragrance literally envelopes their bodies. This is a land of flowers. I've never been so aware of their desirable presence.

Fruit is just as abundant. Mangoes are recently out of season, but I had my fill last month. Papaya are, I believe, still common. Bananas are perennial. To me, the greatest enigma of all is how rice can be consumed with such voraciousness day in and day out, year in and year out. After only a half dozen visits I'm thoroughly tired of it.

I'll be watching a show in rain tonight. Now to bundle up to keep dry. The tedium of recent days demands that I be entertained.

8/23/45

Dear Mom,

By now you're back from camp [at a lake]. I have your letter referring to your arrival, and that you are considering a permanent place is just what I want to hear.

There seems to be a problem getting the eligible boys back home. As we feared, transportation has developed a bottleneck. I've resigned myself to being one of the last to leave. If I could enter college in the fall of '46 I'd be happy, and probably lucky. In the back of my mind there's a sense of discomfit at entering college so late.

It would be fine to spend summer at home. The returning boys aren't enthusiastic about the prospect of arriving home during a frosty autumn. On a bus in New York City last winter the patrons were suffocating from the infernal heat. After discovering that the heater was on full blast, they also learned that the driver was a dischargee fresh from the S.W.P.A. and quite comfortable. Better stock up on coal this winter, just in case.

The rain is still falling, our fifth day of it. The farmers will put it to good use. Their fields will be easily flooded. Along one section of the highway, the flood has torn up the surface exposing its rocky foundation. Ignoring the roadside ditches, the water just sweeps across it. On such days the caribou are able to work for longer stretches. The hot, sunny days exhaust them so that they must be allowed to cool off in the streams or water-filled ditches at regular intervals.

The dredge hasn't operated for several nights. Still, I must remain on duty to maintain the water level in the boilers which are in constant operation. I take catnaps in between calls. It's amazing how well I can sleep on a hard, wooden deck and think nothing of it. Time to be on duty is near. First a snack — a toasted cheese sandwich, a remnant from supper.

8/28/45

Dear Mom,

Apparently the week of the Jap surrender was frolicsome and joyous for you folks as well, yes, and for many millions more. Everything went right, and from the enthusiasm of Dad's letters and yours, I see your vacation week was ultra-gala. I can't remember anytime that you've taken a long vacation. Successive years should enable you to take more days and weeks off for frivolity and relaxation. Next year you must take a real vacation — both of you.

Once the duration is over an enormous era of construction will begin, and we should be in on it. More than you can imagine, I want us to have our own home now. As you know, in view of the ease with which a house can be paid for in monthly installments, cold cash is unnecessary. Furthermore, you have some cash as a down payment: the nest egg under my name. Consider this seriously, folks, and let me know what you think.

I shouldn't need the money I've saved for my school years. I pretend that I have none cached away. With my veteran's benefits going towards my education, it's unlikely that I'll be able to take advantage of a home loan through the veterans administration. Of course, I'll be in no position to earn money, either. I don't want to abandon my present government insurance policy. The government is offering inducements to keep it in force. Once I'm clear on all the available benefits (I'm slightly confused now) we'll talk it over.

I can lift the curtain somewhat on my present whereabouts: the Subic Bay area of Luzon. Last night I returned from a second trip to Manila. My references to "the city" in previous letters, (July 1-2) were, of course, Manila. I couldn't describe much of what I saw on that excursion for fear of my letter being hacked up and torturing you.

The trip takes a long four to five hours by thumb, part of the way suffocating dusty road, but most of it clean, smooth two lane concrete highway. After crossing a treacherous, bouncing mountain pass, the way leads across a great level plain clear into the city. We pass through numerous small towns and villages, each with its church in the center, a school nearby, and a few houses of architectural distinction, mansions that harbor the landlords and aristocratic set. There may be a movie house in a larger town, always a school, and always the quaint nipa and bamboo affairs that house the clerks, artisans and farmers. Most country towns are clean and colorful, with bushes in blossom, banana and mango trees and vines obscuring the houses from the road. Contrasted with these towns, the towns on the coast are more a melting pot where poverty and filth abound.

The land extends flat as far as the eye can see to a hardly discernible mountain range shrouded in a blue haze on the horizon. Green is everywhere in the form of rice, corn, and sugar cane stalks and clumps of shade trees dotting the land. It's all neat and geometrical, an effect produced mostly by the rice paddies that are laid out in tiered squares.

Approaching the city, the towns appear at closer intervals, gas stations (Socony and Texaco) and railroad crossings are more frequent. At the northern entrance to the city a huge monument towers over the vast panorama. You can see a picture of it on the Jap invasion notes that I've sent you. Following Rizal Avenue, the main drag, you soon enter the hustle and bustle of a dank, hot business district. The buildings, some of slightly Spanish, others of Oriental, design, are old and sorely in need of repair. The streets are filled with G.I. vehicles and a few civilian cars, some in sorrily battered condition, others magnificent and gleaming. I believe that the owners of the imposing Buicks and Packards had to be collaborators; it's the only plausible explanation for the excellent condition of the cars. The sidewalks are crammed with people of all colors and races jostling one another. The brown are Filipino, the white are Mestiso (half breed), then the ruddy G.I.'s, the black American Negroes and the olive Chinese. The girls wear what remains of their pre-war wardrobe, and the men sport G.I. suntans and greens, purchased from mercenary G.I.'s and black-marketeers.

The streets are lined with all kinds of shops, all inadequately stocked, selling whatever they had hidden during the occupation. After all, the Mickey Mouse money of the occupation was worthless. Now, it's used as poker chips which are scarce, for lighting cigarettes, and for er—other purposes of convenience. However, none of the merchants are starving. In these miserable days of rampant inflation, they can sell things at any price. Cabarets and restaurants do a big business. House fronts, store facades, and even abandoned gas stations are cluttered with such signs as "Dew Drop Inn," "Atomic Bomb Cafe," "Soldier's Paradise," and "Three Sisters' Cafe." The food, bought on the black market or from illicit G.I.'s, is meager and mediocre. A tiny scoop of ice cream and a glass of cold water sells for a dollar [less than a quarter in the U.S.]. The favorite habitats of the thirsty G.I.'s are the retail liquor stores and bars, many of which have been found selling poisonous concoctions. The owners are cleaning up, but they are also in the process of being cleaned up by the U.S. military.

Two rather elaborate theaters are operating successfully—too successfully. Admission is high, lines are absurdly long, and the pictures are ancient. One of them has neon lights and air conditioning. The other, at which I watched and tolerated about half of "Dragon Seed,"[1] has an arrangement whereby its patrons sweat so profusely that they must leave. Of course, this leads to a profitable quick turnover.

The city is incessantly hot. An oppressive thickness pervades the atmosphere. The gutters are dirty and damp, and the streets are boiling and dusty. The parks are overgrown, and pocked with stagnant pools of dirty water. Elaborate, modernistic buildings are gutted. Hotels, office buildings, and administration buildings lie in heaps of rubble of plaster and twisted steel. One building, four of whose stories remain intact, leans at a sixty degree angle on a foundation of an indistinguishable mass of wreckage. The bridges, once graceful spans that crossed the Pasig River, the pride of Manila, have been replaced with Army prefabricated affairs. One or two walls of some structures remain, exhibiting their once beautiful modern, romanesque or rococo designs. Of all the cities I've visited in the U.S., none had as many modern buildings as Manila. The administration and college buildings of impressive Greek and Roman architecture are a tragic sight. The modern stadium which also includes a basketball court, a swimming pool, and baseball and football fields the like of which I've never seen in one complex, stands ghostlike scarred by machine-gun bullets. My companion spoke nostalgically of the exciting afternoons under a blazing sun and evenings under floodlights that he had spent there rooting.

I'll continue describing what I saw after the stadium, tomorrow. I know you are anxious to hear from me after a three day lapse, so I'll send this on. Off to work now, then to bed at midnight.

8/30/45

Dear Mom,

The day is beautiful, clear and airy. Our routine flows smoothly and all seems at peace, as it rightly should be nowadays. Unlike you, who impatiently and naively expect me to return immediately, I'm reconciled to an exhausting wait. Even at the peak of enthusiasm I never had a notion like yours.

Yet yesterday's news from the navy offers a lift to my forlorn spirits. I should be discharged within a year—in time to enter college—or, once hostilities are officially over, perhaps in six months. Legally I'm in for the duration plus six months. Meanwhile, I await the announcement of the duration's end. The navy intends to retain a half million men, but it guarantees that even us young whelps in the Seabees will be discharged within a year. With both exultation and a freakish dread I expect to be released this winter. I feel that the warmth of our passionate reunion will tide me over until spring comes. Meanwhile over the weekend we lost five boys to paradise, reducing our tent population to a bachelors' three.

You are both unduly alarmed concerning my interest in and relationships with my country friends. For lack of more important things to discuss, I wrote about them and how they affected me. They know, as I've often repeated to them, that my stay here will be short, and my interests here are passing. They lament that I shall fast forget them once I'm in the bustle of American life and in college. Your advice not to give to them came too late. For I have given too many things that I can easily obtain and which they sorrily lack. They have fed me while food is dear. The attraction I offered was talk, talk which in the main was cultured and constructive. Their daughters and sisters either went about their chores or gathered around us to listen quietly. They had no designs on me, nor I on them. The very idea, at this stage, of taking a future with these people seriously, let alone their daughters, is absurd. Never fear, folks, I have a hard shell. I can't let my sympathy and emotions rage for some time to come. I don't have the time to release them now. I'm not entirely vulnerable.

All of us, regardless of our experience, possess a degree of naivete and innocence. A mother weeping in farewell, "Don't get hurt," is naive, and she well knows it. Sometimes, naivete provides comfort and escape. Often, when I'm naive I'm aware of my ridiculousness. I know exactly which paragraphs I write that you will pass off as childish prattle, but I find relief in their release. Whenever I give someone cause, I hate to be called a kid. So I chuckle to myself and await the day when I wish I were again. Sometimes I am disturbed when my ulterior adult reasoning betrays a frivolous, childish demeanor. But the fleeting of time and the rapid decline of my adolescence have at times appalled me. My awareness that time is irretrievable fosters regret. Let me stay a kid once in a while, folks.

I last left off at the Quezon Stadium on Taft Avenue. After thumbing a few miles farther, I viewed close up for the first time a giant B-29 at Nichols Field, south of the city. Last July, the city's rubble was being disinterred and carted away. By last week a good percentage of it had been cleaned up, but it made no noticeable improvement. Irreparable, gaunt structures loom on the skyline, wringing the hearts of the nostalgic Filipinos who need pride and progress so much. Manila was more than just their city; it was their inspiration.

My guide and devotee was a middle-aged friend, Antonio Rivera. We hiked miles on foot and thumbed when we could, although the civilians who rode in miniature taxis were a hindrance. It was in this grueling fashion that I saw most of what's left of the city during my first visit. I rounded it off on my recent visit with a closer examination of the Intramuros [the old walled portion] and the piers on the waterfront.

Rivera's poor house, built in 1905, is situated on Santa Mesa, not far from President Osmenas's mansion. What a contrast! MacArthur lives in a rigorously guarded white house with columns a few hundred yards away. The Riveras, and their many satellites who live beneath and beside their house, showered me with such overwhelming hospitality that it made my farewell awkward and difficult. In only the short time I was with them, a gradual process of endearment developed between us. Mrs. Rivera shed tears, bidding farewell through misty eyes. I'll tell you more about these charming people in my next letter. Off to work soon.

9/1/45

Dear Mom,

Yesterday, I read in a June *Gazette* that veterans have enrolled in Worcester's colleges, but that Tech has few of them because its courses are highly specialized and the requirements are stiff. It seems, the students are studying under some sort of accelerated program, of which I want no part. The report, stating that the students are having an easy time, is encouraging. Despite my poor power of concentration and impatience, I still feel confident.

Realizing that I lack genuine talent, or fear that I do, I've abandoned any aspirations I've had for a literary career. I've made up my mind to stick to a practical career in engineering, and perhaps, if I have the ability, pure science for which I have a yen. Above all, I want to study something highly specialized in which I can become absorbed. I shall relegate reading the classics for entertainment during my spare moments.

By taking Dante in small doses, I'm doing pretty well with him. More information concerning the atomic bomb has lit a philosophical and scientific flame within me. What little I've learned about its mechanics intrigues me. It concerns knowledge that has always fascinated me and led to no end of wonderment.

After many escape weekends, I'm remaining in camp this one to work. My recent trip to Manila will be my last. The ride is too arduous and the city too depressing. Were it not for my new friends there, I wouldn't have made the second journey.

After I first landed here last May, I met a boy who hadn't seen his folks in three years. Having expected to visit Manila that weekend, I volunteered to deliver a message to his parents there. They had actually thought him dead. I didn't get around to make the trip until the last week in June, but true to my promise I delivered the message. After a warm, and bewildering reception, I was fed, given soap and water and offered a companion (Uncle Rosendo) to show me the town. An array of faces danced before me, young and old, all smiling and curious. You might say the place was a seraglio, because olive-skinned daughters and sisters emerged from every room. After my senses cleared, I counted five teen-agers of serenadable aspect and a flock of youngsters who apparently never saw blue eyes before, and a few oldsters kindly asking me questions.

Middle-aged Antonio was the master and breadwinner of all this brood helped by his older, once widowed, wife. After an evening of general discussion, a night's sound sleep on a hard bed, and a simple but hearty breakfast, I was conducted around the city by the enthusiastic Antonio. He insisted on footing all expenses which by my pocketbook ran uncomfortably high. Over the dinner table in a cool restaurant we talked man to man. He asked for advice, and what I gave pleased him. As with all Filipinos, he was astonished at my disregard for women. He was in exact accord with my intentions. Since I was the first such American he had met, I was assured a temporary residence in his household.

In his bachelorhood Antonio was a sort of playboy until he married the older widowed sister with three children of the girl he was courting. His wife, who had been married to an engineer, was a member of a prominent family of professional people that suffered most during the occupation. At forty-four she looks withered and frail. Memories of a romantic past during the flowering of her womanhood, when she mingled with the elite of Manila, had servants and elegant furnishings, constantly crop up in her disillusioned mind. Now she and her family are nearly destitute. I sympathize a little and try to exhort her.

Their plight is tragic. Antonio was placed on the Japanese punishment list, so they sold everything they owned for a song and fled to the provinces where they lived *incognito* with friends. He returned to his uncle's ramshackle house in Manila three weeks after the city was recaptured to get his job back as an inspector in the office of the Sugar Administration. Recently, he volunteered for an excellent paying job in Japan, the simplest solution, he maintains, to assure his family's survival. He doesn't seem to be bothered by leaving his wife. Money, which goads people here to do unspeakable things, has become an obsession with him. I shall now add Antonio to my list of correspondents, a worthwhile one at that.

9/3/45

Dear Mom,

A threatening typhoon has accommodatingly bypassed us. The dredge is back in operation, in an unconscientious way. Since yesterday, V-J day,[1] a fresh optimism surges through us. It's quite obvious that our unit is simply marking time. Everyone takes his sweet time, and no one cares.

By the way, of the forty-four points required to leave, I have only twenty-three. Under the present system, my age and unmarried status are against me. Under a new forthcoming system, time overseas will count for much, which may help me. Rumors of the disbanding of the Seabees are buzzing around. I keep my tongue well in my cheek.

In a disappointing mail call this evening an issue of *Masada*[2] *News* arrived. I'm not acquainted with this organization, Zionist I believe. The paper had nothing interesting to say. I prefer to steer clear of tying myself to any political group. Groups cost too much, take up too much of one's personal time, and often defeat their own purposes.

Instead of a spirited movement, I've wondered whether I'd like to join a social organization. But I've decided that I'm not cut out for such stuff either. The less conspicuous, the farther in the background, I am, where I can stand by and watch, the happier I shall be. Bear this in mind, Mom. I wish to be inconspicuous in all instances, even within my own family. No, I have no complex, merely the adoption of an easy, uninhibited way to learn faster. It is better to be outstanding to another person, than to a crowd.

Lil wrote again. Her letters are arriving regularly. Soon, the Aronovitz clan will be complete again. It's fortunate, no casualties. I recall Eddie's aloofness, Charlie's taciturnity, Sol's sarcasm, and Bobbie's lack of consideration. All are my cousins, yet I have no social ties to any of them. The truth is I've never felt comfortable in their presence. My grudging, hostile bearing (which you may not have noticed) was probably responsible. They simply weren't the type of people with whom I cared to cultivate a closer acquaintance. I was young and insignificant then, but, suddenly, that has all changed. I was of too little consequence to be invited to Eddie's wedding. And I was too quick to argue with one cousin over the pronunciation of the word "clique." Memories of the minutest details of the past never fail to arise out here. With my new perspective, I believe I'll enjoy meeting all the folks again.

Now, for a little reading while the rain dances on the tent roof. Together, they make for a cozy evening.

9/5/45

Dear Mom,

This letter was postponed from being written yesterday evening after work, my usual hour for writing. I played host to a civilian guest from the country. We watched a show, talked, then retired at a late hour. I felt more civilized last night than I have for a long time. There's something artistic and polished about being a host. You wear your best plumage and act exceedingly considerate.

My friend is middle-aged and of no great importance in his poor community. But he is pleasant, intelligent, and prone to giving long soliloquies, which I find interesting. His religious views are firmly set. Anti-Catholic and an ardent member of the Protestant Church of Christ, he was reared in a seminary whence derives his prejudice against Catholicism. After I revealed my faith, his attitude remained the same. He observed me more closely as if to say, "So that's what they are like," and continued his chatter flavored with a Spanish accent.

Yesterday, I finished reading the lengthy *Philippine History and Civilization*. The book cleared up several customs and manners that I've observed, and brought me closer to an understanding of Filipino motives. I was particularly amused by the writer's distinct anti-American attitude. American sailors are called "whisky smelling gobs," and Americans living in Manila are dubbed "the sophisticated set." Nor did the author spare Admiral Dewey.[1] The book's pictures of prewar Manila and the provinces when contrasted with the deplorable condition of those places today, helped me to more fully realize the sickening destruction that has occurred. FDR[2] and Murphy[3] are hailed as virtual saviours of the islands. Stimpson,[4] Wood[5] and Roosevelt, Jr.[6] are tyrants. The dynamic Quezon,[7] the late president, is lauded in a panegyrical chapter, failing to mention, of course, that he was virtually, if not truly, a dictator.

Presently there's an ongoing political rivalry between the young, energetic Roxas[8] and the old revolutionary, Osmena.[9] Remaining in the islands during the occupation, Roxas was appointed the leader by the Japanese. But the elusive Roxas continually played sick, and any charges that he collaborated seems to have been totally disproved. Osmena, you may remember, escaped to the States, while Quezon held his former office as vice-president of the commonwealth. Beyond the elections, supposedly due in November, the great question is will the U.S. grant the Philippines independence next year in accordance with the Tydings-MacDuffie Act.[10] As would be expected, since the war, the once strong ideal of independence has declined into uncertainty. I think they should have it. The American conception of the Philippines has been distorted by congressional propaganda. Mine was. Having argued Philippine politics with the Filipinos, I can testify that they certainly know their own minds.

You know, I've recently come to the conclusion that there is more money to be made abroad in the undeveloped countries such as China or this archipelago, than back in the frontier-lacking U.S.

I'm thinking.

9/7/45

Dear Mom,

Now that the censorship ban is off I find there's not a great deal to unleash. However, here are a few facts about past and present that you may have wondered about.

Last April I spent a week at a spot between the village of Managarin and the town of San José on Mindoro, an island south of Luzon. It was in Managarin Bay that Wolf received his unfortunate wound. [A Kamikaze attacked the vessel he was on]. From there we made our way to Subic Bay, landing at Olongopo on May 1st. There wasn't much there — a shattered remnant of what was once a naval base — but the construction of warehouses and shops was under way at a terrific pace. We were stationed about a mile or so inland near an outlying barrio (Santa Rita) of Olongopo. In June we moved across the bay opposite the larger town of Subic which was about ten miles from Olongopo. There was an existing rest camp for submarine sailors on this side of the bay and three sub tenders — one British, two American, lay offshore. I got an excellent gander at both tenders and talked with the boys a bit, including the Limeys.[1] The entrance of Subic Bay has been fenced off by an underwater sub net. I suppose that has now been removed. The sub tenders are gone; the Britisher went to Hong Kong and the other two have transported naval dischargees to New York, U.S.A.

The bay is about ten miles long and three and one half miles wide. On the west bank, hills slope down to the water and at the head of the bay are located, on flat portions of land, the towns of Subic and Olongopo, whose houses and shops are hidden from any ship by a palm fringed shore. Our bulldozers and heavy equipment have made several changes to the landscape since we've been here. To the east, which my tent faces, lies historic Bataan and its verdant cone-shaped Mount Merivales which thrusts conspicuously beyond the lower hills of the peninsula. While a part of Bataan shares the central plain of Luzon, most of it is extremely mountainous. The Japs who, during our campaign, have been hiding in its hills and managing to subsist on wild fruit and whatever they could grow, are now coming out in increasing numbers.

The hideous, treacherous pass that I've mentioned several times is aptly called Zigzag Pass. Both sides suffered many casualties during its capture. Artillery and mortar shells were lopped into it from Olongopo, sparing hardly a tree. A portion of the pass lies in Zambales province and the rest in Bataan.

My friends, the Santoses, live on a hacienda in Balsic, Bataan, near the boundary of the sugar and rice producing province of Pampanga. The hacienda is situated immediately near the foothills of the peninsula, a flat, rich, refreshing area. Next to the house there's a lovely, shady grove of mango trees that are always lightly rocking to and fro in the fresh breeze that sweeps across the plain. A concrete national highway, the route of the infamous death march from Bataan,[2] runs in front of the house to San Fernando. I've followed this route numerous times to see my friends in Lubao, Pampanga, and to San Fernando on my way to Manila. I've listened firsthand to people who witnessed the march. The people of the towns and villages lined the streets offering food to the starving Filipino and American soldiers who were prodded to move on by the Japs. Women went into hysterics, but the men only became more resolute. An American, a victim of the march, is buried in Mr. Santos's mango grove. When they found the lad, he was too far gone.

The rest of my provincial friends live in Lubao, the barrio of Santa Catalina, which is surrounded by extensive fields and marshes. So now, you know geographically where I live and roam.

I'm located about eighty miles by land from Manila, the half-way point being San Fernando. Many times I've been inclined to journey to the distant summer capital, Baguio, and the cooler north country. But I hear that former resort city is in ruins, and the roads there are in sad shape. So far I haven't had enough time off to travel that distance, and probably never will.

Someday, I'd like to return and get a closer look. There is fine country here. I envy the Jewish immigrants who have settled on the almost virgin Mindanao. They are practicing homesteading down there.

I think, during the past few years, a yen to wander has taken root in me. I doubt if I could spend all my life in the U.S. What I've seen spurs me on to see more. Of course, it will have to remain latent for many years until I become bored.

9/8/45

Dear Mom,

Two of your long and spirited letters came with your package of delicious victuals. I needed them to compensate for the recent three or four day dearth.

Just as I surmised, when you're not sending a package, you feel you're neglecting me. Please don't. I need little, even books, with so many now lying on my shelf.

One chic suit in twenty-five years! My, what lavish folks we have become. It makes me heartily glad, Mom. Dress like a queen for me. Someday, I shall take pleasure in footing the expense. With one reservation: I dance and you'll be my partner. Well, why not? Of course, we must wait until I return to a proper environment.

So far my hunt for souvenirs has been fruitless. Whatever is decent costs far beyond what I can afford. Even the prices of souvenirs are subject to the ridiculous inflation. I've seen some magnificent carving, but nothing in the way of fancy pottery. Since my term is drawing to a close, I must press my friends. Captains, majors and colonels can more easily afford what I liked in Manila. Many are paying hundreds of dollars for items worth no more than ten or twenty.

Your letter is delightful, Ronnie. Your account is reminiscent of those bewildering days of yore when, by hook or crook, I went through boot. It also sounds like our first days after a landing when all's confusion, orders conflict and everyone's outraged at the treatment he must undergo. Good plain "bitchin'," and, believe me, it's the only appropriate vernacular, is a symptom of healthy contentment. If it isn't the chow or the mail or the work or the living conditions, it's the weather or the tedium or the country. Those of us who have learned to take things in stride are by far the best bitchers. I think it's good to get away from the regular, secure routine that both of us have been raised in—for a while, that is.

When a unit is active, there's no such thing as routine. Almost every action is an unforeseen emergency. In the service, confusion and foul ups have been perfected to an art form. We're pretty sure it's deliberate because it keeps us busy and uncomfortably contented. I've concluded that your state guard provides a brilliant mock replica of the general G.I. routine. You're in the right organization just so long as you play war and exult in parading.

Your persistent prediction that when I fall, I'll fall with a thud, has amusing implications. Variety, the spice of life, also alludes to the vice of life. It would seem that I, abstemious and free of conventional vileness, am goaded by none other than my parents into the clutches of promiscuity. To be frank, I've often suffered a moral conflict, which is nothing unusual for anyone my age. What course I take is out of my hands. It's not ordained. I admit my resistance and my compliance with convention are essentially unhealthy, but I believe in the long run it will lead to a happier conclusion. Your suggestion that I should fall for someone at first glance, or that I should mingle to eliminate my awkwardness and innocence, is a far fetched reproof. I've felt all along that such experience isn't necessary, and in any social emergency, I'm capable of wending my way through it no matter how limited or extensive it might be by keeping my mouth shut, and talking shop only when shop is brought up. The foregoing explains why I have avoided doing what you suggest, in the past and now, and it is driven by my ambition and plans for the future.

I'm not concerned with the sensual and social associations that I'm bound to cultivate as a normal part of moderate living. Even if my case is unique, I believe that things will work out by themselves, that everything will catch up and smooth out.

Again I remain in camp this weekend to work. The dredge has been idle for days, but my job is never idle as long as there's a pound of steam in the boiler. We are dredging muck from near the shore and transferring it to a nearby swampy area in order that a fleet recreation center may be built. The task is almost insignificant.

You may be interested to know that I'm in old Kincaid's[1] Seventh Fleet[2] which has cooperated directly with MacArthur from the beginning. The Seventh Fleet operates along the coast of China, the islands of the Indies and these islands.

A couple of recent *Time* magazines arrived, and I'm anxious to read about what's currently going on in politics, and the arts and sciences. The meager daily reports we receive hardly touch on anything except the peace proceedings.

There, I've just yawned, a sufficient hint to conclude any conversation.

9/10/45

Dear Mom,

Suddenly, the boys are excited about the new overseas credit clause. Under the revised point system, our unit will lose most of its men. The new credits increase my total points to a measly 27 1/4, few enough to assure my spending many more months in the service either here or in the U.S. With the key men gone, what will become of the dredge? If replacements don't arrive, those of us left behind will probably be assigned to maintaining it. But if the contraption is returned to its original Australian owners, then all of us, regardless of how few points we might have, will go home. Therefore, my only hope seems to lie in the prospect that the dredge will be returned to the lender.

Until this point my impatience has been irregular. With so much time behind us, I find it easy now to reconcile myself to the fix that's pending. And I'm mighty glad that some of the older boys are at last getting the breaks.

Since that everlasting topic, Jews and intolerance, has entered into our correspondence so earnestly, I see no harm in expressing my opinions about it more clearly. Your comments, particularly the more recent ones, have been beneficial. I see your slant.

For me, joining the A.Z.A.[1] was a blunder. The boys formed controlling cliques and fast sets. Their attitude was fun-loving and insincere. The organization spent money lavishly without regard for an appreciable return. I felt like an outcast, not only because of my weak financial situation, but also because their irresponsible ways were inconsistent with mine. I began to abhor social contact with them. They were essentially frivolous and playful, while I was serious.

Their girls, and other Jewish girls whom I met, were hardly examples of clever, chaste womanhood that you deceived parents thought they were. Nor were the boys. Actually, they were far less restrained than my Gentile friends. They were artificial and shallow.

As I think back, my behavior must have seemed ridiculous. My peculiar personality may have created a barrier, however, that hasn't changed, and if anything, after two years, its peculiar nature is more so. My failure at corresponding with the damsels from Worcester corroborates this.

What I found most irksome was their constant praise of our people. All were conscious of being Jews, while I preferred to take it for granted and still do. Their pride and sense of superiority was so lofty and delicate, that the merest pinprick sets them to screaming. At the proper time and place, I, too, can be conscious and proud of my heritage. Both the individual and our race would benefit if we would abandon our sensitivity to conflicting racial ideas.

I'm quite aware that stinging sarcasm and contempt from non-Jews is unavoidable. But I let it roll off me, and cling only to those people I can trust. I wish to be tolerant precisely because of the very intolerance practiced against me. This man has progressed since those days at Gulfport when, you may recall, I was so troubled over this issue.

Our people are unified, but for some reason I've developed a hatred for organizations, perhaps due to my selfishness. After I return, no doubt all this will come up. You'll find that I share your sentiments, but I can't live by them in the big world. In varying degrees it remains that we are universally,[2] and individually[3] persecuted, and that's not easy to forget.

9/11/45

Dear Mom,

It will be two years ago tomorrow that we last bid farewell. I don't remember what I wrote last year at this time, but I do remember that I didn't expect events to pan out as they have, and that I'd not see home for a such a long time. And now I can sit back in this crude but comfortable chair of mine and recline in utmost satisfaction. My folks look better now than when I left, they have become more prosperous and happier. The most I have asked of life, to now, has been realized, or is about to be.

Of late, your letters have done more for me than usual. Whether their tone is happier, and their pace has quickened, or whether it's my imagination, I prefer to believe that there's an underlying current of mutual excitement between us.

The turbulence of the recent past has abated, and a serenity pervades my second anniversary away from home, and it's no longer sad because there won't be a third.

Today, a letter from one of our former mates was posted on the bulletin board. He had returned home the middle of August and is now a glorious civilian. He wrote that in the middle of August, mind you, he was mercilessly cold in San Francisco. The prospect is frightening. The boys are anticipating drinking plenty of liquor for warmth and comfort. But I, I'm filled with dread already.

When I mentioned the infrequency of letters from the relatives, it was only an observation. I don't crave their letters, nor do I miss them. It was merely an observation.

I wonder what the sensation would be if my hands were manicured by the hands that manicured the hands of the ex-king of England.[1] These coarse hands of mine aren't worth the bother. I have lived so simply these past nineteen months that anything so extravagant is absurd. I wouldn't enjoy a manicure, nor will I ever. All thanks to [Aunt] Anna, but the polished appearance of a gentleman is not for me.

Mr. Riccius has sent me a fine letter. I feel I have cultivated an enduring friendship with this elderly man. He has taken to Ronnie, and describes him as an author would a book character. His refined demeanor, void of any ostentatious display, is captivating. I'm looking forward to having future talks with him. My short interval at the museum has provided me two worthy friends [Johnson and Riccius].

We have had overcast skies and rain for three days for which I am grateful. It keeps the air cool.

9/17/45

Dear Mom,

I've spent the past three days in the country, in Pampanga province, thus the absence of letters. And for the usual reasons I enjoyed my brief vacation—the utter freedom, and refreshing breezes and conversation.

If I am still here for Christmas—how I hope not—I am invited to participate in a three-day country style celebration. My hosts anticipate that the occasion will be the most gala of festivals in which everyone will be able to gorge lavish quantities of food and drink, and there will be no end of dancing.

Here are a few pictures that were taken in the barrios and are not flattering to the subjects. The Filipinos are not very photogenic. Some of the people in the picture are friends or friends of friends. They appear darker than they actually are. Our skin color is about the same when I sport a heavy tan. As you can see, they are short, shorter than I, and I'm hardly tall. Now you can see how foolish you were to fear that I should be taken by one of the native maidens. Real beauties are rare. By the way, I got a haircut the next day.

Make three prints of each, enlarged of course. They've been asking me for them for some time. And the young ones are at wits end with impatience, and secretly so are the oldsters.

Within the week or perhaps a fortnight, we expect to lose a considerable number of men to home. Meanwhile, we do practically nothing; I work every other day for six hours, which affords me three day vacations. This may be a sample of what our time will be like until embarkation. The situation of us young fellows is uncertain and discouraging. Under present law we could remain here until we're discharged, which for most of us is a good six months or more away. All rehabilitation leaves, for which I am qualified, have been canceled. There's no telling what turn navy policy will take, but I prefer to think that we aren't as abandoned as things suggest.

There have been broadcasts requesting men in the C.B.'s to join the civil service and remain to resume the construction of this base. Civilian status would be immediate, the pay is attractive and the contract would run for two years. But the men are leery and want to go home first. However, this doesn't suggest that the navy personnel will soon be replaced by civilians.

We've had a good share of rain in grand New England style lately. It's raining one hour and beating sun the next. One half a street muddy, the other half dusty and choking. I think the nights are getting cooler, or are they? But not the days, not by a long shot. Friday I went swimming in a stream that was new to me. I was exhausted holding to one spot against the swift current. My companions were pleasant: two baby crocodiles and a group of Filipino youngsters. These are the first crocodiles I've seen here. They are more afraid of us than we are of them. Don't worry, I won't send any home.

9/18/45

Dear Mom,

I feel quite cozy this afternoon as the rain beats hard and steadily on the tent roof, drowning out all other sounds. There is no better time to read, or write a letter.

I sent four books home this morning: Lil's and the Histories. I've accumulated a ridiculous mess of items, many that the local civilians could use. I have a stack of your letters to return and a pile of others to throw away. It's part of a campaign to rid myself of all excess baggage.

Through no fault of his own, Henry Wolf has been having a miserable time of it. Having never had proper care and food as a child, he's not a strong lad. The family had once lived in the Philadelphia ghetto; for a while his father was in the moving business. As times improved before the war, his father began doing well, working at a shipyard, and they moved to a better section of the city. Henry was a lavish spender, and treating the father's ulcerated stomach cost the family dearly. Unlike our family that is cautious with every dollar, Henry's spent as they pleased, including summers at Atlantic City[1] which they could ill-afford. From her letters I gather that Mrs. Wolf is a constant worrier and a cynic.

Henry has not weathered the "experience" as well as I. He has been less fortunate, not having had the gift of good health and the breaks. Please, just because his teeth have deteriorated, don't assume that mine have too. After an examination about a month ago, they were found to be in surprisingly good condition. If Henry has been getting poor food, on the contrary, ours has been good.

Henry and I correspond at lengthy intervals, he promptly, and I shamefully belatedly. Many of the boys who participated in the Mindoro assault[2] have come out fine. You may recall that I volunteered for my present job. Fate must pass its verdict; not all do well by it, while others succeed magnificently. There's one lad, my friend from Frisco, who returned home healthy on a survivors' leave, married while there, and landed a comfortable position at the Frisco naval base.

In her recent letter Mrs. Wolf states for the second time that she suspects that the navy is prejudiced against Jewish boys in several respects, including discharge. Malter's Irish wife wrote of a similar suspicion regarding his discharge proceedings. You know, when things fail to go our way, and others appear to be given preferential treatment, we search for the simplest excuse: our racial suffering. It's wrong, completely wrong. It's too handy an excuse for negative situations. The services release a man when they're good and ready. Why should Wolf be released for the observance of the holidays? I believe we are too quick to blame prejudice as the reason for our failures. Anyway, whether the reason we suspect is genuine or false, it does little good to brood.

Because I have stated the hard, unromantic facts concerning the possibility of my going home, don't think I'm griping. I want to be realistic and not cynical. My impatience is perfectly natural. I'm like a bull that wants to be let out of its pen into the unfenced world. You would be surprised at how calmly I am facing the prospect of another six months out here. It doesn't in the least terrify me.

I didn't think you would wear the coin bracelet. Frankly, Mom, I think it's a horrid ornament. Australian coins will be hard to find, but Philippine coins (American made) are plentiful. What few Australians were here have since been evacuated.

Notice, and I quote, "The Veterans Administration will pay the educational institution cost of tuition and such laboratory, library, infirmary and similar payments...and may pay for books, supplies, equipment and such other necessary expenses...as are required." The state as well as the federal government is giving a mustering out bonus that should take care of my clothing for some time to come. I think I shall do better than you figured.

We will have so much to talk about, such an enormous maze of subjects to cover, that you mustn't be surprised if I'm struck silent for a time. My letters are always inadequate.

9/21/45

Dear Dad,

Of all the letters I've received from you, the one I received this afternoon is the most important. Every ounce of it imparted your thoughts beautifully and weighed into my groping soul. You bridged ten thousand miles and swept me up into your fatherly embrace. Both pride and shame mingle within me for what I have done by you. On looking back, I'm happy to see that my revolt was nothing unique, but that my love for you and our companionship were, for we have spent more time together than most fathers and sons. Not until I was away from home for a while, did I become aware of our strong mutual feelings. When, mellowed by time and distance and the unfolding of the world, these feelings thrust themselves into my consciousness, I'm uplifted, and they have helped me weather the past couple of years unscathed. They go beyond the material support you've given, in itself a manifestation of your devotion. Over the miles and months your reassertions have been the rungs of my ascent. I owe it to you and Mom to make good. And by all that exists in the world and the mind, I will.

Soon, very soon, compared with the time we've been apart, we shall be together and brimming with all that we've poured out in our hundreds of letters. I am often gripped in the tremors of such a soul-shaking event. I can only write here what you wrote: "It's grand, glorious, and happiness."

My soul to you, Hughie

9/21/45

Dear Mom,

The dates on my last two letters are wrong. This letter and yesterday's, both dated the twenty-first, should have been dated the twentieth, and today's as above. Somewhere, I lost a day, which is a terrible thing, because they are too precious.

Coincident with your joining the temple, I, too, have acquired a sudden consciousness of our people. Until now in the service, I've associated intimately with only one Jewish boy, and that because of how (not what) he was. The other Jewish boys lacked what I sought for in a friend. I've cultivated only two close friendships, perhaps a third which was brief, during the experience. Although I may have been attracted at first to a boy who was Jewish, I felt no other need to make his acquaintance.

The battalion has a fairly good representation of Jews. Some isolate themselves, other cling to their own kind. By chance, I thought, until I learned that it was intentional, I met two Jewish lads, one from New York, the other from Chicago, twenty-three and twenty-four years old respectively. Not until they were told by a mysterious third party, did they know I was Jewish. At first, I assumed a challenging, hostile air, but the boy from New York, a little man and prolific talker, met my challenge and invited himself to my tent. Later, we visited the other boy's tent and listened to classical records, and talked about our prejudices. Although these boys aren't college educated, they have keen intellects and are better read than I. I often found them more than my match. While with these boys, one, then the other, dominated the conversation. Having been accustomed to solely dominating the conversation with my other friends, I found this confusing and often frustrating.

So now they have found me, and I them. If they had their way, we would spend all our time in intellectual discussion. I don't call on them; they call on me. Since I work nights, they wake me to go to dinner and supper. I don't feel pursued, but rather encouraged. Having spent the past three days entirely with them, I feel that they have impaired my freedom to read and write. I've just sent one of them packing to a show, a show that I've already seen, which is why I'm able to write this.

Our discussions have been profound. We have covered subjects from the mechanics of radioactivity and the atomic bomb to the philosophical question of mankind's purpose on earth. We have dealt with Judaism at length. Having known little about it, I now know a lot more. Of course, girls have been a popular topic. Having had many WAC friends at Hollandia (Jewish girls), and many in Manila, they are familiar with the nature of the American girl. My view of girls is opposite theirs and, much to my embarrassment, they've openly analyzed my deplorable situation. This being hardly the time or place to meet girls, I've turned down my new friends' offers. The fact is, I've learned much from these intelligent boys in a short time, and my opinion that all young Jews are snobs is diminishing. I am often guilty of generalizing. I'm anxious to meet more lads such as these.

P.S. If you have a mathematical wizard thereabouts, I have a problem that has stumped everyone I've put it to. In your next letter let me know if you want it. It's a corker.

9/25/45

Dear Mom,

My new companions have so monopolized my time that I must more than hint to them that I desire some solitude for writing and reading. The three of us spent the afternoon, which was clear and sunfilled, swimming and paddling a banca. I enjoyed it, especially the stream, which was transparent and pure, and we plan to do it often.

Through my association with these boys (Michaelberg from N.Y.C. and Aaron Hollander from Chicago) I have met most of the Jews in the battalion. One of them, a Ben Feldman (age 31) from Long Island, has visited my tent and often joined us to see a show. After a show the four of us would talk into the night. But I'm unaccustomed to this. Mass friendliness, I call it; in the past I always confined myself to only one companion at a time. Otherwise, it's thoroughly delightful.

Mike, a scholarly and systematic individual, has scheduled cultural topics for certain evenings. I've been assigned to teach the use of the mathematical slide rule; Mike, the Hebrew language; and Aaron, Jewish history. Although, having always been a freelancer and private, and I'm not enthusiastic about this way of learning, I plan to string along.

Aaron is dark and rather handsome, has a smooth, pleasant voice and talks sensibly. He's eager to learn and make up for the schooling he's had to miss. But he hardly lacks knowledge because he has read and thought a lot. As you might suspect, women are his favorite objects. In fact, he is presently in a common-law marriage for the duration of his stay here.

Like most small men, Mike makes lots of noise. As if charged with unlike charges, his lips are constantly flying apart, uttering both sense and nonsense. He has read much and, with keen perception, has thought about what he has read. This lad is a likable chap from whom there is much to be learned. His Jewishness is evident from his face, the way he constantly waves his hands, and the inflections in his speech. He admits to being shy with women because of his miniature condition.

Both men would like to settle in Palestine. Mike is determined to become a farmer there. And both are obsessed with Zionism.[1]

I'm the youngest of the lot, although this really doesn't count for or against me. We are all mature enough to talk intelligently and argue logically. Even so, I don't encourage any sort of intimacy with my new friends. I'm wary, even unfriendly at times, for reasons that I can't fathom.

The dredge remains idle, still. During my six hours of duty I have practically nothing to do. Boys that have forty-eight points, four more than required to leave, are still waiting for transportation. The navy has proven to be inefficient at demobilization. Replacements, mostly young fellows wearing glasses, have arrived. The dregs are taking over.

10/1/45

Dear Mom,

You may well wonder why the sparse week, for which I'm sorry. I've been somewhat under the weather; in fact, I'm in a sick bay ward for jaundice patients. The crisis, what there was of it, is long past. The doctor has found my case unique. From beneath my tanned and Atabrine-yellowed complexion, a golden sheen should shine through, and the whites of my eyes should have the hue of withered autumn leaves, but these symptoms have been barely perceptible. However, I've been overcome with nausea and a general weariness, concerning which the doctor has only my word. So after extracting blood with their infamous square hooked needle, they found that the old stream contained a minimum quantity of some foreign polywog and that I best remain a sack commando for a few days. All in this ward would be especially suitable for spearheading an assault on Bunker Hill[1] in which the defenders would be waiting in vain for the whites of their opponents' eyes[2] to show. Most are well on their way to a rapid recovery, and already their rowdyism which has been pent up for weeks is being furiously unleashed.

I couldn't quite believe that I was sick. My usually voracious appetite seriously subsided, (although now restored to its former gusto) and this called for some research. After being officially informed of the malady I had contracted, I, who could boast about having good health, was damn mad. Still, I'm triumphant. My case is slight; the epidemic just brushed me.

Yesterday morning, after I had been gorging fruit juice, and delightfully dozed and slumbered for a few days, the doctor eyed my eyes, gave my stomach a good drubbing, all this amid impressive rumblings of consternation, and announced that I'm just about fixed. I wasn't sure whether to be happy or not. For the past two consecutive dinners ice cream and my favorite brew of fruit juices have been served. After I return to the sanctuary of my tent I plan to rest up from this rest. I haven't done a real stick of work for months, and the tedium of it all certainly calls for some sort of vacation.

At the instigation of my Jewish friends, I read Michael Steinberg's[3] *As a Driven Leaf.*[4] Essentially philosophical and well written, it offered some interesting ideas and revelations. Aside from learning more about our magnificent heritage, I found many of its explanations familiar.

All of you seem suddenly to be aware of the spiritual and social aspects of life which I attribute to your improved circumstances. This pleases me. I, however, remain an infidel, because, until now, I've needed no faith beyond a belief in goodness and truth. I find the vagaries of ritualistic religion unnecessary. The power of the Rabbi's [Olan's] sermons, the simplicity of his service, and the glamour of the congregation, have touched off your enthusiasm, which I think is a fine thing. For your sake I would attend services with you but for reasons other than yours. If you think I would enjoy the rabbi, I would go.

In spite of our confinement we manage to see shows. If our temperature is normal, after supper we are allowed to go. Those other creatures whose temperature reads a few tenths of a degree above normal have only themselves to blame. They didn't keep the thermometer out of their mouths long enough while the corpsman's[5] back was turned. So far I haven't had to resort to such knavery.

A couple of days ago the dredge lost about a dozen men who are now Stateside bound. As a consequence its operation has been halted. On all lips is the question, what next? Now on the brink of our twentieth month, the word we hear most is "home" which is so close that our hearts quicken at its very mention. For me and derelicts like me, the unconsoling word is patience.

10/2/45

Dear Mom,

I'm cured and now well and raring to dash out as soon as my corpuscles are approved. That should be tomorrow. This being cooped up has been an ordeal. My continual dozing and gluttony hardly measure up to weekend meanderings or cold showers and wieners and sauerkraut. Freedom, even under the shackle of the navy, doesn't include confinement in a jaundice ward—not if I can help it.

Today, the navy announced another startling innovation to the point system: all men with three or more children may go home. Now that's just fine and dandy. We have few men here who have been industrious enough to sire such a brood. If the navy continues taunting us and beating around the bush of just deserts, even my patience will wane—which wouldn't really matter. Regardless of the preposterous concessions made, it remains that there's no transportation. Reportedly Manila is jammed with men waiting. A few *West Points*[1] would do the trick.

I can imagine the fuss that [Cousin] Charlie has had to endure. Gifts are all very well, but any understanding person realizes how unnecessary such tokens are. Have no regrets, Mom. Your gifts are priceless; they come from your heart. Yes, and your tears will be exquisite, your eyes elegantly bejewelled with them, a matchless gift guaranteed for life.

When I have much to say, yet my mind is too barren to say it, I resort to the weather. So wait until I send a more ambitious letter. In typical tropical fashion, heavy, windswept rain is now pelting us. The past month is the wettest I've ever encountered—and the coolest in nineteen months, and that isn't cool by your standards.

Unlike mine, your letters have been regular. My heart grows woozy when I hear that mine are held up. I suspect you worry. But now you know that the worst that can happen to me is a silly case of jaundice.

10/4/45

Dear Mom,

I wonder if different members of the clan will be sponsoring frolicsome festivities as each of us return. Of course, Charlie's arrival being the first, he has been greeted with a fresh and novel fervor. Bobbie's is somewhat dampened as a result of his lingering presence during occasional leaves. From the looks of things both Eddie, and, on your side of the family, Billy, will be honored by dinners as frequent as Russian toasts. Not only, as you say, has the war brought loved ones closer together, but from your letters, I can see it has revived the family spirit. Your visits to relatives are more frequent, and the hospitality and warmth with which you are greeted is more profuse. Your common prosperity certainly has helped, but underlying it is an empathy for each other's experience of a love sundered by distance.

Maybe due to time and distance I'm reading into your letters more than is there. Maybe you are no closer together than before.

I left sick bay yesterday fully recuperated and have nothing more to do than read and relax in the breezy shade. On the heels of my last letter in which I upbraided the navy for its inefficiency at demobilization, it was announced that all eligible boys should prepare to leave before week's end. Close to three hundred from an already sadly depleted battalion will leave in this batch. Meanwhile, by the middle of the month, the forty-one personnel (of the original fifty-five) remaining on the dredge will be reduced to a meager twenty-two. Our commanding (and only) officer will also be discharged. I'll most likely be transferred to another unit, as it's inevitable that the dredge will be abandoned.

Most of the remaining fellows, especially those my age, are in a quandary. We don't relish the idea of remaining here until next summer, especially when men with a fraction of our time overseas are being returned. It's discouraging indeed to contemplate the prospect of another six months or a year here under present rules. Our only hope lies in a revision of the regulations, which we hope will be urged by the folks at home. Congress is now under pressure from the public to do so. The navy insists on retaining its "kids" regardless of how much time they have out here. Without dependents, the only alternative is to have accumulated a number of years in the service. The army has done better, retaining the novices and releasing "the old timers" even those who are young. The discrepancy here is that life and procedure in the Seabees differs from that in the shipboard navy. The young fellows say, "Treat us all, married and unmarried, alike as individuals. Wives have gotten along so far. The young have equal responsibilities. Don't favor a man because of what's back there, but rather by what he's done out here."

Oh, things will pan out, and soon so will I.

10/5/45

Dear Mom,

Remarkable, indeed! It is remarkable what a soothing soprano voice, dainty, delicate features, a pearly complexion, and ravishing golden hair, can do for a man when done for a woman. Especially when a man hasn't gazed upon such human splendor for an age.

Last evening I saw the U.S.O. production of "Kiss and Tell."[1] You may recall from ramblings through your "cultural" magazine literature mention of the vivacious, irrepressible Corliss Archer[2] and her antics. She wreaks in her adolescence both happiness and tragedy in a hilarious plot. The show was good, providing wholesome entertainment, an accomplishment in view of the less than ideal conditions here.

The central figure was a comely blonde, who, in her budding, contagious state, was a pleasure to look at. Even I, who tend to be severely critical of most females, had to concede that she was special. In fact I was taken aback by her. And coincidentally, that very evening proved to be by far the most pleasant evening I've had in twenty months—that is, after my insignificant role as a member of the audience changed to that of a more social and obtrusive one.

After the show, as was my habit, I lingered at the theater to converse with my companion in the balmy darkness. I like to remain behind after the crowd has cleared and the lights have been extinguished to enjoy, while still under the spell of the stage, the soothing, contrasting silence.

Eventually, Mike and I proceeded to the chow hall for a snack. He poured his coffee, I my water, and, paying little heed to those around us, we sat at an available table. Only then did I become aware of the performers seated about and talking to the boys. It so happened that seated behind me was the blonde.

I grew absurdly fidgety, recovering gradually as Mike and I fell into a controversy concerning the status of the actors. The only way to settle our argument was to ask one of the actors, but neither of us, awed by their performance I suppose, had the courage.

Simply and spontaneously, such that I was quite astonished, the object of every male's eye, turned toward us and delivered a molten hello. At this invitation, and after gaining my composure with titanic effort, I put the question that led to our stalemated argument before her. And as simply as her pleasant advance was spoken, she then invited us to join her at her table to talk, and, I think, rescue her from the dreary conversation she was having with the "old timers." So there I was, comfortably sitting strangely composed, opposite a charming creature worthy of any *Coronet* cover, indulging in intelligent, inspiring conversation.

It is not easy, after being deprived of the sight of alluring, American womanhood for twenty months, to face such a beauty, at least until she speaks. But once that happens it's refreshing and delightful. The girl brimmed with crystal effervescence, a delicate vivaciousness. Her personality had been nurtured and cultivated by education and art. She won me over completely, even during those moments when I was aware of her insincerity, and she asked probing questions, and attempted to win our admiration.

After she departed, to her regret at that, I pondered what had happened. What had I extracted from that hour or so that had banished the intolerable moods of depression under which I have been laboring of late? I realized she was entirely oblivious of the big impression she made on me, owing not to her desirable contours but rather to her training and inbred wholesomeness. It wasn't an infatuation by a long shot. In that hour she gave me what I needed, and I was completely satisfied. Now that my thirst has been adequately slaked, I shall never see her again, nor do I particularly care to.

This is a typical example of the sort of people the U.S.O. is using. At my prodding she volunteered much information about herself. She would be twenty in twelve days, she said with a blush, hails from Omaha, Nebraska (and called us gentlemen for not quipping "Oh, corn fed, eh."), graduated from the University of Nebraska, studied radio theatrics (that is, radio acting and similar tasks before a microphone), went to New York, was offered the lead role in "Kiss and Tell," grabbed it, fully realizing the marvelous opportunity it was and the experience to be gained.

A good deal of the cast were from the original Broadway production. One of the ladies in it hails from Springfield, Mass., right near home, but, unfortunately, she was indisposed so I failed to get any hot two month old Mass. news by direct word of mouth.

Today, I've returned to languishing in the stark reality of biding my time. It has been only temporarily alleviated by the memory of last night. Last night was a boon to me; that little girl had done her duty well for her employers. I'm sure my companion derived as much from it as I did, but I confess, I gave little chance for anyone to get a word in edgewise. Now I'm branded a veritable Don Juan[3] that uses a technique of feigned innocence. And I can't say that I mind.

10/10/45

Dear Mom,

Five days ago (last Saturday) Michaelberg (from Brooklyn) accompanied me on one of my periodic visits to my provincial (Lubao) friends. Relaxed after the freedom and jolliness of the previous days, we returned only yesterday.

Catching rides is no problem, and we were unusually lucky the entire way. Our first stop to see the Santoses at Balsic, Bataan, was a disappointment. The home, which for weeks and months had offered round welcomes and scrumptious dinners, was desolate, utterly abandoned. So we moved on to the barrio of Santa Catalina in the town of Lubao, where I introduced the magnetic Mike to all my friends, even the Santoses, who, it turned out, had evacuated to the barrio.

It seems like the Socialists, whom the populace dubs Communists, have been resorting to terrorism and violence. One night they fired shots into the Santoses' Balsic house. The trouble here is principally agrarian: the tenants want seventy percent of the crop for themselves, thirty percent for the landowner. At present they split it fifty-fifty. The Socialist party is surprisingly active. Whether they are endorsing the ongoing terrorism is not confirmed, but certainly Santos, a supervisor and sympathizer of his landlord, Erastia, has been driven from his home.

A group of my friends, myself in the middle, tried to thrash out the problem, but to no avail. Siding with the destitute tenants, I opposed Santos, although I wouldn't sanction terrorism. Some insisted that a loan from the U.S. would bring prices down, thus nullify the tenants' grievances. I supported the more radical solution, accusing the present leaders and the party in power of being incompetent and that any money borrowed by the government would be handled poorly and soon lose its value.

Here I am, dashing off into politics when, more important, I have my experience to relate.

We first visited Alehandro (Ando) Quiboloy, the school teacher I may have mentioned at one time or another, whose flair for poetry and intelligent discussion is special. His brother Constantino (Tino) who lives close by, and his brother Delfin, a wisp of a fellow, aspire to the literary, one of short stories, and the other, plays in dialect. Both later carried on a conversation that amazed the prolific and well read Mike. Again, no one was at home, except their teen-age sister, who, being shy, offered no explanation of where they were. On to Lucio's then, where everyone was at home which eased Mike's initial disappointment. Soon Anita and Dolores appeared, and with them a frivolity and naivete that delighted all.

Dinner at Lucio's was hearty Filipino fare, including a dessert of sweet papaya, the season's first from Lucio's grove. Early that afternoon we found Ando at his house, where, after I introduced Mike, we talked briefly; thence, to Reverend Sangco's, where we did the same; thence, to a fast volley ball game in which Mike and I played on opposite sides. When the score was twenty to nineteen, I made a crucial blunder by touching the net which mandated that my side forfeit the winning point to the opposition. The stake, three packs of cigarettes which are at a premium, was given to the winners, while I moaned that I had been ignorant of the rule. Having a carton of Chesterfields in my bag at Lucio's, and feeling solely responsible for losing the game, I dashed off to the house and dashed back waving three packs amid the acclamation of both spectators and players. And we won the next game.

With bare feet blistered from sliding and jumping on the bare ground, but comfortably weary and elated, I limped back with Mike to Lucio's. After a refreshing bath at the cool artesian well and a substantial supper of eggs, soup, fish, rice (which replaces our bread), and fruit, we visited next door where the Santoses now live.

Political talk commenced. Meanwhile, the girls had captivated Mike with their song, and by the time Ando called for me to join the Reverend in discussion that evening, Mike was obviously enjoying their sweet company and pleasant voices. Mike was my instrument; I played him dirty. I purposely tossed him onto the girls so I could take leave and not offend their sensitive feelings. Until nigh on midnight the four of us, the two Quiboloy brothers, the Reverend and myself, talked, while Mike was pleasantly steeped in women and song in another part of the barrio.

After the hard afternoon, Mike slept at the Santoses, and I, soundly, at the Quiboloys. Breakfast was simple but good: rice, eggs, crabs, milk and bananas. Afterwards, I met Mike at Lucio's, having Tino's invitation in hand to be his guests for dinner. We were also invited to attend the Protestant services, but decided against it in favor of going to Tino's small hacienda, where we could see how the tenants live. Who could blame them for revolting? They dwell in bare nipa huts in which they hardly have room to stand. Nothing has changed for centuries. Both people and their abodes were in a primitive state, except that now they know better. They don't speak English, the old men not even Tagalog, and speak in the provincial Pampango. They laughed at my mispronunciation of their words, and offered us seats on a bamboo shelf set two feet off the dirt floor. Having used up all the words I knew and our curiosity grown ragged, we bid them paalam, adios.

Back once more to Sta. Catalina, we had dinner [lunch] at Tino's that was simply elegant. His wife was a shy, handsome, Spanish-looking girl who apparently has mastered the culinary art. There, set before us, was fried chicken, eggs (sunnyside up), string beans, fresh tomatoes, a delicious sauce, chicken soup, rice and a bunch of tender, tasty bananas. Again that night we had supper there, a full supper consisting of pork steak, shrimp and crab salad, a variety of novel tropical sprouts and fruit. Mike was astonished. He hadn't expected to eat so well and so much.

Between our scrumptious dinner and supper, we visited the largest town thereabouts, Guagua (pronounced Gwagwa) to witness the gaudy victory day celebration at the Plaza. As planned, Lucio and his family, and the Santos girls joined us, and together we meandered through the crowd along paved concrete sidewalks and asphalt streets, watching various exhibitions. The bandstand was jammed to the gil's with spectators, a situation perfectly acceptable since the band played on the sidelines. As is typical of Filipino bands, each musician plays solo and only by chance do all the musicians play together. I imagine that were a single instrument isolated from the confusion, you might recognize the semblance of a melody. For instance, sporadic, energetic fits of "Stars and Stripes Forever"[1] were occasionally recognizable before dying away to a tinkling murmur only to blast away again. It was like someone singing a barely familiar song in which the familiar lines are sung extra loud to compensate, I suppose, for the unsung, only murmured lines. However, one instrument was consistently clear, a vestige of inspiration for the rest of the band, the base drum whose reverberating boom lingered in the air.

Mike, who is of embarrassingly minute stature, finally climbed on my shoulders to peer over the crowd. As my shoulders were being put to this worthy purpose, a Reverend Semiento, whom I had often talked to in Lubao, shook my encumbered hand and Mike's on high, and invited us to his house nearby after the parade was over.

As the parade began, throngs of brown people lined the street. Floats made of cardboard and paper, drawn by caribou or rickety cars, depicted Japanese atrocities such as a child pinned down by a bayonet, Uncle Sam's victory, and a caged Jap prisoner. Dressed in costumes of red, white and blue the marchers slowly wended their way down the narrow street. Every float had a martial flavor, even the one on which the beauteous queen, begowned in white, and bedecked with flowers and silk finery, stood.

Rather than hold this letter over another day, I'll stop here and continue tomorrow.

10/14/45

Dear Mom,

While on the graveyard shift I do little more than sleep. It's a struggle to remain awake doing nothing for eight hours, and the day's infernal heat hardly encourages slumber. So I have little ambition to write, even to the point of postponing the continuation of my account of last weekend.

This afternoon I dozed with my companions Mike and Aaron, while lying beside a babbling stream. Between napping, we took pictures then returned to camp for supper, after which I made tail for bed, and they took in a show. Bear with my laxity until next week when I'll have civilized working hours.

The dredge isn't operating and I just put in time standing watch. Tomorrow, we will, lose eight more boys, which now brings our complement to one half what it was. Since the skipper himself is due to be discharged, he views this with consternation, and he has sent a letter to the authorities to learn of our fate. If by chance, a possibility far too good to be true, we are decommissioned, all of us would have priority status to go home.

The air is comfortably cool at this half-hour past midnight. Even the hard deck looks inviting, so with a heavy head I shall stretch out and relax in a semi-sleep. Good morning, folks.

1:00 AM on the job, 10/18/45

Dear Mom,

Four days ago I began writing a letter home that I should have written the day before that. Not until now—and I can't guarantee that I won't doze off before this is finished—have I been able, at least momentarily, to overcome a recent state of delirium and mental depression. While in the tropics no man should work the graveyard shift, especially during the dry season when the days are stark blue, the blazing sun is oppressive, and the thick, sultry heat causes the sweat to soak the mattress.

My job requires that I while away the time awake. What I do cannot be considered work. Men from our reduced unit and others nearby are sporadically leaving for Stateside. The other units receive replacements but not ours. Our status and our fate are hanging fire. Now that the number of points necessary to leave has been dropped to forty today, our complement will be drawn down to a bare minimum. Accordingly, I expect to remain here at least another four months, who knows how many more, for sure. I don't relish it, and I'm mad. More than a discharge, my objective is Stateside and home.

With so much time on my hands, I mostly sleep. In the torrid, breezy afternoons I walk two miles through woods and fields to a sparkling stream where I bask in the shade and doze some more. In the early evening I go to a show then sleep again. As you can see, sleep dominates my life and will continue to do so until next week. Your sweet letters arrive regularly. I know I've been cruel these past two weeks. Believe me, I suffer as much. My inability to write weighs on me. I'm tired.

10/22/45

Dear Mom,

This week my hours change, and now I shall make up for the past poverty-stricken, destitute weeks. My depression has been exacerbated by my worry that you would worry. But now you needn't worry when such lapses occur, for all suspicion of danger should have been banished at war's end—at least I would hope so.

During the sultry, glaring afternoons I've been swimming a lot. Mike regularly accompanies me as we lose ourselves in conversation while walking and swimming. Brown as betel nuts, we find that the walk and the swim tone us up; the very beauty of the landscape soothes our senses.

My mind is stacked with material to write about. Of the nine or so monkeys, two miraculously have survived the rat poison that has been spread throughout the area. Let me tend to the happy batch of unanswered letters before me.

I'm glad that, unlike in my case, you could persuade Ronnie to learn how to dance. Now when will he begin to use his art training? I've just gone through a similar ordeal. One afternoon my companions, finding me idle, taught me the box step. A few nights earlier they dragged me off to a Filipina's[1] sweet sixteen birthday party in which there was dancing to an orchestral ensemble and more girls than boys—and refreshments. Turning the page back five years, I reminisced over a scene at the Coronado[2] where at a dance I spent the evening in the lobby and the men's room. I didn't dance at the Filipina's party, only brooded over forfeiting a good show for Aaron H.'s and Mike's sake.

There was one incident that was both amusing and not amusing. Among many uninvited guests who had attended the party, a number of them were women smeared with gaudy makeup, a sure mark that they were "business women," that is, whores. They monopolized the floor until the virgins' patience exploded. Unified into a single force, they subtly ousted the harlots who, daring to venture no farther, then had to gaze from the sidelines exhibiting grimaces of envy.

When I was last in Pampanga, I informed Carolina of her letter's final arrival. The civilian mails are too slow for carrying on an exciting correspondence. I don't know the girl well. I've visited with her father and her brother, rather infrequently at that, and I have only a passing acquaintance with the rest of the family. If Beverly has seen fit to encourage the correspondence, she might tell me a thing or two about these people.

The navy, in attempting to maintain our morale, has so far failed miserably. With ships pulling out on a regular basis, the transportation bottleneck has abated. After a batch leaves, those left behind become only more impatient. The young fellows, having put in the same amount of time either overseas or in the service as the departees, are as weary of being here as the husbands who are constantly leaving. If no one were to leave, there would be far less complaining, but when any group, husbands for instance, are favored, our ire is aroused. We claim that time spent in the service, especially time overseas, should count for more than it does. As long as regulations remain lax as they have been, I'm reconciled, but I fear that boot camp regulations may be in the offing. The peacetime navy doesn't normally tolerate the murder we have been getting away with.

There you go, anticipating my objections to your plans. How can I object when you silence me before I can open my mouth? So, without my sanction, you do as you please. You're the boss, Mom. Believe me, I succumb with pleasure to your loving domination.

When I was up before the skipper of the 113th last year, I had the choice of working on the dredge or elsewhere in the battalion. A volunteer has a choice. I'm aboard the dredge as much by my own will as by the will of my former C.O.

Al Malter met his present wife while he was in an S.F. hospital recovering from a brain operation. She was a special assistant to the operating surgeon. Her professional interest eventually became personal. Love, Mom, pays little heed to one's heritage and so forth.

I have an aunt whom I don't dislike, but there are things about her that I don't like. For a woman her age, her body, decked in a dress, appears slender and youthful. Her face, after constant kneading with oils and creams and touched up with powders and paint, doesn't betray her age. Her peroxide hair is a lustrous blonde, and perhaps fast disappearing. When I last saw her, she looked like a hen that had extended the appearance of a chick. But she was ailing, and I wondered how long she would remain a chick as inevitably a chick, like lightning renting the darkness, must reveal its drab plumage.

For all the pretentious glamour, and prettiness that some women prefer, I hope, Mom, that you remain conservative and well. I look forward to this "new improved" Mom. It's impossible to spoil her.

As damp as it is here, it was damper in New Guinea. The wet season has noticeably passed. Every day is mostly clear. The rising moon is a large, white spectacle, that only the tropics offers. The sunrise is fiery, and the sunsets are subdued and colorful. The nights are becoming cooler. I must wear a shirt now, sometimes also a jacket. All shades of perennial green can be seen everywhere, amongst the tan sunburnt grass and in the dark woods. The days are growing shorter. The shows begin now at 7:30, a half hour earlier than before when the light still annoyingly lingered. Day breaks very late around 6:00 or 6:30. These are the telltale signs of approaching winter in your lovely northern latitudes. They are sufficient to remind us of falling leaves and swirling snow, and sufficient to make us suddenly more homesick than ever.

10/23/45

Dear Mom,

It's pouring and the sun is shining; half the sky is silvery blue, the other half dark and heavy. Having just come to the dredge from the dock on the LCVP to report to work, I barely missed a soaking. By even the laziest man's standards, my work couldn't be called work. Here on the bridge reading and writing letters, then down below chewing an aimless rag, interrupted occasionally by a hasty tending to one or two pumps, hasn't the slightest resemblance to work, has it? But whatever you call it, it's time spent. According to rumor, new developments concerning the dredge are expected this week. Perhaps the futility of hoping the past few months is about to give way, slightly, to a flicker of optimism.

I have your week old letter that coincides with my recently revived melancholy. Home is on the minds and lips of those for whom a voyage is imminent, and its contagion has caught the rest of us. The other night in the chow hall I overheard buddies delightfully pondering what New York bar they would first visit. Some fellows, the losers and winners who during the past twenty months bet drinks on the date of their returning, are joyously reminding each other to pay up or be paid up. I owe and I'm owed many a chocolate malted, but the final outcome is too far off.

Memories of my visit to Pampanga two weeks ago, which I stopped telling you about plumb in the middle of my account, has, due to the onslaught of recent events and my state of mind, diminished in fervor and fascination. With details no longer vivid, the freshness and vitality are gone. So I'll mention only one major incident: Delfin Quiboloy has elected me to be the godfather of his son Dante. What and when the ceremony will be, what role I shall play, though I hear the occasion is steeped in gaiety, are yet unanswered questions. I nervously await the whole ordeal. I feel wizened and manly to be so honored. Now Delfin and his family will address me as "compadre, an august, respected Spanish designation indeed.

I feel grateful to all these people who have brought me into their homes and given me the best they could afford, and beyond, but I'm embarrassed. Perhaps, after I return, I can send them something to show my appreciation. No perhaps about it. I intend to.

Among all the errors that I have made in my letters, some of which I was aware but too late to correct, I can't let go by one in particular concerning a crocodile.[1] I learned later that they weren't crocodiles but enormous lizards. The combination of my myopic vision and the confirming nod by a Filipino lad to the word crocodile convinced me that what I saw slithering by the stream's bank was truly a crocodile. After many more visits to the spot, and having the living daylights scared out of me, I discovered that they were only lizards that were having the living daylights scared out of them.

10/26/45

Dear Mom,

The scuttlebutt concerning the dredge sounds good. Whether rumor becomes fact or not, the earlier dismal outlook is brighter, and we are thrilled with might happen. I'm still idle, yet working and yearning for a day off, but with no one to replace me I must stay in camp.

Last night I managed to see "The Affairs of Susan,"[1] after swapping shifts, although in doing so I got the bitter end. But it was well worth it, for I was royally entertained.

With a fund of literature overflowing my shelf, despite all the time I have, I'm making slow progress. Right now I'm reading Havelock Ellis's[2] *The Dance of Life*,[3] a philosophical tract that proclaims rhythm governs life and that art is absolute and fundamental. And his tangential remarks are as interesting as his main theme. After reading the chapter on the art of dancing, I'm quite ready to bust my britches to learn. He describes dance as powerful, so utterly basic and full of significance, that I'm sad that I never learned. However, I have been dancing if less obviously, because my thoughts and inner pulsations and energy releases all operate in a rhythmic pattern. So says H. Ellis and I say he has something there.

Before starting, and in contrast to *The Dance* I finished reading Hawthorne's[4] *The Scarlett Letter*.[5] I read as I fancy, choosing books to read on impulse, in defiance, I suppose, of the regimented reading I had to do in school. But I haven't nearly as much as I'd like to. My power of concentration, that major prerequisite, is deplorably weak.

I've rarely touched on the subject of my relationship with the "gang" in my letters. Almost from the beginning, rather after a preliminary period of bewilderment, the subject was not so much sore as sensitive. I'm definitely not one of them, which from a practical point of view, is more bad than good. To be an extrovert, mingle freely and, you know, be one of the boys, is no great task, but the course I choose to follow is difficult and at times frustrating. My perhaps egotistical and obvious indifference to most and my preference for reclusiveness draws more interesting flies than if I had conducted myself otherwise. My friends who know me, and those who don't classify me as being "different," which is not meant to be laudatory. Yet my closer friends tolerate my faults and fancies with a certain enjoyment and amusement, I think, and have assimilated some of my quirks more than I have theirs. In my rather infrequent reflective moods of self-analysis, I believe I know the "why" of my actions. It's my indecision and self-doubt. Are my choices ultimately the best ones?

So profusely do we perspire that in less than a week without exposure to the sun the yellow pallor of our skin returns. Rinso[6] (the best Rinso ever made) could do no better. Next week I shall be lounging in the fields and at the stream again. By the way, this is the stream from which we get our drinking water. The Doc okayed the water with an additional splash of approval: it's fit to drink right from its bed. And, Mom, I didn't have malaria. It was the jaundice, pure and yellow, so help me.

Now, this report on Ronnie concerning his marvelous dancing accomplishments describes something that needs to be reckoned with. In this day, when females no longer flee to entice their admirers, nor even remain stationary as they used to back in the civilized era, tch, tch, Ronnie, I can tell already, will be the object of many a heart, poor lad. And Dad, you must acquaint him with the methods you used so often to shake off the great number of pursuing damsels.

This dreadful routine you have, this, this, commercialized torture chamber [exercise salon] you visit, far surpasses anything I've ever inflicted upon myself. I have a friend here who will tell you that a healthy quart of Calvert Reserve has the identical effect. But if it does you any good, even psychologically, I think it's far more admirable than anything Dad, whom you say is wallowing in obesity, (and who used to suffer from sporadic pins and needles in his arms) has been doing. We should never have sold the bike, eh, Mom?

10/28/45

Dear Mom,

It's a sultry, silvery Sunday afternoon with an Alabama/Georgia game resounding from the P.A. system and off to work at 3:00. I'm in the library surprised at the fluorescent lights above, which I hadn't noticed before. In the tent the boys are drinking beer, Ballantines 6% light, and making too much noise for me to write letters. My old tent was commandeered by the replacements, so I had to move to the one next door. This tent houses a noisome Jewish lad from the Bronx, a Polish landsman from Delaware, and a Hoosier who's due to return home next week, and good riddance, because he broadcasts his affection for his state more intensely than any Texan for his. The tent which has a white ceiling is cool and bright, a light at every bunk, an electric fan, and real running water on its porch.

A large batch will leave next week. Few of the original men remain, only the young but wizened. I hear most of the 113th has left Mindoro and is now located near Nichols Field just south of Manila. I must skip down there to pay them a visit. A few of the original members are left and doing practically nothing.

A refusal to work is not necessarily confined to the States. It's almost universal in the service, beginning when the war ended, and intensified by the slow removal of personnel. Shifts are still working night and day but producing little. The old-timers, especially those about to leave, feel no obligation to work. Since they are the only ones who know the machinery and the techniques of construction, after they leave (next week) things will grind to a near standstill. The replacements are mere moppets, with little incentive and less knowledge. The braid is attempting to get as much work done as possible by those who know how, but having a hard time doing it. Some bluntly refuse to report to work, others just feint working, while a good many grace the sack or take off for Manila. No one cares, nor are they expected to. It's the brass hats' move now.

Last weekend Mike and Aaron and "Count" Grassi (A big time New York Italian contractor) and I simultaneously felt the impulse to listen to some good music. Spearheading the invasion of Radio City (our radio shack), Mike convinced the fellow on duty that it was music or his blood. So we got music: Ravel,[1] Shostakovich,[2] Tchaikovsky,[3] Grieg,[4] Gershwin, Kern and a few more obscure but equally excellent composers. And now that the drone of the ballgame is over, I'm listening to more good music over the P.A. system. Ever since I've been overseas, I've been ardently gripped by an unprecedented yearning for music despite there being nothing to stimulate that yearning. I can't recall ever developing a taste for music; yet, when I listen the melodies are familiar, as if I know them, although not by name. Apparently, my mind must have recorded the music in its recesses without my being aware of it. More and more of what I hear rings familiar; more and more I want to hear.

I've received the prints you had made, but I'm afraid I'll need a couple more sets. I owe them to several people, mostly pictures of myself. My Filipino friends lambaste me when I have none to exchange for theirs. Enclosed is a better picture of Anita, [It's among the photographs herein] and even this one is hardly flattering. This and the other pictures were taken in August and early September at Lubao, Pampanga.

I forgot to mention that a dog freely inhabits our tent. A buxom, willful female, she is mostly German Shepherd, but smaller. Her fur is black and shiny except that her head and lower legs are yellow. Bosco (an odd name for a girl or any beast, we know) has been with us since leaving Hollandia. Apparently sired on Moratai where her mother came aboard, she was one of five pups on the Liberty ship. Bosco is very clever, very lovable and for unaccountable reasons dislikes Filipinos, who, upon her initiative, for their own obvious reasons, dislike her. But Bosco brings a feminine quality into our tent—that she does. When we vigorously call her down for misbehavior, she wags her tail until it whips up a breeze, slants her ears back, and cuddles up to you for a petting and forgiveness. Just like a woman, so we have observed.

10/31/45

Dear Mom,

I've interrupted my reading of *The Dance of Life* to write this. I'm almost finished with it, and in its conclusion I just read a passage which I consider climactic. It confirms what I have long felt but never voiced. It's a perfect point to stop in contemplation and to experience the joy of finding ideas sympathetic with your own. Here H. Ellis is great. His self-confidence is magnetic, and his flamboyant lambasting of his revered contemporaries is exhilarating. I plan to read this book again more thoroughly in the future when I'm more mature, and no doubt, more capable of understanding portions than I am now, and when I'm less susceptible to the convictions of others while mine are still weak. Nevertheless, reading this book now is a means towards that end.

In most cases arrivals are so much better than departures, but here both are good. Which will be the more enthusiastically celebrated is open to question, as the wild gang leaving for Stateside tomorrow is doing it up royally. We are losing an appreciable lump of our own fellows in this draft. Sunday we lost our commanding officer which leaves us, as someone remarked, like chicks without a mother hen. It is generally predicted that the unit will soon be deactivated. I lay my greater hope in the fairly sound rumor that beginning next month a new rotation policy will enable all having eighteen months or more over here to be sent home.

Last night, I attended one of the battalion's farewell parties, stag according to regulations, and got good and stuffed on crispy french fried potatoes. Leaving early, I found my new tent a haven for more celebrants who kept me hilariously wide awake for hours. As you'd expect, benevolence, beer, and whisky were profuse. The fellows in the next tent who were vigorously complaining (in a profane sort of way) ended up joining us and partaking of the refreshments and entering into the nonsensical chatter. Again, I had more french fries and some ice cream, and had to push away the roast beef sandwiches. Our method for procuring such delicacies is rather farcical. Assuming a bearing of authority, one of our representatives strolls nonchalantly into the chow hall and demands a certain quantity of food for a detail that is so hard at work that food must be taken to it. Such a procedure inevitably produces favorable results as demonstrated last night. One fellow got away with procuring a case of eggs while he was at it.

The subject of the blonde in one of my letters was purely happenstance. Don't assume I prefer blondes. Don't you dare become one. I like harmonious blends, not gaudy contrasts. Let her be, Dad.

11/1/45

Dear Mom,

Last night and this morning were filled with sad joy and farewells. We shook hands over and over as I earnestly said goodbye to friends and acquaintances with longing, and they, in turn, with sympathy for my staying behind. Those of us left behind are suffering. Only twenty-three men remain on the dredge, not enough to keep it in operation. Of the original battalion of eleven hundred men, only sixty remain. We question why, in fairness, we should be left behind. The *Anthedon* broadcast her departure with a loud blast, weighed anchor, and glided out of the harbor with the last vestige of the old gang and old spirit waving from her deck. We on shore waved and wished her well to her destination, New London,[1] Connecticut.

And now, with the tension and excitement over, we are once again settling down and waiting. To us the "boots" (a term applicable to anyone with less than a year overseas) seem infantile and awkward. They lack our confident air and strut of indifference. We reign by doing as little as possible and setting a poor example.

Everyone on the dredge is doing more than his job to keep her afloat. A letter is due any day informing us that we are officially deactivated. We are optimistic enough to assume that our leave papers will follow. But, hard though it is, I like to retain a grain of pessimism. A less desirable course of events is possible. Such sweet reality can't cease in my life to be fantasy.

However, the hundred dollar money order enclosed is real.

11/4/45

Dear Mom,

The wind was whipping, heavy clouds scudded overhead, and typhoon warnings were broadcast, but now the sky is aglitter with stars. Whatever it was, it is probably off to somewhere else.

The dredge is now anchored way out in the bay—a precaution against the storm. Three of the remaining twenty-three men live ashore, the rest aboard the dredge. To report to work in the morning I must first contact the dredge to send a boat. To do this, I go through a routine similar to my setting-up exercises of yore. I swing my arms, and prance up and down until someone aboard notices me. Someday, according to certain inquisitive observers, instead of a boat an ambulance may well pick me up. If not for insanity, I would be retrieved for exhaustion.

All this, and anything else concerning the dredge, will soon be over. The orders are to deactivate her, but—a disagreeable "but" indeed—along with those orders came orders to report to a unit down at Manus in the Admiralties.[1] However—a most agreeable "however"—the commander of the 102nd battalion with whom we now live is trying, and I think will succeed, to absorb us into his unit to remain until we leave. Nothing is definite, and our fate hangs in the fire for a few more days.

After my good night's sleep, it's a beautiful morning of the 5th. I had a breakfast of hotcakes, tomato juice, an orange, bread and butter, then delightfully hit the sack afterwards. Now it's pretty nearly dinner [lunch] time.

New boys fresh from the States are piling in. They are swarming over our old 1082 area in which we had built luxurious tents last June. Most of the arrivals are kids, or men not yet past that stage, and all are inexperienced at being overseas. Questions such as "When's inspection?" "Is the water rationed?" are typical boot questions and show their innocence. Although living in screened-in-tents, they use mosquito nets, many have beards, all signs of the novice. Recalling Finschaven almost twenty-one months I ago, I see that I was as awkward and naive. The 78th and 46th were there then, with a good part of their units at Los Negros and finding it hot (not in a meteorological sense). I also recall that after being in Finschaven only 1 1/2 months, we were talking of going home by Christmas at least. Lord help us, if we had known that we'd be here twenty-one months. If our optimism was our sustenance, it was also our greatest folly.

I hardly recognized Al Barios he has become so round and fat. Mrs. Myles from Hollywood has written. I fear I'll not see the West Coast for several years, and if I do, only for an instant. The boys are being shipped either through the Canal to the East Coast or to Frisco and immediately out. If I'm discharged I'd like to stop off on the West Coast, but I realize how anxious you are to see me. No doubt my own eagerness would get the better of me too.

11/6/45

Dear Mom,

Yesterday the discovery of a new person, in fact two new persons, relieved the emptiness of these days. In the chow hall at supper, I noticed a shirt on which "Worcester" was stencilled. On inquiring, I learned that the shirt had been borrowed from a fellow named Gilrein, who was handy. A lad about my age, Gilrein lived on Piedmont Street and knows most of the South High crowd I went to school with. Then a tall, dark fellow entered who, Gilrein pointed out, also came from Worcester, originally the east side, and now established on Somerset Street. A Jewish fellow, his name is Micky (Dick) Bell. His father operates the Tech Tailors, and knows [Cousin] Sol quite well. This Bell chap had chummed around with [Norman] Edinburgh, knew B. [Burton] Chase and Harold Ketcoff, and a host of others who ring familiar, some of whom you and Dad know. These fellows are part of the new group that arrived a few weeks ago. Gilrein is due to go home on the next ship, while Bell (who left for overseas from Gulfport four days after I did) is in the same miserable fix as I. Both are originally from the 118th battalion which was stationed at Gulfport through November 1943, while I was also there. I had never known or met either of them before. Ah, the unpredictable twist of fate.

We talked until one this morning about this, that, and the other thing. Bell rattled off all the acquaintances he knew, including some people we knew in common. He also browsed through an amazing gallery of his female admirers. Some I knew by sight, others more closely. The name of Rhoda Cutler was familiar, and though he knew her far better than I, our opinions of her coincided. Bell's probably the antithesis of me and more like what Ronnie will become, and we would like him to become. He's tall, dark and broad, amiable, and quite handsome. Until now a superficial thinker, he labors under a mental inferiority complex which he succeeds at hiding. He professes to have a flair for writing, and an appreciation of literature which I discern needs more development. Indeed, he's an extrovert for whom the social whirl and an abundance of girls is the greater part of living. I liked him from the first, and expect that it will continue. Like myself, he encourages our new friendship for similar reasons but for opposite things. I'm on a cultural pedestal, and he is on a social one. I've read more about life and he has experienced more.

If our friendship thrives, it will be the most convenient of any. We live only a fifteen minute walk apart back home. We are scheduling some hiking and swimming together, and maybe a trip to Manila. You may well hear more on this later.

11/9/45

Dear Mom,

Tomorrow morning I leave for Manila for a two day sojourn, mostly to see one or two close 113th mates. Four of us (all ex-113th boys) are taking the dredge's weapons carrier which is the first time on any trip that I'll be sure of transportation to and from my destination. In the old days, I'd take off for Manila, a carbine slung over my shoulder, wearing a blend of army and navy clothing. Boot restrictions, that seem ridiculous and aggravating after the freedom I've had, are now rigidly in effect. Each man must carry an array of documents, and our truck can have no liquor, firearms, women, or civilians aboard. We wear a suit of whites, and carry a fund of patience. But the Seabees, who always got away with more than anyone else, flatly refuse to dress up like Astor's stallion, so we wear only our G.I. issue greens. Dirty Manila does not call for wearing clean whites.

Rumors, all favorable, are furiously wafting about. You'd think that after twenty-one months we'd have learned to ignore them. At this stage we pretend to, where once we listened with obvious earnestness, but still listen and ponder. Still those 21 months have taught us to dismiss them more quickly.

After work at three this afternoon a couple of Filipino friends and I took the skiff and rowed to the mainland on the opposite shore. We talked, an endless delight when in their tongue. My Tagalog speech has become more fluent, although my vocabulary could be broader. Since few Americans, in fact almost none, know what little I know of the language, I'm rather an attraction to both young and old Filipinos. They goad me on, enjoying my mistakes, and so do I. Whenever a group of Americanos mingle with the people, I eventually end up as their spokesman. Sometimes, I put my knowledge to more subtle use. One of my mates has been unhappy over having broken up with an attractive damsel. Often, when a damsel rebukes her confused Americano, I pipe in with a Tagalog phrase that surprises her so completely, causing her to ring with laughter, that all is made just divine again. By God, she's won—and inquisitive. The fellows rib me good and proper. They call me Flip, and get as great a kick out of my conversations in Tagalog as do the Filipinos. At times a Filipino, forgetting in his enthusiasm that he's talking to a novice, accelerates his speech to that of a tobacco auctioneer. By then, I shake my head in despair and agree to everything said. Meanwhile, the Americano and Filipino bystanders think that I understood everything. So I've acquired a reputation as a linguist. Actually, when I listen to the people, it's like catching a leaf in the wind on a windy autumn day.

We struck a squall while coming back across the bay. Oh, what rowing and bailing and tossing about there was, so that I'm now comfortably weary. Now I have a spring under my sack for no other reason than to prepare myself for the luxuriousness of that so imminent bed back there.

An interesting book lying on my shelf is Milton Steinberg's[1] *The Making of the Modern Jew.*[2] Before retiring I think a chapter or two would be fine. Oh yes, I play pinochle now. One such game is in progress an arm's length away.

11/12-11/14/45

Dear Mom,

You shouldn't be writing to C.B.D. 1082 much longer. Before our leaving for Manila Saturday afternoon, a verbal order was issued stating that a good number (about a dozen) of the dredge crew would be sent to Samar[1] to fill the complement of another dredge (the *Indianapolis*). After returning this afternoon, we hear that the dredge will be beached and its entire crew (some twenty men) will be quartered here with the 102nd, either awaiting transfer into the 102nd, or to Samar, or home. All are in a quandary, which is nothing new.

Our weekend in Manila and vicinity was great. We saw those who remained of the 113th gang. Our arms are sore from the vigorous handshaking and our bodies are weary from the tiring ride home. I drove to just outside Nielson Airfield (over 100 miles) where the 113th was located and was dubbed Barney Oldfield[2] even though I never went over fifty. "Irish" Hurley, who drove back, went out of his way to find every hole and rut. There were four of us including Al Basil from, yep, Winchendon, Mass. and Tony (Guinea) Gianno from Staten Island.

After we got settled in Manila, the weapons carrier was available for anyone who wanted it for his personal use. So my old friend Ray Albrecht of the 113th, my host there, accompanied me to Sta. Mesa to visit my friends, the Riveras. After being used to thumbing on dusty roads and riding in everything, including dump trucks, it was quite wonderful having transportation so handy—just hop in and drive away.

The four of us received an ultra-cordial reception from the boys. When the usually reserved Raymond saw me drive up to the chow hall, he screamed and talked incessantly all evening. I stayed in his tent during the visit; we were continually together, going to chow, to a show, and visiting with my other friends. Most of the boys, many of whom I'd have liked to see, had already gone home. Like the 102nd, the 113th consists of the youngsters of the outfit, a mere remnant of what there once was. The officer staff was unrecognizable and few. No one worked, nor did they intend to.

I said my last goodbye to the Riveras. Again, they overwhelmed me with a marvelous reception, making it hard to leave. I doubt if I'll ever visit Manila again. For me everything there is done.

There goes the dredge. As I look down the bay, I can see a tug pulling her over to Olongopo for beaching. Very shortly I expect to be working for the 102nd.

Yesterday afternoon Mickey Bell (from Worcester) joined me on my short back country excursion to the swimming hole. We wandered barefoot through the fields, followed mysterious paths, and talked to the strangers who lived in huts that were scattered about. My mastery of the local dialect is now sufficient enough to carry on an interesting conversation. It has been very helpful breaking the ice with strangers.

I just ate and now for a siesta.

11/15/45

Dear Mom,

Something is about to break. Talk has us transferred to Guam, which is plausible. Whatever, the tension hereabouts forebodes something in the wind. And again, it doesn't look like home which is annoying. So many are leaving, so many, we hear, will be leaving. We meet very, very few now who have as much time here as ourselves. And almost boots are arriving, talking already of going home, then actually going. Our impatience, our griping, and our aggravation may be foolish, but can't be just turned off. They will be with us until our time to leave. Both you and I, Mom, are laboring under the weight of an oppressive absence. Our feelings are necessarily pent up. Contrary to how you expected me to react to the news, I don't enjoy reading that thirty-six veterans have entered Tech.

I have to let myself go a little. Instead of reading books, I play pinochle, and I write only you. I go to shows, regardless of their quality. Rules mean little to me. Everyone's morale is disintegrating.

With no mind to work, and not working, I'm beginning to show a few extra pounds. My friends in Manila brought it to my attention. At this rate, I'll soon regain all the pounds I lost between California and a month ago. No wonder, I eat bananas between meals, and have potatoes, butter, oranges, apples and meat twice daily. My stomach is continually full. Then there's little physical activity. All this has gone to extra deposits around my waist and on my face.

I was caught by surprise in the photos I sent two letters ago. The paper in my hand could be called "bathroom literature." My friend who took it has the negative. You may have observed that in all pictures of the past year my hair is parted. I've been grooming it that way since the summer of '44 in Hollandia. It seems that's how my dome wanted it, and with a little nurturing it has taken quite well. I'm sorry that you don't approve, but nothing can be done about it now.

Last week I sent home a package of books and some papers and some size 34 underwear, with more to come soon.

I believe I had written you about spending time with Ted Bagdikian down in Hollandia. We talked night after night of old times and familiar places. Well, he's made it. Good boy! I'm happy that he called you. If someone can bring me closer to you, you become closer to me.

There is a possibility that Ronnie may go to an extreme. So far I delight in your telling me about his good times and happy affairs. It's difficult at his stage. All you can do is watch and wait and hope, for your advice will merely glance off him. Yes, that's how you reared us boys, one the antithesis of the other. Have you forgotten, Dad, that you had a finger in the pie?

11/18/45

Dear Mom,

The awaited news has suddenly broken. Tomorrow morning 218 of us (18 from C.B.D. 1082) will board a navy A.P.A. transport to go to Guam. Packed and ready, I'm jotting this down before hitting the sack.

We are members of what is called a casual draft, for what purpose and to what ultimate destination is a mystery to officers and enlisted men alike. Only men with more than eighteen months overseas are included. Most like to think that we're actually headed U.S.-ward via Guam, but at best it's an optimistic guess. But there's some consolation in knowing that we'll be 1500 miles nearer home. The direction is right. Maybe we'll have enough momentum to carry us onward to the U.S.

Two close friends aren't leaving, one of them being Mickey Bell of Worcester. For some mysterious reason, men with general service rates—seamen, cooks and yeomen—(mine is a C.B. rate) must remain behind. We've agreed that whoever arrives home first will contact the other's folks. Micky is feeling pretty low now, but no one knows what will happen from here. His chances of going home are as good as mine.

I must get some sleep. We'll be off first thing in the morning. My old address, C.B.D. 1082, is now obsolete. I have no idea what my new one will be. Better not write until you hear from me.

Guam

Dear Mom,

After a hectic week aboard ship (USS *Oconto*), I'm on Guam, in the 53rd C.B. camp overlooking the much publicized (*Life* magazine) Apra harbor. The going was tough for the nearly two thousand aboard —tough, dirty and miserable. Now I'm fresh, clean, and shaven, sitting outside the tent cooled by a sea breeze. I'm the cleanest and coolest I've been for a week.

A week ago today we loaded body and gear at Subic, knowing our destination, but not what we would do there, or why we were going. Even our commanding officers seemed genuinely ignorant. The eighteen of us of C.B.D. 1082 were tagging along with the 102nd C.B.'s who had been our hosts since June. What a surprise to find Ray Albrecht, my old crony, and the rest of what was left of the 113th on board. The *Oconto* picked them up at Manila three days before arriving at Subic and they were as perplexed as we were. Everyone hoped that we'd bounce off Guam and head for a west coast port, but had a premonition that it wouldn't happen.

Second deck down, fourth bunk up, (of five bunks high) I bunked with the 113th boys in the bow of the navy troopship. The compartments were stuffy, unless you were fortunate enough to be near a wall to receive the weak waft of a breeze from fans located here and there on the bulkheads. Being near one, I slept well every night, but awoke each morning feeling clammy. By assignment, I was supposed to be in another compartment below the galley, but the heat there was infernal—96 degrees, 100% humidity. That and my desire to be with Ray sent me rushing to find a vacant bunk in the cooler bow compartment which I claimed without an argument. The deck below us, quartering Negroes, was still hotter and more crowded. Bothering no one by their actions, they stayed by themselves, and bothered many by their presence. There were a few words, all spoken by stupid whites, but aside from that all went smoothly.

The chow was excellent. We had never eaten so well aboard ship. There were three meals instead of the usual two that we had on the *West Point* and the succeeding *Libertys*, and the meals were wholesome and fresh: fresh meat, butter, eggs, and good bread without the accustomed weevils visible in the grain. But the chow lines were blasted long. No sooner were you through the breakfast line than you were forming the dinner line, that is if you could find the end of it. Many, becoming discouraged, waited for the confusion to clear and suffered the mortal pangs of hunger. Most, having been miserably seasick, hadn't eaten for two or more days and were hungry. The boots mooch into the line. Overseas living had taught most of us to go to the end. Then again, lines overseas haven't been nearly as bad as the infinite queues in the Stateside camps.

You may have noticed that my penmanship is back to its illegible scrawl. You see, I lost my guideline sheet, my comfortable chair, and the board that used to span its arms.

I know about the temperature of troopship compartments from my job on the dredge. A good many of us were assigned K.P., sweeping decks or to compartment cleaning details. Considering that not a passenger had a rate below third class P.O., in army terms not lower than a sergeant, my measly eagle offered no security against assignment to a dirty job. But my job turned out to be fine. During the hours from 8:00 AM to noon I had to take the air temperature in the dozen or so compartments. My superior was a C.P.O.[1] who had this done at the direction of the ship's doctor. Two on each shift performed this tremendous job, one to hold the thermometer, and the other to hold a pen and a piece of paper. We finished the entire business in less than an hour, and each succeeding day we managed to cut the time down still more by entering, should I say, exaggerated, if approximately reliable, data. After all, it was damned hot in every compartment no matter where it was. Eventually the Doc asked for no more data.

Two decks below the chow hall, in the very bottom of the hold, the men lived with the rats. But both preferred the night's rain and the penetrating tropical sea chill. One deck above the main deck were neat, airy staterooms for the officers and CPOs. Such luxury so close to such misery on the same boat, but not "in the same boat" was nothing new to us. I believe there were also railroad tracks on the *West Point*, one side for us, the other side, luxurious and comfortable where liquor flowed and smiling women and lounge chairs, and three squares, were a cursed spectacle to taunt us. It's no use talking like this; it accomplishes nothing. Your magazines and fancy advertisements and general news reports say nothing of these truths, such small things they are, so ridiculous, trivial, and rotten that they hardly deserve mention. It is for this reason that we yearn so persistently to be free once more to founder in the river of unknowable destiny where no orders are given that fate or one's will have not imperceptibly dictated.

And too there's comfort and virtue to be found in being a spectator. It's better for peace of mind. The G.I. has spectated a lot.

The second day out was ill-fated. The *Oconto* had no cargo in her holds other than us flimsy humans. And, having a fleet of Higgins' boats[2] laid across her decks, she was top heavy and bobbed around like a cork. As the season would have it, the sea was heavy so that even the straits through the P.I.'s[3] were not the usual glassy calm that we had witnessed seven months ago. Few were spared the demoralizing malady. The deck rails became sloppy and sour smelling, and the decks had to be hosed down frequently. Every bowl in the lavatory swam with vomit; even the urinals were plugged. Toilet troughs were unusable. What a gory, stinking mess everything was!

My first heave was comical. I was shaking the hand of a former mate whom I hadn't seen since last year. After returning to the States with Wolf's unfortunate outfit, he came back out again. Cutting our clasp short, I uttered "Excuse me," dove for the rail and retched out every undigested particle that was left in my stomach. I just missed a poor soul on the rail below, but who cared about aiming? I felt better after that. As I was lying in the bunk with a heavy head and feeling as low as I possibly could, my gorge swelled as the ship plunged deep again and I jumped from the height of four bunks to the deck, dashed up the stairway [companion way] and just made it to the lavatory where I vomited all that was left, a bitter, searing, green bile. Then, too weak to feel the toss and roll of the ship, I slept. When I awoke, my body ached and my mouth tasted foul, but my head and stomach were dormant. From then on things went better. I'll tell more about the voyage next letter.

Now, you and I are more concerned with my grand homecoming. Recently, the situation looked dark, but when things are darkest, actually, they are often bright. Usually, once impatience reaches its limits, a finale is imminent. Until now, going home has been an abstraction, an intangible—like a horizon. You can see it, but never reach it. Beautiful, stirring to the imagination, torturing, it recurs over and over like a sweet dream until finally it becomes real; it exists.

When they say that I'm due to go home soon, I'm unmoved. According to reliable talk, here are the facts. A plan of rotation is in effect on Guam. Those with eighteen or more months out here are being speedily sent home. We are supposed to be waiting for a Stateside-bound ship. We are told to do nothing, just wait. According to yesterday's Guam Navy Newspaper, before our arrival only a few were waiting. So, my folks, I expect next month, the month after or the month after that will do it. Were my mates to read the above statement, they'd dub me crazy because all believe in only a matter of days we'll be on board ship again.

Chester's [Nimitz][4] isle of Guam (although no longer his) is different from anywhere we've been. It's more like Stateside than we've seen in twenty-one weary months. The roads are white and smoothly paved. Mile on mile of Quonset huts are laid out in a geometrical pattern. Quaint houses have grass plots around them, the docks are concrete, there are stop signs, and Marine traffic cops, and only Americans are seen. Everywhere typical American primness, methodical efficiency, and planning are visible. The base is gigantic, dwarfing anything we've seen or heard of. It's truly the Pacific colossus beyond Pearl. Just behind our company area is a mound of a hill overlooking Apra and most of the base below. After climbing it this afternoon, I gazed in wonderment at what had been accomplished in less than a year and a half since it was recaptured.

I have a few duties to attend to. In case we suddenly embark in a hurry, I should wash all my clothes. I haven't washed clothes since the first week at Finschaven. It will be not only a task, but not done nearly as well as my laundry girl did it. She creased my trousers, folded my shirts neatly and smiled nicely when I paid her. That was a sweet kid. Sure, that bucket of clothes has me worried.

P.S. I don't know where to tell you to write. We have been given no new address.

11/27/45

Dear Mom,

The days have been gorgeous. The bad season is past. On this second day, after a full night of clean, sound sleep, I already feel very much at home. I had a much needed haircut (closer than usual), gorged myself on ice cream and Coke from the store, repacked my seabag more firmly, and read a portion of *The History of Rome Hanks*.[1] We're still not working, unusual for newly received Seabees. We hear that tomorrow we must move to what is called a receiving area. Widespread talk of our embarkation within a fortnight,[2] which seems to have a basis, has me in an internal dither.

I haven't seen hide nor hair of the 113th since Friday when they left the ship, and we stayed behind until yesterday (Monday). It was a great relief after they debarked. When all were aboard, since everyone preferred to sit on deck, finding a place to sit was a wait-and-pounce proposition. Sitting on winches and boats was prohibited. Once you secured a convenient spot, even if hard as steel to your rear and back, you hated to leave it and give it up. Sunday night I squatted through a show Indian fashion. I'd never have endured the ordeal were the show not as good as the one we watched, "The Keys to the Kingdom."[3] After standing, I ached and creaked all over, although during the show I wasn't aware of my tiring limbs.

Unlike the Philippines, where the natives were free to roam our camp, there are hardly any natives about here. I suppose they are confined to their own section of the island. However, a few youngsters do wander through the camp. Looking exactly like Filipinos, they have less of an accent. You probably know as much about them as I do. They're called Chamorros.[4]

The 200 boys of the 102nd (including ourselves of 1082), all with twenty-one months overseas, are raising havoc with the 53rd boys who have only eighteen to six months overseas. We've created a run on the ship's store, invaded the other concessions, refused to take orders from superiors who have less time in, and taunted the comparative boots. The height of annoyance has occurred in sick bay where fifteen "clapped up" (gonorrhea infected) boys marched in, demanding attention. The disease had never appeared on the island before. Philippine whoredom has certainly left its mark and reputation on Guam. Back on Luzon the disease was considered no more serious than a common cold, although concentrated, of course, in an awkward region. So the 102nd has acquired the reputation of being a rough, tough lot, unmanageable, wilful and deserving to be sent home.

This afternoon we were informed that C.B.D. 1082 no longer exists. I have no idea what my address is. I doubt if we have one which may indicate that we're slated to embark. But my letters should be reaching you regularly. I'll make every effort to write daily until I leave, and, if I remain, I'll advise you when to resume writing. Please don't write until I let you know.

My bag is packed and ready. When I left Hollandia, I had a bulky footlocker, two seabags, and a handbag full of clothes and personal articles. Like Dad, I'm a collector of ridiculous items. Now, I'm down to one bag, and it's doggone convenient. I gave my clothes away, threw a mess of junk into a barrel, and now carry only slightly more than regulation requires.

Well, folks, with a sigh that comes after a job is done, I'm just waiting, and so are you. Yes, it's about over and done. The greater portion of my experience is past, suitable for idle reminiscing and retelling. How lucky I am that I can reminisce without fear of horror. How lucky I am!

11/28/45

Dear Mom,

Our camp lies in a miniature valley. Tonight at the show, as I looked through the tropical evening mist at the low hills under a brilliantly white moon, it was easy to imagine the land was snow-covered. But this time it was a delight, because I shall see that blanket of snow before the year is over. We embark by week's end — so we are told.

It's both a day and night dream about to become real — impossible to believe, even after being told. I can't help lacking faith in such a sweet fate. Not until I feel steel decks and a ship's roll will I truly believe it's happening.

Tonight, after hearing the news of going home, I sat through a showing of "Since You Went Away" a second time for nostalgia's sake. You can imagine how much more I enjoyed it this time. I laughed much harder at the wholesome humor, and tears came easier during the happier episodes.

In a way, going home is cruel. In past months when I watched the boys leaving, I had the satisfaction of knowing that at least I wouldn't have to endure the cold. But endure it I will; I welcome it; it's a meager sacrifice. Our warmth for each other is bound to reduce those wintry blasts to torrid breezes. But to play safe, though I assure you I doubt if I'll have to, I plan to withdraw enough cash to buy a warm suit and an overcoat.

Well, my folks, it's time to sleep and dream those near-far dreams of imminent reality.

[Hughie's 21st birthday] 11/30/45

Dear Mom,

This, I think, will be my last letter from overseas. Exactly two years ago tomorrow — I remember it distinctly — I was on a train pulling out of Gulfport wondering where I'd be in a year or two. Back home today is only the 29th. Three years ago this week were the Cocoanut Grove tragedy,[1] the B.C. upset,[2] and Uncle Bill and Grandma visited us. Do you remember? And now, two, three years later, the happiest moments of my life are about to be realized.

This entire week, during which I've been idle and bored from the unnerving tedium, like a man, yes, a man now with his job done, I've been reexamining my work and pondering the questions of the past now answered.

I haven't seen much of the island in the five days I've been here. When at any moment we may be called to pack up and leave, we'd rather not risk leaving camp. Yesterday, there was a false alarm. After we packed, the orders were changed; however, most of us are remaining ninety percent packed anyway. We are allowed one seabag and a handbag. Our duffel bags which have been with us since boot must be discarded along with our mattresses and pillows.

News that there will be an excess of servicemen stranded on the West Coast through Christmas made many jolly chins drop. "By God, we'll hitchhike, then," is the common threat, and by golly, I predict that's the way it will be. There's a picture of snow-bound cars from Wisconsin in the Navy News sheet. We don't know whether to enjoy or abhor the prospect.

I'm both happy and sad that this will be the last letter of a comforting series of letter writing. Every letter came from my heart and was addressed to yours (via the M.U. Co.) simply and dearly as M&O&M.

My love again, Hughie

STATESIDE

Seattle, Washington

Telegram from Seattle, Washington:

1945 Dec 15 AM 7:15

To Mrs B AARON
67 KING ST PHONE 2-0255 WCSTR
DREAM OVER STOP ANOTHER COMING TRUE SOON STOP STILL A
WHILE TO WAIT HERE STOP ALLS WONDERFUL STOP
MY LOVE STOP HUGHIE

Morning 12/15/45

Dear Mom,

Being here is a sweet thing to contemplate. Though weary from standing in line, pushing about, and anxiety, I couldn't get to sleep right away. My mind brimmed with the happiness of realization. And now it's not so hard to wait when waiting is only a matter of days. What are days when compared to months and years of waiting? My patience is drained because these are such crucial days, but this impatience is far more bearable than the nearly futile impatience over there.

Of course, everyone would like to be home for Christmas. There's a real effort being made to get us there by then. However, we don't know what or when transportation will be available. Meanwhile, we reside in warmly heated naval barracks just ten blocks from the heart of the city. And quite a city this is — more impressive than New Orleans. Compared to what we've been used to, the facilities are heavenly. The chow is elegant. Before I left Subic Bay I weighed 169 when tropically nude. [pre-Seabees weight: 150] Last night in full uniform I also weighed that, indicating that I probably lost a few pounds on the voyage. With milk flowing liberally and foods long since missing from our diet plentiful, I should thrive and be able to combat the cold more easily.

It seems that the Seattle natives find the cold as repugnant and hard to take as we. The weather has been unusually frigid, not only for this region, but for the entire nation. Wherever I've been — from Gulfport to the P.I.'s — the weather has been unusual. I now assume that the unusual is usual, what else? But the cold hasn't been as fearful as I expected. The fourth and fifth days out were the worst. A wool lined jacket borrowed from Ray which I wore over a tropical jacket over a velvety sweat shirt over a regular shirt over a skivvy shirt, sustained me beautifully. Now I feel invigorated and at home in the Seattle air.

We are being issued a pea jacket free of charge today. Last night I wore my blue uniform, still intact through it all, and my infamous army jacket. Strictly against regulation, it was an appalling combination but mighty necessary.

I walked down the street dreamily gazing and smiling at the civilians, curious and awed by the beauty of the delicate white complexions of American girls. It was almost as if I had never seen such creatures before. Everything was both strange and familiar: strange in my recent life, familiar from a life more distant and nostalgic. At times it was as if I had never left the country, as if I went to sleep in L.A. and woke up in Seattle and the South Pacific was only a dream, or some concoction of the imagination. There's a kind of continuity between L.A. and Seattle with no interim. Except that now I see things with a strange, childlike awe. This awe, which applies to everything I see, is a distinct pleasure. Last night, I was ridiculously overwhelmed by it and had no idea how to handle it. So I returned to the barracks in time for taps, instead of staying out until reveille, discouraged with myself, overcome with unfathomable pangs of sorrow.

We are permitted to leave camp every night and our daily duties are academic. Despite arriving here weary early in the afternoon, I had to go out last night to telegraph home on the same day I arrived. Although there's a pay station in the barracks, I elected not to phone, not because of the expense, but because I couldn't deal with the presence of your voice and not you. After I adjust to things, I may yet muster up enough courage to phone.

Under the circumstances the voyage was fine—extraordinarily short and comfortable. The ship was big, bigger by 110 feet than the *West Point*, and fast and famous. Constantly ahead of schedule, we had to slow down to an agonizing 14 1/2 knots not to arrive too soon. So we had big, fast ships both ways. We aren't pikers, that's for sure. Examining the armored splendor of the *Hornet* [an aircraft carrier, the second by that name] kept us occupied the first few days and the monotony was considerably relieved by three movie showings a day and frequent games of pinochle. I listened earnestly to a roundtable discussion presided over by the captain on the current labor squabbles. Managing to take a hot shower every day, easy to do on this ship, I kept clean which is essential to being comfortable.

I have no address because my station here is temporary. I'll do all the writing and avidly.

My love to all of you, Hughie

AFTERWORD

On reading the letters that so openly and honestly delineate the dreams, frustrations, confusions, ambitions and hangups of my springtime, I've been fascinated from the vantage point of one who is approaching winter. As I traveled through life, the driving forces of my youth faded and seemingly became lost, so that over the years I had the illusion that the things I did and the choices I made were of the moment and had no basis in the past. But, of course, they did. The letters have resurrected them, such that I can now clearly see many of the hidden reasons behind my later actions.

Perhaps you are curious to learn what did happen to this callow lad after he became an adult civilian and had to make his own way. After discharge in February 1946, he lived at home and in the fall entered Worcester Polytechnic Institute to become a chemical engineer, but after the first year the curriculum was too narrow for him. As much as he loved science, he yearned to learn more. And, as his letters indicated that he thought he would, he found living at home stressful.

Confused and directionless, he spent the summer as an assistant waterfront counselor at a boys' camp in Maine, where he met an older fellow counselor, Curt Edgett, a social studies teacher at the Laboratory School of The University of Chicago. After Curt described the exciting broad curriculum being taught at the university under Chancellor Robert Hutchins'[1] aegis, he took the entrance exam as soon as his term at the camp was over and was accepted along with thousands of other ex-G.I.'s who were flooding into the nation's colleges. Having matured from their war experience, they were a serious and hard-working lot, just as his letters predicted they would be, and in making many friends among them, he was in his element.

Coming to love the city of Chicago and the university, he had several Nobel prize winners either in class or in the lecture hall, including Enrico Fermi[2] in freshman physics. Among scores of great works, he studied firsthand Dostoyevsky,[3] Forster,[4] Aristotle,[5] Marx[6] and Toynbee,[7] had Anton Carlson[8] in biology, Reuel Denny[9] (who encouraged him, in vain, to write) in composition and Norman MacLean[10] (author of *A River Runs Through It*) in Shakespeare. He attended David Riesman's[11] and Robert Redfield's[12] lectures. And the city of Chicago, its Art Institute, Museum of Science, symphony orchestra, ballet, opera and foreign film theaters fed his need for culture.

His inability to concentrate, which he complained about in the letters, continued to dog him. Every exam was an ordeal. He managed to pass each time, but he sought psychological help to discover the root of his problem and after a lengthy stint of therapy was able to regain control over his will and his future course.

What about girls, his avoidance of women? Well, he got over that at the university where he became smitten in succession with two women students, (including a girl of Greek descent whose parents tried, unsuccessfully, to break up the relationship), and after graduating, a third young woman. But he didn't marry until he was past thirty, and after returning East.

And what about his lack of vices? College life quickly changed that as he took up drinking coffee, beer, and wine, smoked a pipe, later graduated to cigarettes, and ceased being a virgin.

After graduating, he got a job in the mail room of the *Chicago Sun-Times*, where he rubbed elbows with the editors and the local columnists. Soon, he graduated to writing the weather reports and was in line to become a cub reporter, when he began dating the managing editor's secretary who convinced him that in order to maintain their relationship, that is her expensive taste, he must earn more money than the measly stipend paid by the *Sun-Times* or any other newspaper. Forthwith, he secured a better paying job in industry as an order picker for a large manufacturer of lampshades. Being an efficient and conscientious worker, he quickly moved up to become supervisor of an 80 woman department. It was here that he discovered his ability to lead and develop innovative methods for increasing productivity. But after a year he grew disenchanted with the president of the company who had an unpredictable temper and an on-the-job drinking habit.

He then went to work in the national office of a large building materials corporation in the Loop,[13] which bored him, but there he met a brilliant, attractive Catholic co-worker (whose parents wouldn't allow him to enter their home) and fell in love. She eventually moved to her own apartment where he stayed over on weekends. The relationship continued after he moved to a plastics packaging company as supervisor of a flexographic printing (on plastics) operation. Meanwhile, back home his father had had a heart attack, and his parents asked him to return to take over the upholstering business, a possibility that he had considered in several letters. He agreed, provided his brother Ronnie, by then a trained interior decorator, join him.

From the letters it's obvious that he had a keen understanding of how business works, which he had learned by helping his father. Having worked for others for almost four years, he ached to be independent and on his own. His parents' proposal seemed a good opportunity, especially since he knew the business. On his proposal of marriage to his paramour, she accepted, provided that they not leave Chicago. Unwilling to pass up his father's offer, he left for the East, hoping that she would soon follow. But her career and position in the corporation were too important to her, and their relationship waned. One year later he met a Jewish girl, of whom his parents approved, and married her.

Within six months of his son's taking over the business, his father, fully recovered, became active in the business again. But father and son clashed. The father, a product of the Great Depression, having limited capital, refused to spend money on advertising and investing in a better property for displaying their wares. He gradually took over more of the responsibilities that his son had initially taken on. It was then, in a bitter argument, the son learned that his parents had had an ulterior motive when they asked that he come East and take over the business: their real purpose was to break up the relationship with his Catholic girlfriend.

He left for a job that took him to a neighboring state, with a company that had poor labor relations and was badly managed. For the next five years, now married, he held one job after another, seemingly unable for a variety of reasons to find one that made him happy. It was obvious that he had to be on his own, but without capital or connections, or knowledge of a particular field, no opportunity would or could present itself.

During periods of unemployment he filled his time by writing plays and movie reviews, gratis, for a local weekly. His reviews received a favorable public response, but the paper still wouldn't pay. When CBS's "Playhouse 90" expressed an interest in one of his plays, he refused to make the changes they requested, bringing the possibility of a new career to an end before it began. Soon after his first child was born, unable to meet his mortgage payments, he became desperate and joined the management program of a restaurant chain. This involved cleaning bathrooms, mopping floors, cooking, waiting on the trade and putting in long hours. His morale was at a low ebb. He was baffled as to when and how things went wrong.

Through friends he secured a job as an expediter of a coated fabric manufacturer, a job that bored him, which lasted a year, then as manager of a factory that made plastic toys. This job extended the knowledge of plastics that he had acquired earlier on jobs in Chicago and in the Northeast. The owner, his boss, was difficult, and they strongly disagreed on several moral issues concerning business practices. However, since part of his job was purchasing, it gave him the connection he needed to join an up-and-coming plastics materials company for whom he became their first New England salesman. At last, he had found the niche that made him happy, and a field at which he could become expert. Six years later, at the age of 42, having learned the ins and outs of a booming business in a young industry, he joined three others in a plastics materials venture that eventually grew to two plants and over one hundred employees.

After almost twenty years as CEO of his company, and ultimately the sole majority owner with his employees as partners, he felt that he had had enough of business and, were he to sell, enough money to live out the rest of his life. He could have expanded the business — the potential was still enormous — but he wished to return to doing what he insisted he couldn't do as a young man in letter after letter: write. Three years before the business was sold (to one of his former employers), and with day to day responsibility delegated to his employees, he wrote his first short story which he dedicated to his oldest (of three children) daughter on her wedding day, and began writing a novel based on his experience overseas in the Seabees. Each evening after work, from seven to nine, he holed up in his study and wrote. The novel and short story (as part of a collection) have been published.

His wife and friends were skeptical of his retiring. Wouldn't he be bored? Wouldn't he miss all the excitement of running a business, of being in charge of things? What will he do with his time? "Write," he replied, convincing no one.

After retiring to Cape Cod at age 60 with his wife of thirty years, his marriage, which had, during its last twenty years, been at best a truce for the sake of the kids, fell apart, and a divorce ensued. Still he kept on writing, having produced a couple of dozen short stories, another novel, and several long and short non-fiction pieces; all have been published.

I find it ironical that I have come full circle and taken up writing. I had forgotten those early days as a correspondent when my father proposed having the letters published and Helen Lyon Malter importuned me to make use of my "talent." Of course, I considered it absurd, because, as the letters said, I thought my ability fell short, compared with that of others whose works I was reading. During my years of struggle to make a living, I had writer's block, but that ended once I succeeded in business and began to feel that I had worth after all. Perhaps this offers others a clue to the cause of that universal malady.

In hindsight, I now understand that my consummate drive to succeed, to be the best in whatever I did, got me off the more risky track of becoming a writer. Having learned how to run a business from my father, it was an option that seemed to offer a surer road to success. I also see, with a certain sadness, why I failed to take advantage of the generous opportunities that the Malters and others had offered me. I had to win by myself, refusing consideration of any help. The very self-publication of this book bears witness to such a compulsion, even into my older years. (I rejected the idea of submitting the manuscript to commercial publishers, although several likely candidates were suggested by friends and relatives.) Clearly, what we end up doing is the confluence of the many facets of our personality.

Although fiction challenges me more, non-fiction concerning a subject that I know from long experience, business, turns me on. After writing a letter to the editor of *The Wall Street Journal*, the newspaper called and asked for permission to use the letter as an article in their Manager's Journal column—and compensate me. Of course I was flattered, and when the editor asked if there were more whence that came, I said I thought there were, and subsequently for the next three years inundated him with scores of articles, of which, at this time, nineteen have appeared in print.

Of the many articles that the paper has chosen not to publish for one reason or another, often having nothing to do with the merit of the piece, the editor suggested that I put them into a book. After working up a manuscript, I submitted it to several publishers who found it wanting, especially its narrative format, which the readers of *The Wall Street Journal*, many of whom call and write after each article appears, tell me they enjoy so much. So I self-published the book, (*Business Not As Usual*) and despite little effort and less desire to promote it, it has made a profit.

In addition to finding the career that for so long I had dismissed because of my feelings of inadequacy, I also found the woman of my dreams, an artist, a painter of landscapes and portraits in oil, who like a sister-in-arms supports my work and encourages me to publish it myself. She has decided that the proceeds from the sale of her paintings be put to that cause. Although her paintings are wonderful, and my writing is ordinary, she insists that one art must sustain the other. I have agreed to this, but the benefit is secondary to the love that her gesture reveals. It is her way of repaying me for providing the environment that makes her art possible. Whether my material is ordinary or not, I must write. I'm driven to do it much as I seemed to be driven to write in the springtime of my life when I had no idea that a half century later those words would be read again.

It was upon my mother's death in 1979 that I found among her possessions a box containing the letters, and not one missing from the nearly one thousand that I had written home. For years I had stored the box away, assuming them to be mediocre at best; after all, I was a boy of 18 — how worthwhile could they be? Two summers ago, during a gap in my fiction writing, I began reading them and was stunned to find letter after letter well written, painfully honest, and deeply expressive. Indeed, I had used words whose meanings I've since forgotten and had to look up. I wish I could write in the same vein today, but I was a different person then, a third person whom I hardly know except from what he has written. And for all this, for keeping my words safe, for my very life, I owe it all to my mother.

July 1996
Cushing, Maine

[In the August 31, 1995 issue of *The Wall Street Journal* the author's 19th article in that publication, entitled "Witness to the Good War," appeared. Rebutting the revisionist version of World War II, the article quoted, in part, several of the letters herein.

The author's second novel (1995), and a non-fiction travel journal (1996) have been published under a pseudonym.]

ACKNOWLEDGEMENT

Given the nature of researching the NOTES, some information, except where specifically cited, has been paraphrased from various sources. The editor, however, would especially like to thank—for their invaluable assistance, expertise, and patience—the following research librarians at the Arlington (Massachusetts) Public Library: Jennifer De Remer, Nancy Gentile, Rosalind Kantrowitz, Catherine Kiah, Robert James, Oree Malio.

NOTES TO LETTERS BY DATES

by Ramon de Rosas

(with assistance from members of
the Arlington Public Library and the author)

Williamsburg, Virginia

7/6/43

1. A .30 caliber, breech-loading, magazine-fed rifle, operated by a bolt, adopted by the U.S. Army in 1903 and replaced by the Garand rifle (M-1) in World War II.
2. U.S. Marine base, Virginia, used mostly for training Marine officers. The F.B.I. also uses it for various training operations.
3. City in central Massachusetts, population about 130,000 in 1943.

7/8/43

1. A covering for the lower leg, in the form of a cloth or leather gaiter or cloth strip wound spirally.
2. Wooden sandals used in the common shower.

7/9/43

1. Accompanied by a stirring bugle call.
2. Absent Without Official Leave.

7/10/43

1. Made of heavy green cloth in herringbone, introduced in early 1940s for use by Marines in combat.
2. United Service Organizations, providing social services and entertainment for military personnel for purposes of bolstering morale.
3. In 1943 a top-rated comedian of theater, radio, and film. He was tireless in his entertainment of troops in World War II (and later in Korea and Viet Nam).
4. Premier dancer of theater and film (from 1920s to 1960s), noted for his classic movies teamed with Ginger Rogers, dancer and film star.
5. Allied invasion of Sicily in July 1943 was geared toward freeing Mediterranean shipping from Axis harassment, diverting German strength from the Russian front, and increasing pressure on Italy to desert. It proved to be some of the fiercest fighting of the war. (Source: C.L. Sulzberger *et al, The American Heritage Picture History of World War II,* 1966.)
6. Wartime security imposed strict censorship on all military information on troop deployment or movement.

7/12/43

1. Clean-cut.
2. Leading Worcester newspaper.
3. Kitchen Police (i.e. performing various duties in kitchen).
4. Noted for its intensity and—some would say—its harshness. Marines swear by it; others notably enemies on the battlefield swear at it.
5. For purposes of obtaining instant obedience, the military must needs mold the collective mind.

7/13/43

1. Labeled "The King," Clark Gable was one of the most popular cinema actors in Hollywood history, from the early 1930s until his death in the late 1950s. Women loved him and men admired him for his virile movie roles. He was awarded the Distinguished Flying Cross for combat action in World War II.
2. "Hell Divers," 1932
3. A light semi-automatic or automatic .30 caliber rifle of relatively limited range.
4. Popular young singer and actress with operatic voice. A child discovery in the 1930s, her film career lasted into the 1950s.
5. "The Amazing Mrs. Halliday" (or "His Butler's Sister"), 1943.

7/14/43

1. A friend back home. The author is unable to recall him.
2. Located in East Virginia; it is about forty miles long and flows into Chesapeake Bay.
3. North American quail with distinctive call, which inspired lyrics for Johnny Mercer to a 1930s Hanghen tune of the same title: "Bob White."

7/16/43

1. A U.S. Naval Reserve officer training program through which volunteers received military training while completing their bachelor's degree.
2. Small island in San Francisco Bay: site of a Federal prison (1943-1963), incarcerating the most hardened criminals such as Al Capone.

7/17/43

1. Largest island in the Solomon Islands in the SW Pacific, where the 1st Marine Division inflicted—in fierce jungle fighting—the first loss to the Japanese in World War II, setting in motion Japan's irreversible slide toward defeat.
2. Aunt Henrietta, the author's father's younger sister, a dark haired beauty.
3. Sadie, the author's aunt, his mother's half sister, a most congenial person.

4. Bill, the author's uncle, his mother's half brother, a tall, good looking, good natured man.

5. Grandma, the author's mother's mother, a controlling woman, wife of four husbands. After she had pawned Mom's diamond ring that had been used as collateral for a loan to Dad, Dad refused to visit her forever.

6. African-American, whose hostility against them by white southerners dates back to slavery and the Civil War.

7. Before and during World War II the U.S. military was segregated by race.

7/18/43

1. Town in SE Virginia: scene of the surrender of the British general Cornwallis to George Washington in 1781 that ended the Revolutionary War.

2. Means "Sons of the Covenant," the oldest and largest Jewish service organization.

3. The whole body of Jewish religious literature, including the Scripture and the Talmud, among others.

7/19/43

1. Philanthropist (1874-1960) who constructed Rockefeller Center and donated the land used by the United Nations in New York.

2. College in Virginia, named after William III of Orange (Netherlands), King of England (1689-1702) and Mary II, Queen of England (1689-1694). They ruled jointly.

3. The first permanent colonial settlement in America (1607), named after James I, King of England (1603-1625).

7/20/43

1. Webster Lake, a large lake in Webster Massachusetts, also known by a long Indian name meaning "You fish on your side and I'll fish on mine."

2. The largest, and most elegant hotel in Worcester, later made into apartments.

3. Aunt Pearl, Mom's younger sister, a remarkable pianist who could play a song after first hearing it. She was always interested in, and supportive of the author.

7/21/43

1. Aunt Ida, wife of the author's uncle, his father's older brother, Hyman.

2. The Gallants, the Catholic family—mother, father, daughter and son— of the author's best friend in high school, Lionel (Lenny).

3. Uncle Louie, the author's father's older brother who operated a small department store in downtown Boston. Father of Evelyn, the author's older, beauteous, raven-haired cousin.

4. Bob, the author's first cousin, Ida's and Hymie's son, born six months before the author in 1924. The two cousins had little in common and were never friends.
5. A system of signaling by the use of two flags, one held in each hand: The letters of the alphabet are represented by the various positions of the arms.

7/22/43

1. Removal of the gallbladder due to gallstones.
2. Johnson Fulgoni, a close friend, and commercial artist, several years older than the author. He was a young man with a marvelous sense of humor and a positive attitude toward life. A victim of an auto accident, he walked with a severe limp.

7/23/43

1. Lionel (Lenny), the author's closest friend while in high school. Always exhibiting an artistic flair, after the war he went on to become a commercial artist in Worcester.
2. Aunt Anna, Dad's younger sister, an accomplished pianist, and a manicurist who worked in the Park Plaza Hotel, Boston's largest at the time. A beauty, she never married, but had many boy friends.
3. Designating or of a movement in Judaism that seeks to normalize rationalist thought with historical Judaism, stressing its ethical aspects and not requiring strict observance of traditional Orthodox ritual.
4. A late 1930s abbreviated handshake in which palms touch quickly, accompanied by the expressions "Give me some skin man!"

7/24/43

1. The author's father operated a small custom upholstering shop.
2. A widely recognized art school, located in Boston, Massachusetts.

7/26/43

1. Lil, the author's much older first cousin, daughter of his father's oldest brother. Keenly interested in the author's future, she was his mentor, the person to whom he confided when he was troubled. It was she that advised the author's mother to name him Hugh after his great-grandmother, Hannah. Wife of Sol, she had two sons, Nason and Mark, and a daughter, Isa.
2. Herman Riccius, an unmarried man in his sixties, (he shared an apartment with his sister) an executive with a textile manufacturing company, befriended the author in the shower room of the local YMCA. A lover of music and art, he often invited the author to accompany him to concerts (the fall Worcester Music Festival held in the Worcester Memorial Auditorium) and to view his newly acquired paintings.

7/27/43

1. A hot breakfast cereal.
2. Well known laundry soap of the time.
3. Commonly called a "G.I. Shower," in which a non-bather was pounced upon by other members of his unit who "scrubbed" him with dry brushes.

7/28/43

1. The author does not recall this person.
2. Often the author took advantage of his brother's smaller size during boxing bouts.

7/31/43

1. Prices for haircuts in the 1990s range from $7-$10.

8/1/43

1. Sol, Cousin Lil's husband, an orthodox Jew, and a pharmacist who owned a successful Worcester neighborhood drugstore. After classes during his high school years, the author worked behind Sol's soda fountain.
2. Harold, a young pharmacist, and friend, in Sol's drugstore. The author and Harold often went canoeing together on Lake Quinsigamond.
3. Cousin Lil's mother, widowed when a middle aged woman..
4. Shirley, wife of the author's cousin Eddie, Lil's younger brother.
5. Eddie, Cousin Lil's brother, son of Morris, the author's father's oldest brother, and his wife Eva.
6. Joe Ducharme, a man in his late fifties at the time, also a pharmacist at Sol's drugstore. He was always kind to and solicitous of the author.

8/3/43

1. The author does not recall who this was.

Camp Endicott
Davisville, Rhode Island

8/7/43

1. Women Appointed for Voluntary Emergency Service, the women's branch of the U.S. Navy during World War II.

8/11/43

1. Wartime restrictions on train, travel, gas rationing, combined with the rubber shortage, curtailed greatly both public and private transportation.

8/18/43

1. The author does not recall this person.

8/22/43

1. The author does not recall this person.

8/23/43

1. All service personnel when on leave had to wear their uniforms during World War II. A famous cartoonist of the time, Virgil Partch, has an army M.P. addressing a naked man sitting on a stool in a bar: "Why aren't you in uniform?" he barks.

8/25/43

1. Although the author doesn't recall the details of either letter, he would expect that Mr. Aldrin's letter would be warmer and more personal, reflecting his personality. Mr. Aldrin was magnetic, charming and well liked, while Mr. Beeber, much respected and also liked, was mostly business and formal. Both men were prime leaders for their teachers and the student body.
2. In the military, personnel are invariably addressed by their last names.
3. Famous radio news broadcaster and world traveler, who, among his other achievements, documented in dispatches and on film the exploits of T.E. Lawrence (Lawrence of Arabia) during WW I.
4. "Take it Hugh," was Thomas's expression when turning over the microphone to his announcer, Hugh.

8/29/43

1. A popular, low priced cafeteria chain.
2. Musical comedy.
3. One of the great character actors of the American cinema, noted for his unflappable demeanor, clipped mustache, and rapid fire speech, delivered with clarity and emphasis.
4. Leading lady of the time, who combined grace, charm, and beauty.
5. At a time when over 30 million people a week attended the cinema, the movie houses were built in splendor as secular cathedrals to accommodate the motion picture worshipers.
6. Starring Joseph Cotton and Deanna Durbin, who sings the patriotic song "Say a Prayer for the Boys Over There."
7. The term "wolf" was used to describe a womanizer. Here it is applied to overly flirtatious women.

8/30/43

1. Daily and Sunday paper published in Boston, Massachusetts.
2. Named after Antonio Stradivari (1644-1737), violin maker whose violins, because of their incomparable tone, have become priceless.
3. Latin for "Hail, Mary," a prayer—here set to music—to the Virgin Mary, used in the Church.
4. An opera by the French composer Georges Bizet (1838-1875), set in Spain, famous for its stirring music and passionate themes.

5. Metropolitan Opera diva who starred in Hollywood operettas of the time.
6. A popular orchestra leader who featured a large choral group — "Fred Waring and His Pennsylvanians."

8/31/43
1. During World War II for security reasons, mail, especially from war zones or facilities of vital importance, was routinely censored.

En route To Parts Unknown

6:40 PM 9/15/43
1. Huge body of water in the Midwest. One of the Great Lakes.

5:10 PM 9/16/43
1. Slang for African-American who worked the cotton fields.

2:30 PM 9/17/43
1. Nightly band presentation, featuring the big name orchestras of the era, sponsored by Camel cigarettes.
2. Radio show "spotlighting" top bands of the era.

Gulfport, Mississippi

8:10 PM 9/18/43
1. Seaport in Texas, on an island (Galveston Island).
2. A constant concern during World War II.

9/19/43
1. Popular radio soap opera of the era.

9/20/43
1. Entertainers of radio, cinema, and music sold war bonds at rallies throughout the country.
2. A WWII thriller, starring Bette Davis and Paul Lukas, who, as an anti-Nazi living in the U.S., is hunted by German agents bent on returning him to Germany.

9/21/43
1. Movie biography of the late New York Yankee legend Lou Gehrig.
2. Cinematic icon whose career from the late 1920s to the early 1960s embodied the American virtues of stoicism, integrity, and quiet — inarticulate — courage.

3. An Academy Award winning character actor whose range of roles is both brilliant and astonishing.
4. Small technical engineering college, located in Worcester, Massachusetts.
5. Ted Bagdikian, son of a minister, striving to make a career in piano, a contemporary and good friend of the author's.

9/22/43

1. Newly invented in WWII, ra(dio) d(etecting) a(nd) r(anging): using transmitted and reflected radio waves for detecting a reflecting object such as air or seacraft, determining its direction, speed, distance, or height.

9/23/43

1. Commonly called "close order drill" in which a platoon moves in unison to the commands of the drill instructor.
2. The "trick" is to squeeze the trigger, never pulling it.

9/26/43

1. All African-American cast in an exuberant musical.
2. Jazz singer, fabulously beautiful, gifted with a velvet voice, still active.

1:00 PM 9/28/43

1. Prolific American woman writer of historical and philosophical novels.
2. Miss Caldwell's first novel (1938).

7:15 PM

1. Jewish New Year, celebrated on the 1st and 2nd days of Tishri (the first month of the Jewish year).
2. One of the Jewish High Holidays, the Day of Atonement, a fast day observed on the 10th day of Tishri: Leviticus 16:29-34.

9/31/43

1. Mr. Cleavitt, a man in his forties, gym instructor at the Worcester YMCA. The author often assisted him instructing young boys.
2. Miss Phillips, high school teacher of English with whom the author often clashed, causing him to become discouraged and resulting in the only C grade received during his high school career of receiving almost all As.
3. A Jesuit college, located high on a hill in Worcester, Massachusetts.
4. Ivy League college, located in Hanover, New Hampshire.

10/8/43

1. The prayer of atonement recited in synagogues at the opening of the Yom Kippur eve services (also the traditional music to which this is sung).

1. Young Men's Hebrew Association.
2. One can see how long ago this was.

1. The author does not recall this person.
2. A meeting place exclusively for servicemen who danced with movie actresses and socialized with movie stars who served snacks and washed dishes.
3. "I Left My Heart at the Stagedoor Canteen."
4. Popular radio singer of the era, noted for her patriotic renderings, especially "Good Bless America."

1. Joe Ducharme, friend of the author's, Cousin Sol's pharmacist, who was diagnosed as having terminal cancer.
2. Mr. Harlow Lazott was the author's high school physics teacher and mentor. He encouraged the author to take up science as a career. While recovering from an operation for a brain tumor, he was visited by the author at his home, and a few weeks later died. It was the author's first experience with the death of someone whom he admired and cared for.
3. Mr. Arthur Ringer, husband of Goldie, an active World I veteran who, for years, marched in Worcester parades, was a good friend and contemporary of the author's parents. He lived to be in his nineties, and was visited by the author and his wife, in Worcester, only weeks before his death in 1994.
4. A style of jazz piano in which repeated bass figures in 8/8 rhythm accompany melodic variations in the treble.
5. 32nd president of the U.S. (1933-1945).
6. "Two Tickets to London" (Universal, 1943), starring Alan Curtis and Michele Morgan.
7. French movie actress who played mostly in films about France during its Nazi occupation in WWII.

1. Wife of President Franklin D. Roosevelt, who as First Lady was a political and social activist. She had her own newspaper column "My Day."

Gulfport, Mississippi

1. A dance for couples of the era, involving fast, acrobatic movements to swing music.

4:15 PM 10/25/43

1. A WWII Rommel-in-the-desert movie starring Anne Baxter, Akim Tamiroff, and Franchot Tone, as a British soldier, spying on Erich Von Stroheim (as Field Marshall Edwin Rommel, General of the German Afrika Corps).

2. Gene Tunney, a former undefeated heavyweight champion of the late 1920s, was a WWI Marine and WWII naval officer who directed a physical fitness program for the U.S. Navy (1942-1945).

5:30 PM

3. WWII rationing allotted so many "points" for food distribution and consumption of certain items.

4. Mrs. Mann, a neighbor living in the apartment next door of a six apartment three decker.

5. The author's colleague who had earlier advised him how to behave to be accepted.

10/26/43

1. A vitamin supplement advertised for over 30 years and satirized—as here—for just as long.

2. Based on an Arnold Bennet novel in which Monty Wooley takes the place of his deceased valet (Eric Blore) and marries Gracie Fields.

3. Bearded character actor, usually playing a pompous theater critic or a principled college professor, which he once was, at Yale.

4. Hollywood actress whose career proved brief.

5. A handsome, well spoken actor, usually playing the part of a good person.

10/28/43

1. An army training depot, 30 miles northwest of Boston.

2. A day in which the navy celebrates its own existence.

10/29/43

1. Popular but controversial governor of Louisiana, assassinated in 1935.

2. George Gershwin (1899-1937), virtuoso American composer of stage and screen.

3. Hauntingly beautiful concerto of blues and jazz orchestration.

4. U.S. writer on etiquette.

10/31/43

1. Musical extravaganza, highlighting Miss Henie's brilliance as a figure skater.

2. Olympic Gold Medalist (1928-1932-1936), who became an instant success in the 20th Century Fox musicals of the late 1930s and early 1940s.

11/1/43

1. Paramount movie of the Spanish Civil War, starring Gary Cooper and Ingrid Bergman, adapted from Ernest Hemingway's novel of the same name.

11/2/43

1. MGM musical, starring Betty Grable ("America's Pin Up Girl") and Robert Young.
2. Movie actor from the late 1930s to late 1950s, later becoming a household name on TV as Doctor Marcus Welby in the 1960s.

11/3/43

1. Musical of WWII flying ace, home on leave to spark Joan Leslie. The film features Astaire singing and dancing to Harold Arlen's hit song "One More for the Road."

11/5/43

1. At the time, the author was unaware that his father, over the objections of his brothers, had seen to it that Aunt Anna, who had lived with and cared for their mother, received all the proceeds of the mother's estate after her death. Despite not speaking a word of English, the mother owned considerable real estate in Boston.
2. William Wadsworth Longfellow (1807-1882), American (New England) Romantic poet.

11/6/43

1. Hired at low wages to build America's railroads in the West during the 19th century.

11/7/43

1. Another patriotic all star musical with Bette Davis singing the woman-whose-man-is-in-the-service lament: "They're Either Too Young or Too Old."
2. Beloved comedian and recording star of stage, screen, and radio for over 4 decades.

11/8/43

1. A once-thriving drugstore chain in the U.S.

11/14/43

1. "Above Suspicion" (MGM, 1943), starring Fred MacMurray and Joan Crawford.
2. Popular actor, both in comedy and drama, whose career spanned the mid-1930s to the mid-1960s, when he played the role of the father on TV's "My Three Sons."

3. A successful actress who played self-reliant, determined, even hard-boiled women.

11/15/43

1. Al Barios, a boyhood friend of the author's who, realizing a dream, became a fighter pilot.
2. A navy pilot during WWII, he was a matinee idol from the late 1930s to the early 1960s, when he died prematurely from lung cancer.

11/16/43

1. Routine melodrama of the era.
2. American actor with a cultured speaking voice, who played debonair, somewhat decadent character roles.
3. Character actor, with heavy Scandinavian accent, playing a Partisan in WWII patriotic films.
4. American actress, once married to William Holden.
5. Bill Hannon, an employee of the author's father, a highly intelligent and responsible young man from a poor family.
6. The 1940 Republican presidential candidate (and "dark horse"), whom Franklin D. Roosevelt defeated.
7. 4-F: WWII medical designation: unfit for military duty.

11/17/43

1. Anatol Kanef, a once well liked and respected man, owner of the neighborhood drugstore near the author's father's upholstering shop, was involved in a scandal regarding theft from a local pharmaceutical wholesaler.

11/18/43

1. A cartoon character portraying the typical G.I.

11/19/43

1. Wallace Beery plays a tough, former Marine sergeant-major, who, when the Japanese attacked the Philippines, organizes a resistance movement, is killed, and awarded a medal posthumously.
2. A consistent box-office star, who mainly portrayed a rough and ready pugnacious character, invariably with a gentle and good heart.
3. Colonel Lemuel Q. Stoopnagle (F. Charles Taylor), and Budd (William Budd) Hulock, comedy team.
4. Classic horror film of a symphony violinist, horribly disfigured, whose unrequited love for an aspiring young opera singer spells his ultimate doom. Originally made as a silent movie with the great Lon Chaney ("The Man of a Thousand Faces"), it was reprised in 1943 with Claude Rains, whose intensity made the character both believable and pitiable.
5. "Blues in the Night," music by Harold Arlen, lyrics by Johnny Mercer.

6. George's Luncheonette, a small grocery story and lunch counter next to the author's father's upholstering shop, frequented by him daily. The owner, George Kalajian, a Communist sympathizer at the time, and the author's father, were fast friends despite their political differences.
7. On September 1, 1939, Germany attacked Poland from the West and the Soviet Union attacked Poland from the East, setting off the war in Europe.

11/22/43

1. Also called "Trolley Cars," which ran on steel tracks in most cities and towns in the U.S., until replaced in the mid-1950s by buses.
2. Until the late 1950s goal posts, made of wood, were torn down by the fans of winning teams. Injury, and fear of injury, however, precipitated the replacing of wooden posts with iron, encased in cement formulations.
3. A WWII patriotic movie of a group of American and British members of a tank corps holding off, and then capturing, a German battalion in North Africa.

11/23/43

1. Former heavyweight champion in the early 1930s.

11/27/43

1. Inventor of the telephone.

11/28/43

1. A civilian.
2. No longer in operation.

Port Hueneme, California

12/7/43

1. A U.S. fighter plane with two propellers, one on either side of the cockpit.

12/7/43

1. Island chain in SW Pacific, where U.S. forces, especially at Bougainville, met fierce Japanese resistance.
2. The place upon which the United Artists' movie "Stage Door Canteen" was based and previously mentioned.
3. Popular actress of the 1930s and '40s, who also entertained troops in war zones in WWII.
4. Appealing and talented actress (who won an Academy Award 3 years later in "To Each His Own"), whose leading men included Errol Flynn ("The Adventures of Robin Hood") and James Cagney ("The Strawberry Blonde"), among others.

12/8/43

1. Sentimental, yet hard-bitten, portrayal of two women who finally reconcile after years of estrangement.
2. One of the best, and most impersonated, actresses in Hollywood history, noted for her crisp enunciation and petulant — even exaggerated — mannerisms.
3. A hard-edged actress, whose soft Southern accent, could not conceal a flinty temperament.
4. Absent Over Leave.

12/9/43

1. Metro-Goldwyn-Mayer film starring Hedy Lamarr.

12/11/43

1. Popular bandleader, whose Southern drawl, gentle wit, and "Kollege of Musical Knowledge," made him known nationwide.
2. One of the famous Marx Brothers, and one of the wittiest comedians ever.
3. One of the great talents of the American cinema, whose acting range is incredible.
4. An endearing, wise-cracking ventriloquist's dummy, created by Edgar Bergen, usually — with others — playing foil to Charlie's sarcastic wit.
5. Comical radio show, sponsored by Chase and Sanborn Coffee.
6. A movie actress of average talent, best known as a dark haired beauty with a foreign accent.
7. Dorothy Shay ("The Hollywood Hillbilly").
8. Swing trumpeter, popular in the Benny Goodman band, before forming his own, married to Betty Grable.
9. Arguably the greatest bandleader of the Swing Era, who created the Glenn Miller "sound," missing — as a major in the Army — on a flight across the English Channel to lead his Army Air Corps Orchestra, in December 1944.
10. Noted bandleader of radio and cinema.
11. A top Hollywood nightclub.
12. Hollywood restaurant, a landmark (now demolished) which catered to the stars of the era, and which was shaped like a huge brown derby (hat).

12/14/43

1. Warner Brothers star in the late 1930s and '40s, specializing in crime melodrama, one of the first and last of the hard-bitten anti-heroes.
2. Radio and movie singer and comedienne, who contorted her mouth into a "buck teeth" smile for effect.
3. A radio program, featuring top Hollywood stars weekly, who re-created a movie in dialogue for the radio audience.

4. Legendary movie director of Paramount Pictures, noted for his epic productions such as "The Ten Commandments."
5. Famous Broadway producer of *Earl Carroll's Vanities*, a musical variety show, featuring beautiful, usually skimpily clad, women.
6. A popular nightclub and movie comedian.
7. As indicated, a routine western.
8. A behemoth of the American cinema, noted for his rugged, no nonsense, swing-first-ask-questions-later type of character roles.

12/16/43
1. Meaning "Yes, sir," a saying made popular by bandleader and radio personality of the 1930s Ben Bernie, who opened his show with "Yowsah, Yowsah, Yowsah."
2. John Greenleaf Whittier (1807-1892), 19th century American Romantic poet, brought closer to earth by someone's remarking that though another poet was witty, "John Greenleaf was Whittier."
3. Goldie Ringer, wife of Arthur, mother of Beverly and Fay, a delightful woman, best friend and once a neighbor of the author's mother.

12/17/43
1.Magazine illustrator who portrayed gorgeous, nubile women in provocative poses, and every year in calendar form
2. At the time, a men's magazine with a wide range of topics.
3. Taken from a big-selling 1941 novelty recording "The Hut Sut Song" (Killion, McMichael, Owens).

12/19/43
1. Uncle Hy: Hyman, older brother of the author's father, mother of Cousin Bobby, husband of Aunt Ida, an upholsterer and installer of theater seats.

12/21/43
1. Long running radio show, featuring the lives of an inter-faith married couple, a Jewish man and an Irish woman, the conflicts light, the comedy bright, based on a long-running Broadway play of the same name.

12/23/43
1. Irving Berlin's classic song from the Paramount movie "Holiday Inn," sung by Bing Crosby, whose recording of the song is the largest selling single in recording history.
2. Fabulous star of the silent cinema, called "America's Sweetheart."
3. Joseph E. Davies, U.S. Ambassador to Russia (1943).
4. English novelist and essayist (1894-1963), lived in the U.S. from 1935.
5. Variety magazine, popular for about 30 years.

12/26/43

1. Blockbuster musical, directed by the incomparable Busby Berkeley, featuring Benny Goodman and his orchestra.
2. Popular 20th Century Fox star, featured as both a singer and actress. She retired in the late 1940s.
3. Master of ceremonies of a highly successful radio show called "The 64 Dollar Question," which, for a time, became a national slogan.
4. Palace Theater, typical of Loew's ornate and plush edifices, the largest and most elegant theater in Worcester.
5. A Warner Brothers film, starring Olivia De Havilland.
6. Based on the book of the same name by war correspondent Richard Tregaskis, of the 1st Marine Division's invasion of the Japanese-held island.
7. A musical revue.
8. Radio show, spotlighting big bands and celebrities, sponsored by Fitch's Shampoo and Hair Tonic.

12/27/43

1. A popular morning radio show featuring celebrity interviews, broadcast nationally.
2. Comedienne who played "dumb blonde" parts with affecting skill.
3. The dog belonging to Dagwood Bumpstead and his wife Blondie, a famous comic strip.
4. Movie based on the comic strip, starring Arthur Lake and Penny Singleton.
5. Popular, versatile actor of great charm, who could lull movie audiences with a low, soft voice, or make them blink with a staccato, riveting eloquence.
6. Popular radio soap opera of the era.

12/28/43

1. 20th Century Fox drama of a father, Don Ameche (popular actor of the era), reconciling his son's death in WWII.

1/1/44

1. Nationally famous editor and essayist from the 1920 to the 1950s.
2. Emporia, Kansas.

1/3/44

1. Radio show, featuring movie personalities.
2. Samuel Goldwyn war propaganda movie of the peerless Russians with excellent performances, however, from Walter Huston and Erich Von Stroheim.
3. Former child star of the 1930s.

4. Popular actor whose stately demeanor and sand-pit voice made him a natural for the movies, one of which, some years later, "The Treasure of Sierra Madre," won him great, critical praise. He was the father of director John Huston.

5. A breathy-voiced actress, who also, later, won an Oscar for her role in "The Razor's Edge" (1946).

6. Farley Granger.

7. An MGM war drama (1943), starring Jean Pierre Aumont, playing a French soldier who stays in France to fight the Nazis.

1/5/44

1. Popular character actress of the era.

2. Warner Brothers' musical extravaganza of men in uniform, featuring almost a score of Irving Berlin song hits, including the satirical title song.

3. The most talented and lovable of all child actors in the 1930s, whose performances saved a faltering studio (20th Century Fox) during the Depression and enchanted audiences everywhere.

4. A capable character actor, who a year or so later was to win an Academy Award for his performance in "A Tree Grows in Brooklyn."

5. As described, and an erstwhile and talented musical comedy actress of the 1940s.

6. Metro-Goldwyn-Mayer studio.

7. A 1941 stage musical hit, turned into a 1943 film musical, starring Lucille Ball and featuring the rousing song "Buckle Down, Winsocki" (Hug Martin, Ralph Blane).

8. Sex appeal to the nth power.

9. Les Brown ("and His Band of Renown") toured with Bob Hope in 3 wars (WWII, Korea, Vietnam); his vocalist Doris Day, before her movie career, sang the classic mid-1940s "Sentimental Journey."

1/6/44

1. Italian opera by Giuseppe Verdi (1813-1901).

2. Browning Automatic Rifle.

1/7/44

1. Gas-rationing cards indicating priority.

1/10/44

1. In this salute to the Seabees, John Wayne leads C.B. heavy equipment against Japanese tanks and soldiers.

2. A sultry and competent actress, usually playing impulsive and tempestuous women.

1/15/44

1. Popular big band leader, whose orchestra included strings, uncommon for the time.
2. California Institute of Technology.
3. Usually hosts the two top college teams in the country, game played New Year's Day.
4. Lavish parade, featuring myriad floats, marching bands, and celebrities.
5. In Worcester, Massachusetts, the first public park in the U.S. When a young child, the author sailed his model boats on its ponds, and when older, during the winter, skated on them.
6. Named for the legendary General Douglas MacArthur, famed for fighting a holding action on Bataan and Corregidor in the Philippines against invading Japanese forces.
7. One New Year's eve when the author was a child his father got high with the neighbors of the upper floors of the three decker in which the author lived.

1/16/44

1. Character actress, whose films included "Pigskin Parade" (1936), Judy Garland's debut.
2. Character actor in numerous films.
3. Actor, married to Jeanette MacDonald.
4. Operetta star, whose singing voice, especially when teamed with baritone Nelson Eddy in over 5 films, charmed audiences of the 1930s.
5. University of California at Los Angeles.
6. A closed, two-door automobile with a body smaller than that of a sedan.
7. One of Hollywood's top directors.
8. The film, starring Robert Taylor, Lloyd Nolan, and Thomas Mitchell, depicts the heroic—but futile—efforts of an outnumbered army unit to repulse the invading Japanese forces in late 1941 and early 1942.
9. Most likely "The Cross of Lorraine" (December 1943).
10. Character actress in musicals.
11. A then thriving dance instruction enterprise that gave use to the saying "Arthur Murray teaches dancing in a hurry."
12. A former boxer, whose cauliflower ear, broken nose, and vocabulary reduced to words of one syllable made him a lovable and natural character actor in American films.
13. Band leader, actor, radio personality, and song writer ("That's What I Like about the South"), who radiated roguish charm and was married to Alice Faye.
14. Universal musical (1941) based on a zany 1938 Broadway revue starring Olsen and Johnson, two uninhibited vaudeville comedians.
15. Slang for money.

1/18/44

1. A terse and accurate commentary of this film and so many other wartime patriotic movies.
2. U.S. Naval base in Hawaii, bombed by Japanese aircraft December 7, 1941, in a sneak attack that plunged America into WWII.

1/22/44

1. Musical (1943), also starring Michele Morgan, Leon Errol, and Jack Haley. Sinatra sang two fine songs "The Music Stopped" and "I Couldn't Sleep a Wink Last Night."
2. After leaving Tommy Dorsey's band in 1942, Frank Sinatra became an instant hit with the young girls (called "Bobby Soxers") in the country. His fine voice, impeccable taste in songs, and dreamy delivery made the girls yell "Frankeee!"

1/23/44

1. Slang for a devotee of swing music.
2. Slang for "going well."
3. Based on a 1939 Broadway musical, featuring Jerome Kern's memorable "All the Things You Are."
4. Popular actor, song and dance man, who, as a senator from California in later years proclaimed that the voters liked him, because he was "always good to Shirley Temple."
5. Vocalist with the Kay Kyser band, also featured in the film.
6. Gruff-voiced character actor, usually playing a grandfatherly curmudgeon, or a harmless—but derelict—barfly.
7. Character actor, comedian, and dancer.
8. One of the famous "Dorsey Brothers" (Jimmy Dorsey also had a successful orchestra), Tommy was an ace trombonist, leading a popular swing band that featured—at various times—Bunny Berrigan on trumpet, Buddy Rich on drums, and Frank Sinatra as vocalist.
9. Obviously, the author had a crush on Gloria DeHaven.

1/24/44

1. Written and directed by George Seaton.

1/28/44

1. One of Hollywood's most famous entertainers and baritone "crooner," once billed as "the most listened to voice in the world," who influenced a generation of singers, while pleasing fans for over 4 decades.
2. The Kraft Music Hall.
3. Blonde, voluptuous actress, once advertised as the "Sweater Girl," and a favorite of servicemen during WWII (died January 1996).
4. *This* was risqué in 1944.
5. Early silent movie producer and director, who not only provided zany, slapstick gags in his movies but also introduced Bing Crosby in the early

1930s as a featured singer, who showed a surprising knack for light comedy.

1/29/44

1. The news of the infamous "Bataan Death March," in which American and Filipino POWs were shot, clubbed to death, and denied water in the blazing sun on a sixty mile forced march, reached the U.S. about this time. Other Japanese atrocities surfaced throughout the war.

2. William Randolph Hearst, editor, and empire builder in journalism.

3. Dad's leg was injured in a bicycle accident while he was a messenger boy working for the Postal Telegraph Company in Boston. The leg bothered him, causing him to walk with a limp, for the rest of his life.

4. A monthly feature magazine that conveniently fits the hand, has a circulation of over 27 million, and proclaims itself the "World's Most Widely Read Magazine."

5. Once popular, but now defunct, monthly feature magazine, hand sized.

1/30/44

1. Legendary Queen of Egypt whose charms charmed—or ensnared—both Julius Caesar and Mark Anthony.

2. A classic example of never believing everything you hear and only half of what you see.

3. A sublime symphonic suite by the illustrious Russian composer Nikolay Rimsky-Korsakov (1844-1908).

4. Ludwig Von Beethoven (1770-1827), one of the greatest classical composers who ever lived, and who wrote his greatest symphonies after being stricken stone deaf; "to be reduced to a philosopher at age 29," he wrote a friend.

(I) 2/1/44

1. Hollywood hostess (died November 1951).

2. Wife of famous director, whose films include "Boys Town" (1937).

3. Exquisitely beautiful Hollywood actress of Spanish descent.

4. Wife of successful Hollywood director.

5. Wife of popular actor, whose father gained stardom as an athletic-acrobatic performer in silent films.

6. Wife of world-renowned Academy Award winning director.

7. Academy Award winning actress of the late 1930s.

8. Wife of famous movie director.

9. Beautiful Hollywood actress, noted for her role as the wife of "Nick Charles" (William Powell) in "The Thin Man" film series.

10. Tart tongued comedienne of the 1930s and '40s.

11. Talented comedienne of the era.

12. English actress in American films, possessing porcelain beauty and a Mona Lisa smile.

13. Wife of one of the greatest of all film actors.

14. Dramatic and brilliant light-comedy actress, whose career spanned over three decades (1930s-1960s).

15. Wife of prolific director, whose work includes "The Country Girl" (1954).

16. Wife of one of Hollywood's most famous actors.

(II) 2/1/44

1. Mascot Pictures (Nat Levine), based on Louisa May Alcott's novel of the same name.

2. Distinguished actor, gifted with one of the most resonant and identifiable voices in American cinema.

3. Irish actress, noted for her WWII role as "Mrs. Miniver," a stalwart British wife and mother, who — like England — came under siege.

4. A late 1942 movie with Coleman playing a WWI shell-shocked amnesiac, who falls in love with Miss Garson, a music hall performer, neither knowing that he is already married.

(III) 2/1/44

1. While a teen, the author, a gymnast, swimmer, and body builder, had a well developed physique, and often modeled for the Worcester Art Museum school. Having seen the author at the YMCA, a man approached the author asking to take photographs of him in the nude. He agreed, but during the session, the author came to suspect him of being a homosexual, and having ulterior motives.

2. Primarily a radio actor with an exasperated voice, when playing "Baby Snooks's" father.

3. The name of Blondie and Dagwood's son (who for years before had been called "Baby Dumpling").

4. The sound effects man who simulated action (opening of creaky doors, creating stormy winds, etc.) on radio shows.

2/2/44

1. A hilariously bratty character, played by former Broadway musical comedy star Fanny Brice.

2. The penitentiary (prison).

3. Emlyn Williams's stage play (a year later made into a movie starring Bette Davis) about a young English teacher who establishes a school in a Welsh mining town, and her prized pupil.

4. One of the leading ladies of the Broadway theater and the cinema, Miss Barrymore (1879-1959) was the sister of two brilliant, and troubled, actors Lionel and John Barrymore.

5. Starring (in her screen debut) Jennifer Jones, playing the role of Bernadette Soubirous, a young French peasant girl, who in 1858, claimed to see visions of the Virgin Mary at Lourdes, where, ever since, miraculous claims of curing have been made from the water there.

6. V-Mail: mail to or from the armed forces of WW II, reduced to microfilm to conserve shipping space, and enlarged to 4 x 5 inches per page.

7. Traditionally the day the groundhog emerges from hibernation to see his shadow (if the sun is shining).

8. Sigmund Romberg—Oscar Hammerstein II operetta, concerns a patriotic desert bandit, featuring the classic "Riff Song" and the romantic "One Alone."

9. Durable and talented screen actress and comedienne, whose Hollywood career spanned three decades.

10. Singer-actor, who played in some of Warner Brothers' most appealing musicals.

2/3/44

1. Wartime comedy-drama in which Spencer Tracy, playing a deceased fighter-pilot ghost, makes his former love, Irene Dunne, see the reality of finding another love.

2. Starring Greer Garson in the title role and Walter Pidgeon (stalwart dramatic actor for thirty years) as Madame Curie's husband Pierre, the discoverers of radium. The real Madame Curie eventually died of radiation poisoning.

3. Hollywood comedienne and radio personality of the era.

4. Starring Victor Moore (a splendid, creaky-voiced character actor) and Dorothy Lamour (noted for her skimpy sarong roles and as the love interest in the Bing Crosby-Bob Hope "Road" pictures) not to be confused with the 1950 Frank Capra film (about horse racing, starring Crosby also) of the same title.

2/5/44

1. A summary session held by a commanding officer (U.S. Navy) to try minor offenses, hear requests, or award commendations.

2. A downtown Boston entertainment district, now demolished, noted for its seedy burlesque houses and run-down ambience.

2/7/44

1. The author does not recall this person.

2/9/44

1. The Great War (WWI 1914-1918).

2. While skiing down Newton Hill in Worcester, the author had broken his first set of skis.

3. Alfred Hitchcock thriller, starring Tallulah Bankhead, John Hodiak, William Bendix, and Walter Slezak, in which survivors of a German U-Boat torpedoing must survive a Nazi infiltrator, as well as the open sea.

4. Probably George Krikorian, a high school friend—a grade higher— and neighbor of the author's.

2/10/44

1. Underrated Universal musical (1943), starring Deanna Durbin, Pat O'Brien, and Akim Tamiroff, among other fine actors.
2. Probably Jesse Tronic, a dentist and army officer, married to one of Cousin Lil's cousins on her mother's side.
3. By 1944 American and Australian troops, commanded by General Douglas MacArthur, were sweeping the Japanese from New Guinea, while the Marines, under Admiral William F. Halsey's naval command, were driving the enemy out of the Marshall Islands.
4. Controversial Roman Catholic radio-priest of the 1930s, whose fiery oratory was directed at Franklin Roosevelt, Communism, and Jewish Bankers, during the Depression. The church ultimately silenced him, and he apologized for his anti-semitic remarks. The author's father, considering him dangerous, both feared and despised him.
5. Charles Lindberg, first human to fly across the Atlantic Ocean (1927) alone, making him one of America's authentic heroes. Like most Americans during the 1930s, he didn't want the U.S. to get involved in the war in Europe and lectured against it.
6. Stay out of the war in Europe.

2/14/44

1. The author's father, a hard working and dedicated man, often returned to his shop after supper to prepare the next day's work for his employees.
2. Comedy panel show in which the moderator tells a joke sent in by a member of the radio audience. If the panel (Senator Ed Ford, Harry Hershfield, Joe Laurie Jr.) cannot "top" the joke (on the same subject) the contestant wins $10.00.
3. Phil Moore wrote the lyrics and music.

2/15/44

1. During high school, for a short time the author worked in a Worcester laboratory measuring the butterfat content of milk. To the consternation of his employer, his measurements were occasionally found to be in error. When confronted with this, he denied being at fault, and was ultimately dismissed.
2. MGM drama of a foundling (child star Margaret O'Brien), brought up by two wrong-headed psychologists, who themselves, have to learn the nature—and value—of love.

2/16/44

1. Landing Ship, Tank.
2. One of the silent screen's greatest comic geniuses, and a controversial figure socially and politically, after the war.

2/18/44

1. Charles Dickens, noted 19th century social novelist.
2. Dickens's novel of Ebenezer Scrooge and his moral regeneration, now a Christmas classic.

2/19/44

1. MGM (1943) A Wartime "Home Front" comedy about a small-town storekeeper frustrated by wartime restrictions.
2. Lovable, cross-grained character actress, whose gravelly voice and no-nonsense manner intimidated intimidating characters out of their shoes.
3. Paramount Pictures, directed (and written) by Preston Sturges.
4. Called the "Blonde Bombshell" for her wild and irrepressible personality, especially in this film as the girl who, after going out with five soldiers, gives birth to quintuplets, the "miracle" of Morgan's Creek.
5. Comic character actor, superlative as Miss Hutton's wimpy suitor, ineffectual in everything.
6. Paramount Pictures (1940), written and directed by Preston Sturges, who satirizes big city political machines.
7. Top-rated, flinty eyed actor, who played a shrewd bum who rises to become governor on a crooked political ticket.
8. Capitol Theater, the second most elaborate theater in Worcester, at the time. Its ceiling simulated a night sky of clouds and stars.
9. Newton Hill, one of the seven hills of Worcester, located near Elm Park; after the war, part of it was made the site of a high school.
10. Columbia (1944), starring Alexander Knox and Marsha Hunt, in a melodrama about a Nazi officer on trial for war crimes.
11. Dark-haired, slender actress of the era, later blacklisted in the 1950s.

2/20/44

1. USS *West Point*, before conversion into a troopship, the largest U.S. luxury liner afloat, christened the S.S. America by Eleanor Roosevelt.

Overseas in the Pacific Theater
En Route to Islands Unknown

Censored V-Mail 2/26/44

1. Described in an earlier note: Mail to or from the armed forces in World War II, reduced to microfilm to conserve shipping space, and enlarged and printed for delivery.

Finschafen, Papua, New Guinea

3/26/44

1. Australians.

2. A pejorative term, reflecting the white prejudice against blacks prevailing in the U.S. WWII navy.

3. A famous animal hunter, who did not kill the beasts but caged them for zoos in the U.S. His slogan was "Bring them back alive."

3/31/44

1. Hollywood musical of the late 19th century era.

2. Popular radio and movie personality.

3. MGM (1943) propaganda film, starring Robert Taylor, extolling the virtues of Mother Russia's collective system.

4. School grades.

4/2/44

1. Margaret Mitchell's sprawling novel of the ante-bellum South, the Civil War, and its effects on various members of Southern society.

4/4/44

1. Related to Cousin Lil.

2. Norman Edinberg, about the author's age, and an acquaintance.

4/5/44

1. The letter is incorrect: The VFW is not a federal institution.

2. A Jewish holiday (Pesach) celebrated for eight days beginning on the 14th of Nisan and commemorating the deliverance of the ancient Hebrews from slavery in Egypt (Exodus 12:2).

4/6/44

1. Possibly the son of Rabbi Sherman who taught the author Hebrew in preparation for his Bar Mitzvah (confirmation).

2. One of the author's battalion friends, and later a battalion censor. He and the author went on liberty to New Orleans together. Their friendship has endured for over 50 years.

3. Charles Goodness, another battalion friend, from Worcester. A delightful, good natured man.

4. Harold Greenberg, with his wife Janet, rented a room from the author's parents during the Depression. When the author was a boy, Harold often took him kite flying. Their friendship lasted for years after the war.

4/9/44

1. Exaggerated men's apparel, a fad of the early 1940s: broad-brimmed felt hat, wide-shouldered jacket, trousers tapered to the ankle, with a long key chain dangling from the pocket.

2. Clean or fit to eat according to the dietary laws of the Jewish faith.

3. A Broadway play

4. Phrase used by comedian Red Skelton, playing "The Mean Widdle Kid": "I get a lickin' if I dood it. I dood it!"

4/10/44

1. Members of religious orders sent to preach, teach, and proselytize inhabitants of foreign lands, especially those considered heathen.

4/17/44

1. Universal (1941), Charles Laughton plays Cupid for Deanna Durbin, who sings sporadically throughout.
2. Versatile dramatic-comedy actor, whose puffy-faced dialogue, delivered in fluent-breathy gasps, made his performances memorable.
3. Al Martin, also the author's companion on many trips to Hollywood.
4. Radio singer, classical, of the era.

4/25/44

1. James Palais, the author's cousin, Henrietta's son and only child.
2. Harry Palais, the author's uncle, toy manufacturer, later, after retirement, winner of a national award as a SCORE counselor for the Small Business Administration.
3. Edward Aronovitz, the author's cousin, Lil's brother, a pharmacist and later owner of a small drugstore chain in central Massachusetts.
4. Music and lyrics by Cole Porter.
5. Music and lyrics by Irving Berlin.
6. Music by Jimmy McHugh, lyrics by Frank Loesser (1943).
7. Eva Aronovitz, mother of Lil, Edward and Charlie, wife of Uncle Morris.
8. Al Barios, boyhood friend of the author's, dreamed of being a pilot.
9. At that time the word "gay" meant happy, not homosexual.
10. Medford, Massachusetts, a Boston suburb.
11. An international service club of business and professional men.
12. Music by Harry Warren, lyrics by Leo Robin (1943) introduced by Alice Faye in the 20th Century Fox musical "The Gang's All Here."

5/2/44

1. Atabrine was taken daily to prevent the occurrence of malaria symptoms. It did not prevent the contraction of the disease.
2. B gas card: gasoline was rationed according to a priority based on need. A B card carries a high priority.
3. Burton Chase, a boyhood friend of the author's, and member, with the author, of Worcester Boy Scout Troop 36.
4. Mrs. Rome, a friend of the author's mother.
5. Harriet Rome, Mrs. Rome's daughter.
6. Mrs. Lynn, friend and neighbor of the author's mother .

5/4/44

1. Cousin Evelyn, a raven haired beauty, then in her twenties, daughter of Uncle Louie living in Boston.

5/6/44

1. Charles Albright, geologist, native of L.A., a calm, quiet spoken member of the battalion.
2. Clark University, a liberal arts college in Worcester, formerly specializing in geography, where Professor Goddard, the American rocket scientist, taught, and the only U.S. college in which Sigmund Freud lectured.
3. Worcester Polytechnic Institute described in an earlier note.
4. Dashes represent deleted portions of a letter which the censor had cut out.
5. Variety magazine, now defunct.
6. Monthly publication featuring current novels and books.

Hollandia, New Guinea

5/14/44

1. The censor was in error. Revealing the identity of past locations was allowed.

5/15/44

1. Passover.
2. Famous tenor, a prolific radio performer.
3. Whalom Park, an amusement park, once owned by the author's great uncle, William "Bill" Berger, and also the location of a playhouse.
4. Small city in Massachusetts, 35 miles northwest of Boston.

5/22/44

1. The author returned several of Johnson Fulgoni's letters home for safe keeping, but they were eventually lost.

5/25-5/26/44

1. Time flies (Latin).
2. Title of a CBS radio serial drama, the announcer's quoting (in part) John Ruskin's "When getting and spending happiness is our aim, life can be beautiful," opened the show.

5/28/44

1. Beverly Ringer, the author's contemporary, daughter of Goldie and Arthur, the author's parent's best friends.
2. Aleph Zadek Aleph, a Jewish young men's social organization.

3. Miss Chase, the young correspondent, doing what so many young women did to keep up the morale of men overseas.
4. Avoiding or neglecting duty.

5/30/44

1. A faithful follower or efficient helper, from Daniel Defoe's 18th century novel *Robinson Crusoe*.
2. The Emperor of Japan (considered a god by the Japanese people).
3. Capital of Japan.
4. Dad worked as a telegrapher and manager for the Postal Telegraph Company when a young man, and often was required to do line work.
5. Characteristic of the infernal darkness and gloom of the River Styx in Hell.

6/2/44

1. MGM blockbuster (1939), starring Clark Gable and Vivien Leigh (British actress).

6/4/44

1. Longtime popular movie character actor, best known perhaps as the Wizard in MGM's classic "The Wizard of Oz."
2. Music and lyrics by Meredith Wilson (1941).

6/6/44

1. Formerly school hours were from 8:45 AM to 1:00 PM.
2. Overseas the men in the army did not live as well as those in the navy. Food was poorer and quarters more primitive.

6/10/44

1. The Allied invasion of France at Normandy, June 6, 1944.

6/11/44

1. Famous radio and cinema comedian, whose *persona* as a parsimonious roué made him a perennial favorite for 3 decades.
2. One of the most popular radio shows ever, featuring Mary Livingston (Benny's wife), Dennis Day, Eddie "Rochester" Anderson, Phil Harris (the orchestra leader), and Don Wilson (the announcer).

6/14/44

1. MGM musical (1943), based on a novel by Booth Tarkington.

6/17/44

1. Though the Germans were fighting a two-front war against the Soviet armies in the East and the Allied armies in Normandy, their obdurate resistance proved incredibly tenacious.

6/20/44

1. As a teen, the author modeled in the semi-nude for the Worcester Art Museum school which was attended mostly by young women. Since most young men were in the service, few were available for modeling.

6/22/44

1. Four days before, on 18 June 1944, in the Battle of the Philippine Sea, U.S. Navy pilots, while losing but 29 aircraft, had destroyed some 300 Japanese planes, giving the battle the unofficial name of the "Great Marianas Turkey Shoot."

6/23/44

1. Nason Hurowitz, the author's cousin once removed, older son of Lil's.
2. Actually, the Japanese are an assiduously clean people, whose communal baths were something of a ritual.

6/26/44

1. Radio broadcaster.
2. Thomas E. Dewey, governor of New York and former District Attorney who had broken the infamous "Murder Incorporated."
3. Henry A. Wallace, vice president of the U.S. (1941-1945), former Secretary of Agriculture, considered by many to be a Socialist, on whose ticket he ran in 1948.
4. John William Bricker (1893-1986), governor of Ohio and Republican candidate for vice-president in 1944.
5. Leverett Saltonstall (1892-1966), whose son Peter, a Marine Sergeant, was killed on Guam in 1944, served 3 terms as governor of Massachusetts and 3 terms in the U.S. Senate.

6/27/44

1. Small peninsula at the southern tip of Spain, extending into the Mediterranean, consisting mostly of a rocky hill (Rock of Gibraltar).
2. The Japanese invasion forces of Port Moresby (southeast New Guinea) was thwarted, when, in the air battle of the Coral Sea (May 7-8, 1942), Vice Admiral Shigeyoshi Inouye, Chief of the Fourth Fleet, had one carrier sunk (and another badly damaged), losing two-thirds of their carrier planes and half their airmen.
3. 20th Century Fox musical about a saloon singer (Betty Grable) on the way to Broadway stardom at the turn of the century.
4. Promising leading man of the early 1940s with pleasing Southern drawl, who, after military service in WWII, became an acclaimed wood carver.
5. Leading man-character actor, who for 3 decades entertained movie audiences with his suave Cuban good looks, tall frame, and genuinely good-natured persona.

7/1/44

1. The Allied Forces, spearheaded by General George Patton's 3rd Army, had fought through stiff German resistance and the liberation of Paris was two weeks away.

7/2/44

1. Screwball Warner Brothers' comedy (1941) about airplane pilot (Cagney) who abducts eloping heiress (Davis) to return her to her father for money.
2. James Cagney, by many considered the greatest American cinema actor, who, when he wasn't machine-gunning half the cast in gangster roles, and being the most impersonated actor ever, was singing and dancing in musicals like "Yankee Doodle Dandy," for which he won an Academy Award (1942).
3. "Pappy" Collins, a good-natured man then in his fifties.
4. Jefferson, a rural suburb of Worcester.

7/5/44

1. Dramatic and musical comedy star, who could — and did — steal scenes from Cary Grant in movies like "His Girl Friday."
2. A comedy-farce in which Miss Russell (as a high-powered executive) hires MacMurray, as her personal secretary, and, after conflicts and misunderstandings, they fall in love.
3. called a joey.

7/6/44

1. Fifty years ago this word meant "light-heartedly happy."
2. This expression was used by a movie comedian who did short subjects, sporting a suit at least one size too small, while making the observation that "Monkeys are the cwaziest people."

7/8/44

1. MGM (1939).
2. Popular blonde, dramatic actress of the 1930s and early '40s, once married to silent screen star John Gilbert.

7/10/44

1. Japanese-held island in the Marianas, where vicious fighting (15 June-9 July) resulted in 23,000 dead enemy, while the joint U.S. Army-Marine Corps forces lost close to 3500.
2. Used as a vital airstrip on bombing raids against the Japanese homeland.

7/13/44

1. MGM movie series on the simple virtues of American home town life, starring Micky Rooney as the exuberant, yet respectful son, who worships

his tolerant, yet firm father, Judge Hardy (Lewis Stone, granite rock character actor).

2. Companies that supply goods and supplies to upholsterers. Cross makes upholsterers tacks.

3. During college the author smoked a pipe. After college he took up cigarettes and, occasionally, cigars to celebrate a hearty meal. At age 40 he quit tobacco cold turkey.

4. Lowell Thomas's radio news broadcast signoff.

Thurs. Night 7/13/44

1. The era 1890-1900 in America.

2. Pie Alley, a short, narrow, downtown, Boston street.

3. Washington Street, a downtown, Boston commercial street.

4. 20th Century Fox drama of a young starlet who initially gets rejected but later becomes a success through determination.

5. Leading man of 20th Century Fox musicals and dramas of the late 1930s and '40s, whose easy charm and competent acting ability made him quite popular.

6. Gorgeous raven-haired 20th Century Fox dramatic actress, who, though young in her screen debut, remained a top line performer until her tragic death in a fire some years later.

7/14/44

1. An American outpost in the South Pacific, manned by a small detachment of Marines, Guam fell quickly to the Japanese after Pearl Harbor. It was retaken in 1944.

2. The Western Front, the Italian/North African Front, and the Russian Front.

3. Made impossible, however, by the allied policy of "unconditional surrender" (Casablanca Conference January 24, 1943), a phrase that most believe stiffened enemy resistance.

7/17/44

1. Massachusetts Institute of Technology in Cambridge, Massachusetts.

2. United Soviet Socialist Republic (to the surprise of some it was neither socialist nor a republic, but rather a totalitarian state).

7/19/44

1. Music by Richard Rodgers, lyrics by Lorenz Hart (1929).

7/21/44

1. Pigeons trained to find their way home from distant places, usually with messages.

2. From the sobriquet for the Brooklyn Dodger baseball team of the era.

7/22/44

1. The author's father, who was born in Lithuania and came to the U.S. as a steerage passenger in his mother's arms, shortened his birth name Aronovitz to Aaron when he became a U.S. citizen. However, most in the family retained the Aronovitz name.
2. Usually a voluptuous movie queen, whose photo was "pinned up" on a barracks wall or tent.

7/24/44

1. A white stripe on the shoulder around the top of the sleeve signifies S 1/c.

7/26/44

1. Popular beach resort located in Maine.
2. Based on Charles Darwin's 19th century controversial theory on the natural selection of the origin of the species.
3. Eleanor Roosevelt, known for her constant traveling while in the White House as First Lady.
4. Two beach resorts in Massachusetts, at that time.
5. Aunt Pearl's husband, a former lightweight New England boxing champion known as "Kid" Butler.
6. Walter "Kid" Butler was also a cigar maker who would give most of his cigars away to would be constituents in an effort to win political office on the Republican ticket in an overwhelmingly Democratic community. Obviously, he was never elected.
7. A popular comic strip character of the day.
8. Hughie's responsibility each Sunday morning was to brush the lint off the living room sofa whose freize fabric attracted lint and dust like a magnet.

7/30/44

1. A twin engine attack bomber.
2. Bomber.
3. Bomber, named after WWI flying ace and pioneer for U.S. air power General Billy Mitchell, who, though ignored and ridiculed by an unobservant military and an indifferent public, predicted Japan's sneak attack on Pearl Harbor.
4. People, six inches tall, in Lilliput, the land visited in Gulliver's first voyage in Jonathan Swift's 17th century satire *Gulliver's Travels*.

8/1/44

1. Sales, liberal arts, and chemical engineering are fields also mentioned in previous letters as career choices.
2. The author does not recall "the trick" referred to, but clearly it was not to the author's father's benefit.

3. One of the most influential—and intimidating—gossip columnists in the history of journalism from the 1920s to the early 1950s.

4. Grandma was considered selfish, self-centered and uncompromising by her family, and heartily disliked by the author's father.

5. Beverly Ringer, the daughter of Goldie and Arthur, was the author's first date at 16. They attended a dance in which the author virtually ignored her.

6. Helen Lyon, who lived in San Fancisco at the time. Malter had an elaborate figure of a lion's head painted on the hood of his Jeep in honor of his girlfriend.

8/3/44

1. Betty Smith's best selling novel of a family living in tenement poverty in turn-of-the-century New York City, focusing on their frustrations, dreams, and love for one another.

8/4/44

1. Bernarr McFadden, an extreme proponent of physical fitness.

2. Clym Yeobright.

3. Thomas Hardy, one of the 19th century's greatest novelists and poets, wrote of strained and painful relations between men and women in a Victorian society, traditional and unforgiving.

4. Eleanor Roosevelt's syndicated column.

8/5/44

1. Autobiography ("gay" in this era meaning lighthearted, happy, carefree)

2. Influential Hollywood gossip columnist of the era.

3. Autobiography.

4. An opera singer.

5. Biography of John Barrymore.

6. Gene Fowler was the author.

7. Written by Bennet Ames Williams.

8. Novel of an unjustly convicted felon hounded by an obsessed police inspector during the time of the French Revolution.

9. Magnificent 18th century French novelist.

10. Washington investigative reporter, widely-read and controversial.

8/6/44

1. An army cartoon character, always finding bad luck.

2. Bill providing returning war veterans subsidies to buy a home, open a business, or pursue a college education.

3. British author (1593-1683) of the *Compleat Angler* (1653).

4. Roman statue of Venus, goddess of love, noted for its representation of feminine beauty and form (even with its arms broken off).

5. 20th Century Fox (1943) drama of a boy and his horse, starring child actor Roddy McDowell.

8/10/44

1. Warner Brothers (1944), starring Thomas Mitchell as the father of the 5 Sullivan brothers who lost their lives on the *Juneau*, at Guadalcanal.
2. Helen Lyon.
3. Joseph Goebbels, minister of propaganda for the Nazis, who is reputed to have said, "Tell the people a lie long enough and they will begin to believe it." After his wife poisoned their 6 children, he had an S.S. officer shoot him and her on April 30, 1945, in a Berlin bunker, as the Russian army closed in.

8/12/44

1. Nickname for the fighting men of the U.S. armed forces.
2. Harry S. Truman, who became Franklin Roosevelt's vice-presient in 1944.
3. South West Pacfific Area.

8/16/44

1. Vintage Hollywood musical, in a gesture toward the classical.
2. Gifted Viennese composer (1797-1828).
3. Symphony Number 8, in B Minor, a hauntingly beautiful piece that Schubert, in 1822, left uncompleted, the reasons for which remain a mystery.

8/18/44

1. Mr. Bloom, Aunt Libby's father, an optometrist who fitted the author with glasses by having him read letters and symbols mounted on a closet door in his apartment.

8/23/44

1. Bob Hope.
2. NBC radio program, running from 1934, sponsored by Pepsodent tooth paste.
3. Popular blonde vocalist and radio and movie personality of the era.
4. Pop-eyed, zany comedian of movies and radio, starring with Hope for a number of years.
5. Popular radio and orchestra vocalist.
6. George Holas.
7. Bob Hope's theme song.

8/24/44

1. Bing Crosby's 4 children (by his first wife Dixie Lee) were a constant source of comedy material for Hope.

1. Endlessly (Latin).
2. Percy Durgin, the author's father's first boss and mentor, manager of the Boston Postal Telegraph office. In 1969, upon the death of the author's father, Mr. Durgin, then retired in Vero Beach, FL., wrote the author relating how admirable a man his father was.
3. Al Martin
4. A narrow road through the Berkshires in the northwest corner of Massachusetts.
5. Located in the White Mountains of northern New Hampshire.

8/28/44

1. Woodrow Wilson, 28th president of the U.S. (1913-1921), whose proposal for America's entry into the League of Nations, was voted down by the U.S. Congress.
2. Renowned stage and screen actress, whose Lady Macbeth is world-acclaimed.
3. Popular recording, radio, and movie singer, who, years later, had a long run as a T.V. hostess.
4. World famous Spanish classical pianist and conductor, who also played in MGM musicals.
5. Shakespeare's tragedy of the fall of greatness through ambition.

9/1/44

1. William L. Shirer, war correspondent, who had been stationed in Berlin during Hitler's rise to power, and about which he wrote years later in his memorable *The Rise and Fall of the Third Reich.*

9/5/44

1. Best selling novel by Franz Werfel.
2. A column by Al Banx in the *Worcester Telegram.*
3. Morgan Construction Company, Worcester designer of steel mills and other manufacturing facilities.

9/7/44

1. *Earth and High Heaven,* (1944), a novel by Gwethalyn Graham about a wealthy Canadian Protestant girl in love with a poor, but talented, Jewish lawyer who, though they wish to marry, are opposed by her anti-semitic father.
2. President of Motion Picture Association (1944).

9/8/44

1. James V. Forrestal, Undersecretary of the Navy.

9/9/44

1. Famous war correspondent, covering the European campaign, who, in April 1945, was shot dead by a Japanese sniper on the Pacific island of Ie Shima.

9/12/44

1. Controversial novel (1944) of a tragic outcome of an interracial romance in the South.

9/18/44

1. Tatassit was a small, private beach and picnic area on the eastern shore of Worcester's Lake Quinsigamond. Coes Pond is a small lake in Worcester whose private and public beaches the author often frequented. As a young boy he often fished in its waters.

2. MGM (1944), comedy-drama "Marriage is a Private Affair," starring Lana Turner (see also letter of 10/27/44).

3. For obvious reasons Lana Turner was called "The Sweater Girl." (see letter of 1/28/44, note 3).

4. Brilliant young actor, writer, director, whose controversial movie "Citizen Kane" based on the life of publisher William Randolph Hearst, caused him problems till the end of his long and troubled career.

5. On October 30, 1938 Orson Welles presented on CBS radio a fantasy invasion of men from Mars entitled "The War of the Worlds," which many Americans—panicked and fearful—took for actual fact.

9/20/44

1. Academy Award winning performance (1942).

2. From the turn of the century to the late 1930s one of America's greatest musical comedy composers and playwrights, whose rousing songs like "Give My Regards to Broadway" and patriotic "I'm a Yankee Doodle Dandy" thrilled Americans.

3. Warner Brothers' film biography (1942) of George M. Cohan, his partner Sam Harris, and the equally famous Cohan family.

4. Massachusetts.

5. Born July 4, 1878, Providence, R.I., died November 5, 1942.

6. Worcester, Massachusetts.

7. The author was declared the "most argumentative" in his high school year book.

9/24/44

1. Literally, one who seeks refuge (as millions did before, during, and after WWII) from one's war-torn country.

2. Malevolent dictator of Germany (1933-1945), who created a police state (enforced by the dreaded Gestapo—vicious secret police), orchestrated

the genocide of 6 million Jews and others, and plunged the world into World War II.

3. A fanatical and hateful program established by the Nazis to indoctrinate the youth of Germany into blind subservience to the National Socialist state in general and to the Fuhrer (the Leader) Adolph Hitler in particular.

9/28/44

1. Strong winds carrying heavy rains.

10/1/44

1. William Saroyan (1908-1981), American writer.

2 MGM sentimental drama of a typical American family in a typical American town, dealing with the reality of battlefield death while extolling the virtues of good-neighbor unity among nations, starring Micky Rooney, Frank Morgan, and child actor Jack Jenkins.

3. David O. Selznick production of Home-Front wartime drama, also starring Claudette Colbert, Jennifer Jones, and Joseph Cotten.

10/2/44

1. William Shakespeare.

10/3/44

1. Worcester's Superintendent of Schools at the time.

2. American poet (1819-1892).

3. Book of poems, considered profane — certainly controversial for the time for sexual references in some of the selections.

10/6/44

1. Hall of Fame ballplayer (1886-1961) with the Detroit Tigers and Philadelphia Athletics, who, besides his fearless and fearsome personality, holds the highest lifetime batting average in baseball, .367.

10/9/44

1. Italian composer Amilcare Ponchielli.

2. Wendell Willkie (1892-1944).

3. Willkie supported the Roosevelt Administration during WWII.

10/10/44

1. Allied conference in Georgetown, Washington, D.C. (Aug.21-Oct.7, 1944) with China, Soviet Union, Great Britain, and the U.S. to form the U.N. Organization.

2. Thomas Dewey (Republican) running against the incumbent president Franklin Roosevelt.

3. Generals Dwight Eisenhower and George Patton in the European Theater; Admiral Chester Nimitz, William Halsey, and General Douglas MacArthur, Pacific Theater, and General "Hap" Arnold of the Army Air Corps.

4. Wildcat strike in Pennsylvania coal mines, 4/43 (President Roosevelt invoked war power to stop it); Roosevelt forced rubber strikers back to work, 5/43; Roosevelt stopped United Mine Workers strike and seized the mines, 5/43; 60,000 went on strike in the Pennsylvania coal mines, 6/43; Pennsylvania transportation strike, 8/44.

5. Political Action Committees?

6. In Europe, the Allied ground action in France and Germany and the incessant bombing of enemy vital supplies (and incendiary bombing of cities); in the Pacific, the island hopping sieges, jungle fighting, and low-level incendiary bombing of Japanese cities.

10/13/44

1. Legendary silent screen actor, whose comic skill in daring stunts, hilarious chases, and acrobatic zaniness remains unmatched.

2. Buster Keaton was noted for his deadpan expression, no matter what the circumstances.

10/15/44

1. Women's Army Corps
2. Navy language for toilets.
3. Seasickness (French).

10/16/44

1. William Shakespeare's depiction (tragedy? comedy? history?) of a world in chaos during the Trojan War.
2. Shakespearian character in the comedy *A Midsummer Night's Dream.*
3. 3. 2. 15.

10/17/44

1. A purplish-red color.

10/19/44

1. American opera (music by George Gershwin, lyrics by DuBose Heywood), with all African-American cast, concerning a cripple's frustrated love in a poverty-stricken area in the Deep South.

2. Johann Strauss (1825-1899) wrote some of the world's most beautiful waltzes, including the incomparable "Blue Danube."

3. American operetta composer (1859-1924) of enduring melodies such as "March of the Toys" and "Oh, Sweet Mystery of Life."

4. Opera in 2 acts (1840), libretto by Bayard and Jules H. Vernoy, music by Gaetano Donizetti.

5. Lily Pons (1898-1976), French-born coloratura soprano
6. Andre Kostelanetz (1901-1980), noted musical conductor, married at that time to Lily Pons.
7. Italian opera, composed by Leon Cavalho (1825-1897).
8. Enrico Caruso (1873-1921), magnificent operatic tenor, whose quality of voice many consider never to have been equalled.
9. Felix Mendelssohn (1809-1847), German composer of 19th century Romanticism.
10. Overture to Shakespeare's *A Midsummer Night's Dream* (first composed as a piano duet in 1826).

10/20/44

1. Gertrude Gordon, a tall, beautiful, dark-haired woman, is Cousin Lil's cousin on her mother's side.
2. See Letter 9/18/44, Note 2.
3. Having to do with Miss Turner's ample endowments.
4. Will Hays (1879-1954), head of the "Hays Office," which regulated motion picture content.
5. My mother (French).
6. Al Smith, a Catholic, former governor of New York, an influential machine politician.

10/22/44

1. Musical reference.
2. Johann Sebastian Bach (1685-1750), great German classical composer.
3. Igor Stravinsky (1882-1971), noted Russian modern composer.
4. Wolfgang Amadeus Mozart (1756-1791), musical genius in the composing of the symphony, opera, chamber music, and concerto, buried in a pauper's grave.
5. Universal Studios (1943), a follow-up to their 1941 hit "Hellzapoppin."

10/27/44

1. Cousin Edward Aronovitz and his wife Shirley on the birth of their son Richard.
2. Maguire's old store, operated by the Mazur family at the corner of Chandler & Queen streets, contained the largest private lending library in Worcester County.
3. Maguires store also contained a soda fountain behind which the server stood on a raised platform.
4. Mrs. Mazur was a pleasant, large, tall woman as was her sister who often worked in the store.
5. The Volstead Act (1920-1933), commonly called Prohibition, a law named after its sponsor Andrew Volstead (1860-1942), which prohibited the sale or consumption of alcoholic beverage in the U.S.

6. Commonly called the Great Depression (1930-1941), precipitated by the Wall Street stock market collapse of 1929, plunging 13 million people out of work and into harsh, even desperate times.
7. Cousin Lil was Hughie's mentor in whom he often confided his troubles.

11/1/44

1. Universal Studios (1944), starring Deanna Durbin as an innocent young singer who falls in love with Gene Kelly, a scoundrel.
2. Versatile and acrobatic singer and dancer, whose brilliant choreography ran the gamut from tap to ballet.
3. William Somerset Maugham (1874-1965), British novelist, playwright, and short story writer.
4. Kelly, sometimes to advantage, liked to play—at various stages in his career—against type.
5. Music that is similar to classical music but less complex, with a more common appeal.

11/3/44

1. One of Broadway's greatest musicals (1924), with music by Jerome Kern and lyrics by Oscar Hammerstein II, featuring "Old Man River," "Only Make Believe," and "Can't Help Loving That Man of Mine."
2. One of the most successful Broadway musical shows (1943) ever with music by Richard Rodgers and lyrics by Oscar Hammerstein II, featuring the title song "Oklahoma!" and "O, What a Beautiful Morning."
3. Stage musical (1943), based on Georges Bizet's opera (from a novel by Prosper Merimée) *Carmen*, it features new lyrics by Oscar Hammerstein II.
4. Rudolph Friml operetta (1912), featuring enduring musical gems as "Giannina Mia" and "The Donkey Serenade."
5. Written by the brilliant Russian classical composer Nikolay Rimsky-Korsakov (1844-1908).
6. October 20, 1944, General Douglas MacArthur landed on Leyte, fulfilling his 1942 promise, "I shall return."

11/7/44

1. Universal Pictures (1944), about a fugitive killer posing as a Free French hero in Equatorial Africa.
2. French actor with a powerful, understated style.
3. Franklin Roosevelt's 1932 campaign slogan and ultimate political policy in combating the devastating economic times of the Depression.
4. Herbert Clark Hoover (1874-1964), 31st president of the U.S. (1928-1933), whom Roosevelt had defeated in the 1932 election and whom many blamed—perhaps erroneously—for the Depression.

11/8/44
1. MGM (1944), drama of a German anti-Nazi who escapes from a concentration camp, starring Spencer Tracy, Hume Cronyn, and Agnes Moorehead.

11/13/44
1. German novelist and dramatist (1884-1958).
2. Viking Press (1940).
3. Massachusetts Institute of Technology in Cambridge.

11/19/44
1. While in High School Hughie took an aptitude test which determined that he was not mechanically inclined.

11/22/44
1. Historical novel (1943, Farrar & Rinehart) of the Colonial period. The author, Hervey Allen, died before its completion.

11/23/44
1. Located on Main Street, a combination bar on one side of a partition, and a restaurant with booths on the other side.
2. Noted for its raucous sports fans.
3. MGM (1944) a home town drama, starring Brian Donlevy, Ann Richards, and Walter Abel.

11/28/44
1. Alfred Lord Tennyson (1809-1892), poet laureate of England (1850-1892), considered one of the giants of Victorian poetry.
2. Sigmund Freud (1856-1939), Austrian physician and neurologist, founder of psychoanalysis.

12/1/44
1. Cousin Sol often badgered Hughie by telling him that he was "tied to his mother's apron strings."
2. A briss, Jewish ceremony conducted during the circumcision rite performed by a rabbi.
3. A cotton or linen cloth somewhat like canvas but finer and lighter in weight.
4. Considered America's greatest playwright, O'Neill (1888-1953), probed the darker side of human relationships.
5. Paramount Pictures (1944), based on an O'Neill one-act play of the same title, about a doomed stoker, a gorilla, and a society girl.
6. A competent character actor who usually played heavy villains or best friends to leading men.
7. Gorgeous and skilled leading actress, noted for sultry roles.

8. RKO Radio Pictures (1944).

9. Welsh novelist (1906-1983).

10. A Hollywood icon, whose screen *persona* radiated wit, charm, and grace, though in this film he gives a deft performance as a cockney in a London slum.

11. Irish-born American character actor, who stole every scene he ever played, Academy Award recipient (1944), playing a priest opposite Bing Crosby in "Going My Way."

12/1/44

1. The author was confined to a hospital, and, upon contracting scarlet fever there, was quarantined for weeks, unable to see his parents.

12/3/44

1. Muriel Bergstrom, Hughie's much admired, attractive, and intelligent contemporary, and neighbor.

2. Hughie, having received mostly A grades in high school, was honored by qualifying as a Horace Mann Student.

12/4/44

1. RKO Radio Pictures (1944), starring George Murphy, Frank Sinatra, Gloria DeHaven, based on the play *Room Service* by John Murray and Allen Boretz.

12/5/44

1. Universal Pictures (1943), comedy about Park Avenue domestic staff, starring Pat O'Brien, Deanna Durbin, and Franchot Tone.

12/7/44

1. Warner Brothers' film about a spoiled, willful woman who leaves her husband for a hedonistic life, only to be reconciled to him years later when he goes blind.

2. Evelyn Aaron, Hughie's cousin on his father's side, a beautiful, raven-haired young woman.

12/9/44

1. Henry Wolf was wounded in the hand while a member of a detachment of the battalion that was assigned duty in a hot area farther north. His vessel was struck by a Jap Kamikaze.

2. W. Somerset Maugham's novel (1944, Doubleday) of a disillusioned WWI veteran, seeking a spiritual life.

12/12/44

1. Slob (Yiddish).

12/14/44

1. MGM (1944), drama covering both World Wars in which a woman loses her husband in the First and her son in the Second, starring Irene Dunne and Alan Marshall.

12/17/44

1. To the astonishment and consternation of his Reform congregation in Worcester, Rabbi Levi Olan stated, in a sermon, that he would not object to his daughter marrying a black.
2. Up to this time, Boston, still anchored in its puritanical history, had a rigid censorship code, which generated in our language the phrase "Banned in Boston," meaning a strict moral standard.
3. 20th Century Fox, costume drama of the loves of an English courtesan in the 17th century, starring Linda Darnell, George Sanders, and Cornel Wilde, based on a novel by Kathleen Winsor.

12/21/44

1. Hughie was a short man, 5 feet 7 inches.

12/23/44

1. Conover Models were — if their publicity was correct — the most beautiful models in the world.
2. Cole Porter (1893-1964), music composer for Broadway and Hollywood, noted for his memorable tunes (like "Begin the Beguine") and witty, clever lyrics.
3. Jerome Kern (1885-1945), musical composer of greatness on Broadway and in the cinema, whose melodies such as "Long Ago and Far Away," "Smoke Gets in Your Eyes," and "Why Was I Born" remain American classics.

12/24/44

1. Famous watch brand name.
2. High school friend, and son of Gregory Pincus, co-discoverer of the birth control pill.
3. Slang expression of the era, meaning "all right," "going well."

12/26/44

1. Warner Brothers (1944), "Jamie," based on a play of the same title by Josephine Bentham and Herschell V. Williams, teenage girl has problems with the army.
2. After submitting "A Cat's Tale" as his own, in an English class, brother Ronnie received an A, and the story was printed in the school newspaper.
3. Best selling novel by Bennet Ames Williams, about an obsessed wife-murderess, who, after coldly watching her crippled brother-in-law drown, takes poison, hinting before her death that it was her husband's doing.
4. Paramount Pictures (1944), comedy-drama about love in WWII.

5. Paulette Goddard, strikingly beautiful dramatic actress, once married to Charlie Chaplin.

6. Sonny Tufts, a pleasant Hollywood actor, whose career, though brief, was not without merit.

7. Paramount Pictures (1944), a French nun aids an American airman in escaping the Nazis.

8. Ray Milland, British-born American cinema actor, who enjoyed an over 30 year career, including an Academy Award playing an alcoholic writer in Billy Wilder's "The Lost Weekend," (1945).

9. Popular actress, whose career proved brief.

12/29/44

1. A mixed language or jargon with simple vocabulary and grammar.

2. Well known Hollywood gossip columnist of the era, rival of Louella Parsons.

12/31/44

1. Mrs. Rome was Mom's friend and Bridge partner.

2. Mrs. Rome's daughter.

3. Large New England department store located in Boston.

1/1/45

1. *Romeo and Juliet*, William Shakespeare (tragedy).

2. "O Romeo, Romeo, wherefore art thou Romeo?" (2.2.33)

3. Popular novelist of the era.

4. Novel based on the seamless robe Christ wore at the crucifixion, and for which the Roman soldiers threw dice.

1/11/45

1. British novelist (1900-1954).

2. Written as a tribute to his British schoolmaster father, this short novel (1934) portrays the life of a modest teacher, who wins the love of a vibrant young woman and the admiration, affection, and devotion of 3 generations of students.

3. Preeminent German novelist (1875-1955), who wrote in the U.S. after fleeing Germany.

4. Book 3 of a tetralogy (1933-1943), based on the biblical story of Joseph in the Old Testament.

5. 20th Century Fox (1944), a drama of harness racing, starring Lon McAllister.

1/17/45

1. Australians.

2. Capital city of New South Wales, Australia.

1. Benjamin Disraeli (1804-1881), 1st Earl of Beaconsfield, British statesman and writer; prime minister (1868; 1874-1880).

1. The longest running serial drama in radio history, telling the story of the Barbour family, who lived in San Francisco.
2. Worcester Tech.

1. *Count Von Luckner, Knight of Sea,* by Edwin P. Hoyt, a story of World War I.

1. Publius Cornelius Tacitus (55AD-117AD), Roman historian.

1. Edward Hagerup Grieg (1843-1907), Norwegian composer.
2. Helen McInnes, Scottish born author of the novel *Above Suspicion* (1941).
3. Fritz Kreisler (1875-1962), U.S. violinist and composer, born in Austria. In 1935 Mr. Kreisler, a virtuoso violinist, acknowledged that because of modesty he had been playing his own composed pieces while passing them off as Baroque classics. He had also written in 1919 a successful operetta "Apple Blossom."
4. An Ivy League school, located in Manhattan.

1. George Gordon, Lord Byron (1788-1824), British Romantic poet, noted for his exquisite love poems.

1. A novel by Ernest Hemingway (1899-1961), U.S. novelist and short story writer, about an American adventurer Richard Jordan, who fights against the Fascists during the Spanish Civil War (1936-1939).

1. Weiner was in the army infantry, a hardier duty than that of the Seabees.
2. Moderator of the long-running radio panel quiz show "Information Please," whose opening had a rooster crowing and an announcer exhorting, "Wake up, America! It's time to stump the experts."
3. The Allied invasion of Anzio in Italy, in January 1944, stalled by initial inaction, resulted in almost 60,000 casualties, ultimately.

2/2/45

1.Warner Brothers film, directed by Frank Capra from the Joseph Kesselring smash Broadway play. The movie version—of two brothers, one normal, one maniacal—was played for great laughs by Cary Grant and Raymond Massey, among others.

2/3/45

1. MGM (1944), a costume drama of the 17th century in which a bored wife of an aristocrat runs off with a French pirate, starring Joan Fontaine and Arturo de Cordova, based on a novel by Daphne Du Maurier.

2/6/45

1. The author does not recall this ingenue actress' name, and does not know whether she made good.
2. 20th Century Fox (1944), comedy of a professor, who before he marries, discovers he has a baby from a previous marriage, starring Gary Cooper and Frank Morgan.
3. Bud Abbot and Lou Costello, popular radio and movie comedians, masters of slick repartee ("Who's on First") as well as sight gags and slapstick (a holdover from their vaudeville days).
4. Universal Pictures (1944). Two backward plumbers destroy a mansion.
5. Lawrence Tibbett (1896-1960), American baritone, successful in both opera and in the movies.
6. A popular variety radio show, whose masters of ceremonies included Major Bowes and Ted Mack and whose vocalist Belle Silverman later emerged as the fine soprano Beverly Sills.
7. Radio comedy show, featuring adept character actor Jack Carson and great voice master Mel Blanc, with Freddie Martin's orchestra.
8. Radio variety show, featuring Frank Morgan, Cass Daly, and the splendid character actor Eric Blore.
9. Smash hit radio comedy show, starring Bob Hope and Jerry Colonna, sponsored by Pepsodent tooth paste with Irium ("Poor Miriam, neglected using Irium"), featuring Bob's theme: "Thanks for the Memory."
10. A radio variety show, starring Rudy Vallee, a popular singer and movie comedy actor, who was a forerunner of the "crooners" of the 1930s and '40s.
11. All friends and neighbors, or former neighbors, of the family.
12. A cobblestone street lined with an assortment of food stores, from bakeries to meat markets to delicatessens, etc., selling Jewish and kosher foods. So named because the Blackstone River runs beneath it.

2/8/45

1. MGM (1944), costume drama in which an oriental magician bests a villainous vizier, starring Ronald Coleman and Marlene Dietrich.

2. Metaphysical poet (1572-1631), one of the great poets of the 17th century, whose lines, in part, from his prose work *Devotions upon Emergent Occasions* (Meditation 17) Hemingway used as a preface to his novel: "Any man's death diminishes me, because I am involved in mankind, and therefore never send to know for whom the bell tolls; it tolls for thee."

3. Pearl Sydenstricker Buck (1892-1973), American novelist and Nobel Prize winner for literature (1938).

4. Margaret Mitchell, author of *Gone with the Wind.*

5. New York City Post Office Building.

2/12/45

1. "A non-tropical farce in three acts," written by Mark White Reed (1927).

2. Comedy in 3 acts, written by Lawrence Riley (1927).

3. Radio broadcast panel discussion group, emanating from the University of Chicago.

4. Anti-semitism.

2/15/45

1. Dante Alighieri (1265-1321), greatest poet of Renaissance Italy.

2. An elaborate narrative poem in Italian (1307-1321) consisting of the poet's journey (both symbolic and spiritual) through Hell (The Inferno), Purgatory (The Purgatorio), and Heaven (The Paradiso), inspired by his ideal love, Beatrice.

3. Henry David Thoreau (1817-1862), American writer and philosopher, whose book *Walden* details the simple life of living close to the land.

4. A picture or symbol representing a word, symbol, or sound, used by the ancient Egyptians instead of letters of the alphabet.

5. A repository for all the ills befalling military personnel; take your troubles to the chaplain (a priest, a minister, or a rabbi), because no one else will listen to your complaint.

2/17/45

1. Worcester Polytechnic Institute.

2. Federal Agency that administers all laws governing benefits for veterans of the armed forces.

3. At the time, WPI was a first-rate engineering school, with a narrowly focussed curriculum.

4. Nazi Germany in early 1945 was in its death agony, besieged by American and British forces on the West and Soviet forces on the East; Japan, though fanatically resistant, was faltering badly.

5. In English grammar the verb has 4 principal parts: the present, the present participle (always ending in "ing"), the past, and the past participle.

6. The next war, dubbed the "Cold War," was, indeed, a different kind of war.

2/25/45

1. Jefferson and Holden, suburbs north of Worcester, Massachusetts.
2. A member of the battalion, then in his fifties, a resident of Jefferson.
3. Paramount Pictures (1944), starring Bing Crosby as Father O'Malley, a trouble-shooting priest, sent by the Bishop to bail out St. Domenic's parish and its aging pastor, played by Barry Fitzgerald.
4. Crosby is the efficient, yet pleasant and understanding padre, who, while getting the parish solvent, forming a glee club for delinquents, and selling songs (with Rise Stevens, Metropolitan opera soprano), sees the warmth, character, and love in the old priest.
5. David O. Selznick (1944), wartime drama of the women who stay home, coping with the absence of loved ones at the front, starring Claudet Colbert, Jennifer Jones, and Shirley Temple. (See Letter of 10/14/1944, note 3.)
6. Nation-wide bus company.
7. A French luxury liner, converted to wartime use, which burned mysteriously in New York harbor (February 9, 1942).
8. Viscountess, born Nancy Witcher Langhorne, in the U.S., (1879-1964) was the first woman member of the British House of Commons (1919-45).
9. Brilliant French actress (1844-1923).
10. U.S. politician, playwright, and diplomat (1903-87).

3/2/45

1. Universal Studios (1944), gothic drama of a young opera singer, hypnotized by a mad physician, starring Boris Karloff and Susanne Foster.
2. MGM (1944), a costume drama set in the Edwardian age (1901-1914), starring Greer Garson, Walter Pidgeon, Edward Arnold, Gladys Cooper.
3. The war against Japan was still raging as the Marines invaded Iwo Jima (February 19, 1945) at great cost, but getting closer to the Japanese home islands.
4. The war.

3/4/45

1. A collection of literary essays by contemporary writers.
2. Published 1943.
3. Published 1943.
4. The family routinely did its food shopping on Saturday nights on Water Street, a street where Jewish vendors congregated (delicatessens, bakeries, meat markets, etc.), and where Hughie's mother usually met and gossiped with her women friends.
5. *Reader's Digest.*

1. Distinguished university, located in South Central England.
2. Worcester Musical Festival, then held each evening during an entire week in the Memorial Auditorium, performed by prestigious visiting symphony orchestras.
3. See Shakespeare's *Romeo and Juliet*, in which the "star-crossed" lovers of the title suffer a tragic end.

3/9-3/10/45

1. "I Miss You Most of All" (1913), music by Joseph M. McCarthy, Sr., lyrics by James V. Monaco.
2. It would have been a good bet. Ronnie did, indeed, marry first.
3. Warner Brothers (1944), melodrama about international intrigue in WWII, starring Hedy Lamarr, Paul Henreid, Sydney Greenstreet, Peter Lorre.
4. The most famous, most lingering lullaby ever composed.

3/13-3/14/45

1. "Comedy" in Dante's time meant "long narrative."

3/17/45

1. Charles Boyer, one of cinema's all time popular suave lovers, with a French accent, who immortalized "Come with me to the Casbah."
2. Joan Fontaine, popular actress of over 3 decades and Academy Award recipient in Alfred Hitchcock's "Suspicion" (1941).
3. Warner Brothers (1943), romantic drama of a composer leaving his rich wife for a young girl, also starring Alexis Smith, Charles Coburn, Peter Lorre.
4. Columbia Pictures (1945), music-drama of the life and death of Chopin and his love affair with George Sand.
5. Paul Muni, a consummate actor, whose cinema achievements include the classics as Scarface and Louis Pasteur. Though sometimes accused of overacting, he won an Academy Award for "The Life of Louis Pasteur" (1935).
6. Frederic Chopin (1810-1849), Polish composer and pianist, in France after 1831.
7. Merle Oberon, longtime leading lady with waxen beauty.
8. Pseudonym of Amandine Aurore Lucie Dupin, Baronne Dudevarri (1804-1876), French novelist, who dressed scandalously in men's clothing and smoked thin cigars.
9. New Guinea.
10. Hughie's normal weight as a civilian was 150 to 155 lbs.
11. By mid-February U.S. forces had liberated Manila and recaptured Bataan and Corregidor; by early March the Marines had secured Iwo Jima and the U.S. Army had crossed the Rhine River at Remagen.

3/19/45

1. Giovanni Casanova (1725-1798), an adventurer, noted for his *Memoirs*, citing many love affairs as a libertine.

3/20/45

1. Commemorated the end of WWI, November 11, 1918, in France; now called Veterans Day, which commemorates all the wars America has fought.

3/23/45

1. The Nazis under Hitler exterminated 6 million Jews and at least a million others; the Soviet Union under Stalin starved to death at least 10 million Kulaks in the Ukraine, among others.

3/24/45

1. Warner Brothers (1944), drama based on an Ernest Hemingway novel of the same title, *To Have and Have Not*, concerns a fishing boat owner (Humphrey Bogart), who outwits Nazis in Marseille, while romancing a young woman, street savvy and sexy.
2. Humphrey Bogart ("Bogie"), one of the most popular "tough guy" actors ever, who had a remarkable speaking voice, a wide range in both theater and the cinema, and a long career, including an Academy Award (1952) for "The African Queen."
3. Introduced in this film, she informed Bogart that if he wanted her, just whistle, "just pucker up your lips and blow." She was — in words of the ace cinema critic James Agee — "one hot number," who continues her career — and is the widow of Bogart — to this day.
4. 20th Century Fox (1944), a drama based on the struggles of President Woodrow Wilson to unify European thought among the victorious allies after WWI, his futile efforts to convince the U.S. to enroll in the League of Nations, and his breakdown from his failure to do so, starring Alexander Knox in the title role.
5. United Artists (1944), romance about a shell-shocked soldier and a woman thief, starring Joseph Cotten and Ginger Rogers.

3/27/45

1. Two act musical comedy (1943) by Dorothy and Herbert Fields with music and lyrics by Cole Porter.
2. The movie version featured Leon Errol.
3. Popular cartoon character in a then futuristic 21st century.

En Route to Parts Unknown

4/6/45

1. Popular amusement park in Brooklyn, New York.

2. One half of a portable tent.

3. Located in Boston.

4. April 1, Easter Sunday. On June 21, 1945, the bloody battle—which took over 100,000 Japanese and over 9,000 American lives and featured suicide Kamikaze air attacks on the American fleet—ended.

5. 350 miles from Japan proper.

6. "I'll Walk Alone" (1944), music by Jule Styne, lyrics by Sammy Cahn.

7. (1927), music by Jerome Kern, lyrics by Oscar Hammerstein II.

8. (1938), music and lyrics by Cole Porter.

4/19/45

1. Northern coast of New Guinea where General Douglas MacArthur had made a successful and brilliant invasion (150 men lost) against Japanese forces.

2. By the Japanese forces.

5/1/45

1. An apparatus operated by hand or machine, for hoisting or hauling.

2. Main island of the Philippines.

Subic Bay, Luzon, Philippine Islands

5/8/45

1. Germany surrendered unconditionally on May 7, at Rheims to representatives of the U.S., the U.S.S.R., France, and Great Britain.

5/13/45

1. In Judaism the feast commemorating the exodus of the Jews from Egypt, observed in the home by the reading of the Haggada on the eve of the first day of Passover.

5/14/45

1. Sawyer's, a successful Worcester building and hardware supply firm, had offered the author's father the job of running its newly opened home decorating and upholstering department.

2. Flips, a slang term not meant to be derogatory, but somewhat condescending.

5/16/45

1. Charles Boyer.

2. Irene Dunne.

3. Columbia Pictures (1944), comedy of a widow of a small town official and a statue in his memory, also starring Charles Coburn, Mona Freeman.

4. MGM (1944), sentimental story of a young girl whose sister plays in José Iturbi's orchestra, starring Margaret O'Brien, Jimmy Durante.

5. George Frederick Handel (1685-1759), English composer, born in Germany.
6. When General MacArthur invaded Hollandia, he bypassed over 20,000 Japanese troops at Wewak, cutting them off from supplies as well as reinforcements.
7. Chase lost a leg in the war.
8. Bennett Ames Williams.

5/19/45
1. U.S. writer (1874-1946) who lived in France after WWI and is widely known for her repetitious—some say confusing—style, as in her phrase "a rose is a rose is a rose."

5/21/45
1. Warner Brothers (1945), screwball comedy about an eccentric father and his oddball schemes.
2. Anti-aircraft.

5/24-5/26/45
1. "When in Rome do as the Romans do;" or, "When thou art at Rome, do as they do at Rome," from *Don Quixote* by Miguel de Cervantes (1547-1616).
2. So young looking was the father, that he and his son were often taken for brothers.

5/29/45
1. Lottie Simon, distantly related on the author's father's side, operated a toy store in Worcester with her husband.
2. John Garfield.
3. Warner Brothers (1943), WWII drama of a Flying Fortress bomber and its crew, also starring Gig Young, Arthur Kennedy, George Tobias.

5/31/45
1. Music and lyrics by Irving Berlin.

6/2/45
1. Natalie Gordon, a cousin to Cousin Lil, attended, a grade or two ahead, the same high school as the author.
2. 20th Century Fox (1945), a sequel to "My Friend Flicka," a family drama concerning love of a horse by a young boy.

6/7/45
1. The motto of Maxwell House Coffee: "Good to the last drop."
2. Fibber McGee and Molly (Jim and Marian Jordan) were radio and motion picture favorites for two decades, whose radio show featured phrases like "T'aint funny, McGee," which became household familiarities.
3. In the show's comedy broadcasts, Fibber McGee would open his closet and the sound effects man would make noises and sounds as if

everything—including the kitchen sink—were falling out, with a final clink of a bell at the end. McGee would then say something like "I'll have to clean that closet out one of these days."

4. "That's war" (French).

5. "The Picture of Dorian Gray" (MGM, 1945), starring George Sanders, Hurd Hatfield, Angela Lansbury, based on Oscar Wilde's novel of a decadent whose face remains young while his hidden portrait disintegrates.

6/8/45

1. Cousin Charlie came home after a long stint overseas and was discharged from service.

2. Ground potato, with ground onions, garlic, chicken fat, and several "secret" ingredients added, baked in the oven. A favorite of the entire family.

3. Harry Palais, husband of Aunt Henrietta, a toy manufacturer, tended to assume a superior attitude.

4. Betty, Goldie Ringer's beautiful, and highly intelligent, younger sister.

6/10/45

1. Warner Brothers (1945), drama of a widow who refuses to mourn long for her deceased husband, also starring Jerome Cowan, John Ridgely.

2. Barbara Stanwick (1907-1990) ran the range of performance from earthy reporter ("Meet John Doe") to ice-cold killer ("Double Indemnity"), and all roles in between, winning and wonderful in all—a 50 year career.

3. Irish-born actor (1904-1979), whose rich voice made him a Hollywood star for three decades.

6/11/45

1. In 1945 in San Francisco representatives of 50 nations adopted the UN Charter.

2. Robert Frost (1874-1963), American poet.

6/18/45

1. Austrian by birth (1882-1965), associate justice, U.S. Supreme Court (1939-62).

6/23/45

1. Warner Brothers (1944), WWII presentation of Hollywood stars helping out the war effort by entertaining the men in uniform.

6/24/45

1. Commonly called "The Roaring Twenties" (1920-29).

6/26/45

1. Yalta Peace Conference (February 1945) involved the "Big Three" world powers with Winston Churchill, the prime minister of Great Britain; Joseph Stalin, dictator of Soviet Russia; and Franklin Roosevelt, president of the U.S., meeting to plan how to divide post-war Europe into zones of political influence. From this meeting Russia locked up Eastern Europe in its communist embrace.

6/30/45

1. A Jewish money-lender, who, in Shakespeare's play, tried to exact a pound of flesh—not without some justification—from his hated debtor and so-called Christian antagonist Antonio (who had spit on him and kicked him in public).
2. William Shakespeare's dark (often misinterpreted) comedy (1596-7).

7/6/45

1. Shortly after Pearl Harbor, Japanese bombers (stationed on Formosa, a base General MacArthur's advisers urged him to bomb on December 8, 1941) destroyed almost every U.S. fighter plane and bomber—on the ground and massed together to discourage sabotage—thus leaving the U.S. Army forces in the Philippines at the mercy of the invading Japanese, who relentlessly pursued the retreating American soldiers.

7/7/45

1. Universal (1944), Deanna Durbin singing the songs of Jerome Kern as she pursues her lover to California in the mid-1800s.
2. Posing at the Worcester Art Museum school as a model, Hughie wore only a jock strap.

7/20/45

1. Published 1943.
2. Published 1936.
3. Published 1944.

7/22/45

1. Going overseas (Navy term).

7/26/45

1. George Kalajian operated, with his wife, the convenience market and lunch bar next door to the author's father's shop on Lincoln Street. The two men were good friends and often indulged in humorous, sometime uproarious, conversation.

7/31/45

1. Your Hit Parade—radio broadcast (mid-1930s—late 1940s) featuring—at various times—top singers (Frank Sinatra, Lanny Ross,

Buddy Clark, Bea Wain) introducing the ten song hits of the week, concluding with the number one in the country, sponsored by Lucky Strike cigarettes.

2. See Letter of 8/16/44, note 3.

3. Charles Gounod (1818-1893), French composer, whose *Ave Maria* is a vocal meditation on Bach's Prelude in C major from *The Well-Tempered Clavier.*

4. Opera (1850) by Richard Wagner (1813-1882), German composer.

5. Do not touch (French).

8/1/45

1. Raven-haired actress, said to have had the most beautiful overbite in Hollywood; the mystery movie could have been the classic "Laura" (20th Century Fox, 1944).

2. Competent actress of the 1940s who played in John Wayne westerns as well as Preston Sturges comedies.

8/3/45

1. Singer sewing machine.

8/8/45

1. On August 6, 1945, the first atomic bomb was dropped on Hiroshima, Japan, killing 60,000 civilians outright, with many more dying of radiation.

2. The fear of nuclear war has been a permanent legacy of the post-war world.

3. 20th Century Fox (1945), comedy in which a new maid civilizes a crotchety old man, also starring Reginald Gardiner.

4. John P. Marquand (1893-1960), U.S. novelist.

5. Published 1937.

6. Simultaneously attacking Manchuria.

7. Seeing that Japan was doomed and could not retaliate, the Soviet Union attacked, trying to seize as much Japanese-held territory as possible in China and Korea and outlying islands.

8. The U.S. War Department had intended to invade the Japanese home islands sometime in 1946, estimating one million American casualties.

8/15/45

1. MGM (1945), a wartime romance of a girl and a soldier who meet under the huge clock in Grand Central Station, starring Judy Garland and Robert Walker.

8/16/45

1. Capital of Northern Territory, Australia.

8/17/45

1. The Lowes had lived on a large estate (Ellis) in Worcester in which Mr. Lowe served as a chauffeur and handyman. On the death of the matron, they were left $10,000, a large sum in those days, which eventually resulted in the separation of husband and wife.

8/21/45

1. "Billy Rose's Diamond Horsehoe" (20th Century Fox, 1945) musical of backstage love, starring Betty Grable, Dick Haymes, Phil Silvers.

8/22/45

1. Adolph Hitler's retreat in Southeast Germany, in the Bavarian Alps.

8/28/45

1. MGM (1944), melodrama of WWII Chinese peasants resisting the Japanese, starring Katherine Hepburn, Walter Huston, Akim Tamiroff.

9/3/45

1. Victory over Japan. In a twenty minute ceremony General Douglas MacArthur, representing the Allied command—on the deck of the American battleship *Missouri*—accepted the formal declaration of surrender by the representatives of Japan.
2. Masada was an ancient Jewish fortress in Israel near the Dead Sea, site of a prolonged Roman siege (A.D.72-73), resulting in mass suicide by the Jews to avoid capture.

9/5/45

1. George Dewey (1837-1917), U.S. admiral in the Spanish-American War, the war between the U.S. and Spain (1898), the outcome of which Spain ceded the Philippines to America.
2. Franklin Delano Roosevelt.
3. Frank Murphy (1890-1948), governor general (1933-1935) and U.S. high commissioner (1935-1936) in the Philippines, where he supported the independence movement.
4. Henry L. Stimson (1867-1950), U.S. secretary of war (1911-13; 1940-1945).
5. Leonard Wood (1860-1927), U.S. general who, as newly appointed governor of the Philippines (1923) proved so unpopular that the Filipinos demanded his recall.
6. Theodore Roosevelt, Jr. (1887-1944), governor general of the Philippines (1923-33).
7. Manuel Quezon (1878-1944), first president of the Philippines (1935-1944).
8. Manuel Roxas (1892-1948), political leader and first president of the independent Republic of the Philippines (1946-48).

9. Sergio Osmena (1878-1961), founder of the National Party and president of the Philippines (1944-1946).
10. Bill passed by Congress (1934), aimed at minimizing the Philippine competition in trade.

9/7/45

1. Slang for "British."
2. See Letter of 1/29/44, Note 1.

9/8/45

1. Thomas Kincaid (1888-1972), admiral U.S. Navy.
2. In support of General MacArthur's invasion of Leyte, Admiral Kincaid's Seventh Fleet destroyed the Japanese Southern Force—poised to annihilate the invading forces on the beachhead—in the battle of Leyte Gulf.

9/10/45

1. See Letter of 5/28/44, Note 1.
2. In Europe, for centuries, Jews lived in isolated ghettos, suffering, at various times, societal exclusion and government persecution.
3. In the U.S.—before the war, and for some years after—certain fraternal organizations refused Jews membership, hotels refused their business, and colleges and medical schools set up quota systems, allowing only a small number of Jewish applicants admission.

9/11/45

1. Edward VIII abdicated the British throne on December 11, 1936, becoming the Duke of Windsor.

9/18/45

1. A resort city on the Atlantic Ocean, in New Jersey.
2. December 15, 1944.

9/25/45

1. A movement at that time for reestablishing—now for supporting—the Jewish national state of Israel.

10/1/45

1. In the Battle of Bunker Hill (actually fought on nearby Breed's Hill) in 1775, the British defeated colonial forces.
2. One of the commanders of the colonial troops told his men not to fire upon the advancing British until "You see the whites of their eyes."
3. American philosopher.
4. Published in 1939.
5. Enlisted man in a medical corps, attached to a combat unit.

10/2/45

1. The *West Point* was the troopship that took the author overseas.

10/5/45

1. Original Broadway play (1945), written by F. Hugh Herbert.
2. Herbert's play is based on this irrepressible female character, featured in a series of his short stories.
3. In Spanish legend a dissolute nobleman and seducer of women, the hero of many poems, plays, and operas.

10/10/45

1. Stirring march by John Phillip Sousa (1854-1932), U.S. Marine Corps bandmaster and composer of marches, namely "The Stars and Stripes Forever" and "The Semper Fidelis March."

10/22/45

1. A female Filipino.
2. The Coronado, a hotel on Franklin Street in Worcester where dances and weddings were often held.

10/23/45

1. Actually referred to as crocodiles in previous letters.

10/26/45

1. Paramount Pictures (1945), comedy of four suitors, each with a different perspective on the woman pursued, starring Joan Fontaine, George Brent, Walter Abel.
2. English psychologist and writer (1859-1939), especially on human and sexual behavior.
3. Published 1923.
4. Nathaniel Hawthorne (1804-1864), U.S. novelist and short story writer.
5. Hawthorne's novel (1850) of a woman's being condemned to wear a scarlet letter A for adultery in Puritan New England, beset by sin, hypocrisy, and revenge on one hand and enlightened by redemption on the other.
6. Popular powdered laundry soap of the time ("Rinso White" was its slogan).

10/28/45

1. Maurice Ravel (1875-1937), French composer.
2. Dmitri Shostakovich (1906-1975), Russian composer.
3. Peter Illich Tchaikovsky (1840-1893), Russian composer.
4. Edvard Grieg (1843-1907), Norwegian composer.

11/1/45

1. On Long Island sound, site of the U.S. Coast Guard Academy.

11/4/45

1. A group of small islands in the Bismarck Archipelago, northeast of New Guinea, part of Papua, New Guinea.

11/9/45

1. American author (1903-1950).
2. Published 1943.

11/12-11/14/45

1. An island southeast of Luzon.
2. Famous race car driver of the early 20th century, breaking speed records at 25 miles an hour.

11/26/45

1. Chief Petty Officer.
2. Landing craft.
3. Philippine Islands.
4. Chester Nimitz (1885-1966), Admiral, U.S. Navy, commanded U.S. Pacific Fleet in WWII.

11/27/45

1. A popular novel of the time.
2. Two weeks.
3. 20th Century Fox (1944), drama of a troubled but rewarding life of a Catholic missionary priest in 19th century China, starring Gregory Peck, Thomas Mitchell.
4. They speak the Indonesian language.

11/30/45

1. On November 29, 1942, the Cocoanut Grove nightclub, in Boston, burst into flame, killing almost 500 patrons who were virtually trapped when they found exit doors locked and then doomed themselves by pouring into the revolving front door, jamming it.
2. Holy Cross College with a mediocre season defeated Boston College (10-0, with a Sugar Bowl bid) 55-12, in a stunning upset between the two Jesuit schools. The Boston College football team, certain of their impending victory, had booked a celebration at the Cocoanut Grove the night of the tragic fire. Since they lost, however, the team canceled the engagement, saving many—if not all—of their lives.

Afterword

1. Robert Maynard Hutchins (1899-1978), U.S. educator, dean of the Yale law school, president of the University of Chicago (1929-1951), and chancellor (1945-1950), later president of The Fund for the Republic.

2. Nuclear physicist (1901-1954), Italian born, created the first self-sustaining nuclear reaction under the stands of Stagg Field at the University of Chicago.

3. Fyodor Dostoyevsky (1821-1881), prestigious Russian novelist. His *The Brothers Karamazov* has been considered one of the greatest novels ever written.

4. E.M. Forster (1879-1970), British novelist whose theme concerned the need for freedom of action and thought in British society.

5. Greek philosopher (384-322 B.C.), pupil of Plato, noted for his works on logic, metaphysics, ethics, politics.

6. Karl Marx (1818-1883), German social philosopher, founder of modern socialism (Communism).

7. Arnold Toynbee (1889-1975), British historian.

8. Anton J. Carlson (1875-1956), a colorful professor of biology, used to demonstrate the scientific method in class by dipping a finger into a test tube of urine, and tasting it to confirm its identity. After calling on a student to perform the same test, he pointed out that the student failed, because he did not observe that the finger he, Carlson, had tasted was not the finger he dipped into the tube.

9. Reuel Denny left his editorship at Fortune Magazine to teach and write; he co-authored with David Riesman a ground-breaking observation of our society, *The Lonely Crowd.*

10. (1902-1990), professor of literature.

11. (1909-), sociologist, Harvard professor emeritus.

12. (1897-1958).

13. The main business and shopping district in downtown Chicago.